Eighth Edition

Assessment of Exceptional Students

Educational and Psychological Procedures

Ronald L. Taylor

Florida Atlantic University

PEARSON

Upper Saddle River, New Jersey
Columbus, Ohio

Library of Congress Cataloging-in-Publication Data

Taylor, Ronald L.
   Assessment of exceptional students : educational and psychological
procedures / Ronald L. Taylor.—8th ed.
          p.   cm.
   Includes bibliographical references and index.
   ISBN-13: 978-0-205-60839-3 (pbk.)
   ISBN-10: 0-205-60839-6 (pbk.)
   1. Children with disabilities—Education—United States.   2. Children with disabilities—
Psychological testing—United States.   3. Educational tests and measurements—United States.
4. Special education—United States.   I. Title.
   LC4031.T36 2009
   371.90973—dc22

                                                      2008013984

Series Editor: Virginia Lanigan
Editorial Assistant: Matthew Buchholz
Senior Marketing Manager: Krista Clark
Production Editor: Gregory Erb
Editorial Production Service: Omegatype Typography, Inc.
Composition Buyer: Linda Cox
Manufacturing Buyer: Megan Cochran
Cover Designer: Linda Knowles

This book was set in Palatino by Omegatype Typography, Inc. It was printed and bound by Bind-Rite
Graphics. The cover was printed by Phoenix Color Corporation/Hagerstown.

Pearson Education Ltd.
Pearson Education Singapore Pte. Ltd.
Pearson Education Canada, Ltd.
Pearson Education—Japan

Pearson Education Australia Pty. Limited
Pearson Education North Asia Ltd.
Pearson Educación de Mexico, S.A. de C.V.
Pearson Education Malaysia Pte. Ltd.

Merrill
is an imprint of

www.pearsonhighered.com

10 9 8 7 6 5 4 3 2 1
ISBN 13: 978-0-205-60839-3
ISBN 10: 0-205-60839-6

As always, I would like to thank my parents,
my wife, Yvette, and my sons Mike and Danny,
for their constant love and support.

About the Author

RONALD L. TAYLOR, Ed.D., is currently a professor of exceptional student education at Florida Atlantic University. He received his bachelor's and master's degrees in psychology at Austin College and Trinity University. He received his doctorate in special education from the University of Houston. Prior to coming to Florida Atlantic University, Dr. Taylor was a school psychologist and consulting teacher for a Title III grant that focused on working with culturally diverse students. He also served on the faculty in special education at Boston University. Dr. Taylor has published extensively, including eight books (eighteen counting various editions) and over twenty chapters and ninety articles. He recently co-authored an introductory special education text, *Exceptional Students: Preparing Teachers for the 21st Century*, published by McGraw-Hill. Dr. Taylor has received over 2 million dollars in grant funding. He is active in several professional organizations, having made over sixty presentations, and was editor of *Diagnostique*, the journal for the assessment division of the Council for Exceptional Children.

Contents

Preface

Assessment is a constantly changing area. New laws, philosophies, and assessment instruments and techniques quickly make information in this field obsolete. A tremendous amount of change has occurred in the three years since the publication of the seventh edition of this book. This eighth edition contains information that reflects those changes. Specifically, this edition includes:

- More information on accommodations.
- More information on alternate assessment.
- Information about the role of assessment in No Child Left Behind (NCLB), including additional information on high-stakes assessment.
- Updated references and reviews of literature on the norm-referenced tests.
- Description of several new tests and deletions of lesser used ones.
- Additional examples of determining basals and ceilings using real tests.
- More emphasis on application, interpretation, and decision making. This is accomplished through two new features:
    1. For all chapters in Parts III to V, test data are presented for the student described in the vignette at the beginning of the chapter. Those data are then interpreted.
    2. A running case study, "June," is presented in each chapter. This asks students to make decisions as more cumulative information is presented.
- Reflection questions are provided in each chapter that allow the student to think about topics presented. These can also be used by instructors as assignments.

Other changes have also been made, and many of the procedures or instruments that are outdated have been eliminated (or greatly reduced if they are outdated but still used). The eighth edition has, however, kept most of the general features of previous editions.

The text is divided into six major parts. Part I, Introduction to Assessment: Issues and Concerns, begins with a chapter that traces the historical, philosophical, and legal foundations of assessment. The second chapter serves as a general introduction to assessment. It poses several questions that must be answered before assessing any student, and it also proposes an assessment model. Chapter 3 addresses practical considerations that should be taken into account during the assessment process. Part II, Informal Procedures: Basic Tools for Teachers, includes chapters on observation, including functional behavior assessment (Chapter 4), criterion-referenced testing and curriculum-based assessment (Chapter 5), and portfolio and other alternative assessment procedures (Chapter 6).

Part III, consisting of Chapters 7 through 10, provides a discussion and overview of the instruments and procedures most widely used to assess an individual's underlying *abilities*. This includes chapters on the assessment of intelligence (Chapter 7), adaptive behavior (Chapter 8), behavioral and emotional status (Chapter 9), and language (Chapter 10). Part IV focuses on the assessment of *achievement*, including general achievement (Chapter 11), reading (Chapter 12), mathematics (Chapter 13), and written expression (Chapter 14). The following format is used to describe the instruments in these two parts: A general description is followed by a more specific description of subtests or other components of each test; a discussion about how the scores are interpreted; a subsection focusing on technical characteristics including standardization, reliability, and validity; and a review of the relevant research (discussed later). Finally, for each test described, an overview box summarizes the information and suggests uses for the tests.

The Review of Relevant Research section for each major test is a feature unique to this textbook, and it describes the literature that practitioners will find useful for test selection, administration, and interpretation. Specifically, these reviews highlight studies dealing with the reliability and validity of the instruments, as well as their use with special education students. The research studies were located by a computer search. The information yielded by the search was cross-checked against the following periodicals: *Assessment for Effective Instruction, Learning Disability Quarterly, Remedial and Special Education, Journal of Learning Disabilities, Journal of Special Education, Exceptional Children, Psychology in the Schools, Journal of School Psychology, Education and Training in Developmental Disabilities, Intellectual and Developmental Disabilities, American Journal of Mental Retardation, Gifted Child Quarterly,* and *Educational and Psychological Measurement.* For the eighth edition, literature from 2005 through 2007 was updated.

Part V, Special Assessment Considerations, includes chapters describing assessment procedures and instruments relevant for early childhood (Chapter 15) and for older students with vocational/transitional needs (Chapter 16). The book concludes with two case studies (Chapter 17) in which the assessment process is followed from initial identification through the development of an Individualized Education Program (IEP).

A number of unique features have been retained in the eighth edition:

1. A pragmatic approach to assessment is emphasized.
2. A summary matrix is provided for most chapters. This matrix presents information about specific instruments and techniques in a format that allows easy comparison of the instruments for suggested use and target population. The matrix also includes a statement of any special considerations of which a user should be aware. Finally, for each instrument or technique, the matrix gives the educational relevance for exceptional students. The matrices are directly related to the assessment model proposed in Chapter 2.
3. Both informal and formal assessment procedures are included, with emphasis on how each kind of procedure fits into the assessment process.
4. A thorough review of relevant research is provided for each major norm-referenced instrument. The review emphasizes the use of the test with exceptional students.
5. An overview box is provided for each test. The overview summarizes the age range, technical adequacy, and suggested use for the test. This feature adds to the value of this book as a reference text.
6. The book examines instruments and techniques both for students with mild disabilities and for students with severe disabilities. The two case studies in Chapter 17 reflect this emphasis.
7. An instructor's manual that includes test questions and activities is available.

Needless to say, many individuals deserve my sincere appreciation. I would like to thank Dr. Steve Richards, University of Dayton, for his assistance in the preparation of Chapter 16. I would also like to thank the following reviewers of this edition for their time and effort: Stephen Byrd, Elon University; Diane

Giannola, Rider University; Carolynne Gischel, Florida Gulf Coast University; Linda Gronberg-Quinn, Community College of Baltimore County; Joan G. Henley, Arkansas State University; Patty Kohler, University of Central Arkansas; Sandra Manning, University of Southern Mississippi; Theresa M. Nowak, Eastern Kentucky University; Michael F. Shaughnessy, Eastern New Mexico University; Denise A. Simard, SUNY-Plattsburgh; Delar K. Singh, Eastern Connecticut State University; and Marcee M. Steele, University of North Carolina, Wilmington.

Helpful Supplementary Material to Accompany this Edition

For the Instructor

Instructor's Manual with Test Items. The Instructor's Manual has several useful features. These include:

- An overview of each chapter that provides a concise summary of the content included as well as specific points that should be highlighted.
- In-class and out-of-class activities that the instructor can assign. Many of these require the students to apply course content. Examples are establishing basals and ceilings and conducting error analyses.
- A test bank of over 600 items. These include multiple-choice, true-false, and discussion items. Each item is also cross-referenced to the page in the text where the content is located.
- Materials such as math worksheets to be used with many of the activities.

ACCESS: The Instructor's Manual/Test Bank may be accessed for immediate download by logging in at our *Instructor Resource Center*. Your one-time registration to our Instructor Resource Center opens the door to Pearson Higher Education's premium digital resources.

1. Go to the Pearson Higher Education Website (www.pearsonhighered.com).
2. Click on the "Educators" link on the home page.
3. Click on the "Download instructor resources" link.
4. Either log in using the password provided to you by your Pearson representative, or choose the "Register" option. (Note: We suggest you contact your local Pearson rep for the fastest service.)
5. Follow the instructions for using the "search" menus to locate Taylor's *Assessment of Exceptional Students,* Eighth Edition.

For the Student

Companion Website
The Companion Website is an online study guide that provides additional information and interactive experiences. The following links are provided for each chapter:

- **Overview.** Provides a brief overview of the chapter.
- **Objectives.** Act as a guide for the student to understand what is important.
- **Terms to Know.** The specific terms and the page numbers where they are discussed.
- **Multiple-Choice Questions.** For student check of understanding.
- **True-False Questions.** For student check of understanding.
- **Essay Questions.** For student check of understanding.

- **Assessment-Based Activity.** Many of these parallel the activities in the Instructor's Manual to provide additional practice.
- **In-Depth Case Study: June.** This unique feature is an interactive case study. Information about June is introduced in each chapter. For example, prereferral assessment information is provided in Chapter 2, intelligence test data in Chapter 7, achievement test data in Chapter 11, and so on. Students are given questions as well as suggested answers. Information in this section is cumulative, resulting in a complete file with questions/answers in Chapter 17.
- **Web Destinations.** Provides links to other Websites that have important information on the chapter topic.

ACCESS: Go to www.prenhall.com/taylor8e.

part one

Introduction to Assessment

Issues and Concerns

Assessment is a critical component of the educational process. It allows educators and other professionals to make relevant educational decisions. Some individuals downplay the importance of assessment, believing that time spent assessing would better be spent teaching. If, however, appropriate assessment procedures are conducted, the information obtained can be used to enhance the teaching process.

In this part, several issues important to the establishment of appropriate assessment procedures will be discussed. The potential uses as well as the limitations of assessment will be considered. Assessment does not occur in a vacuum; neither is it left totally to the discretion of the assessor. Many important historical events and philosophical movements have shaped the assessment procedures found in today's schools. Similarly, there have been significant court cases and legislation that mandate certain assessment practices. These areas, discussed in Chapter 1, will provide the reader with the *historical framework* for developing assessment procedures.

Assessment should also be practical and efficient. One important issue is knowing when to apply what assessment procedure. This requires, among other things, understanding the types and purposes of various assessment sources. Such information is provided and an assessment model is presented in Chapter 2. This will give the reader a *conceptual framework* for developing assessment procedures.

Assessment certainly is more than the simple administration of a test. Nonetheless, testing is an integral part of the assessment process. Because tests supply only a *sample* of a student's behavior, it is important to understand all the variables that can affect test performance. More important, these variables must be considered when making decisions based on that test performance. Everyone involved in the assessment process must be extremely aware of the ethical responsibilities. The ethical use of test information, confidentiality, and even the choice of tests or other assessment procedures based on ethical considerations are just a few issues that must be considered. The practical considerations related to the testing process and the test themselves, as well as ethical considerations, are discussed in Chapter 3.

AFTER READING PART ONE
You Should Be Able To:

- Identify historical events, philosophical movements, litigation, and legislation that have had an effect on assessment procedures in today's schools.

- Identify important questions that should be asked before initiating any assessment, resulting in a more efficient and practical process.

- Identify factors that can affect assessment results, including those related to the examiner, the examinee, and the test itself.

- Identify ethical considerations that should be addressed during the assessment process.

chapter one

Assessment

Historical, Philosophical, and Legal Considerations

Assessment refers to the gathering of relevant information to help an individual make decisions. The educational and psychological assessment of exceptional students, specifically, involves the collection of information that is relevant in making decisions regarding appropriate goals and objectives, teaching strategies, and program placement. The assessment process should include the general education teacher, special education teacher, school psychologist, specialists, therapists, parents, and any other individuals involved in a student's educational program. Assessment should be an active, ongoing process that has a clearly specified purpose. Further, it can and should be an individualized process, as individualized as instructional strategies are. Not only is it inappropriate, it is also practically impossible to use the same group of tests with all exceptional students; by definition, this population has unique characteristics and concerns that require an individualized approach.

> **ASSESSMENT**
> The gathering of relevant information to help an individual make decisions.

> Assessment should be individualized based on each student's characteristics.

Although educational and psychological assessment has been considered by some to be synonymous with testing, it involves much more than the simple acts of administering and scoring tests and reporting test scores. It includes the careful analysis of the information provided by various instruments and techniques (including tests), which should result in functional, relevant, appropriate decisions. The choice of which instrument or technique to use and the decision about which method of analysis or interpretation is best depends largely on the goal or purpose for the assessment. This textbook focuses on this pragmatic issue that emphasizes the appropriate use of various instruments and techniques, depending on the specific purpose for the assessment.

included
IN THIS CHAPTER

Historical Events and Philosophical Movements
- Early Twentieth Century
- 1920s–1950s
- 1960s
- Early 1970s
- Late 1970s and Early 1980s
- Mid-1980s–Early 1990s
- Early 1990s–2000
- The New Millennium

Relevant Assessment Litigation
- *Hobson v. Hansen* (1968)
- *Diana v. State Board of Education* (1970)
- *Larry P. v. Riles* (1971)
- *Guadalupe v. Tempe* (1972)
- *PASE v. Hannon* (1980)
- *Luke S. & Hans S. v. Nix et al.* (1982)
- *Jose P. v. Ambach* (1983)
- *Marshall v. Georgia* (1984)
- *Gerstmyer v. Howard County Public Schools* (1994)

Relevant Legislation
- P.L. 94-142
- P.L. 99-457
- P.L. 101-476
- P.L. 101-336
- P.L. 103-382
- P.L. 105-17
- P.L. 107-110
- P.L. 108-446

Before addressing these pragmatic issues that will shape the assessment process, it is important to discuss other factors that have had, and will continue to have, an effect on assessment policies and procedures used in the schools. These include historical events and philosophical movements, court cases (litigation), and legislation that directly or indirectly affect assessment practices. In this chapter, a chronology of the historical, philosophical, and legal events that have influenced assessment practices is presented, followed by a summary of the legislation that has led to, or has been a result of, those events.

Historical Events and Philosophical Movements

Early Twentieth Century

Alfred Binet had a major impact on early assessment efforts.

Before special education became a formal field, most assessment issues were related to the measurement of the areas of intelligence and personality. This reflected the beginnings of the special education field with its roots in medicine and psychology. Alfred Binet had perhaps the first major influence on the use of assessment instruments with exceptional individuals. He and Theodore Simon were asked by the Ministry of Education in France to develop an intelligence test that could be used to differentiate individuals with and without mental retardation. Their test was translated into English in 1908 and was revised by Terman in 1916 and called the *Stanford-Binet*. This marked the first formal attempt to provide an objective measure of intelligence.

1920s–1950s

Attempts at measuring personality characteristics and emotional status were popular over the next three decades, using a variety of instruments tied primarily to the fields of psychology and psychiatry. These included the development of projective tests such as the *Rorschach Ink Blot Test* (Rorschach, 1932), thematic picture tests such as the *Thematic Apperception Test* (Murray, 1943), and personality inventories such as the *Minnesota Multiphasic Personality Inventory* (Hathaway & Meehl, 1951). These tests are still used today, although their relevance in education has been questioned (see Chapter 9 for a discussion). Also during this period, there was increased interest in the measurement of achievement. Many group achievement tests such as the *Metropolitan Achievement Tests* were developed more than fifty years ago and continue to be revised as educational demands and curricula in the schools change.

1960s

PROCESS TESTS
Instruments designed purportedly to measure how a student processes information.

In the 1960s, the role of assessment, particularly through standardized testing, became increasingly popular. When the term *learning disabilities* was coined in 1963, the door opened for the development of tests that went beyond the measurement of intelligence, personality, and achievement. During this period, primarily as a result of the application of the medical/neurological model, **process tests** became very popular. These included perceptual-motor tests and other instruments designed to measure how a student processed information. Examples of such tests were the *Illinois Test of Psycholinguistic Ability* (Kirk, McCarthy, & Kirk, 1968) and the *Developmental Test of Visual Perception* (Frostig, Lefever, & Whittlesey, 1966). Interestingly, both instruments were revised three decades later (Hammill, Pearson, & Voress, 1993; Hammill & Wiederholt, 2001). The overemphasis on perceptual-motor testing, in particular, had quite an influence on the field of assessment.

Misuses of Perceptual-Motor Tests.   Perceptual-motor theorists such as Kephart, Cratty, and Frostig were partially responsible for the movement toward perceptual-motor testing during the 1960s. These theorists emphasized the importance—in fact, the necessity—of perceptual-motor skills in the acquisition of academic skills. The problem was that many professionals stressed perceptual-motor development to the exclusion of academic-skill development. In other words, people assumed that development of perceptual-motor skills would "generalize" to academic areas, because such skills were considered a crucial component of the academic skills. Historically, this movement led to (1) the use of perceptual-motor tests to predict achievement, (2) the use of perceptual-motor tests to help determine "modality strengths and weaknesses" for teaching purposes, and (3) the development of remedial programs designed specifically for perceptual-motor skills. Unfortunately, subsequent research did not support the use of perceptual-motor tests for any of these three purposes (e.g., Arter & Jenkins, 1977; Hallahan & Cruickshank, 1973; Larsen & Hammill, 1975).

It should be noted that more modern approaches to process assessment have abandoned the emphasis on perceptual-motor skills. For example, the *Process Assessment of the Learner* (Berninger, 2000) focuses on skills such as phonological processing and orthographic coding.

Early 1970s

Partially as a result of the backlash against perceptual-motor testing, the 1970s brought a somewhat negative view of standardized testing in special education. This negativism was fueled by court cases accusing the schools of discriminatory use of assessment information and charging that many of the tests themselves were discriminatory (discussed later in this chapter). Also at this time, the behavioral model became prominent; included in this model was an emphasis on observation and a de-emphasis on the use of test data on which inferences had to be made. Indeed, there was almost a moratorium against the use of many standardized tests in special education; certainly there was a widespread acknowledgment of their limitations.

Late 1970s and Early 1980s

To further cloud the issue, the passage of Public Law (P.L.) 94-142 (discussed later in this chapter) mandated certain assessment procedures (e.g., nondiscriminatory evaluation) and implied the need for various types of assessment procedures. For example, P.L. 94-142 required that students receive a specific label in order to receive funding; this implied the need for standardized norm-referenced tests. Conversely, the requirement of an Individualized Education Program (IEP) suggested the need for more precise informal measures. Suffice it to say that in the late 1970s and early 1980s there was a shift in emphasis to more informal assessment tempered by the realization that more formal assessment procedures would need to be used as well. The philosophy stated in Chapter 2 and applied throughout this book is that *both* types of assessment procedures can and should be helpful. The appropriate use of both types occurs when the purpose for the evaluation is matched to the type of assessment procedure and when the strengths and limitations of both approaches are recognized.

Mid-1980s–Early 1990s

In the mid-1980s, a major philosophical movement called the **Regular Education Initiative (REI)** affected the field of education and its assessment practices. In an article entitled "Educating Children with Learning Problems: A Shared Responsibility," Madeleine Will (1986) summarized several reasons why and how the concept of special education might be changed. Will, who was assistant secretary of the Office of Special Education and Rehabilitative Services in the U.S. Office of Education, was in a unique position both to evaluate the state of special education and to suggest any necessary changes. She noted, for example, that the current system separated regular[1] and special education, stigmatized certain students as being handicapped, and addressed failure of students rather than prevention of problems. She also noted that whereas approximately 10 percent of the school population might be eligible to receive special education, another 10 to 20 percent had significant problems in school yet did not qualify for special education. Will's recommendation was to have regular educators and special educators "collectively contribute skills and resources to carry out individual educational plans based on individualized educational needs." Specifically, she suggested that assessment and intervention strategies be employed before the referral for special education to try to prevent the identification of a child as handicapped. Figure 1.1 shows a model for *prereferral intervention* that emphasizes the amount of assessment and intervention that should take place before a referral is made. Will also suggested that we need to emphasize the *curriculum-based assessment* procedures discussed in Chapter 5.

Early 1990s–2000

Partially as an extension of the REI, educational reform efforts continued in the 1990s. The most notable, as well as controversial, was **full inclusion**. Proponents of full inclusion believe that *all* students, regardless of the type or severity of their disabilities, should be taught in the general education classroom at their home school. Their reasoning is that these students are a minority group, and denying them access to the general education classroom violates their civil rights (e.g., Stainback & Stainback, 1992).

Critics point out that full inclusion violates the concept of the *least restrictive environment* mandated by federal law, which suggests that a continuum of placement options should be available (discussed later in this chapter). Regardless of the various attitudes toward inclusion, however, its effect on assessment is straightforward. It means that the general education teacher is much more involved in the overall process.

Another visible movement was the shift toward *alternative assessment* procedures. This category includes authentic, performance-based, and portfolio techniques. Their common link is that they provide direct measurements of student learning and progress and focus on the process rather than the product of learning (Rivera, 1993). Wolf, LeMahieu, and Eresh (1992) noted that these approaches tap higher-level thinking and problem-solving skills that emphasize the critique of the student work as part of a dynamic, ongoing process. For example, instead of a teacher determining how many words a student can read compared with others (traditional assessment), he or she might determine the student's attitude

REGULAR EDUCATION INITIATIVE (REI)
An initiative that advocated the integration of general and special education into one educational system for all students; resulted in the widespread use of curriculum-based assessment and prereferral assessment.

The Regular Education Initiative had an impact on assessment practices.

FULL INCLUSION
The belief that all students should be taught in the general education classroom at their home school.

Full inclusion resulted in the general education teacher's becoming involved with assessment.

Alternative assessment procedures have increased in popularity.

[1]Although the term *regular education* was preferred during this time period, the more accepted term *general education* is used throughout the remainder of this book.

FIGURE 1.1   A Model for Prereferral Intervention

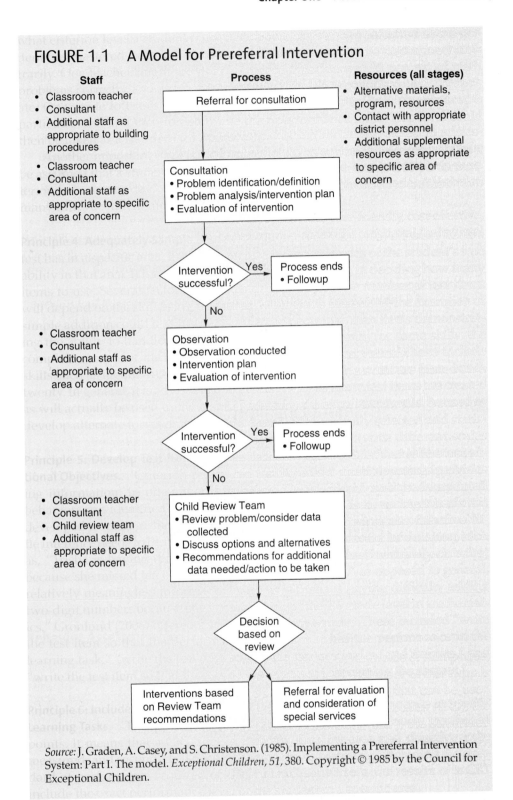

Staff	**Process**	**Resources (all stages)**

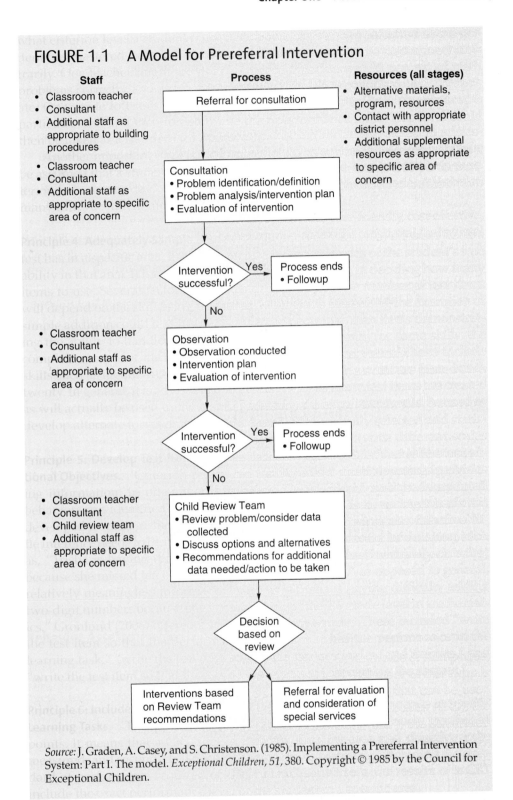

Source: J. Graden, A. Casey, and S. Christenson. (1985). Implementing a Prereferral Intervention System: Part I. The model. *Exceptional Children, 51,* 380. Copyright © 1985 by the Council for Exceptional Children.

toward reading, develop a list of the books the student has read, create a tape of the student reading, and obtain the student's self-evaluation (portfolio assessment). Portfolio assessment and other alternative assessment approaches are discussed in depth in Chapter 6.

The New Millennium

Two other areas currently are receiving considerable attention as a result of recent legislation (Individuals with Disabilities Education Improvement Act of 2004 (IDEA 04), discussed later in this chapter). First, the law requires that students with disabilities must be included in large-scale state and districtwide testing (with appropriate *accommodations,* when necessary). Further, *alternate assessments* must be developed and implemented for those students who cannot participate in the regular testing programs, even with accommodations. These alternate assessments might include, but are not limited to, the alternative procedures described above. This issue will be discussed later in this chapter. IDEA 04 also places an emphasis on *functional behavioral assessment.* Functional behavioral assessment, among other purposes, is used to evaluate a student's behavior within an environmental context that leads directly to an intervention plan. For example, an assessment of a student's disruptive behavior might include the determination of when it occurs, where it occurs, around whom it occurs, what happens right before it occurs, what happens right after it occurs, and so forth. Functional behavioral assessment is discussed in Chapter 4. The third area that IDEA 04 addressed that has an impact on assessment practices is the use of **response to intervention (RTI)** to assist in the identification of students with learning disabilities. RTI is described later in this chapter.

> **RESPONSE TO INTERVENTION (RTI)**
> A tiered model of increasing levels of intervention that can be used to help identify students with a learning disability.

Relevant Assessment Litigation[2]

The majority of the court cases related to assessment practices, particularly the earlier ones, focused on the discriminatory use of tests with ethnic-minority children. Many of these cases also helped lead to the nondiscriminatory evaluation of P.L. 94-142 that, in turn, is infused in current evaluation requirements under IDEA 04 (discussed later in this chapter). Those cases included *Hobson v. Hansen, Diana v. California, Larry P. v. Riles, Guadalupe v. Tempe, PASE v. Hannon,* and *Marshall v. Georgia.* Later cases focused more on assessment practices such as the timely delivery of assessment procedures. These included *Luke S. & Hans S. v. Nix et al., Jose P. v. Ambach,* and *Gerstmyer v. Howard County Public Schools.* Each of these cases is summarized next.

Hobson v. Hansen (1968)

This was the first major case focusing on the misuse or discriminatory use of test scores. The plaintiff charged that test scores were being used to "track" minority students, particularly black students, into the lower track of the educational programs. The court found the grouping of students for tracking purposes to be unconstitutional because of its discriminatory nature.

Diana v. State Board of Education (1970)

This case was filed in California on behalf of nine Spanish-speaking children who were placed into classes for students with mental retardation based on their

---

[2]In the section on litigation and legislation, terminology specific to each case or law is used to maintain historical integrity. Throughout the remainder of the book, current terminology is used (e.g., "student with a disability" instead of "handicapped student").

scores from intelligence tests administered in English. Among the consent decrees from this case, several had particular relevance: (1) language competence should be assessed, (2) tests in the student's primary language should be subsequently administered, (3) more emphasis should be placed on nonverbal measures for students whose primary language is not English, and (4) students who were placed incorrectly should be appropriately reevaluated.

Larry P. v. Riles (1971)

The *Larry P.* case focused on the alleged cultural bias of intelligence tests. This is perhaps the best known and certainly the most complex court case that has dealt with assessment issues. In fact, the case surfaced and resurfaced for more than fifteen years in appeals and was the basis for another court case, *Crawford v. Honig* (1988). The *Larry P.* case was first filed in 1971. Several injunctions were imposed until 1977, followed by an eight-month trial. Finally, in 1979, Judge Peckham reached the following conclusions: (1) intelligence tests are biased, (2) the use of intelligence tests to classify black children as having mental retardation was prohibited, and (3) the overrepresentation of black children as having educable mental retardation must be eliminated. The state of California appealed the decision, but it was upheld by a two-to-one vote in 1984. In 1986, the *Larry P.* plaintiffs again went to court, charging that overrepresentation of black students had not changed markedly since the early 1970s, although the label had changed to "learning handicapped" (Reschly, 1991). The result was the complete prohibition of intelligence tests for the purpose of identifying or placing black students into special education. Further, an intelligence test could not be used with a black student *even with parental consent*. This last point is the basis for the previously mentioned *Crawford v. Honig,* in which black parents argued discrimination because their children *could not* be evaluated using an intelligence test. One can clearly see the impact that the *Larry P.* case has had on assessment procedures overall and in California in particular.

Larry P. v. Riles: Important California case addressing bias in intelligence testing.

Guadalupe v. Tempe (1972)

This case was similar to the *Diana* case with similar conclusions. In addition, however, this case noted the importance of evaluating adaptive behavior before labeling a student as having mental retardation. (Adaptive behavior is discussed in Chapter 8.)

PASE v. Hannon (1980)

Ironically, another court case almost identical to the *Larry P.* case was heard in the state of Illinois with the opposite conclusions. Provided with similar evidence, Judge Grady ruled that intelligence test bias had an insignificant influence on psychoeducational assessment and that the overrepresentation was not regarded as discriminatory (Reschly, 1991). Clearly, this confused the overall issue of test bias. It did, however, help formulate the professional question of whether the right issue is being debated. Is it the tests that are biased, or are tests being used in a biased fashion (Taylor, 1997)?

Luke S. & Hans S. v. Nix et al. (1982)

This case was similar to that of *Jose P.*, which is discussed next. There were estimates that as many as 10,000 students were not being evaluated within the sixty-day period after referral noted in Louisiana's guidelines. The court agreed with the plaintiffs and noted that the state should provide greater assessment *before* the referral is made (prereferral assessment). The case also resulted in more training of both general and special educators in the area of assessment.

Jose P. v. Ambach (1983)

This suit filed against New York City was concerned with the appropriate delivery of services. Specifically, the plaintiffs noted the delays in providing services to students referred for special education. The judge sided with the plaintiffs and, among other things, charged that the district must provide a *timely evaluation* after a student is referred. This was defined as a maximum of thirty days from referral to evaluation.

Marshall v. Georgia (1984)

In this case, the plaintiffs alleged that overrepresentation of black students in special education was caused by violations of procedural regulations and improper interpretation of state and federal guidelines regarding classification and placement. Although the issues of intelligence tests and IQs were discussed, they clearly took a subordinate role. Again in this case the defense of the school district was supported, although procedural violations were acknowledged and prereferral intervention guidelines were established (Reschly, 1991). It would appear that, for the most part, the specific allegations against test bias will probably be debated outside the courtroom in the future.

Gerstmyer v. Howard County Public Schools (1994)

This case demonstrated the importance of a timely evaluation. The school district had been informed of the need for an evaluation four months before a child entered the first grade. The evaluation, however, was not conducted until six months after the referral. The parents sued the district for the costs of private schooling and tutoring caused by the delay in evaluation. The court sided with the parents and made the district reimburse the costs.

Students have the right to a timely evaluation.

Relevant Legislation

Along with philosophical movements and litigation comes legislation. Interestingly, although in some cases the philosophical movements and litigation have led to legislation, in others the legislation has led to philosophical movements and litigation. Among the relevant legislation that affects assessment practices is P.L. 94-142 (the *Education for All Handicapped Children Act*), as well as various amendments to that law including P.L. 99-457, P.L. 101-476 (the *Individuals with Disabilities Education Act* [*IDEA*]), P.L. 105-17 (IDEA 97), and the latest reauthorization of IDEA in 2004. Others include P.L. 101-336 (the *Americans with Disabilities Act*) and P.L. 107-110 (the *No Child Left Behind Act*).

Public Law 94-142: Education for All Handicapped Children Act (EHA)

The law that had perhaps the most impact on the field of special education was the Education for All Handicapped Children Act (P.L. 94-142). Although this law has been amended several times, it remains the basis for changes in special education that have had a profound effect on assessment practices. The law emphasized the following six principles (*Federal Register*, 1977):

1. **Zero reject:** All handicapped children should be provided with a free, appropriate public education.
2. **Nondiscriminatory evaluation:** This principle was defined as avoiding discrimination in the

    . . . procedures used . . . to determine whether a child is handicapped and the nature and extent of the special education and related services that the child needs. The term means procedures used selectively with a child and does not include basic tests administered to or procedures used with all children in a school, grade or class. (*Federal Register*, 1977, p. 42494)

3. **Individualized Education Programs (IEPs):** All students with disabilities must have an IEP; among other components, IEPs should include (1) documentation of the current level of performance, (2) annual goals, (3) short-term objectives, and (4) evaluation procedures and schedules for determining the mastery of short-term objectives. Other requirements included documentation of the type and duration of the planned services, and information related to the extent of general education programming.
4. **Least restrictive environment:** This was (and continues to be) perhaps the most publicized and least understood principle of P.L. 94-142. Although it implies that children with disabilities should be educated with children without disabilities to the maximum extent possible, it is not necessarily synonymous with full inclusion. The idea of the law is that, ultimately, a child with a disability should be included; however, the law does not require that a child be included if the type or severity of the disability precludes the child's successful performance in an inclusive environment. As was mentioned earlier, the current emphasis on full inclusion has challenged the least restrictive environment concept.

    > P.L. 94-142: Law having the greatest effect on special education assessment.

5. **Due process:** This principle referred to a system of checks and balances that seeks to ensure the fairness of educational decisions and the accountability of both the professionals and the parents who make those decisions (Strickland & Turnbull, 1993).
6. **Parental participation:** This principle ensured that parents were informed of decisions made about their children and encouraged their participation in the decision-making process.

In reality, all of these principles addressed by P.L. 94-142 indirectly affect or are affected by assessment. The two principles that had the most direct relevance were *nondiscriminatory evaluation* and *parental participation*. These areas will be discussed in more depth later in this chapter when current regulations and requirements are cited. In subsequent years, P.L. 94-142 was amended and reauthorized, and other laws were passed that had a direct impact on individuals with disabilities.

Public Law 99-457: EHA Amendments of 1986

Of the several amendments to P.L. 94-142, the one that had the greatest impact on the area of assessment was P.L. 99-457. Among the recommendations in this amendment was the need to identify and establish programs for infants and toddlers (children from birth through age 2) with disabilities.

> P.L. 99-457: Law impacting assessment of children from birth to age 5.

This increased emphasis on early intervention created a need for more and improved diagnostic procedures for young children from birth through age 5. This resulted in the creation of new developmental tests and the revision of several older ones. Chapter 15 addresses infant and early childhood assessment.

Public Law 101-476: Individuals with Disabilities Education Act (IDEA)

In 1990, President George H. W. Bush signed the Amendments to the Education of the Handicapped Act, which changed its name to the Individuals with Disabilities Education Act (IDEA). All of the references to *handicaps* noted in P.L. 94-142 and subsequent amendments were replaced by the term *disabilities*. For example, the phrase "handicapped infants and toddlers" was replaced with "infants and toddlers with disabilities."

IDEA: Added autism and traumatic brain injury as disability categories.

Although the most sweeping changes in IDEA dealt with the authorization of grants for special programs and services, a few of the changes did have some influence on assessment practices. Among them were an emphasis on transition services that includes vocational evaluation (discussed in Chapter 16) and a requirement for an *Individual Transition Program (ITP)* by at least the age of 16. Another change was the inclusion of *traumatic brain injury* and *autism* as separate categories of disability. All of the categories under IDEA are listed in Chapter 2.

Public Law 101-336: Americans with Disabilities Act (ADA)

Another major piece of legislation passed in 1990 was the Americans with Disabilities Act (ADA), which is essentially a civil rights act for individuals with disabilities. The law requires that accommodations must be made by schools, employers, and government agencies to allow persons with disabilities to participate to the fullest extent possible in daily living activities. This includes elimination of physical barriers (e.g., requiring ramps for wheelchair access) and modification of equipment (e.g., providing a relay service with an interpreter for an employee with a hearing impairment).

Unlike IDEA, which is relevant only until a person is age 21, ADA covers individuals of all ages. Thus, it is relevant to postsecondary settings and assessment of adults with disabilities. Implicit in this law is accommodation for individuals with disabilities when they are being assessed. For example, a college student with a learning disability might need extended time to complete an exam. Similarly, a student with a visual impairment might need to be evaluated using an enlarged print version of the test. Also unlike IDEA, the ADA does not provide funding to help address its mandates.

Public Law 103-382: Improving America's Schools Act

In 1994, the Elementary and Secondary Education Act of 1965 (ESEA) was signed into law as the *Improving America's Schools Act*. One of its main provisions was to require states to set standards for student achievement and develop and administer assessments to measure students' progress.

Public Law 105-17: Reauthorization of the Individuals with Disabilities Education Act (IDEA 97)

In 1997, IDEA was reauthorized by Congress, resulting in several changes. In general, the intent of the law was maintained, but some requirements were modified and several were added. Some of the language was new and some was retained from previous legislation. For example, in the description of appropriate evaluation procedures in P.L. 105-17 (IDEA 97), the *concept* of nondiscriminatory evaluation was maintained but was subsumed under a more general section called "Conduct of Evaluation" (*Federal Register*, 1997, pp. 81–82). In addition to the general and specific requirements that must be addressed when conducting an evaluation, two other areas that specifically affected assessment procedures were *parent participation* and *participation in assessments*. This latter issue focuses on the inclusion of students with disabilities in statewide or district-level assessment programs.

Public Law 107-110: No Child Left Behind Act

The 2002 reauthorization of ESEA, *No Child Left Behind* (NCLB), increased the emphasis on standards and accountability even more by requiring annual assessments in reading and math for all students in grades 3–8 beginning in the years 2005–2006 and the addition of science assessment in 2007–2008 (although the science assessment will be initially mandated for only three grade spans as in the 1994 law). Interestingly, there is a caveat that the implementation of the new assessments may be deferred if Congress does not appropriate specified levels of funding for the testing. Another change is that the NCLB now requires reading assessments using tests written in English for any student who has attended school in the United States (excluding Puerto Rico) for three or more consecutive years. This has obvious implications for students from multicultural backgrounds. NCLB has had a major effect on all students, including those with disabilities by emphasizing "high-stakes assessment" (as opposed to "low-stakes assessment.")

NCLB emphasizes high-stakes assessment.

Low-stakes assessment refers to the use of assessment data for individual diagnostic purposes or for evaluating the effects of instruction. The use of high-stakes assessment, usually statewide assessment, on the other hand, might result in student promotion or retention, the teacher's evaluation, a basis for school funding and teacher raises, or perhaps a school district's certification. Particularly in the current educational atmosphere of standards and accountability, high-stakes assessment has become routine at the district and state levels. For example, in 1999, the state of Florida began its system of grading schools (A–F) based largely on a high-stakes assessment instrument called the Florida Comprehensive Assessment Test (FCAT). The school's grade has serious implications in areas such as funding.

High-stakes assessment has received considerable criticism.

Although there are many supporters of the current standards and accountability atmosphere, there also has been considerable backlash against high-stakes assessment by many parents and professionals. In some school districts, students have been kept home by their parents in an attempt to protest the pressure put on their children to succeed on these tests. One well-publicized event occurred in Scarsdale, New York. Almost 200 of the 290 eighth graders were encouraged by their parents to stay home to protest a statewide science test. The parents were concerned about the amount of classroom time that was being spent for test preparation. Similar boycotts were conducted in other states, including Massachusetts and Michigan. There is also evidence that teaching practices are largely determined by the content of high-stakes assessment (Boardman & Woodruff, 2004).

Another issue related to high-stakes assessment concerns the **adequate yearly progress (AYP)** required by NCLB for all students, including students with disabilities. Schools and districts that fail to make AYP are subject to

ADEQUATE YEARLY PROGRESS (AYP)
A measurement defined by the No Child Left Behind Act that allows the U.S. Department of Education to determine how every public school and school district in the country is performing academically.

corrective action. The goal is for all students to meet the requirements of proficiency by the 2013–2014 school year. One problem is that the state systems and the system used by NCLB are not always consistent. In other words, the systems used by the states to monitor and measure AYP might not be aligned with the AYP guidelines in NCLB. As an example, in 2003 in the state of Florida, 95 percent of elementary schools made a grade of A, B, or C based primarily on the statewide test, yet only 35 percent met U.S. AYP standards. The discrepancy was larger as the students got older (middle schools, 89 percent vs. 10 percent; high schools, 71 percent vs. 3 percent).

The underlying question in high-stakes assessment should be "Are higher test scores just higher test scores, or are they a true improvement in student learning?" Mehrens (2002) acknowledges that test scores clearly have improved in high-stakes assessment programs but questions whether this is a result of "teaching to the test." He noted that when states initiate graduation tests, the initial failure rates in the eighth and ninth grades are as high as 30 percent but decrease significantly to less than 5 percent by twelfth grade using remediation and sometimes biannual retests (Pipho, 1997). Mehren's interpretation is that the increase in scores represents a true improvement on the domain that the test samples but not necessarily a true improvement in the students' education. In other words, by limiting instruction just to specific domains that the test measures, scores likely will increase. This again gets into the issue of test preparation time and the possibility that other areas important to education are not being covered.

At the time of the completion of this book, NCLB was scheduled to be reauthorized, although it appears that it will take some time before differences in Congress will be worked out. Most of the principles of the original NCLB were recommended. There still is the lofty goal of having students read and do math on grade level by the year 2014. The states will also still be required to calculate and report AYP. Also proposed were several controversial provisions for students with disabilities. The major one was the introduction of the concept of **modified achievement standards.** The intent is to develop and use these modified standards for those students who are receiving an academic curriculum and are working toward a regular high school diploma but who are struggling. Essentially, it would allow states to use modified achievement standards for up to 2 percent of the students tested. Another 1 percent could be given an alternate assessment based on alternate standards, usually used with students with severe cognitive impairments. Thus the following assessment assessment options would exist for students with disabilities in the proposed reauthorization:

MODIFIED ACHIEVEMENT STANDARDS
Permits a limited group of students with disabilities who may not be able to reach grade-level achievement standards within the same time frame as other students.

1. Take the test with no accommodations (regular administration based on grade-level academic standards).
2. Take the test with appropriate accommodations.
3. Take the test using alternate assessment based on grade-level academic standards.
4. Take the test using alternate assessment based on modified academic standards (up to 2 percent).
5. Take the test using alternate assessment based on alternate academic standards (up to 1 percent).

Flexibility would be allowed in that states could determine the actual percentage of students who receive 4 and 5, as long as the total does not exceed 3 percent. These students could also take the assessment more than once, and the state could use their highest score when calculating and reporting AYP. Funds would be available that could assist the states in developing technically adequate assessments for students receiving the modified academic standards. As noted previously, these are only recommendations and, most likely, compromises will be made.

Public Law 108-446: Reauthorization of the Individuals with Disabilities Education Act (IDEA 04)

In general, IDEA 04 maintained most of the same requirements as IDEA 97 regarding the area of assessment, although some of the language was modified. There were, however, some changes. These include:

1. The establishment of a sixty-day time line from receipt of parent consent for eligibility evaluation to the actual determination of eligibility and educational needs of the student.
2. Changes in the frequency of occurrence of reevaluations (discussed later in this chapter).
3. Elimination of short-term objectives and benchmarks in students' individualized education programs except for those taking alternate assessments aligned with alternate achievement standards (discussed in Chapter 2).

Specifically, IDEA 04 states that in conducting the evaluations the local educational agency shall

> (A) use a variety of assessment tools and strategies to gather relevant functional, developmental, and academic information, including information provided by the parent, that may assist in determining whether the child is a child with a disability and the content of the child's individualized education program, including information related to enabling the child to be involved in and progress in the general curriculum or, for preschool children, to participate in appropriate activities.

This requirement, initially mandated in IDEA 97, represents a significant change in evaluation procedures under federal law. Several points are worthy of note. First, the emphasis is on functional, developmental, and academic information. Second, the law specifically states that information from the parents should be included in the evaluation. Third, the purpose of the evaluation is twofold: eligibility determination and IEP development. In the past, the initial evaluation too often leaned toward eligibility determination. Finally, the impact of inclusion and other philosophical positions can be seen in the requirement that the evaluation must provide information about how the student can best succeed in the general education classroom.

IDEA 04: Emphasizes use of assessment for developing educational programs.

> (B) not use any single measure or assessment as the sole criterion for determining whether a child is a child with a disability or determining an appropriate educational program for the child.

This point, found in previous legislation, was to ensure that students were not placed into special education based on the results from one instrument. Several of the previously discussed court cases that focused on the use of a single IQ to determine eligibility led to this mandate. The concept has been extended to the development of the IEP to make sure that those important decisions are made using several sources.

> (C) use technically sound instruments that may assess the relative contribution of cognitive and behavioral factors, in addition to physical or developmental factors.

This requirement makes two points. First, issues such as reliability and validity must be considered when choosing assessment instruments (see Chapter 3).

Second, the evaluation should focus on multiple areas; in fact, all areas related to the suspected disability should be assessed.

In addition to the three requirements just discussed, IDEA 04 listed several others that must be met. These include many of the nondiscriminatory evaluation requirements noted in earlier legislation. The requirements state that each local agency shall ensure

(A) tests and other evaluation materials used to assess a child—
   (i)   are selected and administered so as not to be discriminatory on a racial or cultural basis.

The search for nondiscriminatory evaluation procedures has been frustrating. Several proposed solutions have been attempted. Saenz and Huer (2003) discussed several, including renorming tests for a specific population, using nonstandardized measures, and using dynamic assessment procedures that measure how quickly a student learns new information (see Chapter 7). Others that have been tried include the development of culture-free or culture-specific tests, translation of existing tests, alteration of administration procedures, and a moratorium on testing. Unfortunately, none of these approaches has been a panacea. The Council for Exceptional Children (CEC, 1997) noted four concerns with attempts at nondiscriminatory evaluation. First, few instruments typically are published in languages other than English; therefore, they have to be translated. Second, the translation of a test is not always equivalent to the original because of language and dialect differences. As a good example of this point, consider an intelligence test item in which the examiner shows his or her thumb and asks, "What do you call this finger?" The formal word for thumb in Spanish is *pulgar,* but this word is rarely used; most Spanish-speaking children would probably respond "dedo gordo," a common colloquial phrase meaning "fat finger." This answer would be scored as incorrect, according to the scoring criteria in the manual (Padilla & Garza, 1975). Third, CEC observed that all but a few instruments are standardized on the North American culture and that making comparisons to individuals outside an individual's culture invalidates the results. Acevedo-Polakovich et al. (2007) pointed out that, in addition to instrument selection, there are many cultural factors to consider when evaluating Latino students. Finally, the CEC noted that although many schools use interpreters, this is not really a good solution. The interpreter might not translate properly, or there may be language distortion when certain words have no equivalent in another language. If these previously mentioned attempts at nondiscriminatory testing have been criticized, an important question arises: Can we at least maximize unbiased assessment if we can't eliminate bias altogether? (See Focus on Diversity.)

Unfortunately, inappropriate assessment of culturally and linguistically diverse students persists. Consider the following research findings:

- In an investigation of close to 150 school records of English-language learners referred for special education, only half were evaluated in their native language in the area of cognition (Yzquierdo, Blalock, & Torres-Valezquez, 2004).
- Over 80 percent of assessment personnel made eligibility decisions about a student based on insufficient data (Overton, Fielding, & Simonsson, 2004).
- School psychologists typically do not use legal and professional guidelines when assessing English-language learners (Figueroa & Newsome, 2006).

   (ii)   are provided and administered in the language and form most likely to yield accurate information on what the child knows and can do academically, developmentally, and functionally, unless it is not feasible to so provide or administer.

Nondiscriminatory evaluations are required.

focus on
Diversity

How Can We Maximize Nonbiased Assessment?

Several suggestions for maximizing nondiscriminatory assessment have been offered. For example, Leung (1996) noted that any test results obtained should be cross-validated with other sources such as observation and interviews. Also, Rogers (1998) argued that individuals who administer tests should receive considerable training to obtain cross-cultural competence. Others have suggested that examiners should have cultural and linguistic competencies. These include the examiner's self-awareness of his or her own cultural background as well as the child's cultural background (Quintana, Castillo, & Zamirripa, 2000). They also noted that there are many cultural characteristics that might impact testing behavior and that the examiner should be knowledgeable about these to make any necessary modifications. They also pointed out that test directions might be too difficult for an "on the spot" translation and that translated test items rarely reflect their true meaning.

The American Education Research Association (AERA), the American Psychological Association (APA), and the National Council on Measurement in Education (NCME) collaborated on the *Standards for Educational and Psychological Testing*, published by the AERA (1999). This document provides eleven standards related to testing individuals with diverse linguistic backgrounds. For example, when a test is translated, the methods used should be described and technical information (e.g., validity and reliability, discussed in Chapter 3) should be provided. In addition, necessary qualifications for test interpreters are given.

Considerable research points to the unfairness of using inappropriate tests with certain populations. Examples include using intelligence tests requiring motor responses for individuals with cerebral palsy or tests using visual input for children with low vision and auditory input for persons with hearing impairment. Similarly, using tests in English for children whose primary language is not English is clearly inappropriate as noted above. Although these examples are obvious, they demonstrate the need to ensure the measurement of skills using the appropriate language and form.

> (iii) are used for purposes for which the assessments or measures are valid and reliable.

The reliability and validity of tests and other assessment materials is an absolute prerequisite for a meaningful evaluation (see Chapter 3).

> (iv) are administered by trained and knowledgeable personnel; and
> (v) are administered in accordance with any instructions provided by the producer of such tests.

The *Standards for Educational and Psychological Testing* (AERA, 1999) specifically states that test users must have the proper training, professional credentials, and experience to handle that responsibility. At the very least, persons involved in evaluation should be thoroughly familiar with the instrument used and should be knowledgeable about the general area of assessment. The degree of expertise necessary, at least in terms of test administration, depends somewhat on the test used. To administer some tests (such as intelligence tests like the WISC-IV and the Stanford-Binet 5), certification and licenses are necessary.

Individuals must have proper qualifications to administer tests.

The amount of preparation required to administer most tests, however, often is left to the examiner's discretion. Such factors as test length, type of test, and degree of subjectivity in the scoring criteria should be considered in determining when an examiner is considered to be trained. Because of differences in length of administration and sophistication of scoring, for example, more preparation is required to administer a test such as the *Wechsler Individual Achievement Test II* than to administer the *Wide Range Achievement Test–4*, even though they are both individual achievement tests (see Chapter 11). Most test manuals will also give some indication of examiner qualifications.

(B) the child is assessed in all areas of suspected disability.

Previous legislation specified those areas that should be considered including health, vision, hearing, social and emotional status, general intelligence, academic performance, communicative status, and motor abilities. It also emphasizes the need for multidisciplinary evaluation procedures.

(C) assessment tools and strategies that provide relevant information that directly assists persons in determining the educational needs of the child are provided.

This again emphasizes that assessment information should be meaningful, functional, and directly related to the child's educational needs.

Another change in IDEA 04 was in the area of reevaluation. The importance of reevaluation was noted in an early court case, *Hoffman v. Board of Education* (1979), in which a student in kindergarten was evaluated in 1956 and placed in a class for children with retarded mental development. The psychologist, however, was unsure of the findings because the student had a severe speech problem and recommended retesting within a two-year period. The student was not evaluated until twelve years later. When he was retested, it was determined that he had an IQ of 94 and therefore did not have mental retardation. The Court decided that the student had been inappropriately placed all those years (Rothstein, 2000; Underwood & Mead, 1995). IDEA 04 indicates that reevaluation cannot occur more than once a year unless both the parent and the local education agency agree it is necessary. Also, it must occur at least every three years unless both parties agree that it is unnecessary. This approach requires that the existing evaluation data (including parent input, teacher input, and classroom-based assessment) be reviewed to determine whether additional data are necessary to address four questions. These are (1) Does the child continue to have a disability? (2) What are the present levels of academic achievement and related developmental needs? (3) Does the child continue to need special education and related services? and (4) Are additions and modifications in the educational program needed to meet the goals in the IEP? If no additional data are deemed necessary to answer these questions, the child does not have to be *formally* reevaluated unless the parents request that this be done.

(D) assessments of children with disabilities who transfer from one school district to another school district in the same academic year are coordinated with such childrens' prior and subsequent schools as necessary and as expeditiously as possible, to ensure prompt completion of full evaluations.

IDEA 04 addressed the need for coordination of assessment services for the first time.

Parental Participation and Due Process.   Public Law 94-142 initially mandated that parents have more input and active participation in the assessment process. IDEA 04 extended those rights. Among the procedural safeguards related to assessment afforded to parents are the following:

1. An opportunity to examine all their child's records.
2. An opportunity to participate in meetings about the identification, evaluation, and educational placement of their child.

3. The right to obtain an independent evaluation of their child. *Note:* The issue of the cost of the independent evaluation has been the source of litigation and debate. In general, if the parents have the evaluation conducted before the school district's evaluation, the district is *not* responsible for the cost. If, however, the parents disagree with the results of the school district's evaluation, then the cost of a subsequent independent evaluation is the responsibility of the district. An exception is if the issue is brought to a hearing and the hearing officer determines that the independent evaluation was erroneous or duplicative (Underwood & Mead, 1995). However, Rothstein (2000) noted that the cost and distraction of a due process hearing, in effect, forces the school to agree to pay for an independent evaluation. She also pointed out that this could be countered by the fact that many parents might not go to court because of the attorney's fees if they do not win their case.

4. The requirement that they be given written notification (in the parents' native language) for any change in the evaluation procedures or educational placement of their child.

5. The requirement that the parents give consent to the evaluation and educational placement. If the parents disagree, this could result in a due process hearing, in which a hearing officer makes an impartial judgment.

6. The opportunity to present complaints about the evaluation and the educational placement of their child.

In general, this law establishes that parents have the right, if not the obligation, to be aware of all steps in the special education process. In addition, it provides parents with due process options if they disagree with decisions made by the school district about their child. This involves an impartial hearing between the parents and the school district. In a survey of due process hearings, Havey (1999) reported that the majority were held over assessment issues and the appropriateness of the placement. One addition to IDEA 04 was procedural guidelines that require the appointment of a surrogate for students who are wards of the state or are homeless.

Participation in Assessments and Alternate Assessment.   As noted previously, the pressure and requirement for accountability have led states and school districts to develop large-scale, high-stakes assessments to document student competencies and progress. With the development of these assessment programs came the debate of whether students with disabilities should be involved and whether or how their scores should be included for reporting purposes. When IDEA was reauthorized a specific mandate was provided. Specifically, IDEA 04 stated:

(A) IN GENERAL—All children with disabilities are included in all general State and districtwide assessment programs, . . . with appropriate accommodations and alternate assessments where necessary and as indicated in their respective individualized education programs.

(B) ACCOMMODATION GUIDELINES—The State (or in the case of a districtwide assessment, the local educational agency) has developed guidelines for the provision of appropriate accommodations.

These provisions mean that every attempt should be made to include the student with a disability in the state or districtwide testing program and that accommodation guidelines must be developed. These accommodations might include, among others, increased time, a different setting, different response type (e.g., oral vs. written), and revised formats (e.g., enlarged print). CTB/McGraw-Hill (2004) grouped test accommodations into three categories based on their

Parents should be active participants in the assessment process.

potential influence on appropriate interpretation of the test scores. The categories are

1. Accommodations not expected to alter standard interpretation. An example is taking the test alone or in a study carrel.
2. Accommodations that may have an effect on standard interpretation. An example is allowing extra time for a timed test.
3. Accommodations that are likely to alter standard interpretation. An example is allowing a calculator for a math computation test.

Evidence does exist that accommodations can improve performance on large-scale tests. For example, Tindal, Heath, Hollenbeck, Almond, and Harniss (1998) found that students' performance on a statewide mathematics test improved when the students were read the items, thus eliminating the reading component. More information on testing accommodations is provided in Chapter 3. Table 1.1 provides some guidelines for using test accommodations.

> (C) ALTERNATE ASSESSMENTS
>   (i) The State (or in the case of a districtwide assessment, the local educational agency) has developed and implemented guidelines for the participation of children with disabilities in alternate assessments for those children who cannot participate in regular assessments . . . with accommodations as indicated in their respective individualized education programs.
>   (ii) REQUIREMENTS FOR ALTERNATE ASSESSMENTS—The guidelines shall provide for alternate assessments that—
>   (I) are aligned with the State's challenging academic content standards and challenging student academic achievement standards; and
>   (II) if the State had adopted alternate academic achievement standards permitted under the regulations promulgated to carry out section 1111(b)(1) of the Elementary and Secondary Act of 1965, measure the achievement of children with disabilities against those standards.

All students must participate in statewide tests or be given an alternate assessment.

The requirement for alternate assessment (initially in IDEA 97) came about because many students with disabilities were being excluded from large-scale state and district testing. These data have been monitored since 1990 by the National Center on Educational Outcomes (NCEO), which was funded by the Office of Special Education Programs. One of their responsibilities is to monitor the participation rate of students with disabilities in these assessment programs. As noted earlier, No Child Left Behind requires that all students, including those with disabilities, participate in these assessments. More recent data indicate that there has been much improvement in participation rates. Muller (2007), synthesizing data reported by the NCEO, stated that all fifty states reported general information for students with disabilities in the 2004–2005 academic year. She noted that the NCEO still made several recommendations for areas of improvement.

There have been numerous reports of different states' attempts to provide alternate assessments. For example, Kleinert, Haig, Kearns, and Kennedy (2000) described the performance-based portfolio approaches that Maryland and Kentucky have taken (see Chapter 6 for a discussion of performance and portfolio assessment). Florida has developed the *Performance Assessment System for Students with Disabilities* (PASS-D), which is a performance-based approach that focuses more on functional skills. In reality, the choice of an alternate assessment is usually based on the specific characteristics and needs of the student. Examples might include observation, interviews, different tests or types of tests, and, as noted previously, portfolios and performance assessment. The NCEO

TABLE 1.1   Guidelines for Using Accommodations

Accommodation	Considerations	Cautions
Read-aloud administration (teacher, audiotape, computer, videotape)	• When questions contain large amounts of text. • With students who have poor decoding skills but relatively high listening comprehension. • When assessing skills other than decoding, e.g., solving math problems.	• This accommodation can inflate test scores, especially when assessing reading skills. • The difficulty of some types of test items can increase with read-aloud administration.
Student read-aloud	• When assessing reading skills of students with learning disabilities.	• Research has focused on individual administration, which is time-consuming.
Dictated response (including use of speech-to-text software)	• When trying to measure written expression or composing skills.	• This accommodation has been used more frequently with younger students. • The quality of high school students' writing does not tend to improve. • Dictated response may inflate test scores for spelling, usage, and grammar.
Extended time	• When using special testing formats (e.g., Braille and oral administration) that require more time. • When predictive validity is a consideration (e.g., college placement tests).	• Extended time can inflate scores if not carefully controlled. • Students who do not manage time well do not benefit from this accommodation.
Multiple testing sessions (nonwriting)	• Breaking a test into shorter sessions has been helpful with low-achieving students.	• Multiple testing sessions have not been tested empirically on students with disabilities.
Multiple testing sessions (writing)	• More helpful with elementary-aged students than with adolescents.	• Benefits of this accommodation vary with age of student and specific instrument.
Large print	• Primarily for students with visual impairments. • Some students with learning disabilities may benefit.	• Studies of effect for this accommodation for students with learning disabilities have been contradictory, showing both a positive effect and no effect.
Change in setting	• Small-group accommodation (resource room) may actually be the most normal setting for some students. • Taking a test with a familiar teacher can have a positive effect.	• Little empirical basis exists for using or not using this accommodation on large-scale assessments for students with disabilities.

Source: E. Edgemon, B. Jablonski, and J. Lloyd. (2006). Large Scale Assessments: A Teacher's Guide to Making Decisions about Accommodations. *Teaching Exceptional Children, 38*(3), p. 9. Copyright 2006 by The Council for Exceptional Children. Reprinted with permission.

reported the results of a survey on states' use of alternate assessments. The procedures used the most were performance-based measures, analysis of IEPs, and other miscellaneous approaches. The majority used portfolio or performance assessment (Thompson & Thurlow, 2001). The NCEO also reported that there was some consensus on what outcomes should be evaluated. Five domains noted were academic and functional literacy, personal and social adjustment, contribution and citizenship, responsibility and independence, and physical health (Ysseldyke & Olsen, 1999). Four challenges have been identified for those developing alternate assessment policies and practices: deciding who should participate, deciding what should be assessed, creating reliable and valid assessments, and deciding what should be considered proficiency (Roach, 2005). Browder et al. (2003) reviewed the existing literature and concluded that the data were insufficient to determine if alternate assessment has lived up to its promises.

It is clear that states must have a clear rationale for *not* including students in assessment programs. The assumption is that they will participate unless it is not feasible to do so. Reasons for exemptions might be if the student's disability is severe enough that the assessment would not provide pertinent information on his or her progress or if the student was working toward some type of special diploma that did not include the test content in the curriculum. The law is also clear that if a student cannot participate, an alternate, more appropriate assessment must be given in its place. The alternate assessments, as mentioned earlier, might include performance-based, authentic, or portfolio assessment (see Chapter 6).

Response to Intervention (RTI).   IDEA 04 also mandated that states must be allowed to consider a student's response to scientific, research-based intervention as part of the evaluation procedures for the determination of a learning disability. This recommendation was made, in part, to avoid a "wait to fail" situation that was associated with the previous criterion of having to have a severe discrepancy between achievement and intelligence. There is still some disagreement about how RTI is best carried out and, to date, there is no single, accepted model. Figure 1.2 shows one model that has been suggested. In this model, *all* students are initially screened (Universal Screening). This might involve monitoring statewide testing results or administering some initial screening measure. For those who appear at risk, more intense instruction is given (Tier 1). Those who still struggle will get even more intervention (Tier 2). Finally, for those who still don't respond, an even more intense intervention is used (Tier 3). The following example describes this process.

> RTI has been recommended as one procedure to consider for the identification of a learning disability.

Of the thirty-five students in Ms. Bianco's third-grade class, eight were identified as having problems in reading based on their performance on the statewide assessment (Universal Screening). Those students stayed in her class but were given more instruction in phonics skills. Their progress was monitored for several weeks, and three of the eight responded favorably (Tier 1). The special education teacher, Ms. Caravella, consulted with Ms. Bianco and suggested some more intense strategies for the five struggling students. After a few weeks, all but two students were making acceptable progress (Tier 2). At that point the reading specialist began to work with the two students for an hour a day. One student did much better, but the other did not (Tier 3). At this point that student would be eligible for a diagnosis of learning disability.

FIGURE 1.2   Three-Tiered Response to Intervention (RTI) Model

UNIVERSAL SCREENING: All students are given a screening measure. Students at risk for academic failure are identified.

Tier 1
Students receive effective instruction in the general education setting, using validated practices. Student progress is monitored on a weekly basis. (In some approaches, universal screening is considered part of Tier 1.)

Tier 2
Students whose progress is less than desired receive different or additional support from the classroom teacher or another educational professional. Student progress continues to be monitored.

Tier 3
Students whose progress is still insufficient in Tier 2 may receive even more intensive instruction, which can be provided in a variety of ways. Then, depending on a state's or district's policies, students may qualify for special education services based on the progress monitoring data, or they may receive either an abbreviated or a comprehensive evaluation for the identification of a learning disability.

Source: http://iris.peabody.vanderbilt.edu/rti01_overview/rti01_03.html. Text courtesy of the IRIS Center, Peabody College.

Depending on the criteria used by the state, the fact that the first student didn't respond might by itself result in the diagnosis, although this practice has been questioned (Vaughn & Fuchs, 2003), with some suggesting that it is necessary to combine information from the RTI process with norm-referenced testing before identifying a student as having a learning diability (Flanagan, Ortiz, Alfonso, & Dynda, 2006). For example, the student might be administered an intelligence test to rule out an intellectual disability. Similarly, the Council for Exceptional Children (CEC, 2006–2007) recommended that the use of RTI by itself *cannot* determine a learning disability, and the National Association of School Psychologists (2007) pointed out that a comprehensive evaluation should be used to rule out other possible reasons for the lack of progress and that eligibility decisions should never be made on "any single method, measure, or assessment" (p. 5).

Although RTI has great potential to address the "wait to fail" phenomenon, there are still several concerns and unanswered questions. For example, teachers will need to take on different roles and will need to decide how long the interventions should be in place. There is also the issue of what constitutes responsiveness and nonresponsiveness, and there is no guarantee that a student who does respond will continue to progress (CEC, 2006–2007). There is also some question about how RTI (particulary the earlier tiers) differs from prereferral assessment and intervention (Bender & Shores, 2007).

CASE STUDY *June*

In this case study you are introduced to June, who will appear throughout this textbook. By following June's story and participating in the activities accompanying her case, you will have the opportunity to be involved in the assessment process that is used when a student is referred for consideration for special education services.

Two points need to be stated at the outset of this case study. First, because the purpose of this continuing case study is to provide you with many opportunities to participate in the analysis and decision making that typically accompanies a referral, June's case will involve more assessment procedures than are usually required.

Second, for some chapter activities involving June's evaluation, you will need to refer to the test scores and results from previous chapters. So that you will not have to flip back and forth between chapters to find the information, a Cumulative Assessment File is available in the Companion Website for those chapters where it may be needed. The file is available as a separate link. You will be cued to refer to the Cumulative Assessment File.

On the Website, Chapter 17 contains June's complete file. This will be your opportunity to put all the information together and determine whether June meets the eligibility criteria for special education. If she does, you can then determine appropriate programming and educational goals for her.

June: The Beginning

Your neighbors have a daughter, June, who is 10 years old and in the fourth grade. She has been having "difficulties" in school. Her teacher reports that she is falling too far behind the rest of the students. June's parents know that she has been reluctant to go to school. She has also been struggling with many homework assignments, far too many of which are either not returned to school or are left incomplete. The parents have been notified by their daughter's school that "interventions" are to be tried, but they do not understand the notice that they have received from the school about "interventions."

- Explain to your neighbors the purpose and process of prereferral intervention.

Reflections

1. What do you think were some of the reasons the Regular Education Initiative was not completely successful?
2. Why do you think the *Larry P.* case has had such an impact on assessment practices?
3. What do you think are the implications of the Response to Intervention model?

Summary

A number of historical, philosophical, and legal events have played an important role in shaping the assessment policies and procedures that are used in schools today. Historically, interest in the development and use of standardized tests, particularly in the areas of intelligence, personality, and achievement, grew in the first half of the twentieth century. In the 1960s, with the development of special education as a formal field, the interest in standardized testing increased, particularly in tests designed for use with students with learning disabilities. The 1970s, however, brought a somewhat negative attitude toward testing, partially as a result of discriminatory test practices and overreliance on certain types of standardized tests (e.g., process tests). In the mid-1980s, proponents of the Regular Education Initiative reemphasized the limitations of standardized testing and stressed the importance of informal measures, particularly curriculum-based assessment. There is general agreement that both types of assessment have their place if used appropriately. With the current emphasis on inclusion, the role of the general educator in the assessment process has become an extremely important one. It is necessary for the general educator and the special educator to work collaboratively to design and refine the assessment process.

Legally, the area of assessment has been affected by both litigation and legislation. Most court cases have dealt with the discriminatory use of tests (e.g., *Diana* and *Larry P.*) or with timely delivery of assessment services (e.g., *Jose P.*). The most historically significant legislation was P.L. 94-142, with its specific requirements for (among other things) the development of an Individualized Education Program, the use of nondiscriminatory procedures, and the delineation of parents' rights in the assessment process. Other legislation that has affected assessment are P.L. 99-457, which increased emphasis on infants and preschool children, and P.L. 101-476 (IDEA), which emphasized the importance of the assessment of a student's need for transitional services and added the categories of traumatic brain injury and autism. In addition, the ADA ensured that there can be no discrimination against individuals with disabilities. This implies that the necessary accommodations must be made during any assessment. P.L. 107-110 (NCLB) emphasized the importance of standards-based, high-stakes assessment that has had a significant impact on students with disabilities. P.L. 105-17, the 1997 reauthorization of IDEA, clarified and extended many of the assessment practices noted in earlier legislation, strengthened the areas of parental participation and due process, and mandated guidelines for participation in large-scale assessments for students with disabilities. Finally, P.L. 108-446, the 2004 reauthorization of IDEA, aligned itself with NCLB and increased the call for accountability and the participation of students with disabilities in testing programs. It also maintained most of the assessment guidelines from previous versions of IDEA and introduced the option to consider response to intervention as a criterion for the identification of learning disabilities.

chapter two

The Assessment Process

A Proposed Model

Before any assessment procedure is initiated, the prerequisite questions listed to the left must be addressed. The answers to these serve as a basis for an assessment model discussed later in this chapter. A discussion of each of these questions and possible answers follow.

Why Assess?

Any person who is involved in the assessment process should know why the assessment is being conducted. There are many purposes for assessment and, with careful planning, more than one purpose can usually be addressed. Among the many purposes for assessment are (1) initial identification or screening, (2) determination and evaluation of teaching programs and strategies, (3) determination of current performance level and educational need, (4) decisions about eligibility, (5) development of individualized education programs, and (6) decisions about program placement.

Initial Identification (Screening)

Typically, individuals who might require special services or special education are initially identified through assessment procedures. These can be either informal procedures (such as observation or analysis of work products) or more formal procedures (such as achievement or developmental screening tests). In other words, assessment can be used to identify individuals who warrant further evaluation.

Assessment can also be used to screen individuals who are considered to be at high risk for developing various problems. These individuals do not yet demonstrate deficiencies requiring special attention, but they do demonstrate behaviors that suggest possible problems in the future. Identification of such individuals allows the careful monitoring of those potential trouble areas and occasionally implies the use of a program designed to "prevent the problem." For instance, children who lag behind in language skills before entering kindergarten might be monitored closely after they enter school to make sure that they do not fall behind in language-oriented areas. It might also be possible to initiate a language-stimulation program before kindergarten as a preventive measure. Assessment can also be used to make screening decisions using the Response to Intervention (RTI) model allowed by IDEA 04 for the identification of learning disabilities. In one RTI model, the first step is *universal screening* involving school-wide assessment to determine those students who need more intensive instruction.

Assessment for initial identification purposes, therefore, is used to identify individuals who might need additional evaluation or who might develop problems in the future. Assessment can also identify those students for whom some type of immediate remedial program is warranted. In other words, assessment can be used to determine those students for whom prereferral intervention is necessary or who will need more intensive instruction within the RTI model.

Determination and Evaluation of Teaching Programs and Strategies (Prereferral Assessment)

One of the more important roles of assessment is to help determine appropriate teaching programs and strategies. For this purpose, assessment information can be used in four ways. First, before a student receives special education, it can assist the general education teacher in determining what to teach and the best method for teaching it. Second, assessment procedures can evaluate the effectiveness of the particular teaching program or strategy that is implemented. Many times a formal referral for special education can be avoided if assessment information is used in this way. In other words, assessment data gathered before a referral is made (prereferral assessment) can be used to develop and evaluate prereferral intervention programs. Suppose, for example, that a teacher, Ms. Jones, had a student, Jim, who was performing inconsistently in the area of spelling. The teacher, before referring Jim for formal assessment to determine if he was eligible for special education services, decided to assess him informally. On the basis of the assessment, she determined that Jim was sounding out and spelling words purely on their phonetic representation. For instance, "decision" was spelled "dasishun," and "enough" was spelled "enuff." Ms. Jones then initiated an appropriate remedial program that, among other things, emphasized spelling rules. She reevaluated Jim periodically and determined that her teaching program had been effective, thus avoiding an unnecessary referral for a special education program.

Third, prereferral assessment can provide information to document the need for a formal referral. Suppose, for instance, that the remedial program in the preceding example did not work. The documentation from that experience could be used to help justify a referral for possible special education services. Fourth, this information can be incorporated into the individualized education program for students who are eligible for and who ultimately receive special education. Particularly relevant is information that documents which teaching strategies or approaches have been used, both successfully and unsuccessfully. Fifth, prereferral assessment can be used to monitor students' progress in the various tiers of the Response to Intervention model.

> Prereferral assessment is an important component of the assessment process.

Some states, such as Pennsylvania, have developed statewide instructional support teams to provide prereferral assessment and instruction. Kovaleski, Gickling, Morrow, and Swank (1999) found that when schools made high use of these teams, the academic performance of students was improved. Some school districts have even developed formal attempts to promote the acceptability of prereferral interventions so that they will be used even more (McDougle, Moody-Clonon, & Martens, 2000). It is important to note that in most cases prereferral assessment and intervention are the responsibility of the general education teacher.

Commercial products to assist prereferral assessment are available.

The importance of prereferral assessment and intervention has become so apparent that commercial products are available to help teachers in this process. For example, the *Academic Competence Evaluations Scales* (ACES; DiPerna & Elliott, 2000) and the *Academic Intervention Monitoring System* (AIMS; Elliott, DiPerna, & Shapiro, 2000) offer a comprehensive system. Among other things, ACES provides teachers with a standardized measure to summarize their perceptions of academic skills, interpersonal skills, academic motivation, study skills, and classroom engagement. AIMS provides information to help develop interventions and a way to identify and evaluate appropriate goals. Another example is the *Prereferral Intervention Manual and Prereferral Checklist* (McCarney, 1993). This instrument aids identification of the most common learning and behavioral problems and provides intervention strategies and activities for each. A computerized version is also available.

Determination of Current Performance Level and Educational Need

Since the mandate of P.L. 94-142 over thirty years ago, students who receive special education must have a clearly identified need that is not being currently met by their programs. This is accomplished by evaluating each student's current level of performance and could involve, among other things, measurement of developmental, functional, preacademic, academic, or social skills. By using information for this purpose, the teacher or examiner can document the subject(s) and skill(s) for which each student needs special assistance. This information would also include the student's strengths and weaknesses and possible teaching strategies. In other words, assessment data for this purpose are used (1) to identify general areas in which the student needs additional help, (2) to identify both strengths and weaknesses of the student, and (3) to determine possible teaching strategies and remedial approaches for the student. The current mandate of IDEA 04 also requires documentation of how the disability will affect the student's progress in the general education curriculum (for preschoolers, involvement in appropriate preschool activities).

Decisions about Eligibility

Labeling students, although controversial, is required by IDEA 04 to receive funding.

The use of assessment data to determine eligibility for special education services is controversial because it involves the process of labeling or classifying students. The pros and cons of labeling have been argued, debated, and analyzed for years. The major goals and purposes of labeling and classifying in special education are to identify children with significant educational problems, to indicate similarities and relationships among the educational problems, and to provide information that allows professional communication within the field (Hardman, Drew, & Egan, 2005). The use of labels, however, has been criticized by many professionals for a number of years. Among their criticisms have been that the various disabilities lacked acceptable definitions; that the number of minority students labeled was disproportionately high; that not enough appropriate, identifiable educational programs were available to prescribe after classification; and that labels had a possible stigmatizing effect, resulting in negative attitudes and lowered teacher expectations.

Despite these controversies, the process of labeling and classification has continued, primarily as a means of establishing priorities and obtaining funds for educational programming. IDEA 04 carefully defined those children for whom special education is warranted:

> The term "child with a disability" means a child with mental retardation, hearing impairments (including deafness), speech or language impairments, visual impairments (including blindness), serious emotional disturbance (in this title referred to as emotional disturbance), orthopedic impairments, autism, traumatic brain injury, other health impairments, or specific learning disabilities.

These are essentially the same disabilities noted in P.L. 94-142, except for autism and traumatic brain injury (TBI), which were added in IDEA.

Not all exceptional children in the aforementioned categories are initially identified through educational and psychological assessment. Many children with disabilities, such as those with orthopedic impairments, hearing impairments, or TBI, are identified through medical and other procedures. Even in these situations, however, assessment data are used to document the need for special education and to establish specific goals. The categories that rely heavily on educational and psychological assessment for eligibility determination are specific learning disabilities, mental retardation, and emotional disturbance. In addition, although not included in IDEA 04, the category of gifted and talented is usually identified using those types of assessment data.

Definition and Assessment Profile for Selected Exceptionalities.   Each of the previously mentioned exceptionalities will be defined, and a "sample assessment profile" will be presented in the areas of intelligence (Chapter 7), achievement (Chapter 11), adaptive behavior (Chapter 8), and emotional and behavioral characteristics (Chapter 9). The profiles are based on the definition and available research on each category. The actual profile will depend on the specific eligibility criteria used by a particular state.

Learning Disabilities.   Since the term *learning disabilities* was introduced in 1963, professionals have disagreed about its definition. The following IDEA 04 definition provides a general description as well as an indication of which disorders can and cannot be considered as a learning disability. The IDEA 04 definition reads:

> Specific Learning Disability—
> (A) In General—The term "specific learning disabilities" means a disorder in one or more of the basic psychological processes involved in understanding or in using language, spoken or written, which disorder may manifest itself in imperfect ability to listen, think, speak, read, write, spell, or do mathematical calculations.
> (B) Disorders Included—Such term includes such conditions as perceptual disabilities, brain injury, minimal brain dysfunction, dyslexia, and developmental aphasia.
> (C) Disorders Not Included—Such term does not include a learning problem that is primarily the result of visual, hearing, or motor disabilities, of mental

retardation, of emotional disturbance, or of environmental, cultural, or economic disadvantage.

Apparent from the above definition is that learning disabilities is an *exclusionary* category. In other words, the disability cannot be due to several factors that must first be ruled out. One requirement noted in previous legislation was a discrepancy between intelligence and achievement, or an aptitude-achievement discrepancy. This requirement was criticized by many professionals and led to the current IDEA 04 recommendation that this discrepancy model is no longer required. IDEA 04 did, however, support the use of a process that determines if a student responds to scientific, research-based intervention when identifying a student as having a learning disability. Various Response to Intervention models are currently being researched.

Sample Assessment Profile: Learning Disability (LD)

Intelligence: Average or low average performance

Achievement: Variable or low average performance

Adaptive Behavior: Average or variable performance

Emotional and Behavioral Characteristics: Variable performance

---

Mental Retardation. The term *mental retardation* has been challenged by many professionals and professional organizations. For example, the Division on Mental Retardation changed its name to the Division on Developmental Disabilities, and in 2007 the American Association on Mental Retardation became the American Association on Intellectual and Developmental Disabilities. However, the term *mental retardation* is still used in IDEA 04 and in the majority of states. Perhaps the most widely used definition is one proposed by the American Association on Mental Retardation (AAMR; Luckasson et al., 2002). According to the AAMR:

> *Mental retardation* is a disability characterized by significant limitations in both intellectual functioning and in adaptive behavior as expressed in conceptual, social, and practical adaptive skills. This disability originates before age 18.

Sample Assessment Profile: Mental Retardation (MR)

Intelligence: Low performance

Achievement: Low performance

Adaptive Behavior: Low performance

Emotional and Behavioral Characteristics: Variable performance

---

Emotional Disturbance. Emotional disturbance is extremely difficult to define. In fact, there is little agreement about what term to use to refer to individuals with emotional or behavioral problems. *Emotional disturbance, behavior disorder,* and *emotional/behavioral disorder,* among other terms, have all been used. There is also a considerable amount of subjectivity about what constitutes an emotional or behavioral problem. The following is the IDEA 04 definition of emotional disturbance:

(i) The term means a condition exhibiting one or more of the following characteristics over a long period of time and to a marked degree, which adversely affects educational performance.

    A. An inability to learn that cannot be explained by intellectual, sensory, or health factors.

    B. An inability to build or maintain satisfactory interpersonal relationships with peers and teachers.

    C. Inappropriate types of behavior or feelings under normal circumstances.

    D. A general pervasive mood of unhappiness or depression.

    E. A tendency to develop physical symptoms, pains, or fear associated with personal or school problems.

(ii) The term includes children who are schizophrenic. The term does not include children who are socially maladjusted unless it is determined that they are seriously emotionally disturbed.

Sample Assessment Profile: Emotional or Behavior Problems

Intelligence: Average or low average performance

Achievement: Variable or low average performance

Adaptive Behavior: Variable performance

Emotional and Behavioral Characteristics: Low performance

Gifted and Talented.   In recent years, gifted and talented students have been receiving more and more attention. In a certain sense, however, definitions of *gifted and talented* are just as ambiguous as definitions of other exceptional categories—if not more so. The most recent definition came from a report called *National Excellence: A Case for Developing America's Talent*. This definition eliminates the term *gifted* and substitutes the term *outstanding talent,* partly to emphasize that these students should not just be those with high IQs. Interestingly, however, a survey of the states indicated that IQ was still the most widely used criterion (Stephens & Karnes, 2000). That definition reads:

> The term *gifted* has been replaced with *outstanding talent.*

> Children and youth with outstanding talent perform or show the potential for performing at remarkably high levels of accomplishment when compared with others of their age, experience, or environment. These children and youth exhibit high performance capability in intellectual, creative, and/or artistic areas, possess an unusual leadership capacity, or excel in specific academic fields. They require services or activities not ordinarily provided by the school.
>
> Outstanding talents are present in children and youth from all cultural groups, across all economic strata, and in all areas of human endeavor. (*National Excellence,* 1993)

Sample Assessment Profile: Gifted and Talented

Intelligence: High performance

Achievement: High or variable performance

Adaptive Behavior: Average or high performance

Emotional and Behavioral Characteristics: Average or variable performance

The following Test-Profile Matrix summarizes the various assessment profiles of the different areas of exceptionality. This is an oversimplification, and all the factors that can affect assessment discussed in Chapter 3 also will ultimately affect the individual profile of a given student.

Test-Profile Matrix

	Learning Disability	Mental Retardation	Emotional Disturbance	No Disability	Gifted and Talented
Intelligence	A–LA	L	A–LA	A	H
Achievement	V–LA	L	LA–V	A	H–V
Adaptive Behavior	A–V	L	V	A	A–H
Emotional and Behavioral Characteristics	V	V	L	A	A–V

A = Average; L = Low; LA = Low-average; H = High; V = Variable

It should be noted that IDEA 04 includes a special rule for eligibility determination. A child shall not be determined to be a child with a disability if the determinant factor is—

A. lack of appropriate instruction in reading, including in the essential components of reading instruction
B. lack of instruction in math
C. limited English proficiency

Development of the Individualized Education Program

If a student receives formal special education services and receives federal funding, he or she must have an individualized education program (IEP), another requirement mandated by IDEA 04. The IEP functions as a "contract" to identify goals, objectives, and time lines for delivery of services. Public Laws 101-476 (IDEA) and 99-457 also mandated the development of individualized transition programs (ITPs) and individualized family service plans (IFSPs). IDEA 97 and IDEA 04, however, incorporated the student's transition needs directly into the IEP. IFSPs are still mandated.

Currently, the following information must be included in an IEP:

> IDEA 04 requires that transition needs be identified in a student's IEP by age 16.

> Short-term objectives and benchmarks are no longer required for the majority of students.

1. A statement of the child's present levels of academic achievement and functional performance, including
   A. How the child's disability affects the child's involvement and progress in the general education curriculum.
   B. For preschool children, as appropriate, how the disability affects the child's participation in appropriate activities.
   C. For children with disabilities who take alternate assessments aligned to alternate achievement standards, a description of benchmarks or short-term objectives.
2. A statement of measurable annual goals, including academic and functional goals, designed to
   A. Meet the child's needs that result from the child's disability to enable the child to be involved in and make progress in the general education curriculum.

   B. Meet each of the child's other educational needs that result from the child's disability.

 3. A description of how the child's progress toward meeting the annual goals will be measured and when periodic reports on the progress the child is making toward meeting the annual goals (such as through the use of quarterly or other periodic reports, concurrent with the issuance of report cards) will be provided.

 4. A statement of the special education and related services and supplementary aids and services, based on peer-reviewed research to the extent practicable, to be provided to the child, or on behalf of the child, and a statement of the program modifications or supports for school personnel that will be provided for the child
   A. To advance appropriately toward attaining the annual goals.
   B. To be involved in and make progress in the general education curriculum and to participate in extracurricular and other nonacademic activities.
   C. To be educated and participate with other children with disabilities and nondisabled children.

 5. An explanation of the extent, if any, to which the child will not participate with nondisabled children in the regular class.

 6a. A statement of any individual appropriate accommodations that are necessary to measure the academic achievement and functional performance of the child on state and districtwide assessments.

 6b. If the IEP Team determines that the child shall take an alternate assessment on a particular state or districtwide assessment of student achievement, a statement of why
   A. The child cannot participate in regular assessment.
   B. The particular alternate assessment selected is appropriate for the child.

 7. The projected date for the beginning of the services and modifications, and the anticipated frequency, location, and duration of those services and modifications.

 8. Beginning not later than the first IEP to be in effect when the child is 16, and updated annually thereafter
   A. Appropriate measureable postsecondary goals based upon age-appropriate transition assessments related to training, education, employment, and, where appropriate, independent living skills;
   B. The transition services (including courses of study) needed to assist the child in reaching those goals; and
   C. Beginning not later than one year before the child reaches the age of majority under state law, a statement that the child has been informed of the child's rights under this title, if any, that will transfer to the child on reaching the age of majority.

Although assessment data (either directly or indirectly) are used for all of these purposes, they are used primarily for

 1. Documentation of the student's current level of performance (item 1 above).
 2. Indication of the specific services and type of program to be provided (item 4 above).
 3. Determination of annual goals and benchmarks/short-term objectives (items 1 and 2 above).

The first two areas were discussed earlier; the third is discussed next. Also addressed is the requirement for a statement of how the student's progress toward the goals will be evaluated and how the parents will be notified of the progress.

Determination of Goals and Benchmarks/Objectives.   Assessment data can help determine realistic goals for students. Typically, the goals identified for students are annual; that is, they project approximately one year in advance what a student should be doing. Goals are, as a rule, fairly general; they more or less delineate those major areas for which more specific and short-term objectives will be identified. An example of a goal might be, "Student will correctly add two-digit numbers with carrying." By no later than age 16, the student's goals should also reflect transition needs.

Assessment data are also important in determining appropriate objectives for students. As noted earlier, however, short-term objectives and benchmarks are only required for students who are taking alternate assessments tied to alternate achievement standards. This means that they are *not* required for the vast majority of students with disabilities. Nonetheless, they deserve some discussion. Objectives are essentially a sequential breakdown of those skills that provide a link between the student's current performance level and the projected annual goals. Assume, for example, that a student with a severe disability was dependent on others for feeding him and the goal was to have him eat from a spoon. The objectives might be

1. Student will feed himself a cracker or cookie.
2. Student will feed himself small pieces of food such as raisins.
3. Student will put spoon in mouth (with physical guidance).
4. Student will put spoon in mouth independently.

These objectives serve as "steps" that link the student's current performance level with the goal. Figure 2.1 is a checklist that can be used to ensure that goals and objectives are appropriately determined.

Benchmarks can also be developed to measure progress between a student's current performance level and the annual goals. Typically objectives are used when the goal can be divided into discrete skill components (as above). On the other hand, benchmarks describe outcomes that reflect the amount of progress that the student is expected to make and may be thought of as milestones (Lignugaris-Kraft, Marchand-Martella, & Martella, 2001). For example, different developmental age levels for a specific skill might be selected that link the student's current developmental age and the developmental age identified in a goal.

IDEA 04 requires parents be apprised of their child's progress.

Monitoring and Reporting Progress (Evaluation of Goals and Objectives). It is extremely important that a student's progress toward annual goals (which should be developed to enable the student to be involved in the general education curriculum) be carefully documented. This basically refers to the evaluation of goals and objectives and, essentially, has three major aspects: (1) the determination of objective criteria, (2) the determination of appropriate evaluation procedures, and (3) the determination of evaluation schedules (Strickland & Turnbull, 1993).

The *determination of objective criteria* suggests that the goals and objectives be stated in terms of standards of time and accuracy. The following example, for instance, clearly states the criteria: "Given a worksheet with ten problems of two-digit addition (without carrying), the student will correctly solve the problems in twenty minutes or less with at least 90 percent accuracy." This aspect (determining objective criteria) can be addressed, therefore, by carefully writing the goal to include time and accuracy standards.

The *appropriate evaluation procedure* depends on a number of factors. In practice, more formal procedures are used to evaluate goals, whereas informal procedures are often used to measure objectives. In general, the *schedule for evaluating goals and objectives* should be determined when the IEP is developed. Also, it is helpful to determine who is responsible for the evaluation. Ideally, the evaluation

FIGURE 2.1   Checklist for IEP Goals and Objectives

1. Does the goal statement refer to target areas of deficit?

   OR Have I written a goal that is unrelated to remediation needs described in present level of performance and assessment information?

2. Given the assessment data, is it probable that this goal could be achieved in a year (i.e., annual period for the IEP)?

   OR Is the goal so broad that it may take two or more years to accomplish?

3. Does the goal contain observable terms with an identified target-area for remediation?

   OR Have I used words that fail to accurately describe the problem area or direction I am taking?

4. Have goals been written for each area of deficit?

   OR Do I have dangling data (data that indicate a need for remediation but have been overlooked)?

5. Is the scope of the objective appropriate?

   OR Have I written any objectives that encompass the entire year, thus making them annual goals?

6. Do the objectives describe a subskill of the goal?

   OR Have I failed to determine the hierarchy needed to teach the skill?
   - Did I simply rephrase the goal statement?
   - Did I describe a terminal skill, but only less of it?

7. Are the objectives presented in a sequential order?

   OR Have I listed the objectives in random order, unrelated to the way the skill would logically be taught?

8. Do the objectives show a progression through the skill to meet the goal?

   OR Do the objectives emphasize only one phase of a particular skill?

9. Does the objective contain an appropriately stated condition?

   OR Have I failed to describe the exact circumstances under which the behavior is to occur?
   - Have I described irrelevant or extraneous materials?
   - Does the condition refer to an isolated classroom activity?

10. Does the objective contain an appropriately stated performance using observable terms?

    OR Is the mode of performance (e.g., oral) different from the desired goal (e.g., written)?

11. Does the objective contain an appropriately stated standard?

    OR Is the standard unrelated to the assessment information and level of performance?
    - Am I using the performance statement as a standard?
    - Am I using percentages when the behavior requires alternative ways to measure?
    - Have I chosen arbitrary percentages?

Source: Barbara Tymitz-Wolf. (1982). Guidelines for Assessing IEP Goals and Objectives. *Teaching Exceptional Children, 14,* 200. Figure 1. Copyright © 1982 by the Council for Exceptional Children. Reprinted by permission.

of the goals and objectives should be a continuous process, based on the student's classroom performance.

The importance of notifying parents of their child's performance cannot be minimized. IDEA 04 recommended that one way to address this requirement is through the use of periodic report cards that indicate the student's progress toward the annual goals and the likelihood that the goals will be met. Another approach might be through the use of portfolios or other informal measures that demonstrate progress.

Decisions about Program Placement

Assessment information should also be used to make a decision about the most appropriate educational placement for a student with a disability (i.e., the placement in which the IEP will be implemented). As noted in Chapter 1, P.L. 94-142 required that students be placed in the least restrictive environment (LRE). In the past, this has traditionally resulted in deciding (using assessment information) which "least restrictive" placement would be best for a student on a continuum from, for example, a separate school, a separate classroom, or a part-time separate classroom to a general education classroom. Also as noted in Chapter 1, there is a current emphasis on inclusion, in which all students, regardless of type or severity of disability, are placed in the general education classroom. The need for a continuum of available services, however, is still strongly supported by many. These positions (inclusion vs. continuum of services) are represented in the definition of LRE included in IDEA 04. That definition states:

> To the maximum extent appropriate, children with disabilities, including children in public or private institutions or other care facilities, are educated with children who are not disabled, and separate classes, separate schooling, or other removal of children with disabilities from the regular educational environment occurs only when the nature or severity of the disability of a child is such that education in regular classes with the use of supplementary aids and services cannot be achieved satisfactorily.

Essentially, this allows for placement in noninclusive settings but requires considerable documentation if that placement is made. For example, there must be documentation of why a student is not participating in the general education curriculum with peers without disabilities (as mentioned in the last section on individualized education programs).

Assessment information can help determine a student's LRE.

How Is the Process Initiated?

After a student has been initially identified as having some type of problem or potential problem, decisions must be made about what to do next. As previously discussed, one option and, in many cases, requirement, is to gather prereferral information and initiate a prereferral intervention program. In other words, the student is further assessed by the teacher who made the initial identification. In other situations, a formal referral is initiated to obtain the necessary assessment service. Each school or school district has different procedures for referring individuals for assessment. All those involved in assessment should be thoroughly familiar with the referral procedures used in their school district. If the Response to Intervention model is used, the process is initiated schoolwide and, in some models, eligibility may be determined without a referral. In other models, a student going through the various tiers without responding to the instruction will be referred for evaluation.

Three points regarding referrals deserve further comment. The first is that, as a rule, an individual should not be referred until preliminary assessment data have been collected (including information gathered during the RTI process). For instance, instead of simply referring a child who is "acting up" in class, the documentation should include information about the type of behavior, the frequency or duration of the behavior, and the conditions under which the behavior occurs (time of day, behavioral antecedents, and consequences). In other instances, however, more extensive assessment can be done, including academic testing. As previously mentioned, many times a formal referral might be avoided by collecting this prereferral information and implementing a prereferral intervention program. As noted, although policies differ from state to state, prereferral assessment and intervention are frequently required. Usually the severity of the problem dictates when, and if, a formal referral is necessary. In reality, students who receive special education provided by federal funds go through the formal referral process.

The second point is that although referrals are typically the first step in determining eligibility for special education services, they can also be made to request assistance in other areas (e.g., help with prereferral intervention strategies). The referral for eligibility should include the prereferral assessment data and other specific information such as the type and effectiveness of any prereferral intervention strategies. Nothing is more frustrating than to refer a student for assessment, find out that the student is not eligible for special education, and receive a recommendation to implement an intervention program that you have already tried. This unnecessary situation can be avoided by carefully communicating what is already known about the individual and specifying clearly why you want the assessment.

The third point is that if a student is referred, there is a very good chance that he or she will be found eligible for special education. Ysseldyke, Vanderwood, and Shriner (1997) found that 90 to 92 percent of referred students were tested and that almost 75 percent of those tested were placed in special education. These data stress the importance and significance of making a referral. It obviously should not be done casually.

Referring a student usually results in special education placement.

What Procedures Should Be Used?

Typically, people think of "giving tests" when they think of assessment. Although tests are usually included in the assessment process, the two terms are certainly not synonymous. Tests are merely a means of obtaining behavioral samples that give examiners a *quantitative* measure in a specific area. Thus, we might find out that Jorge has an IQ of 102, Bill scored at the 3.6 grade level in reading, or Kim correctly completed 89 percent of her two-digit addition problems. In short, *tests are simply devices to which individuals are exposed that give a quantitative characterization of one or more traits of those individuals.* Nevertheless, tests are used extensively in the assessment of exceptional students. They can be classified in various ways. For educational purposes, however, three comparisons are most relevant. These are norm-referenced versus criterion-referenced tests, speed versus power tests, and group versus individual tests.

Norm-Referenced Tests: Types of Scores, Scoring, and Interpretation

A **norm-referenced test** is one in which a person's score is compared to a specific reference group. The reference group is also called the *normative* or *standardization sample* and provides the norms on which to base the comparison. Norm-referenced tests are typically used when a person is interested in how a student

NORM-REFERENCED TEST
A test in which a person's score is compared to a specific reference group.

performs in a certain area relative to other individuals. Because norm-referenced tests compare an individual's performance to individuals in the normative sample, it is important to know the makeup and characteristics of the sample. These tests address the question of *how much* rather than *what* a person knows or can do and are normed on either an age scale or a point scale. In an *age scale,* a person's performance on a test is compared to a typical performance by a person of the same age. This is determined by the percentage of individuals at various age levels who respond correctly to a test item. For instance, a particular test might be norm-referenced for 3- through 8-year-old children. Certain items on the test will be scaled for each age level. Thus, for those items scaled for 6-year-old children, some 4- to 5-year-old children should answer them correctly, about half the 6-year-old children should, and most 7- to 8-year-old children should.

Point scales are more common and include test items that are of different levels of difficulty but that are not specifically tied to age-related percentages. In such a scale, items passed are added (this figure becomes the *raw score*). The raw score can then be converted to one of a variety of *derived scores* that compare the raw score to the performance of the normative group that has known demographic characteristics, such as age, gender, race/ethnicity, parental income, and parental educational level.

Types of Scores.   A number of derived scores are used in educational and psychological testing. The most common are age equivalents, grade equivalents, quartiles, deciles, percentiles, and standard scores. These scores are briefly defined in the next sections. Other types of scores are defined in later chapters that provide descriptions of the specific norm-referenced tests.

Age and Grade Equivalents.   Age and grade equivalents are both considered *developmental scores.* Both types of scores indicate the "average" performance of a particular age group or grade level. Age equivalents are expressed in years and months. For instance, suppose that during the standardization of a particular intelligence test, the median (middle) number of correct responses was 80 for all individuals 6 years, 6 months old. Any person taking that test who obtained a raw score of 80 would have an age equivalent of 6 years, 6 months (6–06).

Grade equivalents are expressed in years and tenths of years. The calendar year is actually divided into ten parts, nine of which represent the nine months of the academic year, and the last of which represents the summer months. Thus, a 7.2 would be interpreted seventh grade, second month. Like age equivalents, grade equivalents are based on the median performance of the standardization sample. Grade equivalents are often used inappropriately to measure gains in achievement and to identify exceptional students. For instance, a student with an average IQ in grade 6.7 who scores at the 3.2 grade level in achievement might be considered as having a learning disability. The use of grade equivalents has certain intuitive appeal, because educators often think in such terms regarding academic ability. For teaching purposes, however, a grade equivalent (e.g., 4.1) indicates a *student's performance relative to the standardization sample of the test, not to placement within a curriculum.* In other words, one should not assume that the student who receives the 4.1 grade equivalent should be placed in a beginning fourth-grade curriculum.

Grade equivalents do not indicate a student's placement within a curriculum.

This emphasis on grade equivalents (as well as age equivalents) has been seriously questioned. For example, Lee (2003) found that two forms of a group achievement test yielded different grade equivalents. In an interesting study, Hishinuma and Tadaki (1997) reported that it is possible for a first-grade student to have an average standard score (discussed later) on a popular achievement test yet have a grade equivalent on the same test that is one-half year below his or her actual grade placement.

Quartiles, Deciles, and Percentiles.   Quartiles, deciles, and percentiles are all indications of the percentage of scores (determined from the standardization sample) that fall below a person's raw score. Quartiles divide the distribution of scores from the standardization into four equal parts, deciles into ten equal parts, and percentiles into one hundred equal parts. Thus, for example, the first quartile (Q_1) is the point at which 25 percent of the scores fall below; the eighth decile (D_8) is the point at which 80 percent of the scores fall below; and the twenty-third percentile (P_{23}) is the point at which 23 percent of the scores fall below. Suppose that three students' raw scores on a test were at Q_1, D_8, or P_{23}. These scores would indicate that 75 percent, 20 percent, and 77 percent of the individuals in the standardization sample scored higher than the three students. Of these three types of scores, the most widely used is the percentile. The score itself is often referred to as a *percentile rank*.

Standard Scores.   Standard scores are transformed raw scores with the same mean and standard deviation. The **mean** represents the average score, and the **standard deviation** reflects the variability of a set of scores. In the standardization of a test, approximately 34 percent of the subjects score within 1 standard deviation of the mean; approximately 14 percent score between 1 and 2 standard deviations; only about 2 percent score between 2 and 3 standard deviations. Thus, approximately 68 percent of the subjects score between ±1 standard deviations, and approximately 96 percent score between ±2 standard deviations. For instance, assume that a test has a mean of 100 and a standard deviation of 15. This means that the average score of those subjects in the standardization sample was 100 and that 68 percent scored between 85 and 115. Similarly, 96 percent scored between 70 and 130. Because of its statistical base, standard deviation plays an important role in the determination of extent of strength or weakness in a student's abilities.

There are many types of standard scores whose distributions have different means and standard deviations. Perhaps the most basic is the *z* **score**. A *z* score has a mean of 0 and a standard deviation of 1. In other words, the score is presented in standard deviation units such as -1.46 or $+.59$ that indicate how far away the score is from the mean. The *z* score is used frequently in statistics but less so in assessment. More frequently used standard scores that are yielded from tests are **deviation IQs, scaled scores,** and ***T* scores**. The deviation IQ, used in the aforementioned example, has a mean of 100 and a standard deviation of 15. This is perhaps the most widely used score for norm-referenced instruments. The scaled score is frequently used when an instrument provides scores in a number of areas (usually called subtests). Scaled scores usually have a mean of 10 and a standard deviation of 3. The *T* score is frequently used with behavior rating scales (discussed in Chapter 9). It has a mean of 50 and a standard deviation of 10. Obviously, it is very important that the type of standard score be known before any interpretation is made. For example, a standard score of 70 could represent 2 standard deviations below average (deviation IQ) or two deviations above average (*T* score).

Figure 2.2 gives a visual representation of a variety of standard scores and compares them with percentile ranks. Note that the standard scores are equally distributed (e.g., the distance between 100 and 115 is the same as that between 115

It is important to know the mean and standard deviation of a test when interpreting standard scores.

MEAN
The average score on a norm-referenced test.

STANDARD DEVIATION (SD)
Reflects the variability of a set of scores; approximately 68% will score ±1 SD from the mean.

Z SCORE
A score with a mean of 0 and a SD of 1.

DEVIATION IQ
A standard score with a mean of 100 and an SD of 15.

SCALED SCORE
A score that usually has a mean of 10 and an SD of 3; frequently used with subtests.

***T* SCORE**
A score with a mean of 50 and an SD of 10.

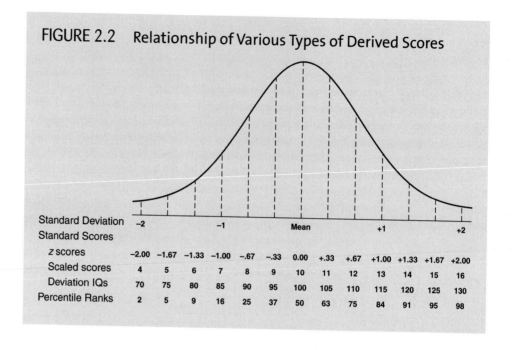

FIGURE 2.2   Relationship of Various Types of Derived Scores

Standard Deviation	−2			−1			Mean			+1			+2
Standard Scores													
z scores	−2.00	−1.67	−1.33	−1.00	−.67	−.33	0.00	+.33	+.67	+1.00	+1.33	+1.67	+2.00
Scaled scores	4	5	6	7	8	9	10	11	12	13	14	15	16
Deviation IQs	70	75	80	85	90	95	100	105	110	115	120	125	130
Percentile Ranks	2	5	9	16	25	37	50	63	75	84	91	95	98

and 130 for the deviation IQ). In contrast, percentile ranks are clustered more toward the center of the distribution. In general, although percentile ranks are easier to understand and explain, standard scores are preferable for making important educational decisions.

Related types of standard scores are the **stanine** and the **normal curve equivalent (NCE).** A stanine is actually representative of a band of standard scores. In other words, the distribution of scores noted in Figure 2.2 is divided into nine parts with each part essentially representing .5 standard deviations. The following can be used to interpret stanines.

Stanine 1: More than 1.75 standard deviations (SDs) below the mean.
Stanine 2: Between 1.25 and 1.75 SDs below the mean.
Stanine 3: Between .75 and 1.25 SDs below the mean.
Stanine 4: Between .25 and .75 SDs below the mean.
Stanine 5: Between .25 SDs below the mean and .25 SDs above the mean.
Stanine 6: Between .25 and .75 SDs above the mean.
Stanine 7: Between .75 and 1.25 SDs above the mean.
Stanine 8: Between 1.25 and 1.75 SDs above the mean.
Stanine 9: More than 1.75 SDs above the mean.

Normal curve equivalents are, in a sense, a combination of standard scores and percentile ranks. An NCE is expressed as a standard score with a mean of 50 and a standard deviation of 21.06. The atypical standard deviation results from dividing the normal curve into 100 equal intervals.

Scoring Norm-Referenced Tests.   After a norm-referenced test has been administered, a *raw score* is obtained. This score, by itself, has no real meaning. As discussed previously, this score can then be transformed into a variety of derived scores that compare the raw score to the normative sample. This is accomplished by using conversion tables that are usually found in the test manual. A specific test might allow a comparison based on the age of the student tested (age norms), the grade of the student (grade norms), or both.

STANINE
A score that represents a band of standard scores; there are nine stanines, representing more than 1.75 SDs below the mean to more than 1.75 SDs above the mean.

NORMAL CURVE EQUIVALENT (NCE)
A combination of a standard score and a percentile rank.

The scoring of many norm-referenced tests can be tedious and frequently results in errors including computational mistakes and the misuse of statistical tables. For this reason, it is important that test examiners are properly trained and careful when doing mathematical calculations and using tables to convert raw scores to derived scores. For this reason also computer scoring programs are available for many tests. Maddux and Johnson (1998) noted that the computer serves several purposes in assessment. They believe that perhaps the most appropriate use of computers in assessment is the simple arithmetic manipulation or transformation of scores. This includes such things as calculating a child's chronological age, adding the number of correct items, or transferring raw scores to standard scores using extensive tables. They did point out, however, that one objection to computerized scoring is that it does not allow the expert judgment that is sometimes allowed to determine the correctness of a response.

Also available are computer-based test interpretation programs. As the name implies, these programs go beyond scoring and into the area of interpretation of test performance. There has been some ethical debate about the appropriateness of such approaches. After all, the computer does not "see" the student and is not able to put the information in proper context. Maddux and Johnson (1998) pointed out that of all the uses of computer application in assessment, interpretation is the most questionable. They felt that automated interpretation programs take away an examiner's ability to use clinical judgment or professional expertise. McCullough (1995) questioned, "Have you laid awake nights wondering about that ethical standard that says you are responsible for assuring the accuracy, reliability, and validity of a computer-based test interpretation program?" (p. 1). In fact, the *Standards for Educational and Psychological Testing* (AERA, 1999) include a standard indicating that test users should not use computer-generated interpretations unless they have the expertise to consider its appropriateness in a given case.

Interpreting Norm-Referenced Tests.   When interpreting results of norm-referenced tests, the derived score(s) are first reported. This information will show the student's relative performance compared to the normative sample. The following example shows the interpretation of several derived scores obtained in a test administration.

Danny, age 10 years, 5 months, obtained a raw score of 133 on Form A of the *Peabody Picture Vocabulary Test–4 (PPVT-4)*. On the PPVT-4, Danny had to choose, among four pictures, the one represented by a vocabulary word read by the examiner (see Chapter 10). His raw score of 133 represents the number of correct responses. By using the tables in the test manual, the examiner compared Danny's raw score to the standardization sample by age (age norms). He received:

- An age equivalent of 8–04. This means that Danny's performance (133 raw score) is equivalent to the average performance of those in the standardization sample who were 8 years and 4 months old. This does not necessarily mean that Danny is performing like an 8-year, 4-month-old student.
- A percentile rank of 16. This means that Danny scored equal to or higher than 16 percent of those individuals of his age in the standardization sample. Conversely, 84 percent scored equal to or better than Danny.
- A standard score of 85. Because the PPVT-4 has a mean of 100 and a standard deviation of 15; this means that Danny's performance was 1 SD below average compared to others his age.

When interpreting results, examiners should do more than simply report derived scores, whether they are determined through hand scoring or computer

Ask "Exactly what did the
student have to do to obtain
this score?"

scoring. For example, suppose that a person obtained a percentile rank of 52 on a spelling test. This would indicate that he or she performed slightly above average in spelling compared to the normative sample. To really understand what that means, however, it is necessary to *consider the task demands of the test itself*. In other words, what did the student have to do to obtain that score? Did he or she have to spell words orally? Write words from dictation? Identify the correct spelling of a word from four choices? Each of these skills might be called "spelling"; it is possible, however, that one might make a mistake in assuming that the student with a 52nd percentile rank is about average in the area of written spelling if the score is based on a multiple-choice format of seeing four choices and indicating the correct spelling. Often the name of a test or subtest does not imply the specific task demands. Frequently, in fact, the name of the test or subtest has little to do with what the examinee actually has to do. It is therefore imperative that those task requirements be determined and considered when interpreting the results. This can be one of the drawbacks of computer-generated test reports.

It is also important to consider the nature or composition of the normative sample. Because an individual's score on a norm-referenced test is derived through comparison with the standardization population, it is extremely important that the nature of that population is known. Are you comparing a student's performance to a random sample of children across the United States? Males from lower-socioeconomic, rural areas? Students with severe disabilities living in residential facilities? Obviously, the score that the student receives needs to be interpreted relative to those who comprise the normative sample. An "average" score would be interpreted differently when compared to the three populations just mentioned, for example. It is best to have a representative sample that considers characteristics such as gender, race, geographic region, and parents' education. It is important to remember that the norm does not necessarily refer to normal, but to the types of individuals included in the standardization sample. According to the *Standards of Educational and Psychological Testing* (AERA, 1999), test publishers should provide specific information about the nature of the population that was sampled and the sampling procedures used. It also indicates that test users should choose tests whose norms include individuals to whom they want to compare their examinee's performance. For example, if you were testing an African American student from a rural area, the test chosen should include students with those characteristics in the standardization sample.

Criterion-Referenced Tests and Curriculum-Based Assessment

**CRITERION-REFERENCED
TEST**
A test that measures an individual's mastery of content.

A **criterion-referenced test (CRT),** as opposed to a norm-referenced test, does not specifically compare an individual's score to other people's scores. Rather, it measures an individual's mastery of content. For instance, instead of discovering that Joan scored at the 63rd percentile in math (norm-referenced test), you might find that she can add and subtract one-digit numbers correctly 100 percent of the time, but she can add and subtract two-digit numbers correctly only 25 percent of the time (criterion-referenced test). In a criterion-referenced test you learn specifically *what a person knows*, rather than *how much a person knows compared to others*. Criterion-referenced tests are often "teacher-made" and thus pinpoint the exact areas included in an individual's curriculum. In fact, many criterion-referenced tests are developed based on specific educational objectives. This is accomplished by sequencing the objectives (task analysis) and developing test items that measure each objective (discussed in Chapter 5). There are also, however, a number of commercially prepared criterion-referenced tests that measure both academic skills and developmental skills.

For teaching purposes, the advantage of using criterion-referenced tests is that they usually provide more specific information about a person's ability level than do norm-referenced tests. In fact, IEPs can usually be developed much more easily from criterion-referenced test data. The disadvantages of criterion-referenced tests are that you do not get comparative information and, unless you use a commercially prepared test, you must take the time to develop the instrument.

An area that has received considerable attention in the past decade is *curriculum-based assessment (CBA)*. CBAs use the expected curricular outcomes of the school as their content. One type of CBA is very similar in nature to criterion-referenced tests and is called a criterion-referenced CBA. If, for example, a school were using the Macmillan reading series, then a criterion-referenced CBA would use the content of that series for the test items. Another type of CBA, referred to as *curriculum-based measurement (CBM)*, has also become popular. CBM includes a more standardized methodology and typically focuses on items representing an entire annual curricular area. Chapter 5 discusses criterion-referenced CBAs and CBMs in greater depth and provides examples.

Power versus Speed Tests

Norm-referenced and criterion-referenced tests can measure power or speed. A *power test* is one designed to measure a full range of skills or abilities without a time limit. In a power test you are more interested in how much a person knows than in how fast he or she can perform. Usually, test items are of increasing difficulty, so that a person taking the test will answer some but not all correctly. A *speed test* is one in which the time element becomes important. With speed tests, the examiners are more concerned with how many test items a person can complete within a specific time limit. Usually the level of difficulty for each item is such that, given unlimited time, all the items could be completed. In reality, many tests in special education are a combination of speed and power.

Individual versus Group Tests

Norm-referenced and criterion-referenced tests can also be individually or group administered. Certain advantages and disadvantages are inherent in each type of test. Group tests yield information in a shorter amount of time. For instance, it might be possible to obtain achievement scores for an entire class in two or three hours. However, you lose the opportunity to observe an individual's approach to a certain task. In short, group tests are usually administered for screening, and individual tests are administered for diagnostic, eligibility, and program-placement purposes. Certainly, both types of tests have their place in the assessment process.

Other Assessment Procedures

As previously mentioned, assessment involves more than simply the administration, scoring, and interpretation of tests. Any and all *relevant* information about an individual should be gathered. This information can be meaningful in

There are many sources of assessment information other than test scores.

its own right, and it can also help put the test data into proper perspective. Although the sources of such information are virtually limitless, several specific sources are frequently used in assessing exceptional individuals. These include the use of *checklists* and *observation*. Both formal and informal checklists can be used to help identify behavior that can be observed later or assessed in depth. Checklists provide a great deal of flexibility. They can be designed to measure student behaviors or to indicate academic material that a student has mastered. Further, checklists may be completed by a variety of individuals, including parents, teachers, peers, or even the student. In addition, checklists can either be developed for use or can be selected from a number that are commercially available (Bigge & Stump, 1999). Observation is an invaluable tool that is always used but not always systematically. (Observational assessment and its very important role in the overall process are discussed in Chapter 4.) Other sources of assessment information involve the study of school records, interviews with students and parents, medical and developmental histories, error analysis of specific work samples, and portfolio and other alternative assessment.

School Records.   School records can and should be more than a collection of meaningless data accumulated in a file folder or stored in a computer. They should contain relevant information about previous assessments, specific documentation of behavioral observations, and information relating to teaching strategies or intervention programs that have been implemented. This type of knowledge can eliminate a tremendous amount of duplication of services if the school records are used as a central data bank. Also, use of the information in the school records can help avoid wasted time in recommending or implementing a program that has already been tried and found ineffective.

Direct Interviews.   In many cases, valuable information can be gathered by interviewing the student directly. The interview can be more open-ended and informal, or can be more formal, using a specific set of questions. One nice feature of the direct interview is that it can be used for a variety of purposes. For example, a student might be interviewed about the method he or she uses to solve a math problem. This way, you might better understand the process being used and can correct any inappropriate step. Another reason might be to ask questions about the referral problem. For example, if a student is having difficulty with written expression, you might ask questions about motivation and interest and could probe further to determine if there is an identifiable reason for the problem. Often, in fact, a student might open up and give information totally unrelated to the reason for the interview (e.g., problems at home or with peers). If the student had only been given conventional tests, then that opportunity probably would not have presented itself. One issue that must be considered, however, is the developmental level of the student. Chittooran and Miller (1998) noted that oftentimes adolescents might be hesitant about sharing information (or even resent the adult intrusion). Also, young children might need considerable rapport building and may be very distracted.

Parent Interviews.   Parent interviews can also be very helpful because, in most cases, the parent knows the student better than anyone else (although you should be aware of the possibility of biased information). Nonetheless, parent interviews are an excellent way of supplementing more conventional assessment techniques. Beaver and Busse (2000) identified three types of interview

Parent interviews are an excellent method of gathering additional information.

formats used with parents. The first is an **omnibus interview,** which is designed to gather a wide range of information. This type of interview is usually unstructured and allows the greatest flexibility. The second type is the **behavior-specific interview,** which is narrower in scope and focus. This allows you to ask specific questions about the student's behavior. The third type of interview is the **problem-solving interview,** in which the goal is to develop an intervention plan. In addition to unstructured interviews there are also structured interviews such as the *Diagnostic Interview for Children and Adults—Revised* (Reich, 1996), which is used for students with emotional or behavioral problems. There also is a semistructured interview in which specific questions are asked but you can also "probe" or ask follow-up questions based on the responses of the person interviewed. Beaver and Busse (2000) argued that this approach allows more flexibility than the structured interview yet provides more reliable information than the unstructured interview. Some tests (e.g., the *Vineland Adaptive Behavior Scales-II*, discussed in Chapter 8), in fact, use a semistructured interview format. Regardless of the type of interview you use, you should receive appropriate training.

In addition to obtaining valuable information about the specific nature of an individual's problem, interviews also let you obtain a historical perspective. For example, you might discover whether any factors in the student's home life have suddenly changed. You might also find out whether the primary language spoken in the home is the same as that used in school. In addition, you can determine whether the child behaves differently at home from at school. If, for instance, a child has problems at school but not at home, certain conditions can often be identified in the home environment that can be replicated in the school environment. Interviews with parents and analyses of the home environment are sensitive areas. Care must be taken not to imply blame or in any manner make the parents feel threatened or uncomfortable. To avoid this, a more structured approach is usually helpful unless the interviewer has had specific training. Also avoid asking questions that are irrelevant to the student's problem or situation. Any information gathered should serve a useful purpose.

Medical and Developmental Histories.   Another source of information is the medical and developmental history of an individual. Again, this is a sensitive area, in which only information that is potentially relevant to the assessment process should be obtained. Most medical and developmental histories are used in the early identification or prediction of some type of special problem or in the search for a cause or prognosis for a particular type of problem (particularly for more severe problems). If one of these is the goal for the assessment, an in-depth evaluation of developmental milestones and pre-, peri-, or postnatal infections, intoxications, or other events might be relevant. You must keep in mind, however, that knowing the cause of a problem does not necessarily imply an appropriate treatment program. Also, asking this information of a parent of a 7-year-old child with spelling problems probably would be unnecessary and might cause undue anxiety in that parent. ("Why are they asking me these questions? Do they suspect brain damage?") In other words, collect the information if there is a reason, but do not collect it if you are not going to use it or do not know what to do with it.

Error Analysis.   A great deal of information can be determined from the type of error a student makes in routine school work products that are easily obtained. Similarly, when test results (CRT or NRT) are examined, the type as well as the

---

OMNIBUS INTERVIEW
An interview designed to gather a wide range of information.

BEHAVIOR-SPECIFIC INTERVIEW
An interview focused around a student's particular behavior.

PROBLEM-SOLVING INTERVIEW
An interview in which the goal is to develop an intervention plan.

Don't overlook work products as an excellent source of information.

number of errors can provide meaningful information. Suppose, for example, that a student gave the following answer to an addition problem:

$$
\begin{array}{r}
1 \\
48 \\
+97 \\
\hline
155
\end{array}
$$

The student knew to carry the one to the tens place but made an error in adding $1 + 4 + 9$. This information would indicate that additional instruction in renaming might not be necessary but that addition of three one-digit numbers might be warranted. Suppose, however, that the student gave this answer:

$$
\begin{array}{r}
48 \\
+97 \\
\hline
1315
\end{array}
$$

This would indicate that the student *does* need instruction in renaming, because the student added the ones and tens columns separately. Figure 2.3 provides additional examples of types of errors that could be made on a simple arithmetic worksheet. The first problem in Figure 2.3 is an example of the use of a wrong operation; the person added instead of subtracting. The second example contains an obvious computational error. The third problem is an example of a defective algorithm; this means that procedural errors were made in an attempt to apply the correct process (in this example, subtracting the smaller number from the larger, regardless of placement). The answer to the last problem appears to be a random error. Clearly, each type of error requires a different remedial strategy.

Gable and Hendrickson (1990) provided several suggestions for maximizing the usefulness of error analysis. For example, they suggested that at least five items are necessary for a given skill before error analysis is used. They also noted that as a first step, a teacher should choose one subject area and one student rather than attempting to analyze errors for an entire class. Error analysis is discussed in later chapters that focus on academic assessment.

Use of Portfolios.   More recently, a number of *alternative assessment procedures* have been gaining popularity. One particularly helpful procedure is portfolio assessment. Using this approach, the student and teacher compile representative examples of the student's work. For example, a portfolio in the area of reading might include classroom tests, audiotapes, the teacher's observational notes, the student's self-evaluation, progress notes, and a list of books the student has read. The intent is to focus on both the process and the product of learning. Valencia (1990) compared portfolio assessment of academic areas to artists' portfolios, in

FIGURE 2.3   Examples of Error Analysis in Arithmetic

$$
\begin{array}{r}
38 \\
-21 \\
\hline
59
\end{array}
\qquad\qquad
\begin{array}{r}
53 \\
\times\ 2 \\
\hline
116
\end{array}
$$

Wrong operation   Computation error

$$
\begin{array}{r}
685 \\
-497 \\
\hline
212
\end{array}
\qquad\qquad
\begin{array}{r}
463 \\
\times 25 \\
\hline
185
\end{array}
$$

Defective algorithm   Random error

which samples of work are used to exemplify the breadth and depth of their expertise. Portfolio assessment as well as other alternative assessment procedures are discussed in Chapter 6.

In summary, a number of techniques and types of instruments are available to assess exceptional students. In general, these approaches are thought of as being *informal procedures* or *formal procedures*. Informal assessment procedures include observation, teacher-made criterion-referenced tests, error analyses, and the use of portfolio assessment. Formal assessment procedures include norm-referenced tests, as well as commercially prepared criterion-referenced inventories and tests. In addition, the dichotomy of **summative assessment** and **formative assessment** is sometimes used. Instruments and procedures used for summative assessment are those that summarize student performance or indicate what the student has learned as a result of instruction. These might include more formal tests such as norm-referenced instruments. On the other hand, instruments and procedures used for formative assessment are more informal and are used to help determine the best method of instructional practice. These might include observation, criterion-referenced testing, curriculum-based assessment, and portfolio assessment (Bigge & Stump, 1999). The choice of procedure depends largely on the purposes for the assessment. Table 2.1 matches the purposes with recommended formal and informal procedures.

Three points should be made about Table 2.1. First, these are merely *suggestions* for types of assessment procedures that can be used for various purposes. There are times when other tests or measures are more beneficial for the purpose stated. Conversely, not all the procedures mentioned need to be used in

SUMMATIVE ASSESSMENT
Summarizes what a student has learned as a result of instruction.

FORMATIVE ASSESSMENT
Designed to determine the best method of instruction.

TABLE 2.1   Matching the Purposes and Types of Assessment Procedures

	Type	
Purpose	*Formal*	*Informal*
1. Initial identification (screening).	Screening and readiness tests; achievement tests.	Criterion-referenced tests; observation; curriculum-based assessment.
2. Determination and evaluation of teaching programs and strategies.	Depends on area of need.	Criterion-referenced tests; error analysis; curriculum-based assessment; portfolios.
3. Determination of current performance level and educational need.	Achievement or diagnostic academic tests; other tests (depending on area of need).	Criterion-referenced tests; observation; curriculum-based assessment.
4. Decisions about eligibility and program placement.	Intelligence, achievement, adaptive-behavior and classroom-behavior measures.	Observation and criterion-referenced tests, used to supplement formal testing.
5. Development of IEPs (goals, objectives, teaching strategies).	Commercially prepared inventories and criterion-referenced tests.	Criterion-referenced tests; observation; error analysis; portfolios.
6. Evaluation of IEPs.	Some norm-referenced tests.	Criterion-referenced tests; observation; portfolios.

all situations. Second, you should determine whether to use informal procedures, formal procedures, or a combination of the two. For many purposes, either type will give the desired information. Third, there is a great deal of overlap in the types of procedures used; in other words, results from specific assessment procedures can often be used for more than one purpose (e.g., an error analysis of norm-referenced test results). Acknowledging this point and planning the procedures in advance will result in a more efficient, more practical assessment.

Who Should Assess?

The question "Who should assess?" raises the question of why the assessment is needed and how the results will be used. As noted previously, assessment can and perhaps should be performed by everyone involved with the education or training of an individual. This might include general education teachers, special education teachers, specialists, therapists, school psychologists, and parents. Each has a unique perspective that might prove invaluable. This does not mean that everyone should always be involved. Sometimes a teacher's assessment in the classroom is all that is needed. Other instances call for in-depth assessment by a number of professionals. Again, to a large extent, the purpose for assessment will determine who assesses.

Teachers should always be involved in the assessment process.

With the current emphasis on inclusion, it has become almost mandatory to involve both the special education teacher and the general education teacher in the assessment process at all times. Teachers are perhaps in the best position to assess their students effectively. First, there is a strong rapport between the teacher and student that might bring out the student's best effort. Second, the student can usually be assessed in the classroom, which typically reduces the common fear of testing. Third, the teacher can assess at the most appropriate times and not have to wait for an outside evaluator who often is working under a tight schedule. If the Response to Intervention model is used, the general education teacher will be actively involved.

When Should Assessment Be Conducted?

Time of assessment depends largely on the answer to the question "Who will assess?" which, in turn, depends on the question "Why assess?" Suppose, for example, that a student is being assessed to determine eligibility for special education. In addition to the teacher, a school psychologist and other diagnostic specialists are usually involved. Therefore, the issue of when to assess becomes one of scheduling. In other words, the student is usually pulled out of class and evaluated at a time that fits into both the examiner's and the student's schedule. Clearly, this is not always the most appropriate or beneficial time but is dependent on a number of factors, such as case loads or priorities for assessment. For this reason, it is even more important that teachers use discretion in referring students for further assessment and that they help in establishing priorities regarding who needs assessing the most. If many children in a class are referred for assessment, chances are that some students who do not really need this service will be evaluated, whereas others who need it will not be evaluated until later.

If a student is evaluated for a reason that can be solely addressed by the teacher (e.g., prereferral assessment or assessment for the RTI process), the issue of scheduling takes on new meaning. The student will not usually be taken out of the classroom, and so assessment time is either incorporated into or separated from teaching time. For example, it might be possible to administer an informal test to a student before and after group instruction in a certain academic area. It might also be possible to assess individually during the day when the rest of the class is busy doing some other type of assignment (such as individual seat work, workbooks, or small-group projects). As noted previously, it is also possible to evaluate all or some of the students in the class based on the content of the curriculum (CBA or CBM). Finally, materials for a portfolio can be routinely gathered and assembled for later analysis.

One way of looking at assessment in the classroom (and anywhere else, for that matter) is to think of a filtering process in which you begin with information for a number of individuals and gradually collect more on those who need more assessment. This is consistent with the Response to Intervention model currently being used to help identify students with learning disabilities. For instance, a group achievement test or curriculum-based assessment might be given as a first step to an entire class of thirty. The assessment at this stage could be incorporated into the teaching time. From these results, the teacher might identify 10 percent, or three students, who need further testing. As a second step, a more individualized achievement test could be given to that 10 percent to determine specific areas of academic strengths and weaknesses. This test could be given while the rest of the class is working on other assignments. Suppose one person performed poorly in math and another in spelling, while another had some minor problems in reading. As a third step, the teacher or other evaluator could then test the first two students' academic areas through diagnostic testing and find out what the students know within the area and possibly determine why the students are having problems. This assessment could be done either within or outside the classroom setting, depending on who assesses. For the third student, a prereferral intervention program could be initiated. Steps one and two could easily be administered by the teacher and, *if necessary,* by other professionals. It is at this point that the teacher typically makes the referral decision. It should be noted that parental permission should be obtained for steps two and three.

This is only an example of a sequence in which assessment might occur. Many times these specific steps will not be followed. If a teacher has a student who is clearly having serious problems—academic, emotional, or physical—then a referral is usually made with observational and supporting data but not necessarily with formalized test results.

What Should Be Done with the Results?

In a certain sense, this should be the first question asked. If you cannot answer it, you probably should not initiate the assessment. Too much time and energy are wasted on testing students and writing reports that are filed in folders and never used. If assessment data are collected, there should be a clearly specified means of using the results. What happens with the results depends largely on the purpose for assessment. For example, if you are assessing for initial identification purposes, the results might be used to determine the need for and type of further assessment or to monitor certain kinds of behavior that are considered high risk. Conversely, data for eligibility and program-placement decisions will be used

You should always know what to do with assessment results that are collected.

more formally, evaluated by a multidisciplinary team of professionals. Information for program planning might be used informally by a teacher to initiate or modify a teaching strategy, or it might be formally used to develop an IEP or IFSP. Whoever is involved in assessment should take the time to learn the policies governing dissemination of assessment data in his or her school or other educational setting. Knowing this information can expedite the effective use of assessment data and can increase communication among the various professionals involved in assessment.

An Assessment Model

Assessment should be a dynamic, continuous process undertaken with a clearly specified goal in mind. The process should be monitored and should be flexible enough to be modified if necessary. One way to view assessment is to break it down into two components: prereferral and postreferral (Figure 2.4). The goal of

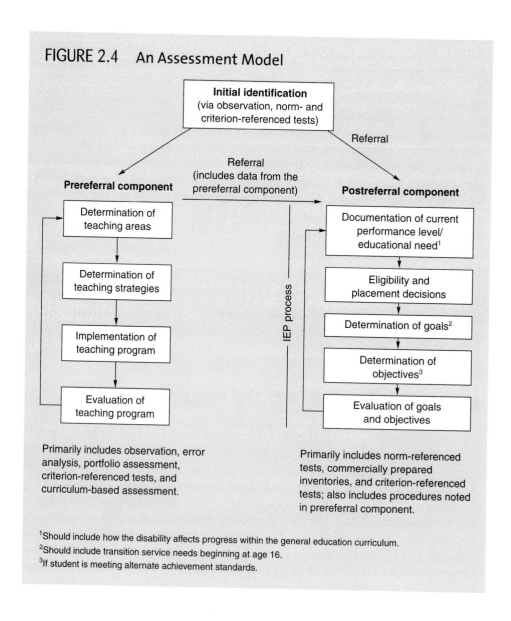

FIGURE 2.4 An Assessment Model

Initial identification (via observation, norm- and criterion-referenced tests)

Referral

Prereferral component

Referral (includes data from the prereferral component)

Postreferral component

Determination of teaching areas

Determination of teaching strategies

Implementation of teaching program

Evaluation of teaching program

IEP process

Documentation of current performance level/educational need[1]

Eligibility and placement decisions

Determination of goals[2]

Determination of objectives[3]

Evaluation of goals and objectives

Primarily includes observation, error analysis, portfolio assessment, criterion-referenced tests, and curriculum-based assessment.

Primarily includes norm-referenced tests, commercially prepared inventories, and criterion-referenced tests; also includes procedures noted in prereferral component.

[1]Should include how the disability affects progress within the general education curriculum.
[2]Should include transition service needs beginning at age 16.
[3]If student is meeting alternate achievement standards.

the *prereferral component* is to develop and implement a teaching or remedial program and to monitor the effectiveness of the program by observing the student's progress. Assessment in this component is conducted before making a referral for special education services and will, it is hoped, result in no referral at all. This component is heavily weighted toward informal assessment procedures, such as observation, error analysis of work products, portfolio assessment, curriculum-based assessment, and teacher-made tests. Note that the *purposes* for assessment are closely tied to the assessment model. If the purpose is identified, the appropriate steps in the model can be followed. Norm-referenced tests are also used occasionally. The prereferral component is usually implemented by the teacher within the student's current educational setting.

The *postreferral component* includes the documentation of an educational need and usually results in decisions about eligibility and program placement. It also might result in the development of a formalized IEP that includes the goals, objectives, instructional strategies, and time line for implementing and evaluating goals and objectives. This component includes both formal assessment (norm-referenced tests, also commercially prepared criterion-referenced inventories and tests) as well as informal assessment procedures. A multidisciplinary approach (including the teacher) is used during this component.

> All students receiving services under IDEA 04 go through the postreferral component.

It is entirely possible that *both* components might be included in the assessment of a particular student. Where possible, it is better to go through the prereferral assessment first. In fact, this is a requirement in many states. This will often yield enough information to deal with the situation that required the assessment. If further assessment is necessary, important prereferral information can be incorporated into the assessment at the time of the referral. On the other hand, with certain students, a referral may be justified as the first step, as soon as a problem has been identified. This is particularly true for children whose problems are severe and who definitely need supplementary or alternative programming. *Note that the procedures used and the information gathered in the prereferral component are of great value in the postreferral component.* In a sense, the entire prereferral component could also be considered as part of the postreferral component (particularly the documentation of educational need and IEP development steps).

CASE STUDY *June*

Following is more information about June, whom you met in Chapter 1. Read the information and respond to the questions that deal with the assessment issues presented in this chapter.

June's teacher, Mrs. Dunn, is concerned that June is not able to keep up with the requirements in fourth grade, particularly with the increased emphasis in the content areas of literature, science, and social studies. Because it is early in the school year, Mrs. Dunn has not determined what is causing the problem or how far behind June actually is. Her concern is based on June's poor performance on weekly in-class tests and assignments in language arts, science, and social studies. June frequently does not complete independent assignments in these subjects. However, when she is called on in social studies or science, June's oral comments show a good understanding of the subject matter. Mrs. Dunn also notes that June does not volunteer to read orally in her reading/literature group. When she does read orally, it is very slow, choppy reading, with many words misread. The only subject in which June is actually doing well is math. Behaviorally, Mrs. Dunn reports that June seems to be avoiding some tasks and often appears to be off-task or daydreaming. Mrs. Dunn has decided to collect information to help develop a prereferral intervention program.

- Develop a list of informal assessment techniques that Mrs. Dunn could use with June to gather more information as part of the prereferral process, and give a rationale for using these techniques with June.

Reflections

1. Do you think prereferral assessment is important? Why or why not?
2. Why do you think error analysis can be helpful for teachers?
3. Do you think students need to receive a label in order to receive special education services? Why or why not?

Summary

It is essential that the legal and philosophical factors that relate to special education be considered when planning assessment strategies. It is also important to answer several questions before any assessment begins. These questions are: (1) Why assess? (2) How is the process initiated? (3) What procedures should be used? (4) Who should assess? (5) When should assessment be conducted? and (6) What should be done with the results? Answering these questions will save time and avoid unnecessary or irrelevant assessment. It is possible, and in fact probable, that the answers to these questions will change once the process begins. It is necessary to keep thinking about them *throughout* the process. One way to do that is to think of assessment as a continuous, dynamic process, requiring constant monitoring and modification. When assessment is looked at in this way, who should be involved and how the results should be used will be clear. An assessment model was proposed that ties directly into this pragmatic philosophy. Once the specific purpose for the assessment was identified in the model, the procedures and steps to follow were delineated.

chapter three

Practical and Ethical Considerations

Several practical considerations must be addressed when conducting any type of assessment procedure. Although these considerations are relevant for all formal as well as informal assessment procedures, they are primarily related to norm-referenced testing. This relevance lies in the format and types of questions as well as in the kind of emphasis placed on the scores of norm-referenced tests. Another extremely important area is ethics. Everyone involved in the assessment process should be very aware of their ethical responsibilities. In this chapter, the practical factors that can affect test results and the ethical responsibilities of participants will be discussed. In reality, knowledge of the factors that can affect assessment leads to more ethical decisions about the use of the information that is obtained.

Practical Considerations: Factors Affecting Test Results

Three principal classes of factors can affect an individual's performance on a test and can minimize the meaning of, and in some cases invalidate, the test results. They are factors related to (1) the person being tested, (2) the examiner and the examiner–examinee interaction, and (3) the test itself. Each will be discussed separately.

Factors Related to the Examinee

Anxiety and Motivation. The first major potential source of error consists of factors related to the examinee. Among these are such factors as anxiety and motivation. All of us have probably experienced test phobia or test anxiety and know how it can affect performance. Zeidner (1998) noted the pervasive effect that test anxiety can have. "Indeed, many students have the ability to do well on exams, but perform poorly because of their debilitating levels of anxiety. Consequently, test anxiety may limit educational or vocational development as test scores and grades influence entrance to many educational or vocational training programs in modern society" (p. 4). Haladyna (2002) notes that about one of four students have some degree of test anxiety that will result in lower test scores. Several researchers have investigated the tendency for specific groups to be test anxious. Among those findings were:

- Stress behaviors during testing were noted as early as kindergarten (Fleege, Charlesworth, Burts, & Hart, 1992).
- Test anxiety was reported to be 41 percent among a sample of African American children (Turner, Beidel, Hughes, & Turner, 1993).
- Gifted students demonstrated considerable test anxiety (Polotsky, 1992).
- Students with learning disabilities and behavior disorders were more test anxious than their peers without disabilities (Swanson & Howell, 1996).
- Female college students reported higher levels of test anxiety than their male counterparts (Baker, 2003).

Some attempts at reducing test anxiety have resulted in reduced anxiety but no improvement in test performance (Kass & Fish, 1991), whereas others have reported both anxiety reduction and improved test performance (Giordano, 2000; Schweiker-Marra & Marra, 2000). There is also some evidence that eliminating time pressure reduces anxiety and improves test performance (Plass & Hill, 1986) and that a pretest review can minimize anxiety (Mealey & Host, 1992).

Similarly, lack of motivation may suggest that an "I don't know" response to a test question means "I don't care." Anxiety and motivational factors might be minimized by ensuring that a test environment is positive, supportive, and nonthreatening. Extra time spent establishing rapport might also help eliminate this source of error.

Students shouldn't be penalized for unfamiliarity with test formats.

Test Wiseness.   Another factor that may influence the student's performance on tests is the effect of practice, that is, repeated administrations of the same test or same type of test. Practice can occur through routine test taking or coaching. Johns and VanLeirsburg (1992) pointed out that students from different cultural groups as well as special education students could benefit from test-taking strategies.

There is evidence suggesting that test performance can be improved through practice of test-taking skills (Flippo, Becker, & Wark, 2000; Putnam, 1992). Yang (2001) found that test-wise students performed better than test-naïve students on the Test of English as a Foreign Language. Morse (1998) indicated that test-taking strategies such as eliminating irrelevant alternatives or selecting the answer having the most information were helpful and relatively easy to employ. One example of a strategy for improving math problem-solving performance was offered by Beattie and Enright (1993). They suggested that the student use the following five-step blueprint with the acronym SOLVE:

Study the problem.
Organize the facts.
Line up a plan.
Verify the plan.
Examine your answer.

In fact, books and manuals including strategies and exercises for improving test-taking skills have been developed (e.g., Ciardi, 1990; Gall, 1990). Rogers and Yang (1996) went so far as to suggest that training programs aimed at increasing test wiseness should be a regular part of the school curriculum. Haladyna (2002) suggested that teachers offer their students practice in all types of item formats, thereby increasing their sophistication in overall test taking. This type of approach also avoids possible violations of ethical principles.

There are also some data to support the idea that certain types of test performances are more amenable to coaching than others. In a series of studies (Scruggs & Mastropieri, 1986; Scruggs, Mastropieri, & Tolfa-Veit, 1986), it was found that students with learning disabilities and behavior disorders improved more on tasks such as word-study skills and mathematical concepts than on reading comprehension after coaching (consisting of teaching them to attend to the appropriate stimulus, mark answers correctly, use time wisely, and avoid careless errors). They hypothesized that two factors led to this result. First, the word-study and mathematical concepts have complicated formats that would ordinarily confuse students. Second, continued poor performance in reading comprehension was the result of problems in deductive reasoning and other deficits not related to the coaching per se. Enright, Beattie, and Algozzine (1992) also found that mathematics test performance could be improved by including a systematic review of the content as well as the format of the test during math instruction.

A "test to test test-wiseness" was even developed to identify students who lack test-taking skills (Parrish, 1982). The interesting question that must be asked is whether students should be trained if they are identified as having these deficiencies. On the one hand, if the goal is to get an accurate picture of how much a person knows, any disadvantage a person might have that is unrelated to the test content should be eliminated. On the other hand, training students might result in test scores that are not reflective of their true classroom performance. It seems that, once again, the *purpose* of the testing is important in that decision. Regardless of the purpose, the specific test items should not be taught; only instruction in test-taking skills should be considered.

Health and Emotional State.   Other factors that can affect the test taker's performance are health and emotional state. Time should be spent to determine whether a student is performing "typically" at the time of evaluation. A teacher is perhaps in the best position to make this judgment, and this is one of the many advantages of teacher assessment. If examiners other than the teacher (or another person familiar with the child) administer the tests, they should consult with the teacher to get this important information.

Type of Disability.   Depending on the type of disability that a student has, a number of factors might bias test results. For example, a student with a reading problem would be at a disadvantage on a timed math test that included story problems. Similarly, a young student with cerebral palsy would have difficulty on an intelligence test that included block building and other fine-motor tasks. As noted in Chapter 1, IDEA 04 mandated that students with disabilities be allowed accommodations during state- and districtwide testing. There has been considerable research since that mandate (initially in IDEA 97) on what accommodations should be given to students with disabilities and how effective these might be.

Thurlow, House, Scott, and Ysseldyke (2000) noted that the decision on what specific testing accommodations are made for a student is usually determined by the IEP team. Frequently, accommodations noted in the IEP for classroom assessment and instruction are also used in large-scale assessments. In fact,

The IEP team typically determines the assessment accommodations.

Ysseldyke, Thurlow, Bielinski, and colleagues (2001) noted that many instructional accommodations were the same as the assessment accommodations for students with disabilities involved in a statewide assessment program. They added, however, that some assessment accommodations were used that were not included in the students' IEPs as instructional accommodations.

There has been some research on the effects of certain test accommodations on test performance of students with disabilities. Some of that research is summarized below.

- When students with learning disabilities were read the math problems on a statewide test, their performance improved (Johnson, 2000), although reading the items on a reading test is obviously inappropriate (McKevitt & Elliot, 2003).
- Students with learning disabilities did not benefit from extended time nor a large-print edition of the test (Fuchs, Fuchs, Eaton, Hamlett, & Karns, 2000).
- Extended time might be helpful, depending on the students' age. Crawford, Helwig, and Tindal (2004) found that it significantly improved performance on a high-stakes writing assessment for students in grade 5 but not for students in grade 8.
- Simplifying the language on a large-scale math test helped special education students but did not help English Language Learners (Johnson & Monroe, 2004) (see Focus on Diversity).

Apparently, the *type of task* might effect the type of accommodation. Bolt and Ysseldyke (2006) found that the read-aloud accommodation had fewer measurement problems for the math portion of a large-scale math test than for the reading/language arts section. Fuchs and colleagues (2000) found that extended time did not help students with disabilities in math computation or math concepts but did help them with math problem solving. Figure 3.1 shows a model for making decisions about the appropriateness of an accommodation.

---

focus on
Diversity

What Accommodations Are Allowed for Students with Limited English Proficiency?

Rivera, Stansfield, and Sharkey (2000), cited in Duran, Brown, and McCall (2002), investigated the use of accommodations for students with limited English proficiency (LEP) in their statewide assessment program. They reported that there was considerable variation in the types of accommodations that were used. During the 1998–1999 school year, only thirty-seven states allowed accommodations for LEP students, and four types of accommodations were mentioned. Approximately half of the states allowing accommodations permitted changes in the presentation and response format of the test. All thirty-seven states allowed the adjustment of the assessment setting, such as administering the test in small groups, individually, or in an isolated area. Twenty-four states permitted the students to have extra time. Other accommodations included the use of a bilingual word list or bilingual dictionary and the use of translated tests. Although the most predominant language for translated tests was Spanish, others included Chinese, Haitian Creole, Hmong, Korean, Vietnamese, and Russian. As discussed earlier, however, there are problems with translated tests.

FIGURE 3.1 Decision-Making Process for Accommodations

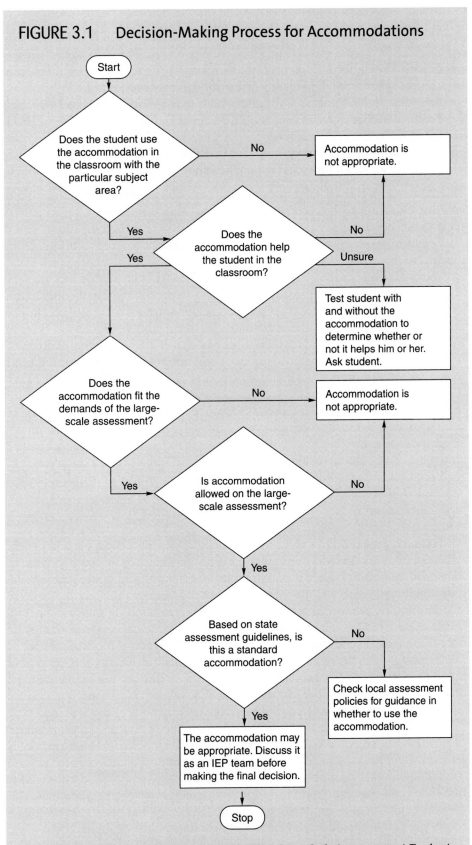

Source: E. Edgemon, B. Jablonski, and J. Lloyd. (2006). Large Scale Assessments: A Teacher's Guide to Making Decisions about Accommodations. *Teaching Exceptional Children, 38*(3), p. 10. Copyright 2006 by The Council for Exceptional Children. Reprinted with permission.

Elliott and Roach (2002) conducted a study to determine the impact of providing testing accommodations to students with disabilities. Among their findings were

- Students with disabilities participate in large-scale assessments at a significantly higher rate when testing accommodations are available.
- The majority of students with disabilities, perhaps 50 percent to 70 percent, produce higher test scores when given accommodations compared to their scores without accommodations.
- Some students without disabilities, perhaps 15 percent to 20 percent, also score higher when provided testing accommodations.

They also reported that both educators and states themselves are finding it difficult to include all students in testing programs and to document the accommodations that are used.

Computer-based accommodations have been attempted.

For those looking for a more data-based procedure for determining accommodations, a commercially prepared product, *Dynamic Assessment of Test Accommodations* (Fuchs, Fuchs, Eaton, & Hamlett, 2003) is available. To use this approach, students are administered brief tests with and without testing accommodations. Those scores are then compared to a normative sample of students without disabilities. When the score indicates that a student would benefit from the accommodation more than would be expected in the normative sample, direct accommodation is recommended. Computer-based test accommodations have also been attempted. Calhoun, Fuchs, and Hamlett (2000) found that there was no difference between teacher-read or computer-read administration, but that both improved test performance over no reading at all. It is clear that the accommodations in these large-scale assessments present practical psychometric and legal challenges that need continued research (Johnson, Kimball, Brown, & Anderson, 2001). It does appear that systematic training of teachers about legal requirements and possible IEP modifications result in more appropriate testing accommodations (DeStefano, Shriner, & Lloyd, 2001). Testing accommodations have been supported by parents, teachers, and the students themselves (Lang et al., 2005).

Jayanthi, Epstein, Polloway, and Bursuck (1996) surveyed over 700 general education teachers to determine their perceptions of testing adaptations for students with disabilities. They found that the most helpful adaptations were giving individuals help with test directions, reading the test questions to the students, and simplifying the wording of the questions. Interestingly, approximately two-thirds of the teachers felt that adaptations should be made for all students, not only those with disabilities. It should be noted that the most recent *Standards for Educational and Psychological Testing* (AERA, 1999) includes a separate chapter on testing accommodations used with individuals with disabilities. Included is a discussion of modifying presentation format, response format, timing, and test setting as well as using only portions of a test.

One approach that can be used to eliminate the need for accommodations, particularly for high-stakes assessment, is to design the instruments based on the concept of *universal design.* IDEA 04 indicates that universal design is the concept or philosophy that products and services should be designed and delivered so that they can be used by individuals with the widest range of capabilities. Universal design can also apply to assessment. The following questions have been recommended to consider when developing a universally designed test:

1. Do all visuals (e.g., images, pictures) and text provide information necessary to respond to the item?

2. Is information organized in a manner consistent with an academic English framework with a left–right, top–bottom flow?
3. Can booklets/materials be easily handled with limited motor coordination?
4. Are response formats easily matched to question?
5. Is there a place for taking notes (on the screen for computer-based tests) or extra white space with paper and pencil? (Johnstone, Thurlow, Moore, & Altman, 2006; p. 3)

Factors Related to the Examiner and the Examiner–Examinee Relationship

Differences in Administration.   The next major factor affecting test results relates to the examiner and the examiner–examinee relationship. One of the most common sources of error is differences in test administration and test interpretation. Assessment instruments, particularly norm-referenced tests, are designed to be administered in a standard, similar manner. However, many factors during the assessment process make this difficult to do. For example, although it is usually not recommended, a third party might be present during the testing session (e.g., if a young child has difficulty separating from the parent). However, there is some evidence that the presence of the other person affects attributes of the examinee's behaviors such as attention and verbal fluency (Kehrer, Sanchez, Habif, Rosenbaum, & Townes, 2000).

Differences in test administration can affect test results.

As noted previously, accommodations under certain conditions (particularly during group testing) are acceptable. However, examiners who evaluate students individually often differ in the amount of variation to the standard instructions and conditions. One reason for such variation is that examiners' personalities and methods of interacting with examinees result in differences in rapport and amount of feedback given, both of which can greatly affect the testing situation.

One method that has been used to address the concern about administration differences is *computer administration.* Maddux and Johnson (1998) noted that there are two general types of computerized testing: computer-based tests and computerized adaptive tests. A computer-based test means that the computer is used to administer a conventional test that has been simply transferred to the computer screen. On the other hand, computerized adaptive testing refers to tests "in which choice of the next item to be administered is made by reference to the examinee's performance on earlier items" (p. 94). There is some evidence that computerized adaptive testing can save considerable time over conventional administration without significantly affecting the overall scores or their validity (Forbey & Ben-Porath, 2007). Maddux and Johnson (1998) also summarized several reasons why computer-administered tests are used.

1. Computer administration can save time.
2. Assessment personnel will be freed from routine data gathering.
3. Test takers will gain a greater sense of control.
4. Precisely standardized administration procedures will be guaranteed.
5. Examinees will have more flexibility.
6. Most examinees have a good attitude toward computerized testing.
7. Examinees may receive their scores immediately.
8. Computers will permit the development of new kinds of tests.

We are all familiar with computer administrations of tests such as the *Scholastic Aptitude Test,* which is used for admission to university programs. Computerized tests are also available commercially, including the *Nelson-Denny*

Computerized administration is available for many tests.

Reading Test CD-ROM (Brown, Fishco, & Hanna, 2000). The Nelson-Denny is a computer-administered reading survey test designed to measure achievement and progress in vocabulary, reading comprehension, and reading rate. This program allows the test administrator to group test takers, monitor test sessions, allocate security information, and print different forms of reports, including a narrative report and a longitudinal report.

Although computer administration appears to solve some of the problems associated with differences in test administration, it does have its drawbacks. Maddux and Johnson (1998) noted, for example, that the computer version of a test cannot be assumed to be equivalent to the original paper-and-pencil edition and that computerized testing could dehumanize the assessment process. Kveton, Jelinek, Voboril, and Klimusova (2007) reported that computerized tests frequently do not provide psychometric properties or demonstrate that they are equivalent to their traditional counterparts. Another problem with computer-administered tests is that using a computer keyboard to answer the questions might be different from the method required to answer questions in the classroom (Gettinger & Seibert, 2000). Thus the computer version might not provide an accurate picture of the student's classroom performance. In one interesting study, Bridgeman, Lennon, and Jackenthal (2003) found that the size of the screen resolution affected scores on computer-administered verbal measures. It appears that technological issues related to both software and hardware need to be considered.

Differences in Interpretation.   In addition to differences in administration, there can also be differences in interpretation. Differences of interpretation are especially obvious when more subjective scoring systems are used. In many situations, a question has no right or wrong answer, but the answers have varying degrees of correctness, such as when test examiners are confronted with a unique, atypical, or ambiguous answer. Consider the following example of an interaction between the examiner and examinee on the comprehension subtest of the WISC-R:[1]

> *Examiner:* What are you supposed to do if you find someone's wallet or pocketbook in a store?
> *Examinee:* I'd give it to the person behind the counter.
> *Examiner:* What should you do if you see thick smoke coming from the window of your neighbor's house?
> *Examinee:* Call the police and call an ambulance.
> *Examiner:* What are some reasons why we need policemen?
> *Examinee:* Because people are always fighting and there are drugs around here.

If these answers are scored according to the criteria stated in the WISC-R manual, the student would receive a 2 (indicating best response) for the first two questions and a 0 (indicating an incorrect response or no credit) for the last question. What if, however, the student comes from a tough neighborhood where fighting and drugs are associated with the police? Would you score the response as incorrect in accordance with the test's scoring criteria? Would you give some credit because the response was correct, given the student's environment? No doubt, many examiners would respond differently to this example, depending

---

[1]The WISC-R is an earlier version of the Wechsler Intelligence Scale for Children—IV (WISC-IV) discussed in Chapter 7.

on their philosophy of assessment and the reason for the evaluation. Because standardized tests imply a standard format for administration and scoring, violations result in invalid findings. One guideline is to adhere strictly to the standard administration and scoring criteria and to state precisely why and where you differ if it is necessary to do so.

Examiner Bias.   Another examiner-related source of error is examiner bias. This is not necessarily conscious bias. Depending on the information you have heard about a particular student, you might have a tendency to give the benefit of the doubt or to be somewhat more conservative with the scoring. For example, empirical evidence suggests that the evaluator's knowledge of special education placement, race, gender, social class, and cultural background significantly affects diagnostic decisions (McDermott, 1981). One general guideline is to make use of the information that you have about an individual but make a conscious effort to avoid being biased. Also, it helps to be aware that some bias will probably still exist.

There are many sources of unconscious examiner bias.

The reason for testing can also affect the scoring. If you know that good students are being routinely evaluated, there might be a tendency to give them positive scores for ambiguous answers. If, however, you know that the "class troublemaker" is being evaluated for possible special education placement, you might not be as liberal in your scoring. Again, these are not necessarily conscious biases but, rather, biases that are tied into expectations.

Race of Examiner.   The racial differences between examiner and examinee have received widespread attention. For years, it was assumed, for instance, that African American children would score higher on tests if the examiner was also African American. An analysis of the research, however, suggested that the race of the examiner does not have a significant effect on test performance. Sattler and Gwynne (1982) reviewed twenty-seven published articles in which the race of the examiner was explored empirically; in twenty-three of the twenty-seven studies, no significant effect was found. They concluded that

> Some writers have simply declared by fiat that white examiners impair the intelligence test scores of black children. Unfortunately, this declaration is not justified by the available research, as the present review and as past reviews have shown. In everyday clinical and school encounters, there are probably individual cases in which a white examiner adversely affects a black person's performance on intelligence tests, but the research suggests that these situations are infrequent. (p. 207)

Lack of familiarity with the examiner may affect test results.

Similarly, Graziano (1982) reviewed fifteen years of research and found no biasing effect of examiner race. Smith, Bradham, Chandler, and Wells (2000) and Terrell, Daniloff, Garden, Flint-Shaw, and Flowers (2001) also reported that the race of the examiner was not a significant factor when evaluating African American students on language tests. Fuchs and Fuchs (1989), however, found that *familiarity* with the examiner did have an effect on Hispanic and African American children's test performance.

Culture and Language of the Examiner.   The cultural, language, and dialect differences of the examiner and the examinee have been explored to determine if they affect test performance. Padilla and Garza (1975) noted that:

> When a Spanish-surnamed examinee and a non-Spanish–surnamed examiner sit across from each other in a testing situation, there is often a wider gulf separating them than just the table. Typically, there is a linguistic, cultural, and socioeconomic

gap between them, associated with their different sets of life experiences. An examiner who is not sensitive to these differences will surely have a negative influence on the outcome of the child's performance. (pp. 55–56)

Hilton (1991) suggested that school personnel involved in assessment should be trained in cultural awareness. Hing-McGowan (1994) even developed a test data collection form that can be used to analyze tests for cultural fairness. The available research suggests that the effect of the language differences of both the examiner and test diminishes as the Spanish-speaking child spends more time in English-speaking schools (Clarizio, 1982). Wolfram (1990) also reported on the important role of dialect differences and its biasing effect on testing. Hilton (1991) went so far as to say that incorrect answers that reflect dialect differences should be accepted as correct responses.

Scoring errors can significantly affect test interpretation.

Scoring Errors.   Another source of examiner error is scoring errors. Although this is an area in which extra care can and should be taken, scoring errors do exist. These include errors such as computation mistakes, using the wrong conversion tables, or miscalculating the chronological age of the examinee. If the age of a student is miscalculated, it is highly likely that the incorrect conversion tables will be used and the wrong derived score will be reported. Although it would seem that determining a student's age shouldn't be a problem at all, it is actually quite a pervasive problem. The example below indicates the appropriate method to determine chronological age.

Problem

Danny, born September 17, 1995, was tested June 8, 2008. Exactly how old is he? (Many tests require exact year, month, and day.) Try to determine before reading the solution.

Solution

1. First step is to put date of testing in a year, month, day format.

Date of Testing	2008	6	8

2. Next step is to put the date of birth in the same order. *Note:* Most test protocols have a place for entering date of testing and date of birth.

Date of Birth	1995	9	17

3. Subtract the days.

Date of Testing	2008	5	38	
Date of Birth	1995	9	17	
			21	(Need to "borrow" 30 days [one month] from the months column. Unless noted otherwise in test manual, use 30 days)

4. Subtract the months.

Date of Testing	2007	17	38	
Date of Birth	1995	9	17	
		8	21	(Need to "borrow" 12 months from the years column)

5. Subtract the years

Date of Testing	2007	17	38
Date of Birth	1995	9	17
	12	8	21

Danny was 12 years, 8 months, and 21 days old when he was tested.

Scoring errors can cause problems leading to incorrect educational programming and, in some cases, incorrect eligibility decisions. As a rather dramatic example, Sherrets, Gard, and Langner (1979) analyzed thirty-nine examiners' scorings of 200 intelligence test protocols, and noted that 90 percent of the examiners made some kind of scoring error. The largest error would have raised the student's IQ by nine points or lowered it by seven points. Interestingly, 32 percent of the protocols included some type of simple addition error. The tendency to make scoring errors apparently begins early in a professional's career. One study reported that graduate students in training made scoring errors on 98 percent of the protocols examined, averaging almost 26 errors per protocol (Loe, Kadlubek, & Marks, 2007). There is some evidence, however, that the lack of significance of training programs to reduce scoring errors that has been reported in the literature is due to methodological problems in the research (Platt, Zachar, Ray, Underhill, & LoBello, 2007). Interestingly, the *Standards of Educational and Psychological Testing* (AERA, 1999) actually address scoring errors, noting that test users should be alert to their possibility and rescore if appropriate.

Factors Related to the Test: Technical Characteristics and Other Issues

The last factor that can affect test results relates to the test itself. This involves the test's technical adequacy (e.g., validity and reliability) or its possible bias against certain types of students.

Validity.[2] Validity refers to the extent to which a test measures what it purports to measure. Three major types of validity are included in a discussion of assessment instruments: criterion-related validity, content validity, and construct validity.

> Validity: Does the test measure what it purports to measure?

Criterion-related validity refers to the extent to which a person's score on a certain test correlates with a criterion measure (usually that person's score on another test). The correlation coefficient that this comparison yields is called a **validity coefficient.** Correlation coefficients indicate the degree of relationship between two variables. They range from a −1.00 (perfect negative correlation) to +1.00 (perfect positive correlation). A +1.00 correlation means that as the values of the first variable change, the values of the second variable change in the same direction. Alternatively, a −1.00 correlation means that as the values of the first variable change, the values of the second variable change in the opposite direction. Very rarely, however, do correlations reach −1.00 or +1.00. Usually,

> **CRITERION-RELATED VALIDITY**
> Refers to the extent to which a test correlates with a criterion measure (usually another test).

> **VALIDITY COEFFICIENT**
> A correlation coefficient ranging from −1.0 to +1.0 that is used in establishing criterion-related validity.

[2]The *Standards of Educational and Psychological Testing* (AERA, 1999) actually suggest that validity should not be discussed in terms of *types*, but rather in terms of *lines of evidence.* For example, instead of *criterion-related validity*, the term would be *criterion-related evidence of validity.* For this discussion, however, the more commonly reported types of validity will be used. As noted in the discussion, there is no such thing as a purely valid or invalid test; rather, there are degrees of validity, based on the evidence to support it.

correlations are expressed as a positive or negative two-digit decimal, such as .63 or −.86 or .75. In assessment, positive correlations are used almost exclusively. In measuring criterion-related validity, the closer the decimal is to +1.00, the more valid the instrument is with respect to the criterion measure. No cutoff point exists that makes a test either valid or not valid; in general, however, a validity coefficient of less than .70 for individual tests and less than .60 for group-administered tests probably should be interpreted with caution.

An example of establishing criterion-related validity is shown in Table 3.1, giving the data from two intelligence tests. By using the formula for determining correlation coefficients, you can determine that Intelligence Test 1 (test to be validated) correlates .86 with Intelligence Test 2 (criterion measure). This type of criterion-related validity is called **concurrent validity,** and it quantifies the degree to which a test correlates with a criterion measure administered at roughly the same time.

The other type of criterion-related validity is **predictive validity,** which refers to the extent to which test results correlate with a criterion measure that is given at some future time. To establish the predictive validity of the *Scholastic Aptitude Test* (SAT), for instance, the SAT scores (test to be validated) of individuals in high school might be correlated with these individuals' grade-point averages (criterion measure) after their senior year in college. The closer the correlation is to +1.00, the greater the predictive validity of the SAT.

Regarding criterion-related validity, it is important to be aware that a test is only as valid as the criterion measure. If authors report high correlations between their test and a criterion test that is not considered valid, this correlation does not

CONCURRENT VALIDITY
Quantifies the degree to which a test correlates with a criterion measure that is given roughly at the same time.

PREDICTIVE VALIDITY
The extent to which a test correlates with a criterion measure that is given at some future time.

TABLE 3.1   Example of Criterion-Related Validity

Subject	Intelligence Test 1 (Test to Be Validated)	Intelligence Test 2 (Criterion Measure)
Ron	97	94
Roni	89	96
Muriel	109	113
Mark	78	85
Juanita	98	95
Ruth	116	110
Helen	93	89
Stuart	100	109
Jay	100	97
Sherri	84	89
Scott	97	99
Randi	98	104
Sonny	102	99
Michael	108	112
JoAnn	89	90
Daniel	93	98
Evan	87	85
Erin	97	107
Lauren	108	110
Eric	111	106

make the authors' test valid. Therefore it is important to look not only at the magnitude of the correlation coefficient, but also at the *criterion measure itself.* Suppose, for instance, that you were interested in establishing the validity of a new intelligence test. You chose as your criterion measure the Terrible Test of Intelligence, a technically inadequate test in its own right. A high correlation would indicate that the new test measures areas similar to those measured in the historically inadequate Terrible Test.

Content validity refers to the extent to which a test accurately measures the sample of behaviors under consideration. Salvia, Ysseldyke, and Bolt (2007) noted three factors that should be considered in establishing content validity:

> **CONTENT VALIDITY**
> Refers to the extent to which a test accurately measures the sample of behaviors under consideration.

1. Appropriateness of the content (i.e., are the items appropriate in age level and content?)
2. Completeness of the content (i.e., does the test include a broad sample of tasks in the measured area?)
3. How content is measured (such as multiple choice, fill in the blank, or true–false)

Suppose, for example, that a test was developed to measure spelling for students in first through sixth grades. If the test had a number of extremely difficult items (e.g., *pulchritude, unctuous*), it would not be *appropriate.* If the test only included simple two-letter words (e.g., *do, an, of*), it would not be *complete.* If it required an examinee to indicate whether a word was spelled correctly using a true–false format, it might not be measuring spelling in an *appropriate way.*

Establishing content validity is extremely important, yet doing so is not as straightforward as determining criterion-related validity. One way to maximize content validity is to consider what needs to be measured and how it will best be measured during test construction. The determination of content validity usually involves some type of expert judgment. In the above example, a group of teachers familiar with spelling curricula might be asked to judge the content validity of the spelling test.

Construct validity has to do with the extent to which a test measures some type of theoretical characteristic or concept. Self-concept and reasoning ability are two examples of these relatively abstract constructs that are difficult to define and subsequently difficult to measure. In general, the establishment of construct validity includes the careful identification and definition of the construct and then the derivation and verification of hypotheses concerning test performance related to the construct (Gronlund, 2006).

> **CONSTRUCT VALIDITY**
> Refers to the extent that a test measures some type of theoretical characteristic or construct.

Construct validity is usually established through careful empirical studies using certain statistical procedures. Two procedures are frequently used for this purpose. The first involves the intercorrelation among test items to determine if the test measures the construct(s) it purports to measure (factor analysis). The second involves procedures to establish a positive correlation of the test scores with other measures that supposedly measure the same construct and a negative correlation with other measures that supposedly do not (convergent/discriminant validity). The *Standards for Educational and Psychological Testing* (AERA, 1999) list twenty-four standards related to test validity. Interested readers are encouraged to refer to those standards.

Reliability. Another important quality of a test is reliability. Reliability refers to the consistency of a test. If a test is not reliable, it is not dependable, stable, predictable, or accurate (Kerlinger & Lee, 2000). Lack of these traits is obviously undesirable in an assessment instrument designed to identify educational needs.

> Reliability: Does a test produce consistent results?

If a test is not reliable, by definition it cannot be valid. However, just because a test is reliable, it is not necessarily valid; in other words, results on a test could be consistent, but they could consistently measure the wrong thing. Five kinds of reliability are most commonly reported: test–retest, equivalent form, test–retest with alternate forms, internal, and interscorer.

Test–retest reliability quantifies the extent to which results from a test remain consistent over time. Test–retest reliability is established by correlating the test results of a group of individuals with the same individuals' test results after a relatively short period of time (usually about two weeks, but time varies with the type of test). Table 3.2 gives hypothetical data demonstrating the test–retest reliability of an intelligence test. The resulting correlation coefficient is .92, a figure that indicates a generally high test–retest reliability. Usually, a reliability coefficient of at least .90 is desirable for individual diagnostic tests, .80 for group-administered tests, and .80 for screening tests (Salvia, Ysseldyke, & Bolt, 2007).

Equivalent-form reliability is established by using alternate forms of an instrument that measure the same skills. For example, a test might have two forms, A and B, that measure the same skills but have different items. The correlation of scores quantifies the similarity of the two forms and gives some indication of the degree to which they are interchangeable. For example, two forms of a mathematics test might include different test items to measure knowledge of the same concepts. Equivalent-form reliability would be established by administering the two forms to the same population and correlating the resulting scores. In establishing equivalent-form reliability, it is important that the time between

> **TEST–RETEST RELIABILITY**
> Quantifies the extent to which results from a test remain consistent over time.

> **EQUIVALENT FORM/ ALTERNATE FORM RELIABILITY**
> Reliability is established by using alternate forms of an instrument that measure the same skills.

TABLE 3.2   Example of Test–Retest Reliability

Subject	Score on Intelligence Test (First Administration)	Score on Intelligence Test (Second Administration)
Ron	97	89
Roni	89	87
Muriel	109	109
Mark	78	80
Juanita	98	96
Ruth	116	119
Helen	93	99
Stuart	100	103
Jay	100	100
Sherri	84	82
Scott	97	93
Randi	98	99
Sonny	102	105
Michael	108	104
JoAnn	89	90
Daniel	93	97
Evan	87	84
Erin	97	104
Lauren	108	110
Eric	111	107

administration of the two forms be as short as possible. This eliminates the possibility that other factors might affect the test performances. Equivalent-form reliability is also referred to as *alternate-form reliability.*

Another method of establishing reliability that is, in a sense, a combination of the two previously discussed approaches is *test–retest with alternate forms.* This involves administering one form of a test to a group of individuals at a given time and then administering the alternate form of the test to the same group after a short period of time has passed. Many argue that this is the best method of estimating test error (e.g., Urbina, 2004). One should note, however, that the resulting correlation coefficient is lower than those yielded by the test–retest or alternate-form techniques.

Internal reliability is determined using a variety of procedures. This type of reliability refers to the internal consistency of a test and is computed using statistical procedures such as coefficient alpha and Kuder-Richardson formulas. Another procedure, called *split-half,* involves the correlation of one-half of a test with the other half (e.g., odd-numbered items vs. even-numbered items).

Interscorer reliability and **interrater reliability** are concerned with how consistently a test is scored or a behavior is rated by two examiners. In the first type, a test might be administered to a group of students and given to two individuals to score. The results of the two individuals' scoring of the tests for the student could be correlated to provide a reliability coefficient. In the second type, usually involved in behavioral observation, the percentage of agreement between two individuals observing the same behavior is computed. The previously mentioned *Standards of Educational and Psychological Testing* (AERA, 1999) also include twenty standards related to a test's reliability and standard error of measurement (discussed next).

> **INTERNAL RELIABILITY**
> Refers to the internal consistency of a test and is computed using statistical procedures.

> **INTERSCORER/INTERRATER RELIABILITY**
> Refers to how consistently a test is scored or a behavior is observed by two separate raters.

Standard Error of Measurement. A reliability-related characteristic that is often reported is the **standard error of measurement (SEM).** The SEM represents an attempt to account for the possible variability or error involved in the scoring and interpretation of a test. Because no tests are absolutely reliable, a person's **true score**—score on a test if the test were totally reliable—is never known. Individual scores on tests, therefore, can be thought of as estimates of true scores. The greater the reliability of a test the smaller the SEM (and vice versa).

The SEM provides a range that more accurately reflects how closely scores on a test approach the true scores. For instance, if Tyrone scored 110 on a given test whose SEM was 3, then approximately two-thirds of the time his true score would fall somewhere between 107 and 113 (± 1 SEM). Similarly, his true score would fall between 104 and 116 approximately 96 percent of the time (± 2 SEM). In general, the lower the SEM, the more confident you can be that a person's score on a test is an accurate estimate of the true score. Conversely, the larger the SEM for a test, the less confident you can be. The SEM is extremely important when eligibility decisions are considered. Many tests include **confidence bands** that are determined from the SEM. This allows the user to see the range of scores that represent the student's true score. The 90 percent range is frequently used. In other words, a test user can plot both the student's obtained score and the range that indicates where the student would score 90 percent of the time.

> **STANDARD ERROR OF MEASUREMENT (SEM)**
> Represents an attempt to account for the possible variability or error involved in scoring and interpretation of a test.

> **TRUE SCORE**
> A person's score on a test if the test were completely reliable.

> **CONFIDENCE BANDS**
> The range of scores that includes the true score, based on the SEM of the test.

Other Test Characteristics. Many tests also have basals and ceilings. Although not considered technical characteristics in a traditional sense, basals and ceilings are important to understand for both correct administration and interpretation. Basals and ceilings are used in power tests in which the difficulty level of the

> Basal and ceiling rules can vary from test to test.

BASAL

The point on a test at which the examiner assumes that the student could answer easier items.

CEILING

The point on a test at which the examiner assumes that the student would miss more difficult items.

items progresses from easy to hard. The **basal** of a test is the point at which the examiner assumes that the student could answer easier items. The **ceiling** of a test is the point at which the examiner assumes that the student would miss more difficult items. The use of a basal and a ceiling allows the examiner to save time by not administering items that are probably too easy or too difficult for the student. The following two examples of applying basal and ceiling rules are based on subtests from popular tests, the *Key Math–3* (KM-3) and the *Peabody Individual Achievement Test–R* (PIAT-R). For the KM-3, the basal is considered the four consecutive responses immediately preceding the easiest item missed; the ceiling is four consecutive errors. The following example is from the Numeration subtest from the KM-3. The first item administered was item 10 (as noted in the manual based on grade level of the student). Item 10 was correct so item 11 was administered. Because this item was missed, the examiner worked backward (as noted in the manual) starting at item 9 to establish the basal. That item was missed although the next four were correct, thus establishing the basal at item 6. Next, item 12 was administered and was correct although the next four items (13–16) were incorrect so the ceiling was established. The raw score is 10 (number of correct responses giving credit for items prior to the basal).

Item

1.

6. Administered after Item 7; Answer was correct; Basal established; Go to Item 12.

7. Administered after Item 8; Answer was correct; Go to Item 6.

8. Administered after item 9; Answer was correct; Go to Item 7.

9. Administered after Item 11; Answer was incorrect; Go to Item 8.

10. STARTED TESTING here; Answer was correct; Go to Item 11.

11. Administered after Item 10; Answer was incorrect; Go to Item 9.

12. Administered after Item 6; Answer was correct; Go to Item 13.

13. Administered after Item 12; Answer was incorrect; Go to Item 14.

14. Administered after Item 13; Answer was incorrect; Go to Item 15.

15. Administered after Item 14; Answer was incorrect; Go to Item 16.

16. Answer was incorrect; Ceiling established; STOP TESTING.

24.

Raw Score is 10.

The next example is from the General Information subtest from the PIAT-R. The basal rule for this test is the highest five consecutive correct responses, and the ceiling rule is the lowest seven consecutive responses containing five errors. The first item administered was item 30 (as noted in the manual based on grade level of the student). Item 30 was correct so item 31 was administered. Because this item was also correct, the examiner administered item 32, which was also answered correctly. At this point the examinee had three in a row correct. Item 33 was missed, however, so item 29 was administered to establish the basal. When the examinee answered that item and the next item (28) correctly, the basal was established and item 34 was administered to begin establishing the ceiling. Items 34 and 35 were correct. When the examinee missed the next four items

(36–39), the ceiling criterion of five (33, 36–39) out of the last seven answers (33–39) being incorrect was established. The raw score is 34 (number of correct responses giving credit for items prior to the basal).

Item

1.

⫻

28. Administered after Item 29; Answer was correct; Basal established; Go to Item 34.

29. Administered after Item 33; Answer was correct; Go to Item 28.

30. STARTED TESTING HERE; Answer was correct; Go to Item 31.

31. Administered after Item 30; Answer was correct; Go to Item 32.

32. Administered after Item 31; Answer was correct; Go to Item 33.

33. Administered after Item 32; Answer was incorrect; Go to Item 29.

34. Administered after Item 28; Answer was correct; Go to Item 35.

35. Administered after Item 34; Answer was correct; Go to Item 36.

36. Administered after Item 35; Answer was incorrect; Go to Item 37.

37. Administered after Item 36; Answer was incorrect; Go to Item 38.

38. Administered after Item 37; Answer was incorrect; Go to Item 39.

39. Administered after Item 38; Answer was incorrect; Ceiling established; STOP TESTING.

⫻

100.

Raw Score is 34.

Note that basal and ceiling rules vary from test to test; it is very important that an examiner be familiar with them. For example, the criteria for the basal and ceiling can be different, and the method of administering the test to establish them can vary.

Possible Test Bias. A test is often considered biased when individuals with certain characteristics (such as different ethnic groups, geographic regions, economic levels, or gender) consistently score differently when it is administered under similar conditions. For example, a test might be considered biased if, when administered in a consistent fashion, Hispanic students score lower than white children, males lower than females, or rural children lower than urban children.

There are actually several possible reasons why individuals with certain characteristics might score lower on a particular test. One explanation is that the differences in test scores are a result of bias in the test itself. For example, Abedi (2003) reported that science and math test items that were highly language-loaded introduced measurement error and resulted in lower scores for students with limited English proficiency. Abedi (2006) also reiterated that language factors not related to the content of tests may negatively affect their validity with English Language Learners and warned against their use when determining special education eligibility in this population. Another explanation is that the differences in test performance reflect true differences and therefore are not the result of test bias. These differing interpretations of the same phenomenon have resulted in heated debate regarding test bias, particularly in the area of intelligence testing. Considerable attention was addressed in the 1970s to the bias of intelligence tests against ethnic minority students (see Hobbs, 1975; Mercer, 1972, 1973; Samuda, 1975). A number of court cases investigating the discriminatory nature of intelligence testing resulted from this attention. Unfortunately, the results from litigation have provided little additional insight into the issue of bias in testing. As noted in Chapter 1, in some cases, such as *Larry P. v. Riles*, the decision implied bias in the tests, whereas in others (*PASE v. Hannon*), the decision did not support test bias.

What is evident from the history of contradiction regarding test bias is the need for a clear definition of bias or at least a delineation of the types of bias that can be empirically explored. Reschly (1980) identified nine common definitions, four of which are particularly relevant to this discussion. These are mean-difference bias, item bias, psychometric bias, and factor-analytic bias.

Mean-difference bias is perhaps the most common definition of bias and is the one described in the previous discussion. It asks the question, Do individuals with different characteristics score differently on the same test? Because certain groups do score lower on certain types of tests, those tests have been considered biased against those groups. As discussed previously, the causes of those differences in scores are subject to considerable controversy. Edwards (2006) argued that the existence of mean differences does not constitute test bias per se. However, if a test is chosen that is known to result in lower scores for students with certain characteristics (that are the same as the student being tested), then bias does exist. In fact, according to the *Standards for Educational and Psychological Testing* (AERA, 1999), mean differences of various subgroups should be considered when an examiner is choosing a test.

Item bias refers to the situation in which specific items on a test are considered to be outside the life experiences of certain individuals. For example, a potentially biased item for a lower-socioeconomic, rural child might be "How far is it from New York to Los Angeles?" (from the WISC-R, one of the tests involved in litigation). Other items might be considered biased if a certain type of typical, stereotyped response is considered the correct answer. For example, one item that appeared in the WISC-R is, "What is the thing to do if a boy (or girl) much smaller than yourself starts to fight with you?" The answer that receives the most credit is to "walk away," although many individuals have argued that this would not be an appropriate response (or behavior) of an inner-city child in a dangerous neighborhood.

Williams (1972) developed a test to illustrate the point that administering a test that includes items to which a person has not been exposed results in biased decisions. His test, called the *Black Intelligence Test of Cultural Homogeneity*, included 100 vocabulary words that he thought would be a better predictor of learning ability for African American children than traditional intelligence test items. Figure 3.2 shows examples from this test. The difficulty with deciding which items on a test are biased is that it requires subjective judgment, a problem that has resulted in experimental investigation and criticism.

Other types of bias include **psychometric bias** and **factor-analytic bias.** Psychometric bias is determined by asking the question, Are the technical characteristics (e.g., validity and reliability) similar for individuals with different characteristics? Factor-analytic bias involves the use of a statistical procedure in which items (or subtests) are grouped together because they correlate highly with one another and have low correlations with other factors identified by the same process. To determine this type of bias, one would see if similar or different factors on a test were identified for the groups of individuals under investigation.

MEAN-DIFFERENCE BIAS
Addresses the question, Do individuals with different characteristics score differently on the same test?

Test bias is a complex and multifaceted issue.

ITEM BIAS
Refers to the situation in which specific items on a test are considered outside the life experience of certain individuals.

PSYCHOMETRIC BIAS
Determined by asking the question, Are the technical characteristics (reliability and validity) similar for individuals with different characteristics?

FACTOR-ANALYTIC BIAS
Involves the use of a statistical procedure in which items or subtests are grouped together because they correlate highly with one another and have low correlations with other factors identified by the same process.

FIGURE 3.2   Examples from the Black Intelligence Test of Cultural Homogeneity

1. Alley apple
   a. Brick
   b. Piece of fruit
   c. Dog
   d. Horse

2. Deuce and a quarter
   a. Money
   b. A car
   c. A house
   d. To like

3. The eagle flies
   a. The blahs
   b. Movie
   c. Pay day
   d. Deficit

Correct answers:
   1. (a)
   2. (b)
   3. (c)

This type of bias is related to psychometric bias, because it essentially focuses on the issue of construct validity.

Clearly, the issue of test bias raises important questions and, once again, should make us look carefully at the uses and limitations of test scores. For example, IQs are relatively good predictors of academic abilities but should not be used to measure "intellectual potential." These important points are discussed in depth in Chapter 7.

Ethical Considerations

Individuals involved in the assessment process must be aware of their ethical responsibilities. Significant decisions about a student's current educational program and his or her future are made on the basis of assessment information. In a survey of ethically challenging situations encountered by school psychologists, Jacob-Timm (1999) found that those involving assessment issues were second only to administrative pressure to compromise ethics. These issues included inappropriate assessment resulting in questionable findings or misdiagnosis, inadequate interpretation of test results, and poor quality psychological reports (e.g., signing and submitting a computer-generated report as if it was the evaluator's interpretation). Careful consideration of the factors noted earlier in this chapter and answering the prerequisite questions noted in Chapter 2 will certainly help to avoid these types of situations.

Ethical standards are one of several sources that guide the conduct of assessments by school personnel. Other sources (discussed in Chapter 1) are federal and state constitutions and federal and state case law and statutes (McGivern & Marquart, 2000). Many professional organizations have developed ethical codes to provide guidelines for their members. For example, the Council for Exceptional Children, American Psychological Association, National Association of School Psychologists, the American Counseling Association, the

Many professional organizations have ethical codes and standards.

National Association of Social Workers, and the National Education Association, among others, have developed such codes (although not all have standards related to assessment). Several of these organizations, however, do have ethical guidelines related to assessment. The following standards are adapted from the American Psychological Association Code of Ethics (2002). The term *psychologist* was replaced by *examiner,* as the latter term is relevant for all individuals involved in the assessment process.

902 Use of Assessments

(a) Examiners administer, adapt, score, interpret, or use assessment techniques, interviews, and teaching instruments in a manner and for purposes that are appropriate in light of the research on or evidence of the usefulness and proper application of the techniques.

Essentially, this means that examiners should use assessment techniques appropriately and for the purposes for which they were intended. Also, any research on these procedures should be considered. That research is highlighted throughout this text.

(b) Examiners use assessment instruments whose validity and reliability have been established for members of the population tested. When such validity or reliability has not been established, examiners describe the strengths and limitations of test results and interpretation.

This point is particularly relevant for students with disabilities and for students from culturally and linguistically diverse backgrounds. This information, when known, is reported for specific tests and procedures in this text.

(c) Examiners use assessment methods that are appropriate to an individual's language preference and competence, unless the use of an alternative language is relevant to the assessment issues.

This standard reinforces the importance of nondiscriminatory evaluation. As noted in IDEA 04, tests and other evaluation materials are "provided and administered in the language and form most likely to yield accurate information."

9.06 Interpreting Assessment Results

When interpreting assessment results, including automated interpretations, examiners take into account the purpose for the assessment as well as the various test factors, test-taking abilities, and other characteristics of the person being assessed, such as situational, personal, linguistic, and cultural differences, that might affect examiners' judgments or reduce the accuracy of their interpretations.

Variables that might affect test results (e.g., fatigue or stress) should be considered. In addition, issues such as dominant language, ethnic background, and educational opportunities should be considered. (Again, these issues were discussed earlier in this chapter.)

9.07 Assessment by Unqualified Persons

Examiners do not promote the use of psychological assessment techniques by unqualified persons except when such use is conducted for training purposes with appropriate supervision.

This point is also made in IDEA 04 and the *Standards for Educational and Psychological Testing* (AERA, 1999). Clearly, examiners should not administer and interpret assessment procedures for which they are not trained.

9.08 Obsolete Tests and Outdated Test Results

(a) Examiners do not base their assessment or intervention decisions or recommendations on results that are outdated for the current purpose.

As mentioned several times in this text, revised versions of tests typically yield different scores (usually lower) than their predecessors. Unless there is a reason, the most recent version should be used.

(b) Examiners do not base such decisions or recommendations on tests and measures that are not useful for the current purpose.

CASE STUDY *June*

In Chapters 1 and 2 you learned that June's teacher, Mrs. Dunn, is concerned about her performance in fourth grade, particularly in reading and several content areas. June is also somewhat inattentive. Mrs. Dunn gathered informal assessment information and provided a prereferral intervention program that was unsuccessful. June eventually was referred and was evaluated to determine special education eligibility.

- Indicate factors specifically related to June that should be considered in her assessment, and indicate how each might be addressed.

Reflections

1. Why do you think IDEA 04 allows accommodations for students with disabilities for high-stakes assessment?
2. Why do you think it is important to establish rapport with a student before beginning any assessment?
3. Why do you think it is important for everyone involved in the assessment process, not just psychologists, to be familiar with ethical standards?

Summary

Several considerations must be addressed during assessment. These include practical considerations or factors that pertain more to formal assessment procedures, although they can also provide guidelines for informal procedures.

The first factor that could affect test results is related to the person being tested (the examinee). Included in this category are such factors as anxiety, motivation, previous test experience, health and emotional status, type of disability, and attitudes of the person being tested. The second major factor relates to the examiner. In this category, test administration and interpretation differences, styles of interacting with the examinee, bias, language or cultural differences between the examiner and examinee, and scoring errors were discussed. The last major factor is in the test itself, including its validity, reliability, standard error of measurement, and possible bias. All three of these factors should be considered throughout the assessment. Acknowledging these factors will help reduce some of the error and put assessment data into proper perspective. Specifically, these factors should be considered during test selection, administration, and interpretation. Such consideration should give a test user some idea of the limitations of assessment information and, when relevant, some idea of appropriate generalization of assessment data.

The ethical responsibilities of those involved in the assessment process, in part, have to do with acknowledgment and understanding of the previously discussed factors and the resulting decisions regarding the administration of assessment results. For example, understanding the technical characteristics of tests, identifying factors related to the examinee that might affect test performance, and acknowledging cultural and linguistic factors are all ethical issues that must be considered when administering assessment instruments and interpreting assessment information.

part two

Informal Procedures

Basic Tools for Teachers

Most assessment can and should be incorporated into the students' "routine" daily schedule. In other words, teachers should be aware of the importance of gathering information that is provided during the instructional process. In many cases, such data can be routinely collected through observation (discussed in Chapter 4). In other cases, the teacher can use the curriculum or a student's individualized education program (IEP) to develop a criterion-referenced instrument (discussed in Chapter 5) or a curriculum-based assessment instrument (also discussed in Chapter 5). These types of tests provide the teacher with relevant information on which to base instructional decisions. The teacher might also use alternative assessment procedures, such as portfolio assessment, to gather meaningful educational information (discussed in Chapter 6).

As noted in Chapter 2, all of these informal procedures are important throughout the assessment process. They are crucial to the prereferral component and can provide much-needed information for developing prereferral intervention programs and documenting referrals of students for special education. They can be used by those who use the Response to Intervention model. These approaches are also invaluable in developing and evaluating educational programs after a student has been identified as needing special education services (postreferral component).

For each technique that is described in this section, the following information is provided:

1. A summary matrix that presents information about specific techniques in a format allowing easy comparison of the techniques for suggested use and target population. The matrix also includes a statement of any special considerations of which a user should be aware. In addition, for each technique, the matrix gives the educational relevance for exceptional students. The matrices are directly related to the assessment model proposed in Chapter 2.

2. An introduction box for each technique identifying the suggested use and the suggested user.

AFTER READING PART TWO
You Should Be Able To:

- Identify the components involved in observational assessment, including the appropriate recording procedures.

- Identify the steps involved in conducting a functional behavior assessment.

- Identify the steps involved in developing a criterion-referenced test.

- Identify the steps involved in developing a criterion-referenced curriculum-based assessment instrument.

- Identify the similarities and differences between criterion-referenced curriculum-based assessment and curriculum-based measurement.

- Identify several types of alternative assessment procedures.

- Identify the uses and limitations of portfolio assessment.

- Identify the steps in developing a portfolio assessment.

chapter four

Observation and Functional Behavior Assessment

Observation is perhaps the most pervasive and widely used method of assessment. It also is generally thought of as the most direct method of obtaining assessment data with the least amount of inference by the evaluator. Virtually every second spent during a day in the classroom yields a tremendous amount of observational data. The key, however, is to use the observational data in a systematic and meaningful way. Observational data can be used for a variety of purposes. As mentioned in Chapter 2, the collection of prereferral information is important in determining the course and method of evaluation. Observational data certainly fit into this category of prereferral assessment. Such data can be used to determine and evaluate a teaching or behavioral program that in turn can be used to identify those students who will need more in-depth formal evaluation. Observation can also be helpful in developing and monitoring Individualized Education Programs (IEPs) for both academic and nonacademic behavior. On the other hand, observation of the instructional environment can also provide important information for making educational decisions. Observation is also a crucial component of functional behavior assessment (FBA). FBA is now required if there is a change in placement for a student with a disability because of problem behavior.

When most people think of observation as an assessment tool, they think about observing student behavior to obtain information that will aid in educational decision making. However, as noted previously, observation of the educational or instructional environment can also provide valuable information.

Observational techniques can be classified as either formal or informal. Formal approaches include observational packages that usually include specific coding and scoring systems. Informal approaches—by far more commonly used—include observation with the observer already present in the setting, observation with an outside observer in the setting, and observation with the observer not present in the setting. These types of informal approaches are particularly relevant when student behavior is being observed.

Student Observation—Informal Systems

Why Use Informal Student Observation?

Screening and identification; informal determination and evaluation of teaching programs and strategies; documentation of need for further evaluation or referral; development and evaluation of IEPs; assist in FBAs.

Who Should Use It?

Primarily teachers; also school psychologists and parents.

In the most widely used of the three informal procedures, the observer is already present in the natural environment. In this approach, many times the teacher is the primary evaluator or observer. It is also possible that peers—or even the target child—could perform these observations. Theoretically, the primary advantage of observation by someone already present is that in the absence of an external observer, the observed child should "act naturally." Observation of the child's behavior in the natural setting, with no changes in the schedule or routine or environment, should give a truer measure of the observed behavior. This procedure also has disadvantages. First, it is often difficult to manage (or find) the time to collect observational data. This is particularly true for the teacher. It is possible to have teachers' aides collect this information, but again, the time element is extremely crucial.

The second type of informal procedure uses an external or outside observer in the natural setting. The observer can be a psychologist, parent, volunteer, principal, or any school staff member who does not routinely work with the child in that setting (usually the classroom). The advantage of this procedure is that it allows the teacher to continue in the routine daily schedule. The observers can work at times that are appropriate both for the child and for themselves. The disadvantage of this approach is that it may cause **reactivity** (the effect of an observer on the behavior of the observed individual) that might bias the results.

REACTIVITY
The effects of the observer's presence.

Many researchers (e.g., Boehm & Weinberg, 1997) have discussed the issue of reactivity and its effects on observational assessment. Skinner, Dittmer, and Howell (2000), in fact, summarized a number of ways that reactivity could be reduced. These included providing students with a vague explanation for the presence of the observer, decreasing the conspicuousness of the observer, and having the observer enter the room prior to the student.

The third informal procedure involves an observer who is not present in the natural setting. This approach usually includes an artificial apparatus such as a one-way mirror or a videotape or audiotape that can later be transcribed. The advantage of this approach is that the child sees no observer, so that reactivity becomes less of an issue. The apparatus itself, however, can have some reactive effect on the child (Boehm & Weinberg, 1997). Obviously, the less obtrusive the apparatus, the more "naturally" a child will behave. This approach can be time-consuming (particularly using tapes) or restrictive (not every classroom has one-way mirrors).

Another approach, although technically not direct observation, is **analogue assessment.** Using this indirect observation procedure, the observer sets up a hypothetical or simulated situation that mirrors the real-life situation in which the behavior occurs (Hintze, Stoner, & Bull, 2000). This usually involves role playing in which the observer interacts with the student (Norton & Hope, 2001). This might be used, for example, when a behavior occurs in a situation that would make direct observation difficult (e.g., interaction between student and bus driver). It should be pointed out, however, that limited research has been conducted on the use of analogue assessment with students with behavior problems (Mori & Armendariz, 2001).

With each of these informal observation procedures, it is extremely important to obtain reliable, valid information. For maximum reliability in obtaining information, observers should use specific operational definitions and collect inter-rater reliability data—that is, more than one person should observe the behavior until all observers reach agreement. For maximum validity, information should be collected by observing the behavior in the environment in which it is a concern. Also, the observation must measure a representative sample of the person's behavior. In general, ensuring the reliability and validity of informal observation is often overlooked, an unfortunate oversight that could have a negative effect on the decisions made about the observed student.

> **ANALOGUE ASSESSMENT**
> An indirect procedure that uses a simulated or hypothetical situation for observation.

Goals of Observing Student Behavior

There are several specific uses of observation for educational decision making. These include (1) early detection of problems, (2) making decisions about entry behaviors, and (3) making instructional decisions (Cartwright & Cartwright, 1984). Another important goal of observation that incorporates many of the previously mentioned uses is to provide a model to allow teachers to increase, decrease, or maintain certain academic or social behaviors of their students.

Early Detection of Problems.   Observation to detect problems is an informal way of screening. It simply means that the observer notes that a student is starting to experience difficulty in some area. This observation is usually based on the observer's knowledge of "typical" or "expected" development or on a comparison to other individuals who have similar characteristics (e.g., same age and gender). This can lead to more formal assessment to determine the extent and possible cause of the problem.

Making Decisions about Entry Behaviors.   In a sense, making decisions about entry behaviors is similar to determining a student's current level of performance. In other words, it allows an observer to determine what behaviors in a given area a student already possesses. This requires that the observer critically analyze the student's needs to determine which behaviors should be observed. This usually involves some type of ecological assessment, or analyzing the environments within which the student exists or will exist to determine those behaviors necessary to function as independently as possible. These might be academic skills for younger students with mild disabilities, more functional "survival" skills, such as recognizing danger signs or completing job applications, for older students with disabilities, or independent living skills for students who have more severe disabilities. By determining a student's entry level in specified areas, the observer will have a good idea where to begin a more in-depth evaluation.

Making Instructional Decisions.   Another use of observation is to help make instructional decisions. As Cartwright and Cartwright (1984) noted, "If you have been able to collect information about a child's history of successes with different instructional materials, then you are better able to select appropriate teaching methods and materials that can be used with some assurance of effectiveness with the child." Using observation for this purpose is important in planning pre-referral intervention strategies.

Student Observation: A Model

One important goal of observational assessment is to provide information that will enable a teacher to increase, decrease, or maintain specific academic and nonacademic behaviors. Put another way, observation should be used to improve instructional decision making (Daly & Murdoch, 2000). This can be easily accomplished if a four-step model is followed. Those four steps are

1. Careful identification of the target behavior
2. Precise and appropriate measurement of the target behavior
3. Systematic introduction of intervention or remedial program
4. Evaluation of program effectiveness

Identification of the Target Behavior.   The success of any program designed to change behavior will depend largely on how well the target behavior is defined. It is extremely important that behaviors be identified in terms that are precise, observable, and measurable. Terms such as *aggression, hyperactivity, poor self-concept,* and *academically slow* are too vague and general to have any practical value. These terms also mean different things to different people, making it difficult to obtain reliable measurement. In general, behaviors presented in terms of traits or personality characteristics are too general to be of much value. If behaviors are defined objectively, few or no inferences are necessary to detect behaviors when they occur. For example, aggression might be defined as "strikes out at others with fists or objects" or "verbally abuses others by using curse words or a loud tone of voice." Similarly, poor self-concept might be defined as "makes negative statements about self," and hyperactivity might be considered as "gets out of seat at inappropriate times."

In the above examples, the behaviors are precise, observable, and measurable; yet even these could be still further defined to include the setting and a clarification of terms. For example, it might be acceptable for a child to raise his or her voice on the playground. It also might be necessary to indicate at which times or in which situations getting out of a seat is considered inappropriate. In every instance when the behavior is defined, the student, the situation, and the anticipated goal or outcome should be kept in mind. For every child labeled distractible, the term *distractibility* might be defined differently. You should strive to be specific enough so that if other people were to observe and measure the behavior they would be able to obtain the same or similar results. It is also important to be aware of the possibility of "observer drift," a situation in which the observer gradually shifts from the initial definition of the target behavior (Alberto & Troutman, 2006).

Measurement of the Target Behavior.   The accurate, careful recording of behavioral data is extremely important. Informal observational assessment requires the evaluator to develop and implement a unique measurement system. Typically, lack of time or misunderstanding of the importance of objective data leads to the use of some type of subjective system. Subjective systems include evaluations such as, "Dmitri seems to be doing much better in the area of self-help skills," or "Sally appears to be getting out of her seat less often than she used to."

Observational data are usually recorded as frequently as possible, ideally daily, thus giving the observer a much better idea of the changes in behavior as a function of environmental interventions and of the teaching program. The observational data are usually recorded on a graph or chart, thereby presenting a visual display of the change in behavior over time.

Initially, data are collected when no specific intervention program is in effect (or when the current, unsuccessful program is in effect). These preintervention data are called **baseline data** and correspond roughly to a pretest in traditional assessment measures. Usually baseline data are collected until they stabilize or show a consistent pattern. If a consistent pattern does not emerge, further definition of the target behavior might be necessary.

> **BASELINE DATA**
> Information collected prior to an intervention.

Before initiating an observational assessment, it is necessary to choose both the recording devices and the recording procedures that will be used. The choice of recording procedure is particularly important and is largely dependent on the type of behavior that is being observed. The general issue of recording devices and several specific recording procedures are discussed next.

Recording Devices.   Three basic tools are necessary to observe and record behavior: a timer, a counter, and a graph or chart. For all the observational approaches, the issue of time is important. Certain recording procedures, however, require more exact timekeeping devices. The most common are the stopwatch, the clock or watch with a second hand, and the calculator with a stopwatch or timer. Devices for counting behaviors include wrist counters, abacus beads, and the basic pencil-and-paper technique. The wrist counter is worn like a watch. By pushing a button on the counter, the observer keeps a cumulative tally. Abacus beads can also be worn on the wrist. They consist of rows of beads that represent place values (ones, tens, hundreds). Pencil-and-paper tallies are widely used. There are a limitless number of pencil-and-paper techniques, although Tukey (1977) developed a standard system over thirty years ago. Alessi (1980) described Tukey's system:

> In this system, dots and lines are used to tally counts. The first count is represented by a single dot (.), the second by two dots (. .), the third by three dots (. :) and the fourth by four dots (: :). The dots are placed so as to outline a box. The numbers five, six, seven, and eight are then represented by completing the box sides with lines, in any order: Five = ⊡, six = ⊡, seven = ⊔, eight = ⊡, nine = ⊠, and ten = ⊠ . Fewer errors in both tabulation and summation are likely using this system as compared with others (such as |, ||, |||, ||||). The dot and box system also takes much less space on the protocol. (pp. 36–37)

More expensive and sophisticated devices are also available. For example, *Datamyte* (Electro General Corporation) and *MORE* (Observational Systems, Inc.) are handheld data collectors that include a measure of time and a counter. These systems also have solid-state memory and optional features that allow interface with a computer for data storage and analysis. Computer software is also available to aid in recording data. One example is the *Direct Observation Data System* (DODS; Johnson, Blackhurst, Maley, Cox-Cruey, & Dell, 1995). The DODS actually includes a remote recording device so that the observer does not have to enter the data directly on the keyboard. Another example is *Behavior Evaluation Strategies and Taxonomies* (BEST) published by Sage Publication Software (Scolari). BEST includes not only a means to collect observational data but also a means to analyze the data. Also available is the *Behavioral Observation of Students in Schools* (Shapiro, 2003). This software records, times, and calculates frequencies and percentages of targeted behavior. Limitations of computer-assisted data collection have also been noted. Ice (2004) noted the possibility of battery failure, computer error, or operator error.

The last basic tool is the graph or chart, which offers a visual representation of observed behaviors. In the most common graph, the data are plotted along a vertical line (ordinate) and a horizontal line (abscissa). The ordinate usually represents the unit of behavioral measure (such as frequency or percentage), and the abscissa represents the unit of time (Alberto & Troutman, 2006). Figure 4.1 demonstrates this approach. Graphs such as this are usually drawn on plain or graph paper. More sophisticated charts are also available. One example is the **standard behavior chart (SBC)** that is used in precision teaching. The SBC is a semilogarithmic chart that is based on a ratio rather than an interval scale (Figure 4.2). Essentially, this means that the vertical axis is scaled proportionally so that, for instance, the distance between 1 and 5 is the same as the difference between 100 and 500. This allows the plotting of behavior that occurs as frequently as 1,000 times per minute or as infrequently as one time in 1,000 minutes on the same $9\frac{1}{2}$-by-11-inch chart. The SBC uses *frequency* (defined as number of behaviors divided by number of minutes observed) as its primary measure. The advantage of a system such as this is that it is interpretable by all who are familiar with the chart (an advantage that is rare when individuals develop their own systems). The SBC also allows a standard measure of learning rate (called *celeration*) and variability (called *bounce*). Software also has been developed that will generate graphs. Behavioral Graphing 99 (Clinical Solutions, Inc.) allows for quick data entry, produces graphs with available trend lines, and includes data decision rules.

STANDARD BEHAVIOR CHART (SBC)
A standard chart for recording data; is used in precision teaching.

Recording Procedures.   One important issue is the choice of recording procedures. Clearly, certain recording procedures are more appropriate for certain types of behavior. A description of each type of recording procedure follows, with examples of appropriate use.

EVENT RECORDING
Involves counting the number of behaviors that occur within a certain time period.

1. *Event Recording.* **Event recording** involves counting the number of behaviors that occur within a certain time period—for instance, the number of times

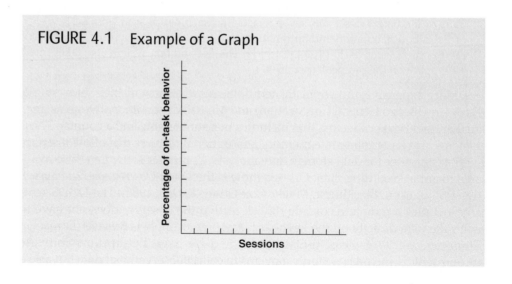

FIGURE 4.1   Example of a Graph

FIGURE 4.2 The Standard Behavior Chart

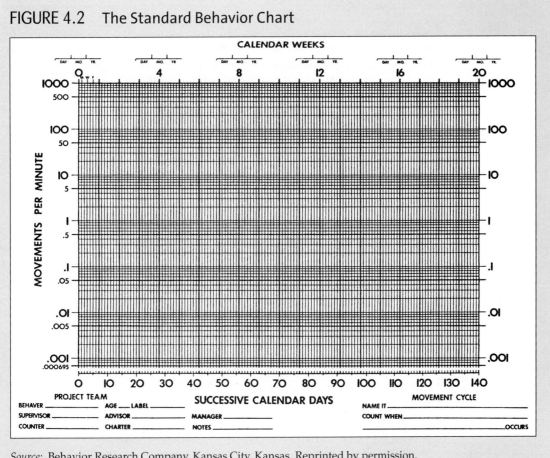

Source: Behavior Research Company, Kansas City, Kansas. Reprinted by permission.

Shanikah gets out of her seat during a fifty-minute science period, or the number of correct problems Alex completes during a fifteen-minute mathematics session. By including both the number of behaviors and the time interval, it is possible to convert the data to a standard metric. This is accomplished by using the following formula:

$$\text{frequency} = \frac{\text{number of behaviors observed}}{\text{number of minutes or hours spent observing}}$$

This allows the observer to record for different time periods without misrepresenting the data. For instance, suppose a teacher noted that Karl was getting more aggressive because he kicked his playmate seven times during recess on Monday and ten times on Tuesday and Wednesday. If, in fact, recess was twenty minutes on Monday and thirty minutes on Tuesday and Wednesday, then Karl decreased, not increased, his frequency of kicking.

Event recording is best used when the behavior has a discrete beginning and ending and when occurrences can be easily counted, particularly if a permanent product is left (such as the number of words spelled correctly). It is not a good method to use if the behavior occurs at an extremely high rate (e.g., pencil tapping) or for an extended period of time (e.g., staring out the window). The example of Sandy demonstrates the use of event recording.

Use event recording when a behavior has a discrete beginning and end.

Example: Sandy

Mr. Gonzalez, a third-grade teacher, is concerned about his student Sandy, who is beginning to hit her peers on their arms, primarily to get their attention. She also seems to think it is funny. Mr. Gonzalez has told her to stop, but this hasn't been effective. Mr. Gonzalez has decided to implement a behavior-change program aimed at decreasing her hitting behavior. The following preintervention or baseline data were collected:

	M	Tu	W	Th	F
Time observed (in minutes)	5	8	6	6	7
Number of behaviors	6	9	7	8	8
Frequency	1.20	1.13	1.17	1.33	1.14

Next, he implemented his behavior-change program, and the following data were collected:

	M	Tu	W	Th	F
Time observed (in minutes)	7	8	6	7	5
Number of behaviors	7	4	3	2	1
Frequency	1.00	0.50	0.50	0.29	0.20

Figure 4.3 is a graph of these data.

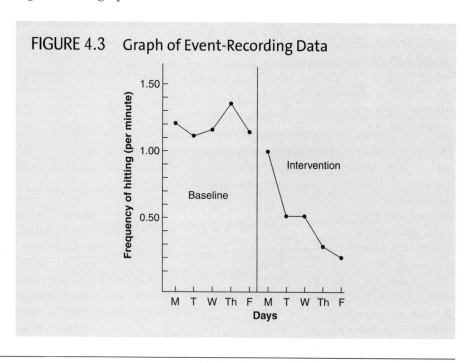

FIGURE 4.3   Graph of Event-Recording Data

Use duration recording when amount of time is important.

2. *Duration Recording.* Suppose you had a student who would get out of his or her seat at the beginning of an instructional period and stay out until the end. In this case, the frequency of the behavior would be irrelevant, and event recording would not be the most appropriate method for measuring the behavior. For a problem in which the important factor is the amount of time a person spends engaging in the target behavior, **duration recording** should be used. Because duration measures require constant attention and monitoring of the time, a stopwatch or clock with a second hand is almost a must. This need for a constant monitoring of the time is a major disadvantage of duration recording, and it usually dictates that only one child at a time be observed. The example of Antoine represents the use of duration recording.

> **DURATION RECORDING**
> Used to document the amount of time a student spends engaging in a behavior.

Example: Antoine

Ms. Lambert was concerned that her student Antoine would frequently be off task during individual seat work. Typically, he would start his work but lose interest rather quickly. At that point, he would tap his pencil, look out the window, or in some other way avoid completing the task. Ms. Lambert decided to implement a program designed to increase Antoine's on-task behavior. First, she would measure the amount of time Antoine actually spent on task. She defined on-task behavior as keeping his eyes on his paper. She decided to observe him for a ten-minute period each day. The following baseline data were recorded:

	M	Tu	W	Th	F
Minutes spent on task	3	2	3	4	3

She then implemented her behavioral program with Antoine, and it resulted in the following data:

	M	Tu	W	Th	F
Minutes spent on task	6	7	9	10	10

Figure 4.4 is the visual representation of these data.

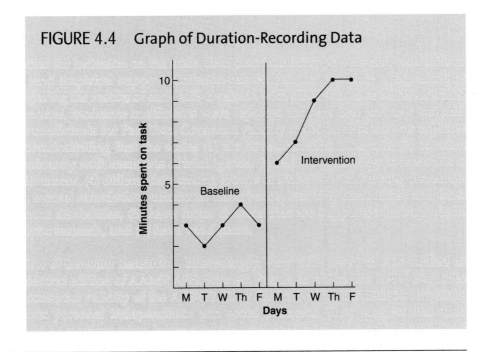

FIGURE 4.4   Graph of Duration-Recording Data

LATENCY RECORDING
Involves an observer measuring how long it takes for a behavior to begin after the signaling of a stimulus (e.g., a verbal request).

Latency recording is helpful in compliance training.

3. *Latency Recording.* Suppose you had a student who typically wandered around the room and visited with his friends even after the bell rang, signaling him to sit in his chair. In this situation, both event recording and duration recording would be inappropriate. **Latency recording** would be the recording procedure of choice. Latency recording measures the amount of time that elapses between the signaling of a stimulus (such as the sound of the bell) and the initiation of a behavior (sitting in a chair). Latency recording, like duration recording, has the basic disadvantage of requiring constant attention to the time. Latency recording is often used in compliance training (getting the student to do what he is asked). The example of Les demonstrates the use of latency recording.

Example: Les

Ms. Lee was concerned about one of her students, Les. When she instructed the class to begin solving written math problems, Les would drop his pencil, stare out the window, or demonstrate other avoidance behaviors. She wanted to develop a program to minimize the amount of time he took before he started writing his answers. She, therefore, chose a latency-recording procedure to measure the amount of time it took him to start writing after she gave the instructions. The following baseline data were collected:

	M	Tu	W	Th	F	M
Number of seconds elapsed	42	30	36	41	39	44

She then developed a program for Les and put it into effect. The following data were then recorded:

	Tu	W	Th	F	M	Tu	W	Th
Number of seconds elapsed	25	15	20	14	12	10	10	5

Figure 4.5 shows these data.

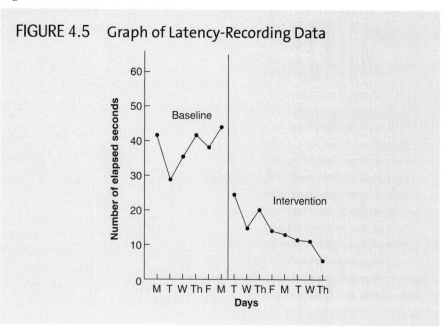

FIGURE 4.5   Graph of Latency-Recording Data

4. *Interval Recording.* Another useful procedure for recording observations is **interval recording.** Interval recording measures the occurrences or nonoccurrences of the target behavior during specified time intervals marked off within an overall observation period. This procedure is appropriate for behaviors that occur at a high frequency or for extended periods of time, and it indicates the pattern of behavior. Suppose, for instance, that Nguyen is off task a considerable amount of time during her five-minute workbook session. Interval recording would make it possible to determine if a pattern exists (such as primarily at the beginning or end of the session) as well as to specify the percentage of off-task behavior. (Of course, the term *off task* would need to be carefully defined.) To set up an interval-recording system, the overall observation period can be divided into smaller time intervals. A five-minute period divided into fifteen-second intervals, for example, would yield twenty time intervals. The observer simply indicates whether the behavior occurs during any portion of each time interval. The length of the interval is also important. For example, Repp and colleagues (1988) noted that smaller intervals are more accurate than large intervals. Typically, a plus (+) is given for the presence of the behavior and a minus (−) for the absence. In this example, the target behavior (off-task behavior) was observed during the first, second, third, fifth, sixth, seventh, and eighth intervals:

+	+	+	−	+	+	+	+	−	−
−	−	−	−	−	−	−	−	−	−

These data indicate that Nguyen was off task during approximately 30 percent of the intervals, primarily during the beginning of the session. This might suggest that the teacher increase the length of Nguyen's instructional sessions since it seems that it takes Nguyen some time to get on task but then stays on task.

5. *Momentary Time Sampling.* **Momentary time sampling** is similar to interval recording. During momentary time sampling, the individual is observed at a given time (e.g., every fifteen seconds). The observer must indicate whether the target behavior is exhibited *at those particular times.* One advantage of both interval recording and momentary time sampling is that more than one child can be observed at one time. One potential disadvantage of both interval recording and momentary time sampling is that some type of cue must signal the time to record. A number of cuing systems are available, such as a kitchen timer or an audiotape with a signal prerecorded at certain intervals. Another disadvantage of momentary time sampling is that only limited conclusions can be drawn on the behavior recorded. For example, it might be possible that the behavior occurs frequently but not at the specific time that it was observed (Alberto & Troutman, 2006). Similarly, a behavior might occur infrequently but consistently, giving a false impression when using interval recording.

Introduction of the Intervention Program. As noted in the examples of Sandy, Antoine, and Les, after a specific behavior or skill has been carefully identified, defined, and recorded, it is time to systematically introduce some type of intervention or remedial program in an attempt to change the behavior in the desired direction. Using whatever information is available, including observational data, the teacher (or other change agent) will make the decision on the nature of the intervention procedure. The key is to attempt to demonstrate that changes in the

INTERVAL RECORDING
Involves observing whether a behavior occurs or does not occur during specified time periods.

In interval recording, the smaller the interval, the more accurate it is.

MOMENTARY TIME SAMPLING
An individual is observed at predetermined times (e.g., every fifteen seconds). The observer must indicate if the behavior is occurring at those particular times.

target behavior are related to the introduction of the intervention program. If an effective procedure can be found for a specific behavior for a given individual, that same procedure might also be effective for other behaviors in the same individual or for the same behavior with different individuals. For this reason it is important to be specific and not attempt to change too many behaviors or introduce a "shotgun approach" to intervention. It is possible that behavioral changes might occur, but the value of the data for assessment purposes will be minimized.

Evaluation of the Intervention Program.   This is an important step in the observational model and, coincidentally, one that is often overlooked. It essentially involves recording (using the same procedures as were used in the collection of baseline data) to determine if the initiation of the intervention program had an effect on the target behavior. If change occurs in the desired direction, the information can be used to plan future instructional programs. If the behavior does not change, or changes in the opposite direction, it signals the need for trying a different approach, or perhaps the need to identify a different target behavior that might be within the student's behavioral repertoire. For example, it might be possible that a target behavior identified for a student might be too difficult, and an easier or prerequisite behavior would be more appropriate as a target. The previously described SBC is used in a system called precision teaching (Lindsley, 1964), which incorporates the previously described four-step observation model to make instructional decisions.

Student Observation—Formal Systems

Why Use Formal Student Observation?

Screening and identification; informal determination and evaluation of teaching programs and strategies; documentation of need for further evaluation or referral; development and evaluation of IEPs.

Who Should Use It?

Primarily teachers; also school psychologists and parents.

Formal observation frequently involves coding systems.

In addition to the informal observation procedures used to assess student needs and instructional programs, more formal observational systems are also available. These systems usually include some type of coding or notational procedure so that behaviors can be categorized in some meaningful way. For example, Bramlett and Barnett (1993) described a system, called the *Preschool Observation Code,* that was specifically developed for use with young children. Similarly, Rotholz, Kamps, and Greenwood (1989) developed a system called the *Code for Instructional Structure and Student Academic Response–Special Education* (CISSAR-SPED) that is used with students with autism or developmental disabilities. Prasad (1994) also described an observational system that stresses social interactions; these include initiating the interaction, turn taking, and responding to the interaction.

In fact, many formal systems allow for the coding of behavioral interactions rather than the behavior of the student in isolation. For example, the *Behavioral Coding System* (Patterson, Reid, Jones, & Conger, 1975) includes fourteen behavior categories. In this system, numbers are assigned to the target child and those who interact with him or her. For example, 2YE*-1IG* might represent an interaction in which the mother yelled and the target child ignored the outburst. The advantage of formal systems is that they allow for greater communication among individuals observing a student. For example, if a student were being observed at home by her parents and at school by her teacher, the coded results would allow each of the observers to understand what was happening in the other environment.

Other systems have been developed exclusively for the school environment but retain the coding systems for behavior interactions. One example is the *Manual for Coding Discrete Behaviors in the School Setting* (Cobb & Ray, 1975). This system uses nineteen behavior categories; both the behaviors of the target child and his or her peers are alternately observed in six-second intervals. Figure 4.6 shows an example of the interaction for the following sequence.

Albert is a fourth-grade student with a learning disability who is in an inclusive classroom. He is involved in a structured individual task of using the dictionary to define certain vocabulary words. The following sequence is observed during the six-second intervals:

1. Albert is talking with a student about a television show. The student responds.
2. Peer 1 is looking at the dictionary.
3. Albert is looking at the dictionary.
4. Peer 2 is staring out the window.
5. Albert is asking the teacher about alphabetizing.
6. Peer 3 is writing a definition.
7. Albert is banging his dictionary on the desk. The teacher tells him to stop.
8. Peer 4 is reading the dictionary.
9. Albert leaves his seat to visit a friend. His friend gets mad and tears a page out of the dictionary.
10. Peer 5 is pulling the hair of his friend.

This sequence indicates that Albert's behavior is inconsistent. He displayed a different type of behavior during each interval.

FIGURE 4.6   Example of Coded Behavior Interactions

Observer_____ Sheet No._____ Subject_____

Date_____ Academic Activity_____

Structured_____ Unstructured_____ Group_____ Individual_____ Transitional_____

Subject	AP	CO	TT+	IP+	VO	AT	PN	DS	DI	NY	NC	PL	TT−	(IP−)	IL	SS	LO	NA	IT
Peer 1	AP	CO	TT+	IP+	VO	(AT)	PN	DS	DI	NY	NC	PL	TT−	IP−	IL	SS	LO	NA	IT
Subject	AP	CO	TT+	IP+	VO	(AT)	PN	DS	DI	NY	NC	PL	TT−	IP−	IL	SS	LO	NA	IT
Peer 2	AP	CO	TT+	IP+	VO	AT	PN	DS	DI	NY	NC	PL	TT−	IP−	IL	SS	(LO)	NA	IT
Subject	AP	CO	(TT+)	IP+	VO	AT	PN	DS	DI	NY	NC	PL	TT−	IP−	IL	SS	LO	NA	IT
Peer 3	AP	CO	TT+	IP+	VO	(AT)	PN	DS	DI	NY	NC	PL	TT−	IP−	IL	SS	LO	NA	IT
Subject	AP	CO	TT+	IP+	VO	AT	PN	DS	DI	(NY)	NC	PL	TT−	IP−	IL	SS	LO	NA	IT
Peer 4	AP	CO	TT+	IP+	VO	(AT)	PN	DS	DI	NY	NC	PL	TT−	IP−	IL	SS	LO	NA	IT
Subject	AP	CO	TT+	IP+	VO	AT	PN	DS	DI	NY	NC	PL	TT−	IP−	(IL)	SS	LO	NA	IT
Peer 5	AP	CO	TT+	IP+	VO	AT	(PN)	DS	DI	NY	NC	PL	TT−	IP−	IL	SS	LO	NA	IT

Note: IP− = inappropriate interaction with peers, AT = attending, TT+ = appropriate talking with teacher, LO = looking around, NY = noisy, IL = inappropriate locale, and PN = physical negative.

Observation of the Instructional Environment

Why Use Observation of the Instructional Environment?
Analysis of instructional environment.

Who Should Use It?
Teachers.

Although assessment of student behavior is the primary use of observational data, the assessment of the student's instructional environment is another role of observation. Both types of observation have a common goal of improving instructional practices that will positively affect the student.

According to Cartwright and Cartwright (1984), four components of the instructional environment should be considered. These components (which actually interact constantly) are teacher behaviors, space and objects in the environment, time variables, and the management and teaching procedures that are used within the instructional environment. For example, it might be possible to observe teachers and provide feedback on their behavior. It might be observed that a teacher is inadvertently reinforcing an annoying student behavior by attending to it whenever it occurs. It might also be possible that a student is much more distractible when placed in an open classroom setting, thus implying that moving him to a more structured setting would be advisable. Time variables are important in setting up schedules that optimize the chance for student success. Borich (2007) developed a number of informal rating scales that address the learning climate in the classroom. These include classroom control and classroom warmth.

Although most observation of instructional environments is done informally, and sometimes inconsistently, a few formalized approaches and instruments have been designed to achieve this goal. For example, Ysseldyke and Christenson (1992) developed *The Instructional Environment Scale II* (TIES-II), which is described as a comprehensive methodology for assessing an individual student's instruction.

TIES-II is a set of observation and interview forms used with teachers and parents. Specifically, information is gathered through observation of the student in a classroom setting and through interviews with the student and the student's teacher and parents. The following is a list of the twelve Instructional Environment components used to analyze the classroom environment.

> TIES-II can be used to observe the instructional environment.

Instructional Match: Instruction is clear and effective; directions are presented in sufficient detail.

Teacher Expectations: Expectations of student performance are realistic yet high.

Classroom Environment: Classroom is positive and supportive; time is used effectively.

Instructional Presentation: Instruction is presented in a clear and effective manner.

Cognitive Emphasis: Thinking skills necessary to complete tasks are communicated to the student.

Motivational Techniques: Teacher uses good strategies to increase student interest and effort.

Relevant Practice: Student is given adequate opportunities for practice.

Academic Engaged Time: Student is actively engaged in tasks and is redirected by teacher if not.

Informed Feedback: Student receives appropriate feedback for correct and incorrect performance.

Adaptive Instruction: Curriculum is modified to meet student needs.

Progress Evaluation: Teacher uses direct and frequent measures of student progress.

Student Understanding: Student knows what to do in the classroom.

In addition, five Home Support for Learning components in TIES-II involve a parent interview. Those components are Expectations and Attributions, Discipline Orientation, Effective Home Environment, Parent Participation, and Structure for Learning.

Technology has also been used to facilitate the observation of the instructional environment. One example is the *Ecobehavioral Assessment Systems Software* (EBASS; Greenwood, Carta, Kamps, Terry, & Delquadri, 1994). The EBASS can be used with a portable notebook computer so that data entry and analysis can be done on site. It includes three different observation instruments: *Ecobehavioral System for Complex Analysis of Preschool Environments* (ESCAPE), *Code for Instructional Structure and Student Academic Response* (CISSAR), and a special form of CISSAR designed for inclusion classes (MS-CISSAR). As one example of its use, the EBASS was used to evaluate such variables as academic engagement and inappropriate behavior of students in over 100 inclusion classes (Wallace, Anderson, Bartholomew, & Hupp, 2002).

Functional Behavior Assessment

Why Use Functional Behavior Assessment?

To determine purpose or function that a behavior serves; to help develop a behavior intervention plan.

Who Should Use It?

Teachers, school psychologists; parents should be involved.

One of the most controversial issues brought up in IDEA 97 and later revisited in IDEA 04 had to do with discipline. The primary concern related to issues focused around changing a student's educational placement as a result of his or her behavior (e.g., violence). What is required by law is a **manifestation determination;** in other words, was the behavioral act in question a result of the student's disability? This is a particularly important issue for students identified as having an emotional or behavioral disorder. Also required is the development of a **behavioral intervention plan (BIP)** to address the specific problem and a **functional behavior assessment (FBA)** to assist in developing the BIP.

Functional behavior assessment, contrary to many professionals' beliefs, is not new and does not require a great deal of specialized training. In fact, FBA has been discussed in the behavior analysis literature for over twenty years (e.g., Carr & Durand, 1985; Touchette, MacDonald, & Langer, 1985). An FBA involves the determination of the function or purpose that a behavior serves and leads directly to an intervention plan. For example, if a student, Frank, frequently is disruptive in math class when he should be doing worksheets, he may be trying

MANIFESTATION DETERMINATION
A legal requirement to determine if a disciplinary infraction by a student was a result of the student's disability.

BEHAVIORAL INTERVENTION PLAN (BIP)
A positive behavior plan resulting from observation, data collection, and analysis of targeted behaviors.

FUNCTIONAL BEHAVIOR ASSESSMENT (FBA)
Observation and interview data used to develop a behavioral intervention plan.

to gain attention (negative) from the teacher or to gain attention (positive) from his peers. The disruption might result in his being placed in time-out or sent to the office. In that case, the disruption might serve the purpose of avoiding the task at hand. Once the purpose of the behavior is determined, the intervention plan is developed. There are many possible intents or purposes for a behavior. Neel and Cessna (1993) listed several: power/control, escape/avoidance, attention, acceptance/affiliation, expression of self, gratification, and justice/revenge. Interventions based on FBA have been shown to be effective with a variety of populations including students with learning disabilities (Burke, Hagen-Burke, and Sugai, 2003), mental retardation (Hetzroni & Roth, 2003), behavior disorders (March & Horner, 2002), and young children with challenging behaviors (Gettinger & Stoiber, 2006). FBA, however, is subject to the same scrutiny as other assessment techniques regarding reliability and validity. Gresham (2003) noted that, to date, evidence of these technical characteristics has not been sufficiently provided and more investigation is needed in this area.

Direct observation is a crucial component of FBA.

There are many sources of information that can be used to gather information for a FBA. For example, interviews of parents, teachers, and other individuals who interact with the student as well as an interview of the student can provide valuable information (see Chapter 2 for a discussion of interviews). In addition, more formal instruments have been developed. For example, the Psychological Corporation has published the *Functional Assessment and Intervention System: Improving School Behavior* (Stoiber, 2003). This system includes general guidelines, a specific protocol for documenting performance-based information, and a list of resources and materials to help develop intervention programs. In addition, the *Behavioral Intervention Planning—Third Edition* (McConnell, Patton, & Polloway, 2007), available commercially, generates functional behavior assessment and subsequent behavioral intervention plans. Direct observation, however, is perhaps the most widely used approach to gather information for the FBA. Skinner and colleagues (2000) pointed out that direct observation is very helpful in determining the various functions of behavior.

Although there are slight variations on the components of a functional behavior assessment, the following steps should generally be included. The case study of Cynthia will be used to illustrate each step. Note that the FBA of Cynthia relies very heavily on observation.

Case Study: Cynthia

Cynthia is a third-grade student who is currently receiving special education services under the category "emotionally disturbed." She occasionally has problems with her academic work but is only slightly below grade level in most areas. Her teacher reports that she is "in her own world" and will sometimes become aggressive, particularly toward her peers, for no particular reason. At her initial IEP meeting, the IEP team decided that a FBA should be conducted and a behavior intervention plan initiated. The IEP team also felt that Cynthia could control her aggression, and she was placed in an inclusion class with a behavioral consultant available.

---

1. Carefully define the behavior(s). For this step, the procedures previously described for identifying a target behavior should be followed. The description of the behavior should be precise, observable, and measurable. In addition, if more than one behavior is identified, it is important to prioritize the behaviors for the functional assessment and determine if the behaviors tend to occur at the same time. The general education teacher observed that the two behaviors that were the most problematic for Cynthia were pinching her peers and scratching her peers. She also reported that they occasionally occurred together.

2. Identify variables that predict or occur immediately before the behavior (antecedents). The person performing the FBA can determine the antecedents of the behavior from direct observation, interviews with the child's parents and teachers, or other available sources of information. When directly observing the student in school, the observer should choose the appropriate recording procedure discussed earlier in this chapter. Several questions should be asked when observing behavior such as "When does the behavior typically occur?" "Where does the behavior typically occur?" and "Around whom does the behavior typically occur?" One technique used to address these issues and determine when and where a behavior occurs is the *scatterplot*. The observer can adapt this technique to determine the persons around whom the behavior occurs as well. Figure 4.7 shows an example of a scatterplot for Cynthia.

If an interview is given, there are formal functional assessment interview forms (e.g., O'Neill, Horner, Albin, Storey, & Sprague, 1997). Areas addressed in the interview form include ecological events (e.g., medication, sleep and eating patterns) that might affect the behavior, and the setting, time of day, and activities in which the behavior is most likely and least likely to occur. Also important to determine are teacher or parent factors (e.g., reprimand, lack of attention), peer

FIGURE 4.7   Scatterplot for Cynthia

Name: Cynthia   D.O.B.: 6/1/99
Grade: 3rd   Age: 9-3
Target Behavior: Pinching and scratching her peers

ACTIVITY	TIME	10/9	10/10	10/11	10/12	10/13	10/16	10/17	10/18	10/19	10/20
Social Studies	8:30–9:15				■						
Art	9:20–10:05										
English	10:10–10:55							■			
PE	11:00–11:45										
Lunch	11:45–12:15										
Science	12:20–1:05	■				■	▲2				
Music	1:10–1:55				■2						
Math	2:00–2:45	■		▲2				▲			■2

■ Target Behavior Occured Once   ▲ Target Behavior Occured Twice or More   2 Occured in Small-Group Activities factors (e.g., positive or negative attention), or setting factors (e.g., elevated noise levels, presence of an unfamiliar adult) that appear to precede the behavior (Maag, 2004). On the basis of direct observation in her inclusion classroom (including the use of the scatterplot) and an interview with Cynthia's referring teacher and her mother, the observer found the following antecedents:

- Difficult task demands.
- Elevated noise level in the class.
- Small, crowded groups.
- The end of the school day.

3. Identify variables that occur immediately after the behavior (consequences). Using the techniques previously described, the observer should identify the consequences of the behavior. These again could include teacher factors (e.g., teacher warning, time-out) and peer factors. Using the observational and interview data, the following consequences were identified:

- Teacher immediately reprimands then sends her to time-out.
- Receives negative attention from peers.

Remember: (A)ntecedents, (B)ehavior, (C)onsequence.

4. Develop a hypothesis. Based on the information obtained in Steps 2 and 3, the IEP team must develop a hypothesis about the possible function or purpose of the behavior. Forms such as the ABC (**A**ntecedents-**B**ehavior-**C**onsequences) Observation Forms (see Figures 4.8 and 4.9) can be used to organize observations and other data. The IEP team met and discussed the information gathered about the function that Cynthia's pinching and scratching seems to serve. They developed their

FIGURE 4.8   Example of an ABC Observation Form

Student Name: _____   Observation Date: _____

Observer: _____   Time: _____

Activity: _____   Class Period: _____

Behavior: _____

Antecedent	Behavior	Consequence

Source: Center for Effective Collaboration and Practice, *Addressing Student Problem Behavior,* 1998. Office of Special Education and Rehabilitative Services, U.S. Department of Education.

FIGURE 4.9   Example of an ABC Observation Form

Student: _____   Observer: _____

Date: _____ Time: _____ Activity: _____

Context of Incident:

Antecedent:

Behavior:

Consequence:

Comments/Other Observations:

Source: Center for Effective Collaboration and Practice, *Addressing Student Problem Behavior,*
1998. Office of Special Education and Rehabilitative Services, U.S. Department of Education.

hypothesis: "When given difficult tasks in a crowded setting, Cynthia will pinch
and scratch her peers to be removed from the situation."

5. Collect observational data to support the hypothesis. A hypothesis is an educated guess; to test it, additional data should be collected. Subsequently, the next
step is to collect observational data that support the hypothesis. For Cynthia, this
involved observing her in large-group instructional periods when she was given
difficult task demands and observing her in small groups performing easy tasks.
The data indicated that she did not pinch or scratch during either situation. Subsequently, the hypothesis was supported. If, however, Cynthia engaged in the
target behavior in the small groups even when given easy tasks, the hypothesis
would have to be amended. In that case, it would indicate that the small-group
setting and not the interaction of the small-group setting and difficult task de-
mand was the "cause" of the problem. Similarly, if she engaged in the behavior
in large-group instruction when given a difficult task, the hypothesis would have
to be amended. As a rule, enough accurate, relevant information can be collected
in the FBA to develop a valid hypothesis. When there is no consistent pattern of
behavior, a *functional analysis manipulation* (O'Neill et al., 1997) can be conducted.
For Cynthia, if it was unclear what type of task was initiating the behavior, this
might involve an alternation between easy tasks and difficult tasks in the small-
group setting. If she became aggressive only during the difficult tasks, it would
clarify the issue. This has some ethical issues because the environment is being
set up to initiate the negative target behavior. Clearly, the behavior should be

stopped immediately. O'Neill and colleagues (1997) recommended that such a manipulation be conducted only when necessary.

6. Develop an intervention plan. As noted, the goal of FBA is to provide information that will directly lead to an effective intervention program. In addition to determining the intended functions of the targeted behavior, a good FBA should also identify possible *replacement behaviors* and possible reinforcers. A replacement behavior is one that is appropriate and can serve the same function as the target behavior. Possible reinforcers help increase the probability of the replacement behavior. The replacement behavior identified for Cynthia was to have her ask to be moved when she started feeling agitated. The intervention plan included two components. The first was prevention, in which Cynthia was not placed in small-group settings when given difficult tasks. The second was counseling in the recognition of the early signs of anger so that Cynthia could let the teacher know.

In summary, observation is a crucial component of FBA. It is used to help provide information related to the identification of the target behavior, as well as the antecedents of, and consequences for, the target behavior. Observation can be used to identify replacement behaviors that are appropriate and can determine possible reinforcers. For example, it is possible to identify high-preference activities (those in which the student voluntarily spends time doing) that might be used as reinforcers. The Appendix provides a comprehensive form that summarizes the information gathered in the FBA. Clearly, observation is one of the main sources of information for this form.

The Appendix provides a comprehensive FBA form.

Finally, the four-step observational model discussed previously has direct relevance to FBA. In fact, it can be adapted to be a five-step model. The additional step would be the use of observational assessment to *help develop* the intervention plan. The implications of the five steps to FBA are

1. *Carefully identify the target behavior.* This is the first step of the FBA. It will determine the high-priority behavior(s) for which intervention is necessary in precise, measurable terms.

2. *Precisely and appropriately measure the target behavior.* Data can be collected to serve as a baseline to determine the effectiveness of the eventual intervention plan. Because the effectiveness of the intervention plan is best determined through direct observation, it makes sense that the baseline data also be based on direct observation. Interview data could be used—"Do you think Cynthia's behavior is improving?"—but they lack objectivity and accountability.

3. *Develop an intervention plan.* Observation can identify the antecedents and consequences of the target behavior. This information should help determine the intended purpose of the behavior. This information, in turn, should lead to the development of prevention strategies. In addition, observation can identify appropriate replacement behaviors that would serve the same purpose as the target behavior. Finally, observation can identify possible reinforcers to use in the intervention plan. This could include, for example, noting what types of activities the student engages in during free time.

4. *Systematically introduce the intervention plan.* Both the prevention strategies for the target behavior and the strategies for developing the replacement behavior should be implemented.

5. *Evaluate the intervention plan.* As noted previously, recording the target behavior after the intervention program has been initiated is an important, yet often overlooked, process. When implementing a behavior intervention plan, the criteria for discontinuing the program should be specified.

CASE STUDY *June*

As previously reported, June usually does not complete her individual seat work, which is given during the morning instructional sessions for reading, language arts, and math. Students are expected to complete independently the work in the twenty minutes allowed for each subject. Mrs. Dunn has decided that observational data needs to be collected during the three instructional sessions for one week. She wants to measure the time that June is off task. She has defined *off task* as not working at the task, either writing or computing. Mrs. Dunn has a weekly routine regarding the types of activities assigned students each day. It is as follows:

Language Arts

M/T/W	Practice spelling, usually writing sentences and copying words
TH/F	Write paragraphs based on readings from social studies

Reading

M/T/W/TH/F	Silent reading and responding to written comprehension and vocabulary questions

Math

M/T/TH/F	Computation practices
W	Solving math word problems

Below is a chart with the data that Mrs. Dunn collected while observing June's off-task behavior. Study the chart and then answer the questions that follow. Remember to keep in mind the weekly routine that was described.

Observational Data Chart

Subject	Mon	Tues	Wed	Thurs	Fri
Lang. Arts	4	4	4	7	7
Reading	7	8	8	7	7
Math	1	1	6	1	1

Minutes off task

- What type of recording system did Mrs. Dunn use?
- What patterns emerged?
- What should Mrs. Dunn do after gathering and analyzing the data?

Reflections

1. Why do you think it is important to collect data when you are observing student behavior?
2. Why do you think individuals use formal observational systems?
3. Why is it important to consider both antecedents and consequences when conducting a functional behavior assessment?

Summary Matrix

The summaries for all chapters that describe instruments or techniques will be in the form of a *summary matrix.* This matrix will allow the reader to compare and contrast the instruments or techniques in terms of their suggested use, target population, and relevance for exceptional students. The matrix includes the following specific components (and their definitions):

A. Suggested use
   1. *Screening and initial identification (prereferral):* Use of assessment data to identify individuals who need further evaluation, remedial help, or both.
   2. *Informal determination and evaluation of teaching programs and strategies (prereferral):* Use of assessment data
      a. To assist the general-education teacher in identifying and evaluating appropriate objectives and teaching strategies.
      b. To help document the need for a formal referral.
      c. To assist in the development of IEPs for students who receive special education.
   3. *Determination of current performance level and educational need (postreferral):* Use of assessment data to determine
      a. General areas in which a student needs remediation or assistance.
      b. Strengths and weaknesses.
      c. Possible teaching strategies and approaches.
   4. *Decisions about classification and program placement (postreferral):* Use of assessment data to determine special education eligibility and to identify the most appropriate program setting for the student.
   5. *Goals of IEP (postreferral):* Use of assessment data to identify annual goals.
   6. *Objectives of IEP (postreferral):* Use of assessment data to identify appropriate objectives (if objectives are included).
   7. *Evaluation of IEP (postreferral):* Use of assessment data to monitor student progress toward meeting the identified goals and objectives and progress in the general education curriculum.
B. Target population
   1. *Mild/moderate:* Refers to individuals whose special needs are usually met within an inclusive classroom, resource room, or self-contained classroom. This category may include students with mild or moderate mental retardation, learning disabilities, behavior disorders, or other types of disabilities whose problems are not considered severe.
   2. *Severe/profound:* Refers to individuals whose special needs might be met within an inclusive classroom, self-contained classroom, special school, or residential setting. This category may include students with severe or profound mental retardation, multiple disabilities, sensory disabilities (vision or hearing impairments), or other individuals who have significant impairments.
   3. *Preschool:* Includes individuals from birth through approximately age 5.
   4. *Elementary age:* Includes individuals from ages 6 through approximately 12 (kindergarten through grade 6).
   5. *Secondary age:* Includes individuals from approximately ages 13 through 18 or 20 (grade 7 through grade 12).
   6. *Adult:* Includes individuals who because of their age no longer receive public-school services (usually older than 18 or 21).
C. *Special considerations:* Includes a brief statement of any particular advantage or disadvantage, technical characteristic, or other consideration that is relevant to each instrument or technique.
D. *Educational relevance for exceptional students:* Provides a rating of the relative applicability of each instrument or technique for exceptional students. The ratings are "very limited," "limited," "adequate," "useful," and "very useful." This rating is based on information such as the type of data yielded, the technical adequacy of an instrument, and research related to the instrument or technique.

Summary Matrix

Instrument or Technique	Suggested Use							Target Population						Special Considerations	Educational Relevance for Exceptional Students
	Prereferral			Postreferral											
	Screening and Initial Identification	Informal Determination and Evaluation of Teaching Programs and Strategies	Determination of Current Performance Level and Educational Need	Decisions about Classification and Program Placement	IEP Goals	IEP Objectives	IEP Evaluation	Mild/Moderate	Severe/Profound	Preschool	Elementary Age	Secondary Age	Adult		
Event Recording	X	X	X		X	X	X	X	X	X	X	X	X	Use when the frequency of a behavior is important; behavior should have a discrete beginning and ending.	Useful
Duration Recording	X	X	X		X	X	X	X	X	X	X	X	X	Use when the amount of time during which behavior occurs is important; requires constant monitoring.	Useful
Latency Recording	X	X	X		X	X	X	X	X	X	X	X	X	Requires constant monitoring.	Useful
Interval Recording	X	X	X		X	X	X	X	X	X	X	X	X	Use for behaviors that occur at a high frequency or for an extended time.	Useful
Momentary Time Sampling	X	X	X		X	X	X	X	X	X	X	X	X	More than one person can be observed at a time; requires a cue to signal when to record.	Useful
Behavioral Coding System	X						X	X	X	X	X	X	X	Use in home and school; codes behavioral interactions; has a complex scoring system.	Adequate
Manual for Coding Discrete Behaviors in the School Setting	X	X					X	X	X	X	X	X	X	Use in the school setting; requires observation of the target subjects and control subjects.	Adequate
The Instructional Environment Scale–II		X						X			X	X		Provides qualitative evaluation of learning environment; also looks at teacher behaviors.	Useful
Functional Behavior Assessment		X			X			X	X	X	X	X	X	Use to determine the function that a behavior serves; leads to a behavior intervention plan.	Very Useful

chapter five

Criterion-Referenced Testing and Curriculum-Based Assessment

included
IN THIS CHAPTER

Criterion-Referenced Tests
   An Overview of Principles
   Development of Criterion-Referenced
      Tests: Procedures and Examples

Curriculum-Based Assessment (CBA)

Criterion-Referenced CBA (CR-CBA)
   Development of a CR-CBA
      Instrument: An Example
   Uses and Limitations of CR-CBA
      Instruments

Curriculum-Based Measurement (CBM)
   Computer-Based CBM
   Uses and Limitations of CBM

CR-CBA and CBM: An Integrated Model

Criterion-Referenced Tests

Why Use Criterion-Referenced Tests?

Determination and evaluation of objectives and teaching strategies; gathering of prereferral information; development and evaluation of IEPs.

Who Should Use Them?

Teachers.

When people refer to tests used in schools, they usually think of traditional norm-referenced instruments such as achievement tests or intelligence tests. These instruments can be helpful in making certain types of decisions including screening, eligibility, and the determination of strengths and weaknesses. These types of traditional assessment instruments have some shortcomings, however. As noted in Chapter 2, norm-referenced tests (NRTs) show how an individual performs compared to others but provide little information that can be used for the development of specific instructional programs. The instruments typically used for those decisions are criterion-referenced tests (CRTs). Gronlund (2006) noted that whereas there are many similarities in the development of NRTs and CRTs, there are also some basic points of difference. For example, in a NRT the intended learning outcome may be described in either general or specific terms; in a CRT the intended outcome tends to be described in more specific terms. Second, a NRT usually covers a broad range of areas with few items per area; a CRT usually measures a more limited domain with numerous items per area. Finally, a NRT is designed so that the items can *discriminate* among students, whereas a CRT is designed so that the items will *describe* student performance on specific learning tasks.

An Overview of Principles

CRTs are particularly helpful in determining *what* to teach. For this reason, they are frequently used to determine appropriate goals and objectives for a student. Many CRTs have been developed and published commercially and will be discussed elsewhere in this textbook. This chapter, however, will focus on the principles and procedures that teachers and diagnosticians can use to develop their own CRTs. As mentioned in Chapter 2, CRTs focus more on an individual's mastery of content (e.g., John can complete 90 percent of his two-digit addition problems correctly) than on a comparison of that individual with others (e.g., John scored at the 63rd percentile in arithmetic).

CRTs are helpful in determining *what* to teach.

By developing your own test, you can ensure that relevant objectives and items are included in the instrument; however, it is necessary to design and construct the CRT in a systematic, meaningful fashion. Gronlund (1973) suggested the following six principles to follow in developing a CRT. Criterion-referenced testing requires

1. A clearly defined and delimited domain of learning tasks.
2. Instructional objectives clearly defined in behavioral (performance) terms.
3. Standards of performance clearly specified.
4. Student performance adequately sampled within each area of performance.
5. Test items selected on the basis of how well they reflect the behavior specified in the instructional objectives.
6. A scoring and reporting system that adequately describes student performance on clearly defined learning tasks. (pp. 3–5)

Each of these six principles will be discussed in greater detail.

Principle 1: Clearly Define and Delimit Domain of Learning Tasks. Criterion-referenced testing is most effective when it focuses on a specific set of instructional objectives. Identifying the skill or skills for which a CRT will be developed is simplest if certain procedures are kept in mind. First, certain skills are more amenable to this type of testing. For example, the basic skill areas (e.g., arithmetic computation) are easier to measure than loosely structured areas (e.g., social studies or history). In either case, however, the skills should be broken down into manageable units. This is usually accomplished through a task analysis of the instructional objective to be measured.

Task analysis refers to the identification and sequencing of behaviors that are necessary components of the skill required for an individual to complete a task. Figure 5.1 gives an example of a task analysis. Note that each step is a prerequisite for later steps in the task analysis.

Two issues concerning task analysis should be mentioned. The first concerns the determination of how small or incremental the steps should be. For instance, it might be possible to have two equally valid task analyses, one with twenty-five steps and another with ten steps. The choice of which task analysis you would use as the basis for a CRT would depend largely on the type of student for whom the test was designed. A student with a profound intellectual disability, for example, might need a much more sensitive sequential breakdown than a student with a learning disability. In addition, the task analysis for the student with a profound intellectual disability would focus on a narrower set of skills than one for the

TASK ANALYSIS
The identification and sequencing of behaviors that are necessary components of the skill required for an individual to complete a task.

Task analysis is important in developing CRTs.

FIGURE 5.1   Example of a Task Analysis

Task Analysis of Objective: The child is able to alphabetize the following list of words, each of which has been placed on a separate card: stop, ask, dinner, name, boy.

1. Child can write the alphabet in the correct order.
2. Given a stack of 26 flash cards, each containing a different letter of the alphabet, the child can place the cards in alphabetical order.
3. Given a stack of 26 flash cards, each containing a word beginning with a different letter of the alphabet, the child can place the cards in alphabetical order *with* the help of an alphabet chart.
4. Given a stack of 26 flash cards, each containing a word beginning with a different letter of the alphabet, the child can place the cards in alphabetical order *without* the help of an alphabet chart.
5. Given a stack of 15 flash cards, each containing a different letter of the alphabet, the child can place the cards in alphabetical order *with* the help of an alphabet chart (therefore, some letters of the alphabet are missing).
6. Given a stack of 15 flash cards, each containing a different letter of the alphabet, the child can place the cards in alphabetical order *without* the help of an alphabet chart.
7. Given a stack of 15 flash cards, each containing a word beginning with a different letter of the alphabet, the child can place the cards in alphabetical order *with* the help of an alphabet chart.
8. Given a stack of 15 flash cards, each containing a word beginning with a different letter of the alphabet, the child can place cards in alphabetical order *without* the help of an alphabet chart.
9. The child is able to alphabetize the following list of words, each of which has been placed on a separate card: *stop, ask, dinner, name, boy.*

Source: A. R. Frank. (1973). Breaking Down Learning Tasks: A Sequence Approach. *Teaching Exceptional Children, 6.* Figure 3, p. 19. Copyright © 1973 by the Council for Exceptional Children. Reprinted with permission.

student with a learning disability. The second issue concerns the kind of skill for which a task analysis is planned. It is much easier to task-analyze nonacademic skills (such as tying a shoe or dialing the telephone) than academic skills (such as identifying words by sight or multiplying two-digit numbers).

Principle 2: Define the Objectives in Behavioral Terms.   This principle requires that an objective be defined in such a way that its mastery must be observed in student behavior. In other words, students must demonstrate that they have met an objective. "The student must complete correctly arithmetic problems involving the multiplication of three-digit numbers by two-digit numbers with carrying" is an objective that requires a specific behavioral performance. "Understands multiplication" does not. Swezey (1981) further noted that a good objective should specify the conditions and standards. The condition refers to the situations under which a student's performance is evaluated. The standard refers to the level of performance required (discussed next).

Principle 3: Specify Standards of Performance.   One extremely important issue in the development of CRTs is to determine what the criteria should be—that is, what criterion level a student must meet if an observer is to assume that the student has mastered that skill. Unfortunately, criteria tend to be determined arbitrarily. One teacher might feel that a student must answer 90 percent of math problems correctly, and another teacher might feel 95 percent is more appropriate. One guide to use is to identify which students appear to have mastered a particular skill and then to determine their performance level. This level could then be taken as a standard for mastery.

Another important issue is *maintenance* of the behavioral performance. Can it be assumed that a student has mastered a skill if he or she meets a 90 percent criterion for only one day? In defining mastery, it is also important to indicate how many times a student must meet the criterion level.

It is necessary to identify the performance level required for mastery.

Principle 4: Adequately Sample Student Performance.   As a rule, the more items a test has in a specific area, the better picture the test provides of the student's true ability in that area. It is necessary to be practical, however, in deciding how many items to use. Several factors affect this decision. First, the number of test items will depend on the skill being measured. More items measuring the execution of simple addition could feasibly be included, for example, than items demonstrating the ability to handle money and make change. Second, for some skills, the complete sample of the skill can be described in the test items. These include skills such as identifying letters of the alphabet or writing numbers from one to twenty. In general, it is advisable that at least twice as many test items are created as will actually be used in the test. If necessary, the extra items could be used to develop alternate forms of the test (Swezey, 1981).

Principle 5: Develop Test Items That Reflect the Behavior Specified in the Instructional Objectives.   Criterion-referenced testing uses a direct approach in obtaining information. In other words, a specific instructional area is determined, behaviors are identified that are associated with that area, and test items are developed to measure those behaviors. In evaluating the test results, therefore, little inference needs to be made. The test yields specific, relevant information, such as, "Trisha is having difficulty adding two-digit numbers requiring carrying, because she missed ten out of ten problems of this type," as opposed to general, relatively meaningless information, such as, "Trisha is having difficulty adding two-digit numbers because she is functioning at the 1.6 grade level in mathematics." Gronlund (2006) offered guidelines for item writing. These included "write the test item so that the performance it elicits matches the performance in the learning task," "write the test item so that the test task is clear and definite," and "write the test item so that there is no disagreement concerning the answer."

Principle 6: Include a Scoring System That Describes Student Performance on Specific Learning Tasks.   This principle incorporates many of the previously mentioned points. It means that a CRT should indicate, first, the area and objective to be measured, and second, the specific behavior to be measured, including the standard of performance required of the student. Conversely, the results of a CRT include the exact performance level of the student in a specific area.

Development of Criterion-Referenced Tests: Procedures and Examples

The following steps can act as guidelines for developing a CRT. An example is also provided for each step in the process for a student named Susie.

Step 1: Identify Skill to Be Measured

Task.   Determine the skill to be measured.

The IEP might identify the skill areas to measure.

Comments.   The skill that should be measured can be determined in a number of ways. Hopefully, a student's individualized education program (IEP) will reflect his or her educational needs and will indicate those areas that need to be specifically assessed. However, if the student is not receiving special education services and no IEP is available, a careful analysis of the areas covered in the curriculum will identify a number of goals. In some situations, school or district policy will determine the skills to be covered.

Example.   After analyzing standardized test information and classroom work products, Susie's teacher decided to develop a CRT based on the following skill: subtraction of three-digit whole numbers (with renaming).

Step 2: Identify Objectives

Task.   Identify the specific subskills or objectives to be measured.

Comments.   Again, objectives can be identified in a number of ways. Since the passage of IDEA 04, most IEPs no longer include objectives. As a result it may be necessary to perform a task analysis of the skill.

Example.   The following objectives were determined from a task analysis of the skill.

1. Given problems requiring the subtraction of one-digit numbers from one-digit numbers, Susie will provide the correct answers.
2. Given problems requiring the subtraction of 0 from numbers 1 to 10, Susie will provide the correct answers.
3. Given problems requiring the subtraction of a one-digit number from a two-digit number without renaming, Susie will provide the correct answers.
4. Given problems requiring the subtraction of a two-digit number from a two-digit number without renaming, Susie will provide the correct answers.
5. Given problems requiring the subtraction of three-digit numbers from three-digit numbers without renaming, Susie will provide the correct answers.
6. Given problems requiring the subtraction of a one-digit number from a two-digit number with renaming, Susie will provide the correct answers.
7. Given problems requiring the subtraction of a two-digit number from a two-digit number with renaming, Susie will provide the correct answers.
8. Given problems requiring the subtraction of a three-digit number from a three-digit number with renaming, Susie will provide the correct answers.

Step 3: Develop Test Items

Task.   Develop materials and test items for each objective.

Develop representative test items that measure each objective.

Comments.   If the objective is associated with a finite, easily manageable number of behaviors (such as counting from one to ten), *each* behavior can be included in the test. If this is not possible, the test should cover as many items as feasible. In general the evaluator should ask several questions such as, "Does each item present a clearly formulated task?" "Is the item stated in simple, clear language?" and "Is the item free from extraneous clues?" (Gronlund, 2006). If the answer is not yes to all the questions, the items should be modified. Figure 5.2 also provides a series of questions based on the *type* of item that is developed. After the items have been developed, they must be put together in a meaningful way. Gronlund (2006) suggested that items be grouped together that measure the same learning outcome, and be arranged in increasing level of difficulty.

Example.   The following test items were developed for each objective resulting in a CRT with eighty items.

1.	7	8	6	7	4	9	4	5	9	9
	−3	−4	−1	−1	−3	−6	−2	−3	−5	−7
2.	9	5	3	8	1	4	7	2	6	10
	−0	−0	−0	−0	−0	−0	−0	−0	−0	−0
3.	17	14	26	48	79	23	65	89	55	96
	−5	−2	−4	−6	−8	−2	−1	−7	−3	−5
4.	28	39	45	13	86	64	78	57	92	40
	−16	−17	−22	−11	−45	−32	−23	−34	−81	−10
5.	865	752	279	370	143	666	478	607	191	754
	−652	−241	−124	−230	−121	−351	−352	−506	−180	−322
6.	18	55	62	27	76	91	36	44	82	17
	−9	−7	−8	−9	−8	−3	−9	−5	−4	−8
7.	84	28	31	82	65	97	56	33	41	92
	−35	−19	−22	−64	−17	−38	−29	−16	−25	−83
8.	985	257	381	973	444	543	674	278	626	552
	−796	−179	−193	−588	−255	−358	−596	−179	−337	−274

Step 4: Determine Standard of Performance

Task.   Determine criteria for evaluating performance.

Comments.   In developing a CRT, it is important to establish criteria to indicate when a student has mastered a particular skill. Although the criteria could relate to *speed* (e.g., can read twenty sight words in two minutes), they usually involve *accuracy*, specifically the percentage of items passed. Although determining the criteria or the standard of performance is usually left up to the teacher's (or other testmaker's) discretion, certain standards are typically used more than others. Frequently, 90 or 95 percent of the items must be passed before mastery is assumed. As noted previously, however, there is a great deal of flexibility in determining those criteria. When establishing the standards of performance, it is also important to keep the number of items in mind. For example, if ten items are used to measure each objective (as in Susie's CRT), a mastery level of 95 percent would be inappropriate (she would have to answer nine-and-one-half items correctly).

FIGURE 5.2   Questions to Ask before Developing CRT Items

A. Multiple-Choice Items
1. Does the stem of the item present a single, clearly formulated problem?
2. Is the stem stated in simple, readable language?
3. Is the stem worded so that there is no repetition of material in the alternatives?
4. Is the stem stated in positive form, wherever possible?
5. If negative wording is used in the stem, is it emphasized (by underlining or caps)?
6. Is the intended answer correct or clearly best?
7. Are all alternatives grammatically consistent with the stem and parallel in form?
8. Are the alternatives free from verbal clues to the correct answer?
9. Are the distracters plausible and attractive to the uninformed?
10. Is the relative length of the correct answer varied, to eliminate length as a clue?
11. Has the alternative "all of the above" been avoided and "none of the above" used only when appropriate?
12. Is the position of the correct answer varied so that there is no detectable pattern?

B. True–False Items
1. Does each statement contain one central, significant idea?
2. Is the statement so precisely worded that it can be unequivocally judged true or false?
3. Are the statements brief and stated in simple language?
4. Are negative statements used sparingly and double negatives avoided?
5. Are statements of opinion attributed to some source?
6. Have specific determiners (such as always, sometimes, may) and other clues (such as length) been avoided?

C. Matching Items
1. Does each matching item contain only homogeneous material?
2. Is the list of items short with the brief responses on the right?
3. Is the list of responses longer or shorter than the list of premises, to provide an uneven match?
4. Do the directions clearly state the basis for matching and that the responses can be used once, more than once, or not at all?

D. Interpretive Exercises
1. Is the introductory material relevant to the learning outcomes to be measured?
2. Is the introductory material new to the examinees?
3. Is the introductory material as brief as possible?
4. Do the test items call forth the performance specified in the learning outcomes?
5. Do the test items meet the criteria of effective item writing that apply to the type of objective item being used?

E. Short-Answer Items
1. Is the item stated so that a single, brief answer is possible?
2. Has the item been stated as a direct question wherever possible?
3. Do the words to be supplied relate to the main point of the item?
4. Are the blanks placed at the end of the statement?
5. Have extraneous clues (such as "a" or "an," and length of the blank) been avoided?
6. Where numerical answers are to be given, have the expected degree of precision and the units in which they are to be expressed been indicated?

F. Essay Test
1. Is each question restricted to the measurement of complex learning outcomes?
2. Is each question relevant to the learning outcome being measured?
3. Does each question present a clearly defined task?
4. Are all examinees directed to answer the same questions (unless the outcome requires a choice)?
5. Has ample time been allowed for answering, and has a time limit been suggested for each question?
6. Have adequate provisions been made for scoring the essay answers?

G. Performance Test
1. Have the performance outcomes to be measured been clearly specified?
2. Does the test situation reflect an appropriate degree of realism for the outcomes being measured?
3. Do the instructions clearly describe the test situation?
4. Are the observational forms well designed and appropriate for the performance being evaluated?

Source: Norman E. Gronlund. (1988). *How to Construct Achievement Tests* (4th ed). Copyright © 1988. Reprinted with permission of Pearson Education, Inc., Upper Saddle River, New Jersey.

One also should keep in mind that identifying a cutoff for mastery will create an artificial dichotomy. In other words, if 90 percent correct is determined to be the criterion level for mastery, a person who correctly answered 89 percent of the items on a 100-item test would not have "mastered" the skill involved, whereas a person who answered one more correctly would have.

Gronlund (1988, pp. 119–120) noted that when a testmaker is setting the performance standards, several considerations should be taken into account. Those are:

1. Set mastery level on a multiple-choice test at 85 percent correct.
2. Increase the level if essential for next stage of instruction.
3. Increase the level if essential for safety (e.g., mixing chemicals).
4. Increase the level if test or subtest is short.
5. Decrease the level if repetition is provided at next stage.
6. Decrease the level if tasks have low relevance.
7. Decrease the level if items are extremely difficult.
8. Adjust the level up or down as teaching experience dictates.

Standards can also be calculated empirically by determining the performance levels of students who, in the testmaker's eyes, have already mastered a particular objective. It is also a good idea to indicate how many times a student must reach criterion level before mastery is assumed.

Example.   The teacher decided that Susie must correctly answer at least nine out of ten problems (90 percent) before mastery is assumed. Further, she must reach criterion level for three consecutive days before mastery is assumed.

Step 5: Administer the Test

Task.   Administer the CRT.

Comment.   After the test has been developed carefully, it can be administered to the student(s) for whom it was intended. One frequently overlooked area has to do with ensuring that the student is given proper instructions on how to take the criterion-referenced test. Swezey (1981) indicated that general test instructions should include the following types of information:

> Don't forget to develop test instructions.

1. The purpose of the test
2. The time limits for the test
3. A description of the test conditions (e.g., "You may use scratch paper if you wish.")
4. A description of the test standards (e.g., "In order to receive credit you must get the exact answer.")
5. A description of the test items (e.g., "Reduce fractions in your answers to the lowest common denominator.")
6. The general test regulations (e.g., "Continue to the next page when you see a finger pointing at the bottom of a page; stop when you see a stop sign at the bottom of the page.")

> It is not always necessary to administer the entire CRT.

Suppose that in the measurement of a specific skill, ten subcomponents or objectives were determined. For each of these ten objectives, ten test items were developed, resulting in a CRT of 100 items. Is it necessary to administer all 100 items? Probably not. The goal of a CRT is to provide specific information for instructional purposes. Two approaches might be appropriate. First, on the basis of the information available about a student (e.g., work products, results of tests to document educational need), the test user might know that the student has mastered some of the earlier objectives and can therefore skip them. Another approach might be to administer the items for objective 10 (goal) first, and work backwards to the items for objectives 9, 8, 7, and so on. If a student reaches mastery for the items for objective 5, for instance, it could be assumed that the student also has mastery over items in objectives 1 through 4. Thus, a teacher might gain from the test an indication of the immediate short-term objective (objective 5) as well as a list of sequential objectives (6 through 9) leading to the goal (objective 10). The problem with the latter approach is that the student might become frustrated when beginning with so many difficult items.

Example.   On the information gathered prior to the administration of the CRT (e.g., test data to document educational need, work samples), the teacher was able to determine that Susie knew her basic number facts and had no problems with one-digit numbers. Therefore, the criterion-referenced testing began with objective 3—subtraction of a one-digit number from a two-digit number without renaming.

Step 6: Score and Interpret the Test Results

Task.   Score and interpret the CRT.

Comment.   After the test has been developed and appropriately administered, it is necessary to score and interpret the test. This usually will involve determining the number of correct and incorrect items for each skill area and determining the percentage of mastery. Obviously, scoring the instrument will depend on the type of items used and the purpose for the testing. For example, if rate were more important than accuracy it might only be necessary to count the correct responses (e.g., the number of words read in a one-minute period). The test results should indicate what the student has already mastered as well as what should be appropriate instructional objectives.

Example.   The following percentages of correct answers were obtained for the three administrations of the CRT.

First Administration	*Second Administration*	*Third Administration*
1. Not administered (NA)	1. NA	1. NA
2. NA	2. NA	2. NA
3. 90%	3. 100%	3. 90%
4. 20%	4. 40%	4. 30%
5. 10%	5. 20%	5. 20%
6. 0%	6. 0%	6. 0%
7. NA	7. NA	7. NA
8. NA	8. NA	8. NA

These results suggest that Susie has mastered objectives 1 to 3, is having difficulty and is somewhat inconsistent with objectives 4 and 5, and does not know how to do objectives 6 to 8. The immediate objective for Susie would be to subtract multidigit numbers without renaming. The goal would be to teach the concept of renaming. The teacher would progress from objectives 4 to 8 and reevaluate using the CRT as skills are taught.

Curriculum-Based Assessment (CBA)

Why Use Curriculum-Based Assessment?

Determination and evaluation of objectives and teaching strategies; gathering of prereferral information; development and evaluation of IEPs.

Who Should Use It?

Teachers.

During the past two-and-a-half decades, *curriculum-based assessment (CBA)* has received widespread attention in the area of special education. The Regular Education Initiative discussed in Chapter 1, for instance, placed heavy emphasis on the use of CBA. Idol, Nevin, and Paolucci-Whitcomb (1999) noted that interest in CBA seemed to develop as a means of coping with low-achieving and special-needs learners who were mainstreamed into general education. They further noted that the CBA model fits nicely into a noncategorical model in which the emphasis is on testing curricular-based skills instead of testing for labeling purposes. Clearly, the current emphasis on full inclusion of students with disabilities in the general education classroom has led to increased use of CBA procedures. In fact, in one survey, school psychologists rated CBA as more acceptable than norm-referenced testing and felt it was particularly helpful for developing intervention strategies (Chafouleas, Riley-Tillman, & Eckert, 2003).

> CBA gained popularity in the 1980s.

CBA involves the measurement of the level of a student in terms of the *expected curricula outcomes of the school* (Tucker, 1985). In other words, the assessment instrument is based on the content of the student's curriculum. CBA actually refers to a variety of different procedures. Some types of CBA are relatively informal, others are more formal and standardized (Fuchs & Fuchs, 2000). In fact, there has been some confusion as to what professionals are talking about when they refer to the term CBA. Peverly and Kitzen (1998) discussed five different models of CBA that are reported in the professional literature. These were:

1. **Curriculum- and instruction-based assessment (CIBA).** Addresses the adequacy of children's performances in the curriculum and tries to ensure that students are placed appropriately (Shapiro, 1989).
2. **Curriculum-based assessment for instructional design (CBA-ID).** Focuses on controlling the level at which instructional material is presented (Gickling & Thompson, 1985).
3. **Curriculum-based evaluation (CBE).** Analyzes students' errors and identifies missing skills (Howell, Fox, & Morehead, 1993).
4. **Criterion-referenced curriculum-based assessment (CR-CBA).** Focuses on measurement of student mastery of objectives derived from classroom performance (e.g., Blankenship, 1985)
5. **Curriculum-based measurement (CBM).** Provides measurements that teachers can use to alter or modify instructional programs based on student progress (Deno, 1985).

The last two, CR-CBA and CBM, are the most widely used and researched and will be discussed in greater depth.

Criterion-Referenced CBA (CR-CBA)

Similar to CRTs, most criterion-referenced CBA procedures are based on a task-analytic model. A number of guidelines have been suggested for developing an informal CBA instrument. Blankenship (1985) suggested that the first step should be to list the skills presented in the curriculum, write an objective for each skill, develop items for each listed objective, and then administer the test before and after a structured program has been initiated. Cohen and Spence (1990) identified a five-step process that involved identifying the purpose of the CBA, developing the test specifications for curriculum objectives, constructing and revising the test items, administering the CBA instrument, and finally, graphing the student's performance. Similarly, Salvia and Hughes (1990) expanded somewhat on these previously mentioned steps and suggested the following:

1. Specify reasons for decisions.
2. Analyze the curriculum.
3. Formulate the behavioral objectives.
4. Develop appropriate assessment procedures.
5. Collect data.
6. Summarize data.
7. Display the data.
8. Interpret data and make decisions.

The steps outlined by these various authors are similar to the steps for developing a criterion-referenced test (CRT) noted earlier in this chapter. In fact, this type of CBA is essentially a CRT with the content of the curriculum dictating the content of the instrument.

CR-CBA instruments can be developed for any type of curriculum. Usually, the content of the test reflects several levels of the curriculum. For example, if the curriculum area were reading, it would be desirable to develop tests that would include passages selected from each level of the reading series. If the test were focused on spelling, items could be randomly chosen from each lesson at each level in a spelling series. A teacher can then choose to give the entire CR-CBA or only portions related to a given skill area.

A student should be evaluated on three separate days using three separate forms of the test (Idol et al., 1999). In other words, three forms should be developed that cover the same content but that have different items. By administering these three forms, one can get a better picture of the student's true ability and help to control sporadic performance. CR-CBA instruments are also frequently group administered. By reproducing the tests, it is possible to administer them to an entire class to find out where each student is in relation to the curriculum.

CR-CBA instruments are frequently group-administered.

Development of a CR-CBA Instrument: An Example

Using the procedures previously described for developing a CRT for Susie, an example of how to develop a CR-CBA instrument in the area of math for a student named Mark follows.

Step 1: Identify Skill to Be Measured. The first step was to look at Mark's mathematics curriculum and determine the skill areas included in that curriculum. Suppose that Mark's teacher, Ms. DiLorenzo, uses the Scott, Foresman, and Co. mathematics curriculum. Ms. DiLorenzo would analyze that curriculum and determine what specific skill areas it covered. (Note: For this example, only a portion of the mathematics curriculum was analyzed, for ease of discussion.) Analysis showed that the following skills were included in the part of the mathematics curriculum selected:

digit writing
place value
greater than/less than concept
addition
subtraction
missing addends

If the entire curriculum had been analyzed, a chart could have been developed that included all of the skill areas covered, the sequence of the skills, and even the page numbers in the curriculum on which the skills are explained.

Step 2: Identify Objectives. When breaking down skill areas into objectives, a *summary sheet* is sometimes used that allows the teacher to determine the specific concepts to be tested as well as the number of items that measure each objective and the standards of performance, that is, Mark's performance that is required to assume mastery. Table 5.1 shows the summary sheet for this CBA instrument.

A summary sheet helps organize the information.

Step 3: Develop Test Items. Figure 5.3 displays the test developed from the portion of the mathematics curriculum analyzed. Note that the "problem numbers"

TABLE 5.1   Summary Sheet for a Mathematics CBA

Concepts	Problem Numbers	Day 1	Day 2	Day 3	Total Score 5/6	Mastery 5/6
Writing digits	1,2	/2	/2	/2	/6	/6
Place value	3,4	/2	/2	/2	/6	/6
Comparing numbers	5,6	/2	/2	/2	/6	/6
Add basic facts 0–10	7,21	/2	/2	/2	/6	/6
Add basic facts 11–20	8,22	/2	/2	/2	/6	/6
Add 2 digits (no renaming)	9,24	/2	/2	/2	/6	/6
Add 1 (renaming)	10,26	/2	/2	/2	/6	/6
Add 3 digits (no renaming)	11,28	/2	/2	/2	/6	/6
Add 2 (renaming)	12,30	/2	/2	/2	/6	/6
Add 3 or more numbers	13,32	/2	/2	/2	/6	/6
Add 4 digits (renaming)	14,30	/2	/2	/2	/6	/6
Subtract basic facts 0–10	15,23	/2	/2	/2	/6	/6
Subtract basic facts 11–20	16,25	/2	/2	/2	/6	/6
Subtract 2 digits (no renaming)	17,27	/2	/2	/2	/6	/6
Subtract 2 digits (1 renaming)	18,29	/2	/2	/2	/6	/6
Subtract 3 digits (no renaming)	19,31	/2	/2	/2	/6	/6
Subtract 3 digits (1 renaming)	20,33	/2	/2	/2	/6	/6
Missing addends (1)	35,36	/2	/2	/2	/6	/6

Source: Adapted from L. Idol. (2007). *Models of Curriculum-Based Assessment: A Blueprint for Learning* (4th ed., p. 98). Copyright 2007 by PRO-ED, Inc. Adapted by permission.

FIGURE 5.3 Sample Math CBA

Give the number:
1. 9 tens, 6 ones   2. 3 thousand, 7 hundred forty-one

_____   _____

Tell what place 7 holds:
3. 271 _____   4. 8,726 _____

Compare the numbers. Use > or <:
5. 32 _____ 49   6. 2×3 _____ 10

Add:

7.	2	8.	7	9.	42	10.	76	11.	231
	+6		+5		+21		+17		+243

12.   373   13. $7 + 2 + 5 =$ _____   14.   3692
      +147   +2345

Subtract:

15.	8	16.	11	17.	87	18.	76	19.	588	20.	349
	−7		−4		−43		−59		−164		−187

Add or subtract:

21.	4	22.	6	23.	9	24.	55	25.	15
	+3		+3		−4		+31		−8

26.	24	27.	79	28.	401	29.	82	30.	242
	+36		−25		+296		−37		+369

31.   865   32. $4 + 4 + 6 =$ _____   33.   824   34.   4654
      −321   −717   +1975

Fill in the missing number:
35. $3 +$ _____ $= 9$ 36. $57 -$ _____ $= 39$

Source: L. Idol. (2007). *Models of Curriculum-Based Assessment: A Blueprint for Learning* (4th ed., pp. 101–102). Copyright 2007 by PRO-ED, Inc. Adapted with permission.

heading in Table 5.1 relates to the items in the test itself. The test in Figure 5.3 would be one of three tests developed that measure the same areas.

Step 4: Determine Standards of Performance. Table 5.1 indicates that Mark is required to correctly answer five out of six items for each objective to reach mastery. The criteria are based on Mark's performance on the three tests together.

Step 5: Administer the CBA Instrument. Each of the three tests was administered on consecutive days to the entire class.

Step 6: Score and Interpret the Test Results. Table 5.2 shows the test results for Mark. These results indicate that he was having no problems with writing digits,

TABLE 5.2   Results from the CBA

Concepts	Problem Numbers	Day 1	Day 2	Day 3	Total Score 5/6	Mastery 5/6
Writing digits	1,2	2/2	2/2	2/2	6/6	6/6
Place value	3,4	2/2	2/2	2/2	6/6	6/6
Comparing numbers	5,6	2/2	2/2	2/2	6/6	6/6
Add basic facts 0–10	7,21	2/2	2/2	2/2	6/6	6/6
Add basic facts 11–20	8,22	2/2	2/2	2/2	6/6	6/6
Add 2 digits (no renaming)	9,24	2/2	1/2	2/2	5/6	5/6
Add 1 (renaming)	10,26	0/2	0/2	0/2	0/6	0/6
Add 3 digits (no renaming)	11,28	2/2	2/2	1/2	5/6	5/6
Add 2 (renaming)	12,30	0/2	0/2	0/2	0/6	0/6
Add 3 or more numbers	13,32	2/2	1/2	2/2	5/6	5/6
Add 4 digits (renaming)	14,30	0/2	0/2	0/2	0/6	0/6
Subtract basic facts 0–10	15,23	2/2	2/2	2/2	6/6	6/6
Subtract basic facts 11–20	16,25	2/2	2/2	2/2	6/6	6/6
Subtract 2 digits (no renaming)	17,27	1/2	2/2	2/2	5/6	5/6
Subtract 2 digits (1 renaming)	18,29	0/2	0/2	0/2	0/6	0/6
Subtract 3 digits (no renaming)	19,31	2/2	2/2	2/2	6/6	6/6
Subtract 3 digits (1 renaming)	20,33	0/2	0/2	0/2	0/6	0/6
Missing addends (1)	35,36	1/2	1/2	1/2	3/6	3/6

Source: Adapted from L. Idol. (2007). *Models of Curriculum-Based Assessment: A Blueprint for Learning* (4th ed., p. 98). Copyright 2007 by PRO-ED, Inc. Adapted with permission.

understanding place value and comparing numbers, and addition and subtraction of single- and multiple-digit numbers without renaming. Mark, however, apparently had no idea how to "carry" or "borrow" when adding and subtracting and had not mastered how to supply missing addends. It would be possible, therefore, to have a good idea which skill—renaming—to teach Mark. Further, the teacher could group the students in the class according to performance, so that students with similar deficits could be taught together.

Uses and Limitations of CR-CBA Instruments

Overall, the research support for CBA procedures has been positive. Among the noted strengths of CBA are its ability to lead to student improvement (Galagan, 1985) and its use as an effective communication tool with parents (Marston & Magnusson, 1985). Clearly, its primary advantage is in allowing increased instructional decision making (Howell & Morehead, 1987).

Although the majority of information about CR-CBA is positive, proponents and critics alike agree that CBA procedures have certain limitations. For example, Heshusius (1991) argued that the CBA model was simplistic and did not consider the learning process itself. He further argued that CBA use creates a situation in which the teacher is virtually teaching the test. He instead argued for holistic evaluation that emphasizes process and ecological testing. One also has to consider the validity and appropriateness of the curriculum on which the CBA instrument is based.

Consider the validity and appropriateness of the curriculum itself.

Curriculum-Based Measurement (CBM)

One of the more widely researched models of CBA is CBM, developed by Deno and his associates at the University of Minnesota (Deno, 1985; Deno & Fuchs, 1987). Whereas CBA is a more generic term that usually refers to informal and nonstandardized assessment (including the previously discussed criterion-referenced CBA), CBM is a standardized, empirically derived version. CBM differs from informal CBA in at least two ways: First, it focuses measurement on the annual curriculum so that the items represent an entire school year's content. For example, spelling might include a twenty-word test drawn randomly from the entire pool of words for the year. Second, it uses a standardized methodology with documented reliability and validity (Fuchs & Fuchs, 2000). Shinn and Bamonto (1998) described CBM as "a set of standard, simple, short duration fluency measures of reading, spelling, written expression, and mathematics computation." Shinn and Bamanto went on to say that CBMs act as "academic thermometers" to monitor student growth in relevant skill domains. Colón and Kranzler (2006) emphasized the importance of using a standard set of instructions when using CBM procedures.

Fuchs and Fuchs (1990) noted the following characteristics of the CBM model:

1. Selection of one long-term goal instead of a series of short-term curricular steps
2. Measurement of standard behaviors that have documented reliability, validity, and sensitivity
3. Use of prescribed measurement methods
4. Incorporation of rules that provide systematic procedures for summarizing and evaluating the information
5. Accommodation of any instructional paradigm

Allinder, Fuchs, and Fuchs (1998) provided a description of the CBM procedures used in a number of academic areas. For *spelling,* words would be chosen that represent the entire school year's spelling curriculum. Twenty of those words would be randomly chosen for the test. These would be dictated to the student who attempts to write the correct spelling. The words would be dictated for two minutes, allowing ten seconds to spell each word. The number of correct letter sequences (pair of letters in the correct sequence) would be counted and graphed. This same procedure would be repeated twice weekly. For *mathematics,* a student would be provided with single problem probes (e.g., all subtraction), mixed problem probes (e.g., a combination of computation problems), or application probes (e.g., time or money). Again, the student is given a specific time period to solve as many problems as possible. The number of correct numerals in the correct place value would be counted and graphed. Espin, Shin, Deno, and colleagues (2000) described a procedure to measure *written expression.* They reported that determining the correct minus incorrect word sequences in a written passage resulted in a reliable and valid measure using teacher ratings and districtwide writing tests as comparison measures. Another CBM measure of written expression that has been used is the number of correct punctuation marks (Gansle, Noell, VanDerHeyden, Naquin, & Slider, 2002). In general, CBMs of written expression have been found to have sufficient technical adequacy (Gansle, VanDerHeyden, Noell, Resetar, & Williams, 2006).

Several procedures have been used to measure *reading.* Allinder and colleagues (1998) described a procedure in which passages of approximately

300 words are chosen from end-of-year-curriculum. The student is asked to read the passage orally for one minute (after three seconds without a response the word is provided to the student). The number of correct and incorrect words are noted and the number of correct words are graphed. This is sometimes referred to as the *oral reading rate* approach or the *oral reading fluency* approach; it is a common curriculum-based reading measure that has been shown to have good technical characteristics (Madelaine & Wheldall, 2004). Christ (2006) also pointed out that although oral reading fluency CBMs are sensitive to the effects of instruction, they also are sensitive to the conditions present, including the characteristics of the examiner, the setting, and incentives for performance. Wheldall and Madelaine (2000) described the *Wheldall Assessment of Reading Passages (WARP)*, which are five 200-word standardized passages that have been used to determine reading rate and have discriminated between good and poor readers. Bradley-Klug, Shapiro, Lutz, and DuPaul (1998) noted that the oral reading rate approach was useful for students being taught in literature-based reading series. Madelaine and Wheldall (1999) also felt that oral reading fluency was a good predictor of both general reading ability and reading comprehension. There has been some research, however, indicating that oral reading fluency is not a particularly accurate predictor of reading comprehension (Kranzler, Brownell, & Miller, 1998). Similarly, Foegin, Espin, Allinder, and Markell (2001) found that teachers were more positive about the utility of the oral reading fluency approach than its perceived validity, particularly related to comprehension skills. Another CBM approach used for reading is the *maze procedure* (discussed in Chapter 12). In this procedure, every *n*th word (e.g., every tenth word) is omitted and in its place are three choices. The student must indicate which of the three choices is correct. For example,

went

After the long school day, Sue work home.

gone

Shin, Deno, and Espin (2000) reported that CBM maze tests had good reliability, sensitivity, and validity. Faykus and McCurdy (1998) specifically compared the sensitivity and acceptability of the oral reading rate approach and the maze procedure. They found that although the teacher acceptability of the two approaches was equal, the oral reading approach appeared to be a more sensitive measure of reading progress.

One of the hallmarks of the CBM model is the importance of instructional decision making based on the student's progress within the curriculum. Therefore, when CBM procedures are used, it is important to determine the *trend line* or *progress line* of the student's performance (based on graphed data points) and compare that with the goal established for the student. If the trend line indicates that progress is slower than expected (in relation to the goal), an instructional change is suggested. If the trend line indicates that progress is faster than expected, the goal is modified accordingly. The progress line can be determined informally by visually drawing a line through the data that appear to best fit the trend. The accuracy of this approach, however, has been questioned (Richards, Taylor, & Ramasamy, 1999). Some relatively simple approaches can be used to increase the reliability of the trend line. Examples of these approaches are the *quarter-intersect method* and a modification of this procedure called the *split-middle method* (White & Haring, 1980). In addition, software is also available for graphing data and determining trend lines. An example is Behavioral Graphing

It is important to determine a student's trend line.

99 published by Clinical Solutions (www.clinicalsolutions.com). The following steps describe the quarter-intersect and split-middle procedures. In addition, the steps are depicted visually in Figure 5.4.

Step 1. Divide the data into two equal parts. With an odd number of data points, the line will be through the middle (median) data point going from left to right. With an even number the line will be between two data points.

Step 2. For each half, draw a vertical line at the mid-date. This will be the middle data point from left to right for an odd number of data points or between the middle data points for an even number.

Step 3. For each half, draw a horizontal line through the mid-rate line (the middle data point or between the two middle data points counting from bottom to top).

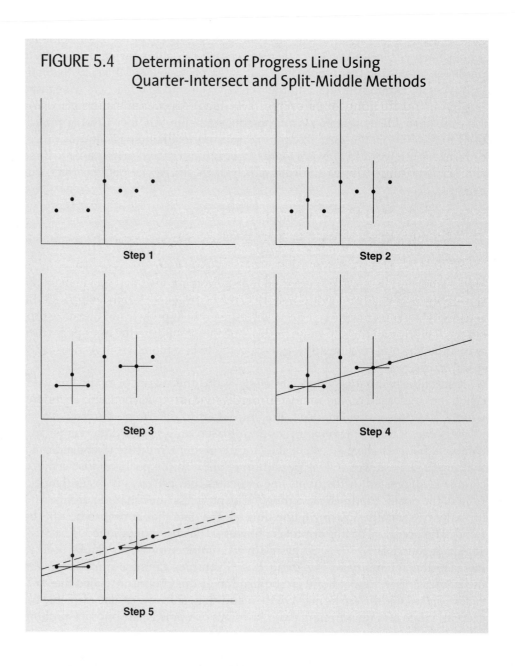

FIGURE 5.4   Determination of Progress Line Using Quarter-Intersect and Split-Middle Methods

Step 4. Draw a line that passes through the intersection created in steps 1 and 2. This is the *quarter-intersect method.*

Step 5. Move the line (always in a parallel fashion) up or down until there are equal numbers of data points on or above the line and on or below the line. This is the *split-middle method.*

Fuchs and Fuchs (1990) provided an excellent description of the use of CBM in the area of reading that demonstrates the important role of the trend line. The following example summarizes their description.

1. The teacher determines that by the end of the year the student should be proficient at third-grade-level material (proficiency defined as reading at least ninety words per minute correctly with no more than five errors). This constitutes the long-term goal.

2. The teacher assesses the student at least twice weekly, each time on a different passage, randomly sampled in the third-grade curricular text. The teacher states a standard set of directions, has the student read orally for one minute from the text, and scores the number of correctly and incorrectly read words.

3. The teacher charts the student's performance on graph paper, with the performance criterion of ninety words per minute placed on the graph at the intersection of the goal date and criterion level. A goal line connecting the baseline level and date and the goal criterion and date is drawn onto the graph. Figure 5.5 shows an example of such a graph in which the student correctly read twenty-nine words in the first week of September, with the goal set at ninety words correct by the end of May.

4. The teacher provides an instructional program and continues to assess and graph the student's performance.

5. Whenever at least eight scores have been collected, the teacher analyzes the adequacy of the student's progress and then draws a line of best fit through the student's data.

> Educational decisions are based on the trend line.

6. At this point the teacher determines the effectiveness of the teaching program. If the student's actual progress is steeper than the goal line, the teacher

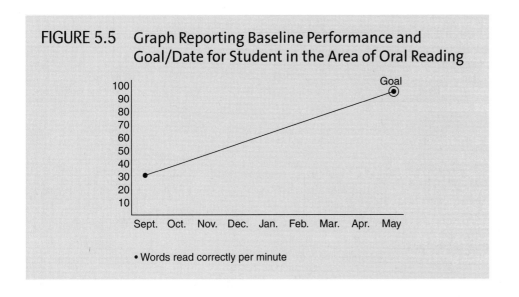

FIGURE 5.5 Graph Reporting Baseline Performance and Goal/Date for Student in the Area of Oral Reading

• Words read correctly per minute

increases the goal (Figure 5.6). This would indicate that the date of the goal could be moved to mid-January. If the student's progress is less steep than the goal line, the teacher changes the instructional program to address the student's instructional needs (see Figure 5.7). This figure shows that the student's improvement was not consistent with the projected goal.

Note that the CBM procedure relies heavily on decision making based on visual inspection of the data. In other words, the assessment information is used continually to monitor progress and to aid the teacher in instructional decision making.

Computer-Based CBM

The use of computers to monitor and assist in CBM decision making has become increasingly widespread. Computers are helpful in the mechanical aspects of scoring and in helping teachers with analysis. They lead to more accurate

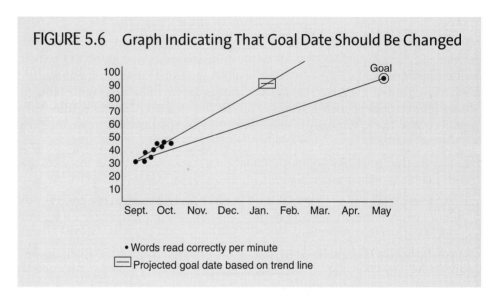

FIGURE 5.6   Graph Indicating That Goal Date Should Be Changed

• Words read correctly per minute
▭ Projected goal date based on trend line

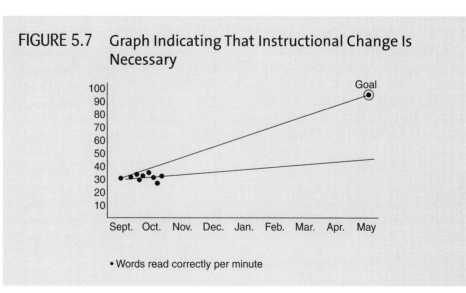

FIGURE 5.7   Graph Indicating That Instructional Change Is Necessary

• Words read correctly per minute

information that enhances teacher decision making (Fuchs, Fuchs, & Hamlett, 1993). Specific programs have been designed to help teachers score, graph, and analyze student performance data (Hasselbring & Moore, 1990). Students can also complete the CBM tasks directly on the computer.

Do computer-generated CBMs yield similar results as other types of CBM? In one study, Swain and Allinder (1996) compared oral reading probes with a computer maze procedure. The subjects were second-grade students with learning disabilities. The results indicated that the students performed better on the oral reading procedure than the computer maze procedure after repeated reading. The authors suggest that there are two possibilities to explain these results. The first is that the oral reading procedure is more sensitive and the second is that due to their age, the children were not competent enough with computer skills to perform adequately. Interestingly, however, the students preferred the computer maze procedure over the oral reading approach.

An example of a computer-based measurement technique is *Monitoring Basic Skills Progress,* a computer program package that is available for reading and mathematics.

> MBSP is a computer-based version of CBM.

Monitoring Basic Skills Progress (MBSP).   Monitoring Basic Skills Progress (MBSP) is comprised of three software programs that were designed using the CBM model. As such, they allow the student to take a series of short tests at a given grade level that are automatically scored by the computer. It also provides feedback to the student and saves the student's scores and responses. Finally, it summarizes the performance for the teacher by providing a graph of the student's scores across the school year and a profile.

The three programs are Basic Reading, Basic Math Computation, and Basic Math Concepts and Applications. The materials for each program include a manual and a disk. The disk includes a student program that allows the student to take the tests on the computer. There is also a teacher program that allows the teacher to view and monitor the student data, among other things. The MBSP manuals include guidelines to help teachers make instructional decisions by interpreting the graphs and skill profiles that are generated by the computer. The guidelines include suggestions for monitoring goals, adjusting instructional programs, and comparing the relative effectiveness of different instructional components. The skill profile provides such information as the objectives that the student has mastered, partially mastered, not mastered, or not attempted. The graphs provide a visual representation of the student's progress over time. Figure 5.8 shows an example of a student's graph in which performance indicated that an instructional change was necessary.

Basic Reading Tests.   The tests used for Basic Reading (Fuchs, Hamlett, & Fuchs, 1997) use the maze procedure. In the MBSP, the maze procedure is set up so that every seventh word in a 400-word reading passage is deleted and replaced with a blank. The students read the story and when they get to a blank they press the space bar to get three choices to replace the blank. The student indicates the correct choice and then goes to the next blank. It is recommended that the student take a test every week (twice a week for special education students). The test is automatically scored and saved, and a graph similar to that in Figure 5.9 is created.

> MBSP Reading uses a maze procedure.

Basic Math Computation Tests.   The Basic Math Computation Tests (Fuchs, Hamlett, & Fuchs, 1998) include thirty 25-item mathematics tests available for each of six grade levels. The computer automatically administers the tests at the

FIGURE 5.8   Sample Performance Pattern for Recommended Teaching Change

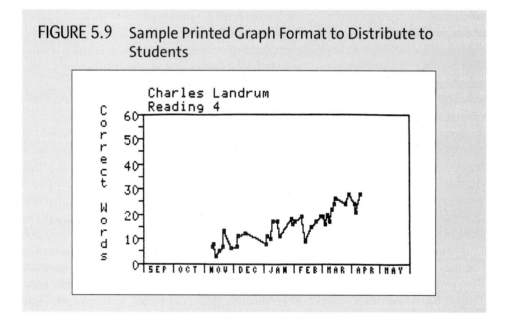

FIGURE 5.9   Sample Printed Graph Format to Distribute to Students

grade level designated by the teacher. The same scoring and feedback features noted in the other programs are available. A separate workbook with 180 mathematics tests (thirty at each grade level) also comes with the package.

Basic Math Concepts and Applications.   The Basic Math Concepts and Applications (Fuchs, Hamlett, & Fuchs, 1999) includes thirty 3-page tests at each of five grade levels (2–6). It has the same features as the other programs.

Uses and Limitations of CBM

Similar to the research on CR-CBA, the professional literature has generally supported the use of CBM procedures, particularly for enhancing instructional decision making. Shapiro and Eckert (1994), in fact, reported that school psychologists significantly and consistently rated CBM as more acceptable than standardized achievement measures. Many have argued that CBM is more appropriate than traditional, norm-referenced tests with minority children, including language minority children (e.g., Baker, Plasencia-Peinado, & Lezcano-Lytle, 1998; Shinn, Collins, & Gallagher, 1998). Bentz and Pavri (2000) also provided a strong argument that CBM is a viable alternative to traditional testing with bilingual students. In fact, Elliott and Fuchs (1997) suggested that CBM was a favorable alternative to both intelligence tests and achievement tests.

Several purposes for CBM have been identified. These include:

- Determining whether a student's educational program is adequate to meet year-end goals (Stecker, 2006)
- Determining eligibility for special education (Bricker, Yavanoff, Capt, & Allen, 2003)
- Screening and placing students (Fewster & MacMillan, 2002)
- Grouping for instruction (Wesson, Vierthaler, & Haubrich, 1989)
- Monitoring progress (Stecker, 2006)

CBM can also be used to identify potential candidates for reintegration into general education. Shinn, Habedank, Rodden-Nord, and Knutson (1993) developed local norms of low-level reading students in general education. When applied to special education students, they found that 40 percent could be reintegrated into the general education classroom. Their model, called the *Responsible Reintegration of Academically Competent Students* (RRACS), provides a systematic, data-based decision-making model (Powell-Smith & Stewart, 1998). Mathes, Fuchs, Roberts, and Fuchs (1998) also found that the use of CBM information resulted in greater likelihood of implementing appropriate academic interventions during reintegration. CBM has also been found to be helpful in identifying students who may or may not do well on both statewide assessments and standardized norm-referenced achievement tests (Shapiro, Keller, Lutz, Santoro, & Hintze, 2006). More recently, CBM has played a significant role within the Response to Intervention model (e.g., Bender & Shores, 2007). Specifically, it has been used to identify students who are initially at risk for failure and to monitor student progress through the different tiers (Hosp, Hosp, & Howell, 2007).

Instructional Decision Making. The majority of research on CBM has been conducted to determine ways to improve instructional decision making. Fuchs, Fuchs, and Hamlett (1989) reported that the appropriate selection of the long-term goal used in CBM procedures has been a problem for teachers. They need specific recommendations on how to incorporate CBM feedback into instructional planning (Fuchs, Fuchs, Hamlett, Phillips, & Bentz, 1994). If they know the actual student responses and not just the graphed responses, teachers can more effectively make instructional decisions (Fuchs, Fuchs, Hamlett, & Allinder, 1991). As a result, skill analysis programs such as that noted in the MBSP have been developed to provide more specific information for the teacher. Fuchs and colleagues (1991), in fact, found that teachers' effective use of CBM data improved when the teachers were provided with skills analyses as well as the graphed performance of the students' skills. Interestingly, Pretti-Frontczak and Briker (2000) found that the quality of IEP goals and objectives were improved after teachers used CBM, and Yell and Stecker (2003) reported that CBM could be used to develop legally correct and meaningful IEPs. Fuchs and Fuchs (2000)

Research has supported the use of CBM to improve decision making.

summarized the role that CBM plays in meeting four requirements for multifaceted decision making. These are (1) molding academic growth, (2) distinguishing between ineffective instruction and unacceptable student learning, (3) informing instructional planning, and (4) evaluating treatment effectiveness.

The important question is, Does the use of CBM improve students' achievement levels? The following summarizes some of the important research in this area:

- Greater academic improvement is noted when consultation (computerized, systematic, and instructional) is provided than when no CBM is used or is used without consultation (Fuchs, Fuchs, Hamlett, & Ferguson, 1992).
- Increased planning time resulted in greater accuracy in teachers' implementing CBM, which in turn resulted in more gains in student achievement (Allinder, 1996).
- Greater achievement gains were noted when teachers' attitudes toward CBM were positive (Allinder & Oats, 1997).
- When teachers monitored their use of CBM, it resulted in more modification of academic programs and greater student achievement gains (Allinder, Bolling, Oats, & Gagnon, 2000).
- Greater gains in math scores were noted when instructional programs were modified based on CBM results (Stecker & Fuchs, 2000).
- CBM was paired with a reading diagnosis analysis to refocus teachers to improve instruction which, in turn, improved student achievement (Fuchs, Fuchs, Hosp, & Hamlett, 2003).
- Greater gains in math computation scores were reported when CBM was paired with peer-assisted learning. Further, both teachers and students reported that CBM increased the students' motivation (Calhoun & Fuchs, 2003).

Deno (2003), almost two decades after introducing CBM, summarized the research support for its various uses. Those uses include (1) screening to identify, (2) evaluating prereferral interventions, (3) determining eligibility and placement in special education programs, (4) evaluating instruction, and (5) evaluating reintegration and inclusion in the general education classroom. He also added that recent research supports the use of CBM to predict success in high-stakes assessment, to measure growth in secondary level content areas, and to evaluate early childhood programs.

There have been some criticisms of CBM with certain populations.

Limitations.   Some limitations of CBM procedures have been noted. One criticism is that CBM emphasizes the isolation of skills rather than the examination of the learning process itself. Also, it tends to view learning in a linear fashion, and the use of the graphs may oversimplify the learning process. Gable (1990) also noted that CBM procedures are not always useful for designing interventions. In other words, although they can effectively indicate when a program change is needed, they do not provide the type of information that would help in determining the nature of an effective program. As an example of this, Frank and Gerken (1990) found that CBM probes were insufficient in making program decisions for students with mild cognitive disabilities. Kranzler, Miller, and Jordan (1999) investigated the racial/ethnic and gender bias of curriculum-based reading measures. They reported that there were both types of bias at certain grade levels. For example, in grade 5, the CBM measures overestimated the actual reading comprehension of girls and underestimated the comprehension of boys. As a result, they cautioned against the use of CBM to make eligibility decisions regarding special education placement. Finally, some general drawbacks of CBM are the time and logistics required to implement it in a practical, meaningful way (Yell, Deno, & Marston, 1992). Fuchs and Fuchs (2000) also acknowledged that CBM can take a great deal of teacher time. In fact, Hasbrouck, Woldbeck, Ibnot, and Parker (1999) reported that there was little evidence that CBM was actually being used by a significant number of teachers. They did note that those who did use it typically were strong advocates for the approach. Mehrens and Clarizio (1993) summarized, "We believe that viewing [CBM] procedures as a *replacement* for current psychoeducational practices is misguided. If by an alternative method CBM procedures are viewed as a *supplement* to existing procedures, we find the position acceptable" (p. 252).

CR-CBA and CBM: An Integrated Model

There are clear similarities and differences in the CR-CBA and CBM procedures discussed in this chapter. Both procedures have many advantages over traditional assessment methods. Cohen and Spence (1990) summarized several of these advantages. First, they provide increased communication for parents, teachers, and students about instructional decisions and student progress. Second, they have increased sensitivity and a direct impact on the student's curriculum. Finally, they noted that the use of these procedures reduces bias in teacher referrals.

Should the CR-CBA and CBM procedures discussed in this chapter be viewed and used in isolation? No. Each provides important information in the evaluation process. In a very real sense, CR-CBA is used for *instructional planning,* whereas CBM is used for *instructional monitoring* and *decision making.* Both clearly have their place in the assessment process. Shapiro (1990), in fact, proposed an integrated model for CBA. He suggested that the first step should be to assess the academic environment through interviews and observation. The second step should be to assess the grade level of the student across the curriculum material. The third step should be to assess the instructional level within the correctly placed grade level. The fourth step should be to determine when instructional modification is necessary as new skills are acquired. The last step should be to assess the student's progress. Given the information presented in this chapter, CR-CBA would be appropriate for step 3 (as a pretest) and step 5 (as mastery tests or probes). CBM would be appropriate for steps 2, 4, and 5.

Another model proposed to help individuals develop effective and meaningful curriculum-based assessment instruments was offered by King-Sears (1994), who suggested naming the model with the mnemonic APPLY. The APPLY model is essentially a combination of the criterion-referenced CBA and the CBM methods already discussed and uses the following steps:

> CR-CBA and CBM can be used together.

> Use the APPLY model.

1. Analyze the curriculum. The first step in developing a CBA is curriculum analysis. Care should be taken to look at the curriculum in collaboration with appropriate professionals. For example, if the student is placed in general education for all or part of the day, the general education teacher should become involved. Similarly, if vocational training is important then collaboration with potential employers might be relevant. The curriculum must be analyzed to determine short-term objectives (as in criterion-referenced CBA) and long-term objectives (as in CBM), and these should be identified considering the individual characteristics of the student who will be administered the instrument.

2. Prepare items to match curriculum objectives. Among the issues involved in preparing items is the consideration of the type of measurement to be used for evaluating a specific objective. The previous discussion regarding item development on criterion-referenced tests would be particularly relevant here. Another consideration is the use both of items that measure basic facts and items that measure higher-level thinking skills. It is important to avoid a simplistic skill-by-skill analysis and to include probes that will ensure that the student can apply or perform this skill in realistic situations. This is a strong basis for the use of alternative assessment procedures discussed in Chapter 6. King-Sears (1994) noted, "All items must (a) match the behavior and conditions stated in the objective, (b) be directly measurable, (c) link student performance to curriculum objectives, and (d) be considered as overall indicators of critical performance necessary for students within a given curriculum."

3. Probe frequently. It is important to probe or to sample frequently students' behavior related to the objectives found in the CBA. Although there is no specific time suggestion regarding how often the student should be tested, the goal of CBA (identification of appropriate objectives and monitoring of progress) dictates that the more frequent the assessment the more valuable the information received.

4. Load data using a graph format. It is important that results from a CBA be visually displayed so that data trends are obvious. Although the specific numerical scores of the CBA can also be meaningful, they often are not interpreted appropriately until a visual analysis is provided.

5. Yield to results—revisions and decisions. Without using the results of the CBA, the whole process is somewhat meaningless. In reality, the data derived from the CBA should dictate the decisions to be made in the classroom; this might include revising the instructional program, changing the method of instruction, using more probes, or changing the behavioral objectives themselves.

CASE STUDY *June*

Mrs. Dunn has decided to collect more data on June's reading by administering a curriculum-based assessment. In Part I below you will review curriculum-based measures. In Part II you will view the data collected from a CBA in reading that June completed with Mrs. Dunn. Then you will answer questions pertaining to these results.

Part I

Answer the following question regarding curriculum-based measures, and then proceed to the data collected by Mrs. Dunn.

- Describe a type of curriculum-based reading measure that is commonly used by teachers to measure a student's oral reading skills.

Part II: Curriculum-Based Data Collected in Reading

June read three passages of approximately 300 words each from the fourth-grade literature series used in her class. She read orally for one minute. The results are listed below.

Passage No.	Words per Minute	No. of Words Incorrect	No. of Words Correct	Percent of Words Correct
1	43	15	28	65
2	40	16	24	60
3	42	16	26	63

Note: The following reading rate guidelines are for grades 4–6:

   Frustration level: 49 words/minute or less with 8 or more errors
   Instructional level: 50–99 words/minute and 3–7 errors
   Mastery Level: 100–150 words/minute or better and 2 or fewer errors

- What conclusions can you make regarding June's performance on this curriculum-based measurement in reading?
- What questions might you and Mrs. Dunn have at this point regarding June's reading level?
- What should be done next?

Reflections

1. Why do you think standards of performance should not simply be set arbitrarily when developing a criterion-referenced test?
2. Why do you think it is advisable to test a student on three tests on three different days when using criterion-referenced, curriculum-based assessment?
3. Why do you think it is important to graph data when using curriculum-based measurement?

Summary Matrix

Instrument or Technique	Suggested Use									Target Population							Special Considerations	Educational Relevance for Exceptional Students
	Prereferral		Postreferral															
	Screening and Initial Identification	Informal Determination and Evaluation of Teaching Programs and Strategies	Determination of Current Performance Level and Educational Need	Decisions about Classification and Program Placement	IEP Goals	IEP Objectives	IEP Evaluation	Mild/Moderate	Severe/Profound	Preschool	Elementary Age	Secondary Age	Adult				
Criterion-Referenced Tests	X	X	X		X	X	X	X	X	X	X	X	X	Can be developed by the teacher on the basis of a student's curriculum; determination of criteria is arbitrary.	Very Useful
Curriculum-Based Assessment (CR-CBA & CBM)	X	X	X		X	X	X	X		X	X	X		A general term referring to a variety of assessment techniques.	Very Useful
Criterion-Referenced CBA	X	X	X		X	X	X	X		X	X	X		Uses the actual curriculum as the content of the testing.	Very Useful
Curriculum-Based Measurement	X	X	X		X	X	X	X			X	X		A more standardized version of CBA.	Very Useful
Monitoring Basic Skills Progress	X	X	X		X	X	X	X			X			A computerized version of CBM; available in reading and math.	Useful

chapter six

Portfolio Assessment and Other Alternative Assessment Procedures

Ironically, two opposing philosophical movements have occurred in the last decade. On one hand, there has been greater emphasis on standardized achievement tests, particularly group-administered tests. On the other hand, there are several alternative assessment procedures, such as portfolio assessment, that have received widespread attention. Both movements have been fueled by legal mandates. The first is the NCLB requirement of high-stakes assessment for accountability purposes. The other is the IDEA 04 mandate that students with disabilities be included in these assessments if at all possible (with accommodations, if necessary). However, if the student cannot participate, then he or she must be given an alternate assessment. The approaches discussed in this chapter actually could be used for both purposes of high-stakes assessment. First, because of the criticism of large-scale standardized testing, they could be used in place of such tests. Some states, such as Kentucky and Maryland, have already gone in this direction. Second, they are all appropriate procedures that might be used to meet the legal mandate of alternate assessment for those who cannot participate in the required district or state assessment.

Another reason for the interest in alternative assessment is the growing criticism of standardized testing because of the lack of information it provides when evaluating an individual student at the classroom level. Among the reasons for the criticism are

- It puts too much value on recall and rote learning at the expense of understanding and reflection.
- It promotes the misleading impression that a single right answer exists for almost every problem or question.
- It turns students into passive learners who need only recognize, not construct, answers and solutions.
- It forces teachers to focus more on what can be easily tested than on what is important for students to learn.

Traditional group-administered achievement tests have been criticized.

TABLE 6.1   Shifts in Instructional Practices

From	To
• Acquisition of pieces of knowledge as an end in itself.	• Embedding knowledge in a conceptual framework and using knowledge as a tool for solving problems.
• Emphasis on separate areas of content.	• Content integration.
• Emphasis on one right answer.	• Emphasis on students' reasoning and problem-solving processes.
• Students as passive participants in learning.	• Students as active participants in constructing learning.
• Teachers as transmitters of knowledge.	• Teachers as facilitators of learning.
• Evaluation as measuring student mastery.	• Evaluation as a means of improving instruction, learning, and programs.
• Students working alone, quietly.	• Cooperative learning.
• Learning to write.	• Writing to learn.
• Computer-assisted instruction in computer labs.	• Classroom-based technology to enhance instructional opportunities.

- It trivializes content and skill development by reducing whatever is taught to a fill-in-the-bubble format. (Hart, 1994, p. 7)

As a result of this dissatisfaction with standardized testing, several changes have occurred in the area of assessment. These changes have been largely a result of changes in curricular and instructional practices (see Table 6.1). Gullo (2006) noted that one of the advantages of alternative assessment is that it reflects the goals of curriculum. It should be noted, however, that traditional norm-referenced tests are still widely used. In a survey of school psychologists, McCloskey and Athanasiou (2000) found that although alternative assessment was used more often than was expected, traditional norm-referenced tests were still the most popular.

Alternative approaches discussed in this chapter are performance assessment, authentic assessment, and portfolio assessment. All of these alternative approaches have several points in common, usually requiring the student to produce, construct, demonstrate, or perform a task. On the other hand, traditional norm-referenced tests require students to select and mark correct responses. Figure 6.1 provides the definitions of many terms currently used in the alternative assessment movement.

Performance Assessment

Why Use Performance Assessment?
Determination and evaluation of objectives and teaching strategies; gathering of prereferral information; monitoring progress; parent conferencing.

Who Should Use It?
Teachers.

> ## FIGURE 6.1   Definitions of Common Terms
>
> **alternative assessment:** Assessments that are not standardized, multiple-choice, or norm-referenced.
>
> **performance assessment:** An alternative assessment that requires the student to *do* (produce, demonstrate, perform, create, construct, apply, build, solve, plan, show, illustrate, convince, persuade, or explain) some task.
>
> **authentic assessment:** A performance assessment that requires the *application* of knowledge to real-life, real-world settings, or a simulation of such a setting using real-life, real-world activities.
>
> **portfolio assessment:** A performance assessment of observable evidence or products completed by the student over time. Portfolio assessment may or may not be "authentic."

Performance assessment can be defined as assessment in which a student *creates* a response to a question, problem, or task. This is in contrast to more traditional, standardized testing in which a student must *choose* a response using, for example, a true–false or multiple-choice format. Perlman (2003) pointed out that performance assessment can be used to measure areas that are difficult to tap with more traditional multiple-choice items including communication abilities, critical-thinking skills, and problem solving. McMillan (2004) noted that performance assessment emphasizes the students' ability to use knowledge and skills to produce their own work. In some cases, this might be demonstrated through actual performance (e.g., playing the piano). In others, a product is developed (e.g., measurement of achievement through a completed project or task). There are many advantages to performance assessment. McMillan also noted that it is particularly relevant for curricula emphasizing applied reasoning skills and integrated subject matter. He also argued that it forces teachers to identify multiple, specific criteria for judging success. McLaughlin and Warren (1995) added that performance assessment can help motivate students by using meaningful, relevant tasks. Performance assessment has even been used to evaluate students' multiple intelligences using Howard Gardner's model (Sarouphim, 1999). It has also been suggested as a potentially beneficial technique with students with moderate mental retardation and severe disabilities (Siegel-Causey & Allinder, 1998).

> **PERFORMANCE ASSESSMENT**
> An alternative assessment that requires the student to create a response to a question, problem, or task.

The following is a description of a performance assessment task in the area of mathematics:

> A group of five families on your block is going to have a garage sale. Your family has twelve items to sell and will need eighteen square feet to display these items; the Hamletts have thirteen items and need twenty square feet; the Phillips, seven items and ten square feet; the Garcias, fifteen items and fifteen square feet; the Nguyens, ten items and thirty square feet. Rental tables measure 6 feet by 2.5 feet and cost $6 per day. The garage where the sale will be held is twenty feet by thirty feet. Newspaper advertising costs $11 for the first ten words and $1.50 for each additional word.
>
> 1. How many tables will you need? Explain how you got this number.
> 2. Draw a diagram showing how the tables can be arranged in the garage to allow the customers to move about with at least four feet between tables.
> 3. Write an ad for your sale that includes enough information.
> 4. How much money do you have to earn from your sale for the families to break even? (Fuchs, 1994)

The students are aware of the scoring system and the criteria used to determine the scores. Their responses will be classified as exemplary, competent, minimal, inadequate, or no attempt, based on a rubric that specifies the characteristics of responses in each of these categories.

This example demonstrates that performance assessment requires the student to do more than simple arithmetic computations. In fact, it taps a number of different areas as the student applies the information in a variety of ways. Elliott (1994) provided several guidelines for teachers to follow to make performance assessment meaningful. These included selecting assessment tasks that clearly relate to what is being taught; providing students with statements, standards, and models of acceptable performance; and encouraging students to complete self-assessments of their performance.

Limitations

Unfortunately, performance assessment is not without its critics. For example, Soodak (2000) felt that more educational reform was necessary than simply changing the format of assessments for students with learning difficulties. In other words, performance assessment might be a move in the right direction, but is probably not enough to address the issue of assessing and instructing exceptional students. Also, as noted previously, one use of these procedures has been to evaluate students in large-scale, statewide testing programs (high-stakes assessment). Mehrens (1992) pointed out that it is difficult, if not impossible, to keep the exact content of these types of exams secure. Thus, new performance assessments have to be developed each year, adding to the costs and making cross-year comparisons of growth difficult. Coutinho and Malouf (1993) also agreed that the expenses of performance assessment are greater than those of pencil-and-paper tasks and that the amount of time involved in the administration, scoring, and interpretation is considerable. McMillan (2004) also pointed out that time is a major concern when using performance assessment. For example, Kleinert, Kennedy, and Kearns (1999) reported results of a statewide survey in Kentucky regarding their state's alternate assessment procedure and found that the main frustration was over the amount of time necessary to complete the assessment.

One must also be aware of the *purpose* for the performance assessment and its subsequent limitations. Baker (1993) argued that although performance assessment has been viewed as equally useful for both accountability (high stakes) and for improving classroom learning (low stakes), the technical aspects of performance assessment must be more stringent when it is used for high-stakes assessment. Coutinho and Malouf (1993), however, pointed out that performance assessment requires subjectivity of scoring and that examiner objectivity and reliability may be a problem. McMillan (2004) and Chittooran and Miller (1998) also noted the low reliability of many performance assessments. As districts and states meet the requirement to have alternate assessments in place, more attention will undoubtedly be given to this area. Baker also noted that we do not know enough about the effectiveness of performance assessment as a stand-alone procedure for its use in low-stakes assessment to determine individual student accomplishments. Finally, Burger and Burger (1994) suggested that whereas performance-based assessment does provide additional information to that yielded from norm-referenced tests, it is unclear if this information is any better. Thus, it appears that the expense and time concerns as well as technical limitations of performance assessment might create some problems for high-stakes assessment. Further, the exact value of the information obtained from these procedures for

Performance assessment can be costly.

Reliability of performance assessment has been questioned.

low-stakes assessment is not clear. Regardless of the specific purpose for the performance assessment, certain recommendations should be considered when developing the measures. Moskal (2003) suggested several, including (1) clearly aligning goals and activities with measurable performance outcomes and (2) avoiding the measurement of extraneous or unintended outcomes.

The exact role of performance assessment when used with individuals with disabilities also is unclear. For example, Fuchs, Fuchs, Karns, and colleagues (2000) found that when students were provided an orientation on the structure and scoring of performance assessments, their prior achievement histories affected their performance on a subsequent assessment. Specifically, they found that the training significantly increased scores on the subsequent performance assessment for students who were above or at grade level, but did not for those students who were below grade level. Thus, the very students for whom many performance assessments have been developed might not be those who will do well on the tests. Coutinho and Malouf (1993) noted three critical issues: (1) What are the significant policy, procedural, and technical considerations regarding students with disabilities and large-scale performance assessment programs? (2) What are appropriate uses of performance assessment with children and youth with disabilities? and (3) How should special education contribute to the productive use of performance assessment in the schools? Although we have come a long way toward answering these questions, there is still more to learn.

Finally, the goal of performance assessment should be to bring assessment and instruction together. The results in this area, however, have not been clear. Fuchs, Fuchs, Karns, Hamlett, and Katzaroff (1999) reported that teachers who used performance assessment modified their curriculum to promote greater problem solving and also reported relying on different strategies to promote problem solving. They also found that students who received performance assessment showed stronger problem-solving skills. The same pattern as noted in the previously mentioned Fuchs, Fuchs, and colleagues (2000) study, however, was also found. In other words, the greatest gains in problem solving were from those students who were performing at or above grade level. On the other hand, Vitali (1993) noted that while teachers do tend to focus instruction on the content of standardized multiple-choice tests, the same was not true when performance-based assessment was used. Vitali concluded that teachers simply did not know how to teach the performance-based assessments, and they did not feel they could do so within the current educational constraints.

Authentic Assessment

Why Use Authentic Assessment?

Determination and evaluation of objectives and teaching strategies; gathering of prereferral information; monitoring progress; parent conferencing.

Who Should Use It?

Teachers.

Performance assessment becomes **authentic assessment** when it requires realistic demands and is set in a real-life context (Poteet, Choate, & Stewart, 1993). However, because the school setting is a major real-life context for many

> **AUTHENTIC ASSESSMENT**
> A performance assessment that requires application of knowledge to real-life or real-world situations.

students, particularly younger students, the distinction between performance and authentic assessment is not always clear. The terms, in fact, are sometimes used interchangeably. Again, authentic assessment is also not new. For example, when an individual is being assessed in the area of vocal music, typically he or she must sing and is evaluated according to various criteria; it is not simply the person's knowledge of the music, the notes, and the tempo. Howell, Bigelow, Moore, and Evoy (1993) noted that whereas a more traditional achievement test might ask a student to spell words or punctuate sentences to measure written language skills, an authentic measure might ask the student to write a story about the pursuit of a dream. The student would first generate details regarding character and plot, then write a rough draft, then read the rough draft to class members to get ideas to improve the work, and finally edit, rewrite, and proof-read the work. Examples of authentic assessment in a variety of areas follow (Poteet et al., 1993):

Reading: Audio- or videotape of reading to a peer
Science: Original investigation and report of findings
Oral Expression: Phone call to request information
Social Studies: Design of museum exhibit on topic of interest
Written Expression: Article for school paper
The Arts: Design and decoration of bulletin board
Mathematics: Monitoring a savings account

The determination of what constitutes authentic assessment requires some degree of value judgment. For example, Coutinho and Malouf (1993) indicated that the task must be considered examples of "valued performances" to be considered authentic. Similar to performance assessment, authentic assessment also has limitations when it is used for high-stakes assessment purposes. Miller and Seraphine (1993) felt that authentic assessment was good for classroom assessment uses but not for accountability purposes. Kerka (1995) summarized several questions that should be asked when designing authentic assessments. These included "What should learners know and be able to do?" "What are the purposes of the assessment?" and "What criteria will be used to evaluate the performance?"

Portfolio Assessment

Why Use Portfolio Assessment?
Determination and evaluation of objectives and teaching strategies; gathering of prereferral information; monitoring progress; parent conferencing.

Who Should Use It?
Teachers.

PORTFOLIO ASSESSMENT
A collection of observable evidence or products completed by the student over time.

The alternative assessment approach that has the most direct relevance for the classroom teacher is **portfolio assessment.** Paulson, Paulson, and Meyer (1991, p. 60) defined a portfolio as "a purposeful collection of student works that exhibits the students' efforts, progress, and achievement in one or more areas. The collection must include student participation in selecting contents, the criteria for selection, the criteria for judging merit and evidence of student self-reflection." In other words, portfolio assessment contains the observable evidence of the products of performance assessment and other sources of information. The portfolio, therefore, can serve as an excellent means of allowing a teacher to discuss progress with a student, parents, or other teachers. This approach moves away from a skill-by-skill approach to assessment, toward a more holistic evaluation that focuses on the *process* of learning, as well as the *product* of learning (Mathews, 1990). Valencia (1990) in describing a portfolio in the area of reading, compared it to an artist's portfolio in which samples of work are used to exemplify the artist's depth and breadth of expertise. Included in a typical reading portfolio might be samples of student work such as classroom tests, audiotapes, teacher's observational notes, the student's self-evaluation, and progress notes. Table 6.2 provides examples of different types of assessment portfolios.

If designed and used correctly, portfolio assessment can be integrated with classroom instruction and can represent significant authentic work that requires complex thinking skills and provides a more sensitive portrait of the student's strengths and weaknesses. It also encourages teachers and students to reflect on

TABLE 6.2   Examples of Assessment Portfolios

Reading Portfolio
- Audiotape of oral reading of selected passages
- Original story grammar map
- Transcript of story retelling
- Log of books read with personal reactions, summaries, vocabulary
- Representative assignments; responses to pre-postreading questions
- Favorite performance
- Journal entries including self-evaluation

Science Portfolio
- Representative work samples
- Student-selected best performance
- Report from hands-on investigation
- Notes on science fair project
- Journal entries including self-evaluation

Writing Portfolio
- Scrapbook of representative writing samples
- Selected prewriting activities
- Illustrations/diagrams for one piece
- Log/journal of writing ideas, vocabulary, semantic maps, compositions, evaluations
- Conference notes, observation narratives
- Student-selected best performance
- Self-evaluation checklists and teacher checklists

Social Studies Portfolio
- Representative work samples
- Student-selected best performance

- Design of travel brochure, packet, or itinerary of trip
- Notes on history fair project
- Journal entries including self-evaluation

Mathematics Portfolio
- Reports of mathematical investigations
- Representative assignments
- Teacher conference notes
- Descriptions and diagrams of problem-solving processes
- Video, audio, or computer-generated examples of work
- Best performance
- Journal entries including self-evaluation

Arts Portfolio
- Best performance
- Favorite performance
- First, middle, and final renderings of projects
- Tape of performance
- Journal entries including self-evaluation

Generic Portfolio
- Learning progress record
- Report cards
- Personal journal
- Tests
- Significant daily assignments
- Anecdotal observations
- Photographs
- Awards
- Personal goals

Source: J. Poteet, J. Choate, and S. Stewart. (1993). Performance Assessment and Special Education: Practices and Prospects. *Focus on Exceptional Students, 26*(1). Reprinted by permission of Love Publishing Company, Denver, Colorado.

the progress and to adjust instruction accordingly (Herman, Gearhart, & Baker, 1993). Similarly, Ezell, Klein, and Ezell-Powell (1999) also reported that portfolio assessment was helpful in fostering self-determination in older students with mental retardation. Morrison (1999) even suggested that a portfolio might be an effective tool for early childhood educators to help enhance the acceptance of young children with disabilities by their peers. Recently, the use of portfolios for individuals with intellectual disabilities has been recommended (Carothers & Taylor, 2005; Klein-Ezell & Ezell, 2005).

Nolet (1992) in reviewing the research on portfolios noted five characteristics that were consistently reported:

1. Portfolios involve samples of student behavior collected over time, rather than during a single testing situation.
2. Portfolio assessment employs data generated from multiple procedures and under a variety of stimulus and response conditions.
3. Assessment portfolios are intended to sample tasks regularly performed in a natural or authentic context.
4. Portfolio assessment typically involves at least two types of data: raw data consisting of student's actual work and summarization data compiled by the teacher.
5. The process of selecting materials for inclusion generally involves at least some degree of student participation.

Bullock and Hawk (2001) also noted consistent characteristics of portfolios. These were (1) They have a specific purpose, (2) they are developed for a specific audience, (3) they contain work samples commonly called evidence, and (4) they include reflections.

Purposes for Portfolio Assessment

As mentioned earlier in this chapter, portfolio assessment has been used in some high-stakes testing. One example is the Vermont Portfolio Project, which initially began in 137 schools. Fourth- and eighth-grade students developed portfolios in the areas of written expression and mathematics. In general, the results indicated that the students' writing skills were good, although their math abilities needed improvement. More important, the results indicated that the students did not present their results clearly; fewer than half of the students assembled their portfolios in a clear manner. This indicated the need for training both teachers and students in the portfolio process. In addition, when portfolios are used for high-stakes assessment, the issue of reliability is crucial. Johnson, McDaniel, and Willeke (2000) reported that at least three raters are required to obtain acceptable reliability with these types of tests. Similarly, the validity of statewide portfolio programs has been questioned (Johnson & Arnold, 2007).

Snider, Lima, and DeVito (1994) made several recommendations regarding portfolio assessment based on their experience with a statewide program. Those included:

- Those involved must share a fundamental belief that all students can learn and achieve at high levels.
- Participants must embrace the concept that good assessment looks like good instruction.
- Students must be ready to take more responsibility for their own learning and be willing to accept the teacher as a facilitator or coach rather than solely as a lecturer.

- School and district administration support must be evident for portfolio assessment procedures to succeed.
- Teachers must be given the time to learn about portfolio assessment, to try out numerous activities, and to experience successes as well as failures.
- Teachers must be provided with adequate technical assistance in portfolio assessment, for the great majority of classroom teachers are neither trained nor experienced in these procedures. (p. 87)

While the use of portfolio assessment on a large scale is becoming more popular, its primary use is for low-stakes purposes. Although there are a variety of consistent descriptions of portfolio assessment for these purposes, there is little consensus regarding the goals or procedures for using portfolio assessment. Nolet (1992) suggested that portfolio assessment is a process of collecting multiple forms of data to support inferences about student performance in a skill or content area that cannot be measured directly by a single measure. He also noted that portfolios have been used for a variety of reasons, including formative and summative evaluation of student's performance in elementary and high schools. Farr and Tone (1994) made the distinction between a **working portfolio** and a **show portfolio.** The working portfolio includes examples of daily work, whereas the show portfolio would have selected samples of the student's work and would be used for conferences and other more formal evaluation purposes. These have also been referred to as the *instructional portfolio* and *assessment portfolio* (Nolet, 1992), and the *master portfolio* and *assessment portfolio* (Hewitt, 1995). Duffy, Jones, and Thomas (1999) discussed four types of portfolios: the *everything portfolio, product portfolio, showcase portfolio,* and the *objective portfolio.* Again each one of these would be used for a specific purpose.

Swicegood (1994) stated five possible purposes for a portfolio. The first is to provide a concrete display of the learner's best work and the learner's development. The second is to obtain multidimensional assessment information over time. The third is to produce a concrete display of the range of learning abilities, and the fourth is to share a tool for student and teacher reflection on learning goals. The last purpose is to encourage dialogue and collaboration among educators and between the teacher and the student. Wesson and King (1992) suggested that portfolio information could be used in conjunction with curriculum-based measurement (CBM) (discussed in Chapter 5). They believed that portfolios could be used for instructional planning and that CBM could be used to evaluate the instructional plans. Portfolio assessment has even been used to identify minority children who are gifted and who are not identified through more traditional measures, such as intelligence tests (Coleman, 1994; Hadaway & Marek-Schroer, 1994).

There are many types of portfolios.

WORKING PORTFOLIO
Includes examples of daily work.

SHOW PORTFOLIO
Includes selected samples of student work to share at conferences and used for more formal assessment.

Diversity

Portfolio Development: Procedures and Examples

Although any number of entries can be included in a portfolio, it is important to be systematic in choosing those that will ultimately be included. As noted previously, the purpose for the assessment to a certain extent will dictate the type of information included.

Salend (1998) identified six guidelines to follow in the development of a portfolio:

1. Identify the goals of the portfolio.
2. Determine the type of portfolio to be used.
3. Establish procedures for organizing the portfolio.

4. Choose a range of authentic classroom products that relate to the portfolio objectives.
5. Record the significance of items included in students' portfolios.
6. Review and evaluate portfolios periodically.

Similarly, Vavrus (1990) suggested that there are five decisions that teachers must make before they develop a portfolio. Each of these five decisions will be identified and discussed. These will be the basis for an example of the development of a portfolio that illustrates each step.

The portfolio was being developed for Mike, a seventh-grade student with a learning disability. At Mike's middle school the teachers worked in teams and had a specified number of students assigned to them. Included on the team were all the content area teachers for the group of students as well as a special education teacher who worked with those exceptional students assigned to the team. Mike's team included his English teacher, Ms. Brewer; history teacher, Ms. Ortiz; geography teacher, Mr. Lee; science teacher, Ms. Novello; mathematics teacher, Ms. Massey; and special education teacher, Mr. Wald. This team approach allowed for collaborative planning and conferencing with parents when appropriate. Mr. Wald wanted to develop a portfolio for Mike in the area of written expression. This had been a difficult area for Mike in the past although improvement was noted in the previous year by his sixth-grade team.

DECISION ONE: What Should It Look Like? (Structure of Portfolio).   A good portfolio should have both a physical structure and a conceptual structure. The physical structure is the actual arrangement of the entries in the portfolio, such as the subject area and the chronological order, whereas the conceptual structure refers to the learning goals that are set for the student and the corresponding portfolio entries that best reflect those goals. Nolet (1992) also noted that *portfolio format* is important and could include some type of expandable file folder, laser disks, or computers. Hewett (2007) highly recommended electronic portfolios (e-portfolios), based on their ease of use, their efficiency, and the ease of transmitting information. As an example of the use of technology in portfolio assessment, Edyburn (1994) described the Grady Profile, an integrated series of Hypercard stacks that serve as an electronic portfolio for students' work. The actual work samples can be stored in three formats: sound (by microphone), graphics (by a scanner), and video. Each student has a complete set of stacks that serves as his or her portfolio and is protected by a password. Figure 6.2 shows one of several screens that can be accessed through the Grady Profile. This screen would allow an individual to review the student's reading skills and hear a recording of the student actually reading. Denham, Bennett, Edyburn, Lahm, and Klienert (2001) described other options of developing electronic portfolios including web-based portfolios. They did note, however, that significant resources and time are necessary to develop them appropriately.

EXAMPLE—DECISION ONE: Determine Structure of the Portfolio

Determine physical structure and format. Mr. Wald decided to coordinate the portfolio; he requested entries from each of the content-area teachers. He chose a simple expandable file folder as the best way to hold and display Mike's work. He separated the portfolio according to content areas and included a section on self-reflections and a section on teacher comments.

Determine conceptual structure. Because Mr. Wald was interested in determining progress in Mike's written expression areas, he requested that each teacher

FIGURE 6.2 Reading Sample Card from the Grady Profile

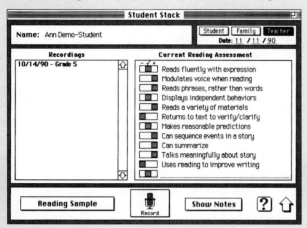

Source: D. Edyburn. (1994). An Equation to Consider: The Portfolio Assessment Knowledge Base + Technology = The Grady Profile. *LD Forum, 19*(4). Reprinted by permission, Council for Learning Disabilities.

provide representative samples of Mike's writing. The determination of the representative samples would be made jointly by Mike and each teacher.

DECISION TWO: What Goes in It? (Content of Portfolio). The second decision is *what goes in* the portfolio. This determination is sometimes totally left up to the student, whereas other times it is teacher driven. Usually there is some joint decision making. Six questions must be answered before deciding what goes into a portfolio (Nolet, 1992).

1. Who is the intended audience for the portfolio?
2. What will this audience want to know about student learning?
3. Will the selected documents show aspects of student growth or will they corroborate evidence that test scores have already documented?
4. What kinds of evidence will best show student progress toward learning goals?
5. Will the portfolio contain best work, a progressive record of student growth, or both?
6. Will the portfolio include more than finished pieces, such as ideas, sketches, and revisions?

Swicegood (1994) investigated the contents of several portfolios and identified four major areas or categories of information that emerged. The first area was measures of behavior and adaptive functioning. This included entries such as observations, interviews about interests, videotapes of student behavior, and social skills and peer ratings. The second was measures of academic and literacy growth. Entry examples included writing samples collected over time, photographs of student projects, classroom tests, informal assessment (such as criterion-referenced tests or curriculum-based assessment), and running anecdotal records. The third area was measures of strategic learning and self-regulation. Examples of entries included student self-evaluations of task performance, interviews with the student about how they approach classroom tasks, student descriptions of strategies

> Content of the portfolio depends on its purpose.

and operations used in observation, and ratings of study skills. The last area was measures of language and cultural aspects. These included entries such as a primary language sample, simulation in role plays, and cultural interviews with the student and parents.

The actual content of the portfolio will depend on the specific goals that are set for the student. Examples for entries for documenting progress in literacy might be samples from writing folders, excerpts from writing journals and literature logs, audiotapes of oral reading, or portions of projects that require reading and writing. In the area of math the student might include samples of computations, explanations of why mathematical processes work, or solutions to open-ended questions. Also included in any portfolio should be documentation of the students' *self-evaluations* and *self-reflections.* Many feel that this is one of the most important components of portfolio assessment. As John Dewey once said, "We learn by doing if we reflect on what we've done." McMillan (2004) suggested that certain, simple questions can be asked initially (e.g., "What did you like best about this sample of your writing?"). Later, more reflective questions could be asked such as "If you could work more on this piece of writing, what would you do?" Some guidelines to follow include creating a safe and supportive environment for honest reflection, and designing prompts to move students toward independence (Fernsten & Fernsten, 2005).

Knight (1992) provided the following excerpt from one of her eighth-grade students' portfolio that indicates the degree of reflection that goes into the selection of portfolio materials.

> I chose these papers for my portfolio because they show my best work and my worst work. They portray both sides of my academic performance in math this last semester. The 45% math test is in my portfolio because it shows that I have some problems in math. It shows my bad work. It shows that sometimes I have a bad day. It shows also that I forgot to study (ha, ha, ha). I can sum up three papers in this paragraph. Those are the Personal Budget, the James project, and the $2,000 lottery project. On all of these papers I did really well. That shows that I tend to do much better on those projects, especially the creative ones. I have a bit more fun doing them rather than doing just normal take-home math assignments, these papers definitely show me at my best. (p. 72)

Interestingly, Ezell and Klein (2003) found that students both with and without disabilities became more internally oriented in terms of locus of control after using portfolio assessment.

EXAMPLE—DECISION TWO: Determine Contents of the Portfolio

Determine purpose of the portfolio. As noted, the purpose of Mike's portfolio was to document progress over time in the area of written expression.

Determine intended audience. Mike's portfolio was developed with several people in mind—included were Mike's parents, all of Mike's teachers, and Mike himself.

Determine audience needs. Based on the intended audience, the portfolio was developed in such a way that both qualitative and quantitative growth could be demonstrated over time. This would allow Mike's parents to see the differences in his written expression throughout the school year, provide the teachers with examples of how Mike was writing in the other content areas, and would also serve as a basis for self-reflection on Mike's part.

Determine type of entries. As noted, the entries were chosen jointly by Mike and each of his teachers. Mike was instructed to vary the types of writing samples that he chose from each classroom. In other words, he was told to take examples of creative work, of responses to essay questions, poems, reports, and so on. This would provide a good variety of writing samples on which to base his progress.

DECISION THREE: How and When Are the Entries Selected? (Selection Process). The third decision that a teacher must make is *how and when to select the entries.* This relates to the *conditions* under which the material is produced. Are typical performances included, or should exemplary work only be included? Again, this ties into the goal for why the portfolio is being assembled. For example, the end of a unit, semester, or school year are good times to select work samples that best demonstrate student growth. Vavrus (1990) also suggested creating a time line and identifying regular times during the year for selecting student work. This also provides a time line for the student who can prepare portfolio entries.

EXAMPLE—DECISION THREE: Determine Selection Process

Every two weeks, on Thursday, Mike's teachers would put all of his written material in a folder and send it home so that he could decide which of the pieces were the most representative of his work. He was told not to pick his best work, or examples where he felt he had not done a good job. In other words, he was told to pick those that represented the most consistent type of writing sample.

Initially, the teachers met with Mike to show him examples of what they thought were representative. It was his responsibility after that point to make the determination. The next day he would meet with his teachers, show them the samples he had chosen, and would confer to determine if, in fact, they were representative. The teachers questioned Mike about his choices. Figure 6.3 shows a sample from science chosen by Mike and Ms. Novello during the beginning of the year. Mike had to write a poem using the science vocabulary words that he was learning that week. Figure 6.4 shows the example of writing chosen from Mike's English class for an entry during the middle of the year. His assignment was to write a brief description of three books that he had recently read and liked best. He also was asked to

FIGURE 6.3   Portfolio Entry from Science Class

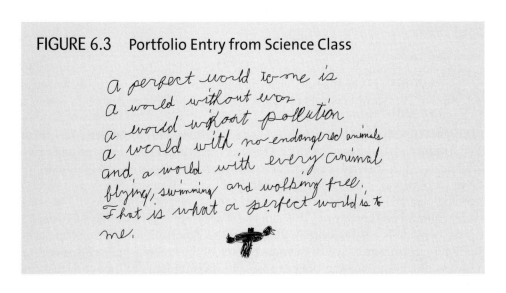

FIGURE 6.4   Portfolio Entry from English Class

Rating scale 1 forget it, 2 poor, 3 fair, 4 good, 5 got to read it

Book ratings from 1 to 5
The three best books I read were Congo, Jurassic Park, and Goosebumps.
Congo is about an expedition sent into the Congo to findout what happend to the first expedition. The first was killed by an unknown predator. With the second expedition is, Amy, the gorilla with a 620 sign vocabulary, and a man looking for the lost city of Zinj and millions of diamonds. I rate this book a 4. P.S. Congo is a real place in Africa.
    Jurassic Park is about a group of people invited to a theme park only to notice they are surounded by prehistoric dinosaurs. Once they finish their tour in the cars, Nedry shuts the dinosaur gates down. The movie is different than the book. I rate this book a 5. P.S. This will probably happen in 48 years.
    Goosebumps is one of many book series It is about 3 kids who go to a carnival but this one is very different with real freaks, a lagoon monster, and a rollercoaster that puts you in another dimension this isn't your everyday carnival. I rate this book a 3. P.S. you choose the story.

develop a rating system and to rate each book. Finally, Figure 6.5 shows an example from his history class in which he wrote about his favorite historical person. This sample was chosen toward the end of the school year.

DECISION FOUR: How Is the Portfolio Evaluated? (Criteria and Procedures). McMillan (2004) indicated four ways by which a teacher can evaluate portfolio contents, two of which are particularly relevant for this discussion. Those are evaluation of individual portfolio entries and evaluation of the overall progress toward meeting learning objectives. To evaluate individual entries, some type of objective scoring system should be developed. This is usually accomplished through the use of a rubric. A *rubric* is a set of criteria that provide a description of various levels of student performance as well as a value to each of the levels. Rubrics also serve as a means of communicating the purpose and requirements of the work that the

A rubric helps to evaluate portfolio entries.

FIGURE 6.5   Portfolio Entry from History Class

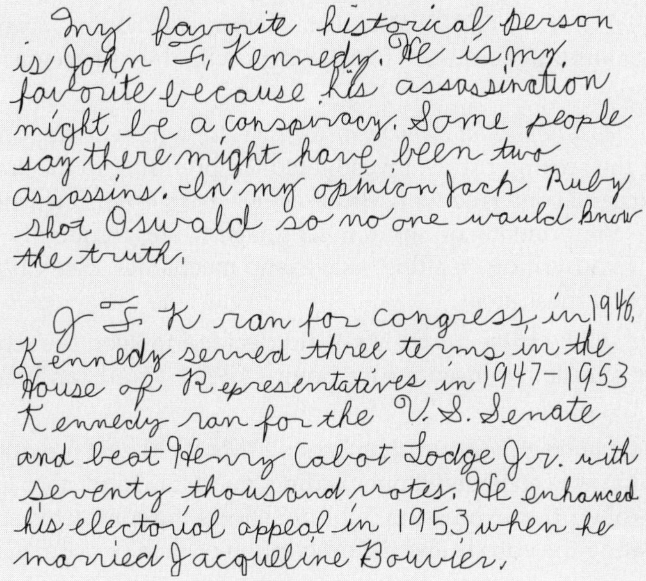

> My favorite historical person is John F. Kennedy. He is my favorite because his assassination might be a conspiracy. Some people say there might have been two assassins. In my opinion Jack Ruby shot Oswald so no one would know the truth.
>
> J F K ran for congress, in 1946, Kennedy served three terms in the House of Representatives in 1947–1953 Kennedy ran for the U.S. Senate and beat Henry Cabot Lodge Jr. with seventy thousand votes, He enhanced his electorial appeal in 1953 when he married Jacqueline Bouvier.

student is completing. Fischer and King (1995, pp. 29–30) provided the following steps for developing a rubric.

Step 1.   Start by making a list of the most important components or expectations of a learning activity. These might include the process, content, mechanics, presentation, variety and number of source materials, neatness, and other factors.

Step 2.   Determine the criteria you will use for a scale. It might start with *Excellent* or *5* and scale down. Write a description or number for as many additional categories as you desire. Rubrics using more than six criteria descriptions are more difficult to use.

Step 3.   Write a description of the performance expected for each criterion. Include the components you previously identified as important to this activity in your description of performance at each level. Some criteria on the scale may have more components assigned to them than others.

The development of a rubric can be somewhat time-consuming, and there is still the issue of reliability to address. One method used to increase reliability is *benchmarking*. A benchmark is an example of a piece of work chosen to illustrate the various levels of accomplishment for each of the criteria (Hewitt, 1995). This provides a guideline by which the students' work can be scored. This determination of benchmarks is, in itself, somewhat subjective and time-consuming.

Benchmarks help increase reliability.

To evaluate overall progress toward meeting learning objectives, a more holistic approach is used. It is important to set standards that relate to the student goals. These standards should be determined ahead of time, and the portfolio can be evaluated in terms of meeting those standards or on growth demonstrated toward meeting those standards. This setting of standards is a difficult and somewhat subjective process and might be facilitated by consulting with other teachers and getting their interpretations of mastery or high performance.

McMillan (2004) suggested that overall progress might be rated on, for example, a 1 (inadequate performance) to 6 (outstanding performance) scale.

EXAMPLE—DECISION FOUR: Determine Evaluation Criteria.   In order to provide a more quantitative measure of Mike's growth, it was necessary to develop a scoring rubric.

Determine most important components. Mr. Wald, who was responsible for developing the scoring rubric, investigated the literature in the area of written expression and conferred with Ms. Brewer, Mike's English teacher. He found that five components of written language were frequently mentioned: ideation, handwriting, spelling, usage, and mechanics. (See Chapter 14 for a discussion of these areas.)

Determine scaling of the rubric. Mr. Wald decided to keep the scoring system relatively simple. He used a four-point scale: 4 = outstanding, 3 = good, 2 = fair, 1 = poor.

Write a description of the expected performance. Mr. Wald next provided a description of what was considered outstanding, good, fair, and poor in each of the five areas of written expression. Table 6.3 shows the completed scoring rubric incorporating the criteria and the description of each performance level.

TABLE 6.3   Scoring Rubric for Written Expression

	Ideation	**Handwriting**	**Spelling**	**Usage**	**Mechanics (e.g., capitalization and punctuation)**
4 Outstanding	Writing style and quality are very appropriate for intended purpose.	Writing is very neat and legible.	Few, if any, errors made.	Use of vocabulary and syntax very appropriate for intended purpose.	Few, if any, grammatical errors made.
3 Good	Writing style and quality relatively appropriate for intended purpose.	Writing is relatively neat and legible.	Some errors are made.	Use of vocabulary and syntax is relatively appropriate for intended purpose.	Some grammatical errors made; starting to affect the meaning of the passage.
2 Fair	Writing style and quality are somewhat inappropriate for intended purpose.	Writing is becoming illegible.	Several errors are made; begin to affect the meaning of the passage.	Use of vocabulary and syntax somewhat inappropriate for intended purpose.	Several grammatical errors made; starting to affect the meaning of the passage.
1 Poor	Writing style and quality are not appropriate for intended purpose.	Writing is illegible.	Frequent errors are made; affect meaning of passage.	Use of vocabulary and syntax is not appropriate for intended purpose.	Frequent grammatical errors made; affects meaning of passage.

Determine evaluation procedures. Because the goal of the portfolio was to document progress over time, a summary sheet was developed that showed Mike's scores throughout the school year (Figure 6.6). This provided a quantitative representation of his progress. The scores presented are an

FIGURE 6.6   Summary Sheet for Rubric

Ideation

English	1.5	2	2	2.5	3	3	3	3	3	3.5	3.5	4	4	4	3.5
Science	2	2	1.5	2	2	2	2.5	3	3	3	4	3.5	3	3	3
History	2	2	2.5	2	3	3	3	3	3	3	3	4	4	3.5	3.5
Geography	2	2	2.5	2	2.5	3	3	3	4	3	3.5	3.5	4	4	4
Mathematics	1.5	1.5	1	1.5	2	2	2	2	2.5	3	3	2.5	3	3	3

Handwriting

English	2	2	2	2	2	2	3	3	3	3.5	3	3	3	3	3
Science	2	2	2	2	2.5	2.5	2	2	3	3	3	3	3	3	3
History	2	2	2	2	2	2	2	22	2	3	3	3	3	3	3
Geography	2	2	2	2	2	2.5	2	3	3	3	3	3	3	3	3.5
Mathematics	1	1	1	1.5	2	2	2	2	2	2.5	3	3	3	3	3

Spelling

English	2	2	2.5	3	3	3	3	3.5	4	4	4	4	4	4	4
Science	3	3	3	3	3	3	3.5	3	3	3.5	4	4	4	4	4
History	3	3	3	3	3	3	3	3.5	4	4	4	4	4	4	4
Geography	2	3	3	3	3	3.5	3	4	4	4	3.5	4	4	4	4
Mathematics	2	2	2	3	3	3	3	3	3	3	4	4	3.5	4	4

Usage

English	2	2	3	3	3	3	3	3.5	3.5	4	4	4	4	4	4
Science	2.5	3	3	3	3	3	3	3	3	3	3	3	3.5	4	3.5
History	3	3	3	3	4	3	3	3	3	4	4	4	3.5	4	4
Geography	3	3	3	3	3	4	3	4	3	4	4	4	4	4	4
Mathematics	2	2	2	2.5	3	2.5	3	3	3	3	3	3	3	3	3

Mechanics

English	2	2	2	2	2	3	2.5	3	3	3	3	3	3	4	3.5
Science	2	2	2	2	2	2	2.5	2.5	3	3	3	4	4	4	3.5
History	2	2	2	3	2	3	3	3	3	3	4	4	4	4	4
Geography	2	2	2	3	3	3	3	3	3	3.5	3	4	3	4	4
Mathematics	1.5	2	2	2	2	2	2	2	2.5	3	3	3	3	3	3

average of the ratings from Mr. Wald and the content area teacher for each subject.

DECISION FIVE: How Is the Portfolio Passed On? (Using Portfolio Data).   The last decision has to do with *how to pass the portfolios on.* A portfolio should not end when the school year ends, but could and should be passed on with the student to the next grade or the next teacher (Wesson & King, 1996). Valencia (1990), in discussing the contents of a portfolio, noted that care must be taken not to simply have a holding file for various unrelated samples of isolated skill tests, but that contents should be related to the district's curricular goals and objectives.

One final suggestion, provided by Swicegood (1994), is that a portfolio should contain a table of contents that groups the pieces included into sections, for example, (1) samples of daily work, (2) interviews and attitudes, (3) behavioral observations, (4) student reflections, and (5) teacher reaction. The table of contents should be based on the nature of the student's portfolio. Figure 6.7 provides a checklist of what constitutes a complete portfolio.

EXAMPLE—DECISION FIVE: Determine Procedures to Utilize Portfolio Data

> Self-reflection is a very important component.

Self-reflection. In addition to making his biweekly choices, Mike was asked to answer a series of questions about his selections. Figure 6.8 shows Mike's responses to several questions about his writing sample.

FIGURE 6.7   Checklist for a Complete Portfolio

A Complete Portfolio Will Include:
- *A completed table of contents,* which may represent the student's current mode of communication; written, pictorial, audiotape.
- *A letter to the reviewer* written or dictated by the student (or a collaborative effort of a student and a peer without a disability) that describes the portfolio and its contents.
- *Seven to ten entries* that represent the breadth of entries (types, contexts, and domain areas). Each entry must include the original question, task, or problem posed, a name, a title, and a date. Entries must be arranged in the order presented in the table of contents.
- *A student's weekly schedule* and description of its use indicating types of activities, opportunities for choice, and interactions with nondisabled peers.
- *A sample of the student's current mode(s) of communication* and description of use. May use as evidence the table of contents, letter to the reviewer, or student schedule.
- *A letter from a family member or caregiver* validating the contents of the portfolio.

An Incomplete Portfolio Fails to Include:
- A table of contents.
- A student letter to the reviewer.
- At least seven entries (not including the letters).
- A student activities schedule and description of its use.
- Validation letter from family member or caregiver.

FIGURE 6.8   Example of Self-Reflection

WRITING SAMPLE SUMMARY

Date: 12/14/95

Subject: English

Choice: Three book reviews

Why did I choose this sample? because I enjoyed the assignment and thought it was pretty good

What is good about this work? I think I gave good descriptions about the books.

What could I do better? I could have read myself and check for spelling. I also could have checked if my commas and periods are there

What was easy about this assignment? Rating the books from one to five.

What was difficult about this assignment? Remembering what happened in the books.

How has my work changed over the year? It has improved because I enjoy writing a lot.

Portfolio conferencing. Twice during the year, at the middle and at the end, Mr. Wald scheduled an appointment with Mike's parents to go over his general progress. As part of that conference, the portfolio was used to indicate his progress in the area of written language. Both the writing samples themselves, as well as the quantitative scoring, were presented and discussed.

Passing it on. When Mike goes to the eighth grade, he will be assigned to a different team; he will also have a different learning disabilities teacher. Mr. Wald plans on meeting with Mike's new teacher in the fall to go over the portfolio and the scoring rubric and to encourage Mike's new team to continue the portfolio process through the eighth grade. Mike responded favorably to the responsibility of determining his portfolio entries and was pleased to be involved in this self-reflection process.

Advantages and Disadvantages of Portfolio Assessment

Generally speaking, the advantages of portfolio assessment outweigh the disadvantages. For example, Wesson and King (1996) noted that it allows both the teacher and the student to monitor progress. They also showed that it emphasizes the breadth and scope of learning and gives students a sense of ownership of that learning. McMillan (2004) also stressed the advantage of student reflection and collaboration between student and teacher. He added that portfolios focus on self-improvement rather than comparisons to other students and provide a continuous assessment over time. Portfolios might also provide a better, more nonbiased assessment for students from culturally diverse and low socio-economic backgrounds. Rueda and Garcia (1997), in fact, reported that results of portfolio assessment were more informative than results from other assessment procedures. Suporitz and Brennan (1997) reported that portfolio assessment was less discriminatory than standardized testing. They cautioned, however, that there were still racial, gender, and socioeconomic differences (albeit fewer than standardized testing), so this issue cannot be ignored.

Portfolio assessment can be time-consuming.

The disadvantages of portfolio have less to do with philosophy and more to do with implementation (although Wesson and King [1996] did note that some teachers might be resistive to the student-centered approach). The two major limitations of portfolios appear to be related to time and technical characteristics. Based on the nature of the information and the process for evaluating it, problems in both validity (Day & Skidmore, 1996) and reliability (Rivera, 1993) have been noted. Clearly, the criteria for judging the materials must be very specific and the use of benchmarks can help in this area. Wesson and King (1996) showed that considerable time is needed to collect, share, and evaluate the information. If conferencing is used, this requires additional time. In a survey about portfolio assessment of over 200 teachers, time needed to design and implement was listed as one of three most serious concerns. The other two were lack of adequate training and support and difficulty in evaluating the results (Harris & Curran, 1998). Finally, Beigel (1997) noted that portfolios can sometimes be large and materials can be lost or misplaced. The solution to this problem, he argued, is to use electronic portfolios (similar to the Grady Profile).

CASE STUDY *June*

Mrs. Dunn has decided that a portfolio will be an appropriate means of collecting and assessing June's reading and language arts work during the prereferral stage. Guide Mrs. Dunn through the process of creating a portfolio by following the steps outlined in the text. List each step and describe the action taken by Mrs. Dunn.

Reflections

1. Why do you think alternative assessment procedures are becoming more popular?
2. Why do you think some teachers are hesitant to use performance assessment and authentic assessment in their classrooms?
3. When using portfolio assessment, why do you think it is important to determine the purpose or type of portfolio that will be created?

Summary Matrix

Instrument or Technique	Suggested Use							Target Population						Special Considerations	Educational Relevance for Exceptional Students
	Prereferral		Postreferral												
	Screening and Initial Identification	Informal Determination and Evaluation of Teaching Programs and Strategies	Determination of Current Performance Level and Educational Need	Decisions about Classification and Program Placement	IEP Goals	IEP Objectives	IEP Evaluation	Mild/Moderate	Severe/Profound	Preschool	Elementary Age	Secondary Age	Adult		
Performance Assessment	X	X	X		X	X	X	X	X	X	X	X		Requires the student to apply information instead of selecting the correct response.	Useful
Authentic Assessment	X	X	X		X	X	X	X	X	X	X	X		Application of performance assessment in real-life, meaningful situations.	Useful
Portfolio Assessment	X	X	X		X	X	X	X	X	X	X	X		Collection of student work used for a variety of purposes; usually includes self-reflection.	Very Useful

part three

Assessment of Abilities

One of the hallmarks of educational and psychological assessment is the measurement of an individual's abilities. Ability assessment involves the measurement of hypothetical constructs (i.e., underlying abilities) and is distinguished from the assessment of achievement (discussed in Part IV). As will be discussed, however, there is some question whether this ability/achievement distinction represents a true dichotomy. The abilities and their subsequent assessment that are discussed in this part are *intelligence, adaptive behavior, emotional/behavioral status,* and *language* (Chapters 7, 8, 9, and 10, respectively).

Evaluation of the areas discussed in this section are important to help make eligibility decisions. For example, intelligence and adaptive behavior are measured to help determine the label of mental retardation. Language testing is used to help determine those who are eligible for programs for students with speech and language impairments, whereas emotional/behavioral testing is used with students suspected of such problems (see Chapter 2 for more information about eligibility decisions).

Perhaps more important, these types of tests can also be used to provide information about a student's strengths and weaknesses in each of the areas. They might also be used to identify general educational goals for the student and to identify areas that require further assessment. Finally, they are frequently used to make assumptions about an individual's underlying abilities. Often, ability tests are administered by ancillary personnel such as school psychologists, social workers, or speech-language clinicians (depending on the area tested). Teachers, however, do administer many of the tests discussed in this section. Further, teachers must be familiar with these areas because they will see assessment information about them.

Both formal and informal tests and procedures are included in these chapters. For most tests described in this section the following information is included:

1. A summary matrix is provided that presents information about specific instruments and techniques in a format that allows easy comparison of the instruments for suggested use and target population. The matrix also includes a statement of any special considerations of which a user

AFTER READING PART THREE
You Should Be Able To:

- Identify critical issues related to the assessment of intelligence.

- Identify alternative methods of measuring intelligence.

- Identify the various uses of adaptive behavior testing.

- Identify the various philosophical approaches of measuring emotional/behavioral status.

- Identify the advantages of using language samples.

- Identify the strengths and weaknesses of the major instruments used to measure intelligence, adaptive behavior, emotional/behavioral status, and language.

should be aware. In addition, for each instrument, the matrix gives the educational relevance for exceptional students. The matrices are directly related to the assessment model proposed in Chapter 2.

2. A thorough review of relevant research is provided for each major norm-referenced instrument. The review emphasizes the use of the test with exceptional students. The terminology used in this section is that used by the authors in the original research.

3. An overview box is provided for each test. The overview summarizes the age range, technical adequacy (for norm-referenced tests), and suggested use for each instrument.

In addition, information is presented about how each type of test best fits into the overall assessment process.

chapter seven

Assessment of Intelligence

STUDENT PROFILE

Tommy

Tommy is a 6-year-old boy who has been receiving speech and language services since he was age 4. Tommy's mother had a difficult pregnancy; he was born a month prematurely and had a low birth weight. Although he appeared to be doing well developmentally, his parents began noticing problems when Tommy was 3 years old and had him evaluated on the recommendation of his pediatrician. The preschool evaluation indicated that Tommy would qualify for services as a child with developmental delays. Now his parents and first-grade teacher are particularly concerned because Tommy seems to be falling further and further behind his peers in a number of areas. Up until this time it appeared that the problem was primarily a language delay. However, his teacher did some informal assessment and started a prereferral intervention program for three targeted goals. When the followup assessment indicated minimal progress for all three goals, she recommended that Tommy be reevaluated to determine his current status.

Think about These Questions as You Read This Chapter:

1. Why assess Tommy? (There could be more than one reason.)
2. Who should assess Tommy? (There could be more than one person.)
3. What procedure(s)/test(s) should be used?
4. What other areas (if any) should be assessed?

   (Suggested answers appear at the end of this chapter.)

Intelligence testing is one of the most debated issues in special education. Intelligence tests have both their staunch supporters and their vehement critics. Legal battles have been fought over whether these instruments have their place in the field of education. Suffice it to say that the debate is far from over and that ignoring the issue will not make it go away.

Historically, intelligence has been an enigmatic concept. It is a much-valued construct or quality that is extremely difficult to define. Is intelligence the same as verbal ability? Analytical thinking? Academic aptitude? Strategic thinking? The ability to cope? Different theorists might argue for each, or a combination, of these abilities. In fact, Gardner (1993) provided a theory of multiple intelligences that has received considerable support. Similarly, one should consider whether intelligence is, or should be, defined in the same way for individuals of different cultural, ethnic, or social backgrounds.

As noted in Chapters 1 and 3, intelligence tests have been the focus of considerable debate because of their alleged bias against ethnic minority students. Research on the presence of bias in intelligence testing is fairly straightforward. Individuals from different cultural, ethnic, and socioeconomic groups do score differently on most measures of intelligence, particularly those that are verbal. Empirical investigation of the tests themselves (much of which was conducted as a result of the court cases regarding discriminatory evaluation) suggests that they are not *statistically* biased. Perhaps educators should be less concerned about whether a test is biased and more concerned about the uses of test data for discriminatory purposes. For instance, it has long been known that verbally oriented intelligence tests are valid predictors of school performance (measured by achievement tests), regardless of the racial or ethnic background of the student (Oakland, 1977; Reschly & Reschly, 1979). The use of these tests to predict teachers' ratings of students is somewhat more speculative, however (Partenio & Taylor, 1985; Reschly & Reschly, 1979). Certainly, test-based statements regarding "intellectual potential" should be avoided. In other words, intelligence tests have been criticized (probably erroneously) because incorrect or inappropriate decisions have been made from intelligence test data. The problem is not necessarily inherent in the test itself; it is more a function of what we, as professionals, are doing with the test results.

Intelligence tests measure performance, not potential.

One reason for this misunderstanding is that a distinction between "potential" and "performance" has not always been made. Many professionals have used intelligence tests as if they measured "intellectual potential." The tests, however, are much more accurate in reflecting what individuals have been taught and the material to which they have been exposed. Even performance on nonverbal analytical tasks is affected by a person's experience with similar tasks.

Alternatives to traditional intelligence testing, however, have been receiving more and more attention, namely, dynamic assessment. These alternative approaches will be discussed briefly, and an analysis of several intelligence measures widely used in special education will then follow.

Alternatives to Traditional Tests

Traditional intelligence tests are considered static measures.

Traditional intelligence testing has been referred to as static assessment; as such, it measures what students have already learned, not the extent to which they would profit from instruction (Campione, 1989). This static approach has been criticized when used to identify students from culturally and linguistically diverse backgrounds. Regardless, Bigge and Stump (1999) noted that currently most types of assessment fall in the category of static assessment. Sternberg (1999) provided a convincing argument that traditional intelligence tests are too narrow, particularly when used with multicultural populations. He felt that intelligence can mean different things to different cultural groups. As a result, he developed the *Sternberg*

Triarchic Abilities Test (Sternberg, 1993), which is a multidimensional instrument including twelve subtests. He argued that this unstandardized test measures a broader array of skills than traditional tests. There are also essay items that stress analytical, creative, and practical thinking. Another criticism of traditional intelligence tests is that they are based on a too narrowly defined concept of intelligence (Naglieri, Das, & Jarman, 1990).

These criticisms have led to a number of attempts to devise alternative techniques for measuring learning potential. One alternative attempt was provided by Plucker, Callahan, and Tomchin (1996). They developed a battery of instruments based on Howard Gardner's multiple intelligence theory. They found that although the battery yielded reliable results, additional evidence of validity was necessary. This battery of procedures used teacher checklists and performance-based assessment activities. Most alternative approaches, however, are usually referred to as **dynamic assessment.** Dynamic assessment is an interactive test–intervention–retest model of assessment (Haywood & Lidz, 2007). In other words, dynamic assessment is used to determine what learning takes place when an individual is provided supports in the form of prompts or cues (Bigge & Stump, 1999). This "assisted assessment" (Gettinger & Seibert, 2000) focuses on the cognitive processes involved in learning. Kirshenbaum (1998) found that dynamic assessment was a particularly useful alternative to traditional intelligence testing for students who are disadvantaged or have limited English language proficiency. Lidz (2002) also discussed the potential advantage of dynamic assessment with preschool children and for gifted students from culturally and linguistically diverse backgrounds. Interestingly, Haney and Evans (1999) found that only 42 percent of the school psychologists in a national survey were "somewhat familiar" with dynamic assessment, and of those familiar only 39 percent reported using the techniques. They argued that more training needs to take place in alternative assessment procedures such as dynamic assessment.

> **DYNAMIC ASSESSMENT**
> Characterized by the use of a test-train-retest paradigm and an emphasis on assessment of process, not product.

Computer-assisted dynamic assessment has also been shown to be effective and systematic (Tzuriel & Shamir, 2002). An example of computer-assisted dynamic assessment was provided by Guthke and Beckmann (2003). They described the *Adaptive Computer-Aided Intelligence Learning Test Battery.* It includes three separate subtests using a dynamic assessment approach. Dynamic assessment has also been combined with curriculum-based measurement (Barrera, 2003; Deno, 2003) and has been found to be effective in predicting reading and mathematics (Swanson & Howard, 2005).

There are, however, limitations to dynamic assessment. For example, Jitendra and Kameenui (1993) noted that dynamic assessment varies in its definition, theoretical foundation, and procedural requirements. Another primary concern of theirs is the large amount of time it takes to conduct dynamic assessment because of the individualized nature of the testing. It is possible, however, that the use of computers will help to minimize this concern. Additionally, dynamic assessment procedures also have been reported to have limited reliability (Laughon, 1990), although it appears that validity data are being generated that support its use (Beckmann, 2006; Guthke, Beckmann, & Dobat, 1997). Dynamic assessment approaches are described next.

Dynamic Assessment Procedures

One of the first to use a test-train-retest paradigm to measure an individual's ability to learn from teaching was Budoff (1973). His *Learning Potential Assessment Strategy* was developed initially for adolescents who had been classified as having educable mental retardation (EMR). Using nonverbal measures (e.g., *Raven's Progressive Matrices, Koh's Block Designs*), Budoff pretested the subjects, trained or coached the subjects on problem-solving strategies, and posttested the subjects twice over a one-month period. He then classified the subjects as *high scorers* (pretest scores are high—gain little from training); *gainers* (pretest scores are low—gain from training); and *nongainers* (pretest scores are low—gain little from training). Budoff supported such a model to identify those students who have *educational* (gainers) as opposed to *mental* (nongainers) retardation.

Feuerstein and colleagues' (1984) approach also uses a test-train-retest paradigm. The *Learning Potential Assessment Device* (LPAD) consists of four nonverbal tasks (including the *Raven's Progressive Matrices*). The training in the LPAD, however, is somewhat different from Budoff's training. Feuerstein encourages the examiner to interact constantly with the examinee to maximize the probability of solving the problem. Feuerstein suggests that results from his measure can be used to identify appropriate teaching strategies as well as to supply information helpful in classifying a student. Frisby and Braden (1992), however, argued that the LPAD lacked the technical adequacy to replace more traditional assessment. More recently, the *Analogical Reasoning Learning Test* (Hessels-Schlatter, 2002) was developed to help determine those with severe cognitive disabilities who would benefit from intensive intervention and cognitive training and those who would not.

> Dynamic assessments use a test-train-retest format.

Intelligence Tests: General Purpose and Description

Why Use Intelligence Tests?
Screening and identification (group tests); decisions about eligibility and program placement (individual tests).

Who Should Use Them?
School psychologists, guidance personnel; information also used by teachers.

As noted previously, intelligence tests are relatively good predictors of school performance (particularly of achievement test scores). They are much less accurate in measuring the "learning potential" of an individual. Thirty years ago, Reschly (1979) reported a type of "surgeon general's warning" that should be used to help avoid misinterpretation of results from intelligence tests:

> IQ tests measure only a portion of the competencies involved with human intelligence. The IQ results are best seen as predicting performance in school, and reflecting the degree to which children have mastered middle class cultural symbols and values. This is useful information, but it is also limited. Further cautions—IQ tests do not measure innate-genetic capacity and the scores are not fixed. Some persons do exhibit significant increases or decreases in their measured IQ. (p. 24)

Intelligence tests fall into two major categories: group-administered and individually-administered. Group-administered intelligence tests are similar in structure and format to group-administered achievement tests. They measure, in fact, similar areas. Group intelligence tests usually have different levels that are used with individuals in certain grades. Typically, they include some combination of measures of language ability, memory skills, comprehension, analogical

> Group intelligence tests should be used for screening only.

reasoning, and reading and mathematics aptitude. The determination and use of IQs on the basis of these group tests is not advised. In fact, the state of California banned the use of group intelligence tests (Law, 1995).

Perhaps the two most widely used group intelligence tests are the *Cognitive Abilities Test* (CogAT) and the *Otis-Lennon School Ability Test, Eighth Edition* (OLSAT 8). The CogAT (Lohman & Hagen, 2001) is a comprehensive test that is organized by levels for students in kindergarten through grade 12. It measures the areas of verbal, quantitative, and spatial (nonverbal) symbols. One advantage of the CogAT is that it was normed concurrently with the *Iowa Test of Basic Skills* and the *Iowa Tests of Educational Development* (see Chapter 11 for their description). The OLSAT 8 (Otis & Lennon, 2003) is similar to the CogAT in that various levels of the test are available for students in grades K–12. It was also co-normed with a group achievement test, the *Stanford Achievement Test, Tenth Edition*. The OLSAT 8 measures the areas of verbal comprehension, verbal reasoning, pictorial reasoning, figural reasoning, and quantitative reasoning. Other group-administered intelligence tests are the *Multidimensional Aptitude Battery–II* (Jackson, 1998) and the *Kuhlman-Anderson Test* (Kuhlman & Anderson, 1997), both of which measure verbal and nonverbal skills.

Individually administered intelligence tests vary tremendously in their format and content. Some intelligence tests (or tests that purportedly measure intelligence) measure only one skill such as vocabulary or visual analogy. Other more popular instruments are multiskilled—that is, they measure many components of the intelligence construct. There are also a number of tests that have been developed for or are used primarily with special populations. For example, the *Perkins-Binet Intelligence Scale*, the *Leiter International Performance Scale–Revised*, and the *Comprehensive Test of Nonverbal Intelligence* are designed in such a way to circumvent the person's specific visual, auditory, or verbal/physical disability.

Individual intelligence testing, until recently, has been a crucial, even mandatory component in the formal assessment process. It is still required to determine eligibility for special education in the vast majority of states. This section focuses on four instruments that are used widely in special education. The *Stanford-Binet–Fifth Edition* is the most recent version of the "grandfather" of intelligence tests. The *Wechsler Intelligence Scale for Children–IV* is the most popular and widely used intelligence scale for school-age children. There are also two other individually administered tests that are commonly used. These tests are the *Kaufman Assessment Battery for Children–II* and the *Woodcock-Johnson–III* (WJ-III). The WJ-III includes a separate achievement battery in addition to the cognitive battery.

Kaufman Assessment Battery for Children–II

The *Kaufman Assessment Battery for Children–II* (KABC-II; Kaufman & Kaufman, 2004c) is designed for use with children ages 3 through 18. The KABC-II is based, in part, on Luria's neuropsychological model of sequential and simultaneous processing that was used in the original K-ABC. It also is based on the Cattell-Horn-Carroll (CHC) model of broad and narrow abilities that resulted in subtests that measure learning, planning, and knowledge. Unlike the original K-ABC, there is no specific Achievement Scale although there are knowledge subtests that are achievement related. Three different combinations of subtests are administered to children age 3, 4–6, and 7–18, respectively. There are both core subtests and supplemental subtests, although some subtests can be either type, depending on the age of the examinee.

Description. The following is a brief description of the core subtests. The age ranges for which the subtest is a core subtest are noted. For children age 3, the subtests are not broken down into the five areas; rather, only global scores are available.

Sequential Processing
Number Recall (4–18). Examinee must repeat a series of digits in the correct order.

Word Order (3–18). Examinee must touch a silhouette of objects named by the examiner in order.

Simultaneous Processing
Conceptual Thinking (3–6). Child must choose from a set of four or five pictures the one that doesn't belong with the others.

Block Counting (13–18). Examinee must count partially or completely hidden blocks.

Rover (4–18). A toy dog is moved on a checkerboard with obstacles to get to a bone in the fewest moves.

Triangles (3–12). Examinee assembles foam triangles to make abstract designs.

Learning
Atlantis (3–18). Examiner teaches nonsense names for twelve objects; examinee must identify each from pictures.

Rebus (4–18). Examinee learns words and concepts associated with different drawings and then must "read" the drawings.

Planning
Pattern Reasoning (4–18). Examinee must identify a missing stimulus from a logical, linear pattern. Note: For ages 4 through 6, this subtest is considered simultaneous processing.

Story Completion (7–18). Examinee must identify pictures that are missing in a row that tells a story.

Knowledge
Riddles (7–18). Examinee must name a concept after the examiner lists several characteristics.

Verbal Knowledge (7–18). This subtest measures receptive vocabulary and general information.

Expressive Vocabulary (3–6). The child must choose one of six pictures that (a) corresponds to a vocabulary word or (b) answers a general information question.

Interpretation of Results. The Examiner's Manual devotes two chapters to scoring and interpretation of the KABC-II. Scores can be interpreted using both the Luria model (yields a global index score called the Mental Processing Index [MPI]) and the CHC model (global index score is called the Fluid-Crystallized Index [FCI]). The MPI does not include the Knowledge subtests. A Nonverbal Index (NVI) can also be determined. Standard scores (mean = 100; SD = 15), percentile ranks, and age equivalents are available. The areas for which scores are available depends on the age of the examinee. For age 3, only the MPI and FCI are available. For ages 4 to 6, the MPI, FCI, as well as scale indexes for Sequential Processing, Simultaneous Processing, Learning, and Knowledge can be computed. For ages 7

Scores can be interpreted using two theoretical models.

to 18, scores are available for all of the above areas plus Planning. Individual subtests have scaled scores with a mean of 10 and a standard deviation of 3. There are also tables that can determine whether the Index scores are normative strengths or weaknesses and/or personal strengths or weaknesses. One interesting feature is a method to determine if an Index score should be interpreted or not, based on the variability of the subtest scores on a given Index.

Technical Characteristics

Normative Sample. The KABC-II was normed on 3,025 individuals ages 3 to 18 from thirty-nine states and the District of Columbia. The sample was stratified by age, sex, parental education, ethnic group, geographic region, and educational placement (type of exceptionality).

Reliability. Internal reliability coefficients for the Global Scale Indexes ranged from the low .90s to the upper .90s. The scale indexes were in the high .80s to the low .90s. The median coefficients for the subtests were in the mid .80s. Test-retest reliability was established using a sample of 205 individuals. The coefficients for the global indexes ranged from the mid .80s to the low/mid .90s for the MPI and FCI but were lower for the NVI, particularly for younger children. The scale indexes had coefficients of approximately .80 except for Knowledge, which was higher. Median subtest coefficients were generally in the low to mid .70s.

Validity. Evidence of construct validity is provided through a series of tables depicting factor analysis data and intercorrelations of the global scales, scales, and subtests. Criterion-relaxed validity was determined by correlating the KABC-II scores with a number of cognitive measures, including the original K-ABC, the WISC-III and WISC-IV, and the Woodcock-Johnson–III. These correlations generally ranged from the .50s to the .80s with lower correlations for the Sequential Processing Index and higher for the Knowledge Index. Correlations with a number of achievement measures were somewhat lower, particularly for younger children. Results of clinical validity studies for nine groups of students with known disabilities are also presented. These were conducted to show that certain types of students (e.g., those with mental retardation) score lower than the normative group whereas others (e.g., gifted) score higher.

Review of Relevant Research. Limited research was located on the KABC-II. There is a book entitled *Essentials of KABC-II Assessment* (Kaufman, Lichtenberger, Fletcher-Jansen, & Kaufman, 2005) that includes case studies and interpretation guidelines. Information on the previous edition can be found at the Earlier Research link for Chapter 7 on the Companion Website (www.prenhall.com/taylor8e.)

Overview: Kaufman Assessment Battery for Children–II
- *Age level*—3 through 18 years.
- *Type of administration*—Individual.
- *Technical adequacy*—Good reliability, adequate validity.
- *Scores yielded*—Standard scores, scaled scores, percentile ranks, age equivalents.
- *Suggested use*—The KABC-II includes several interesting features. The interpretation models (Luria and CHC) provide the examiner with an

A nonverbal scale is available.

option. For example, the Luria model eliminates the highly verbal Knowledge scale, therefore making it potentially useful for students for whom English is a second language or for those with known language disabilities. The Nonverbal Scale allows certain subtests to be administered using pantomine and responded to motorically rather than verbally. This feature would prove helpful to those with hearing impairment and/or speech impairment. In addition, there are Spanish translations of the scoring keys for the subtests that require verbal responses. The authors do note, however, that the KABC-II is not intended to be administered in Spanish. Research on the KABC-II should be forthcoming to determine if the various scales measure their purported areas as well as to explore its use with exceptional students. It should be noted that related instruments include the *Kaufman Adolescent and Adult Intelligence Test* (KAIT) and a screening test called the *Kaufman Brief Intelligence Test–2* (KBIT-2).

Stanford-Binet Intelligence Scale—Fifth Edition

The fifth edition of the Stanford-Binet Intelligence Scale (SBIS-5; Roid, 2003) retained many of the characteristics of the earlier versions yet made some significant changes. The SBIS-5 addressed some criticisms of earlier editions regarding its overemphasis on verbal ability by including both verbal and nonverbal domains. It also increased the number of easy and difficult items so it can be used more confidently with individuals with lower and higher ability levels. In other words, it increased the floor and ceiling of the test. The SBIS-5 also has a linking sample with the *WJ-III Test of Achievement* so that intelligence–achievement comparisons can be determined based on the same standardization sample. It was also co-normed with the *Bender Visual Motor Gestalt Test–Second Edition.*

The SBIS-5 uses routing subtests.

The SBIS-5 includes ten subtests that measure both the verbal and nonverbal domains of five factors. The five factors are Fluid Reasoning, Knowledge, Quantitative Reasoning, Visual–Spatial Processing, and Working Memory (see Table 7.1). The instrument uses a verbal and nonverbal *routing subtest* to estimate the student's ability and subsequently route him or her to the remaining subtests at the most efficient level of difficulty.

TABLE 7.1   Model Used in the Stanford-Binet Intelligence Scale—Fifth Edition

Factor	Nonverbal Subtests	Verbal Subtests
Fluid Reasoning	Nonverbal Fluid Reasoning	Verbal Fluid Reasoning
Knowledge	Nonverbal Knowledge	Verbal Knowledge
Quantitative Reasoning	Nonverbal Quantitative Reasoning	Verbal Quantitative Reasoning
Visual–Spatial Processing	Nonverbal Visual–Spatial Processing	Verbal Visual–Spatial Processing
Working Memory	Nonverbal Working Memory	Verbal Working Memory

Description. The subtests include different activities that are identified by levels. These are described next.

Verbal Domain

Fluid Reasoning. Activities include Early Reasoning, Verbal Absurdities, and Verbal Analogies.

Verbal Knowledge. This vocabulary subtest is the verbal routing subtest.

Verbal Quantitative Reasoning. There are five levels of this particular subtest.

Verbal Visual–Spatial Processing. This involves the activity of Position and Direction at five different levels.

Verbal Working Memory. This includes activities of Memory for Sentences and Last Word.

Nonverbal Domain

Nonverbal Fluid Reasoning. Involves the activity of Object Series/Matrices, which is also the nonverbal routing subtest.

Nonverbal Knowledge. This subtest includes two activities, Procedural Knowledge and Picture Absurdities.

Nonverbal Quantitative Reasoning. This includes four levels of activities.

Nonverbal Visual–Spatial Processing. This includes the activities of Form Board and Form Patterns.

Nonverbal Working Memory. Includes the activities of Delayed Response and Block Span.

Interpretation of Results. Standard scores are available for each subtest (mean = 10; standard deviation = 3), for each of the five factor indexes, and for four intelligence composites: Full Scale IQ, Nonverbal IQ, Verbal IQ, and an Abbreviated Battery IQ (mean = 100; standard deviation = 15). The Abbreviated Battery consists of the two routing subtests. In addition to the standard scores, age equivalents and percentile ranks are also available.

One unique feature is the use of criterion-referenced information called Change-Sensitive Scores that allows comparison of changes in an individual's ability level over time regardless of the IQ that is determined. A computer scoring option is also available that provides very meaningful information and comparisons of the different types of scores.

Technical Characteristics

Normative Sample. This included 4,800 individuals ages 2 through 85+. The sample was representative of the 2000 U.S. census based on age, sex, race/ethnicity, geographic region, and socioeconomic level.

Reliability. The internal consistency reliability coefficients were very high ranging from .91 (Abbreviated Battery) to .98 (Full Scale IQ). The .91 coefficient is actually considered relatively high given that the Abbreviated Battery only consists of two subtests. The reliability coefficients for the five factor indexes ranged from .90 to .92; for the subtests the coefficients ranged from .84 to .89.

Validity. Several studies were conducted to investigate the criterion-related validity of the SBIS-5. Some of them used earlier versions of the *Stanford Binet* as the criterion measure and, as expected, these correlations were relatively high (approximately .90). Other correlations were computed between the various *Wechsler Scales,* the *WJ-III Test of Cognitive Ability* and the *WJ-III Test of Achievement.* Correlations were generally in the high .70 to mid .80 range for appropriate comparative scores.

Review of Relevant Research.   To date, there is limited research on the SBIS-5. In fact, Dombrowski, DiStafano, and Noonan (2004) noted that more research needed to be conducted on the instrument. Some of that research is summarized below.

- Although the Manual staes that test results can be used to develop intervention plans (e.g., IEPs), there are no studies that support this claim (Bain & Allin, 2005).
- In a review of the SBIS-5, Mieko and Burns (2005) noted that it addressed many of the shortcomings of earlier versions, including enhanced nonverbal content and additional measures tapping working memory.
- The Verbal and Nonverbal domains were supported for children age 10 and younger, but for older individuals only a general intelligence factor was identified (DiStefano & Dombrowski, 2006).
- Scores on the SBIS-5 for gifted and talented students were significantly lower than those from another major intelligence test, suggesting that it should not be used to identify that population (Minton & Pratt, 2006).
- Scores on the Verbal Working Memory and the Nonverbal Working Memory subtests correlated highly with reading and math performance, respectively (Pomplun & Custer, 2006).

Information about earlier editions can be found at the Earlier Research Link for Chapter 7 on the Companion Website (www.prenhall.com/taylor8e).

Overview: Stanford-Binet Intelligence Scale–5

- *Age level*—2 years to adult.
- *Type of administration*—Individual.
- *Technical adequacy*—Good standardization, reliability, and validity.
- *Scores yielded*—Standard scores, percentile ranks, age equivalents.
- *Suggested use*—The fifth edition of the SBIS is one of the major individually administered intelligence tests. Certainly the earlier versions of the Stanford-Binet have played an important role in the history of intelligence testing. The fifth edition has retained some of the features of earlier editions but also has made some significant revisions. For example, the inclusion of both verbal and nonverbal domains was a nice addition. Earlier versions of the SBIS yielded different scores than other widely used instruments with certain populations, such as students who are gifted. More research on the SBIS-5 should be forthcoming to determine its strengths and limitations. A separate instrument designed for young children ages 2 through 7 years, 3 months, the *Stanford-Binet Intelligence Scale for Young Children* (Roid, 2005) is also available.

The SBIS-5 now has verbal and nonverbal domains.

Wechsler Intelligence Scale for Children–Fourth Edition

The Wechsler Intelligence Scale for Children–IV (WISC-IV; Wechsler, 2003) is one of three scales developed by Wechsler. The others are the *Wechsler Preschool and Primary Scale of Intelligence–III* (used for children 2½ to 7 years old) and the

Wechsler Adult Intelligence Scale–III. There also is a screening test called the *Wechsler Abbreviated Scale of Intelligence.* The WISC-IV is the most widely used intelligence test in the schools, covering the age range of 6 through 16 years. The WISC-IV provides a general or Full Scale IQ as well as Index scores for four composites: Verbal Comprehension, Perceptual Reasoning, Working Memory, and Processing Speed.

Description.   The WISC-IV includes ten required subtests and five optional supplementary subtests. The subtests that comprise each composite are described below.

Verbal Comprehension
Similarities. This subtest requires the student to identify the common element of two terms (e.g., an orange and a banana).

Vocabulary. Requires the student to name pictures and orally define different words.

Comprehension. Measures social, moral, and ethical judgment (e.g., "Why do we have three branches of government?").

Information (optional). The student responds orally to general information questions (e.g., "Why do bears hibernate in the winter?").

Word Reasoning (optional). The examiner gives a series of clues and the student must guess what is being described (e.g., "You eat this for breakfast" and then "It comes from a chicken").

Perceptual Reasoning
Matrix Reasoning. The student is presented a partially filled grid and must select which item of five choices correctly completes the matrix.

Block Design. The child must reproduce certain designs using red and white blocks.

Picture Concepts. From multiple rows of objects, the student must select the items that go together based on an underlying concept (e.g., animals).

Picture Completion (optional). In this subtest, the student is shown a picture in which an important element is missing. The student must indicate what is missing.

Working Memory (Note: Each item is presented only once)
Letter–Number Sequencing. The student is presented a mixed series of numbers and letters and must repeat the numbers in numerical order and the letters in alphabetical order.

Digit Span. Requires the student to repeat a series of digits forward and another series backward.

Arithmetic (optional). The student is read arithmetic problems that have to be answered without the use of pencil and paper.

Processing Speed (Note: All subtests are timed)
Symbol Search. The student visually scans a group of symbols to determine if a target symbol is present.

Coding. The student must copy geometric symbols that are paired with numbers in a specific time period (see Figure 7.1 for an example of this type of task).

Cancellation (optional). Several target pictures are shown to the student who must then cross them out from an array of pictures).

FIGURE 7.1   Tasks Similar to the Coding Subtest from the WISC-IV

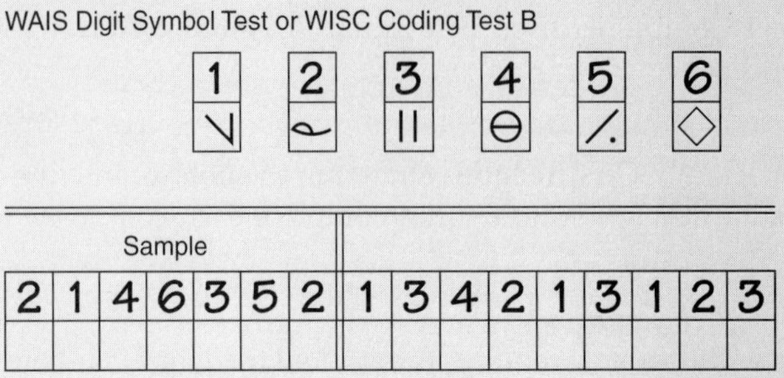

WAIS Digit Symbol Test or WISC Coding Test B

Source: Weschler Intelligence Scale for Children ® Fourth Edition. Copyright © 2003 by NCS Pearson, Inc. Reproduced with permission. All rights reserved. "Weschler Intelligence Scale for Children," "WISC," and "Weschler" are trademarks, in the U.S. and/or other countries, of Pearson Education, Inc., or its affiliate(s). Pearson is a trademark, in the U.S. and other countries, of Pearson Education, Inc., or its affiliate(s).

Interpretation of Results.   Each subtest raw score is converted to a scaled score with a mean of 10 and a standard deviation of 3. This allows for a visual profile of the student's strengths and weaknesses. The WISC-IV also yields a Full Scale IQ and Index scores in the areas of verbal comprehension, perceptual reasoning, working memory, and processing speed. Each of these scores has a mean of 100 and a standard deviation of 15. There are also tables that allow interpretation among both subtest and Index scores to look for significant strengths and weaknesses.

Technical Characteristics

Normative Sample.   The WISC-IV used a nationally representative sample (similar to the 2000 census) of 2,200. Variables considered were geographic region, race/ethnicity, and parent educational level (to determine socioeconomic status). There were equal numbers of boys and girls.

Reliability.   Split–half reliability coefficients ranged from approximately .80 to .90. The average coefficient for Full Scale IQ was .97. Average coefficients of .95 and above were reported for the Index scores. Test-retest reliability and interrater reliability coefficients were also reported.

Validity.   Construct validity of the WISC-IV was established using factor analysis and intercorrelations of the subtests and scales. Correlations with the WISC-III are also presented (.87 for the verbally oriented scores and .74 for the performance-related scores; .89 for the Full Scale IQ). Correlations with the *Wechsler Individual Achievement Test–II* are also reported.

Review of Relevant Research.   The earlier versions of the WISC-IV were researched more than perhaps any other instrument used in special education, although the differences between the WISC-III and WISC-IV should be considered when interpreting that research, which can be found at the Earlier Research link for Chapter 7 of the Companion Website (www.prenhall.com/taylor8e). The results of selected studies on the WISC-IV are described next.

- In a review of the WISC-IV, Baron (2005) noted the significant revisions to the previous edition and also pointed out the generally stronger psychometric characteristics.

- Needelman, Schnoes, and Ellis (2006) also noted the significant differences between the WISC-III and the WISC-IV and the strong psychometric properties of the latest edition.
- When substituting supplementary (optional) subtests for core subtests, the reliability remained high and, in some cases, actually improved (Ryan & Glass, 2006).
- When predicting achievement (reading and mathematics), it may only be necessary to consider the Full Scale IQ and not the composite scores (Glutting, Watkins, Konold, & McDermott, 2006).
- In a sample of thirty-five students classified as having mental retardation (based on the WISC-III), 80 percent were confirmed when the WISC-IV was administered (Launey, Carroll, & van Horn, 2007).
- Based on factor analysis, it seems that the best model of interpretation is to look at the general factor of intelligence (Watkins, Wilson, Kotz, Carbone, & Babula, 2006). This could be interpreted that the Full Scale IQ should be interpreted rather than the Index scores.
- Kaufman, Flanagan, Alfonso, and Mascolo (2006) pointed out that Wechsler was a clinician, not a theoretician, and designed his test to have practical value.
- The WISC-IV measures consistent constructs across all age ranges covered by the test (Keith, Fine, Taub, Reynolds, & Kranzler, 2006).
- Although the manual provides tables to help compare an individual's index scores, it does not provide the cautions of using this approach (Naglieri & Paolitto, 2005).
- The administration time varies considerably depending on factors such as the examinee's age and overall IQ as well as the examiner's experience (Ryan, Glass, & Brown, 2007).

Overview: Wechsler Intelligence Scale for Children–IV

- *Age level*—6 through 16 years.
- *Type of administration*—Individual.
- *Technical adequacy*—Good standardization; adequate reliability for subtests; good reliability for IQ; adequate validity.
- *Scores yielded*—Subtests (X = 10; SD = 3); Full Scale IQ and Index Scores (X = 100; SD = 15).
- *Suggested use*—The WISC-IV measures a number of intellectual skills. Unlike previous editions, the WISC-IV abandoned the concepts of verbal and performance IQs and includes four Index scores in addition to a global, Full Scale IQ. This change was made to be consistent with more recent theory and practice in cognitive assessment, particularly adding more emphasis on working memory and processing speed. Other improvements in the WISC-IV are a potentially shorter administration time and increased sensitivity for students with very low or very high performance levels. Previous editions were the most widely used intelligence test for school-age children; the WISC-IV will probably continue that trend. It is important to know that the WISC-IV yields scores that are 2 to 3 points lower than the WISC-III.

    There are several unique aspects of the WISC-IV. It has a link to the *Wechsler Individual Achievement Test–II* and is part of the *WISC-IV Integrated*. The latter is a system to help determine if the WISC-IV scores are being affected by underlying processing problems. It includes sixteen

The WISC-IV no longer has verbal and performance IQs.

focus on
Diversity

Should We Adjust IQs of Diverse Students?

Padilla (2001) noted that in 1937, over seven decades ago, Mitchell suggested that a corrective factor be added to the intelligence quotients of Spanish-language-dominant children who were tested in English. Although this recommendation was not followed at that time, a similar one was implemented by Mercer and Lewis (1977) in their *System of Multicultural Pluralistic Assessment (SOMPA)*. In that system four sociocultural scales (Urban Acculturation, SES Status, Family Structure, and Family Size) were combined and used to "correct" the IQ obtained from the *Wechsler Intelligence Scale for Children–Revised*, an earlier version of the WISC-IV

described in this chapter. Padilla goes on to suggest that this practice (group-adjusted scoring procedures) is now considered illegal. Based on concerns that such practices were discriminating against white individuals seeking employment, Congress added a provision to the Civil Rights Act (Public Law 102–166) in 1991. That law stated that an employer cannot "adjust the scores of, use different cutoffs for, or otherwise alter the results of employment-related tests on the basis of race, color, religion, sex, or national origin" (Section 106). Padilla argues that since the type of test is not stated in this provision, the ban on adjusted scoring applies equally to all tests.

supplementary processing subtests that include variations of the format of several WISC-IV subtests (e.g., multiple choice). It should be noted that a computerized scoring assistant also is available. (Also see Focus on Diversity.) A Spanish version of the WISC-IV is also available.

Woodcock-Johnson–III (Normative Update)

The *Woodcock-Johnson–III (Normative Update)* (WJ-III-NU; Woodcock, McGrew, Mather, & Schrank, 2007) is a wide-ranging set of individually administered tests designed to measure general intellectual ability, specific cognitive abilities, oral language, and academic achievement. There are separate Cognitive and Achievement Batteries. For each, there is also a Standard and an Extended Battery. Among the various uses of the WJ-III-NU are to diagnose learning disabilities, plan educational programs, determine performance discrepancies, and monitor progress. One nice feature of the WJ-III-NU is the co-norming of the Cognitive and Achievement Batteries. This allows for the determination of both intratest discrepancies and intertest discrepancies. This is important because it allows the determination of a comparison between intelligence and achievement based on the same standardization sample. The authors have provided several methods to assist in this determination. Norms are available for individuals age 2 to 90+; grade norms are available from kindergarten through university graduate school.

The WJ-III has a standard and extended battery.

Description.   The cognitive tests included in the WJ-III are based on the Cattell-Horn-Carroll theory, an extension of the fluid/crystallized model of intelligence. There are seven broad cognitive factors included. These are Comprehension-Knowledge (Gc), Long Term Retrieval (Glr), Visual-Spatial Thinking (Gv), Auditory Processing (Ga), Fluid Reasoning (Gf), Processing Speed (Gs), and Short-Term Memory (Gsm).

Standard Cognitive Battery
   Comprehension-Knowledge
   Verbal Comprehension. This subtest involves identifying objects, completing verbal analogies, and understanding antonyms and synonyms.

Long-Term Retrieval

Visual-Auditory Learning. Measures the ability to associate new visual symbols with words and then read stories by "reading" sentences consisting of the visual symbols.

Visual-Auditory Learning—Delayed. The individual must recall and relearn the visual symbols after at least a thirty-minute time span.

Visual-Spatial Thinking

Spatial Relations. The individual must identify the necessary pieces to form a complete shape.

Auditory Processing

Sound Blending. This is an auditory blending task requiring the synthesis of speech sounds.

Incomplete Words. This is an auditory closure task in which words with one or more missing phonemes are presented for identification.

Fluid Reasoning

Concept Formation. This is a controlled learning task requiring categorical reasoning based on principles of logic.

Processing Speed

Visual Matching. This timed test requires the individual to locate and circle two identical numbers in a row of six numbers.

Short-Term Memory

Numbers Reversed. This requires an individual to remember a random sequence of numbers and repeat them in reverse order.

Auditory Working Memory. Involves remembering a set of words and numbers and reordering them.

Extended Battery

Comprehension-Knowledge

General Information. This involves identifying where objects are found and what people typically do with various objects.

Long-Term Retrieval

Retrieval Fluency. This requires an individual to name as many examples as possible from a variety of categories.

Visual-Spatial Thinking

Picture Recognition. This involves the identification of previously seen pictures from a field of distracting pictures.

Planning. This is a motor test requiring an individual to trace a pattern without retracing or removing the pencil from the paper.

Auditory Processing

Auditory Attention. The individual must identify orally presented words with increasing background noise.

Fluid Reasoning

Analysis-Synthesis. This task involves the presentation of an incomplete logic puzzle for which the individual must present the missing components.

Planning. See previous description.

Processing Speed

Decision Speed. This requires an individual to locate and circle two pictures that are conceptually similar out of a row of pictures.

Rapid Picture Naming. This involves recognizing objects and saying their names as quickly as possible.

Pair Cancellation. The individual must identify and circle repeated patterns as quickly as possible.

Short-Term Memory
Memory for Words. Requires the individual to repeat a series of unrelated words in the correct sequence.

Interpretation of Results.   Hand scoring of the previous editions of the WJ was tedious and afforded the opportunity for numerous scoring errors. As a result, the WJ-III-NU includes computer software, Compuscore and Profiles Program, that eliminates hand scoring. A variety of scores are available for both the individual tests and the clusters, which are various combinations of individual tests that measure the same construct. The scores yielded by Compuscore are standard scores (mean = 100; SD = 15), percentile ranks, age equivalents, and grade equivalents. It also provides instructional range bands, and Relative Mastery Indexes (RMI). The RMI is a score that is presented as a fraction with a constant denominator of 90. This score indicates the percentage of material that the examinee has mastered that a reference group (by either age or grade) has mastered at 90 percent. For example, if a 10½-year-old boy received a RMI of 62/90 in calculation, it would indicate that he has mastered 62 percent of the content in that area compared to 90 percent for the average child of the same age. Scores are also available for General Cognitive Ability (Standard and Extended) and Brief Intellectual Ability. This latter measure is a combination of the Verbal Comprehension, Concept Formation, and the Visual Matching tests.

> Only computer scoring is available.

Technical Characteristics

Normative Sample.   The standardization sample for the WJ-III-NU was 8,782 individuals from over 100 U.S. communities. The subjects were chosen to be representative of the U.S. population across ten variables including community size, race, type of school, and occupational status (for the adult, postschool norms).

Reliability.   For the Cognitive Batteries the internal consistency reliability coefficients ranged from .81 to .92 in the Standard Battery and from .74 to .97 in the Extended Battery. Except for two coefficients in the Extended Battery all coefficients were above at least .80. Test-retest coefficients were also obtained for the five speed tests on the Cognitive Battery using three samples. Coefficients ranged from .78 to .87 for a sample of ages 7 to 11, from .73 to .85 for a sample ages 14 to 17, and from .69 to .86 for an adult sample. As expected, the internal reliability coefficients for the cluster scores were generally higher than those for the individual tests. For the Standard Battery, coefficients ranged from .90 to .97. For the Extended Battery the coefficients ranged from .88 to .98. Twenty-one of the twenty-three coefficients were at least .90.

Validity.   The authors provide a significant amount of information supporting the content validity of the items chosen. Evidence for construct validity was provided through the use of confirmatory factor analyses. These indicated, for example, that almost all of the tests on the Cognitive Battery loaded on a single factor. Criterion-related validity studies were conducted using a variety of criterion measures for both the Cognitive Battery and the Achievement Battery. The correlations for the General Intellectual Ability score from the Standard Battery correlated in the .70s with five different intelligence tests. The correlation was .67 with the *Wechsler Adult Intelligence Scale.*

Review of Relevant Research. Little research was located on the Cognitive battery of the WJ-III. That research is summarized below.

- Data have been reported that support the CHC model (Sanders, McIntosh, Dunham, Rothlisberg, & Finch, 2007; Taub & McGrew, 2004).
- Moderate correlations were reported between several cognitive clusters and math achievement (Floyd, Evans, & McGrew, 2003).
- Statistically significant, moderate correlations were reported between several cognitive clusters and measure of executive functioning for both children and adults (Floyd et al., 2006).
- Although mean scores between African American and Caucasian students are different, the scores have comparable meaning (Edward & Oakland, 2006).
- The WJ-III subtests primarily have inadequate item gradients and/or ceilings for individuals ages 16–25 (Krasa, 2007).

Research on the WJ-Revised might be relevant. It can be accessed on the Earlier Research link for Chapter 7 on the Companion Website (www.prenhall.com/taylor8e).

Overview: Woodcock-Johnson–III–NU

- *Age level*—2 years to adult.
- *Type of administration*—Individual.
- *Technical adequacy*—Good standardization, adequate reliability and validity.
- *Scores yielded*—Standard scores, percentile ranks, relative mastery index (age and grade equivalents also available).
- *Suggested use*—The WJ-III-NU is a comprehensive and wide-ranging set of tests that measure a variety of areas. The Cognitive Battery was developed within a theoretical framework (Cattell-Horn-Carroll) making the interpretation more meaningful. Several changes and improvements in the WJ-III-NU are worthy of mention. These include the addition of new cognitive tests and a brief intellectual ability score that can be obtained in ten to fifteen minutes. Because of the possibility of so many scores, it is necessary that an examiner carefully plan so that the appropriate test(s) can be administered. One criticism of earlier editions was the difficulty in hand scoring. This has been addressed by including a computer scoring program with the instrument that eliminates hand scoring. Another advantageous feature of the WJ-III-NU is the use of continuous-year norms. This means that the standardization occurred throughout the year for the school-age subjects rather than at one or two times. Thus, scores can be compared to individuals of the exact age or grade placement rather than to individuals of an average age or grade. This procedure helps eliminate the error variance associated with grouping students of similar, but not the same, age or grade. In addition to the scoring software included with the WJ-III-NU, there is an expanded program called the *Report Writer for the WJ-III.* This includes an interpretation of the results in addition to the scoring of the tests (see Chapter 3 for cautions regarding computerized interpretation programs). It also contains a series of checklists for the teacher, parent, and the examinee as well as a classroom behavior observation form. These allow background information from a variety of sources to be incorporated into the report. Finally, there is a Spanish version.

Additional Instruments

There are several other less frequently used instruments that provide measures of intelligence. Some have more limited use for a variety of reasons, including heavy reliance on one aspect of intelligence (*Slosson Intelligence Test–Revised 3*). Other tests are a shorter version of the same comprehensive instrument (*Kaufman Brief Intelligence Test–2*). Others, such as the *Das-Naglieri Cognitive Assessment System* and the *Detroit Tests of Learning Aptitude–4*, are instruments with a limited amount of research to validate their use to rival the more popular intelligence tests. A brief description of these instruments follows.

Das-Naglieri Cognitive Assessment System

- *Age level*—5 to 18 years.
- *Type of administration*—Individual.
- *Technical adequacy*—Good standardization, reliability, and validity.
- *Scores yielded*—Scaled scores, standard scores, percentile ranks, age equivalents.
- *Suggested use*—The *Das-Naglieri Cognitive Assessment System* (CAS; Naglieri & Das, 1997) is based on a cognitive theory called PASS—**P**lanning, **A**ttention, **S**imultaneous, and **S**uccessive. The three Planning subtests are Matching Numbers, Planned Codes, and Planned Connections. The Attention subtests are Expressive Attention, Number Detection, and Receptive Attention. The Simultaneous subtests are Nonverbal Matrices, Verbal–Spatial Relations, and Figure Memory. The Successive subtests are Word Series, Sentence Repetition, Speech Rate (ages 5–7), and Sentence Questions (Ages 8–17). These subtests represent the Standard Battery. Eight of the subtests can be used as the Basic Battery. The Achievement Battery from the *Woodcock-Johnson–Revised* (an earlier version of the WJ-III-NU) was also administered to 1,600 individuals from the CAS normative sample to allow for the determination of ability-achievement differences. The authors claim that the CAS is more appropriate than other measures with minority students. Naglieri and Rojahn (2001) did report that it resulted in fewer African American students being classified as having mental retardation compared to the WISC-III. On the other hand, Keith, Kranzler, and Flanagan (2001) found that their data did not support the theoretical model on which the CAS was based. Naglieri (2001) in discussing the CAS noted that it was a good predictor of achievement, is particularly helpful for students with learning disabilities and attention deficits, and was relevant for intervention and instructional planning.

Detroit Tests of Learning Aptitude–4

- *Age level*—6 to 18 years.
- *Type of administration*—Individual.
- *Technical adequacy*—Good standardization, adequate reliability, adequate validity
- *Scores yielded*—Standard scores, percentile ranks, age equivalents
- *Suggested use*—The *Detroit Tests of Learning Aptitude* (DTLA–4; Hammill, 1998) is the third major revision of a test that was originally published in 1935. There are eleven subtests that can be interpreted individually or grouped into three domains: Linguistic, Attentional, and Motoric. Composite

scores within each domain (e.g., Verbal Aptitude and Nonverbal aptitude in the Linguistic domain) are available. A General Mental Ability Quotient is also available by combining all eleven subtests. The Global Composite score is probably the best to interpret as an overall measure of learning aptitude. The authors caution that composite scores from different domains should not be compared. For example, it is acceptable to compare Verbal Aptitude and Nonverbal Aptitude because they are within the same domain. It would be inappropriate, however, to compare Verbal Aptitude with Attention-Enhanced Aptitude from the Attention Domain because the same subtest(s) might be found in each. The manual includes a good chapter that discusses test scores and their interpretation. There is also a *DTLA–Primary* for children ages 3 to 9 and a *DTLA–Adult*. Another related instrument is the *Hammill Multiability Intelligence Test* (HAMIT; Hammill, Bryant, & Pearson, 1998). The HAMIT includes eight of the subtests and was co-normed with the *Hammill Multiability Achievement Test* (see Chapter 11) so that comparisons between intelligence and achievement can be made with the same comparison group.

> Do not compare composite scores from different domains.

Kaufman Brief Intelligence Test–2

- *Age level*—4 to 90 years.
- *Type of administration*—Individual.
- *Technical adequacy*—Good standardization and reliability, adequate validity.
- *Scores yielded*—Standard scores, percentile ranks, descriptive categories.
- *Suggested use*—The *Kaufman Brief Intelligence Test–2* (KBIT-2; Kaufman & Kaufman, 2004a) is a brief screening instrument that uses two subtests. One subtest measures crystallized intelligence through the use of two types of items—Verbal Knowledge and Riddles. The other subtext, Matrices, measures fluid intelligence. Matrices involves nonverbal problem-solving tasks. The KBIT-2 appears to have adequate technical characteristics and can be used confidently as a brief screener of verbal and nonverbal intelligence. Although no research was located on the KBIT-2, the K-BIT was investigated as a possible predictor of WISC-III scores in a number of studies. Although there appears to be a strong correlation between the two sets of scores, the K-BIT and the WISC-III seem to yield different scores. In one study, Seagle and Rust (1996) found that the K-BIT composite IQ was approximately seven points less than the average WISC-III IQ. On the other hand, Grados and Russo-Garcia (1999) found the K-BIT scores were six to seven points higher than the WISC-III IQs. Chin and colleagues (2001) cautioned the use of the K-BIT to predict WISC-III, noting that in individual cases the K-BIT could under- or overestimate the WISC-III IQ by 25 points. Research on the KBIT-2 should be forthcoming to determine if this pattern exists for the revised instrument as well.

Slosson Intelligence Test–Revised 3

- *Age level*—4 through 65 years.
- *Type of administration*—Individual.
- *Technical characteristics*—Adequate standardization, limited reliability, adequate validity.
- *Scores yielded*—Deviation IQ, percentiles, total standard score.

- *Suggested use*—The *Slosson Intelligence Test–Revised* (SIT-R3; Slosson, Nicholson, & Hibpshman, 1998) gives a quick estimate of a person's intelligence. The majority of items are highly verbal, measuring six cognitive domains: Information, Comprehension, Quantitative, Similarities and Differences, Vocabulary, and Auditory Memory. The SIT-R3 should be used for screening only. It can help to identify students for whom intelligence testing in more depth might be necessary. The inclusion of a total standard score in the revised version allows for more meaningful interpretation than for its predecessors. In a review of the SIT-R, Campbell and Ashmore (1995) noted that many of the problems with the original version had been addressed but with varying success. It should be noted that there is also a supplemental manual for individuals who are blind or visually impaired.

BACK TO THE PROFILE

Possible Answers to the Questions

1. **Why assess Tommy?** As Tommy's teacher noted, he is having difficulty in a number of areas and didn't respond to the prereferral intervention efforts. She wanted to determine his current educational status. A comprehensive assessment would more than likely include individual intelligence testing.

2. **Who should assess Tommy?** Tommy would probably be assessed by a number of professionals. An educational diagnostician or trained teacher might be involved in academic testing. The individually administered intelligence test would be given by the school psychologist (or psychometrist in some states). The individual would have to have the appropriate credentials and training in administering and interpreting intelligence tests.

3. **What procedure(s)/test(s) should be used?** The choice of intelligence test is limited somewhat because of Tommy's age. Many of the tests discussed in this chapter (e.g., the WISC-IV) start at age 6. Although technically Tommy could be administered this test, it might not be the best choice. Many professionals feel that the test lacks sensitivity and might give artificially higher or lower scores when administered to individuals in the extreme ends of the age range for a given test (e.g., age 6 and age 16 for the WISC-IV). An option might be the SBIS-5 or the WJ-III-NU, which start at age 2.

4. **What other areas should be assessed?** As noted earlier, his academic level would probably be administered using an individual achievement test (see Chapter 11). Based on the results of the intelligence and academic testing, other areas might need to be assessed if Tommy were to qualify for special education services other than speech and language (which he was already receiving). For example, if both his IQ and achievement levels were low, he might be administered an adaptive behavior scale (see next chapter) to qualify for a program for students with mental retardation. On the other hand, if his IQ was significantly higher than his achievement, additional testing for learning disabilities might be warranted.

STUDENT PROFILE DATA

Tommy

The Standard Cognitive Battery from the Woodcock-Johnson–III–NU was administered to Tommy. The following results were obtained:

Area/Subtest	Standard Score
General Cognitive Ability	90
Verbal Comprehension	102
Visual-Auditory Learning	98
Visual-Auditory Learning-Delayed	85
Spatial Relations	106
Sound Blending	88
Incomplete Words	84
Concept Formation	99
Visual Matching	108
Numbers Reversed	78
Auditory Working Memory	74

These results indicate that Tommy is below average in overall intelligence. He does, how-ever, show certain strengths and weaknesses. His strengths are in visual processing skills and verbal comprehension. He is having difficulty with auditory processing tasks, partic-ularly those that require the use of memory. His General Cognitive Ability Score suggests that he would not qualify for IDEA 04 services under the category of mental retardation. Depending on the individual state's eligibility criteria, Tommy might be evaluated further in areas such as academic achievement and/or language.

CASE STUDY *June*

By now Mrs. Dunn has tried several interventions dealing with off-task behavior and June's problems in reading and writing. Though June's time-on-task has im-proved somewhat, June is still not completing all of the assignments, and she is struggling with the reading assignments in particular. Mrs. Dunn has observed that knowledge expressed verbally by June shows a greater depth of understand-ing than the knowledge she expresses in writing. Mrs. Dunn has also noticed that June worries and is "beginning to get an attitude."

Mrs. Dunn believes that June has the ability to do well, but something is pre-venting her from being successful in reading and written expression. She has de-cided to refer June for further evaluation. She has completed the necessary referral form and attached a file with the informal assessment results including the observational data, the portfolio with work samples, and the CBA. She also in-cluded the results of the prereferral intervention program that was developed and implemented. June's parents have given their written permission for the formal assessment. The evaluation process began.

Review the results of the intelligence assessment shown below. Look for June's relative strengths and for areas of concern. When you have completed the review, answer the questions that follow.

Assessment Profile

Name: June
Age: 10 years, 0 months
Grade: 4th

WISC-IV
Full Scale IQ	99

Verbal Comprehension Index	114
Similarities	13

Vocabulary	11
Comprehension	13
Perceptual Reasoning Index	98
Matrix Reasoning	9
Block Design	10
Picture Concepts	9
Working Memory	80
Letter-Number Sequencing	8
Digit Span	7
Processing Speed	76
Symbol Search	7
Coding	6

- Look at the Full Scale IQ and the four Index scores. What are June's overall intellectual abilities?
- Review the subtests of the WISC-IV. What are June's relative strengths?
- Which subtests indicate deficits for June? Is there a relationship between the tasks required for these subtests?
- What other areas do you think should be assessed?

Reflections

1. Do you think intelligence tests are inherently biased against ethnic-minority students? Why or why not?
2. Why do you think that may professionals argue that intelligene tests measure performance and not potential?
3. What do you think is the advantage of some tests such as the Woodcock-Johnson–III having both a Cognitive battery and an Achievement battery?

Summary Matrix

Instrument or Technique	Suggested Use — Prereferral: Screening and Initial Identification	Suggested Use — Prereferral: Informal Determination and Evaluation of Teaching Programs and Strategies	Suggested Use — Postreferral: Determination of Current Performance Level and Educational Need	Suggested Use — Postreferral: Decisions about Classification and Program Placement	Suggested Use — Postreferral: IEP Goals	Suggested Use — Postreferral: IEP Objectives	Suggested Use — Postreferral: IEP Evaluation	Target Population: Mild/Moderate	Target Population: Severe/Profound	Target Population: Preschool	Target Population: Elementary Age	Target Population: Secondary Age	Target Population: Adult	Special Considerations	Educational Relevance for Exceptional Students
Group Intelligence Tests	X							X		X	X	X	X	Use for screening only; resemble group-achievement tests in format and, to a certain extent, content.	Limited
Kaufman Assessment Battery for Children–II			X	X	X			X		X	X	X		Results can be interpreted using two theoretical models.	Useful
Stanford–Binet Intelligence Scale–Fifth Edition			X	X				X		X	X	X	X	The "grandfather" of intelligence tests; now has verbal and nonverbal domains.	Useful
Wechsler Intelligence Scale for Children–Fourth Edition			X	X				X			X	X		Very widely used, well constructed; profile analyses of subtests should be avoided.	Very Useful
Woodcock–Johnson–III–NU			X	X	X			X		X	X	X	X	WJ-III includes many new features and improvements; computer scoring only.	Useful
Das–Naglieri Cognitive Assessment System			X	X				X			X	X	X	Based on a solid theoretical model; includes a standard battery and basic battery.	Useful
Detroit Tests of Learning Aptitude–4			X					X			X	X		Some question about its validity; needs further research.	Adequate
Kaufman Brief Intelligence Test–2			X	X	X			X		X	X	X		Brief version of the KABC-II; use for screening only.	Useful
Slosson Intelligence Test–Revised 3	X							X		X	X	X	X	Use for screening only; easy to administer; revised version an improvement.	Adequate

chapter eight

Assessment of Adaptive Behavior

STUDENT PROFILE

Mike

Mike is a first-grade student who was new to his school. His teacher, Ms. Capella, felt that he was significantly below his peers in academic and social skills. Routine group-administered intelligence testing resulted in an IQ of 65. Previous educational records from his kindergarten were incomplete. It did seem that he comes from a lower-socioeconomic family environment and that his mother (a single parent) seemed to move a lot. He was also frequently absent from school. Ms. Capella was very concerned and felt that Mike would have considerable problems keeping up in all the academic areas. His reading readiness and math readiness skills were very depressed, and he wrote very little. She did note that Mike seemed to be able to handle himself in nonacademic environments such as the playground or the bus stop, although he was sometimes aggressive.

STUDENT PROFILE

Tamika

Tamika, a 12-year-old girl with mental retardation, is in an inclusion classroom. In addition to her mental retardation, Tamika has significant physical limitations due to cerebral palsy. Both the general education teacher, Ms. Perez, and the special education teacher, Ms. Phillips, felt that Tamika seemed to have potential in a number of areas, including self-help skills and socialization skills. Although these areas were included in a functional curriculum that was used with her, both teachers wanted more information to help establish more sequential objectives for her IEP. It has been almost three years since Tamika was last tested, and that evaluation focused more on reestablishing eligibility and identifying more general goals and objectives. Both teachers also wanted a better method of monitoring Tamika's progress, which must be measured in small steps.

Think about These Questions as You Read This Chapter:

1. Why assess Mike and Tamika? (There could be more than one reason.)
2. Who should assess Mike and Tamika? (There could be more than one person.)
3. What procedure(s)/test(s) should be used?
4. What other areas (if any) should be assessed?

(Suggested answers appear at the end of this chapter.)

In its broadest sense, **adaptive behavior** has to do with a person's ability to deal effectively with personal and social demands and expectations. Boan and Harrison (1997) noted, "Daily, functional skills related to self-care, interaction with others, and participation in the community are necessary for all individuals" (p. 33). Adaptive behavior, in general, is a difficult concept to define and measure. Harrison (1990) offered five elements of adaptive behavior that make it difficult to define. First, it is *developmental*. The content of adaptive-behavior instruments will differ depending on the age range for the test. For instance, adaptive behavior for a 3-year-old child primarily includes motor skills, language skills, and self-help skills. On the other hand, adaptive behavior for a 15-year-old might include social skills and prevocational skills. Second, adaptive behavior *involves many domains*. The American Association on Mental Retardation[1] (Luckasson et al., 1992), in fact, defined ten specific adaptive skill areas: communication, self-care, home living, social skills, community use, self-direction, health and safety, functional academics, leisure, and work. The AAMR (Luckasson et al., 2002) later subsumed these into three adaptive behavior areas: conceptual, practical, and social. Adaptive behavior must also be viewed *within cultural norms and expectations* (see Focus on Diversity) and as *specific to different situations* (e.g., home vs. workplace). Finally, adaptive behavior includes both *ability and performance*. For example, a person might have the ability to clean his room but is viewed as being deficient in that area if he routinely does not clean it.

In general, adaptive behavior instruments can be used for three purposes. The specific purpose for an instrument depends largely on its depth, breadth, and technical characteristics, most notably the nature of the standardization sample. Some instruments are used to help make *eligibility* decisions. The AAMR definition of mental retardation requires a deficit in adaptive behavior, and these instruments play an important role in those labeling decisions. Tests used for this purpose usually measure a number of areas and are usually standardized on populations without disabilities. Other adaptive behavior scales are used more for *developing* and *evaluating specific teaching programs*. Tests used for this purpose usually include specific sequential items that cover functional, independent-living skill areas. Some of these tests are standardized on, and used with, individuals with more severe disabilities (e.g., *Balthazar Scales of*

> **ADAPTIVE BEHAVIOR**
> Adaptive behavior has to do with daily functional skills related to self-care, interaction with others, and participation in the community.

Adaptive behavior is a multidimensional concept.

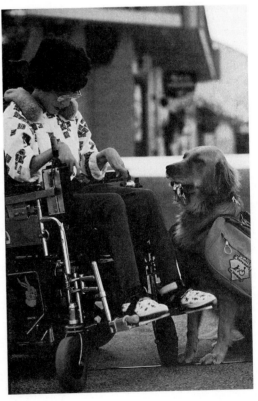

---

[1]The AAMR is now known as the American Association on Intellectual and Developmental Disabilities. The term AAMR will be used in this chapter when referring to the AAMR definitions and AAMR Adaptive Scale, because that term was used at the time of their publication.

focus on
Diversity

Are Adaptive Behavior Scales Culturally Biased?

Adaptive behavior can be defined within a cultural context. For example, what might be considered an adaptive skill in one culture might not be in another. In a study that reinforces this point, van Keulen, Weddington, and Debose (1998) noted that when using European American standards, the adaptive behavior of many African American children was reported to be immature and socially delayed. However, when those same children were rated by African Americans, they were viewed as being typical children having fun and acting age-appropriately. The AAMR acknowledged the importance of considering the issue of sociocultural factors in adaptive behavior assessment in their 2002 *Manual.* Luckasson et al. noted that since it is not possible to obtain standardization samples from all cultural groups to provide specific comparisons, it is necessary for the examiner to consider the sociocultural background of the individual evaluated when clinically interpreting the scores.

The format of adaptive behavior scales is important.

Adaptive Behavior; Balthazar, 1976). Others are standardized on individuals without disabilities and simply include more expanded and detailed items than those instruments used for eligibility purposes. Siegel and Allinder (2005) noted, however, that although adaptive behavior scales may be used for developing a student's IEP, additional assessment, such as criterion referenced testing, should be included. A third purpose for adaptive behavior testing is *screening*. Tests used for this purpose help to identify general goals.

The technical characteristics of many adaptive-behavior scales have been questioned. Pierangelo and Giuliani (2002), for instance, noted that many adaptive behavior scales lack appropriate validity and reliability. Harrison (1987), however, in a review of adaptive behavior research available at that time, concluded that the instruments exhibit adequate reliability and can differentiate individuals with different labels. The format of adaptive behavior scales has also been scrutinized. Some scales allow for direct observation, whereas others require an interview. These two procedures do not always yield similar information or results. In addition, the nature of the informant (if an interview is used) can make a difference. For example, a teacher and a parent might rate the same child differently. For this reason, Boan and Harrison (1997) suggested that multiple raters should be used to determine consistencies and inconsistencies. A discussion of some of the more widely used adaptive behavior instruments follows.

Adaptive Behavior Instruments

Why Use Adaptive Behavior Instruments?

Screening and identification; documentation of educational need; decisions about eligibility and program placement; development and evaluation of IEPs (largely depending on target population).

Who Should Use Them?

Teachers or staff members; social workers and school psychologists (often using interview with parent).

Adaptive Behavior Inventory

The *Adaptive Behavior Inventory* (ABI; Brown & Leigh, 1986) is an individually administered instrument used with individuals ages 6 through 18. It is designed to be completed by the classroom teacher and is relatively simple to score. The respondent must use a four-point scale to indicate the degree to which the examinee can perform certain behaviors (the items).

The primary use of the ABI is to aid in eligibility decisions regarding mental retardation and to determine general strengths and weaknesses in various adaptive behavior areas. The ABI does not provide specific information that could be used for educational programming. The ABI includes 150 items (30 items in each of five areas). There is also a 50-item ABI–Short Form available for quick screening.

The ABI is administered by the teacher.

Description

Self-Care Skills. This scale measures areas such as grooming and personal hygiene.

Communication Skills. This scale measures writing ability as well as expressive and receptive oral language skills.

Social Skills. This scale measures a wide range of skills including responsibility, organizational skills, and leadership ability.

Academic Skills. This scale measures both preacademic and academic reading and mathematics skills.

Occupational Skills. This includes such areas as job responsibility and supervisory skills.

Interpretation of Results. For each of the five scales, percentile ranks and standard scores (mean = 100; standard deviation = 15) are available. The scales can thus be used independently, although a composite quotient (Total Score) is also available.

Technical Characteristics

Normative Sample. The ABI was standardized on both a sample of students with mental retardation and a sample of children with normal intelligence. The sample with mental retardation included approximately 1,100 individuals from twenty-four states. The sample with normal intelligence included approximately 1,300 individuals from those same locations.

Reliability. Internal consistency (coefficient alpha) was generally good for all the age ranges for all five scales (.86–.97). The coefficients for the total score all exceeded .90. Test-retest reliability coefficients for the individual scales and the total score were also above .90. In general, reliability data for the ABI–Short Form were similar.

Validity. In general, the ABI is lacking evidence of validity. Some concurrent validity data are presented (moderate coefficients) using the American Association on Mental Deficiency (AAMD) *Adaptive Behavior Scale* and *Vineland Adaptive Behavior Scales* as criteria. There is also a discussion by the authors regarding the test's content and construct validity. For example, they note the significant differences in the scores of the individuals in the two standardization samples.

Review of Relevant Research.   Although no empirical studies were located, a few reviews of the ABI were found; those reviews were, in general, relatively positive.

- Hughes (1988) believed that the test was highly useful for diagnosis and placement decisions because of the inclusion of the two different normative samples. Ehly (1989) found the instrument attractive as well as quick and easy to administer.
- Smith (1989) considered the test best used to identify general strengths and weaknesses as well as areas for which further assessment to determine instructional goals could be pursued. He added that the total score was better to report than the individual scale scores.

Overview: Adaptive Behavior Inventory

- *Age level*—6 through 18 years old.
- *Type of administration*—Individual.
- *Technical adequacy*—Good reliability, questionable validity.
- *Scores yielded*—Percentile ranks, standard scores.
- *Suggested use*—The ABI is relatively quick and easy to administer. It is designed for use by the classroom teacher or other professional who is familiar with the student. As with most adaptive behavior tests, the ABI should be used to supplement other assessment information, particularly when being used to assist in eligibility and placement decisions. The test appears to be reliable, and the use of two sets of norms is a good feature. More evidence of the test's validity would be beneficial.

AAMR Adaptive Behavior Scale–Second Edition: Residential and Community Edition; School Edition

There are two separate editions of the AAMR ABS-2.

The *AAMR Adaptive Behavior Scales* include the Residential and Community Edition (AAMR ABS-RC:2; Nihira, Leland, & Lambert, 1993), designed for use with individuals between the ages of 6 and 79 years who live in residential and community settings, and the School Edition (AAMR ABS-S:2; Lambert, Leland, & Nihira, 1993), to be used with students ages 6 through 21 years who are receiving services in the public schools. Both scales are used with individuals who have mental retardation, emotional problems, and other disabilities. The School Edition is actually a shorter version of the Residential and Community Edition with some items deleted from the longer version because of their inappropriateness for use with school-age children receiving services in the public schools. According to the authors, the ABS-2 can be used for identifying persons who may be in need of specialized clinical services, identifying adaptive strengths and weaknesses in individuals under different situations, documenting progress in an intervention program, and stimulating research. It should also be emphasized that a deficit in adaptive behavior and cognitive functioning must be documented before an individual is labeled as having mental retardation. The ABS-2, in part, was developed for that purpose.

The ABS-2 consists of two parts: Part One deals primarily with personal independence in daily living skills. Part One of the Residential and Community Edition includes seventy-three items that are divided into ten areas or domains and three factors. Part One of the School Edition consists of sixty-seven items that contribute to nine domains and three factors. Part Two, which concerns the measurement of maladaptive behavior, includes eight domains (seven for S:2) and two factors. The RC:2 has forty-one items, and the S:2 contains thirty-seven items. For the most part, items deleted from the RC:2 involved sexual relations (e.g., "exposes body improperly," "has sexual behavior that is socially unacceptable"). For both parts of the ABS-2, information is collected by one of two methods. The first is first-person assessment. This method is used when the evaluator is thoroughly familiar with the person who is being evaluated. The second method is third-party assessment. In this approach, the evaluator asks another individual (e.g., teacher, parent, or ward attendant) about each item on the scale. This is usually a time-consuming endeavor.

Description

Part One.   This part includes ten domains assessing the degree of independence in daily living skills. Each item in a given domain is scored in one of two ways. For some items, there is a breakdown and description of skills on a dependent–independent continuum. The examiner chooses which behavioral description best fits the individual being evaluated. For the remaining items, a list of behaviors is provided, and the examiner must check all that apply. Descriptions of the ten domains follow.

> Part One focuses on independent living skills.

> *Independent Functioning.* Included in this domain are eating, toilet use, cleanliness, appearance, care of clothing, dressing and undressing, travel, and other independent functioning.

> *Physical Development.* This domain includes items measuring a person's sensory development (vision and hearing) and motor development (gross motor and fine motor skills).

> *Economic Activity.* Items in this domain measure ability in money handling and budgeting and shopping skills.

> *Language Development.* This domain includes measures of expression and verbal comprehension plus two items concerning social language development (e.g., conversational behavior).

> *Numbers and Time.* Items in this domain measure a person's ability to understand and manipulate numbers and to understand time concepts.

> *Domestic Activity.* This domain includes items measuring skills in cleaning, kitchen activities, and other domestic activities (not included in S:2).

> *Prevocational/Vocational Activity.* These items measure work and school habits and job performance.

> *Self-Direction.* These items measure an individual's initiative, perseverance, and use of leisure time.

> *Responsibility.* These items measure an individual's dependability.

> *Socialization.* This domain includes measure of cooperation, consideration for others, and social maturity.

Part Two.   This part was designed specifically to measure the degree of an individual's *maladaptive behavior*. It includes eight domains. For each item in a given domain, several behaviors are listed. The examiner must determine whether each behavior occurs frequently (scored as 2), occasionally (scored as 1), or not at all (scored as 0). Unfortunately, no guidelines are provided that operationally define

> Part Two focuses on maladaptive behavior.

"frequently" and "occasionally." The eight behavioral domains are summarized below.

> *Social Behavior.* This domain includes such items as "threatens or does physical violence" and "reacts poorly to frustration."
>
> *Conformity.* This domain includes questions about impudence, resistance to instructions, and absenteeism.
>
> *Trustworthiness.* These items inquire about the possible presence of lying, cheating, and stealing behavior.
>
> *Stereotyped and Hyperactive Behavior.* These items measure stereotypical and repetitive behaviors, as well as hyperactive tendencies.
>
> *Sexual Behavior.* This domain measures behaviors that relate to physical exposure and/or masturbation (not included in S:2).
>
> *Self-Abusive Behavior.* This domain includes items such as "does physical violence to self" and "has strange and unacceptable habits."
>
> *Social Engagement.* This domain measures inactivity and shyness.
>
> *Disturbing Interpersonal Behavior.* This domain measures such behaviors as "reacts poorly to criticism" and "has hypochondriacal tendencies."

Interpretation of Results.   Each item on the ABS-2 is scored by the methods previously described. Scores for all the items in a given domain are added together to obtain a raw score for that domain. Raw scores for various factors can also be obtained. The factors are Personal Self-Sufficiency, Community Self-Sufficiency, Personal-Social Responsibility, Social Adjustment, and Personal Adjustment. The domain and factor raw scores can be converted to percentile ranks and standard scores. The standard scores are then plotted on a Profile/Summary Sheet (see Figure 8.1) to provide a visual representation of the individual's adaptive behavior functioning. Note that the mean and standard deviation of the domain and factor scores are 10 and 3 and 100 and 15, respectively.

One important consideration in using this instrument is that, for the most part, there are too few items in a given domain to provide adequate information for specific educational programming. The authors do address this issue, however.

Technical Characteristics

Normative Sample.   The RC:2 sample consisted of more than 4,000 persons with developmental disabilities who reside in residential or community settings. The S:2 sample consisted of more than 1,000 students without disabilities and more than 2,000 students with mental retardation. In both instances, the samples' demographic characteristics were representative of the nation as a whole.

Reliability.   Interrater reliability was established in separate studies by having two staff members or a parent and a staff member independently rate clients or students. In most instances, the coefficients for the various domains approach or exceed .80. Internal consistency reliability coefficients for the RC:2 and S:2 domains generally exceed .80 across ages. Factor score reliability coefficients exceed .90 across most ages. Stability reliability coefficients, for the most part, also exceed .80 for the domains and factors.

Validity.   Validity for each version of the ABS-2 was examined in a number of ways. For content validity, a description is provided of how the items were

FIGURE 8.1 Profile Sheet from the AAMR Adaptive Behavior Scale–2

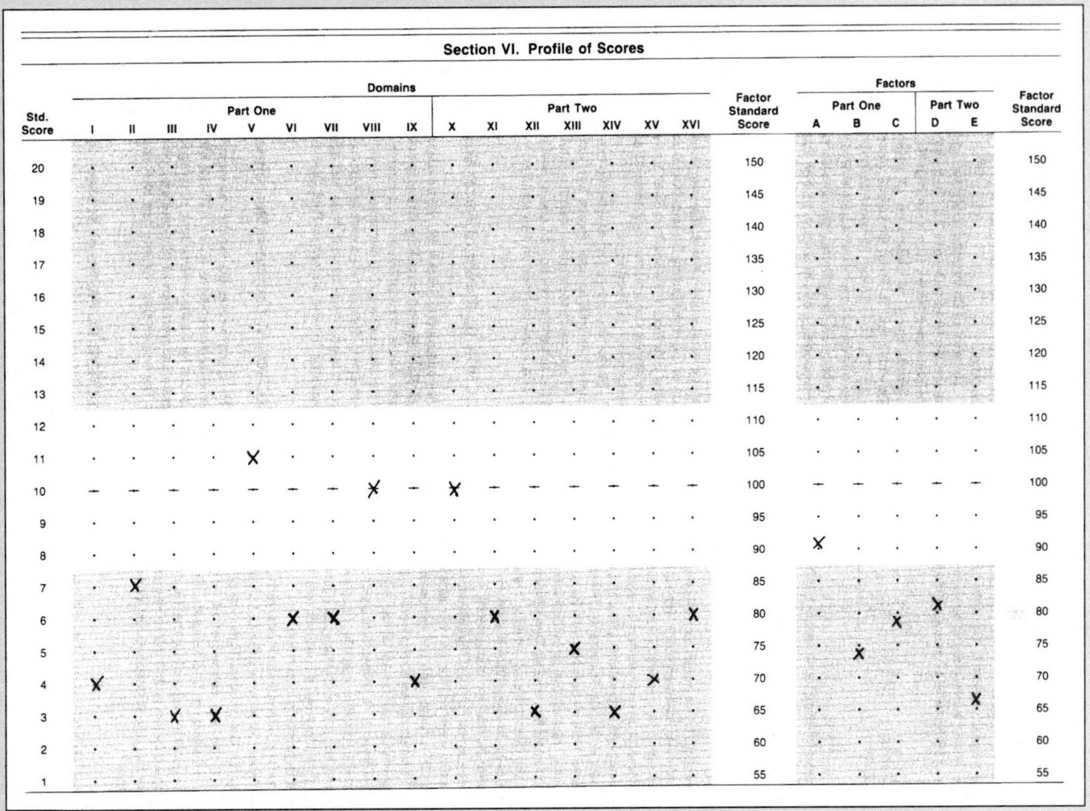

Source: K. Nihira, H. Leland, and N. Lambert. (1993). *AAMR Adaptive Behavior Scale* (2nd ed). Copyright © 1993 by American Association on Mental Retardation. Additional copies of this form (#6194) are available from Pro-Ed, 8700 Shoal Creek Boulevard, Austin, TX 78757, 512/451-3246.

selected for inclusion on the scale. Item discriminating powers and item difficulties lend empirical support. Criterion-related validity evidence is explained by comparing the results of each ABS-2 version with other adaptive behavior scales. In general, moderate coefficients were reported for Part One and low insignificant coefficients for Part Two. Construct validity for both versions was explored by demonstrating that the scales (1) are developmental in nature, (2) correlate significantly with measures of intelligence, (3) relate significantly to measures of achievement, (4) differentiate among groups of students with varying disabilities (i.e., mental retardation, emotional disturbance, learning disabilities) and those without disabilities, (5) have factor clusters that are supported through factor analytic research, and (6) have valid items.

Review of Relevant Research. Interestingly, very little research was located on the second edition of AAMR ABS. Stinnett, Fuqua, and Coombs (1999) examined the construct validity of the ABS-S:2. They found that the test reflects two major factors: personal independence and social behavior. They suggest that users should be cautious when interpreting the results in terms of the five factor model presented by the authors. Watkins, Ravert, and Crosby (2002) agreed with

Research on the AAMR ABS-2 is lacking.

cautions of interpreting the five factors, also finding that the test primarily measures personal independence and behavior.

Stinnett (1997) reviewed the revised school edition. He reported that it is an improvement over previous editions, particularly regarding the standardization and technical characteristics. Despite these improvements, he noted that more validity data are needed and that high-functioning individuals with mental retardation are not well represented in the norms. He also argued that the domains do not align with the adaptive skill areas required in the 1992 AAMR definition of mental retardation. For this purpose, however, other instruments were developed (discussed later in this chapter). In another review, Pierangelo and Giuliani (2002) noted that the ABS-S:2 has an excellent standardization sample and can be used with a wide variety of individuals. They also felt that the instrument's psychometric properties were good.

The second edition of the ABS is similar in format to its predecessors. Thus, a review of the research conducted on the earlier instruments may be of value. Most of that research explored its psychometric characteristics, particularly its reliability and validity. These studies, in general, supported the use of the ABS to identify groups of individuals according to diagnostic category. In other words, there are significant differences among the scores of differently labeled groups of individuals. As with most adaptive behavior instruments, there has been research on the method of gathering the information and the nature of the informant (usually teacher versus parent). Finally, the reliability of the ABS has been questioned, particularly for Part Two. Part Two, in fact, has been criticized for a number of technical inadequacies, although many of these inadequacies have been addressed through alternate scoring methods. It should also be noted that many of these inadequacies were addressed in the revised version. The more limited research on the ABS-SE generally supported its use as an instrument to aid in eligibility decisions. Specific research studies on the earlier versions of the ABS:2 can be found by consulting the Earlier Research link for Chapter 8 of the Companion Website (www.prenhall.com/taylor8e).

Overview: AAMR Adaptive Behavior Scale–2: Residential and Community Edition; School Edition

- *Age level*—6 to 79 years (RC:2) and 6 to 21 years (S:2).
- *Type of administration*—Individual.
- *Technical adequacy*—Reliability of domains is adequate; reliability of factors is good; validity is adequate for Part One, questionable for Part Two.
- *Scores yielded*—Percentile ranks, standard scores.
- *Suggested use*—The ABS originally was developed primarily as a result of the AAMR's emphasis on adaptive behavior in its definition of mental retardation. Although limited research was located on the ABS-RC:2 or the ABS-S:2, it would appear that the instruments are similar enough to the earlier versions to warrant some generalization. For example, the ABS was successful in identifying groups of individuals according to their diagnostic classification. The ABS, however, had several limitations. Generally speaking, the items were not sensitive enough to be useful for individuals with severe disabilities. Technical inadequacies in Part Two, in particular, were criticized. The revised versions have addressed many of the technical limitations of the previous editions, however.

The AAMR ABS-2 is used primarily to assist in eligibility decisions.

Overall, the results from the ABS:2 should be used to aid in eligibility and placement decisions and to identify general areas of programming needs. Important decisions should not be based on the results alone, nor should specific educational plans be developed around the child's adaptive behavior profile. Obviously, more research needs to be conducted to determine the uses and limitations of the two revised versions of the ABS.

Scales of Independent Behavior–Revised

The *Scales of Independent Behavior–Revised* (SIB-R; Bruininks, Woodcock, Weatherman, & Hill, 1996) is an individually administered instrument designed for use with a wide age range (3 months to adult). The SIB-R uses a structured format in which the interviewer makes a statement (e.g., "Picks up and eats food such as crackers" to which the respondent must indicate if the examinee exhibits that behavior "never or rarely," "about one-fourth of the time," "about three-fourths of the time," or "always or almost always." It is also possible for an individual who is familiar with the student to simply read and complete the items directly on the test protocol. The SIB-R consists of fourteen subscales that can be grouped into four larger clusters. In addition, there is a Problem Behavior Scale. Finally, there is a short form consisting of forty items, and an Early Development Scale to use with younger children that also consists of forty questions. Also available are a shorter version of the SIB-R called the *Inventory for Client and Agency Planning* (ICAP) and a related criterion-referenced instrument called the *Checklist of Adaptive Living Skills* (CALS). A correlated curriculum called the *Adaptive Living Skills Curriculum* (ALSC) completes the package.

The SIB-R uses a multiple-choice format.

The SIB-R has several related components.

Description

Motor Skills Cluster
Gross Motor. Items range from "Sits without support for thirty seconds with head and back held straight and steady" to "Takes part in strenuous physical activities on a regular basis that require strength and endurance."

Fine Motor. Items range from "Picks up small objects with hand" to "Sews missing or loose buttons on clothing."

Social Interaction and Communication Cluster
Social Interaction. Ranges from "Reaches for a person whom he or she wants" to "Makes plans with friends to attend activities such as movies or special events outside the home."

Language Comprehension. Includes "Turns head toward speaker when name is called" and "Reads one or more articles in a regular newspaper at least weekly."

Language Expression. Ranges from "Makes sounds or gestures to get attention" to "Explains the terms of a written contract, such as an installment purchase agreement."

Personal Living Skills Cluster
Eating. Ranges from "Swallows soft foods" to "Plans and prepares meals regularly for self and family."

Toileting. Items include "Shows some sign of discomfort when wet" and "Independently replaces emptied roll of toilet paper."

Dressing. Includes "Removes socks" and "Selects and buys appropriate size and style of clothing."

Personal Self-Care. Ranges from "Holds hands under running water to wash them when placed in front of sink" to "Makes appointments for periodic medical or dental examinations."

Domestic Skills. Includes "Places his or her empty dish in or near the sink" and "Cleans refrigerator and throws out food that may be spoiled."

Community Living Skills Cluster

Time and Punctuality. Includes "Points to any number from 1 to 5 when asked" and "States the time on a clock with hands to the nearest minute."

Money and Value. Items range from "Counts from 1 to 5" to "Invests savings to achieve the most favorable conditions and rate of return."

Work Skills. Includes "Indicates when a chore or assigned task is finished" and "Prepares a written summary of work experience."

Home/Community Orientation. Includes "Finds toys or objects that are always kept in the same place" and "Locates his or her polling center at election time."

Interpretation of Results. A variety of derived scores are available for each of the four clusters as well as Broad Independence (a global score combining the clusters). Scores for those areas include age equivalents, standard scores (mean = 100; standard deviation = 15), percentile ranks, and normal curve equivalents. There is also a "Support Score" that combines the scores from the Broad Independence and the Problem Behavior areas. This score indicates the degree of support (e.g., extensive, limited, pervasive) that the individual requires based on the AAMR's levels of support services.

The SIB-R is easy to administer.

Overall, the SIB-R is easy to administer; the use of suggested starting points and basal and ceiling rules decreases the number of items that must be given. Scoring, however, can be tedious because of the number of tables that must be used. There is an automated computer scoring program that is available, however.

Technical Characteristics

Normative Sample. More than 2,100 individuals were included. The authors intended to include subjects in the same proportion as the U.S. population regarding gender, community size, race, socioeconomic status, and geographic region.

Reliability. Split-half reliability coefficients for each subscale for each of thirteen age groups were computed with the median coefficients of .74 to .78 for the subscales, .88 to .94 for the cluster scores, and .98 for the Broad Independence score. Test-retest coefficients are reported for a small sample of thirty-one children between the ages of 6 and 13. A similar pattern to the split-half coefficients emerged with the subscale coefficients lower and more variable (.83 to .97) than the clusters (.96 to .97). The Broad Independence was very high at .98. Interrater reliability with a small sample between mother and father, and teacher and teacher aide, are reported. Again, the same pattern emerges. In addition, reliabilities of the Problem Behavior Scale and the reliabilities of the SIB-R with small samples of individuals with mental retardation are reported in the manual.

Validity. The majority of the actual validity data presented in the SIB-R manual are the results of criterion-related validity studies with the original SIB. Those are generally moderate coefficients with a variety of measures. The authors do report the coefficients with the Broad Cognitive Index of the *Woodcock-Johnson–Revised.* Those were .64 to .81, .75 to .82, and .82 for the subscale scores, cluster scores, and Broad Independence, respectively. The authors also present arguments supporting its content validity and the results of several studies that demonstrate its construct validity.

Review of Relevant Research.   Although the SIB-R has been used to measure treatment effects of intervention programs (Block, 2003) and the relationship with other variables (McIntyre, Blacher, & Baker, 2002), no literature on the SIB-R was located. However, the SIB-R is very similar to the original SIB so that research on the earlier version will probably be relevant. In fact, data presented in the manual indicate that SIB–SIB-R scores correlate .97 to .99. The results of the few studies on the SIB reported in the professional literature have been relatively positive. Overall, the instrument appears to be valid and can help in making eligibility decisions. Research on the SIB-R is necessary. A brief summary of the research studies on the SIB can be found at the Earlier Research link for Chapter 8 of the Companion Website (www.prenhall.com/taylor8e).

Overview: Scales of Independent Behavior–Revised

- *Age level*—3 months to 44 years.
- *Type of administration*—Individual.
- *Technical adequacy*—Adequate standardization, good reliability (adequate for subscales), adequate validity (based on previous version).
- *Scores yielded*—Standard scores, age equivalents, percentile ranks, normal curve equivalents, stanines, several descriptive approaches.
- *Suggested use*—The SIB-R appears to be a reasonably valid instrument to aid in eligibility decisions. The technical characteristics of the instrument indicate that it is more advisable to use the cluster scores or, preferably, the Broad Independence score rather than the individual subscale scores. This is particularly true in tests of a young child or an adult for whom subscales would be of little value (e.g., work skills for infants or gross motor skills for adults).

  Several features of the test and related materials are favorable. One is a short form of the SIB-R that is designed for individuals with visual impairments. The second is the inclusion of the Early Development Scale for a quick estimate of young children's adaptive behavior. The third is the computerized scoring system that is recommended to save time and decrease the possibility of making errors. Finally, the availability of the ICAP, CALS, and ALSC provides a total adaptive behavior package to examiners.

Computerized scoring for the SIB-R is helpful.

Vineland Adaptive Behavior Scales–Second Edition

The *Vineland Adaptive Behavior Scales–Second Edition* (Vineland-II; Sparrow, Cicchetti, & Balla, 2007) is designed for use with individuals from birth through age 90. The Vineland-II has two versions that can be used separately or in combination. The first version includes two survey forms, the Survey Interview Form and the Parent/Caregiver Rating Form. There is also a

Teacher Rating Form. Note: The Teacher Rating Form is used with individuals ages 3–21.

Description.   Both survey forms assess four broad domains of adaptive behavior: Communication (Expressive, Receptive, Expressive), Daily Living Skills (Personal, Domestic, Community), Socialization (Interpersonal Relationships, Play and Leisure Time, Coping Skills), and Motor Skills (Gross, Fine). The Survey Interview Form uses a semistructured interview format in which the caregiver receives a series of prompts to elicit responses and does not have to respond to direct questions. The Parent/Caregiver Form uses a rating scale so that a direct interview is not necessary. In addition, the Survey Forms include a Maladaptive Behavior Domain. The Teacher Rating Form involves a simple rating scale and includes items that measure the same areas as the Survey Forms except that Academic replaces the Domestic subdomain and there is no Maladaptive Behavior Domain. Following is a description of each domain.

> *Communication Domain.* There are three subdomains contained in this section. These are (1) the Receptive subdomain, which measures areas such as "beginning to understand" and "listening and attending"; (2) the Expressive subdomain, with areas such as "prespeech sounds" and "articulating"; and (3) the Written subdomain, which measures reading and writing skills.
>
> *Daily Living Skills Domain.* The three subdomains in this section are (1) Personal, which measures areas such as "eating and toileting"; (2) Domestic, measuring such areas as "housecleaning and food preparation"; and (3) Community, which includes such areas as "safety and understanding money."
>
> *Socialization Domain.* The three subdomains are (1) Interpersonal Relationships (areas such as "recognizing emotions" and "initiating social communication"); (2) Play and Leisure Time (areas such as "playing with toys" and "sharing and cooperating"); and (3) Coping Skills (such as "following rules").
>
> *Motor Skills Domain.* This section includes items divided into gross-motor and fine-motor areas.
>
> *Maladaptive Behavior.* This optional domain allows for the ratings of a number of maladaptive or inappropriate behaviors, including internalizing and externalizing behaviors.

Interpretation of Results.   A variety of scores are available for the Vineland-II. These include standard scores, *v*-scale scores, percentile ranks, adaptive levels, age equivalents, and stanines. For individuals from birth through age 6, all four adaptive behavior domains are combined for an Adaptive Behavior Composite (mean = 100; SD = 15). For individuals ages 7 through 90, the Adaptive Behavior Composite does not include the Motor Skills Domain. The standard scores yielded for each Domain also have a mean of 100 and a standard deviation of 15. The *v*-scale scores are used for the subdomains and for the subscales of the Maladaptive Behavior Index. The *v*-scale scores are standard scores with a mean of 15 and a standard deviation of 3. The Adaptive Levels are descriptive categories ranging from low to high. A computerized scoring and interpretation system, *ASSIST*, is available for both the Survey Forms and the Teacher Rating Form.

Technical Characteristics

Normative Sample.   The Survey Forms were normed using a nationally representative sample of almost 3,700 individuals. The Teacher Rating Form used a representative sample of almost 2,600 individuals ages 3–18.

Reliability.   Internal-consistency (split-half) reliability coefficients were generally above .90 for the majority of the subdomains for the two Survey Forms. Test-retest reliability coefficients for subdomains and domains were generally above .85 and above .90 for the Adaptive Behavior Composites. For the Maladaptive Behavior Index, the internal-consistency coefficients ranged from .85 to .91, depending on the age range. Test-retest coefficients were generally above .85. For the Teacher Rating Form the internal-consistency coefficients for the subdomain scores were .85 or higher for over 80 percent reported. The Adaptive Behavior Composites had coefficients of .97 or higher for every age level. Test-retest coefficients for the TRF were generally in the .80s for the subdomains, the mid-80s for the domain scores, and approximately .90 for the Adaptive Behavior Composite. Interrater reliability for the TRF was noticeably lower, suggesting that teachers rate adaptive behavior differently.

Validity.   Concurrent validity coefficients with the original Vineland Adaptive Behavior Scales were in the upper .80s and .90s. Correlations with the Adaptive Behavior Assessment System–2 were considerably lower. Correlations with the WISC-III and WAIS-III were near zero, although the authors suggest that this is expected since intelligence tests and adaptive behavior tests measure different skills. Finally, modest correlations were reported between the Vineland-II and the Behavior Assessment System for Children–2. The authors also provide a discussion supporting the content and construct validity of the Survey Forms. Correlations between the TRF and the Classroom Edition from the previous Vineland were primarily .80 and higher.

Review of Relevant Research.   The original Vineland (VABS) was the most widely researched adaptive behavior scale. Much of the research focused on its use with students with autism. Some of that research is summarized below. Additional research can be found at the Earlier Research link for Chapter 8 of the Companion Website (www.prenhall.com/taylor8e). Due to the relative recency of the Vineland-II, no literature was located at the time of the completion of this book. Undoubtedly, that research will be forthcoming.

- There is preliminary support for the use of VABS profiles to identify subgroups of children with autism (Stone, Ousley, Hepburn, Hogin, & Brown, 1999).
- Cabrera, Grimes-Gaa, and Thyer (1999) noted the strong technical characteristics of the VABS and recommended its use for clinical social workers. They also noted that users should be very familiar with the methods of administering and interpreting the test.
- Scores from the socialization domain resulted in very accurate classification of children with and without autism (Gillham, Carter, Volkmar, & Sparrow, 2000) and between children and autism and children with mental retardation (Njardvik, Matson, & Cherry, 1999).
- The VABS was used to help establish the relationship of the executive function abilities of children with autism and their deficits in communication (Gilotty, Kenworthy, Sirian, Black, & Wagner 2002).

- Boelte and Poustka (2002) used the VABS to establish the relationship between adaptive behavior and IQ in individuals with autism with and without mental retardation.
- The VABS differentiated individuals with fragile X syndrome who displayed autistic behaviors from those with the syndrome without autistic behaviors (Hatton et al., 2003).
- The Expressive Communication section of the VABS was 80 percent accurate in differentiating children with autism from those with pervasive developmental disorder—not otherwise specified (Paul et al., 2004).

Overview: Vineland Adaptive Behavior Scales—Second Edition

- *Age level*—Birth through age 90.
- *Type of administration*—Individual.
- *Technical adequacy*—Good standardization, good reliability (Survey forms), inadequate interrater reliability (Teacher form), adequate to questionable validity (depending on the criterion measure).
- *Scores yielded*—Standard scores, percentiles, adaptive levels, age equivalents, stanines, and *v*-scale scores.
- *Suggested use*—The Vineland-II is probably the most widely used adaptive behavior instrument. Its standardization and technical aspects are generally good, particularly for the Survey forms. The Vineland-II added many new items to make it appropriate for adults and more sensitive with young children. The Survey Interview form uses a semistructured interview format, whereas the Parent/Caregiver form requires the respondent to complete the form in writing using a three-point scale. Both forms can take up to an hour to administer. According to the manual, the Vineland-II can be used for diagnostic evaluations, developmental evaluations, progress monitoring, program planning, and research purposes. In general, the Survey forms are recommended over the Teacher form.

Additional Adaptive Behavior Instruments

In addition to the instruments previously described, there are others that are used for specific purposes. One instrument, the ABAS–2, is designed to measure the adaptive skill areas noted in the 1992 and 2002 AAMR definition of mental retardation. Some instruments are used more for screening purposes (e.g. N-ABC, K-FAST). Others measure unique aspects of adaptive behavior (e.g., RISA). A brief description of these instruments follows.

Adaptive Behavior Assessment System—Second Edition

- *Age level*—5 to 89 years.
- *Type of administration*—Individual.
- *Technical adequacy*—Good standardization, validity, and reliability.
- *Scores yielded*—Scale scores for ten areas, general adaptive composites, age equivalents.
- *Suggested use*—The Adaptive Behavior Assessment System–2 (ABAS-2; Harrison & Oakland, 2003) addresses the ten adaptive skill areas noted in the 1992 AAMR definition of mental retardation. It also incorporates the three

general areas of adaptive behavior, conceptual, social, and practical, from the 2002 AAMR definition, as the instrument was updated only 3 years after its initial publication (Rust & Wallace, 2004). There are several forms for the ABAS-2: Parent and Teacher for individuals ages birth to 5 and 5 to 21 and an Adult form for older individuals. The Adult form can be self-administered or completed by a caretaker. Boney (2003) suggested the use of multiple informants rather than just one. One notable feature is a series of validity studies with the *Wechsler Scales.* A computerized scoring system is also available.

Kaufman Functional Academic Skills Test

- *Age level*—15 to 85+ years.
- *Type of administration*—Individual.
- *Technical adequacy*—Adequate reliability and validity.
- *Scores yielded*—Standard scores, percentile ranks, descriptive categories.
- *Suggested use*—The *Kaufman Functional Academic Skills Test* (K-FAST; Kaufman & Kaufman, 1995) is a quick measure of functional arithmetic and reading skills. One somewhat unique feature of the K-FAST is that it requires the individual to actually perform each skill (rather than have an informant provide the information). The skills are those that are required in everyday activities outside the classroom (e.g., following directions in a recipe, understanding signs). The test provides scores for Arithmetic, Reading, and a Functional Academic Composite. It was also co-normed with the *Kaufman Brief Intelligence Test.* Thus, a screening measure of both intelligence and functional academics can be obtained using the same normative group. Overall, the K-FAST appears to be a good screening measure for the functional academics component of adaptive behavior. It should also be noted that the K-FAST has been shown to have moderate to strong correlations with more traditional achievement tests such as the *Wide Range Achievement Test–3* (Flanagan, McGrew, Abramowitz, & Untiedt, 1997; Klimczak, Bradford, Burright, & Donovick, 2000).

Normative Adaptive Behavior Checklist

- *Age level*—Infancy to 21 years.
- *Type of administration*—Individual (questionnaire).
- *Scores yielded*—Standard scores, age equivalents.
- *Technical adequacy*—Good reliability, adequate validity; standardized on more than 6,000 individuals.
- *Description and suggested use*—The *Normative Adaptive Behavior Checklist* (N-ABC; Adams, 1986) includes more than 100 items that measure the areas of self-help, home living, independent living, social, sensorimotor, and language and academic skills. It can be used to provide a quick, reliable estimate of a person's adaptive behavior. If a person scores low on the N-ABC, an extended, much longer version, the *Comprehensive Test of Adaptive Behavior,* can be administered to provide more specific information.

Responsibility and Independence Scale for Adolescents

- *Age level*—12 through 19 years.
- *Type of administration*—Individual.
- *Technical adequacy*—Generally acceptable.

- *Scores yielded*—Standard scores, percentile ranks.
- *Suggested use*—The *Responsibility and Independence Scale for Adolescents* (RISA; Salvia, Neisworth, & Schmidt, 1990) is uniquely designed to focus on higher level adaptive behavior skills in older students. It can be used with individuals with mild disabilities or those with no disabilities. As the title suggests, the RISA measures responsibility and independence areas such as money management, transportation skills, career development, self-management, and social communication. Although the RISA is not appropriate for all students, it does serve a useful purpose.

BACK TO THE PROFILES

Possible Answers to the Questions

1. **Why assess Mike?** Ms. Capella is faced with somewhat conflicting information. On the one hand, there is information (e.g., low IQ, poor academic skills) that suggests that Mike might have mental retardation. On the other hand, there also is evidence of environmental factors that might explain it as well as information suggesting that he can function adequately in nonschool environments. The issue of Mike's aggression also needs to be considered. Ms. Capella's first step would be to obtain prereferral assessment data and to design and implement a program. Assuming that this program was not effective, she would refer Mike for eligibility determination, which would require an adaptive behavior assessment based on the referral information. Thus, the purpose for the assessment is twofold: to gather prereferral information and to help determine eligibility.

2. **Who should assess Mike?** The prereferral assessment information would be collected by Ms. Capella. This probably would involve informal assessment of his academic areas to help gather information to develop the prereferral intervention program. It is also possible that a special education teacher might consult with Ms. Capella to assist in the assessment and development of the program. The administration of the adaptive behavior scale used to help determine eligibility for special education would depend on the policies and resources of the particular school district. For example, large school districts might employ social workers to work with the parents and gather the information. Others, however, might require that the school psychologist, psychometrist, or special education personnel administer the test.

3. **What procedure(s)/test(s) should be used?** Chapters 4, 5, and 12 through 14 provide information about the possible procedures that would be used to gather prereferral assessment information for the different academic areas. This might involve observation, criterion-referenced or curriculum-based assessment, and error analysis, among others. For determination of eligibility, the test chosen will, in part, be based on the definition of mental retardation used by a specific state. If a general adaptive behavior deficit is used as a criterion, then the Survey Interview form of the Vineland-II, the AAMR ABS-S:2, or the SIB-R could be used. The choice will largely depend on the amount of training of the individual who will administer it. For example, the semistructured interview of the Vineland-II requires more training than the multiple-choice format of the SIB-R. If a state has adopted the AAMR definition of mental retardation that specifies deficits in specific adaptive skill areas, then the ABAS-2 should be used.

4. **What other areas (if any) should be assessed?** In most states, eligibility criteria for a student like Mike also would require an individually administered intelligence test and a general achievement test (the latter to document that an educational need exists).

1. **Why assess Tamika?** The reason for Tamika's evaluation would be to gather more specific information to help develop Tamika's sequential teaching objectives.

2. **Who should assess Tamika?** As with Mike, the answer to this question will largely depend on the policies and resources of Tamika's school district. In fact, the answer to "who should assess" might drive the decision of which test to use. It would make sense that, if possible, one or both teachers should be involved.

3. **What procedures should be used?** Most adaptive behavior scales do not provide specific enough information to develop small sequential objectives. For example, the AAMR ABS-2, the Vineland-II, the ABI, and the SIBS-R would probably not be the best choice. One possibility might be the use of the criterion-referenced Checklist of Adaptive Living Skills and the associated Adaptive Living Skills Curriculum (parts of the SIBS-R package). Yet another possibility would be to administer the appropriate skill sequences from a commercially prepared criterion-referenced developmental inventory. An instrument such as the *Behavior Characteristics Progression–Revised* (see Chapter 15) would be appropriate.

4. **What other areas (if any) should be assessed?** The vignette does not really indicate that any other areas need to be assessed.

STUDENT PROFILE DATA

Mike

Mike's mother was administered the Scales of Independent Behavior–Revised. The following results were obtained:

Cluster	Standard Score
Motor	90
Social Interaction and Communication	68
Personal Living Skills	78
Community Living Skillls	80
Broad Independence	77

These results indicate that Mike is about 1½ standard deviations below average in overall adaptive behavior. His relative strength is motor skills, and his lowest area is social interaction and communication, which includes social interaction, language comprehension, and language expression. Based on Mike's background and his adaptive behavior scores, it was decided that the next step should be a prereferral intervention program that should be carefully monitored. Based on those results, a decision will be made on whether to pursue additional testing.

CASE STUDY *June*

Should June be given an adaptive behavior assessment? Why or Why not?

Reflections

1. Why do you think adaptive behavior is such a difficult concept to define and measure?
2. What are the advantages and disadvantages of using a parent (as opposed to a teacher) as the informant on an adaptive behavior scale such as the Vineland-II or the AAMR ABS-2?
3. Why is knowing the mode of administration (e.g., interview vs. direct observation) important when choosing an adaptive behavior instrument?

Summary Matrix

Instrument or Technique	Prereferral		Suggested Use (Postreferral)					Target Population						Special Considerations	Educational Relevance for Exceptional Students
	Screening and Initial Identification	Informal Determination and Evaluation of Teaching Programs and Strategies	Determination of Current Performance Level and Educational Need	Decisions about Classification and Program Placement	IEP Goals	IEP Objectives	IEP Evaluation	Mild/Moderate	Severe/Profound	Preschool	Elementary Age	Secondary Age	Adult		
Adaptive Behavior Inventory			X	X	X			X		X	X	X		Easy to administer and score; there is a shorter version for screening purposes.	Useful
AAMR Adaptive Behavior Scale–Second Edition: Residential and Community Edition			X	X	X			X	X	X	X	X	X	Technical aspects of Part Two have been questioned; has limited use for individuals with severe disabilities.	Useful
AAMR Adaptive Behavior Scale–Second Edition: School Edition			X	X	X			X		X	X	X		Potentially useful instrument to aid in classification and placement decisions.	Useful
Scales of Independent Behavior–Revised			X	X	X			X	X	X	X	X	X	There is a screening version, criterion-referenced instrument, and a curriculum that are associated with the SIB-R.	Useful
Vineland Adaptive Behavior Scales–Second Edition			X	X	X	X	X	X	X	X	X	X	X	A useful instrument for the overall measurement of adaptive behavior.	Very Useful
Adaptive Behavior Assessment System–Second Edition			X	X	X			X	X	X	X	X	X	Co-normed with the Wechsler Scales; measures the adaptive skill areas in the AAMR definition.	Useful
Kaufman Functional Academics Skills Test	X							X				X	X	Provides a measure of functional reading and math performance.	Useful
Normative Adaptive Behavior Checklist	X				X			X		X	X	X		Can be used in conjunction with the Comprehensive Test of Adaptive Behavior.	Useful
Responsibility and Independence Scale for Adolescents	X				X			X				X		Designed for individuals with milder disabilities.	Useful

chapter nine

Assessment of Behavioral and Emotional Status

included
IN THIS CHAPTER

Behavior-Rating Scales and Behavior Assessment Systems

Classroom/Home Behavior Instruments
Achenbach System of Empirically Based Assessment
Behavior Assessment System for Children–2
The Devereux Behavior Rating Scale–School Form

Additional Classroom/Home Behavior Instruments
Behavior and Emotional Rating Scale–2
Emotional or Behavior Disorder Scale–Revised
Revised Behavior Problem Checklist

Social Skills Instruments
Social Skills Rating System
Walker-McConnell Scale of Social Competence and School Adjustment

AD/HD Instruments
Attention Deficit Disorders Evaluation Scale–2
ADD-H Comprehensive Teacher's Rating Scale (Second Edition)
Attention Deficit/Hyperactivity Disorder Test
Clinical Assessment of Attention Deficit–Child
Diagnostic Assessment Scales for Attention Deficit/Hyperactivity Disorder

Autism Instruments
Autism Screening Instrument for Educational Planning–2
Childhood Autism Rating Scale
Gilliam Autism Rating Scale-2

Measurement of Emotional Status
Projective Methods
Personality Inventories

STUDENT PROFILE

Tara

Tara is a 6-year-old girl from a single-parent household whose main source of support is welfare. She was sometimes left alone all day when her mother was able to get a temporary job as a housekeeper and never had any type of preschool program. Her mother noted that Tara was often aggressive and noncompliant at home, although she was not overly concerned. When Tara started kindergarten, she immediately began to have problems with her teacher and her peers. She would steal things, ignore teacher requests, become extremely agitated, and talk back to everyone, always having to have the last word. Her teacher, Ms. Duffy, became frustrated and talked with the school psychologist to help her develop a behavior management program. Unfortunately, that program, implemented for three weeks, was not successful. Ms. Duffy tried to discuss the problems with Tara's mother but could never arrange a meeting.

STUDENT PROFILE

Anna

Anna is a sixth-grade student who recently began to throw temper tantrums during some of her classes at the middle school that she attends. At times, the tantrums lead to verbal aggression and sometimes physical aggression. Her mother reported that she thought Anna was moodier than usual and "wasn't acting like herself." No significant events had happened at home that would explain her change in behavior. Her parents were told by their friends that Anna was "just being a teenager," but they were still concerned. When Anna was sent home for fighting during lunch, her parents and the school requested an evaluation.

Think about These Questions as You Read This Chapter:

1. Why assess Tara and Anna? (There could be more than one reason.)

2. Who should assess Tara and Anna? (There could be more than one person.)
3. What procedure(s)/test(s) should be used?
4. What other area(s) (if any) should be assessed?

(Suggested answers appear at the end of this chapter.)

In recent years, there has been increasing interest in the measurement of an individual's emotional and behavioral status. This can be traced to three specific issues. First, the importance and relevance of *social skill development* has become more recognized in the past decade. Second, *autism* was recognized by the Individuals with Disabilities Education Act (IDEA) as a separate disability area; subsequently, there has been a search for reliable methods of screening and identifying children with this condition. Third, although not officially noted as a disability area under IDEA, *attention-deficit/hyperactivity disorder* (AD/HD) remains a highly visible topic within the field of special education. A number of instruments have been developed to help identify children with AD/HD.

Most instruments that measure emotional and behavioral status involve the *indirect measurement* of emotional status or the *direct measurement* of behavior. Measurement of an individual's emotional state usually requires a great deal of inference and subjectivity on the part of the examiner. On the other hand, standardized measures of classroom behavior usually involve direct observation documented by some type of behavior-rating scale. Another option is a behavior assessment system, which includes a behavior rating scale but involves multiple informants.

Both indirect measurement and direct measurement are included.

Behavior-Rating Scales and Behavior Assessment Systems

Why Use Behavior-Rating Scales and Behavior Assessment Systems?

Screening and identification; decisions about eligibility and program placement; establishment of IEP goals.

Who Should Use Them?

Teachers, school psychologists, parents.

Behavior-rating scales are concerned with documenting observable behavior. Typically, these scales are developed for use by the classroom teacher or some other individual who has an opportunity to observe the examinee. Like personality inventories (discussed later in this chapter), behavior-rating scales usually include items grouped according to some categorical characteristic. Theoretically, the grouping of items leads to a profile of a student's behavior patterns. Behavior-rating scales have been criticized, however, on a number of grounds. For example, the technical adequacy of many scales has been questioned. Also, the educational significance of their results is limited. As an example of their limitations, Bracken, Keith, and Walker (1998) reviewed the technical characteristics of the most popular behavior-rating scales and reported that none met their minimum standards for interrater reliability. Similarly, Nickerson and Nagle (2001) noted that low interrater reliability is common for behavior rating scales. Merrell (2000), however, argued that there has been increased acceptance of behavior-rating scales and that technical advances have been made. In addition, Hinshaw and Nigg (1999) noted that for the most part behavior-rating scales have good-to-excellent reliability and are capable of differentiating clinical from comparison samples. They pointed out, however, that a more difficult criterion is a scale's ability to differentiate clinical groups from one another.

Another concern is the well-documented fact that different informants (e.g., teacher and parent) rate the same child differently (Child Assessment News, 1997). For example, Hart and Lahey (1999) reported that the agreement between parent and teacher ratings is generally low, with a correlation of only approximately .30 to .40. What is unclear is which rating is the most accurate. Does the parent have a bias, or simply more opportunity to observe behaviors? Does the child actually behave differently in the two settings? This shows the need to obtain additional information and not to rely solely on the test scores from behavior-rating scales. One solution is to use a behavior assessment system that involves multiple raters. These instruments are more comprehensive and contain multiple components.

In this chapter, the discussion of behavior-rating scales and behavior assessment systems will focus on (1) classroom/home behavior instruments, (2) social skills instruments, (3) AD/HD instruments, and (4) autism instruments.

Classroom/Home Behavior Instruments

Achenbach System of Empirically Based Assessment

The Achenbach System of Empirically Based Assessment (ASEBA; Achenbach, 1991, 1997, 2000, 2001, 2003, 2007) is an integrated set of forms including the popular Child Behavior Checklists designed for parent use. Other components of the ASEBA include measures of teacher ratings, direct observation, interviews, and self-report. The behavior checklists have been extended to include individuals from ages 1½ to 30. A brief description of the components follows.

Description

Child Behavior Checklist and Young Adult Behavior Checklists. These checklists are administered to parents to determine their child's social competency and problem behaviors. There are two separate Child Behavior Checklists (CBCL). One is for ages 1½ to 5. The CBCL/1½–5 measures six cross-informant syndromes: Emotionally Reactive, Anxious/Depressed, Somatic Complaints, Withdrawn, Attention Problems, Aggressive Behavior, and Sleep Problems. Scores for Internalizing, Externalizing, and Total Problems are available as well as a Language Development Survey. A CBCL for ages 6 through 18 is also available. The areas measured are slightly different from the CBCL/1½–5. These are Anxious/Depressed, Withdrawn, Somatic Complaints, Social Problems, Thought Problems, Attention Problems, Aggressive, and Delinquent. Internalizing, Externalizing, and Total Problems are also available as well as Social Competence Scales. There are separate profiles for boys and girls. The Young Adult Behavior Checklist (YABCL) includes scales for Aggressive Behavior, Anxious/Depressed, Attention Problems, Delinquent Behavior, Intrusive, Somatic Complaints, Thought

There are separate profiles for boys and girls.

Problems, and Withdrawn. Adaptive Functioning Scales as well as Internalizing, Externalizing, and Total Problems are included. There also is an Adult Behavior checklist (ages 18–59) and an Older Adult Behavior Checklist (ages 60–90+).

Caregiver-Teacher Report Form (1½–5) and Teacher Report Form (5–18).   Content for these forms closely resembles the content of the CBCL/1½–5 and the CBCL/4–18. However, items have been added that are more teacher related. For example, the TRF provides separate scores for Inattention and Hyperactivity/ Impulsivity.

Direct Observation Form.   The Direct Observation Form is designed for ages 5 to 14. It requires the evaluator to observe the child in ten-minute time samples and then respond to ninety-six items that yield a behavior problem score and an on-task score.

Youth Self-Report and Young Adult Self-Report.   The YSR and YASR essentially mirror the items from the CBCL and the YABC with the items written to reflect the first person: There are several general questions (e.g., "Please list any jobs or chores that you have") and other items (e.g., "I show off or clown") that must be rated "not true," "sometimes true," or "very true." There is also an Adult Self-Report and an Older Adult Self-Report.

Semistructured Clinical Interview for Children and Adolescents.   The SCICA is designed for experienced interviewers working with individuals ages 6 to 18. It includes a series of questions and probes as well as forms to rate the behaviors during the interview. Scoring profiles are available for ages 6 to 12.

Interpretation of Results.   Results of the CBCL, YABCL, and other components are interpreted through the use of the various profiles. The profile shown in Figure 9.1 shows the "normal range" of performance that is based on the T-scores (mean = 50; standard deviation = 10) yielded. Profiles are also interpreted as "borderline" or "clinical." A helpful feature is the Assessment Data Manager, a software program that scores the ASEBA and allows for multisource data comparisons.

A software program generates a visual graph.

Technical Characteristics

Normative Sample.   The CBCL was normed on 2,368 children. Scales were devised from parents' ratings of 4,455 clinically referred children. The YABCL used 1,074 parents.

Reliability.   Interrater reliabilities were primarily in the .90s for the CBCL and from the .70s to the .90s for the Direct Observation Form. Test-retest coefficients were in the .80s to .90s for the Teacher Report Form.

Validity.   Results of several validity studies are reported in the manual. These generally demonstrate moderate correlations with other behavior-rating scales and the instruments' ability to identify children who have been referred for mental health services.

Review of Relevant Research.   Research reported in the professional literature has focused on the various components of the ASEBA. The test publisher has stated that the ASEBA has been used in over 3,500 research studies in fifty countries.

The components of the ASEBA have been widely researched.

FIGURE 9.1 Example of CBCL and Revised Behavior Profile for Boys

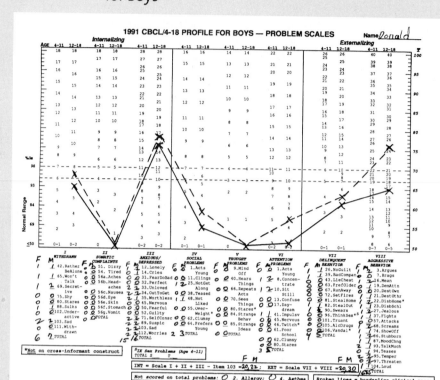

Note: The current version can be found in the *Manual for the ASEBA School-Age Forms and Profiles* (Achenbach & Rescorla, 2001). Additional information can be obtained at www .ASEBA.org.

Source: T. M. Achenbach. *Child Behavior Checklist.* Copyright © 1991 by T. M. Achenbach. Reproduced by permission.

The vast majority of these studies, however, have used it as an outcome measure and have not studied its strengths and weaknesses specifically.

The majority of published research on the ASEBA itself has focused on establishing the validity and reliability of its various components. In general, the technical characteristics of the ASEBA have been favorable. There are also many articles that describe and review the various components of the ASEBA. Examples of research over the past five years follow. Additional summaries can be found at the Earlier Research link for Chapter 9 on the Companion Website (www.prenhall.com/taylor8e).

- Connor-Smith and Compas (2003) found that the CBCL and the YSR were effective in identifying anxiety and mood disorders based on DSM-IV criteria.
- A French-Canadian translation of the YSR was developed and was highly correlated with the English version. However, French-English bilingual adolescents reported more internalizing problems on the French version than the English version (Wyss, Voelker, Cornock, & Hakim-Larson, 2003).
- Adolescents reported more delinquent behavior on the YSR than were acknowledged by parents on the CBCL and by probation records, suggesting that adolescents are truthful when completing the scale (Cashel, 2003).

- The CBCL was effective in differentiating two types of conduct disorders: aggressive behavior and delinquent behavior (Tackett, Krueger, Sawyer, & Graetz, 2003).
- The CBCL has been criticized because it is illness-oriented and requires raters to determine what a child is thinking or feeling (Bulotsky-Shearer & Fantuzzo, 2004).
- The CBCL (administered to parents) and the YSR (administered to adolescents) were used to predict the behavioral outcome of the adolescents four years later. Several discrepancy scores between the two instruments were significant predictors of poor outcome (Ferdinand, van der Ende, & Verhulst, 2004).
- Rescorla (2005) reported that the ASEBA "provides user-friendly, cost-effective, reliable, and valid procedures" when used to assess the emotional/behavioral problems of preschool children.

Overview: Achenbach System of Empirically Based Assessment

- *Age level*—1½ to 30 years.
- *Type of administration*—Individual.
- *Technical adequacy*—Generally good reliability and validity.
- *Scores yielded*—T-scores (type of standard score); results are placed on a Behavior Profile.
- *Suggested use*—Overall, the ASEBA is one of the better behavior-assessment systems available. Items were carefully selected and statistically validated. The idea of separate profiles (with different scales included) for boys and girls at different age levels is an excellent one. In addition, the use of separate forms that allow multiple ratings provides potentially important information. The ASEBA is continually updated through ongoing research by the author. This is advantageous, but it requires test users to keep up with the latest versions of the instruments. Overall, the ASEBA can be used confidently to document the behavioral status of students in a variety of areas. One drawback is that the manual is not "user friendly."

The ASEBA has many positive features.

Behavior Assessment System for Children–2

The *Behavior Assessment System for Children–2* (BASC-2; Reynolds & Kamphaus, 2004) is a multidimensional approach for evaluating the behavior of individuals ages 2 to 25. The BASC-2 includes five separate components that can be used individually or in combination. These are the Teacher Rating Scales (TRS), the Parent Rating Scales (PRS), the Self-Report of Personality (SRP), the Structured Developmental History (SDH), and the Student Observation System (SOS). The BASC-2 is considered multidimensional because it measures many different aspects of behavior and personality.

The BASC-2 has five components.

Description

Teacher Rating Scales.   Three separate forms for the TRS are designed for different age levels. These are the preschool form (ages 2–6), the child form (ages 6–11), and the adolescent form (ages 12–18). Each form can be completed in about ten to twenty minutes. Each of the forms has five composites composed of fourteen separate scales. In addition, an overall composite called the Behavioral Symptoms Index is available. A description of each scale and a representative item in each scale are presented next. The scales are grouped according to their corresponding composites.

Externalizing Problems

Aggression (all forms). "Argues when denied own way."

Hyperactivity (all forms). "Cannot wait to take turns."

Conduct Disorders (Child and Adolescent Forms). "Has friends who are in trouble."

School Problems

Attitude to School (Child and Adolescent Forms). "I don't like thinking about school."

Attitude to Teachers (Child and Adolescent Forms). "Teachers make me feel stupid."

Sensation Seeking (Adolescent Form only). "I like to be the first one to try new things."

Internalizing Problems

Atypicality (all forms). "Sometimes when I am alone I hear my name."

Locus of Control (all forms). "I can't seem to control what happens to me."

Social Stress (all forms). "I am lonely."

Anxiety (all forms). "I feel guilty about things."

Depression (all forms). "No one understands me."

Sense of Inadequacy (all forms). "When I take tests I cannot think."

Somatization (Adolescent and College forms). "My muscles get sore a lot."

Behavior Symptoms Index

Atypicality (all forms). "Hears sounds that are not there."

Withdrawal (all forms). "Avoids other children/adolescents."

Attention Problems (all forms). "Gives up easily when learning something new."

Adaptive Skills

Adaptability (all forms). "Objects to change in routine."

Leadership (all forms). "Attends afterschool activities."

Social Skills (all forms). "Congratulates others when good things happen to them."

Study Skills (all forms). "Asks to make up missed assignments."

Functional Communication (all forms). "Has difficulty explaining rules of games to others."

The TRS and PRS are conceptually similar.

Parent Rating Scales.   The PRS also provides for a comprehensive evaluation of the child's adaptive and problem behaviors. It uses the same response format as the TRS and also takes approximately the same amount of time to complete (ten to twenty minutes). The areas are similar to the TRS with the exception of the School Problem Composite and the Learning Problems and Study Skills Scales, which are not included in the PRS. Also, the Attention Problem scale is included in the Behavior Symptoms Index and Activities of Daily Living Skills replaces Study Skills in the Adaptive Skills Composite.

Self-Report of Personality.   The SRP has three forms for three different age levels: The Child form (ages 8–11), the Adolescent form (ages 12–18), and the College form (ages 18–25). The Child form has fourteen scales, the Adolescent form has fifteen, and the College form has thirteen (see Table 9.1). Some of the items in the SRP are answered as true or false and others are rated on a four-point scale (never, sometimes, often, always). The composites and corresponding scales as well as representative items are listed below.

The SRP uses both a four-point scale and a true-false format.

> **School Problems**
> *Attitude to School* (Child and Adolescent Forms). "I don't like thinking about school."

TABLE 9.1   Composites, Primary Scales, and Content Scales in the SRP

Scale	C 8–11	A 12–21	COL 18–25
Composite			
Emotional Symptoms Index	•	•	•
Inattention/Hyperactivity	•	•	•
Personal Adjustment	•	•	•
School Problems	•	•	
Primary Scale			
Alcohol Abuse			•
Anxiety	•	•	•
Attention Problems	•	•	•
Attitude to School	•	•	
Attitude to Teachers	•	•	
Atypicality	•	•	•
Depression	•	•	•
Hyperactivity	•	•	•
Interpersonal Relations	•	•	•
Locus of Control	•	•	•
Relations of Parents	•	•	•
School Adjustment			•
Self-Esteem	•	•	•
Self-Reliance	•	•	•
Sensation Seeking		•	•
Sensation of Inadequacy	•	•	•
Social Stress	•	•	•
Somatization		•	•
Content Scale			
Anger Control		•	•
Ego Strength		•	•
Mania		•	•
Test Anxiety		•	•
Number of Items	139	176	185

Note: Shaded cells represent new scales added to the BASC-2.

Source: C. Reynolds and R. Kamphaus. *Behavior Assessment System for Children–2.* Copyright © 2004 by American Guidance Service, Circle Pines, MN. Reprinted with permission.

Attitude to Teachers (Child and Adolescent Forms). "Teachers make me feel stupid."

Sensation Seeking (Adolescent Form). "I like to be the first one to try new things."

Internalizing Problems

Atypicality (all forms). "Sometimes I want to hurt myself."

Locus of Control (all forms). "I get blamed for things I can't help."

Social Stress (all forms). "I am left out of things."

Anxiety (all forms). "I feel guilty about things."

Depression (all forms). "I feel sad."

Sense of Inadequacy (all forms). "I am disappointed with my grades."

Somatization (College Form). "My muscles get sore a lot."

Inattention/Hyperactivity

Attention problems (all forms). "I forget things."

Hyperactivity (all forms). "I have trouble sitting still."

Personal Adjustment

Relations with Parents (all forms). "My parents are easy to talk to."

Interpersonal Relations (all forms). "My classmates make fun of me."

Self-Esteem (all forms). "I like the way I look."

Self-Reliance (all forms). "I can solve difficult problems by myself."

Structured Developmental History.   The SDH can either be completed directly by a parent using a questionnaire or by an examiner through an interview with the parent or guardian. The SDH allows for an extensive history of developmental and medical factors that could have an effect on the child's current behavior.

Student Observation System.   The SOS form allows for the direct observation of the student in a classroom setting. It uses a momentary time sampling procedure (see Chapter 4 for a discussion of this procedure). It allows for the observation of both positive and negative behaviors.

> The SOS uses momentary time sampling.

Interpretation of Results.   Each item of the TRS and PRS is rated on a four-point scale from "never" to "almost always." These raw scores can then be converted to T-scores (standard score with a mean of 50 and a standard deviation of 10) and percentile ranks. These scores are available for each scale as well as the composite areas noted above (the exception is the Other Problems composite). In addition, a computer scoring program allows the examiner to enter and score the results in five minutes. A behavior profile is available to display the results visually (see Figure 9.2). The SRP provides T-scores and percentile ranks for the Clinical Maladjustment, School Maladjustment, and Personal Adjustment composites as well as each individual scale. In addition, an Emotional Symptoms Index is available that combines the scores from several scales to give an overall indication of the individual's emotional status. There are also three types of validity scores to determine if the person is "faking bad" or "faking good," or if he or she consistently chooses nonsensical items. The SDH and SOS provide additional information but are not scored in the traditional sense. The authors provide detailed information on the steps to follow in interpreting the results of the TRS, PRS, and SRP.

FIGURE 9.2 Summary Page of a TRS

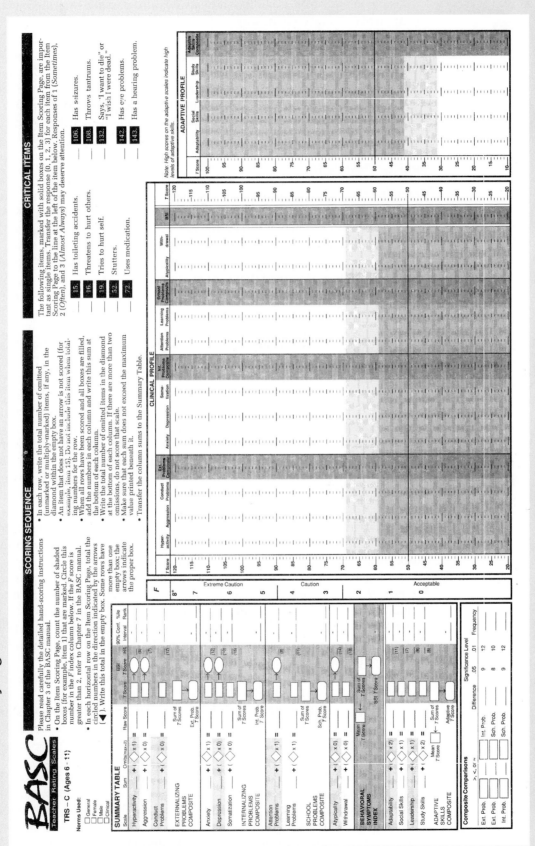

Using the BASC-2 Assist Plus software it is also possible to print out an interpretation of several "content scales." For the TRS and PRS these scales are Anger Control, Bullying, Developmental Social Disorders, Emotional Self-Control, Executive Functioning, Negative Emotionality, and Resiliency. For the SRP the content scales are Anger Control, Ego Strength, Mania, and Test Anxiety (also see Table 9.1). The software also allows for the comparison of up to three different reports to monitor progress as well as a multirater feature that allows a simultaneous comparison of up to five different administrations, which would assist in comparing ratings across settings.

Technical Characteristics

Normative Sample.   The BASC-2 has both general and clinical norms. The general norms included a total of more than 13,000 for the TRS, PRS, and SRP collectively. The subjects were chosen on the basis of sex, mother's educational level, geographical region, race/ethnicity, and the presence of a disability, based on the 2000 census. The clinical norms were made up of children ages 4 through 18 whose parents had identified them as having one or more emotional, behavioral, or physical problems. The clinical norms were based on a combined total of over 5,000 individuals.

Reliability.   The internal consistency reliability coefficients for the TRS scales ranged from a median of .84 (ages 2 and 3) to .88 (ages 4 through 11) for the general norms, and was .85 for the clinical norms. Coefficients for the composites were generally in the low to the mid .90s for the general norms and the high .80s to the mid .90s for the clinical norms. Test-retest reliability was computed using a relatively small sample. The median coefficients ranged from .79 (Adolescent form) to .88 (Child form). The coefficients for the composites were generally in the .80s with the exception of the Child form for which the majority were in the .90s. Interrater reliability coefficients were considerably lower with the median coefficients ranging from .52 (Adolescent form) to .69 (Preschool form).

Median internal consistency reliabilities for the PRS scales ranged from .80 to .86. Coefficients for the composites were primarily in the low to mid .90 range for the general norms. For the clinical norms the median scores for the scales ranged from .85 to .87 and the composites coefficients were primarily in the mid .90s. Test-retest coefficients ranged from .76 (Preschool form) to .84 (Child form). Interrater reliability median coefficients ranged from .76 to .79. Test-retest reliability coefficients for the composites were primarily in the .80 to .90 range. Interrater reliability coefficients for the composites were primarily in the .70s and .80s.

Internal reliability coefficients for the SRP ranged from .79 to .83 for the general norms and .77 to .82 for the clinical norms. For the composites, the correlations were primarily in the .80s and .90s for both the general norms and the clinical norms. Test-retest coefficients ranged from .73 (Child form) to .83 (College form).

Validity.   Content validity for the TRS, PRS, and SRP was maximized by the authors during test development by matching the test content to standard diagnostic systems such as the DSM IV-TE, to expert opinion, and to the perception of teachers, parents, and children. Construct validity was reported using intercorrelations of the scales and factor analysis. Criterion-related validity was determined through correlations with the *Achenbach System of Empirically Based*

Assessment, the *Connors Rating Scales* and the original BASC. The correlations vary considerably with the majority in the low to moderate range. Not surprisingly, the highest correlations were recorded between the BASC-2 and the BASC. The SRI was also correlated with the *Connors-Wells Adolescent Self-Report Scale,* the *Children's Depression Inventory,* the *Revised Children's Manifest Anxiety Scale,* the *Brief Symptom Index,* the *Beck Depression Inventory–II,* and the *Minnesota Multiphasic Personality Inventory–II.* The majority of those correlations were in the .40 to .60 range.

Review of Relevant Research.   Because of the recency of the publication of the BASC-2, no literature was located. The BASC-2 was reviewed favorably. Tan (2007) noted that it is a comprehensive instrument that can enhance assessment of behavior for various educational decisions. In addition, research on, and reviews of, the original BASC do exist. Because of the similarities between the BASC and BASC-2 that research might have relevance, although research on the BASC-2 should be forthcoming. Research on, and particularly reviews of, the BASC were generally favorable. For the most part, the technical characteristics were reported to be good and the multiple sources of information were valued. The TRS and PRS, in particular, seem to have support for their use. The BASC appears to be an instrument with many clinical uses. Recent studies and reviews are summarized below. Additional summaries are available at the Earlier Research link for Chapter 9 on the Companion Website (www.prenhall.com/taylor8e).

- Mothers and teachers rated children with ADHD differently on the parent and teacher rating scales from the BASC (Schwean, Burt, & Saklofske, 1999).
- In a review of the BASC, Hart and Lahey (1999) felt that the advantages were its inclusion of positive items and the use of scales that are clinically relevant and consistent. The disadvantage noted was its lengthier administration time than other behavior rating scales.
- Barton (2000) reported that the BASC was not effective in predicting the presence or absence of depression in adolescents with ADHD.
- The BASC was an effective instrument with children with Asperger's syndrome. In fact, the self-report portion was completed with little difficulty (Barnhill et al., 2000)
- Merydith (2001) found that teacher's ratings of externalizing and attention problems were more stable than the parent's ratings on the BASC.

Overview: Behavior Assessment System for Children–2

- *Age level*—2 to 25 years.
- *Type of administration*—Individual.
- *Technical adequacy*—Good standardization (general norms), adequate standardization (clinical norms), varied reliability (depending on component), adequate validity.
- *Scores yielded*—T-scores, percentile ranks.
- *Suggested use*—The BASC-2 has incorporated many positive features of other instruments. For example, it has several components, including a teacher rating scale, a parent rating scale, and a self-report of personality. It also has different forms for different ages and considers the internalizing/externalizing dichotomy of behavior. There is some evidence that the Teacher Rating Scales and the Parent Rating Scales may be

Several components are
available in Spanish.

more useful than the Self-Report of Personality, the Structured Developmental History, and the Student Observation System. Other components of the BASC-2 are a Spanish version of the Parent Rating Scales, the SDH, the child form of the SRP, and the BASC Monitor for ADHD. The latter component includes both Teacher and Parent Ratings and can be administered in approximately five minutes. One unique feature of the original BASC is a forum via the Internet that allows users of the instrument to interact with other users as well as the authors of the test. In addition, a current bibliography of research on the original BASC is available. There are two computer software packages available for scoring the BASC: the BASC Enhanced Assist for general scoring and reporting purposes and the BASC Plus for more in-depth analysis. A parent feedback report is also available, as is the BASC-2 Portable Observation System, which allows users to conduct behavioral observations using their PDA or laptop computer and also includes the SOS form.

The Devereux Behavior Rating Scale–School Form

The *Devereux Behavior Rating Scale–School Form* (DBRS-SF; Naglieri, LeBuffe, & Pfeiffer, 1993) is the most recent revision of the *Devereux Behavior Rating Scales* that date to the 1960s. According to the authors, the DBRS-SF can be used for a variety of purposes, including the identification of individuals who need more in-depth behavioral evaluation and the determination of which specific aspects of behavior might be more atypical for an individual than for others. The instrument can also be used to identify problem behaviors and to monitor and evaluate behavioral changes over time. The DBRS-SF actually contains two levels or versions corresponding to the age groups 5 to 12 years and 12 to 18 years. Although some of the items were selected from previous Devereux Scales, the 1993 revision is considerably different from its predecessors. For each age level of the DBRS-SF there are four subscales (each with ten items) that correspond to the criteria listed in IDEA regarding the identification of emotional disturbance. The DBRS-SF is also available online through the Psychological Corporation's Assessment Center. This service makes it possible to order, administer, and score several instruments, including the Devereux, online. There is also a longer, more clinical version called the *Devereux Scales of Mental Disorders*.

The DBRS-SF measures the
criteria noted in IDEA.

Description

Interpersonal Problems. This includes ten items such as "annoy others?" (5–12 years) and "disregard the feelings of others?" (13–18 years).

Inappropriate Behaviors/Feelings. This includes items such as "become very upset or emotional if he/she did not get what he/she wants?" (5–12 years) and "failed to control his/her anger?" (13–18 years).

Depression. Items include "fail to participate in activities?" (5–12 years) and "appear discouraged or depressed?" (13–18 years).

Physical Symptoms/Fears. Items include "say that others were picking on him/her?" (5–12 years) and "say that people picked on or did not like him or her?" (13–18 years).

Interpretation of Results.   For each of the forty items on the DBRS-SF the informant is asked to rate the student using a five-point scale (from "never" to "very frequently"). Each item is preceded by the phrase "During the past four weeks how often did the child . . . ?" Raw scores are totaled for each subscale and are converted to a standard score with a mean of 10 and a standard deviation of 3. These conversions are available on the basis of the rater (parent or teacher), age group (5–12 or 13–18), and the individual's gender. It is also possible to obtain a total standard score and percentile rank for the combination of the four subscales. The standard scores can then be classified as being normal, borderline, significant, or very significant. The authors also provide a method to identify problem behaviors that occur in a specific area or areas. In other words, it might be possible for the individual to receive scores in the average range for total and subscale scores, yet have a specific pattern or problems in a certain area. Tables are provided to determine if specific items should be considered significant.

Technical Characteristics

Normative Sample. The DBRS-SF included 3,153 children and adolescents in its standardization sample. The authors detail the procedures used to ensure a representative sample on the basis of age, gender, geographic region, race, ethnicity, socioeconomic status, community size, and educational placement.

Reliability. Internal reliability of the subscales were generally in the .80s range, with slightly lower coefficients for ages 13 to 18. The internal reliability coefficient for the total scale was .94 and .95 for ages 13 to 18 and 5 to 12, respectively. In general, the internal reliability coefficients were higher for teacher ratings than for parent ratings. Test-retest reliability was determined at twenty-four-hour, two-week, and four-week intervals. Not surprisingly, the coefficients were higher given a shorter interval between tests. For example, total scale coefficients decreased from .75 at twenty-four hours to .65 for two weeks to .52 for four weeks. Interrater reliability studies were conducted that resulted in total scale coefficients of .40 between teacher and residential counselor and .53 between teacher and a teacher's aide. Intrarater reliability was also determined in two studies in which a teacher and residential counselor each separately rated the individual two times. Those total scale coefficients were .78 for the teacher and .57 for the residential counselor. For the most part, the subscale coefficients for intra- and interrater reliability were similar to the total scale coefficients.

Validity. Criterion-related validity was determined through the use of six separate studies that investigated the accuracy of the DBRS-SF in differentiating between individuals with serious emotional disturbance and those without. For the 5 to 12 age range, the average percentage of total correct identification was 75.3 percent. The average percentage for ages 13 to 18 was 77.5 percent. Arguments for both content and construct validity are also reported in the test manual.

Review of Relevant Research. The limited research on the DBRS-SF appears to support its use in differentiating among children with and without behavior or emotional problems. There is some question if it is useful in identifying the specific type of problem. In general, however, validity data are limited (Floyd & Bose, 2003). Summaries of three studies follow. Additional summaries are located on the Earlier Research link for Chapter 9 on the Companion Website (www.prenhall.com/taylor8e).

- Gimpel and Nagle (1999) reported a slightly different factor structure from that suggested by the authors. They did note, however, that there was adequate internal consistency reliability and that children classified as having serious emotional disturbance scored higher on all factors and subscales than those children who were not classified.

- Wrightson and Saklofske (2000) found that the Devereux Scales successfully discriminated among children who were mainstreamed, those who attended alternate education, and those who had significant behavior problems.
- Nickerson and Nagle (2001) reported that when general education teachers and special education teachers rated students with and without emotional disturbance there was greater interrater reliability for those without emotional disturbance than for those with emotional disturbance.

Overview: Devereux Behavior Rating Scale–School Form

- *Age level*—5 through 18 years (2 forms).
- *Type of administration*—Individual.
- *Technical adequacy*—Good standardization sample, good reliability (teacher), adequate reliability (parent), adequate validity.
- *Scores yielded*—Standard scores, descriptive profiles.
- *Suggested use*—The DBRS-SF is the newest revision of a series of tests originally published by the Devereux Foundation. There are two separate forms based on age level. The items and factors are consistent with the diagnostic criteria included in the definition of emotional disturbance noted in IDEA. The newest revision appears more technically sound than earlier versions and can be administered in a relatively short period of time. A more lengthy instrument, the *Devereux Scales of Mental Disorders*, is also available that measures more acute or serious psychopathology (Smith & Reddy, 2002).

A lengthier version of the DBRS-SF is available.

Additional Classroom/ Home Behavior Instruments

In addition to the instruments just described, several others are worthy of note. These include the *Behavioral and Emotional Rating Scale–2*, a strength-based instrument, the *Emotional or Behavior Disorder Scale–Revised*, designed to measure emotional and behavior problems based on the proposed definition, and the *Revised Problem Behavior Checklist*, based on Quay's classification system.

Behavioral and Emotional Rating Scale–2

- *Age level*—5 through 18 years.
- *Type of administration*—Individual.
- *Technical adequacy*—Good standardization and reliability (for Total Score); adequate validity.
- *Scores yielded*—Standard scores, percentiles.
- *Suggested use*—The *Behavioral and Emotional Rating Scale–2* (BERS-2; Epstein, 2004) is considered a "strength-based" system that focuses on student's personal strengths. The BERS-2 measures the areas of interpersonal strength, involvement with family, intrapersonal strength, school functioning, affective strength, and career strength. There are three components: the Youth Rating

The BERS is a "strength-based" instrument.

Scale (self-report), the Parent Rating Scale, and the Teacher Rating Scale. Thus, the individual can be rated from several different perspectives. The previous edition was shown to differentiate students with emotional and behavioral disorders from those without (Reid, Epstein, Pastor, & Ryser, 2000) and appears to have good technical characteristics for both younger and older students (Trout, Ryan, LaVigne, & Epstein, 2003), including good cross-informant agreement (Synhorst, Buckley, Reid, Epstein, & Ryser, 2005).

Emotional or Behavior Disorder Scale–Revised

- *Age level*—5 through 18 years.
- *Type of administration*—Individual.
- *Technical adequacy*—Good normative sample, adequate reliability and validity.
- *Scores yielded*—Standard scores, percentiles.
- *Suggested use*—The *Emotional or Behavior Disorder Scale–Revised* (EBDS-R; McCarney & Arthaud, 2003) was designed to meet the criteria specified in the proposed behavior disorder definition by the same name. The behavioral subscales included are Academic Progress, Social Relationships, and Personal Adjustment. The vocational subscales are Work Related, Interpersonal Relations, and Social/Community Expectations. One nice feature of the EBDS-R is an intervention manual that includes more than 400 strategies, goals, and objectives for students with EBD. The EBDS-R can be used in conjunction with other information to meet the criteria for emotional and behavior disorders.

Revised Behavior Problem Checklist

- *Age level*—Kindergarten to grade 6.
- *Type of administration*—Individual.
- *Technical adequacy*—Adequate reliability (limited interrater), acceptable validity (based on research data); limited standardization.
- *Scores yielded*—Profile analysis, T-scores (used cautiously).
- *Suggested use*—The *Revised Behavior Problem Checklist* (RBPC; Quay & Peterson, 1987) is a rating scale that is easy to administer and score. The rater must simply assign a score of zero (does not constitute a problem), 1 (constitutes a mild problem), or 2 (constitutes a severe problem). This instrument follows Quay's classification system for children with behavior disorders. There are major scales in conduct disorders, socialized aggression, attention problems-immaturity, and anxiety-withdrawal. There are minor scales for psychotic behavior and motor excess. A growing body of literature has focused on its technical and interpretive characteristics. The RBPC seems to be a valid measure of classroom behavior problems, although, like many behavior rating scales, it has some problems regarding reliability. One concern is the limited standardization sample.

The RBPC is based on Quay's classification system.

Social Skills Instruments

One criticism of many behavior-rating scales is that they focus more on maladaptive or problem behaviors instead of prosocial behaviors. With the acknowledged importance of social skill deficits in students with disabilities, it is not surprising that instruments have been developed that focus more on social competence and social skills. Two widely used instruments are the *Social Skills Rating System* and the *Walker-McConnell Scale of Social Competence and School Adjustment*.

Social Skills Rating System

- *Age level*—Preschool through secondary level.
- *Type of administration*—Multiple raters (student, parent, teacher).
- *Scores yielded*—Behavior level, standard score, percentile rank.
- *Technical adequacy*—Adequate standardization (Student Form), limited standardization (Teacher and Parent Forms), adequate reliability and validity.
- *Suggested use*—The *Social Skills Rating System* (SSRS; Gresham & Elliott, 1990) allows for multiple ratings that can provide important diagnostic information. The SSRS was built on a solid theoretical framework and does have the advantage of looking primarily at prosocial behaviors as opposed to maladaptive behaviors. An important aspect of the SSRS is the inclusion of an Assessment Intervention Record that allows the development of specific intervention programs based on data obtained on the SSRS. This provides a convenient record to list social skill strengths, social skill performance deficits, social skill acquisition deficits, and problem behaviors. In addition, the record provides a table that links the assessment needs with specific intervention suggestions. The test manual, in fact, devotes a chapter to discussing the development of intervention plans. Although the information presented is cursory, it does emphasize the importance of linking the assessment to a program of intervention strategies. It should be noted that the preschool version of the SSRS is somewhat limited due to the small standardization sample. More research needs to be conducted on the SSRS, primarily to support the validity of the instrument. Its several positive features (multiple ratings, consideration of importance of social behaviors, and assessment–intervention record) make it an attractive instrument. It should be noted that the authors have also published a separate *Social Skills Intervention Guide*, which contains case studies and forty-three lessons for developing prosocial skills. The guide can be used separately or in conjunction with the SSRS.

The Intervention Guide is helpful.

Walker-McConnell Scale of Social Competence and School Adjustment

- *Age level*—Kindergarten through grade 6 (adolescent form available).
- *Type of administration*—Teacher rating (individual student).
- *Technical adequacy*—Limited standardization (poorly described), good reliability, adequate validity.
- *Scores yielded*—Standard scores, percentile ranks.
- *Suggested use*—The *Walker-McConnell Scale of Social Competence and School Adjustment* (W-M Scale; Walker & McConnell, 1995) appears to be a reliable, relatively valid yet quick measure of social skill development of elementary-age students. Its use as a screening instrument appears to be justified, and its short administration time (five minutes) will allow its use in combination with other measures. The W-M Scale is based on a sound theoretical framework, measuring the areas of teacher-preferred social behavior, peer-preferred social behavior, and school adjustment behavior. Its use to make comprehensive diagnostic decisions should be avoided, however. Further studies that focus on the predictive validity of the instrument should be forthcoming.

The W-M Scale is a good screening instrument for social skills.

AD/HD Instruments

Although not recognized as a separate disability area in the Individuals with Disabilities Education Act, attention-deficit/hyperactivity disorder (AD/HD) has been receiving increasing interest. According to the *Diagnostic and Statistical Manual*, 4th edition text edition (DSM-IV-TE), published by the American Psychiatric Association, AD/HD can be either predominantly inattentive (previously termed ADD), predominantly hyperactive/impulsive, or combined.

The following is a synopsis of the DSM-IV-TE (2000) definition of AD/HD. First, certain criteria must be met. The characteristics should be severe compared to others, should manifest at least some symptoms by age 7, be present for at least six months, negatively impact academic or social life, and be present in multiple settings. For the *predominately hyperactive/impulsive* diagnosis, six of the following characteristics should be noted:

- Fidgety
- Difficulty staying seated
- Runs and climbs excessively
- Difficulty playing quietly
- Often "on the go"
- Talks excessively
- Difficulty taking turns
- Blurting out answers
- Interrupting others

For the *predominately inattentive* diagnosis, at least six of the following characteristics must be identified:

- Lack of attention to detail
- Difficulty sustaining attention
- Does not seem to listen
- Does not follow through
- Difficulty with organizational skills
- Avoids or dislikes tasks requiring sustained attention
- Easily distracted
- Loses or misplaces things
- Is forgetful

For the *combined* type, both the predominantly hyperactive/impulsive and predominantly inattentive criteria must be met.

In recent years instruments designed to measure these areas have been published. Among these are the *Attention Deficit Disorders Evaluation Scale–2*, the *ADD-H Comprehensive Teacher's Rating Scale*, the *Clinical Assessment of Attention Deficit-Child*, the *Attention-Deficit/Hyperactivity Disorder Test*, and the *Diagnostic Assessment Scales for Attention-Deficit/Hyperactivity Disorder*.

Attention Deficit Disorders Evaluation Scale–2

- *Age level*—4½ to 20 years.
- *Type of administration*—Individual.
- *Technical adequacy*—Good normative sample (school version), adequate normative sample (home version), good reliability, adequate validity.
- *Scores yielded*—Standard scores and percentile ranks; a profile analysis is also available.

- *Suggested use*—The Attention Deficit Disorders Evaluation Scale–2 (ADDES–2; McCarney, 1995) was developed to help identify individuals with attention deficit disorder (with and without hyperactivity). The scale was designed based on the American Psychiatric Association's (APA) *Diagnostic and Statistical Manual IV* (DSM-IV) criteria. Subsequently, three subscales measure inattention, impulsiveness, and hyperactivity. Both a school version and a home version are available, and each can be completed in approximately fifteen to twenty minutes. In addition to the scale itself, an *Attention Deficit Disorders Intervention Manual* also coincides with the behaviors noted in the school version of the test. A parent guide to attention deficit disorders provides suggestions for interventions based on the behavior noted in the home version. A computerized program is also available for both the scale and intervention manual. In a review of the original ADDES, Silverthorne (1994) noted several positive features, including the ease of administration and scoring and its construction on the basis of ADD criteria established by the APA. She also pointed out that factor analytic studies have indicated the presence of only two factors—inattention-disorganization and motor hyperactivity-impulsivity.

ADD-H Comprehensive Teacher's Rating Scale (Second Edition)

- *Age level*—Kindergarten through grade 8.
- *Type of administration*—Individual.
- *Technical adequacy*—Adequate normative sample, adequate reliability, questionable validity.
- *Scores yielded*—Percentile ranks and a visual profile.
- *Suggested use*—The *ADD-H Comprehensive Teacher's Rating Scale* (ACTeRS; Ullmann, Sleator, & Sprague, 1991) is a brief checklist of twenty-four items that measures the areas of attention, hyperactivity, social skills, and oppositional behavior. The authors recommend that the scale be administered by teachers because the majority of the items on the scale would be demonstrated in the classroom. The ACTeRS is probably best used as a quick screening device, although it might be used with other information to help identify a student as having AD/HD. Computerized scoring is also available for the ACTeRS.

The ACTeRS is completed by teachers.

Attention Deficit/Hyperactivity Disorder Test

- *Age level*—3 to 23 years.
- *Type of administration*—Individual.
- *Technical adequacy*—Good normative sample, good reliability, adequate validity.
- *Scores yielded*—Standard scores and percentile ranks.
- *Suggested use*—The items for the *Attention Deficit/Hyperactivity Disorder Test* (ADHDT; Gilliam, 1995) were selected based on the diagnostic criteria for AD/HD found in the DSM-IV. The ADHDT contains thirty-six items measuring the areas of hyperactivity, impulsivity, and inattention. The instrument is basically used as a screening measure and can be completed by teachers, parents, as well as others who are knowledgeable about the child. The ADHDT is the first instrument to provide national norms based on AD/HD subjects.

Clinical Assessment of Attention Deficit—Child

- *Age level*—8–18 years.
- *Type of administration*—Individual.
- *Technical adequacy*—Adequate standardization; good validity and reliability.
- *Scores yielded*—Standard scores (T-scores), percentile ranks, qualitative classifications.
- *Suggested use*—The *Clinical Assessment of Attention Deficit–Child* (CAT-C; Bracken & Boatwright, 2005) consists of three separate forms, Self-Report, Parent Rating, and Teacher Rating, so that the student can be evaluated by three different informants, including the student. Each of the forms measures the areas of inattention, impulsivity, hyperactivity, personal, academic/occupational, social, internal locus of control, and external locus of control. There is also an adult version of the instrument that measures the same areas.

Diagnostic Assessment Scales for Attention Deficit/Hyperactivity Disorder

- *Age level*—5–18 years.
- *Type of administration*—Individual.
- *Technical adequacy*—Good standardization (both AD/HD and non-AD/HD), good reliability and validity.
- *Scores yielded*—A four-point Likert scale.
- *Suggested use*—The *Diagnostic Assessment Scales for Attention Deficit/Hyperactivity Disorder* (DAS-ADHD; Ryser & McConnell, 2001) are designed using the AD/HD criteria found in the DSM-IV. In addition, the American Academy of Pediatrics Practice Guidelines for the Diagnosis and Evaluation of AD/HD were used. There are three subtests that measure inattention, hyperactivity, and impulsivity; separate forms are available for home use and school use, each with two sets of norms: AD/HD and non-AD/HD. The DAS-ADHD is easy to administer and is relatively brief (fifteen to twenty minutes).

Autism Instruments

Autism has been recognized as a category under IDEA for over fifteen years. During that time there has been increased interest in the assessment of individuals with this disability. Similar to AD/HD, autism is primarily diagnosed using the DSM-IV-TE criteria. In general, a child with autism will have problems with social interactions and difficulties in the area of communication. In addition, repetitive and stereotyped patterns of behavior, interests, and/or activities are displayed. The characteristics must be evident before the age of 3.

One important component in the assessment of students with autism is a developmental history. Not only does it provide valuable diagnostic information, it also allows for the meaningful interaction between the examiner and the family. The areas to assess in the developmental history include those related to physical, family, language/communication, social, behavior, and education (Plotts & Webber, 2001–2002). Also, there are several autism rating scales that are available that assist in the identification of students with autism. These include the *Autism Screening Instrument and Educational Planning–2*, the *Childhood Autism Rating Scale*, and the *Gilliam Autism Rating Scale–2*.

Autism Screening Instrument for Educational Planning–2

- *Age level*—18 months through adulthood.
- *Type of administration*—Individual.
- *Technical adequacy*—Adequate normative sample, reliability, and validity.
- *Scores yielded*—Standard scores and percentiles; summary booklet profile.
- *Suggested use*—The *Autism Screening Instrument for Education Planning–2* (ASIEP-2; Krug, Arick, & Almond, 1993) is a revision of a popular autism screening instrument that includes subtests measuring five areas. Those five areas are a sample of vocal behavior, assessment of interaction, assessment of communication, determination of learning rate, and a behavioral checklist measuring sensory, relating, body concept, language, and social self-help skills. Not all five areas are necessarily administered for each individual; guidelines are provided to assist the examiner in making that decision. In general, the authors provide evidence that the battery is helpful in distinguishing among groups of subjects with a variety of disabilities including autism. One potential drawback is the amount of time (1½–2 hours) that is necessary to obtain basic screening information. It should be noted, however, that this instrument yields more in-depth information than that obtained from other types of screening instruments.

The ASIEP-2 is a lengthy instrument.

Childhood Autism Rating Scale

- *Age level*—2 years and up.
- *Type of administration*—Individual.
- *Technical adequacy*—Adequate normative sample, reliability, and validity.
- *Scores yielded*—A diagnostic categorization system is provided based on the individual's raw score on the fifteen items.
- *Suggested use*—The *Childhood Autism Rating Scale* (CARS; Schopler, Reichler, & Renner, 1988) was originally developed as a means of evaluating children for a statewide program called Treatment and Education of Autistic and Related Communication Handicapped Children (TEACCH). There are fifteen items or areas in which the examiner must rate the individuals on a seven-point scale from 1 (within normal limits for that age) to 4 (severely abnormal for that age). The areas covered are Relating to People, Imitation, Emotional Response, Body Use, Object Use, Adaptation to Change, Visual Response, Listening Response, Taste, Smell and Touch Response, Fear or Nervousness, Verbal Communication, Nonverbal Communication, Activity Level, Level and Consistency of Intellectual Response, and General Impressions. Some research has been conducted on the CARS. Eaves and Milner (1993) found that the CARS correctly identified 98 percent of the approximately fifty subjects who had a firm diagnosis of autism. Stella, Mundy, and Tuchman (1999) also reported that the CARS could be used to distinguish between children with autism, pervasive developmental disorder (not otherwise specified), and those without autism. In a review of the CARS, Volkmar and Marans (1999) noted that it has a tendency to overidentify individuals as having autism, therefore making it more appropriate as a screening instrument than a diagnostic instrument. This observation was substantiated in an empirical study comparing the CARS with another procedure—the *Autism Diagnostic Interview–Revised* (Saemundfen, Magnusson, Smari, & Sigurdardottir, 2003). It should also be noted that the CARS has been translated into Japanese and Swedish, so it has international appeal.

Gilliam Autism Rating Scale–2

- *Age level*—3 through 22 years.
- *Type of administration*—Individual.
- *Technical adequacy*—Adequate normative sample, good reliability and validity.
- *Scores yielded*—Standard scores and percentiles.
- *Suggested use*—The *Gilliam Autism Rating Scale–2* (GARS-2; Gilliam, 2006) was designed for use by teachers, parents, and other professionals. The GARS was based on the information on autism provided, in part, from the DSM-IV-TR manual of the American Psychiatric Association and by the Autism Society of America. The forty-two items are grouped in areas related to stereotyped behaviors, communication, and social interaction. The instrument is extremely quick to administer, requiring only five to ten minutes to complete. The author provides evidence that the original GARS discriminates between individuals with autism and those with other severe behavioral and cognitive problems. There is some evidence, however, that the GARS underestimates the likelihood of the child being autistic. South et al. (2002) found that it consistently underestimated children who had strict DSM-IV diagnoses of autism. Mazefsky and Oswald (2006) also reported that the GARS consistently underestimated the likelihood of autism. On the other hand, Eaves, Wood-Graves, Williams, and Fall (2006) found that the GARS significantly discriminated between individuals with and without autism. One nice addition to the GARS-2 is a separate booklet that ties test results to instructional objectives. It should be noted that the author also has a test called the *Gilliam Asperger Disorder Scale* (Gilliam, 2001). There is also a structured parent interview form, new to the GARS-2, which provides information about a child's early development.

A scale for Asperger's disorder is also available.

Measurement of Emotional Status

Why Use Measures of Emotional Status?

Determination of personality characteristics, and general emotional status; frequently used in nonschool settings for individuals with emotional problems.

Who Should Use Them?

Psychologists.

Ironically, many examiners try to infer a child's emotional state by "analyzing" the observable behavior. For instance, "Because Susan is sitting alone in the back of the classroom, she has a poor self-concept"; or "Because Billy hit his sister, he is having problems with sibling rivalry." Inferences of this type should be avoided; they usually result in some kind of misinterpretation.

Several types of instruments have been used historically to measure emotional status. Most of these procedures are administered only by trained psychologists and psychiatrists. Their relevance to special education is questionable. These instruments include projective tests and personality inventories.

Projective Methods

Projective methods grew out of psychoanalytic and Gestalt psychology. The concept is simple. When presented with an ambiguous stimulus, an individual will "project" his or her "way of seeing life, his meanings, significances, patterns and especially his feelings" (Frank, 1939). Theoretically, the ambiguous stimulus will break down the individual's defense mechanisms; further, the more ambiguous the stimulus, the deeper the penetration into the personality (Haley, 1963). Thus, an ink blot, hypothetically, will penetrate more deeply into the personality than a picture of people engaging in some activity.

The appropriateness of projective testing has been seriously questioned for a number of years. O'Leary and Johnson (1979) noted, for example, that the Society for Projective Techniques and Personality Assessment dropped the words *Projective Techniques* from its title in 1970. Similarly, that organization's journal also deleted the same words from its title. The use of projective tests in special education particularly has been challenged for a number of reasons. As a general rule, projective tests lack reliability and validity. The subjective way in which they are scored tends to lower their reliability. Because the tests measure abstract hypothetical constructs, validity is difficult to establish. For example, Motta, Little, and Tobin (1993) reviewed several studies using human figure-drawing projective techniques and found little support for their validity or use to assess personality or behavior. Petot (2000) also noted that projective techniques are time-consuming and generally lack adequate psychometric properties.

Another problem with projective tests is insufficient standardization or an insufficient normative group. Many times, in fact, norms are not used—the results are interpreted completely subjectively. This is particularly true if the examiner is highly experienced in projective techniques. It can, however, result in a type of "reverse projection." Consider this hypothetical situation:

> *Examiner:* (*shows examinee a card with an ink blot*) Tell me what you see.
> *Examinee:* A bat.
> *Examiner:* Anything else?
> *Examinee:* Just a bat, an angry bat.

After several interactions about various ink blots, the examiner determines that the examinee is "a hostile, impulsive person with hyperactive tendencies." In reality, the examiner's response has been "projected"—the examinee's response was the stimulus! Wiederman (1999), in fact, developed a demonstration that illustrates how prior expectancies can lead interpreters of projective tests to focus on responses that "fit" the initial impression. In other words, the projective test data are used to confirm an initial hypothesis. The message should be clear; if a projective is used, an objective scoring system should be applied. Even though projective tests have been criticized by many, they are still used in the school and are frequently defended. An example of a projective test is the *Rorschach Ink Blot Test* (Rorschach, 1932).

Some projective instruments are called **thematic picture story tests.** These require the examinee to make up stories about pictures that are shown; the examiner subsequently looks for patterns or themes in the responses. The nature of the pictures varies from test to test. One criticism of these instruments is potential cultural bias (see Focus on Diversity). Examples of thematic picture story tests include the *Thematic Apperception Test* (Murray, 1973) and the *Children's Apperception Test* (Bellak & Bellak, 1991).

Projective methods have many critics.

THEMATIC PICTURE STORY TESTS
A projective technique that requires the examinee to make up stories about pictures or photographs.

focus on
Diversity

Is There a Culturally Sensitive Projective Measure?

In general, picture story tests such as the *Thematic Apperception Test* (TAT) and the *Children's Apperception Test* (CAT) have been criticized when used with children from culturally and linguistically diverse backgrounds. Dana (1999), for example, urged that developers of the TAT include pictures that are more culturally recognizable and use scoring variables that are more germane to the culture of different individuals, including interpretations based on more culturally specific variables.

Costantino, Flanagan, and Malgady (2001) also criticized the use of the CAT for a variety of reasons including lack of appropriate technical characteristics and theoretical framework. Clearly, the pictures used to elicit stories in both the TAT and CAT lack multicultural representation. Costantino et al., however, do view another instrument, the *Tell-Me-A-Story* (TEMAS), as an appropriate projective

measure to use with ethnic minority individuals because it has both a majority and ethnic-minority version. They note that it is the only personality measure that offers nonminority and minority norms for four groups (African American, Puerto Rican, other Hispanic, and White). Ritzler (1993) stated that "besides being the most cleverly named psychological test, the TEMAS (in English it is an acronym for Tell-Me-A-Story and in Spanish and Italian it means themes) represents a milestone in personality assessment. . . . It also represents the first time a thematic apperception assessment technique has been published in the United States with the initial, expressed purpose of providing personality assessment of minority (as well as nonminority) subjects" (p. 381). Dana (1996) also lauded the TEMAS as an appropriate multicultural assessment that has psychometric credibility.

Another type of projective instrument is the **projective drawing test.** The examinee draws certain pictures (content depends on the test) that are interpreted by the examiner. Examples include the *Human Figure Drawing Test* (Koppitz, 1968), the *Kinetic Drawing System for Family and School* (Knoff & Prout, 1985), and the *Draw-a-Person Screening Procedure for Emotional Disturbance* (Naglieri, McNeish, & Bardos, 1991).

Theoretically, projective tests are able to measure some underlying emotional characteristic of an individual that he or she cannot or will not verbalize. By using ambiguous stimuli, the individual "projects" his or her feelings and needs. Unfortunately, evaluating the responses usually requires a great deal of subjective interpretation by the examiner. The use of projective testing should be limited to those examiners who have been trained specifically in projective techniques. In a survey of school counselors, Giordano, Schwiebert, and Brotherton (1997) reported that there was a need for additional training in the use of projective tests, particularly those that require specialized training to administer, score, and interpret.

Regardless of the examiner, however, it should be questioned whether projective methods have relevance in the field of special education. Research, in general, has not supported the validity of projective instruments. O'Leary and Johnson (1979) perhaps best summarized the state of the art for projective methods thirty years ago:

> The data are simply not compelling enough to suggest that projective methods be used for clinical purposes. With a few exceptions, the validity coefficients are either inconsistent or so small as to preclude their use in routine clinical work. Most projective methods require substantial time to administer and score and, as important, they require many hours to learn. Since information gathered on projective

PROJECTIVE DRAWING TESTS
Instruments in which the examinee draws certain pictures (content depends on the test) that are interpreted by the examiner.

techniques can generally be obtained from simpler and less expensive methods, it is incumbent upon advocates of projective methodologies to demonstrate their clinical utility in terms of costs in time and training as well as predictive validity. (pp. 218–219)

A review of the publication dates of the projective tests included in this chapter suggests that new attempts of applying this method are limited. Kamphaus, Petoskey, and Rowe (2000) noted that for the most part the use of behavior rating scales (discussed previously in this chapter) has supplanted the use of projective testing.

Personality Inventories

The intent of personality inventories is to measure objectively the emotional and personality characteristics of individuals. Most of these instruments are designed for adolescents and adults. One notable exception is the *Personality Inventory for Children–2* (PIC–2) discussed in the following section. Another is the *Beck Youth Inventories* (Beck, Beck, & Jolly, 2005), which are used primarily for screening anxiety, depression, disruptive behavior, and self-concept. Inventories usually include a large number of items that purportedly measure several personality traits or characteristics. (A group of items referring to a given trait is usually referred to as a *scale* for that trait.) Many times, these items are in the form of a behavioral description (such as "I sometimes hear strange voices") that the examinee must label as true or false. This self-report technique is used in the majority of these instruments, although some of them require a familiar person (such as a parent) to complete the items about the examinee.

In addition to the personality scales themselves, these instruments usually include some type of validity scale to help determine if the examinee is "telling the truth." In general, however, both the reliability and the validity of these instruments have been questioned. Many inventories have also been criticized because the various areas identified for a profile analysis overlap in content. For these and several other reasons, the use of these instruments as tools in the process of education is limited. A brief discussion of the PIC-2 and the *Minnesota Multiphasic Personality Inventory,* perhaps the most popular inventory, follows.

Many personality inventories include "validity scales."

Personality Inventory for Children–2. The *Personality Inventory for Children–2* (PIC–2; Lachar & Gruber, 2001) is one of the few inventories designed to include children in its age range. It can be used with individuals from age 5 through 19. There are both Response Validity Scales (to determine the truthfulness of the answers) and Adjustment Scales. There are 275 items that can be administered in approximately forty minutes. A shorter version, called the Behavioral Summary, consists of ninety-six items that can be administered in fifteen minutes.

The Validity Scales are called Inconsistency, Dissimulation, and Defensiveness. There are nine Adjustment Scales: Cognitive Impairment, Impulsivity and Distractibility, Delinquency, Family Dysfunction, Reality Distortion, Somatic Concern, Psychological Discomfort, Social Withdrawal, and Social Skills Deficit. Each scale also has two to three subscales. For instance, Psychological Discomfort has the subscales of Fear and Worry, Depression, and Sleeping

Disturbance/Preoccupation with Death. Items are presented in a true-false format to the parent or parent surrogate. A computer scoring option is available as well as visual profiles.

The PIC–2 is one of the few available personality inventories designed for children. One must be aware of the possible bias of the respondents (as with any instrument that requires third-party information). The test is more a clinical instrument than an educational instrument; the results will be used more for eligibility purposes than educational programming. A companion instrument, the *Personality Inventory for Youth* (PIY; Lachar & Gruber, 1995), is available. The PIY, designed for individuals ages 9 to 19, uses a self-rating format and includes the same Adjustment Scales as the PIC–2. Also available is the *Student Behavior Survey* (Lachar, Wingenfeld, Kline, & Gruber, 2000), which is essentially a teacher rating scale. Although its content does not mirror that of the PIC–2 and the PIY, it is sometimes used with those instruments to get the teacher's perspective.

> The PIC is specifically designed for young children.

The Minnesota Multiphasic Personality Inventory–2.   The *Minnesota Multiphasic Personality Inventory–2* (MMPI-2; Butcher, Dahlstrom, Graham, & Kaemmer, 1989) is the most recent revision of the extremely popular, widely used MMPI that has been in existence for more than fifty years. The instrument is designed for individuals 16 years of age and older. The MMPI-2 consists of 704 items, 550 of which were from the original version. The items are designed to be answered in a true-false format, and there are scores for ten clinical scales, three validity scales, and seven additional scales. Generally, the *pattern* of scores is used in interpretation. The clinical scales include Hypochondriasis, Depression, Hysteria, Psychopathic Deviate, Masculinity-Femininity, Paranoia, Psychoasthenia, Schizophrenia, and Hypomania. The three validity scales are Lie, Infrequency, and Defensiveness. The additional scales include an Anxiety scale, a Repression scale, an Ego-Strength scale, and an Alcoholism scale, in addition to three scales that focus on variable response, inconsistency, and unusual responding.

Duckworth (1991) noted that the MMPI-2 has many positive features, including updated items and additional validity scales. She also noted that the new norms were an improvement over the original MMPI, although there were still some concerns with the representativeness of the norms. Others have noted that the MMPI-2 has limitations in the areas of both validity and reliability (Rogers & Sewell, 2006).

Personality inventories generally lack supportive data that would establish their reliability and validity. The use of these instruments in special education is questionable and is typically limited to providing information to help make eligibility and placement decisions.

BACK TO THE PROFILES

Possible Answers to the Questions

1. **Why assess Tara?** Tara is obviously having problems with defiance and compliance. The decision by Ms. Duffy to collaborate with the school psychologists to develop an immediate intervention program was a good idea, although the fact that Tara had never

been in any type of formal educational program might explain some of her behavior. When the suggestions of the school psychologist did not change Tara's behavior, Ms. Duffy needed to gather more assessment data to develop a prereferral intervention program. Based on the results of that program, it might be necessary to assess Tara for consideration for eligibility for special education in a program for students with behavioral/emotional disorders (based in part on Tara's mother's report of programs prior to school). Considering Tara's background, the decision to assess for eligibility should be made carefully.

2. **Who should assess Tara?** If Tara is assessed to determine more specific information to help develop a prereferral intervention program, a more formal, data-based collection of information might be initiated by Ms. Duffy and the school psychologist. Certainly, if a decision was ultimately made to refer Tara for eligibility, those two professionals, in addition to perhaps a school counselor and/or social worker, would be involved. The determination of who would be involved would depend on the eligibility criteria for the category that would dictate the personnel involved.

3. **What test(s)/procedure(s) should be used?** For the preintervention assessment data, observational procedures (discussed in Chapter 4) would be most helpful. In particular, a functional behavior assessment (also discussed in Chapter 4) based on specific behavioral incidents would be appropriate. A behavior-rating scale designed for the teacher (e.g., *Devereux Behavior Rating Scale–School Form*) might also be administered to help prioritize behavioral goals. Finally, it would be very important to have information about Tara's background. An interview with her mother would provide necessary information and might help determine if she should be referred at a later time. Assessment for eligibility, if conducted, would involve multiple sources of information and would again depend on the specific eligibility criteria used. For example, a measure of personality, such as the *Personality Inventory for Children–2*, might be required. Certainly, the prereferral assessment information would be incorporated into the process.

4. **What other area(s) should be assessed?** As noted in answers 2 and 3, if Tara was assessed for determination of eligibility into a program for students with emotional or behavior problems, then the areas would be dictated by the eligibility criteria. The vignette does not really suggest any other areas to be assessed other than those noted in the collection of prereferral assessment information.

---

1. **Why assess Anna?** It would be important to determine Anna's overall behavioral/emotional status and to determine if there are any reasons for her change in behavior. It is also possible that she might be evaluated to see if she would qualify for a program for students with behavior disorders.

2. **Who should assess Anna?** There are really two answers to this question. The person who actually administers the tests might be the psychologist or social worker. However, several individuals should provide information for the assessment, including Anna's parents, teacher, and perhaps her peers. Anna herself should also be involved.

3. **What procedure(s)/test(s) should be used?** It would be possible to administer a comprehensive behavioral assessment system such as the BASC-2. If the BASC-2 were used, the parents would provide information for the Parent Rating Scales and the Structured Developmental History. Her teacher would provide the information for the Teacher Rating Scales. Finally, Anna could complete the Self-Report of Personality and be observed using the Student Observation System. If a comprehensive

behavior system is not used, direct observation (Chapter 4) or a behavior rating scale such as the Child Behavior Checklist from the *Achenbach System of Empirically Based Assessment* could be used. Another technique that should definitely be used is a functional behavior assessment (Chapter 4). This would assist in determining the cause of the behavior problems and would provide important information for behavioral intervention. In fact, information from the BASC-2 could be used to supplement the procedures that are used in the FBA.

4. **What other areas (if any) should be addressed?** As with Tara, the answer to this question depends on what information was found in the initial assessment. Hopefully, the FBA would provide the necessary information to develop an intervention program. If it would seem necessary and appropriate to place her in a special education program for behavior disorders, then additional required eligibility procedures might need to be used (e.g., documentation of an educational need).

STUDENT PROFILE DATA

Tara

The first step was to administer Ms. Duffy the *Devereaux Behavior Rating Scale–School Form*. The following results were reported.

Areas	Scaled Score
Interpersonal Problems	6
Inappropriate Behaviors/Feelings	7
Depression	9
Physical Symptoms/Fears	8

These results indicate that Tara is below average in all of the measured areas. Her major problems are in interpersonal relations, followed by inappropriate behaviors and feelings. The school psychologist suggested that the BASC-2 be administered to get others' ratings of her behavior, including those of Tara herself. At that point, either an eligibility decision or a decision to continue evaluating will be made.

CASE STUDY *June*

Earlier in June's assessment her parents completed the Child Behavior Checklist from the ASEBA. All scores were in the normal range except for the Anxious/Depressed Scale, which was Borderline. The questions arose as to whether June is anxious or depressed.

To help answer that question and to provide more information about June's self-perception, June completed the Self-Report of Personality from the

Behavior Assessment System for Children–2 (BASC-2). The results are reported below.

Self-Report of Personality Results

Area/Composite	Percentile Rank
Attitude to School	95
Attitude to Teachers	98
School Maladjustment Composite	**99**
Atypicality	48
Anxiety	85
Locus of Control	80
Social Stress	78
Clinical Maladjustment Composite	**75**
Depression	48
Sense of Adequacy	58
Relations with Parents	65
Interpersonal Relations	52
Self-Esteem	60
Self-Reliance	52
Personal Adjustment Composite	**56**

Note: The higher the percentile, the greater the problem in each of the areas/composites.

- Is June anxious or depressed? What is the basis for your answer?
- What other areas appear to be problematic?

Reflections

1. Do you think it is a good idea for teachers to complete behavior-rating scales? Why or why not?
2. What do you think is the advantage of using a behavior assessment system?
3. Do you think that the use of AD/HD rating scales should be the primary method of identifying AD/HD?

Summary Matrix

Instrument or Technique	Prereferral: Screening and Initial Identification	Prereferral: Informal Determination and Evaluation of Teaching Programs and Strategies	Postreferral, Suggested Use: Determination of Current Performance Level and Educational Need	Postreferral, Suggested Use: Decisions about Classification and Program Placement	Postreferral, Suggested Use: IEP Goals	Postreferral, Suggested Use: IEP Objectives	Postreferral, Suggested Use: IEP Evaluation	Target Population: Mild/Moderate	Target Population: Severe/Profound	Target Population: Preschool	Target Population: Elementary Age	Target Population: Secondary Age	Target Population: Adult	Special Considerations	Educational Relevance for Exceptional Students
Achenbach System of Empirically Based Assessment	X		X	X	X			X			X	X		Has separate forms for multiple raters; different profiles for boys and girls.	Useful
Behavior Assessment System for Children–2	X		X	X	X			X			X	X		Includes several components involving input from multiple sources.	Useful
Devereux Behavior Rating Scale–School Form	X		X		X			X			X	X		Based on diagnostic criteria from the IDEA 04 definition of emotional disturbance.	Adequate/Useful
Social Skills Rating System	X		X		X			X		X	X	X		Assessment-intervention record is a nice feature; preschool version limited.	Useful
Walker-McConnell Scale	X							X			X			A valid screening instrument that can be quickly administered.	Useful
ADHD instruments	X							X		X	X	X		Many are checklists based on the diagnostic criteria of ADHD from the DSM-IV.	Adequate
Autism instruments	X				X			X	X	X	X	X	X	Primarily screening instruments based on the diagnostic criteria of autism.	Adequate
Projective techniques				X				X			X	X	X	Losing popularity in special education; little evidence of reliability or validity for most of these instruments.	Very Limited
Personality Inventories				X				X			X	X	X	Most have limited technical aspects; most are designed for adolescents and adults.	Limited

Assessment of Oral Language

STUDENT PROFILE

Bobby

Bobby is a student in the first grade who recently had his sixth birthday. He was the first born of three boys in his family. His parents did not notice any developmental problems, although his grandparents thought that he "said funny words." For example, he would say "Peese give me the wed ball." His parents took Bobby to his pediatrician, who said that the articulation problems were expected for his age and that he would eventually outgrow them. However, he is still making articulation errors that his teacher, Ms. Goldstein, feels are no longer age-appropriate. His preschool teacher also expressed concern about his "baby talk" or immature speech. He still uses incorrect pronouns ("me want a cookie") and has an immature vocabulary. He also has great difficulty expressing himself and seems to have a difficult time finding the right word to use. In addition, Ms. Goldstein has indicated that often Bobby will just give a blank stare when he is asked questions. She is not sure if Bobby is ignoring her, not hearing her, or not understanding her. A major concern of the teacher is that the other children are starting to avoid Bobby because he has difficulty maintaining conversations. She mentioned the following sequence:

Phillip: (to Bobby and Will) Hi, I went to the movie Saturday, what did you do?
Will: Me too, I saw a really neat movie.
Bobby: (to Phillip) How come you're wearing that hat?
Will: Bobby, why did you ask that?
Bobby: 'Cause I don't like blue.
Phillip: (to Will) Let's go, I have a card I want you to see.

Overall, Mrs. Goldstein is concerned about a number of speech and language areas.

Think about These Questions as You Read This Chapter:
1. Why assess Bobby? (There could be more than one reason.)
2. Who should assess Bobby? (There could be more than one person.)

3. What procedure(s)/test(s) should be used?
4. What other areas (if any) should be assessed?

(Suggested answers at the end of this chapter.)

Although there are many definitions of language, it is generally agreed that communication is its primary function. Language is usually thought of as the use of spoken or written symbols, although manual symbols should also be considered. In education, language, as a way in which we receive and express information, is important for success in virtually all areas of academic life. Reading, writing, spelling, and following directions are just a few of the areas in which language plays an important part. In special education, language assessment is an important area.

Structurally, language can be viewed as having five components: phonology, morphology, syntax, semantics, and pragmatics. Each of these five components involves both reception (or processing) and expression (or production) (see Figure 10.1). **Phonology** involves the use of phonemes, the smallest significant units of sound that are combined into words, or with words, to create meaning. For example, the word *goes* comprises three phonemes: /g/, /o/, /z/. The assessment of phonology involves both the aural discrimination of speech sounds and the articulation of speech sounds. Examples of instruments that measure these areas are the *Auditory Discrimination Test* (Wepman & Reynolds, 1986) and the *Goldman-Fristoe Test of Articulation–2* (Goldman & Fristoe, 2000). Related areas are *phonological processing* and *phonological awareness.* There is increasing evidence that there is a relationship between phonological processing and reading ability. An example of a test in this area is the *Comprehensive Test of Phonological Processing* (CTOPP; Wagner, Torgesen, & Rashotte, 1999). The CTOPP measures phonological awareness, phonological memory, and rapid naming. There are two versions of this test, one for children ages 5 and 6, and the other one for individuals ages 7 to 24. The CTOPP is discussed later in this chapter. Other instruments are the *Test of Phonological Awareness–2* (Torgesen & Bryant, 2004) and the *Test of Phonological Awareness Skills* (Newcomer & Barenbaum, 2003).

Morphology is concerned with how phonemes are put together to give meaning. A morpheme is the smallest combination of sounds that has a meaning. For instance, the word *displacement* has three morphemes: (dis), (place), (ment). Most assessment instruments measure morphology and syntax together because they are both concerned with grammar; one exception is the *Test for Examining Expressive Morphology* (Shipley, Stone, & Sue, 1983).

> Oral language includes both expression and reception.

> There are five components of language.

> **PHONOLOGY**
> Involves the use of phonemes, the smallest significant units of sound that are combined into words or used with words to create meaning.

> **MORPHOLOGY**
> Involves the use of morphemes, the smallest combination of sounds that have meaning.

FIGURE 10.1 Model of Language

Components of Language

Mode of Language	Phonology	Morphology	Syntax	Semantics	Pragmatics
Receptive					
Expressive					

SYNTAX
Involves the relational meanings of language—how words are put together to form sentences.

SEMANTICS
Refers to the meaning of words.

PRAGMATICS
Refers to the use of language for communication.

Syntax involves the relational meanings of language—that is, how words are put together to form sentences. Assessment of syntax involves the measurement of the understanding of the meaning of sentences and the ability to formulate sentences. For the most part, syntax measures are designed for younger children. Examples are the *Test for Auditory Comprehension of Language–3* (Carrow-Woolfolk, 1999a), the *Developmental Sentence Analysis* (Lee, 1974), and the *Carrow Elicited Language Inventory* (Carrow, 1994).

Semantics refers to the meaning of words. The assessment of semantics skills usually involves the measurement of a person's receptive and expressive vocabulary skills. Receptive vocabulary can be measured using instruments such as the *Peabody Picture Vocabulary Test–4* (discussed later in this chapter). Expressive vocabulary measures are included on tests such as the *Expressive Vocabulary Test–2*. There are also quick measures of semantics such as the *Receptive One Word Vocabulary Test* (Brownell, 2000a) and the *Expressive One Word Vocabulary Test* (Brownell, 2000b). The *Comprehensive Receptive and Expressive Vocabulary Test–2* (CREVT-2), discussed later in this chapter, includes the assessment of both receptive and expressive semantics.

Pragmatics refers to the use of language within the communicative context. In a certain sense, pragmatics deals with the most important function of language, that of communication. Although all the other components of language usually must be intact before communication can occur, it is possible that an individual might have all the necessary skills in the areas of phonology, morphology and syntax, and semantics, yet still have difficulty communicating with others. The assessment of pragmatics is a relatively new practice.

The overall area of language assessment is a complex process for a number of reasons. As previously discussed, a number of language components are involved. There is also the issue of the processing/production dichotomy and the fact that language can be transmitted and understood in oral and written form (not to mention manually). Still further, there is the question of whether language tests accurately measure the language skills that an individual actually uses. As a result, informal assessment of language is important; in addition, there are many types of formal tests available. For example, some tests are designed to measure only one component of language and others are designed to evaluate multiple components. For example, the *Test for Auditory Comprehension of Language–3* (Carrow-Woolfolk, 1999b) measures only receptive language but measures the areas of vocabulary, morphology, and syntax. In the discussion of formal instruments in this chapter, both single component and multicomponent language tests will be included.

The discussion that follows focuses on informal oral language sampling and the formal oral language tests typically used by special educators. Also included is a brief discussion of specific language tests that are used more by speech and language clinicians.

Informal Assessment of Language Skills

Why Use Informal Language Skills Assessment?

Screening and identification of language problems; informal determination of objectives and teaching strategies; analysis of spontaneous use of language.

Who Should Use It?

Teachers; speech and language clinicians.

During the past fifty years, the increase in knowledge of language development has resulted in many changes in language assessment with increasing emphasis on evaluating in a naturalistic, interactive context (Lund & Duchan, 1993). In fact, the dynamic assessment technique that involves mediated learning (discussed in Chapter 7) has been successfully applied to language assessment (Pena, Quinn, & Iglesias, 1992). Because formal language testing usually occurs in a contrived situation (sometimes requiring the student to imitate language skills), it is possible that many individuals may be able to exhibit certain language skills that they do not produce spontaneously. Conversely, it is possible that they may fail to exhibit certain skills that they might be able to perform within a naturalistic context.

One approach that can be used to evaluate the spontaneous use of language in a naturalistic setting is **language sampling**. This usually involves eliciting (taping, transcribing) and analyzing an individual's language. Language sampling actually refers to a set of possible procedures for gathering information ranging from a spontaneous unstructured sample to a highly structured sample.

> **LANGUAGE SAMPLING**
> Taping or transcribing language in a natural setting for later analysis.

Eliciting the Sample

In general, the procedures for obtaining a language sample include (1) a spontaneous sample taken during free play or a conversation; (2) an elicited sample asking the child to tell or retell a story; (3) an elicited imitative sample requiring the child to respond to questions, pictures, or activities that are specifically designed to elicit certain language structures; and (4) an imitative language sample asking the child to repeat sentences produced by the examiner.

> Spontaneous samples yield valuable information.

Each procedure for obtaining a language sample provides different types of evaluation information on the child's language abilities. The decision to use one procedure over another is dependent upon the child who is being evaluated and the behaviors to be examined. As noted previously, however, the most meaningful information regarding the individual's actual use of language will be gathered from the spontaneous procedure. If this is the procedure chosen, it is important that the sample represent the highest level of language of which the student is capable (Smiley & Goldstein, 1998). Provided below are suggestions for obtaining a language sample regardless of the procedures (Florida Department of Education, 1989):

1. Use a high-quality recorder to assure a good playback. The tape recorder should have a quality microphone that will result in a quality sample. The speakers are also important during playback. For purposes of transcription, a recorder with a counter will be invaluable, as you will find you need to stop many times, rewind a short distance, and listen again.

2. Use appropriate stimulus materials (e.g., toys, pictures) based on the interests, intellectual level, and disabilities of the child.

3. Present the stimulus material to the child and ask questions about the material that require more than one- or two-word responses from the child. Try to elicit complete sentences from the child and set a conversational climate conducive to eliciting responses from the child.

4. Try to elicit different grammmatical forms such as past tense, plural, and so on, if possible. Encourage this by using them in your own speech. For example, ask, "What will he do next?" "What did he say then?"

5. Repeat what the child says, if possible. This will aid you later in transcribing the tape. This should be done so that the child is unaware of it. If the repeating becomes distracting, discontinue. For example:

Child: He don't goes in.
Examiner: He don't goes in? Why not?
Child: He too big.
Examiner: He too big. Yes, he is.

6. Take notes while the child is talking, including attempts to write out some of the utterances. These notes help when you go back and transcribe the tape. Also, this gives you a good idea of the number of utterances obtained from the child.

7. Transcribe the tape as soon as possible after the session so that you can make use of your own recall of the sample.

Analyzing the Sample

Analyze the form, content, and use of language.

Once the language sample has been obtained from the child, the examiner needs to determine the level of analysis of the sample. This analysis includes (1) form, including phonology, morphology, and syntax; (2) content, including vocabulary; and (3) use, including pragmatics. In addition, the use of any nonstandard dialect should be noted. The specific guidelines to follow are beyond the scope of this discussion. However, Smiley and Goldstein (1998) provided teacher-oriented suggestions for the analysis of both the quantitative and qualitative aspects of language sampling. For example, they noted that the following information should be included, at least when morphology and simple syntax are analyzed:

1. Plural markers, both regular and irregular.
2. Past tense markers, both regular and irregular.
3. Third person singular markers, both regular and irregular.
4. Articles (a, an, the).
5. Copula (linking verb) and auxiliary (helping verb).
6. Modal auxiliaries and emphatic auxiliary.
7. Pronouns.
8. Prepositions.
9. Comparative and superlative markers.

In addition, Smiley and Goldstein (1998) provide examples and suggestions for analysis. Interested readers are encouraged to consult the appendix of their book for additional information.

Formal Language Tests

Why Use Formal Language Tests?

Screening and identification of language problems; informal determination of objectives and teaching strategies; establishment of IEP goals.

Who Should Use Them?

Teachers; speech and language clinicians.

Comprehensive Receptive and Expressive Vocabulary Test–2

The *Comprehensive Receptive and Expressive Vocabulary Test–2* (CREVT–2; Wallace & Hammill, 2002) is an individually administered test of both expressive and receptive oral vocabulary. It has two equivalent forms that can be used for individuals ages 4 through adulthood. The authors note four distinctive features of the CREVT–2. First, both receptive and expressive vocabulary skills are measured; second, those areas are both measured based on the same normative sample. Third, both the receptive and expressive vocabulary items pertain to the same ten categories of words (e.g., animals, transportation). Fourth, the authors note that the CREVT–2 uses color photographs in the receptive vocabulary subtest, unlike other measures that use black-and-white drawings (although color pictures are now more common).

The CREVT-2 has two forms.

The four primary uses of the CREVT–2 are (1) to identify students who are significantly below their peers in oral vocabulary proficiency, (2) to determine any discrepancy between receptive and expressive oral vocabulary skills, (3) to document progress in oral vocabulary development as a consequence of special intervention programs, and (4) to measure oral vocabulary in research studies.

Description of Subtests

Receptive Vocabulary.   In this subtest the student is shown ten plates (e.g., one with animals, one with modes of transportation), each of which has six pictures. The examiner then says a series of stimulus words one at a time. After each word, the student must select the correct choice from one of the six pictures. As noted, each of the ten plates represents a different category of vocabulary words. In this subtest, all students begin with the first item and continue until two items in a row are missed (at which point the testing is discontinued).

Expressive Vocabulary.   This subtest requires the student to provide an oral definition for words that are stated by the examiner. ("What does _____ mean?") The words used in this subtest are based on the same categories used in the Receptive Vocabulary subtest. The basal for this subtest is three in a row correct and the ceiling is three in a row incorrect. This subtest is not administered to children under age 5.

Interpretation of Results.   Raw scores from the Receptive Vocabulary and Expressive Vocabulary subtests are converted into standard scores (mean = 100; standard deviation = 15), percentile ranks, and age equivalents. It is also possible to obtain a standard score for a composite of the two subtests called General Vocabulary. A table is presented in the test manual that also allows the conversion of the CREVT–2 scores to stanines, T-scores, and national curve equivalents.

Expressive and receptive vocabulary are compared to the same norm.

Technical Characteristics

Normative Sample.   The normative sample consisted of 2,545 individuals stratified according to socioeconomic factors, gender, disability, and other factors. The sample was similar to the 2000 census data regarding representation in the United States.

Reliability.   The majority of internal reliability coefficients (coefficient alpha) across age levels for the Receptive and Expressive subtests were .90 and above. The coefficients for the Composites were above average for all age levels except for individuals aged 70–89. Median alternate form reliability coefficients were .94, .88, and .94 for the Receptive, Expressive, and Composite scores, respectively. Test-retest coefficients were determined for a relatively small sample of kindergarten students (.91 to .95), high school students (.93 to .99), and adults (.93 to .99).

Validity.   The authors provide a rationale for the content validity of the CREVT–2 in the manual. They also argue for its construct validity by noting the increase of scores as the age of the examinee increases. Criterion-related validity coefficients were determined using a variety of vocabulary measures. These generally ranged in the .70s and .80s, although some were higher and lower than that range. The coefficients differed slightly depending on the CREVT–2 form (A or B).

Review of Relevant Research.   No research was located on the CREVT–2. Information related to the clinical use of the instrument for the diagnosis and classification, particularly of language problems, is necessary. Bosley (1998) did use the original CREVT as a measure of language maturity in a study designed to look at the relationship of verbal aggression and language maturity. Similarly, the CREVT was reported to have adequate validity using the WISC-III as the criterion (Smith, Smith, Eichler, & Pollard 2002).

Overview: Comprehensive Receptive and Expressive Vocabulary Test–2

- *Age level*—4 through 89 years.
- *Type of administration*—Individual.
- *Technical adequacy*—Adequate standardization, good reliability, adequate validity.
- *Scores yielded*—Standard scores, percentile ranks, and age equivalents.
- *Suggested use*—The CREVT–2 is a potentially valuable instrument that provides scores for both expressive and receptive oral vocabulary based on the same normative sample. The technical characteristics appear to be adequate enough to confidently make decisions regarding a person's vocabulary skills. The receptive portion is also colorful and would be appropriate for younger children. More evidence of validity would be helpful. There is an adult version called the *CREVT–Adult* (Wallace & Hammill, 1997a) and a computer-administered version (Wallace & Hammill, 1997b). The latter is a multimedia, interactive test.

A computerized version of the CREVT–2 is available.

Oral and Written Language Scales (Oral Scales)

The oral language component of the *Oral and Written Language Scales* (OWLS; Carrow-Woolfolk, 1995) includes two individually administered scales. The scales, Listening Comprehension (LC) and Oral Expression (OE), can be administered to individuals from age 3 through 21. Together, they provide a comprehensive measure of both receptive and expressive language. The written language component is packaged separately with its own manual (see Chapter 14 for a discussion). Results from the LC and OE scales can be used to determine broad levels of language skills as well as specific receptive and expressive language skills. Uses noted by the test publisher include meeting the IDEA requirements for learning disabilities assessment and providing a record of growth in language skills over time.

Oral Scales measure listening comprehension and oral expression.

Description

Listening Comprehension Scale.   This scale includes items presented in a multiple-choice format. The examiner reads aloud a verbal stimulus and the student must point to the correct picture (out of four in an easel kit) that represents the stimulus. The items measure areas ranging from comprehension of nouns, verbs, idioms, and so on to the comprehension of figurative language, humor, and meaning from context, logic, and inference.

Oral Expression.   In this scale the student is shown one or more pictures while the examiner reads a verbal stimulus. The student responds orally by answering questions, completing sentences, or generating one or more sentences. The scale measures the same areas as the Listening Comprehension scale plus the area of pragmatic language. The possible correct and incorrect responses as well as the scoring criteria are placed directly on the test protocol.

Interpretation of Results.   Derived scores for both the LC and OE scales include standard scores (mean = 100; standard deviation = 15), percentiles, normal curve equivalents, stanines, and age equivalents. These same options are also available for an Oral Composite (OC), which includes the raw scores of both scales. If the Written scale is administered, an overall Language Composite is also available. For the OE scale a feature called the Descriptive Categories of Responses can be used. For example, this provides the option of categorizing the incorrect answers into grammatically or syntactically/pragmatically incorrect. Finally, it is possible to determine the level of significance of the difference between the scores on the two scales.

Technical Characteristics

Normative Sample.   A total of 1,795 individuals were included in the standardization of the Oral scales. The sample was based on 1991 census data and included variables such as gender, race, geographic region, and parent education level.

Reliability.   Internal reliability coefficients were .84 for LC, .87 for OE, and .91 for the OC. Test-retest coefficients ranged from .73 to .80 for LC, .77 to .86 for OE, and .81 to .89 for the OC. Finally the interrater reliability for the OE scale was reported at .95 (average of four grade levels).

Validity.   Criterion-related validity coefficients of the Oral Composite with various language measures (e.g., the PPVT-R) were primarily in the .70s. One exception was the Total score from the *Clinical Evaluation of Language-Fundamentals–Revised,* which was considerably higher (.91). Coefficients with verbal measures of intelligence and Global IQs were also in the .70s. Coefficients with nonverbal intelligence, as expected, were somewhat lower (.65 to .70). Coefficients with academic measures were variable, primarily in the .60s to .80s range. Differences in scores between nonclinical and clinical (e.g., learning disabilities, language delayed, language impaired) samples were also reported.

Review of Relevant Research.   Interestingly, no specific literature was located on the OWLS although it has been used as an outcome measure in research studies (e.g., Gillam, Crofford, Gale, & Hoffman, 2001). In a review of the OWLS, Bradley-Johnson (1998a) recommended that it not be used for eligibility purposes because of the relatively low test-retest reliability coefficients. She suggested that additional test-retest data by age level are needed. In another review, Goldblatt and Friedman (1998–1999) also noted the limited reliability but offered that the materials are engaging and provide a good sample of various language skills.

Overview: Oral and Written Language Scales (Oral Scales)

- *Age level*—3 through 21 years.
- *Type of administration*—Individual.
- *Technical adequacy*—Good standardization, adequate reliability and validity.
- *Scores yielded*—Standard scores, percentiles, normal curve equivalents, stanines, age equivalents.
- *Suggested use*—The Oral Scales from the OWLS appear to measure a broad spectrum of receptive and expressive language skills. Unlike other measures of receptive and expressive language, it measures more than just vocabulary. The Descriptive Categories of Responses for the Oral Expression scale is a nice feature. As noted by the test publisher, it can also be used to assist in the identification of learning disabilities that are primarily language related. Particularly when used with the Written scale, the OWLS provides a comprehensive overview of an individual's strengths and weaknesses in language. Additional reliability and validity data would give users more confidence in making important educational decisions.

Peabody Picture Vocabulary Test–4

The PPVT-4 is the most popular measure of receptive vocabulary.

The *Peabody Picture Vocabulary Test–4* (PPVT-4; Dunn & Dunn, 2007) is an extremely popular individually administered instrument that measures receptive language ability (semantics: receptive). According to the authors, it is a useful screening device for verbal development and is appropriate for measuring language development among nonreaders and those with expressive language problems, although the PPVT-4 measures only hearing vocabulary. The authors also provide a case for the relationship between vocabulary and reading comprehension and between vocabulary and cognitive ability. Test results should *not* be used solely for measuring those areas, however. The original 1965 edition of the PPVT was frequently used—actually, misused—as an intelligence measure, primarily because it included a table to transform raw scores to IQs. The authors do point out, however, that the test should be used as only one element in a comprehensive test battery of cognitive processes. The test is both easy and quick to administer. It has two forms (A and B) that can be used with individuals from ages 2½ to over 90.

Description.   The 228 PPVT-4 items are presented in an easel kit. The examinee is presented with four numbered pictures on each page. When the vocabulary word is stated by the examiner, the examinee must indicate the correct picture either by pointing or saying the number of the picture. For example, the examiner says the word "feline" and the examinee must indicate the correct answer from pictures of a deer, a cat, a dog, and a donkey.

Interpretation of Results.   The PPVT-4 offers several types of derived scores. These include standard scores, percentiles, normal curve equivalents, stanines, and age and grade equivalents. Also available is a Growth Score Value, which is not a normative score but rather is designed as a score to statistically determine an individual's progress over time.

Technical Characteristics

Normative Sample.   The PPVT-4 has both age norms and grade norms. For the age norms, 3,540 individuals ages 2½ to 90+ were included. For the grade norms, all those in kindergarten through grade 12 from the age norms were included. The sample was representative of the 2004 census in areas such as race/ethnicity, socioeconomic status, geographic region, and gender.

Reliability.   Split-half reliability coefficients averaged .94 for both Form A and Form B for the age norms and .95 (Form A) and .94 (Form B) for the grade norms. Alternate-form reliability was .89. The test-retest reliability was .93.

Validity.   A discussion of content validity is provided in the manual. Correlations with a number of other tests such as the Clinical Evaluation of Language Functions were adequate although the correlations with a reading test, the Group Reading Assessment and Diagnostic Evaluation, were moderate at best, thus questioning the relationship of reading and vocabulary development as measured by the PPVT-4.

Review of Relevant Research.   Because of the recency of the publication of PPVT-4, no research was located at the time of the publication of this book. Because of the similarity between the current edition and the PPVT-III, research on the latter might be relevant. Those studies are summarized below.

- The PPVT-III correlated between .56 to .88 with various IQs and index scores from the WISC-III. Not surprisingly, the highest correlation was with the Verbal IQ (Hodapp & Gerken, 1999). This finding, however, does not indicate that the PPVT-III should be used as a measure of intelligence.
- The PPVT-III is an appropriate instrument to use with African American preschoolers (Washington & Craig, 1999).
- The PPVT-III had weak to moderate correlations with actual language performance, suggesting that caution should be taken when predicting actual conversational language from this test (Ukrainetz & Blomquist, 2002).
- Boys in Headstart programs scored significantly lower than girls in the programs. In addition, boys with behavior problems scored lower than their peers without behavior problems (Kaiser, Cai, Hancock, & Foster, 2002).
- Preschool African American children scored significantly lower on the PPVT-III than the average for the normative sample. This performance could be reflective of socioeconomic status or ethnic patterns of vocabulary usage (Champion, Hyter, McCabe, & Bland-Stewart, 2003).
- African American children from low-socioeconomic areas scored significantly lower on the PPVT-III than on an intelligence measure, the Kaufman Assessment Battery for Children (Campbell, Bell, & Keith, 2001).
- Adults with poor language skills scored scored significantly higher on the PPVT-III than on the PPVT-Revised (Pankratz, Morrison, & Plante, 2004).

Overview: Peabody Picture Vocabulary Test–4

- *Age level*—2½ through 90+ years.
- *Type of administration*—Individual.
- *Technical adequacy*—Good standardization (somewhat limited for adults), good reliability, adequate validity.

- *Scores yielded*—Standard scores, percentiles, normal curve equivalents, stanines, age and grade equivalents, growth-scale values.
- *Suggested use*—The PPVT-4 seems to be a good measure of receptive vocabulary, although it should be used for screening or as a part of a more comprehensive evaluation. The PPVT-4 can be used with individuals who have speech and language as well as (to a certain extent) motor disabilities. Advantages of the newest edition include the use of larger pictures and colored pictures (earlier editions used black-and-white drawings). The PPVT-4 also added more items, particularly for younger students. It should be noted that the PPVT-4 was co-normed with the *Expressive Vocabulary Test–2* (Williams, 2007), so a measure of both receptive and expressive vocabulary using the same comparison group is available. Computerized scoring is also available that provides a variety of report options, including an analysis of the types of errors the individual made (noun, verb, attribute).

Tests of Language Development–3

The *Tests of Language Development–3* (TOLD-3; Hammill & Newcomer, 1997; Newcomer & Hammill, 1997) consist of a primary edition (TOLD-3 Primary) and an intermediate edition (TOLD-3 Intermediate). According to the authors, the TOLD-3 can be used to identify children who have language disorders and to profile individual strengths and weaknesses in basic language abilities. They add that the test is based on a sound theoretical model. This model includes semantics, syntax, and phonology through the receptive, organizing, and expressive channels for the TOLD-3 Primary. The TOLD-3 Intermediate measures both semantics and syntax through the receptive and expressive channels.

> The TOLD-3 has a primary and an intermediate edition.

Description

TOLD-3 Primary.   The primary edition of the TOLD-3 is designed for use with children ages 4 to 8. It includes six subtests that measure syntax and semantics and three optional subtests that measure phonology. The subtests and what they measure follow.

> *Picture Vocabulary.* Understanding the meaning of words.
> *Relational Vocabulary.* Understanding similarities between words.
> *Oral Vocabulary.* Defining words.
> *Grammatic Understanding.* Understanding sentence structure.
> *Sentence Imitation.* Generating proper sentences.
> *Grammatic Completion.* Using acceptable morphological forms.
> *Word Discrimination.* Noticing sound differences.
> *Phonemic Analysis.* Segmenting words into smaller phonemic units.
> *Word Articulation.* Saying words correctly.

TOLD-3 Intermediate.   The intermediate version of the TOLD-3 is designed for use with children ages 8½ to 12. The six subtests and what they measure follow.

> *Sentence Combining.* Constructing compound or complex sentences from two or more simple sentences.
> *Picture Vocabulary.* Identifying pictures that represent a two-word phrase (e.g., face scraper).
> *Word Ordering.* Constructing sentences from a series of randomly presented words.

General Understanding. Identifying abstract relationships of three related words (e.g., Mars, Venus, Pluto).
Grammatic Comprehension. Recognizing grammatical sentences.
Malapropisms. Correcting ridiculous sentences.

Interpretation of Scores.   The TOLD-3 yields several derived scores. These include age equivalents, percentiles, and standard scores for the individual subtests. The standard scores have a mean of 10 and a standard deviation of 3. In addition, the subtests can be grouped into the following composites: syntax, semantics, speaking, listening, organizing (primary edition only), and overall spoken language. Each of these composites yields quotients with a mean of 100 and a standard deviation of 15. A summary sheet and profile chart are also available that display the scores visually.

Technical Characteristics

Normative Sample.   The primary edition was standardized on approximately 1,000 children from twenty-eight states; the intermediate edition used 779 children from twenty-three states. The characteristics of the samples were similar to the national population in 1990.

Reliability.   Internal consistency coefficients for both editions were in the .80s and .90s for the subtests and above .90 for the composites. Test-retest coefficients were generally above .80 for both editions (somewhat higher for the Intermediate).

Validity.   The manual presents evidence to support both editions content and construct validity. Concurrent validity data with a variety of criterion measures are also presented. The composites correlated in the .80s with the TOAL-3 and between .75 and .91 with the *Bankson Language Test* (2nd edition). The coefficients for the subtests with these criterion measures were somewhat lower.

Review of Relevant Research.   No research literature on the TOLD-3 was located; in fact, only one study was found that investigated the TOLD-2. That study indicated that both the primary and intermediate forms had adequate reliability, with the exception of the 8-year-old level (Fodness, McNeilly, & Bradley-Johnson, 1991). The TOLD-3 has been reviewed, however. Bradley-Johnson (1998b) felt that it was a considerable improvement over earlier versions, although the criterion-related validity data were limited.

Overview: Tests of Language Development–3
- *Age level*—4 to 8 years (primary); 8½ to 12 years (intermediate).
- *Type of administration*—Individual.
- *Technical adequacy*—Acceptable reliability and validity.
- *Scores yielded*—Standard scores, percentile ranks, age equivalents.
- *Suggested use*—The TOLD-3 editions are similar to their predecessors, the TOLD-2 Primary and the TOLD-2 Intermediate. Both tests measure a number of language areas in both the receptive and expressive channels (also organizing channel for the Primary edition). This model allows for a profile of a child's strengths and weaknesses in language, using the same comparison group. The value of the tests depends on the extent to which the subtests actually measure the various language components. Clearly, research should be conducted to address this

The TOLD-3 provides a profile of expressive and receptive skills.

issue. One nice addition to the TOLD-3 is the use of colored pictures. This makes them more interesting, particularly for younger children. Interested readers should note that there is another instrument to measure language skills in young children: The *Test of Early Language Development-3* (Hresko, Reid, & Hammill, 1999) is designed for children ages 2 to 7.

Additional Oral Language Instruments

Comprehensive Test of Phonological Processing

The CTOPP measures skills thought to be related to reading.

- *Age level*—5 through 24 years.
- *Type of administration*—Individual.
- *Technical adequacy*—Good standardization and validity, adequate reliability.
- *Scores yielded*—Standard scores, percentiles, age and grade equivalents.
- *Suggested use*—The *Comprehensive Test of Phonological Processing* (CTOPP; Wagner, Torgesen, & Rashotte, 1999) measures the areas of phonological awareness, phonological memory, and rapid naming (a Quotient is available for each of these areas). There are two forms of the CTOPP, one for ages 5 and 6, and the other for ages 7 through 24. The early version includes seven core subtests and one supplemental subtest. The core subtests for this version are Elision (segmenting words into smaller parts), Rapid Color Naming, Blending Words, Sound Matching, Rapid Object Naming, Memory for Digits, and Nonword Repetition. The older version includes six core subtests and eight supplemental subtests. The core subtests are Elision, Blending Words, Memory for Digits, Rapid Digit Naming, Nonword Repetition, and Rapid Letter Naming. The authors note the growing research base suggesting that phonological processing deficits are related to reading problems. In a review of the CTOPP, Bruno and Walker (1998–1999) were generally favorable but noted that the reliability for some of the subtests, particularly for the younger children, were somewhat low. They also suggested that examiners be very familiar with the test items and format of the tests before administering it and that a quality tape recorder with a counter be used to play the audiotape that accompanies the instrument. Two validity studies were located. In both, the CTOPP had moderate to strong correlation with other measures of phonological processing (Havey, Story, & Buker, 2002) and early literacy skills (Hintze, Ryan, & Stoner, 2003).

Expressive Vocabulary Test–2

- *Age level*—2½ to 90+ years.
- *Type of administration*—Individual.
- *Technical adequacy*—Good standardization, adequate reliability and validity.
- *Scores yielded*—Standard scores, percentiles, age equivalents, stanines, normal curve equivalents.
- *Suggested use*—The *Expressive Vocabulary Test–2* (EVT-2; Williams, 2007) is the expressive counterpart of the PPVT-4 discussed earlier in this chapter. Although the two tests were developed by different authors, they share the same standardization sample. Thus, an individual's expressive and receptive vocabulary can be compared to the same normative group. The EVT-2 is

designed for use with individuals ages 2½ through 90 years. It measures expressive vocabulary in two ways: first, through the use of labeling items, designed primarily for younger children. This requires the child to identify the name of a picture (e.g., rabbit, ship, leaf). The second method is the use of synonyms in which the person is shown a picture and given a name (e.g. a chart). A correct synonym (e.g., diagram, graph) must be given. The EVT-2 can be given quickly with an average administration time of fifteen minutes. There are two parallel forms, each with 190 items.

Illinois Test of Psycholinguistic Abilities–3

- *Age level*—5 through 12 years.
- *Type of administration*—Individual.
- *Technical adequacy*—Good standardization and reliability, adequate validity.
- *Scores yielded*—Standard scores, percentiles, age and grade equivalents.
- *Suggested use*—The *Illinois Test of Psycholinguistic Abilities–3* (ITPA-3; Hammill, Mather, & Roberts, 2001) is a recent major revision of a once-popular and controversial test. The original ITPA included twelve subtests that purportedly measured channels of communication (input-output modalities), psycholinguistic processes (reception, association, expression), and levels of organization (representational and automatic). Many critics noted that the ITPA didn't really measure these constructs and was more a measure of verbal intelligence. Unfortunately, this was one of the most popular "process tests" in the early history of learning disabilities.

  The authors of the ITPA-3 acknowledged many of the limitations, particularly the technical adequacy of the original instrument. In response, they developed ten new subtests (they kept two from the original but changed their names) and paid close attention to issues of validity and reliability. The subtests are Spoken Analogies, Spoken Vocabulary, Morphological Closure, Syntactic Sentences, Sound Deletion, Rhyming Sequences, Sentence Sequencing, Written Vocabulary, Sight Decoding, Sound Decoding, Sight Spelling, and Sound Spelling. In addition to the twelve subtests, there are eight specific composites related to both spoken and written language and three general composites: Spoken Language, Written Language, and General Language (see Table 10.1). The ITPA-3 is a vastly different instrument from its predecessors. Care was taken to ensure that the instrument measures only linguistic ability, both oral and written. Only time, use, and research will determine the potential uses and limitations of the ITPA-3.

The ITPA-3 is considerably different from previous editions.

Test for Auditory Comprehension of Language–3

- *Age level*—3 through 9 years.
- *Type of administration*—Individual.
- *Technical adequacy*—Good standardization, adequate validity and reliability.
- *Scores yielded*—Standard scores, percentiles, age equivalents.
- *Suggested use*—The *Test for Auditory Comprehension of Language–3* (TACL-3; Carrow-Woolfolk, 1999a) is a measure of receptive vocabulary, grammar, and syntax. There are three subtests that total 142 items. These are Vocabulary, Grammatical Morphemes, and Elaborated Phrases and Sentences. The format of the test is straightforward. A colored picture plate is presented that includes three drawings. A word or sentence is read to the child, who must indicate which of the three drawings represents the meaning of the word or morphemic or syntactic structure. The child points to the correct response to

TABLE 10.1   Relationship of ITPA–3 Subtests to Composites

ITPA–3 Subtests	Global Constructs			Specific Constructs							
				Spoken Language			Written Language				
	General Language	Spoken Language	Written Language	Semantics	Grammar	Phonology	Comprehension	Word Identification	Spelling	Sight-Symbol Processing	Sound-Symbol Processing
Spoken Analogies	X	X		X							
Spoken Vocabulary	X	X		X							
Morphological Closure	X	X			X						
Syntactic Sentences	X	X			X						
Sound Deletion	X	X				X					
Rhyming Sequences	X	X				X					
Sentences Sequencing	X		X				X				
Written Vocabulary	X		X				X				
Sight Decoding	X		X					X		X	
Sound Decoding	X		X					X			X
Sight Spelling	X		X						X	X	
Sound Spelling	X		X						X		X

Source: D. Hammill, N. Mather, and R. Roberts. *Illinois Test of Psycholinguistic Abilities–3.* Copyright © 2001 by Pro-Ed, Austin, TX. Reprinted with permission.

eliminate the spoken language component. Overall, it is an easy test to administer and score. Ceiling rules are used so that items that are too difficult are not administered.

Test of Adolescent and Adult Language–4

- *Age level*—12 through 24 years.
- *Type of administration*—Individual (small group possible).
- *Technical adequacy*—Adequate standardization, good validity and reliability.
- *Scores yielded*—Standard scores and percentiles.
- *Suggested use*—The *Test of Adolescent and Adult Language–4* (TOAL-4; Hammill, Brown, Larsen, & Wiederholt, 2007) measures both oral and written language for older students and young adults. The TOAL-4 is a significant revision from the previous edition, with virtually all new subtests based on a different theoretical model. There are six subtests: Word Opposites, Word Derivations, Spoken Analogies, Word Similarities, Sentence Combining, and Orthographic Usage. The first three subtests can be combined to provide a Spoken Language Composite, and the last three provide a Written Language Composite. Finally, all six subtests can be combined to form a General Language Composite. The authors state that the test can be used with individuals who have varying degrees of knowledge of the English language.

Tests for Speech and Language Clinicians

Why Use Specialized Language Tests?

Identification; determination of goals and objectives.

Who Should Use Them?

Speech and language clinicians.

Some tests, although useful to the special educator, are typically administered by speech and language clinicians. These tests focus on various aspects of language and are typically used to identify individuals that might have a language disorder in one or more areas. It is recommended that the manuals and test materials be consulted for more information about these tests.

Clinical Evaluation of Language Fundamentals–4

The *Clinical Evaluation of Language Fundamentals–4* (CELF-4; Semel, Wiig, & Secord, 2003) is the latest revision of this popular test. The CELF-4 provides an evaluation of both language processing and production for students from ages 5 to 21. The test provides scores for Core Language, Receptive Language, Expressive Language, Language Structure, Language Content, Language and Memory, and Memory.

The test can be administered in approximately an hour and can provide standard scores, age equivalents, and percentile ranks. There is also a Preschool version, a Screening version, and a Spanish version.

Comprehensive Assessment of Spoken Language

The *Comprehensive Assessment of Spoken Language* (CASL; Carrow-Woolfolk, 1999b) is an orally administered language battery to identify delayed or disordered language. It is designed for use with individuals ages 3 through 21 years. There are two separate record forms, one for ages 3 through 6 and the other for ages 7 through 21. This individually administered instrument can also be used in the determination of language-based learning disabilities. The test includes fifteen subtests that measure four language structure categories: Lexical/Semantic, Syntactic, Supralinguistic, and Pragmatic. A variety of scores are available, including standard scores (mean = 100; SD = 15), grade and age equivalents, percentiles, normal curve equivalents, and stanines. These scores are available for both age-based and grade-based norms. The CASL is a purely oral instrument; no reading or writing is required. Computer scoring software (ASSIST) is available, as well as a video that demonstrates how to administer the test.

Language Processing Test–3

The *Language Processing Test–3* (LPT-3; Richard & Hanner, 2005) was designed to measure an individual's ability to attach meaning to language and to effectively formulate a response. Norms are available for individuals ages 5 to 12, although the authors state that the LPT-3 can be used with older individuals for more informal purposes. The authors further indicated the types of behaviors that might be observed in individuals whose language problems might be identified through the use of the LPT-3. These include word-retrieval problems, inappropriate word usage, neutral or nonspecific word usage (e.g., thingamajig), inability to correct recognized errors, seemingly poor memory, avoidance or no response, repeating what has been asked, and pausing.

There are eight subtests on the LPT-3: (1) Associations, (2) Categorization, (3) Similarities, (4) Differences, (5) Multiple Meanings, (6) Attributes, (7) Labeling, and (8) Stating Functions. Age equivalents, percentile ranks, and standard scores are available for interpretation purposes. There is also an associated Language Processing Kit that includes reproducible activities to remediate deficits noted in the LPT-3.

Test of Problem Solving–3

The *Test of Problem Solving–3—Elementary* (TOPS-3; Bowers et al., 2006) is designed for children ages 6 through 12. It measures thinking skills based on the child's language strategies. The test includes six subtests: (1) Making Inferences, (2) Predicting, (3) Determining Causes, (4), Sequencing, (5) Negative Questions, and (6) Problem Solving. Standard scores, percentile ranks, and age equivalents are available for each subtest and for the total test. There is also a version of the TOPS-3 for older students called the *Test of Problem Solving–2—Adolescent* (Bowers, Huisingh, & LoGuidice, 2007) that is designed for individuals ages 12 through 17. Also available are the *Tasks of Problem Solving*, a book of activities and exercises designed to increase expressive language and problem-solving ability. There are separate books for elementary and adolescent students.

Test of Word Finding–2

The TWF-2 measures a unique aspect of language.

The *Test of Word Finding–2* (TWF-2; German, 2000) is designed to measure the word-finding ability of children ages 4 through 12. There are three forms, a preprimer form for preschool and kindergarten children, a primary form for first and second grades, and an intermediate form for third through sixth grades. There are four different sections that measure the child's word-finding skills. These are Picture Naming Nouns, Sentence Completion Naming, Picture Naming

Verbs, and Picture Naming Categories. In addition, there are five informal supplemental analyses or procedures that can be used to analyze the student's performance. The TWF-2 provides percentile ranks and standard scores for both age and grade comparisons. There is also considerable information in the manual about the types of word-finding skills that can be identified.

BACK TO THE PROFILE

Possible Answers to the Questions

1. **Why assess Bobby?** Bobby appears to have a history of speech and language problems, although they were not severe enough for his parents to do anything other than see his pediatrician. The continued problems, however, have caused his teacher to become concerned. Bobby's description indicates that he might have difficulty in a number of areas including phonology, semantics, and pragmatics in both the receptive and expressive areas. It would seem that a comprehensive language evaluation would be needed to determine the area(s) in which Bobby is having difficulty and to see if he might qualify for speech and language services.

2. **Who should assess Bobby?** Bobby would probably be evaluated by a speech and language clinician. Depending on which test(s) are chosen, another type of diagnostician (e.g., educational diagnostician) might also be involved. Informal assessment could be conducted by the teacher. For example, she could provide meaningful language samples for analysis of Bobby's use of spontaneous language.

3. **What test(s)/procedure(s) should be used?** Because Bobby seems to be having difficulty in a number of areas of both expressive and receptive language, a comprehensive test (or battery of tests) should be given. Another consideration is his age. Although many of the tests discussed in the chapter (e.g., CELF-4, TOPS-3) have norms that begin at age 6, there might not be enough items on those tests that are really relevant for someone that age, particularly since Bobby only recently had his sixth birthday. Two possible instruments to use would be the Oral Scales from the OWLS or the TOLD-3 Primary. Both instruments measure expressive and receptive language in a number of areas. Plus, the norms begin at age 3 for the Oral Scales and age 4 for the TOLD-3 Primary. As mentioned previously, a spontaneous language sample would also provide helpful information. If the language sample and/or comprehensive instrument indicated a particular problem in a specific component (e.g., semantics), a test such as the CREVT-2 could be used to provide additional information. Finally, the speech-language clinician would also probably administer a test of articulation.

4. **What other area(s) should be assessed?** As noted above, other language areas might be probed based on the results of the language sample and the comprehensive language test. An obvious area that should be addressed is hearing. Although Bobby undoubtedly has had a hearing screening, it would be advisable to have an audiological evaluation.

STUDENT PROFILE DATA

Bobby

The Oral Scales from the *Oral and Written Language Scales* were administered to Bobby. The following information was obtained:

Listening Comprehension Scale	87
Oral Expression Scale	72
Oral Composite	79

These results indicate that Bobby is having difficulty with both expressive and receptive language but is having more problems in oral expression. Using the Descriptive Categories of Responses, it was determined that Bobby was having particular difficulty with syntax and pragmatics. He is now seeing a speech and language pathologist twice a week for therapy.

CASE STUDY *June*

As part of the assessment battery, June was given the *Comprehensive Test of Phonological Processing* (CTOPP). Here are the results:

Composite	Standard Score
Phonological Awareness	92
Phonological Memory	80
Rapid Naming	93

- Why was the CTOPP selected?
- What do the results of this test tell you?
- Do the results of this test correlate with the results of any other tests that June has been given?

Reflections

1. Why is the assessment of pragmatics skills so important?
2. Why do you think obtaining a language sample will provide more valuable information than administering a standardized language test?
3. The original Peabody Picture Vocabulary Test included tables that allowed an examiner to determine an IQ. This practice was subsequently dropped. Do you think the PPVT-4 should yield an IQ? Why or why not?

Summary Matrix

Instrument or Technique	Screening and Initial Identification	Informal Determination and Evaluation of Teaching Programs and Strategies	Determination of Current Performance Level and Educational Need	Decisions about Classification and Program Placement	IEP Goals	IEP Objectives	IEP Evaluation	Mild/Moderate	Severe/Profound	Preschool	Elementary Age	Secondary Age	Adult	Special Considerations	Educational Relevance for Exceptional Students
	Prereferral	Prereferral	Postreferral	Postreferral	Postreferral	Postreferral	Postreferral	Target Population							
Language Sampling	X	X			X			X		X	X	X	X	Productive means to determine individual's actual spontaneous use of language.	Very Useful
Comprehensive Receptive and Expressive Vocabulary Test–2	X							X		X	X	X		Includes a measure of both receptive and expressive semantics using the same norms.	Useful
Oral and Written Language Scales (Oral Scales)	X				X			X		X	X	X		Oral Scales include listening comprehension and oral expression.	Useful
Peabody Picture Vocabulary Test–4	X							X		X	X	X	X	Can be used with individuals with speech and motor disabilities.	Useful
Tests of Language Development–3	X	X	X		X			X		X	X	X		Measures a variety of language skills; has a primary and intermediate form.	Adequate
Comprehensive Test of Phonological Processing	X	X			X			X		X	X	X		Measures skills shown to be related to reading ability.	Useful
Expressive Vocabulary Test–2	X							X		X	X	X	X	Co-normed with the PPVT-4 to give a measure of both expressive and receptive vocabulary.	Useful
Illinois Test of Psycholinguistic Abilities–3	X	X	X		X			X		X	X			A major revision of one of the most used (and misused) tests in special education.	Adequate/Useful
Test for Auditory Comprehension of Language–3	X	X								X	X			Measures understanding of vocabulary, grammar, and syntax.	Adequate

(continued)

Summary Matrix (continued)

Instrument or Technique	Suggested Use							Target Population						Special Considerations	Educational Relevance for Exceptional Students
	Prereferral		Postreferral												
	Screening and Initial Identification	Informal Determination and Evaluation of Teaching Programs and Strategies	Determination of Current Performance Level and Educational Need	Decisions about Classification and Program Placement	IEP Goals	IEP Objectives	IEP Evaluation	Mild/Moderate	Severe/Profound	Preschool	Elementary Age	Secondary Age	Adult		
Test of Adolescent and Adult Language–4	X	X	X		X			X				X	X	One of a few tests designed to measure language abilities of older students.	Adequate
Clinical Evaluation of Language Fundamentals–4	X	X	X		X			X			X	X		Measures language processing and production.	Useful
Comprehensive Assessment of Spoken Language	X	X	X		X			X		X	X	X		A purely oral instrument, no reading or writing is required.	Adequate/Useful
Language Processing Test–Revised	X	X						X			X			Used to identify children with language processing problems.	Adequate
Test of Problem Solving–3	X	X						X			X	X		Measures the use of language related to events of everyday living.	Adequate
Test of Word Finding–2	X							X			X			Tests for expressive language problems.	Adequate

part four

Assessment of Achievement

As noted in Part III, one major focus of educational and psychological assessment is the evaluation of an individual's abilities. Another major focus of assessment is the measurement of achievement. This usually involves the basic skill areas of *reading* (Chapter 12), *mathematics* (Chapter 13), and *written expression* (including spelling) (Chapter 14). They are sometimes evaluated together with a *general achievement* test (Chapter 11); at other times they are evaluated separately with a variety of instruments and techniques.

The assessment of achievement is extremely important in making appropriate educational decisions. Evaluation in this area is necessary to document that an educational need exists (a requirement of the Individuals with Disabilities Education Act [IDEA 04]) and to help make eligibility decisions. More importantly, information in this area is used to assist in establishing relevant goals and objectives and to monitor progress in relation to those goals and objectives. The use of the instruments and procedures discussed in this section (along with the techniques discussed in Part II) are primarily the responsibility of the teacher.

As in Part III, both formal and informal tests and procedures will be discussed and information provided describing how each type fits into the overall assessment process; the same format will be used to describe the tests. That includes the following elements:

1. A summary matrix that presents information about specific instruments and techniques in a format that allows easy comparison of the instruments for suggested use and target population. The matrix also includes a statement of any special consideration of which a user should be aware. In addition, for each instrument, the matrix gives the educational relevance for exceptional students. The matrices are directly related to the assessment model proposed in Chapter 2.

2. A thorough review of relevant research for each major norm-referenced instrument. The review emphasizes use of the test with exceptional students.

3. An overview box for each test. The overview summarizes the age range, technical adequacy (for norm-referenced tests), and suggested use for each instrument.

AFTER READING PART FOUR
You Should Be Able To:

- Identify strengths and weaknesses of the major general achievement tests.

- Identify strengths and weaknesses of individual- and group-administered reading tests.

- Identify a variety of informal methods of assessing reading.

- Identify strengths and weaknesses of individual- and group-administered mathematics tests (formal and informal).

- Identify strengths and weaknesses of spelling instruments (formal and informal).

- Identify strengths and weaknesses of tests for written expression.

- Identify strengths of written language sampling.

chapter eleven

Assessment of General Achievement

STUDENT PROFILE

Steve

Taking part in a required "high-stakes" statewide assessment program, Steve scored extremely low in both reading (7th percentile) and math (9th percentile). Steve is a fourth grader diagnosed as having attention deficit/hyperactivity disorder. He is receiving some accommodations in the classroom, such as shortened assignments through a "504 Plan." His teacher has noted that Steve does struggle in class, particularly when he has to listen to lecture material for an extended time or when he is working in a large group. He is easily distracted and frequently will doodle and draw pictures rather than doing his assignment or taking notes. His grades are average at best, and his mother states that she spends two to three hours per day going over his homework and schoolwork that wasn't completed in class. She was, however, very concerned when she received Steve's test scores. The assumption had always been that it wasn't a question of whether Steve *could* do the work but rather whether he *would* do the work. She discussed this with Steve's teacher; they were both unsure whether the scores reflected a true academic deficit or were deflated because of attention problems related to his AD/HD and the fact that the assessment was group-administered.

Think about These Questions as You Read This Chapter:

1. Why assess Steve? (There could be more than one reason.)
2. Who should assess Steve? (There could be more than one person.)
3. What procedure(s)/test(s) should be used?
4. What other areas(s) (if any) should be assessed?

(Suggested answers appear at the end of this chapter).

Probably all individuals have taken some kind of achievement test during their years as students. Typically, group achievement tests are administered periodically to document both the level of academic ability and the progress of individuals in specific academic areas. Individual achievement tests are sometimes administered to yield more specific academic information and to allow the examiner to observe the student's approach to the individual tasks. Many students perform quite differently on group and individual achievement tests, although individual achievement tests are usually required for students who receive special education services. Criterion-referenced inventories are also used to gather more specific information about certain academic areas.

It is absolutely necessary that an achievement test measure the curriculum to which a student is exposed. This requires that the "appropriate" achievement test be carefully selected. In other words, the content of an achievement test must be appropriate and complete in relation to the behaviors (curriculum) being measured. This can best be achieved by choosing valid instruments that measure the content a student has been taught. This is particularly important with group-administered achievement tests used in high-stakes assessment programs. Conversely, it is *not* appropriate to change the curriculum to match the content of the test. It is also important to acknowledge that, similar to intelligence testing, achievement testing often results in lower scores for some types of students, including minority students (see Focus on Diversity).

Although most norm-referenced achievement tests are not really thought of as screening tests, many are used for this purpose. In fact, most achievement tests are used to gather some basic, preliminary information before more in-depth academic assessment is pursued. In some cases, individually administered achievement tests are also used to document that an educational deficit exists in order to meet that requirement of the Individuals with Disabilities Education Act (IDEA 04).

> Achievement tests should reflect the student's curriculum.

Norm-Referenced Tests (Group-Administered)

Why Use Group-Administered Achievement Tests?

Screening and identification of students needing further academic testing; informal determination of goals.

Who Should Use Them?

Teachers.

Group achievement tests usually have different levels for different grades in school. Tests that measure achievement in the elementary grades typically include items related to the basic skill areas of reading, spelling, and arithmetic. The levels for older students are concerned not only with basic skills but also with content areas such as science and social studies. Therefore, not all of the areas measured by each test are used with students of all ages; certain areas are relevant and designed for students at specific grades. Brief descriptions of the most commonly used group achievement tests follow.

Iowa Test of Basic Skills

- *Age range*—Kindergarten through grade 8.
- *Standardization*—Stratified sample of more than 150,000 students (concurrently with the Tests of Achievement and Proficiency).

focus on
Diversity

How Does Social Context Influence Academic Achievement?

Berends and Koretz (1996) discussed six important student-reported social context categories and their impact on test scores of students from different ethnic backgrounds. The information was obtained from large data banks from two national assessments of academic achievement. The categories of social context data were family background, family composition, language use, community characteristics, school characteristics, and curricular differentiation.

Berends and Koretz (1996) used statistical procedures to control for the effects of the social context measures on the achievement test scores of large numbers of white and African American eighth-grade students from the reports of the National Assessment of Educational Progress (NAEP) and the National Education Longitudinal Study (NELS). The differences between the actual reported achievement test scores of the white and African American students were .92 standard deviation (SD) (NAEP) and .77 SD (NELS). After the six social context variables were factored in, the difference between white and African American scores was reduced to .52 SD (NAEP) and .34 SD (NELS). Berends and Koretz do acknowledge that other social context variables might also be important in explaining differences in scores. However, their study shows how social variables can mitigate achievement test scores.

- *Technical adequacy*—Good.
- *Areas measured*—The *Iowa Test of Basic Skills* (Hoover, Dunbar, & Frisbie, 2006, 2007) has ten levels. It includes a complete battery, a core battery, and a survey battery. The complete battery includes the following areas: Vocabulary, Word Analysis, Listening, Reading/Reading Comprehension, Language, Mathematics, Social Studies, Science, and Sources of Information.
- *Types of scores obtained*—Percentile ranks, national stanines, standard scores, grade equivalents, normal curve equivalents.
- *Special features*—Also available in the Iowa series is the *Iowa Tests of Educational Development* (for high school students). A list of accommodations is available, and the test comes in Braille, enlarged print, and Spanish versions. There are three forms of the ITBS—A, B, and C.

Metropolitan Achievement Tests–Eighth Edition

- *Age range*—Kindergarten through grade 12.
- *Standardization*—Stratified sample of approximately 140,000.
- *Technical adequacy*—Good.
- *Areas measured*—The *Metropolitan Achievement Tests–Eighth Edition* (MAT-8; Harcourt Educational Measurement, 2002) has thirteen levels (kindergarten–grade 12) and includes thirteen subtests: Sounds and Print, Reading Vocabulary, Reading Comprehension, Open-Ended Reading, Mathematics, Mathematics Concepts and Problem Solving, Mathematics Computation, Open-Ended Mathematics, Language, Spelling, Open-Ended Writing, Science, and Social Studies. Not all subtests are found on all levels.
- *Types of scores obtained*—Scaled scores, percentile ranks, stanines, grade equivalents, normal-curve equivalents, functional reading levels, proficiency statements, and content cluster performance categories.
- *Special features*—The MAT-8 is the latest revision of an old standby that takes approximately four-and-a-half hours to administer. It provides a complete battery of norm-referenced and criterion-referenced information.

Stanford Achievement Test Series–Tenth Edition

The Stanford Achievement Test Series–Tenth Edition (SAT-10) is actually comprised of three tests. These are the *Stanford Early School Achievement Test*, the *Stanford Achievement Test*, and the *Stanford Test of Academic Skills*.

- *Age range—*
  Stanford Early School Achievement Test: Kindergarten and grade 1.
  Stanford Achievement Test (SAT): Kindergarten 1 through grade 9.
  Stanford Test of Academic Skills: Grades 9 through 12.
- *Standardization—*Stratified sample of almost 200,000.
- *Technical adequacy—*Good.
- *Areas measured—*The *Stanford Early School Achievement Test* (Harcourt Educational Measurement, 2003a) measures sounds and letters, word reading, sentence reading, total reading, mathematics, listening to words and stories, and environment. A total battery score is also available.
- *Areas measured—*The *Stanford Achievement Test* (Harcourt Educational Measurement, 2003b) includes more than twenty subtests that measure the general areas of reading, mathematics, spelling, language, social science, science, and listening skills.
- *Areas measured—*The *Stanford Test of Academic Skills* (Harcourt Educational Measurement, 2003c) measures the following areas for grades 9 through 12: reading vocabulary, reading comprehension, language, spelling, mathematics, science, and social science.
- *Types of scores obtained—*Percentile ranks, stanines, grade equivalents, and standard scores.
- *Special features—*The *Stanford Achievement Test Series* provides a comprehensive evaluation of achievement for students from kindergarten through grade 12. The SAT also has both an edition for use with blind or partially sighted students and one for students with hearing impairments.

The SAT has special editions for students with certain disabilities.

Terra Nova–Second Edition

- *Age range—*Kindergarten through grade 12.
- *Standardization—*Stratified sample of approximately 114,000 (fall standardization) and 150,000 (spring standardization).
- *Technical adequacy—*Limited.
- *Areas measured—*Reading/Language Arts, Mathematics, Science, Social Studies, Word Analysis, Vocabulary, Language Mechanics, Spelling, Mathematics Computation.
- *Types of scores obtained—*A variety of scores including percentile ranks.
- *Special features—*The *Terra Nova–Second Edition* (CTB/McGraw-Hill, 2001) has several versions, including a complete battery, a survey battery, and a multiple assessment battery. The multiple assessment battery includes open-ended items in addition to multiple-choice items. The first four subtests listed above are considered basic and the rest are supplemental. There are also two forms (C and D) of the instrument.

Tests of Achievement and Proficiency

- *Age range—*High school (grades 9 through 12).
- *Standardization—*Stratified sample of more than 150,000 (concurrently with the *Iowa Test of Basic Skills* (ITBS).

- *Technical adequacy*—Acceptable.
- *Areas measured*—For grades 9 through 12 the following areas are measured: Reading Comprehension, Written Expression, Vocabulary, Mathematics, Social Studies, Science, and Information Processing (e.g., reading maps).
- *Types of scores obtained*—National percentiles, national stanines, standard scores, grade equivalents, and normal curve equivalents.
- *Special features*—The *Tests of Achievement and Proficiency* (TAP; Scannell, 1996) are an upward extension of the *Iowa Test of Basic Skills*. This instrument was standardized concurrently with the Iowa Test and the *Cognitive Abilities Test*. Another test, the *Iowa Tests of Educational Development* (ITED; Forsythe, Ansley, Feldt, & Alnot, 2001) is also designed for grades 9 through 12 and was co-normed with the *Cognitive Abilities Test*. The ITED includes more analytic items (e.g., problem solving versus computation).

Norm-Referenced Tests (Individually Administered)

Why Use Individually Administered Achievement Tests?

Screening and identification of students needing further academic testing; documentation of educational need; establishment of IEP goals.

Who Should Use Them?

Teachers; diagnosticians; school psychologists.

Until the 1980s, only two individually administered norm-referenced tests were specifically designed to measure overall academic achievement. Those two tests, the *Peabody Individual Achievement Test* and the *Wide Range Achievement Test*, were frequently used and constantly scrutinized. Other tests were developed, and the two "old standbys" were revised. Descriptions of several of these instruments follow.

Kaufman Test of Educational Achievement–II

The Kaufman Test of Educational Achievement–II (KTEA-II; Kaufman & Kaufman, 2004b) is a revision of a popular instrument that is used with individuals ages 4½ through 25 (grade norms, kindergarten through grade 12). There are two forms of the KTEA-II: the Brief Form that measures the domains of reading, math, and written expression, and the Comprehensive Form that includes fourteen subtests, six of which are supplemental reading subtests. Administration time varies from approximately thirty minutes for younger children to approximately one-and-a-half hours for students in grade 6 and above. According to the authors, the KTEA-II can be used for a variety of purposes including identifying academic strengths and weaknesses, analyzing errors, planning programs, measuring academic progress, evaluating interventions, and making placement decisions. This description focuses on the Comprehensive Form.

Description.   There are eight subtests that are combined into four composites: Reading, Math, Written Expression, and Oral Expression. There are also six supplemental reading subtests. The eight core subtests are briefly described.

Reading

Letter and Word Recognition. Student must orally read letters and words.

Reading Comprehension. The majority of items require the student to read a passage and subsequent questions and respond orally to the questions. One interesting feature is the inclusion of five items at the beginning of the subtest in which the student must read a word and identify the appropriate picture and also seven items that require the student to respond gesturally to commands such as "look at the door." The last four items in the subtest require the student to read five sentences and then put them in the correct order to tell a story and then answer a question about each story.

Math

Math Concepts and Applications. The student is required to answer different types of conceptual and reasoning questions. The items are presented orally, although the student has a visual stimulus (e.g., a table, graph, or word problem) to act as a cue. In addition, the student can use a pencil and paper to aid in computations.

Math Computation. The student must solve traditional addition, subtraction, multiplication, and division problems as well as fractions, algebraic formulae, and other complex types of problems.

Written Language

Written Expression. This subtest is divided into six levels ranging from writing letters and words to providing correct punctuation and capitalization of a paragraph.

Spelling. The student must write the correct spelling of words of increasing difficulty dictated by the examiner.

Oral Language

Listening Comprehension. A CD is used to provide short stories to the student. After hearing the story the student answers questions about it.

Oral Expression. This subtest includes a wide variety of oral tasks requiring the student to demonstrate knowledge of sentence structure, vocabulary, grammar, and pragmatics.

Supplemental Reading Subtests

Phonological Awareness
Nonsense Word Decoding
Word Recognition Fluency
Decoding Fluency
Associational Fluency
Naming Facility

The KTEA-II has six supplementary reading subtests.

Interpretation of Results. The KTEA-II provides a variety of interpretative guidelines to help the examiner get the most out of the test results. Each subtest yields standard scores (mean = 100; standard deviation = 15) based on both age and grade norms. In addition, there are eight composite scores, also with a mean of 100 and a standard deviation of 15. These are combinations of various subtests that measure the same areas. Composite scores are available for Reading, Math, Written Language, Oral Language, Sound-Symbol, Decoding, Reading Fluency, and Oral Fluency. A Comprehensive Achievement Composite is also available that provides a global score of the student's achievement. Overall, the authors suggest a five-step process for interpretation:

1. Interpret the Comprehensive Achievement Composite.
2. Interpret the composite and subtest scores.
3. Identify composite strengths and weaknesses.
4. Identify subtest strengths and weaknesses.
5. Make planned comparisons (this involves tables that show the statistical significance of composite and subtest differences).

Another feature is guidelines and tables that assist the examiner to formally and informally analyze the errors that the student makes. For seven of the subtests, an *item-level classification system* is used. Within this system, each error is automatically classified according to the process, concept, or skill it assesses. For three subtests (Letter and Word Recognition, Nonsense Word Decoding, Spelling), a *within-item classification system* is used that requires more judgment on the examiner's part. The errors made by the student can be compared to norm tables to determine the significance of a particular error. This information can be placed on an Error Analysis Summary (see Figure 11.1 for the Error Analysis Summary for the Spelling subtest).

Error analysis guidelines are available.

Technical Characteristics

Normative Sample.   For the age norms, a nationally representative sample of 3,000 examinees ages 4½ to 25 were used; for the grade norm sample, 2,400 students in grades K–12 were included. The demographic design was based on the population survey of 2001 and was stratified according to gender, parent educational level, nationality, and geographical region. In addition, the educational placement of the students was taken into account to ensure proportional representation of students with different educational classifications or clinical diagnoses. The KTEA-II was co-normed with the KABC-II using a total of 2,520 students.

Reliability.   Overall internal consistency (split-half) reliability coefficients for the composites were all .93 or higher except for Oral Language and Oral Fluency, which were .87 and .85 respectively. The overall split-half coefficients for the subtests were primarily above .90. Two exceptions were Oral Expression (.79) and Association Fluency (.72). For both the composites and subtests, the coefficients were relatively stable across age groups. The pattern for the alternate-form reliability coefficients (based on administrations several weeks apart) was similar to the split-half coefficients with the Oral Language and Oral Fluency composites lower than the other composite scores. Interrater reliability was determined for five subtests that require subjective scoring. All were in the .90s except for Association Fluency and Oral Expression.

Validity.   Evidence of construct validity is provided in the manual through the use of factor analysis and intercorrelations of the subtests and composites and was generally supportive (one exception was the Oral Language domain). Criterion-related validity was established by correlating the scores from the KTEA-II with the original K-TEA, the *Wechsler Individual Achievement Test–II*, the *Woodcock Johnson Test of Achievement–3*, the *Peabody Individual Achievement Test–Revised* and the *Oral and Written Language Scales*. In general, there were relatively high correlations among composites measuring similar constructs (majority in .80s) except for the Oral Language Composite, which had lower and more variable correlations with other instruments. KTEA-II scores were also correlated

FIGURE 11.1 Error Analysis Summary for the Spelling Subtest of Kaufman Test of Educational Achievement–II

Item	Score	Single/Double Consonant	Initial Blend	Medial/Final Blend	Consonant Digraph	Short Vowel	Long Vowel	Vowel Team/Diphthong	R-controlled Vowel	Silent Letter	Prefix/Word Beginning	Suffix/Inflection	Hard/Soft CGS	Unpredictable Pattern	Insertion/Omission	Non-phonetic	Whole Word Error
1 P	0 1																
2 G	0 1																
3 T	0 1																
4 R	0 1																
5 fan	0 1	f n				a											
6 dog	0 1	d g				o											
7 he	0 1	h					e										
8 book	0 1	b k						oo									
9 farm	0 1	f r m							a								
10 pet	0 1	p t															
11 the	0 1				th	e											
12 cat	0 1	c t				a											
13 was	0 1	w s															
14 home	0 1	h m					o							a			
15 you	0 1	y						ou									
16 as	0 1	s				a											
17 bath	0 1	b			th	a											
18 of	0 1	f				o											
19 open	0 1	p					o			e							
20 what	0 1	t			wh							en					
21 very	0 1	v r					y		e					a			
22 went	0 1	w		nt		e											
23 said	0 1	s d				e											
24 dry	0 1		dr				y							ai			
25 don't	0 1	d n					o										
26 phone	0 1	n			ph		o			e		t					
27 would	0 1	w d						ou		l							
28 better	0 1	b tt				e				i							
29 people	0 1	p p										er					
30 graded	0 1	d	gr			a						le		eo			
31 dressing	0 1	ss	dr			e						ed					
32 spoken	0 1	k	sp			o						ing					
33 reached	0 1	r			ch			ea				en					
34 she's	0 1				sh	e						ed 's					
35 waited	0 1	w t						ai				ed					
36 germ	0 1	g m							e								
37 while	0 1	l			wh		i			e							
38 roasted	0 1	r		st				oa		e		ed					
39 wrongly	0 1	r		ng		o				w		ly					
40 bridge	0 1	g	br			i				d e							
41 worried	0 1	w rr							o			ed			i		
42 knocked	0 1	n ck				o				k		ed			i		
43 construction	0 1	c		str		u					con	tion					
44 squirted	0 1		squ	rt					i			ed					
45 physical	0 1										phys	ic al					
46 hungrier	0 1	h r		ng		u						er		i			
47 misfortune	0 1	f r t							o		mis			une			
48 irregular	0 1	r g l				e u					ir	ar					
49 splitting	0 1	tt	spl			i						ing					
50 definition	0 1	d f n				e i i						tion					
51 schedule	0 1	d	sch			e								ule			
52 appreciate	0 1		pr				e				ap	ate		ci			
53 exhaust	0 1			st				au		h	ex						
54 desperate	0 1	r		sp							de			ate			
55 regretted	0 1	tt		gr					e		re	ed					
56 exaggerate	0 1	r				e			e		ex	ate				gg	
57 deceive	0 1	c v						ei		e	de						
58 consensus	0 1	n s s				e u					con						
59 definitely	0 1	f n				i					de	ly		s			
60 accommodate	0 1	c d				o o				e	ac	ate		ite		mm	
Total Errors by Category		Single/Double Consonant	Initial Blend	Medial/Final Blend	Consonant Digraph	Short Vowel	Long Vowel	Vowel Team/Diphthong	R-controlled Vowel	Silent Letter	Prefix/Word Beginning	Suffix/Inflection	Hard/Soft CGS	Unpredictable Pattern	Insertion/Omission	Non-phonetic	Whole Word Error
		CONSONANTS				VOWELS					OTHER						

with scores from several intelligence tests. The Comprehensive Achievement Composite correlated approximately .80 with the global IQs from the intelligence tests.

Review of Relevant Research. In a review of the KTEA-II, Vladescu (2007) pointed out that the Comprehensive Form has both an A and a B form. He also noted that by using the error analysis, the KTEA-II can be used as a criterion-referenced assessment as well as a norm-referenced test. Research on the original K-TEA indicated that it yielded higher scores than other achievement tests; research on the KTEA-II should indicate whether this is true as well. Bradley and Scott (2006) recommended a book, *Essentials of WIAT-II and KTEA-II Assessment,* by Lichtenberger and Smith as a helpful guide to decide which instrument to administer. Research on the original K-TEA can be found at the Earlier Research link for Chapter 11 on the Companion Website (www.prenhall.com/taylor8e).

Overview: Kaufman Test of Educational Achievement–II

- *Age level*—4½ to 25, grade norms kindergarten–grade 12.
- *Type of administration*—Individual.
- *Technical characteristics*—Good reliability and validity (oral language adequate).
- *Scores yielded*—Standard scores, percentile ranks, age and grade equivalents, stanines, error analysis guidelines.
- *Suggested use*—The KTEA-II has added several subtests to the original version, particularly in the area of reading. In addition, subtests have been added to allow the determination of a Written Language and Oral Language Composites. The Oral Language Composite, however, should be interpreted cautiously based on limited technical characteristics. Overall, the KTEA-II appears to be one of the better individual achievement tests. Research should be forthcoming.

The KTEA-II is generally considered to be a well-constructed test.

Wechsler Individual Achievement Test–II

The *Wechsler Individual Achievement Test–II* (WIAT-II; Psychological Corporation, 2001) is a comprehensive update of the original WIAT that was published in 1992. A strong feature of the WIAT-II is a linking sample with the *Wechsler Intelligence Scale for Children–IV* (WISC-IV), the *Wechsler Preschool and Primary Scale of Intelligence–III* (WPPSI-III), and the *Wechsler Adult Intelligence Scale–III* (WAIS-III). As a result, an individual can be compared in the areas of intelligence and achievement using the same standardization sample. The instrument was also designed to measure the areas of achievement in which a student with a learning disability must show problems. Those areas are oral expression, listening comprehension, written expression, basic reading skills, reading comprehension, mathematics calculation, and mathematics reasoning. The WIAT-II subtests reflect these seven areas and includes additional subtests in the area of spelling and pseudoword decoding.

The WIAT-II has a linking sample with the Wechsler Intelligence Scales.

Description

Word Reading. This subtest measures basic word reading ability primarily through sight recognition. Younger students identify and generate rhyming words, identify beginning and ending sounds, and match sounds to letter blends.

Numerical Operations.   This subtest requires the student to perform basic mathematical calculations in addition, subtraction, multiplication, and division. It also measures basic algebra and geometry. Early math calculation skills such as number recognition and number counting are required for younger children.

Reading Comprehension.   This subtest requires the student to read short passages and then respond orally to comprehension questions. There are three types of items: Words, Sentences, and Passages. For the *words,* the student must point to the correct choice of four pictures that represents words read (e.g., "red box"). The *sentences* are read aloud and then questions are asked about their meaning. The *passages* can be read either aloud or silently and a series of questions are asked about the passage.

Spelling.   This written spelling subtest requires the student to spell words that are dictated by the examiner. Early spelling concepts such as sound-to-letter correspondence are also included.

Pseudoword Decoding.   The student must use word attack skills to read a list of nonsense words.

Math Reasoning.   This requires the student to respond by speaking, pointing to, or writing a variety of tasks that require knowledge of mathematic concepts.

Written Expression.   This subtest has five sections: Alphabet Writing, Word Fluency, Sentences, Paragraph, and Essay. For example, the *sentences* section requires a student to write sentences in response to verbal and visual cues and to combine sentences appropriately. Both the *paragraph* and *essay* portions are scored using a rubric in the areas of mechanics, organization, vocabulary, and theme development (for essay only).

Listening Comprehension.   This subtest has three sections: Receptive Vocabulary, Sentence Comprehension, and Expressive Vocabulary. In the *expressive vocabulary* part, the student is read a definition of a word that must be identified.

Oral Expression.   This subtest has four sections: Sentence Repetition (for younger children only), Word Fluency, Visual Passage Retell, and Giving Directions. For example, in *visual passage retell,* cartoon-like pictures are shown in sequence and the student must make up a story about the pictures that goes from beginning to end.

Interpretation of Scores.   Derived scores are available for each subtest, as well as a composite for Reading, Mathematics, Written Language and Oral Language (see Figure 11.2). A total composite score that includes all of the subtests is also available. Standard scores, percentile ranks, age and grade equivalents, normal curve equivalents, stanines, quartile scores, and decile scores are all provided. Tables are available to compare students by their age or grade. One feature of the WIAT-II is the tables that allow the determination of ability (aptitude)–achievement discrepancies that most states have required for the determination of a learning disability (however, this requirement was dropped in the 2004 reauthorization of IDEA). In fact, two different methods of determining a significant discrepancy are discussed in the manual with appropriate tables presented for the examiner's use. A software program, called Scoring Assistant, is also available. Another nice feature is the addition of appendices in the normative booklet that provide detailed

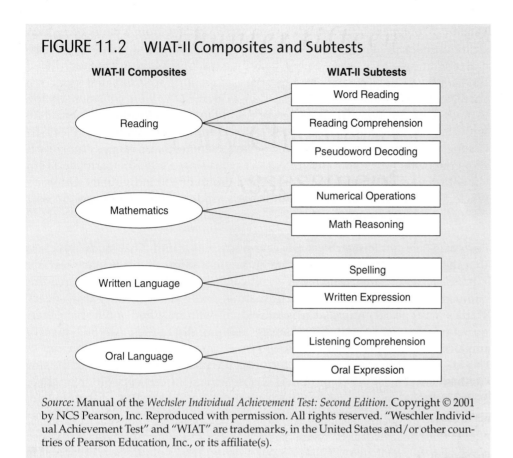

FIGURE 11.2 WIAT-II Composites and Subtests

Source: Manual of the *Wechsler Individual Achievement Test: Second Edition.* Copyright © 2001 by NCS Pearson, Inc. Reproduced with permission. All rights reserved. "Weschler Individual Achievement Test" and "WIAT" are trademarks, in the United States and/or other countries of Pearson Education, Inc., or its affiliate(s).

examples on scoring for the reading comprehension, written expression, and oral expression subtests. These examples act as benchmarks to help decrease the subjectivity in scoring these subtests.

Technical Characteristics

Normative Sample. The WIAT-II went through several stages of development to determine the final normative sample. There are separate age-based and grade-based norms. The grade-based norms included 3,600 participants and the age-based sample included 2,950. The normative samples were stratified on a number of variables including race/ethnicity, geographic region, parent education level, and gender. Data from 1998 U.S. Census were used to provide the basis for stratification.

Reliability. Internal consistency reliability was determined using the split-half procedure and was generally in the .80s to .90s for the subtests and the .90s for the composite scores. One exception was the Oral Language composite, which had a coefficient of .88. Test-retest reliability was determined using a subset of 297 students from four different grade ranges. Again, correlations were primarily in the .80s to .90s for the subtests and .90 or above for the composites. Interscorer reliability was also determined for a limited number of subtests for which this type of reliability would be appropriate. In general, these were high for Reading Comprehension and Oral Expression (.94, .96). However, the Written Expression coefficient was .85.

Validity.   Content validity was determined by a review from a panel of experts. Criterion-related validity was determined by correlating the WIAT-II with several other measures of achievement, including the *Wide Range Achievement Test–3,* the *Differential Ability Scales,* and the *Peabody Picture Vocabulary Test–III.* These coefficients were quite varied. Correlations with the DAS were considerably low (e.g., .28 between WIAT-II Word Reading and DAS Word Reading). Coefficients with the WRAT-3 ranged from .52 to .80 and from .44 to .75 for the PPVT-III. Coefficients with group-administered achievement tests also ranged from low to moderate. One interesting finding was that reading composite correlated only .42 with the school grades in reading for a group of 350 individuals. Other coefficients were mathematics .44 with math grade, written language .57 with spelling, and oral language .24 with English grade.

Ability–achievement discrepancy tables are available.

Review of Relevant Research.   Only one study was found. That study indicated that the reading–writing scores from an English language proficiency test, the *Woodcock-Munoz Language Survey,* significantly predicted the WIAT-II reading composite scores (Dicerbo, 2003). The manual does include the results of several studies with special groups such as individuals who are gifted or who have mental retardation, emotional disturbances, learning disabilities, AD/HD, hearing impairments, or speech and language impairments. This information can be found in the validity section of the technical manual. Because of some of the similarities between the WIAT and WIAT-II, research on the earlier addition might be beneficial. That research generally supported its use but indicated that it yields different scores than other achievement measures. However, one should not overgeneralize this information because of the significant changes that were made in the WIAT-II in some of the subtests. Examples of recent studies on the WIAT follow. Additional summaries can be located at the Earlier Research link for Chapter 11 on the Companion Website (www.prenhall.com/taylor8e).

- Muenz and colleagues (1999) reported that the Written Expression subtest was more valid and reliable than the Written Expression subtest from the PIAT-R.
- Wickes and Slate (1999) found that scores from the WIAT were significantly higher than the counterpart scores on the *Key Math–Revised* and the *Woodcock Reading Mastery Test–Revised* with a population of African American students.
- Separate regression equations have been developed to predict the WIAT's composite scores using the index scores from the WISC–III (Konald, 1999).
- The WIAT Written Expression subtest yielded higher scores than the Writing Samples subtest from the *Woodcock Johnson–Revised* (Brown, Giandenoto, & Bolen, 2000). They suggested that the WIAT would be less likely to identify students for special education services in written expression when a discrepancy between achievement and IQ is required.

Overview: Wechsler Individual Achievement Test-II

- *Age level*—5 through 19 years (adult norms available).
- *Type of administration*—Individual.
- *Technical adequacy*—Good standardization, good reliability (limited for some subtests), adequate validity (questionable criterion-related).
- *Scores yielded*—Standard scores, age and grade equivalents, percentiles, stanines, normal curve equivalents, quartiles, deciles.
- *Suggested use*—The WIAT-II is a well-constructed instrument that was designed, in part, to help identify students with learning disabilities. In

general, the reliability of the instrument is good with some exceptions (e.g., Written Expression). The composites should probably be used for important educational decisions. The validity coefficients with other achievement tests are variable, with some being quite low. The WIAT-II is much more comprehensive than its predecessor, having many more items and more precise starting points. There are also separate age-based and grade-based norms. Research needs to be conducted on this instrument, particularly to establish its validity. The major feature of the WIAT-II is the "linking sample" with the Wechsler Scales that allows the determination of an aptitude–achievement discrepancy based on the same normative group, although this is no longer a requirement for learning disabilities eligibility.

Woodcock-Johnson–III (Normative Update)

The *Woodcock-Johnson–III–NU* (WJ-III-NU; Woodcock, McGrew, Mather, & Schrank, 2007) is a wide-ranging set of individually administered tests designed to measure general intellectual ability, specific cognitive abilities, oral language, and academic achievement. There are separate Cognitive and Achievement Batteries. For each, there is also a Standard and an Extended Battery. Among the various uses of the WJ-III-NU are to diagnose learning disabilities, plan educational programs, determine performance discrepancies, and monitor progress. One nice feature of the WJ-III-NU is the co-norming of the Cognitive and Achievement Batteries. This allows for the determination of both intratest discrepancies and intertest discrepancies. This is important because it allows the determination of a comparison between intelligence and achievement based on the same standardization sample. The authors have provided several methods to assist in this determination. Norms are available for individuals age 2 to 90+; grade norms are available from kindergarten through university graduate school.

> The WJ-III-NU has a standard and an extended battery.

Description. The tests in the Achievement Battery measure six curriculum areas: Reading, Written Language, Mathematics, Oral Language, Academic Knowledge, and Supplemental. A brief description of the tests in the Achievement Battery and their relationship to the factors/areas follow.

Standard Achievement Battery

Reading
Letter Word Identification. This measures the individual's skill in identifying isolated letters and words.

Reading Fluency. This requires an individual to read printed statements very quickly and indicate whether they are true or false statements.

Passage Comprehension. This uses a modified cloze procedure to evaluate a person's comprehension and vocabulary skills.

Written Language
Spelling. This simply involves spelling of verbally presented words.

Writing Fluency. This requires the individual to formulate and write simple sentences as quickly as possible.

Writing Samples. The individual must write meaningful sentences given a variety of purposes.

Mathematics

Calculation. This is a written math calculation test measuring computation skills.

Math Fluency. This requires the individual to add, subtract, and multiply as quickly as possible.

Applied Problems. This requires the individual to perform math calculations in response to orally presented problems.

Oral Language

Story Recall. This requires an individual to listen to a story and remember details.

Understanding Directions. This involves listening to a sequence of instructions and then carrying them out.

Extended Achievement Battery

Reading

Word Attack. This measures the individual's ability to apply phonics and instructional analysis skills using nonsense words.

Reading Vocabulary. This involves reading words and giving their meaning.

Written Language

Editing. This requires the individual to identify mistakes in a typewritten passage and indicate how they should be corrected.

Mathematics

Quantitative Concepts. This is a math knowledge subtest where an individual must identify math terms, formulae, and number patterns.

Oral Language

Picture Vocabulary. The individual must identify specific objects from a choice of several.

Oral Comprehension. This involves a type of oral cloze procedure in which an individual must identify a missing word from an orally presented passage.

Academic Knowledge

Academic Knowledge. This involves questions about science, social studies, geography, and humanities.

Supplemental

Story Recall—Delayed. This involves recalling the details of the stories that were read previously.

Punctuation and Capitalization. This measures the individual's knowledge of English usage.

Spelling of Sounds. The individual must write certain letter combinations typically found in written English.

Sound Awareness. The individual must determine rhyming words and remove, substitute, or reverse parts of words to make new words.

Interpretation of Results. Hand scoring of the previous editions of the WJ was tedious and afforded the opportunity for numerous scoring errors. As a result, the WJ-III-NU includes computer software, Compuscore and Profiles Program, that eliminates hand scoring. A variety of scores are available for both the individual tests and the clusters, which are various combinations of individual tests that measure the same construct. The scores yielded by Compuscore are standard scores (mean = 100; SD = 15), percentile ranks, age equivalents, and grade equivalents. It also provides instructional range bands and Relative Mastery Indexes (RMI). The RMI is a score that is presented as a fraction with a constant denominator of 90. This score indicates the percentage of material that the examinee has mastered that a reference group (by either age or grade) has mastered at 90 percent. For example, if a 10½-year-old boy received a RMI of 62/90 in calculation, it would indicate that he has mastered 62 percent of the content in that area compared to 90 percent for the average child of the same age. Scores are also available for Total Achievement.

Only computer scoring is available.

Technical Characteristics

Normative Sample.   The standardization sample for the WJ-III-NU was 8,782 individuals from over 100 U.S. communities. The subjects were chosen to be representative of the U.S. population across ten variables, including community size, race, type of school, and occupational status (for the adult, postschool norms).

Reliability.   For the Achievement Batteries, internal reliability coefficients ranged from .81 to .94 for the Standard Battery and from .76 to .91 for the Extended Battery. Again, all but two coefficients were at least .80. Test-retest reliability was also determined on the three speed tests from the Achievement Battery. Those coefficients were .76 to .94 for the ages 7 to 11 sample, .80 to .89 for the ages 14 to 17 sample, and .87 to .96 for the adult sample. Again, the cluster reliability coefficients were higher than the individual tests' coefficients. For the Standard Achievement Battery, coefficients ranged from .87 to .98; and for the Extended Battery, from .85 to .95. The Total Achievement cluster score coefficient was .98.

Validity.   The authors provide a significant amount of information supporting the content validity of the items chosen. Evidence for construct validity was provided through the use of confirmatory factor analyses. The Broad Reading cluster score from the Achievement Battery correlated primarily in the .60 to .70 range with six different measures of reading from the K-TEA and WIAT. The Broad Math score correlated between .52 and .70 with the same two tests. Finally, the Broad Written Language score correlated .47 to .67 with written language measures from those same two tests. The lowest coefficients were with the Writing Composite and Written Expression scores from the WIAT.

Review of Relevant Research.   No research was located that focused on the Achievement Battery of the WJ-III-NU.

Overview: Woodcock-Johnson–III–NU

- *Age level*—2 years to adult.
- *Type of administration*—Individual.
- *Technical adequacy*—Good standardization, adequate reliability and validity.
- *Scores yielded*—Standard scores, percentile ranks, relative mastery index (age and grade equivalents also available).
- *Suggested use*—The WJ-III-NU Achievement Battery is a comprehensive and wide-ranging set of tests that measure a variety of areas. Several changes and improvements in the WJ-III-NU are worthy of mention. These include the addition of new achievement tests. Because of the possibility of so many scores, it is necessary that an examiner carefully plan so that the appropriate test(s) can be administered. One criticism of earlier editions

was the difficulty in hand scoring. This has been addressed by including a computer scoring program with the instrument that eliminates hand scoring. Another advantageous feature of the WJ-III-NU is the use of continuous-year norms. This means that the standardization occurred throughout the year for the school-age subjects rather than at one or two times. Thus, scores can be compared to individuals of the exact age or grade placement rather than to individuals of an average age or grade. This procedure helps eliminate the error variance associated with grouping students of similar, but not the same, age or grade. In addition to the scoring software included with the WJ-III-NU, there is an expanded program called the *Report Writer for the WJ-III-NU.* This includes an interpretation of the results in addition to the scoring of the tests (see Chapter 3 for cautions regarding computerized interpretation programs). It also contains a series of checklists for the teacher, parent, and the examinee as well as a classroom behavior observation form. These allow background information from a variety of sources to be incorporated into the report. Finally, there is a Spanish version.

Additional Achievement Instruments

In addition to the instruments previously described, several others deserve mention. These tests, for the most part, are less frequently used and should be used primarily for screening.

Diagnostic Achievement Battery–3

- *Age level*—6 to 14 years.
- *Type of administration*—Individual; possible small group.
- *Technical adequacy*—Adequate standardization and validity; good reliability, particularly for composite scores; technical data based on limited samples.
- *Scores yielded*—Percentiles, standard scores, age/grade equivalents.
- *Suggested use*—The *Diagnostic Achievement Battery–3* (DAB-3; Newcomer, 2001) is a potentially useful instrument to determine individual strengths and weaknesses in a number of academic areas. As with most tests, the composite scores are more stable than the individual subtest scores and should be used for important educational decisions. Research on the DAB-3 is needed before its full potential can be determined. One potential drawback to the test is its administration time. It takes approximately one-and-a-half to two hours to administer the entire test. However, it is possible to administer only portions of the test. A computerized scoring program (PROSCORE) is available.

Hammill Multiability Achievement Test

- *Age level*—7 through 17 years.
- *Type of administration*—Individual.
- *Technical adequacy*—Generally adequate.
- *Scores yielded*—Standard scores, percentiles, age and grade equivalents.
- *Suggested use*—According to the authors of the *Hammill Multiability Achievement Test* (HAMAT; Hammill, Hresko, Ammer, Cronin, & Quinby, 1998), it is one of the most content-driven achievement test of today's school curriculum. The HAMAT consists of four subtests. The Reading subtest uses a cloze procedure in which the student must supply words that are selectively deleted from paragraphs. The Writing subtest measures spelling, punctuation, and

capitalization. The Mathematics subtest primarily measures computation skills. The Facts subtest includes questions in content areas such as science and social studies. The HAMAT includes a set of tables that facilitate the determination of the discrepancy between achievement and IQ since it was co-normed with the *Hammill Multiability Intelligence Test* (HAMIT).

The HAMAT was co-normed with the HAMIT.

Mini-Battery of Achievement

- *Age level*—4 to over 90 years.
- *Type of administration*—Individual.
- *Technical adequacy*—Good standardization, adequate reliability, limited validity data.
- *Scores yielded*—Standard scores, age and grade equivalents, percentiles, normal curve equivalents.
- *Suggested use*—The *Mini-Battery of Achievement* (MBA; Woodcock, McGrew, & Werder, 1994) is actually a short form of the *Woodcock-Johnson–Revised*, an earlier version of the *Woodcock-Johnson–III–NU*. It consists of three reading subtests, two writing subtests, two math subtests, and a subtest on factual knowledge. All the subtests but the last can be combined for a Basic Skills score. Interestingly, there are no norm tables available; rather, there is computerized scoring and reporting. In a review of the MBA, Willis, DuMont, and Cruse (1997) noted that it was one of the best screening measures but should not substitute for a more comprehensive achievement test. Similarly, Flanagan, McGrew, Abramowitz, and Untiedt (1997) noted that the MBA provided the broadest assessment of reading and writing of three screening tests that they reviewed.

Peabody Individual Achievement Test–Revised/Normative Update

- *Age level*—Kindergarten through grade 12, extended norms through age 22.
- *Type of administration*—Individual.
- *Technical adequacy*—Good standardization, limited validity, adequate reliability.
- *Scores yielded*—Age and grade equivalents, percentile ranks, standard scores, stanines, normal curve equivalents.
- *Suggested use*—The PIAT-R is a well-standardized general achievement test designed for kindergarten through grade 12 that should be used primarily for screening purposes. It includes subtests of General Information, Reading Recognition, Reading Comprehension, Mathematics, Spelling, and Written Expression (optional). The majority of subtests use a multiple-choice format that allows a pointing response. Its appropriateness with special education students largely depends on the nature of the disability. For students with language or motor impairments, it would be an appropriate general-achievement test. On the other hand, its use with students with visual or visual-perceptual problems is limited. You must keep in mind the nature of the tasks presented on the PIAT-R. The mathematic and spelling subtests, in particular, measure different aspects of those skills than are measured in typical classroom activities. The addition of the written expression subtest may prove helpful, although Lazarus, McKenna, and Lynch (1990) noted that informal interpretation of the writing samples is probably the best procedure to follow. This is particularly true given the research that has noted some of its limitations. The test publisher for the PIAT-R noted that the

The PIAT-R is primarily a screening test.

updated norms should provide the same or slightly higher scores in reading, spelling, and mathematics for children in the primary grades. For those in grades 5 through 12, the updated norms should provide similar scores to the earlier norms in spelling and reading, but lower scores in mathematics.

Wide Range Achievement Test–4

- *Age level*—5 through 94 years.
- *Type of administration*—Individual.
- *Technical adequacy*—Adequate standardization, reliability, and validity.
- *Scores yielded*—Standard scores and percentile ranks.
- *Suggested use*—The *Wide Range Achievement Test–4* (WRAT-4; Wilkinson & Robinson, 2007) is a much-needed revision of a test that has been around for decades. The last revision was made over twenty years ago. That test and its predecessors were severely criticized for the lack of a reading comprehension measure and overreliance on age equivalents. This new revision has addressed those concerns. The WRAT-4 includes four subtests: Word Reading, Sentence Comprehension, Spelling, and Math Computation. The WRAT-4 has a relatively short administration time and, because it is designed to cover such a wide age range, there are few items appropriate for students of a given age. The WRAT-4 should be used for screening purposes only. It should be noted that even though a reading comprehension measure was added, it still does not have a measure of written language or math comprehension that most comprehensive achievement tests have.

Wechsler Essential Academic Skills Inventory

- *Age level*—5 through 50 years.
- *Type of administration*—Individual or group.
- *Technical adequacy*—Adequate to good.
- *Scores yielded*—Grade equivalents, age equivalents, stanines, progress measures.
- *Suggested use*—The *Wechsler Essential Academic Skills Inventory* (Wechsler EASI; Wechsler, 2007) includes three core subtests and one optional subtest. The core subtests are Reading Comprehension, Spelling, and Numerical Operations, and the optional subtest is Word Reading. The publisher states that the core subtests can be given as a schoolwide screening to identify at-risk students using the Response to Intervention model. It can also be used to monitor progress.

Criterion-Referenced Instruments

Why Use Criterion-Referenced Instruments?

Establishment of IEP goals and objectives; monitoring educational progress.

Who Should Use Them?

Teachers.

Criterion-referenced instruments that measure academic skills are crucial tools for both pre- and postreferral assessment, particularly for students with mild disabilities. Frequently, the use of these instruments (in conjunction with informal techniques) is all that is necessary to evaluate students. Even if a student goes through the formal assessment process, these instruments, typically, are the ones that yield the most functional educational data for instructional purposes. Information from these instruments, for instance, is extremely helpful in developing IEPs. These instruments, usually described as *multicomponent,* are also comprehensive, so that only selected portions are administered.

Multicomponent Instruments: The Brigance Inventories

Over the past two decades, a number of inventories developed by Albert Brigance and published by Curriculum Associates have received widespread attention and use. These inventories consist of lists of skill sequences that cover a large number of areas. For each skill sequence, an objective is provided (see Figure 11.3) that can be used for an IEP or as an informal teaching objective. There are, in fact, CD-ROMs available that create, edit, and print IEPs.

Appropriate use of the Brigance Inventories requires that the teacher or test administrator carefully select those skill sequences that are relevant for a given student. Under no circumstances should any inventory be given in its entirety. Many people, unfortunately, have assumed that "because this is a test, I'll administer it." This has led to criticism of the inventories because of inappropriate use. Another issue relates to content validity. One must be sure that the content of the skill sequences included in the inventories is consistent with curricular goals in the schools. As an example of this concern, Ferguson and Kerstig (1988) noted a lower than .50 correlation between items on the Brigance Inventories and a statewide test administered to all students.

The Brigance Inventories are often referred to by their color rather than their name. These are yellow (*Inventory of Early Development–II*)—discussed in Chapter 15—green (*Comprehensive Inventory of Basic Skills–Revised*), and red (*Inventory of Essential Skills*).

Brigance Comprehensive Inventory of Basic Skills–Revised (Green). The *Brigance Comprehensive Inventory of Basic Skills–Revised* (CIBS-R; Brigance, 1999) is designed for students from kindergarten through grade 9. In all, twenty-three content areas are measured, with 154 total skill sequences or basic skill assessments. One major change in the *Comprehensive Inventory of Basic Skills–Revised* is the addition of a normative/standardized option through grade 6 when such information is wanted or required.

Description.   Following is a list of the twenty-three content areas:

> *Readiness*
> *Speech*
> *Listening*
> *Word Recognition Grade Placement*
> *Reading Comprehension*
> *Word Analysis*
> *Functional Word Recognition*
> *Spelling*
> *Writing*
> *Reference Skills*
> *Graphs and Maps*
> *Math Grade Placement*

Never administer a Brigance Inventory in its entirety.

Normative information is also available for the "Green Brigance."

FIGURE 11.3 Example of an Objective Provided by the Brigance Inventories

G-9 READS WORDS WITH COMMON ENDINGS (*CONTINUED*)

SKILL: Reads words with common endings.

STUDENT RECORD BOOK: Page 16.

CLASS RECORD BOOK: Page 21.

ASSESSMENT METHOD: Individual oral response.

MATERIALS: S-210, S-213, and S-214.

DISCONTINUE: Your discretion, or after failure on two consecutive endings.

TIME: Your discretion, or approximately five seconds per response.

ACCURACY: 3/3 (100%) or 1/1 (100%). (See **OPTIONAL CRITERIA.**)

OPTIONAL CRITERIA: The third word for each common ending is a nonsense word. You may wish to ask the student to pronounce only the nonsense word and give credit if the student responds correctly. Allow for self-correcting. Using this criteria will require less assessment time. (See **NOTE 2** on page 210.) If after evaluating the response to the third word (the nonsense word), you question the student's mastery of the skill, you should administer the remaining two words for the ending sound.

NOTES: (See **NOTES** on pages 210–11.)

DIRECTIONS

This assessment is made by asking the student to read the groups of words with common endings on S-210, S-213, and S-214.

Point to the words on S-214, and

Say: **The words in each group rhyme. They have the same ending. I want you to read the three words in each group of words. The third word in each group is not a real word. Try your best to sound out this word.**

If necessary, give the student help with the initial consonant.

If you wish to have the student pronounce only the nonsense word (the third word in each group of words),

Say: **I want you to read the last word in each group of words. These words are not real words. Try your best to sound out these nonsense words.**

OBJECTIVE

By _____ (date) _____, when shown three one-syllable words with common endings, _____ (student's name) _____ will correctly pronounce the ending sound in each word with 3/3 (100%) or 1/1 (100%) accuracy for _____ (quantity) _____ of sixty common endings.

STUDENT-PAGE FORMAT AND SKILL ANALYSIS FOR S-214

41. **ace** face race nace	46. **ang** bang rang mang	51. **end** bend send dend	56. **ind** kind mind pind
42. **ash** dash hash posh	47. **art** part cart bart	52. **ent** dent tent nent	57. **ip** tip dip fip
43. **ave** cave wave mave	48. **ean** bean lean kean	53. **ice** nice rice fice	58. **oat** coat boat poat
44. **oke** joke poke noke	49. **each** beach reach meach	54. **ig** dig fig nig	59. **ong** long pong fong
45. **ain** main gain fain	50. **eat** seat peat deat	55. **ile** mile pile dile	60. **ug³** dug tug sug

Numbers
Number Facts
Computation of Whole Numbers
Fractions and Mixed Numbers
Decimals
Percent
Time
Money
U.S. Customary Measurement and Geometry
Metrics

Interpretation of Results. The primary reason for using the *Comprehensive Inventory of Basic Skills–Revised* is to identify appropriate objectives for a student. The inventory is designed to facilitate this purpose. Each skill sequence is associated with a stated behavioral objective, so that objectives can be directly determined from a child's performance on the inventory. The normative use of the inventory allows composite scores for general knowledge and language, gross-motor skills, graphomotor, reading, writing, and math (all considered Readiness composites). For grades 1 to 6, scores are available in reading comprehension, written expression, and math. Scores include standard scores, percentiles, and grade equivalents.

> The Inventory is helpful in determining educational objectives.

Overview: Brigance Comprehensive Inventory of Basic Skills—Revised (Green)

- *Age level*—Kindergarten to grade 9.
- *Suggested use*—The *Brigance Comprehensive Inventory of Basic Skills–Revised* covers skills usually taught from kindergarten through middle school. If you are interested in testing students in the late elementary or early secondary grades, this inventory would be a good choice. The addition of the normative option gives this inventory more versatility. The norms, however, only extend through grade 6. In a review of the CIBS-R, Bradley-Johnson (1999b) highly recommended its use for planning individualized instruction. She did note, however, that there is insufficient evidence regarding its reliability. One nice feature is the availability (by subscription) of an online management system that, among other things, track students' progress. There is also an *Assessment of Basic Skills–Revised Spanish Edition* that includes twenty-two skill sequences.

Brigance Inventory of Essential Skills (Red). The *Brigance Inventory of Essential Skills* (Brigance, 1981) is designed for use with students in grades 4 to 12. The inventory basically measures those minimal competencies commonly accepted as important in lifetime experiences. As such, it is one of the few instruments that includes measures of functional academics at the secondary level. Like the *Brigance Inventory of Basic Skills–Revised*, this inventory is used primarily to establish and monitor educational or prevocational objectives.

> The "Red Brigance" includes functional academic skills.

Description. The *Inventory of Essential Skills* includes twenty-six content areas, with a total of 181 skill sequences. Ten informal rating scales are also included. Following is a list of the twenty-six content areas:

Word Recognition Grade Placement
Oral Reading

Reading Comprehension
Functional Word Recognition
Word Analysis
Reference Skills
Schedules and Graphs
Writing
Forms
Spelling
Math Grade Placement
Numbers
Number Facts
Computation of Whole Numbers
Fractions
Decimals
Percents
Measurement
Metrics
Math Vocabulary
Health and Safety (includes two rating scales)
Vocational (includes five rating scales)
Money and Finance
Travel and Transportation (includes one rating scale)
Food and Clothing
Oral Communication and Telephone Skills (includes two rating scales)

Interpretation of Results.   The *Inventory of Essential Skills* primarily yields information related to behavioral objectives, although grade-placement approximations are given in a number of areas. Results from the inventory are often used in secondary-level special education classrooms to identify and help develop prevocational and other survival skills necessary after high school.

The information from the ten rating scales can be used to identify "specific traits, behavior attitudes, and skills that may need to be changed or improved in order to help a student achieve optimal adjustment and success" (Brigance, 1981, 373). These scales should be used with caution, because no validity data exist to support their use. They are, in fact, more similar to checklists than rating scales.

The rating scales should be used cautiously.

Overview: Brigance Inventory of Essential Skills (Red)
- *Age level*—grades 4 to 12.
- *Suggested use*—The *Inventory of Essential Skills* is designed for use with students in grades 4 to 12. The inventory emphasizes minimal competencies and includes measures of "functional academics." This instrument is, in fact, one of the few that includes items for the secondary-level special education student and is a popular instrument for IEP development for older students. Objectives from the Essential Skills Inventory also have been correlated with instructional materials from the Janus Company, although no research is available to support or refute their effectiveness. This test, like all Brigance Inventories, should not be administered in its entirety. Rather, the skill sequences should be carefully chosen by the teacher or other examiner who is familiar with the student to be evaluated. There is another inventory, the *Brigance Life Skills Inventory* (Brigance, 1994), which is also designed to assess basic and functional

life skills in real-world contexts. This inventory is designed for vocational and adult education programs as well as secondary special education programs.

Multilevel Academic Survey Test—Curriculum Level

The *Multilevel Academic Survey Test* (MAST; Howell, Zucker, & Morehead, 1985) is actually comprised of two different types of tests. The first, a *grade-level test*, is a norm-referenced measure of reading and mathematics designed for students from kindergarten to grade 8. The *curriculum-level test* is intended to complement the grade-level test by providing specific information regarding content-skill deficits. Used together, the two provide comparative and curricular information. Much of the information in the MAST evolved from the authors' previous assessment instrument, the *Multilevel Academic Skills Inventory* (MASI) described by Taylor (1984).

> The curriculum-level test provides the most educational information.

Description

Reading.   This section includes eight levels of graded passages that are read aloud by the student to determine decoding skills. The comprehension part also involves graded passages that the student must read silently and then answer questions about. A series of passages that use the maze procedure is also included.

Mathematics.   Included in this section are computation items related to whole numbers, fractions, decimals, ratios, and proportions, as well as a problem-solving test that uses a multiple-choice format.

Interpretation of Results.   The curriculum-level test from the MAST provides specific information for teaching purposes. A decision/activity analysis tree on the record form indicates when a student needs additional testing, instruction, or progression into more difficult content areas.

Overview: Multilevel Academic Survey Test

- *Age level*—Kindergarten to grade 8.
- *Suggested use*—The MAST is a comprehensive assessment instrument that provides both norm-referenced and criterion-referenced information. The curriculum-level test provides the more specific information for teaching purposes. The grade-level test, however, can be used initially to determine the appropriate starting point in the curriculum-level test. Issacson (1988), in a review of the instrument, noted that the MAST had many desirable features.

BACK TO THE PROFILE

Possible Answers to the Questions

1. **Why assess Steve?** Based on the information in the vignette, it is difficult to tell if Steve's scores on the statewide test were due to true deficits in those areas or are more a function of the type of testing (large group). One reason to assess Steve would be to determine how he performs on an individually administered general achievement

test. This should address the question about content deficit versus type of test administration. It is also possible, if Steve did demonstrate specific academic problems, that further testing to determine eligibility for a special education program might be warranted. It would also be possible to determine specific educational goals and possible teaching strategies.

2. **Who should assess Steve?** The individual achievement test could be administered by an educational diagnostician or perhaps a special education teacher. In some districts the school psychologist might do this although he or she wouldn't be involved unless eligibility decisions were made. The teacher could do the assessment for educational programming.

3. **What procedure(s)/test(s) should be used?** Steve might be given the *Kaufman Test of Educational Achievement–II* or the *Wechsler Individual Achievement Test–II*. Another possibility is the *Diagnostic Assessment Battery–3,* although that test is not used as frequently as the other two. The *Peabody Individual Achievement Test–Revised* would probably not be recommended because you would be more interested in his performance on more typical classroom-type tasks. To determine educational programming information, the appropriate skill sequences from the *Brigance Comprehensive Inventory of Basic Skills–Revised* might be administered. Also the error analysis guidelines from the KTEA-II (if administered) would be helpful.

4. **What other areas should be assessed?** The answer to this question largely depends on the results of the individual achievement test. For example, if the results indicate that Steve might benefit from a special education program based on a suspected learning disability, then an individual intelligence test would be suggested. Also, depending on the specific eligibility criteria, other areas might also have to be evaluated. It is also possible that some of the diagnostic academic tests and informal procedures discussed later in this text could provide more detailed educational information on Steve's weak areas.

STUDENT PROFILE DATA

Steve

Steve was administered the *Kaufman Test of Educational Achievement–II* to help determine if his school problems were ability-related or more indicative of his AD/HD behaviors. The following results were obtained:

Subtest	Standard Score
Letter and Word Recognition	102
Reading Comprehension	98
Math Concepts and Applications	99
Math Computation	83
Written Expression	80
Spelling	85
Listening Comprehension	82
Oral Expression	104

These results indicate that Steve is not having problems in reading. His low scores on the statewide assessment test was probably due to his AD/HD. In math, he was about average in concepts and applications but was below average in math computation. That score, along with his low scores in written expression and spelling, suggest that Steve has problems with writing tasks. His low score in listening comprehension reinforces Steve's teacher's observation about his listening skills. Steve's 504 Plan was amended to include his taping lectures (for later playback at his pace) and using a computer for written assignments.

CASE STUDY *June*

The school psychologist also administered an individual achievement test, the *Wechsler Individual Achievement Test–II* (WIAT-II). (Hint: To review the WISC-IV results from Chapter 7, see the Cumulative Assessment File on the Companion Website, www.prenhall.com/taylor8e.) Following are the results of June's performance on the WIAT-II. After reviewing the scores, answer the questions that follow. You may want to refer to the information in this chapter on the WIAT-II.

Wechsler Individual Achievement Test–II Results

Subtests	Standard Score
Word Reading	80
Reading Comprehension	83
Pseudoword Decoding	79
Numerical Operations	98
Math Reasoning	99
Spelling	89
Written Expression	82
Listening Comprehension	90
Oral Expression	102

- Since the WISC-IV was given to measure intellectual ability, why would the WIAT-II be chosen as the achievement instrument?
- Make a statement regarding June's *strengths* as seen in this test.
- Make a statement regarding June's *weaknesses* as seen in this test.
- What *conclusions* can you draw from the results of this test?
- What other areas do you think should be assessed?

Reflections

1. Why is it important that a chosen achievement test reflect the curriculum for a given student? What implications does this have for high-stakes assessment?
2. Do you think commercial group achievement tests (e.g., the *Iowa Test of Basic Skills)* or a test developed by and for a specific state should be used for high stakes assessment?
3. How would you determine what content areas (skill sequences) you would administer to a student on a Brigance Inventory?

Summary Matrix

Instrument or Technique	Preferral: Screening and Initial Identification	Preferral: Informal Determination and Evaluation of Teaching Programs and Strategies	Postreferral Suggested Use: Determination of Current Performance Level and Educational Need	Decisions about Classification and Program Placement	IEP Goals	IEP Objectives	IEP Evaluation	Target Population: Mild/Moderate	Severe/Profound	Preschool	Elementary Age	Secondary Age	Adult	Special Considerations	Educational Relevance for Exceptional Students
Group Achievement Tests	X							X			X	X		Stanford and Metropolitan have good technical characteristics; good for initial screening.	Adequate/Useful
Kaufman Test of Educational Achievement–II	X	X	X		X			X			X	X		Good technical aspects; error analysis helpful; overall one of the better achievement tests.	Very Useful
Wechsler Individual Achievement Test–II	X	X	X		X			X			X	X		Has a linking sample with the Wechsler Scales; subtests are consistent with definition of learning disability.	Useful
Woodcock-Johnson–III (Normative Update)			X	X	X			X		X	X	X	X	WJ-III-NU includes many new features and improvements; computer scoring only.	Useful
Diagnostic Achievement Battery–3	X	X	X		X			X			X	X		Provides a profile of strengths and weaknesses; composite scores most useful.	Adequate
Hammill Multiability Achievement Test	X							X			X	X		Is co-normed with the Hammill Multiability Intelligence Test.	Adequate/Useful
Mini-Battery of Achievement	X							X		X	X	X	X	A short form of the Woodcock-Johnson–Revised Achievement Battery; includes eight subtests.	Adequate/Useful
Peabody Individual Achievement Test-Revised (Normative Update)	X	X	X		X			X			X	X		Adequate technical aspects; revised version has optional written subtest; unique format.	Adequate/Useful

Instrument or Technique	Suggested Use							Target Population						Special Considerations	Educational Relevance for Exceptional Students
	Prereferral				Postreferral										
	Screening and Initial Identification	Informal Determination and Evaluation of Teaching Programs and Strategies	Determination of Current Performance Level and Educational Need	Decisions about Classification and Program Placement	IEP Goals	IEP Objectives	IEP Evaluation	Mild/Moderate	Severe/Profound	Preschool	Elementary Age	Secondary Age	Adult		
Wide Range Achievement Test–4	X	X	X		X					X	X	X	X	Results often overused; best used as a screening measure.	Adequate/Limited
Wechsler Essential Academic Skills Inventory	X				X						X	X	X	Can be used with the RTI model.	Adequate
Brigance Comprehensive Inventory of Basic Skills–Revised		X	X		X	X	X	X			X	X		Now has a normative option; most appropriate for students in later elementary grades.	Useful
Brigance Inventory of Essential Skills		X	X		X	X	X	X				X		Includes objectives for each skill measured, used in IEP development for older students.	Useful
Multilevel Academic Survey Test–Curriculum Level	X	X	X		X	X	X	X			X			Includes both a grade level and curriculum level.	Useful

chapter twelve

Assessment of Reading

STUDENT PROFILE

John

John, a third-grade student, has always struggled with reading. He spent his first two school years in private school so that there would be fewer children in his class. His parents, however, were not happy with his academic progress and decided to send him to public school for third grade and supplement his school program with a private tutor. When he reads, he tries to sound out words but makes frequent errors. It also takes him about five minutes to read one short paragraph. He has to pay so much attention to sounding out the words that he really doesn't remember much about what he has read. His second-grade teacher became very frustrated because John was not making progress. After only about a month, his third-grade teacher, Ms. Gupta, felt that he might have a learning disability in reading and began procedures to have him referred for special education.

Think about These Questions as You Read This Chapter:

1. Why assess John? (There could be more than one reason.)
2. Who should assess John? (There could be more than one person.)
3. What procedure(s)/test(s) should be used?
4. What other areas (if any) should be assessed?

(Suggested answers appear at the end of this chapter.)

Statistics indicate that as many as 40 percent of students cannot read at a basic level and that the percentage is even higher for children from low socioeconomic backgrounds (Brynildssen, 2002). It is important, however, to recognize that many factors might be involved in reading failure (see Focus on Diversity). It is not surprising that there is such an emphasis on reading assessment and instruction. In fact, one important provision of *No Child Left Behind* was the *Reading First* and *Early Reading First* initiatives that provide funding to identify at-risk children and to provide scientifically

focus on
Diversity

Should There Be Special Considerations When Assessing Migrant Students?

Migrant students create a particular challenge when we assess their reading achievement. Factors such as mobility, health, and nutritional status can affect test scores but often go unacknowledged. School attendance may be sporadic, and there may be frequent school changes. These students frequently experience alienation and withdrawal as a response to stress and the change of social and family structures (Cloud, 1991). All of these factors are strong predictors of school failure. It is therefore important to consider this background information when interpreting test scores. More important, one should consider using informal measures and procedures that will not stigmatize these students by attaching a score to their performance that might be attributed to environmental factors.

based reading instruction. One certainly cannot minimize the importance of reading to the overall success of the student during the school years. Reading affects virtually all areas of an individual's life. Reading involves the components of recognition, analysis, and comprehension. Figure 12.1 shows a schematic indicating the various components of reading. Within this model, the overall process of reading is broken

FIGURE 12.1   Components of the Reading Process

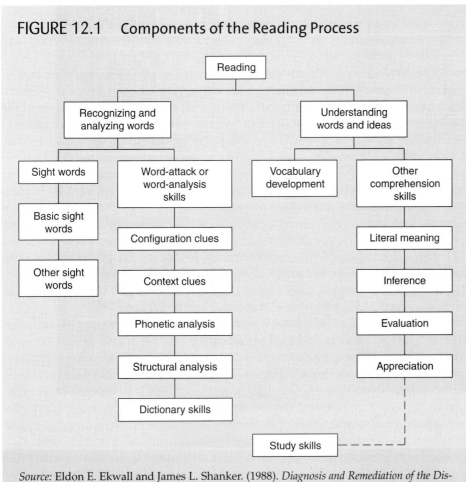

Source: Eldon E. Ekwall and James L. Shanker. (1988). *Diagnosis and Remediation of the Disabled Reader* (3rd ed.). Copyright © 1988 by Pearson Education. Reprinted with permission.

down into two subareas: (1) recognition and analysis of words and (2) understanding words and ideas. This roughly is equivalent to word recognition and reading comprehension. Word recognition can further be broken down into sight word identification and word-analysis skills. Sight word identification involves the immediate identification of a word even though the individual might not understand its meaning. Word-analysis skills are used when a reader does not instantly recognize the word and therefore must use a variety of word attack skills to attempt to read it. As noted in Figure 12.1, word attack involves the configuration or the shape of the word, context cues that a person receives from the way a word is used in the sentence, phonetic analysis, structural analysis (ability to derive meaning from word parts), and dictionary skills, such as alphabetizing and using guide words.

The other main area of reading involves the understanding of words and ideas. According to Ekwall and Shanker (1988), this involves (1) vocabulary development or the understanding of the meaning of words and (2) other comprehension skills or the student's ability to make sense from written material. As noted, this involves such things as literal comprehension (e.g., understanding and remembering the facts presented in a passage) and inferential comprehension (e.g., the ability to understand what might happen next in a passage).

Reading Assessment

As in most areas, the evaluation of the reading process can be done either informally or formally. In a survey of 800 special education teachers, Arthaud, Vasa, and Steckelberg (2000) found that nine of the ten most frequently used reading assessment procedures were informal in nature. They also reported, however, that 67 percent of the teachers used formal, individual testing. One advantage of informal reading assessment is that it provides more of an opportunity to understand the *reading process* rather than simply to analyze the *reading product.* The areas of informal reading assessment that will be discussed in this chapter include the use of informal reading inventories as well as other informal techniques such as the cloze procedure, the maze procedure, retelling, questioning, and error analysis. Other techniques discussed elsewhere in this text are also extremely relevant for reading assessment, including alternative procedures such as portfolio assessment (see Chapter 6). Valencia (1997), in fact, pointed out that authentic assessment was superior to the use of standardized instruments. In addition, observation (discussed in Chapter 4) can provide helpful information in assessing reading. For example, behaviors such as choice of books, willingness to read, staying on task during reading activities, maintaining concentration, and staying engaged during reading can all be observed and can provide valuable information (Keefe, 1999).

As noted earlier, there has been significant interest in identifying young children who are at risk for reading failure. As such, a number of instruments are available that measure *emerging reading skills.* These tests can be either norm referenced or criterion referenced. Those instruments considered more formal tests are usually called *diagnostic reading tests,* although the term *diagnostic* is somewhat a misnomer. The reasons for administering the test is not to diagnose a problem in a traditional sense but to gather specific information about where a problem might exist and how to remediate it. Many of these diagnostic academic tests actually magnify a particular area to determine an individual's strengths and weaknesses. In other words, although these tests are norm-referenced, their primary objective is frequently to obtain important information for remediation and not necessarily to compare the student's performance to others. Most diagnostic reading tests measure such areas as oral reading recognition, reading rate, comprehension, word attack skills, and vocabulary, although not all tests measure all of these areas.

Another type of formal test is the oral reading test. These instruments provide documentation of the child's overall reading ability, considering such areas as speed and accuracy. Some also include measures of comprehension areas.

Informal Reading Assessment Procedures

Why Use Informal Reading Assessment Procedures?

Identification of areas for further evaluation or remediation; informal determination of objectives and teaching strategies; development and evaluation of IEPs.

Who Should Use Them?

Teachers.

Informal Reading Inventories

Informal reading inventories (IRIs) can be developed by a teacher or can be prepared by a publisher to accompany a specific basal reading series (Lipson & Wixson, 2003). When a teacher or other test user develops an IRI, it is usually necessary to select representative passages from various levels of a student's reading program and generate comprehension questions related to those passages. Newcomer (1985) found, however, that teachers frequently had difficulty selecting representative passages, partly as a function of variations of reading levels within the same text. She also noted that teachers often have problems formulating the comprehension questions. In addition, not all reading series are accompanied by IRIs. As a result, commercially prepared IRIs that are independent of a specific reading series are relatively popular.

Although IRIs differ from one another in format and content, most contain graded word lists and graded reading passages that yield a measure of word recognition and comprehension skills. Some IRIs also include a measure of listening comprehension in which graded passages are read to the student, who must answer comprehension questions. Most commercially prepared IRIs construct the reading passages from existing word lists. Among the more popular commercially prepared IRIs are the *Analytical Reading Inventory* (Woods & Moe, 1999), the *Basic Reading Inventory* (Johns, 2001), the *Classroom Reading Inventory* (Silvaroli, 2000), the *Burns-Roe Reading Inventory* (Roe, 2006), and the *Ekwall/Shanker Reading Inventory* (Shankar & Ekwall, 2000). Table 12.1 shows a comparison of four of these IRIs. The term *graded* refers to the approximate grade level associated with the passages. Typically, three levels of reading are determined from an IRI. The *independent* level is identified as the level at which the student can read alone without any help from another person. The *instructional* level is the teaching level at which the student can read relatively comfortably but finds it challenging. The *frustration* level is the level at which the student finds the material difficult and frustrating. Rasinski (1999) also described a method to determine the three levels based on reading rate. As in criterion-referenced tests, criteria are established that indicate how much of the material the student must read correctly (oral reading) and understand (comprehension) to be placed at the various reading levels. Although the criteria for these reading levels vary for different

IRIs typically provide three reading levels.

TABLE 12.1   A Comparison of Four Commonly Used Informal Reading Inventories

Inventory	Grade Levels	Forms of Inventory	Length of Passages	Source of Passages
Analytic Reading Inventory (ARI)	Primary to 9th, 1st to 9th for science and social studies	3 equivalent narrative forms; 1 social studies and 1 science form	Varies 50 words to 352 words	Written for inventory; some science and social studies passages from textbooks
Basic Reading Inventory (BRI)	Preprimary to 8th	3 forms; A for oral, B for silent, C as needed	50 words at preprimary, 100 words primary to 8th grade	Revised from earlier editions; original source not stated
Classroom Reading Inventory (CRI)	Preprimary to 8th	4 forms in all; A and B for students in grades 1 to 6; C for junior high students; D for high school students and adults	Varies; 24 words to 157 words	Written for inventory based on readability
Informal Reading Inventory by Burns & Roe (IRI-BR)	Preprimary to 12th	4 forms; all interchangeable	Varies; 60 words to 220 words	Primarily from graded materials in basal readers and literature books

IRIs, there is at least some agreement on some general guidelines. One widely accepted set of criteria for reading levels is that proposed by Betts (1946), who many people credit for the initial development of IRIs sixty years ago. He indicated that *recognition* of 99, 95, and 90 percent of the words at a specific grade level corresponds to the independent, instructional, and frustration levels. The criteria for *comprehension* for the three levels were 90, 75, and 50 percent, respectively. One could argue that the criteria for recognition are too stringent. Should a student who reads 90 percent of a word list be considered to be reading at the frustration level? Regarding the criteria for comprehension, Lipson and Wixson (2003) pointed out that there is too large a gap between the frustration and instructional levels of comprehension. An interesting position regarding the reading levels included in IRIs was offered by Pehrsson (1994), who felt that the use of frustration levels does a disservice to students. The thought is that attempts to avoid frustrating students fail to challenge students, thus resulting in less progression in reading.

Several researchers have compared the strengths and weaknesses of various IRIs and noted certain limitations. Chittooran and Miller (1998), for example,

Use of Pictures	Use of Purpose-Setting Questions	Number of Comprehension Questions per Passage	Types of Comprehension Questions	Criteria for Instructional Level	Time Needed for Administration
No	Discourages discussion before reading, but allows examiner discretion	6 for levels primary to 2nd; 8 for levels 3rd to 9th	Main idea factual terminology cause/effect inferential conclusion	95% for word recognition; 75% comprehension	Not stated
No	Uses prediction from titles	10 for all levels	Main idea fact inference evaluation vocabulary	95% for word recognition (only "significant" miscues counted); 75% comprehension	Not stated
Yes	Yes	5 for all levels	Factual inferential vocabulary	95% for word recognition; 75% comprehension	12 minutes
No	Yes	8 for all levels	Main idea detail inference sequence cause/effect vocabulary	85% word recognition for grades 1 and 2; 95% word recognition for grades 3 and above; 75% comprehension	40–50 minutes

Source: J. Pikulski. Informal Reading Inventories. *Reading Teacher, 43,* 515. Copyright © 1990 by International Reading Association. Reprinted with permission of the International Reading Association in the format Textbook and Other book via Copyright Clearance Center.

stated that IRIs have significant technical deficiencies. In addition, the usefulness of the comprehension measures has been questioned (Dufflemeyer, Robinson, & Squier, 1989), particularly related to main ideas (Dufflemeyer & Dufflemeyer, 1989) and higher level thinking skills (Applegate, Quinn, & Applegate, 2002). Paris and Carpenter (2003) pointed out that IRIs provide the most information for students who are initially developing reading skills and when they are combined with other assessment data. IRIs appear to have adequate reliability for activities such as selecting reading materials, but not for more serious decisions such as identifying reading problems (Spector, 2005).

Newcomer (1985) also noted a general lack of reliability and validity data for most IRIs and that different IRIs do not necessarily yield similar results when administered to the same student. She found, in fact, that in more than 50 percent of the students tested, the two tests (*Classroom Reading Inventory* and *Ekwall Reading Inventory*) identified different instructional levels. In a comparison of the *Analytic Reading Inventory* (ARI), *Basic Reading Inventory* (BRI), *Classroom Reading*

Inventory (CRI), and *Informal Reading Inventory* (IRI), Pikulski (1990) made the following recommendations:

ARI—Use when longer passages are preferred to sample reading ability.
BRI—Use when information about use and interpretation of IRIs is desired.
CRI—Use when quick, less complete evaluation is preferred.
IRI—Use for older students (forms available above ninth grade).

Other Informal Techniques

A number of other informal techniques are available. Examples are the *cloze* and *maze procedures, retelling,* and *questioning.* Another extremely valuable procedure is *error analysis.*

Cloze Procedure.   The **cloze procedure** consists of a reading passage (usually 250 to 300 words) in which certain words are deleted (usually every fifth or tenth). This *fixed ratio* approach of choosing the deleted words has been criticized. Farhady and Keramati (1996), for example, found that using the fixed ratio method versus other cloze procedure methods resulted in different interpretations of students' reading ability. However, Jonz (1990) found that such an approach was not erratic in choosing deleted words with similar linguistic and content characteristics. Another limitation that has been pointed out is that the cloze procedure is primarily helpful for those students who have strong language ability (Sepassi, 2003).

In the cloze procedure, the student must read the passage and provide the missing words by analyzing the content and its structure. This procedure measures the reader's ability to interpret written passages, and it requires the student to use both comprehension skills and knowledge of linguistic structure. The percentage of correct responses can be determined and can serve as a rough indication of the reading level of the student. This could be viewed as similar to the reading levels found in the informal reading inventories. It would be up to the evaluator, however, to determine the criteria for those levels. Perhaps administering it to a student who the teacher feels is a good reader could provide some guidelines. Figure 12.2 gives an example of a cloze passage. In this example, the student correctly replaced approximately 45 percent of the words (sixteen out of thirty-six).

The cloze procedure can also be used to evaluate spelling. For example, the student might be given a series of sentences such as "I hope mother doesn't b__n the food" and asked to supply the missing letters. Obviously the child's reading ability might also affect the results.

Maze Procedure.   Another technique used to measure a student's reading comprehension and knowledge of linguistic structure is the **maze procedure.** As noted in Chapter 5, the maze procedure is frequently used to evaluate comprehension in curriculum-based measurement procedures. This procedure is similar to the cloze method, except that vertically presented choices are given instead of blanks. The following sentence is an example of the maze procedure:

store
On Tuesday, John went to the corn
on

Parker, Hasbrouck, and Tindal (1992) reviewed twenty years of research on the maze procedure and reported overall support of the technique. They did note that more research is needed on the reliability of the maze procedure.

CLOZE PROCEDURE
Consists of taking a reading passage (usually 250–300 words) and deleting every fifth or tenth word. A student must read the passage by analyzing its content and structure.

MAZE PROCEDURE
Consists of taking a reading passage (usually 250–300 words) and deleting every fifth or tenth word. Choices are presented vertically and students have to choose the correct word to fill the blank.

FIGURE 12.2 Example of the Cloze Procedure

Sir Walter Raleigh

Four hundred years ago, when Elizabeth I was Queen of England, a young man *called* (named) Walter Raleigh once saw *her* (her) crossing a street. It *was* (was) raining hard and the *streets* (streets) were muddy. He took *down* (off) his rich velvet cape *then* (and) threw it down in *front* (front) of the Queen, so *when* (that) she could step on *it* (it) as on a carpet. *The* (The) Queen was so pleased *when* (that) she made Walter Raleigh *the* (a) knight. From then on, *he* (he) was called Sir Walter *Raleigh* (Raleigh,) and he became one *of* (of) the Queen's special friends.

Sir (Sir) Walter Raleigh was very *very* (much) interested in the new *city* (country) of America. He sent *many* (some) Englishmen to the American *city* (Coast) to found a colony, *then* (which) he named Virginia. They *took* (brought) back potatoes and tobacco *for* (to) England, and Sir Walter *Raleigh* (Raleigh) learned how to smoke *like* (as) the Indians did.

The *dumb* (English) people did not know *about* (about) tobacco and they didn't *know* (know) how to smoke. One *time* (day) while he was smoking *a* (his) pipe, a servant saw *much* (the) smoke coming out of *his* (his) master's mouth and thought *Walter* (he) was on fire. He *went* (ran) for a bucket of *water* (water) and dumped it on *his* (his) master's head.

Source: William H. Rupley and Timothy R. Blair. (1979). *Reading Diagnosis and Remediation*, p. 116. Copyright © 1979 by Houghton Mifflin Company, Boston, MA. Reprinted with permission.

Both the cloze and the maze procedures are examples of informal adaptations of curriculum materials into assessment devices. As with the criterion-referenced tests previously discussed, however, it is necessary for teachers to establish criteria that reflect not only the curriculum and objectives for their students, but also the learning abilities of these students. The criteria that others have established as standards may be too strict or too lenient. Pikulski and Pikulski (1977) found, for instance, that in a study of regular fifth graders, the maze and cloze scores were higher than teachers' judgments of the students' reading abilities. On the other hand, Jenkins and Jewell (1993) reported that results from a maze procedure correlated higher with reading achievement test scores than did oral reading ability.

Retelling. One valuable procedure that can be used to help determine a student's comprehension of reading material is **retelling.** This approach allows the reader to provide a free recall of the information read as opposed to responding to structured questions. Lipson and Wixson (1997) noted that retelling allows an individual to obtain a view of the quantity, quality, and organization of the information read. They further point out that text recall does not bias a student to process the information in a specific way as asking specific questions might. Anderson and Roit (1998) cautioned that the retell should be more than simply repeating the story verbatim. They argued that this may not be a good indicator of

> **RETELLING**
> Allows the student to retell a passage in his or her own words, to assess comprehension.

> Retelling doesn't bias the reader.

comprehension for students whose first language is not English. In other words, these students may be able to retell the story but not comprehend its meaning. They also suggested that the students explain the passage in their own words. Another caution that should be taken is to make sure a student does not have some type of expressive language problem that might affect performance and be misinterpreted as a comprehension problem (Carlisle, 1999).

An approach that has been used to measure reading comprehension is the **think aloud** procedure. This approach is particularly helpful in learning the cognitive or metacognitive strategies that a reader employs (Gettinger & Seibert, 2000). According to Meyers and Lytle (1986), this involves having the student read a passage (a sentence or clause at a time) and tell what he or she is thinking about or what might happen next. This procedure has been used primarily with older students but recently has been tried with younger children.

Several approaches to analyzing retellings have been suggested. Marshall (1983) suggested that a checklist be used in which the teacher notes if the retelling includes the theme, setting, character, goal/problem, attempts, resolution, and reactions. Morrow (1989) offered a more structured approach using a point system. The teacher would determine ten important components of the reading selection (e.g., names main character, includes statement about time and/or place) and the retelling would be compared to these to obtain a score of 0 to 10.

Questioning. Questioning a student about what he or she has read can be very useful but should be done after the student has had the opportunity to retell. The reason is that structured questions imply what the teacher thinks is important (Lipson & Wixson, 1997). The previously discussed IRIs often include literal (factual) questions and inferential questions. Teacher-generated questions of reading material can also be of both types. Raphael (1999) suggested three types of question–answer relationships (QARs). The first is *Right There QARs,* in which the answer is explicitly stated in the reading material. The second type is the *Think and Search QAR.* This type of question requires the student to infer what the answer is from information presented throughout the material. The third type is *In My Head QARs.* These require the student to use past information, knowledge, and experiences to answer questions for which the answers are not in the material.

Error Analysis. Error analysis in reading can focus on oral reading, reading comprehension, or both. In addition, a procedure called *miscue analysis* is available that addresses oral reading, comprehension, and word analysis skills.

Oral Reading. Analyzing errors made during oral reading and word recognition can provide important information that can be useful in developing instructional plans for students. For example, a student who substitutes a different word (e.g., *suit* for *shout*) might require different teaching procedures from a student who incorrectly sounds out phonetically a given word (e.g., *tut* for *toot*). Usually, error types such as omissions, substitutions, mispronunciations, repetitions, insertions, reversals, or hesitations are noted when conducting an error analysis of word recognition (Evans, Evans, & Mercer, 1986).

Morsink and Gable (1990) reported a four-step procedure for the analysis of word recognition errors. The first step involves the *actual sampling of the oral reading.* They suggest that the student should read from graded material from a basal series or other instructional material at a level at which the student can comprehend approximately 60 percent of the information. In other words, one should choose a reading passage that is neither too difficult nor too easy for the student.

THINK ALOUD
Measures reading comprehension by having the student read a passage, then tell what he or she is thinking about or what might happen next.

Error analysis can focus on oral reading and reading comprehension.

The second step is to *identify possible error patterns and confirm those patterns through retesting.* To identify error patterns, Morsink and Gable suggested that both qualitative information and quantitative information be gathered. Retesting is important to determine if the problem is consistent or is due perhaps to other factors such as lack of motivation or inattention. It is also possible that retesting might help to determine other relevant diagnostic information. For example, Salvia and Hughes (1990) noted that it is important to distinguish between words that a student can read without time constraints and words that a student cannot read at all. This distinction is important because different teaching procedures are required for increasing word fluency and for teaching unknown words.

It is important that a consistent coding or notation system and perhaps a scoring system be used that allows for greater communication among those who see the error analysis (e.g., the general and special education teachers). Figure 12.3 is an example of a notation system that might be used for coding reading errors. Miller (1986) suggested a scoring system whereby one point is deducted for an error that affects comprehension and one-half point is deducted for minor errors that do not affect comprehension. The points are totaled and divided by the number of words in the paragraph to obtain a percentage of correct words.

FIGURE 12.3 Notation System for Indicating Oral Reading Errors

Error Type	Notation	Example
Omission	Circle the word, words, or part of a word that is omitted.	He did not want to go in(to) his friend's house.
Substitution	Write the substituted word above the correct word.	She put the coins in the bag. [box]
Mispronunciation	Write the mispronounced word above the correct word.	The man is a thief. [thife]
Repetition	Draw a wavy line under the repeated word or words.	He wants a truck for his birthday.
Insertion	Write in the insertion. Indicate with a caret.	The doll has ^dark brown hair.
Reversal	For a letter reversal within a word, write the substituted word above the corrected word.	They were cooking soup in the pot. [top]
	For reversals of words draw a line indicating the transposition of words.	He |looked|quickly| for his homework.
Hesitation	Indicate with a slash mark.	The park was close/to the school.
Unknown or aided	Underline the word(s) after waiting a sufficient time for a response.	The boys were exhausted from their hike.
Omission of punctuation marks	Cross out the punctuation mark that was omitted.	The little girl put on her coat‚ She went outside‚
Self-corrected error	Write the incorrect word and place a check beside it.	He wants a new bike for his birthday. [bake ✓]

Source: S. Evans, W. Evans, and C. Mercer. (1986). *Assessment for Instruction.* Copyright © 1986. Reproduced by permission of Pearson Education, Inc., Upper Saddle River, New Jersey.

The third step is to *interview the student*. This involves asking the student what type of approach to reading he or she is using. For example, an incorrect word could be shown to the student, who is then asked, "Were you trying to sound out this word or were you trying to figure it out by looking at the other words in the sentence?" Information from these types of questions can provide important insight into the method of reading that the student is using. The last step involves *recording the results of the error analysis*. This could be a simple chart in which the type and number of errors as well as instructional priorities are identified.

Reading Comprehension.   Morsink and Gable (1990) suggested the use of the same four-step procedure in evaluating the errors in reading comprehension. For the first step, *obtaining the sample,* they suggest a procedure in which the teacher asks the student to read from a passage and to then tell what the story was all about. The teacher then notes the key thought units recalled and separates these into areas such as main ideas, actual details, sequential events, or inferences.

For the second step, *identifying the errors and retesting,* the teacher should probe further if it is noted that the student is having difficulty with a particular aspect of comprehension. This can be accomplished by asking specific detailed questions. Morsink and Gable (1990) also noted that this is a good time to focus on the student's understanding of vocabulary words. They suggest that for each error made during word recognition, the teacher can indicate that word in text and ask, "What does _____ mean?" This might also provide important informa-tion. For example, Salvia and Hughes (1990) noted that in literal comprehension, the most important areas are related to vocabulary and grammar. In other words, many errors in literal comprehension may be due to the student's lack of knowl-edge of the meaning of the words or the grammatical structure used in the pas-sage. They also note that when the student does understand the words and grammar, lack of comprehension could result from such things as slow reading in which the train of thought is lost.

In the third step, *interviewing the student,* the student is asked directly about the type of strategies or procedures being used to complete the comprehension exercise. To illustrate, "The student with difficulty in simple literal comprehen-sion may say, 'I just try to remember what it says but when there are so many things, I can't remember them all.' This type of response indicates the absence of a workable strategy for recall" (Morsink & Gable, 1990). For the final step, *recording the findings,* they suggest that a chart be developed that includes the type and number of the errors that are made. In the areas of critical reading, for example, the findings may address making inferences, sequence of events, main idea or summary, and recall of factual detail. Again, based on this information, prioritized instruction can be identified.

MISCUE ANALYSIS
An informal process for as-sessing oral-reading deficits by studying error patterns.

Miscue Analysis.   **Miscue analysis** is an informal process for assessing oral-reading deficits. Specifically, miscue analysis yields information on skills in oral reading, comprehension, and word analysis by providing a systematic method for study-ing the patterns of reading errors. Davenport (2002) made it clear that these errors are *miscues* not *mistakes* and can give insight into the reader's use of language and processing of written material. Although any method of analyzing the errors can be used, the *Reading Miscue Inventory* (Goodman & Burke, 1972) is perhaps the most well known. Goodman, Watson, and Burke (1987) described the steps in conducting a miscue analysis. First, an appropriate reading selection is made, the student reads the selection, and the oral reading is audiotaped. Next, the student retells the story. Finally, the pattern of errors are studied both qualitatively and quantitatively. The areas that are addressed are syntactic acceptability, semantic acceptability, meaning change, graphic similarity, sound similarity (does the reading error sound similar to the correct word?), and correction (did the reader attempt to self-correct?).

Emergent Reading Tests

Why Use Emergent Reading Tests?

Screening for at-risk reading problems; informal determination of objectives and teaching strategies.

Who Should Use Them?

Teachers; diagnostic specialists.

Assessment of Literacy and Language

- *Age level*—Preschool to grade 1.
- *Type of instrument*—Norm-referenced and criterion-referenced.
- *Scores yielded*—Subtest scaled scores, Language Index, Emergent Literacy Index, Phonological Index, Phonological Orthographic Index.
- *Areas measured*—The *Assessment of Literacy and Language* (ALL; Lombardino, Lieberman, & Brown, 2005), as the name suggests, measures emergent literacy and language skills in young children. The literacy subtests include Rhyme Knowledge, Letter Knowledge, Sound Categorization, Phonics Knowledge, and Sight Word Recognition. The language subtests include Receptive Vocabulary, Word Relationships, Parallel Sentence Production, and Listening Comprehension. There are also a series of criterion-referenced subtests measuring areas such as word retieval and rapid automatic naming. The ALL is aligned with the instructional components of Reading First and includes a Caregiver Questionnaire that evaluates the child's literacy and language use in the home.

Basic Early Assessment of Reading

- *Age/Grade level*—Kindergarten through grade 3.
- *Type of instrument*—Criterion-referenced.
- *Scores yielded*—Individual profile report and summary report.
- *Areas measured*—The *Basic Early Assessment of Reading* (BEARS; Riverside Publishing, 2002) is a series of four criterion-referenced tests that measure the areas of phonemic awareness, phonics, vocabulary, comprehension, and oral reading fluency. Overall, information on basic reading, oral reading fluency, comprehension, and language arts is provided throughout the school year via an initial-skills analysis (given at the beginning of school year), specific-skill analysis and oral reading fluency assessment (for instructional planning and progress monitoring), and summative assessment (given at the end of the school year). The results can be either hand- or computer-scored. Both individual profiles and class profiles are available.

Many tests are aligned with the Early Reading First Initiative of NCLB.

Dynamic Indicators of Basic Literacy Skills–Sixth Edition

- *Age level*—Kindergarten through grade 3.
- *Type of instrument*—Criterion-referenced.

- *Scores yielded*—Number of correct responses per minute; word use fluency—number correct.
- *Areas measured*—The *Dynamic Indicators of Basic Literacy Skills–Sixth Edition* (DIBELS; Good & Kaminski, 2002) is a set of seven fluency measures used primarily for screening and monitoring progress. It has become a popular measure to use within the Response to Intervention model and lends itself well to curriculum-based measurement. Three general areas are measured—Phonological Awareness (Initial Sounds Fluency, Phonemic Segmentation Fluency), Alphabetic Understanding (Letter Naming Fluency, Nonsense Word Fluency), and Fluency with Connected Text (Oral Reading Fluency, Retell Fluency, Word Use Fluency).

Early Reading Diagnostic Assessment–Second Edition

- *Age/Grade level*—Kindergarten to grade 4.
- *Type of instrument*—Norm-referenced.
- *Scores yielded*—Percentile ranges.
- *Areas measured*—The *Early Reading Diagnostic Assessment–Second Edition* (ERDA-2; Psychological Corporation, 2003a) measures the five components of reading defined in Reading First: phonemic awareness, phonics, fluency, vocabulary, and comprehension. Its primary use is to identify students at risk for reading failure and to provide information about strengths and weaknesses for instructional planning.

Early Reading Success Indicator

- *Age level*—6 through 10 years/kindergarten to grade 4.
- *Type of instrument*—Norm-referenced.
- *Scores yielded*—Variety of derived scores.
- *Areas measured*—The *Early Reading Success Indicator* (ERSI; Psychological Corporation, 2004) addresses the areas of phonemic awareness, phonological processing, rapid automatic naming, decoding, auditory working memory, and verbal comprehension. The ERSI includes selected subtests from other instruments—the *Process Assessment of the Learner, the Wechsler Individual Achievement Test–II,* and the *NEPSY* (a neuropsychological test for children). The ERSI is used to predict the early reading ability of children using a process model; it is recommended that it be used with the *WISC-IV Integrated* to provide a picture of the student's cognitive, processing, and reading abilities.

Pre-Reading Inventory of Phonological Awareness

- *Age level*—4 through 6 years.
- *Type of instrument*—Norm-referenced.
- *Scores yielded*—Percentile ranges (for six-month age groups).
- *Areas measured*—The *Pre-Reading Inventory of Phonological Awareness* (PIPA; Psychological Corporation, 2003b) includes six subtests: Rhyme Awareness, Syllable Segmentation, Alliteration Awareness, Sound Isolation, Sound Segmentation, and Letter–Sound Knowledge. This comprehensive inventory focuses on phonological skills that are used to identify children at risk for reading failure.

Test of Early Reading Ability–Third Edition

- *Age level*—3½ to 8½ years.
- *Type of instrument*—Norm-referenced.

- *Scores yielded*—Standard scores, age and grade equivalents, normal curve equivalents.
- *Areas measured*—The *Test of Early Reading Ability–Third Edition* (TERA-3; Reid, Hresko, & Hammill, 2001) was designed to measure three areas related to early reading. Knowledge of Conceptual Meaning measures skills such as comprehension of words, sentences, and paragraphs. Alphabet measures knowledge of the alphabet as well as related areas such as determination of the initial and final sounds as well as the number of syllables in printed words. Reading Conventions measures such skills as knowledge of spelling, punctuation, and capitalization. There are two forms—A and B—of the TERA-3.

Test of Preschool Early Literacy

- *Age level*—3 to 5 years.
- *Type of instrument*—Norm-referenced.
- *Scores yielded*—Standard scores, percentiles.
- *Areas measured*—The *Test of Preschool Literacy* (TOPEL; Lonigan, Wagner, Torgeson, & Rashotte, 2007) is comprised of three subtests. In the Print Knowledge subtest the child is asked to identify letters and letter sounds. Definitional Vocabulary measures the child's oral vocabulary, and in Phonological Awareness the child says a word and is then asked to say the word again with certain sounds omitted. It also measures the child's ability to blend sounds to form words.

Diagnostic Reading Tests

Why Use Diagnostic Reading Tests?

Screening and identification; informal determination of objectives and teaching strategies; documentation of educational need; establishment of IEP goals.

Who Should Use Them?

Teachers; diagnostic specialists.

Stanford Diagnostic Reading Test–4

The *Stanford Diagnostic Reading Test–4* (SDRT4; Karlsen & Gardner, 1996) is a group-administered and individually administered instrument designed to measure a student's strengths and weaknesses in reading. It is used with students from kindergarten through grade 12. The authors suggest that the results from the SDRT4 can be used to help in grouping students and in developing appropriate instructional strategies. The SDRT4 places special emphasis on the low-achieving student, and it contains more easy items than many reading-achievement tests. The SDRT4 measures four major components of reading: vocabulary, phonetic analysis, comprehension, and scanning. The SDRT4 has eight levels, each designed for different age ranges. The Pink and Teal Levels were recently added to address the early reading components of Reading First.

> The SDRT4 can be group administered.

Pink Level. Used with students from the beginning of kindergarten to the middle of kindergarten.

Teal Level. Used with students from the middle of kindergarten to the middle of grade 1.

Red Level. Used with students from the middle of grade 1 to the middle of grade 2.

Orange Level. Used with students from the middle of grade 2 to the middle of grade 3.

Green Level. Used with students from the middle of grade 3 to the middle of grade 4 and with low-achieving students in grade 5.

Purple Level. Used with students from grades 4.5 to 6.5.

Brown Level. Used with students from grades 6.5 to 8.9 and with low-achieving high-school students.

Blue Level. Designed for use with students from grades 9 through 12.

For each level, several tests are given that measure performance in such areas as auditory vocabulary, auditory discrimination, comprehension, reading rate, and phonetic and structural analysis. There is one form for the first three levels and two forms for the last three.

Description

Pink and Teal Levels. These levels measure the components of reading indicated in Reading First:

Vocabulary
Comprehension
Phonemic Awareness
Phonics
Fluency

Red Level. The Red Level includes eight tests that generally measure phonetic analysis, vocabulary, and comprehension:

Consonants
Vowels
Word Reading
Listening Vocabulary
Sentences
Riddles
Cloze
Paragraphs with Questions

Orange Level. This level includes six tests:

Consonants
Vowels
Listening Vocabulary
Reading Vocabulary
Cloze
Paragraphs with Questions

Green Level. The Green Level includes five tests:

Consonants
Vowels
Listening Vocabulary
Reading Vocabulary
Paragraphs with Questions

Purple Level.   There are three tests for the Purple Level. These are *Reading Vocabulary, Paragraphs with Questions,* and *Scanning.*

Brown Level and Blue Level.   These levels include the same tests as the Purple Level.

Interpretation of Results.   The SDRT4 can be either hand-scored or computer-scored. The raw scores from each test can be transformed into a number of norm-referenced scores. The manual for each level includes tables for percentile ranks, stanines, grade equivalents, and scaled scores. Computer scoring can also provide stanines and percentile ranks compared to both local and national norms. In fact, the computer scoring profile provides much valuable information. The SDRT4 also includes progress indicators, which are essentially cutoff points, determined by the authors, that document whether a student has demonstrated competence in various reading skills. The authors suggest that the cutoff points be used only as guides and that they may need to be modified according to the individual's instructional program. Also included with the SDRT4 is an instructional-placement report that summarizes the results of an entire class by using the scores that are viewed as the most relevant.

SDRT4 results of an entire class can be summarized.

Technical Characteristics

Normative Sample.   A nationally stratified sample of approximately 60,000 was used.

Reliability.   Internal reliability coefficients were generally above .80; many were .90 or above. Alternate-form reliability coefficients ranged from .62 to .88.

Validity.   A discussion of content validity can be found in the manual. Construct and criterion-related data are presented that show high coefficients with the previous edition of the SDRT.

Review of Relevant Research.   No relevant research literature was located for the SDRT4 or any of the previous editions. Lewandowski and Martens (1990) reviewed an earlier version of the SDRT4 and found that it was useful as a screening instrument. They did point out, however, that some of the subtests were inappropriately named and found little rationale presented for its theoretical base.

Overview: Stanford Diagnostic Reading Test–4
- *Age level*—Grade 1 through grade 12.
- *Type of administration*—Group or individual.
- *Technical adequacy*—Good.
- *Scores yielded*—Percentile ranks, stanines, grade equivalents, scaled scores, progress indicators.
- *Suggested use*—The SDRT4 is a well-constructed diagnostic reading test. Its standardization sample was large and representative and the reliability and the validity are good. It can therefore be used as a reasonable measure of vocabulary, phonetic analysis, comprehension, and scanning, particularly for screening purposes. It gives more normative information but less informal information (e.g., error analysis) than other diagnostic reading tests. It should be noted that an online version of the SDRT-4 was made available in 2003.

There are two different forms of the WRMT-R.

Woodcock Reading Mastery Tests–Revised/Normative Update

The *Woodcock Reading Mastery Tests–Revised* (WRMT-R; Woodcock, 1998) includes six individually administered tests and a two-part supplementary checklist designed for individuals ages 5 to 75 and older. There are two forms of the test—Form G contains all six tests and the supplementary checklist, whereas Form H contains only four tests. According to the author, the WRMT-R can be used for a variety of reasons, including diagnosis of reading problems, program planning, and program evaluation. The tests are designed for both criterion-referenced and norm-referenced purposes, although their use as a criterion-referenced tool is somewhat limited.

Description

Visual-Auditory Learning (Form G only).   This subtest requires the examinee to associate new visual symbols with familiar words and then translate sentences using those new symbols.

Letter Identification (Form G only).   This subtest requires the student to identify lower- and uppercase letters presented in common styles (such as cursive) and uncommon styles (such as special typestyles).

Word Identification.   This subtest includes words arranged sequentially according to level of difficulty. The examinee simply has to read the word.

Word Attack.   This subtest measures the ability to pronounce nonsense words (e.g., "gnouthe") through the use of structural and phonetic analysis.

Word Comprehension.   This test is comprised of three separate subtests. *Antonyms* requires the examinee to say a word that is opposite of a vocabulary word. *Synonyms* requires the examinee to say a word that means the same thing as a vocabulary word. *Analogies* requires the person to read a pair of analogous words (e.g., cowboy–horse) and then complete a second analogy (e.g., pilot– _____).

Passage Comprehension.   This subtest uses a modified cloze procedure. The examinee must read a passage in which a key word is missing and must identify the missing word.

Supplementary Letter Checklist (Form G only).   This checklist includes both *capital letter* and *lowercase letter* sublists. These letters are presented in the sans serif typestyle that is common in many beginning reading programs.

Interpretation of Results.   The subtests of the WRMT-R can provide specific information about the examinee or can be combined into various clusters for interpretation. Age equivalents, grade equivalents, percentile ranks, and standard scores (mean = 100; standard deviation = 15) are available in the following areas: Readiness (Visual-Auditory Learning and Letter Identification), Basic Skills (Word Identification and Word Attack), Reading Comprehension (Word Comprehension and Passage Comprehension), Total Reading–Full Scale (Word Identification, Word Attack, Word Comprehension, and Passage Comprehension), and Total Reading–Short Scale (Word Identification and Passage Comprehension). A Relative Performance Index (RPI) is also available that gives an indication of the relative mastery of content at a specific grade level. Scoring of the

WRMT-R is rather cumbersome. Several interesting and potentially valuable features are a word-attack error inventory and tables that allow for the determination of aptitude-achievement discrepancies. Scores can also be placed on a diagnostic profile, a percentile rank profile, and an instructional level profile. The diagnostic profile allows the interpretation of scores from other tests as well as the WRMT-R. Figure 12.4 shows the percentile rank profile. Eaves, Campbell-Whatley, Dunn, Reilly, and Tate-Braxton (1995) also developed a set of tables that allow a comparison of the standard scores taking into account each subtest's reliability.

Hand scoring the WRMT-R can be tedious.

Technical Characteristics

Normative Sample. In 1998, AGS renormed four tests: *Kaufman Test of Educational Achievement* (K-TEA), *KeyMath–Revised* (KM-R), the *Peabody Individual Achievement Test–Revised* (PIAT-R), and the *Woodcock Reading Mastery Test–Revised* (WRMT-R). The format and items are the same as those for previous editions: K-TEA (1985), KM-R (1988), PIAT-R (1988), and WRMT-R (1987). This renorming was somewhat unique. It involved "domain norming," which means that the similar subtests across each instrument was administered to the standardization sample (as opposed to each subject being given the entire instrument). As a result, only approximately 20 percent of the total sample were administered the entire instrument as the "primary test." However, each subject took the relevant subtests from the other three instruments that measured the same domain. The

FIGURE 12.4 Percentile Rank Profile from the Woodcock Reading Mastery Tests–Revised

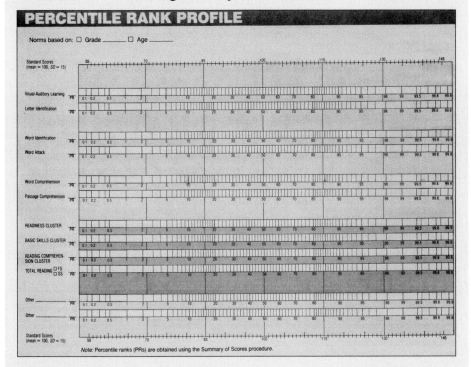

Source: R. Woodcock. *Woodcock Reading Mastery Tests–Revised.* Copyright © 1987 by American Guidance Service. Reprinted with permission.

total sample was over 3,000 individuals although the domain norms ranged from 1,285 (Written Expression) to 2,809 (Math Applications). Careful stratification was used considering a number of variables such as race/ethnicity, region, and parent educational level.

Reliability.   Split-half coefficients were above .90 for all subtests and clusters. A coefficient of .99 was reported for the total reading.

Validity.   Concurrent validity coefficients with the reading tests from the Woodcock-Johnson Psychoeducational Battery ranged from .25 to .91. Total reading scores from one test correlated .85 or above with total reading from the other test. Arguments for the test's content and construct validity are also reported in the manual.

Review of Relevant Research.   Surprisingly, relatively little research on the WRMT-R was found. The studies have generally indicated that it is a widely used test but that its results might be different from those of other reading tests. Reviews of the WRMT-R have been somewhat mixed and have noted the need for additional technical data. In particular, information related to the updated norms needs to be gathered. Summaries of representative studies and a review follow. Additional summaries can be located at the Earlier Research link for Chapter 12 on the Companion Website (www.prenhall.com/taylor8e).

- Wickes and Slate (1999) found that African American students score significantly lower on the WRMT-R than on the reading portion of the *Wechsler Individual Achievement Test.*

> Reviews of the WRMT-R have been mixed.

- Sutton (1998–1999), in a review, questioned the validity of the WRMT-R and noted that the updated norms still have problems with representativeness.
- Arthaud, Vasa, and Stekelberg (2000) surveyed 800 special education teachers about their current reading assessment practices and found that over half were using the WRMT-R.
- Three subtests (Letter-Word Identification, Passage Comprehension, and Word Attack) were successful in differentiating students with and without reading disabilities (Sofie & Riccio, 2002).
- Simpson, Smith, Johnson, and Halpin (2003) applied alternate ceiling criteria to the Passage Comprehension subtest that resulted in a shorter test with no significant change in the scores.

Overview: Woodcock Reading Mastery Test–Revised

- *Age level*—5 to 75+ years.
- *Type of administration*—Individual.
- *Technical adequacy*—Adequate standardization, good but limited reliability (only split-half), somewhat limited validity.
- *Scores yielded*—Standard scores, percentile ranks, age and grade equivalents, relative performance index.

> The WRMT-R is probably the most popular reading test in special education.

- *Suggested use*—The WRMT-R is probably the most popular norm-referenced diagnostic reading test used in special education. The tests are easy to administer and cover a number of abilities. The WRMT-R, however, is tedious to score, requiring the use of multiple tables that could lead to scoring errors. It is important that examiners practice the scoring several times before administering it in a real test situation. For this reason, the computer scoring program is recommended. The meaning and interpretation of the visual-auditory learning subtest and the aptitude–achievement discrepancy tables need to be established. The error inventory is a nice addition. In summary, it appears that the WRMT-R has improved many of the shortcomings of the original test, although the technical characteristics have been questioned. Although the norms are ten years old, the test itself, including the format and items, is over twenty years old. Thus, there may be some questions about the items being consistent with today's curriculum.

Other Diagnostic Reading Tests

In addition to the previously discussed norm-referenced reading tests, four others deserve mention. The first, the *Gray Diagnostic Reading Test–II*, is a significant revision of its predecessor. The second, the *Test of Reading Comprehension–3*, measures various components of silent reading comprehension. The third, the *Test of Silent Word Reading Fluency*, eliminates the oral reading component. The fourth, the *WJ III Diagnostic Reading Battery*, includes ten subtests from the *Woodcock-Johnson–III* (discussed in Chapter 11).

Gray Diagnostic Reading Test—Second Edition

- *Age level*—6 through 13 years.
- *Type of administration*—Individual.
- *Technical adequacy*—Good reliability; adequate validity.
- *Scores yielded*—Standard scores; percentile ranks, age equivalents, grade equivalents, and a descriptive rating.
- *Description*—The *Gray Diagnostic Reading Test–Second Edition* (GDRT-II; Bryant, Wiederholt, & Bryant, 2004) is a significant revision of the *Gray Oral Reading Test–Diagnostic.* There are two alternate forms of the GDRT-II that can be used to evaluate specific reading strengths and weaknesses. The four core subtests are Letter/Word Identification, Phonetic Analysis, Reading Vocabulary, and Meaningful Vocabulary. There are also three supplemental subtests: Listening Vocabulary, Rapid Naming, and Phonological Awareness. The authors state that the revision is based on current research in reading.

Test of Reading Comprehension–3

- *Age level*—7 to 18 years.
- *Type of administration*—Individual (small group is possible).
- *Technical adequacy*—Adequate standardization, good reliability, questionable validity.
- *Scores yielded*—Scaled scores, percentile ranks, Reading Comprehension Quotient.
- *Suggested use*—The *Test of Reading Comprehension–3* (TORC-3; Brown, Hammill, & Wiederholt, 1995) is theoretically a measure of silent reading comprehension. Only a small part of the test actually focuses on traditional comprehension measures (that is, on reading a passage and answering questions about the content). Most of the test is concerned with vocabulary and syntax. For example, four of the eight subtests measure vocabulary (including content areas of math, social studies, and science). This is not necessarily a criticism of

The TORC-3 has many vocabulary and syntax subtests.

the test; however, you should be aware of the test's content if you use the results exclusively to assess a student's comprehension. The TORC-3 is most appropriate for students ages 8 to 14.

Test of Silent Word Reading Fluency

- *Age level*—6½ to 18 years.
- *Type of administration*—Individual or small group.
- *Technical adequacy*—Adequate standardization, good validity and reliability.
- *Scores yielded*—Standard scores, percentiles, age and grade equivalents.
- *Description*—The *Test of Silent Word Reading Fluency* (TOSWRF; Mather, Hammill, Allen, & Roberts, 2004) is designed to screen for poor readers and to monitor their progress. Students are presented with rows of letters that are actually several words without spaces between them (e.g., sadpondcow). They are given three minutes to draw a line to separate the letters into words (sad/pond/cow) for as many letter strings as possible.

WJ III Diagnostic Reading Battery

- *Age level*—2 to over 90 years.
- *Type of administration*—Individual.
- *Technical adequacy*—Good standardization, good reliability (particularly for clusters), good validity.
- *Scores yielded*—Age and grade equivalents, percentiles, standard scores, descriptive reading levels.
- *Description*—The *WJ III Diagnostic Reading Battery* (WJ III DRB; Woodcock, Mather, & Schrank, 2004) is actually a "repackaging" of ten subtests from the *Woodcock-Johnson–III.* The ten subtests can be combined to form eight clusters: Brief Reading, Basic Reading Skills, Reading Comprehension, Phonics Knowledge, Phonemic Awareness, Oral Language Comprehension, Broad Reading, and Total Reading. The WJ III DRB includes measures of the five areas identified in *Reading First,* suggesting it has a strong pre-reading component. A computerized scoring and reporting program is included in each test kit.

BACK TO THE PROFILE

Possible Answers to the Questions

1. **Why assess John?** Given John's situation and Ms. Gupta's concerns that John might have a reading disability, the first reason to assess John probably would be to collect information to develop a prereferral intervention program. As noted in Chapter 2, such a program is prerequisite for a formal referral to determine eligibility for special education. If the prereferral intervention program was ineffective, than a second reason to assess would be to determine eligibility. If he was found to be eligible, then a third reason to assess would be to get additional information for the development of his IEP.

2. **Who should assess John?** Assuming all three types of assessments noted above were conducted, a number of individuals would be involved. First, the general education teacher would be responsible for gathering information for the prereferral intervention program. It is also possible that this would be done in collaboration with a special education teacher (particularly if inclusion was the model followed in the school). To determine eligibility, the area of reading might be evaluated by a reading specialist, psychometrist, or special education teacher (this will vary from state to state). Finally,

the information for the development of the IEP should involve a reading specialist and/or a special education teacher.

3. **What procedure(s)/test(s) should be used?** To gather information for the prereferral intervention program, a variety of informal procedures might be used. First, an IRI may be used to determine John's instructional level. This could also be supplemented by the use of the *Reading Miscue Inventory.* This should provide Ms. Gupta with a good idea of the level of his reading as well as a basic idea of the type of errors he is making. To determine eligibility, an individually administered norm-referenced test should be used. Because John is having trouble in both word identification and reading comprehension, a test such as the WRMT-R could be used.

4. **What other areas (if any) should be assessed?** Because eligibility for special education is one of the purposes for the assessment, other areas will have to be evaluated. This will involve a measure of intelligence (such as the WISC–IV) administered by a school psychologist. In some states, a measure of processing skills might be necessary. This could be the *Comprehensive Test of Phonological Processing* or others that might be used by individual districts.

STUDENT PROFILE DATA

John

John was initially tested by his teacher using an IRI. Those results indicated that he was only performing at the first-grade level instructionally in both reading recognition and reading comprehension. He was, however, on grade level in listening comprehension. John was subsequently administered the *Gray Diagnostic Reading Test–Second Edition.* The following results were reported:

Subtest	Percentile Rank
Letter-Word Identification	45
Phonetic Analysis	29
Reading Vocabulary	35
Meaningful Vocabulary	40
Listening Vocabulary	75

These results indicate that John's primary problem is in phonetic analysis. This apparently affects his word identification and vocabulary skills. This, in turn, probably affects his reading comprehension.

CASE STUDY *June*

Based on the results of several assessments including teacher observations, the CBA, and the WIAT-II, it was determined that June would need a more extensive evaluation in reading. Following are the results of the *Woodcock Reading Mastery Test–R* (WRMT-R). Review the scores of the WRMT-R. As you review these scores, think back to the other assessment information that has been gathered so far on June. Look for links between the previous results and the scores from the reading assessment. (For your convenience, the results of the assessments that have already been completed are available in the Cumulative Assessment File on the Companion Website, www.prenhall.com/taylor8e.) After you have reviewed the WRMT-R results, answer the questions that follow.

WRMT-R

Subtests/Composites	Standard Score
Word Identification (word id)	81
Word Comprehension (word comp)	90
Passage Comprehension (passage comp)	85
Word Attack	76
Basic Skills Composite (BSC)	77
Reading Comprehension Composite (RCC)	86

- The Word Comprehension subtest (SS = 90) is June's best score.

   a. What skills does this subtest measure?

   b. This relative strength for June has also been indicated by what other scores from previous tests?

- What deficit areas are indicated by the scores of the WRMT-R? Do these deficits appear in other assessment results? Explain.

- June was initially referred for assessment because of concerns regarding her struggles in academic areas. Taking into consideration what you now know from the information in her file, write a statement summarizing June's assessment profile to this point.

- What further reading assessment would you recommend in order to more precisely understand June's reading problem? Explain your choices.

Reflections

1. Why is it better to use the retelling approach before the questioning approach when assessing reading comprehension?
2. Why do you think the assessment of emergent literacy is so important, both educationally and politically?
3. What are the advantages and disadvantages of using the SDRT4 and the WRMT-R?

Summary Matrix

Instrument or Technique	Prereferral: Screening and Initial Identification	Prereferral: Informal Determination and Evaluation of Teaching Programs and Strategies	Postreferral: Determination of Current Performance Level and Educational Need	Postreferral: Decisions about Classification and Program Placement	Postreferral: IEP Goals	Postreferral: IEP Objectives	Postreferral: IEP Evaluation	Target Population: Mild/Moderate	Target Population: Severe/Profound	Target Population: Preschool	Target Population: Elementary Age	Target Population: Secondary Age	Target Population: Adult	Special Considerations	Educational Relevance for Exceptional Students
Informal reading inventories	X	X	X		X			X			X	X		Most measure word recognition and comprehension skills.	Useful
Cloze procedure	X	X						X			X	X	X	The reading levels that are determined should be used only as guidelines.	Adequate
Maze procedure	X	X						X			X	X	X	The reading levels that are determined should be used only as guidelines.	Adequate
Retelling	X	X						X			X	X	X	Allows free recall of information read to determine comprehension.	Useful
Questioning	X	X						X			X	X	X	Allows teachers to question comprehension of important information.	Useful
Error Analysis	X	X						X			X	X	X	Provides important information for oral reading and reading comprehension.	Very Useful
Assessment of Literacy and Language	X							X		X	X			Measures emergent literacy and language skills.	Useful
Basic Early Assessment of Reading	X	X						X			X			Series of criterion-referenced tests for instructional planning.	Useful

(continued)

Summary Matrix (continued)

Instrument or Technique	Screening and Initial Identification	Informal Determination of Teaching Programs and Strategies	Determination of Current Performance Level and Educational Need	Decisions about Classification and Program Placement	IEP Goals	IEP Objectives	IEP Evaluation	Mild/Moderate	Severe/Profound	Preschool	Elementary Age	Secondary Age	Adult	Special Considerations	Educational Relevance for Exceptional Students
Dynamic Indicators of Basic Early Literacy Skills–Sixth Edition	X							X		X	X			Often used as CBM measures within the RTI model.	Very Useful
Early Reading Diagnostic Assessment–Second Edition		X						X		X	X			Measures five components of reading defined in *Reading First*.	Useful
Early Reading Success Indicator	X	X						X		X	X			Used to predict early reading ability using a process model.	Adequate
Pre-Reading Inventory of Phonological Awareness	X							X		X	X			Phonological inventory used to identify children at risk for reading failure.	Useful
Test of Early Reading Ability–Third Edition	X	X						X		X	X			Measures three areas related to early reading.	Adequate
Test of Preschool Early Literacy	X							X		X				Measures three areas of preschool literacy.	Adequate
Stanford Diagnostic Reading Test–4	X		X		X			X			X	X	X	Well constructed; can be group administered; does not give specific instructional information.	Useful
Woodcock Reading Mastery Tests–Revised/Normative Update	X		X		X			X			X	X		Earlier version widely used; some improvements in revision; tedious scoring system.	Adequate/Useful
Gray Diagnostic Reading Test–Second Edition	X		X		X			X			X			A significant revision based on current reading research.	Adequate/Useful
Test of Reading Comprehension–3	X				X			X			X	X		Heavily weighted toward vocabulary and syntax.	Adequate
Test of Silent Word Reading Fluency	X	X						X			X	X		Eliminates the oral reading component	Useful
WJ III Diagnostic Reading Battery	X		X		X			X		X	X	X	X	Ten subtests from the Woodcock-Johnson–III packaged together.	Adequate/Useful

chapter thirteen

Assessment of Mathematics

STUDENT PROFILE

Zandra

Zandra is a fourth-grade student who has been receiving services for a learning disability for two years. She is in an inclusion classroom where she works with both her general education teacher, Mr. Bell, and her special education teacher, Ms. Rivera. Ms. Rivera collaborates with Mr. Bell for the four students in the class identified as having disabilities. Zandra's IEP primarily had goals related to reading because that was the area in which she initially had difficulty. Recently, however, she has started to struggle in math as well. Her teacher says that Zandra "seems to be afraid of numbers." She often confuses the mathematical signs and is having particular difficulty understanding multiplication. When given word problems, she frequently does not know which operation to use to solve them, even though the problems are read to her because of her reading deficiency. Mr. Bell noticed that Zandra was beginning to have difficulty applying her math skills as well.

Think about These Questions as You Read This Chapter:

1. Why assess Zandra? (There could be more than one reason.)
2. Who should assess Zandra? (There could be more than one person.)
3. What procedure(s)/test(s) should be used?
4. What other areas (if any) should be assessed?

(Suggested answers appear at the end of this chapter.)

Less attention is given to the assessment of mathematics than of reading. Evaluation of mathematics is important, however, and should be included when conducting a comprehensive basic skills assessment. A look at the general achievement tests discussed in Chapter 11 reveals that subtests that measure mathematics are included in virtually every instrument.

Mathematics assessment usually involves the areas of mathematical concepts, computation, application, and problem solving. *Mathematical concepts* focus on basic information such as the understanding of numeration, mathematical operations, number concepts, and place value. *Computation* involves such areas as addition, subtraction, multiplication, and division of whole numbers, fractions, and decimals. *Application* includes such areas as measurement skills, money skills, and time concepts, whereas *problem solving* involves the ability to (1) determine how to solve a given problem (frequently a word problem) and (2) perform the necessary operation(s) to determine the correct answer.

Over the past two decades, the National Council of Teachers of Mathematics (NCTM) has published several sets of standards that have implications for both the content of math curricula and the type of assessment used in the area of mathematics. NCTM Standards 2000 are ten specific math standards that should be included in today's schools. The NCTM argues that appropriate assessment of mathematical skills requires the use of multiple measures. They stated, "assembling evidence from a variety of sources is more likely to yield an accurate picture of what each student knows and is able to do" (NCTM, 2000, p. 24). They also emphasize the relative importance of each standard based on the grade level of the student. Following are the ten standards of the NCTM (2000).[1]

Standard 1: Numbers and Operations
- Understand numbers, ways of representing numbers, relationships among numbers, and number systems.
- Understand meaning of operations and how they relate to one another.
- Compute fluently and make reasonable estimates.

Standard 2: Algebra
- Understand patterns, relationships, and functions.
- Represent and analyze mathematical situations and structures using algebraic symbols.
- Use mathematical models to represent and understand algebraic symbols.
- Use mathematical models to represent and understand quantitative relationships.
- Analyze change in various contexts.

Standard 3: Geometry
- Analyze characteristics and properties of two- and three-dimensional geometric shapes and develop mathematical arguments about geometric relationships.
- Specify locations and describe spatial relationships using coordinate geometry and other representational systems.
- Apply transformations and use symmetry to analyze mathematical situations.
- Use visualization, spatial reasoning, and geometric modeling to solve problems.

Standard 4: Measurement
- Understand measurable attributes of objects and the units, systems, and processes of measurement.
- Apply appropriate techniques, tools, and formulas to determine measurements.

[1]Reprinted with permission from *Principles and Standards for School Mathematics.* Copyright © 2000 by the National Council of Teachers of Mathematics. www.nctm.org. All rights reserved. NCTM does not endorse these alignments.

Standard 5: Data Analysis and Probability
- Formulate questions that can be addressed with data and collect, organize, and display relevant data to answer them.
- Select and use appropriate statistical methods to analyze data.
- Develop and evaluate inferences and predictions that are based on data.
- Understand and apply basic concepts of probability.

Standard 6: Problem Solving
- Build new mathematical knowledge through problem solving.
- Solve problems that arise in mathematics and in other contexts.
- Apply and adapt a variety of appropriate strategies to solve problems.
- Monitor and reflect on the process of mathematical problem solving.

Standard 7: Reasoning and Proof
- Recognize reasoning and proof as fundamental aspects of mathematics.
- Make and investigate mathematical conjecture.
- Develop and evaluate mathematical arguments and proofs.
- Select and use various types of reasoning and methods of proof.

Standard 8: Communication
- Organize and consolidate mathematical thinking through communication.
- Communicate mathematical thinking coherently and clearly to peers, teachers, and others.
- Analyze and evaluate the mathematical thinking and strategies of others.
- Use the language of mathematics to express mathematical ideas precisely.

Standard 9: Connections
- Recognize and use connections among mathematical ideas.
- Understand how mathematical ideas interconnect and build on one another to produce a coherent whole.
- Recognize and apply mathematics in context outside of mathematics.

Standard 10: Representation
- Create and use representations to organize, record, and communicate mathematical ideas.
- Select, apply, and translate among mathematical representations to solve problems.
- Use representations to model and interpret physical, social, and mathematical phenomena.

A number of both informal and formal approaches to mathematics assessment is available. As with all academic skills, informal assessment can provide extremely important information to assist in educational decision making. For example, the use of error analysis procedures, particularly for computation skills, can be quite valuable. The ease of obtaining written products for error analysis adds to its benefits. Other informal techniques include interviews and authentic assessment.

Norm-referenced tests for the mathematical areas are sometimes referred to as *diagnostic* tests. Similar to diagnostic reading tests, however, these instruments are used to determine strengths and weaknesses and to identify areas for remediation rather than "diagnosing" in a traditional sense. Criterion-referenced instruments in the area of mathematics are used to identify more specific information that might be incorporated into an IEP. Many of these criterion-referenced instruments are now available as software to provide computerized assessment of math (computation) skills.

Informal Assessment

Why Use Informal Math Assessment?

Determination and evaluation of teaching strategies; gathering of prereferral information; development and evaluation of IEPs.

Who Should Use It?

Teachers.

The area of mathematics can be easily assessed using various informal techniques. The sequential nature of most arithmetic skills (particularly computation) allows for the use of both criterion-referenced testing and curriculum-based assessment (discussed in Chapter 5). These approaches can help determine which skills to target for teaching and remediation. Also, because the student usually creates a written product when computing or solving math problems, error analysis can offer important insight about the correct and incorrect strategies the student uses. This information can then be translated into instructional recommendations.

Error Analysis

Written products to analyze are readily available.

Error analyses in mathematics are relatively simple, because, as a rule, a written product is available; thus, the teacher has a tremendous amount of potential information from the students' routine math work in school. Ashlock (2006) has written a widely used book that addresses error patterns in arithmetic computation. The problems in Figure 13.1 are examples of the error types discussed by Ashlock. It is important to do more than just note whether a problem is worked out correctly. The pattern of error can yield meaningful information, particularly in determining the teaching strategy that is most appropriate.

For example, assume a student, Lucy, was making the type of multiplication error noted in Figure 13.1. The following are samples of her work:

$$
\begin{array}{ccccc}
\textbf{1.}\ \ \overset{3}{1}4 & \textbf{2.}\ \ 32 & \textbf{3.}\ \ \overset{2}{1}7 & \textbf{4.}\ \ \overset{1}{2}3 & \textbf{5.}\ \ 41 \\
\underline{\times\ 8} & \underline{\times\ 4} & \underline{\times\ 3} & \underline{\times\ 6} & \underline{\times\ 9} \\
322 & 128 & 91 & 188 & 369
\end{array}
$$

Error patterns can indicate appropriate teaching strategies.

Lucy correctly answered #2 and #5, but missed #1, #3, and #4. Her error pattern indicated that she added the carried digit (crutch) to the number in the tens column before multiplying it instead of after. Ashlock made several suggestions for teaching this skill. For example, the crutch could be placed below the bar to remind Lucy that the number should be added after the multiplication has been conducted.

$$
\begin{array}{ccc}
14 & 14 & 14 \\
\underline{\times\ 8} \ \rightarrow & \underline{\times\ 8} \ \rightarrow & \underline{\times\ 8} \\
{}^{3}2 & {}^{3}2 & 112 \\
 & \underline{+8} & \\
 & 112 &
\end{array}
$$

FIGURE 13.1 Examples of Math Errors

Addition examples:

(1)	82	(2)	68	(3)	45
	+ 41		+ 39		+ 35
	123		917		710

Error Pattern: The student is adding the 1s column and the 10s column independently without carrying or noting the place value in the sum.

Subtraction examples:

(1)	63	(2)	49	(3)	81
	− 37		− 27		− 19
	34		22		78

Error Pattern: The student is subtracting the smaller number from the larger number in each column regardless of their positions as subtrahend or minuend.

Multiplication examples:

(1)	83	(2)	63	(3)	48
	× 4		× 5		× 2
	362		355		106

Error Pattern: The student is adding the carried digit before instead of after multiplying. In the first example, for instance, the student multiplied 3×4, wrote the 2, carried the 1, and added this to 8. The student then calculated 4×9 rather than $(4 \times 8) + 1$.

Division examples:

	13		81		32
(1) 3$\sqrt{93}$		(2) 4$\sqrt{72}$		(3) 6$\sqrt{138}$	
	9		4		12
	3		32		18
	3		32		18

Error Pattern: The student is dividing correctly but is writing down the answer from right to left.

This cue, which eventually would be eliminated, should assist her in remembering the correct sequence. In addition, the familiar acrostic <u>M</u>y <u>D</u>ear <u>A</u>unt <u>S</u>ally could be introduced to indicate the order of operations (<u>M</u>ultiplication, <u>D</u>ivision, <u>A</u>ddition, <u>S</u>ubtraction) to be conducted. Thus, Lucy would know to do all multiplication operations before going on to other operations including addition.

Enright, Gable, and Hendrickson (1988), described a nine-step model for diagnosing and remediating errors in mathematics computation. Each of these steps will be presented with a brief discussion.

Step 1: Obtain Samples. This involves gathering multiple samples of the student's mathematics computation work. Enright and colleagues (1988) recommend that samples should include at least three to five items for each subskill measured.

Step 2: Interview the Student. The diagnostic interview is a helpful technique in math error analysis. Using this procedure, the examiner employs a variety of techniques to determine how a student arrives at an answer for a certain problem (interviews will be discussed later in this chapter).

Step 3: Analyze Errors and Identify Error Patterns.   A variety of major error types have been used in classification. Salvia and Hughes (1990) summarized five distinct types of computational errors. These were a lack of prerequisite skills, wrong operation (e.g., adding instead of subtracting), an obvious computational error, a defective algorithm (when a student tries to apply the correct operation but makes errors in making the necessary steps), and random responses. Gable and Coben (1990) also included grouping errors (mistakes in placing digits in the proper column when regrouping) in addition to those just listed.

To assist in the analysis, Enright and colleagues (1988) suggested the use of a computational error chart (see Figure 13.2) that indicates the type and number of errors made. As an exercise, try to identify the type of error for each of the following examples using the error chart in Figure 13.2.

A computational error chart may be helpful.

1.	**2.**	**3.**	**4.**	**5.**
48	91	35	43	45
+8	× 4	−25	× 6	+23
416	157	60	308	67

Answers

1. Grouping (student correctly added but did not carry).
2. Random (no apparent pattern).
3. Wrong operation (student added instead of subtracting).
4. Defective algorithm (student correctly multiplied but added 1 to 4 before multiplying).
5. Computational error (student added 5 + 3 incorrectly).

Step 4: Select Primary Error Pattern and Show the Precise Error to the Student.   The information presented in Figure 13.2 might be shared with the student as a means of providing corrective feedback.

Step 5: Demonstrate a Correct Computational Procedure as Part of the Corrective Feedback Mechanism.   The teacher should demonstrate the correct computational procedure and leave the completed problem as a permanent model.

Step 6: Select a Corrective Strategy.   At this point, the teacher has determined the error pattern and has provided feedback to the student about why the answer was incorrect and how to determine the correct answer. Now the teacher must determine instructional strategies that might be helpful in teaching the correct procedure. For example, color coding the signs, such as green for plus, red for minus, when a student is using the wrong operation might help draw attention to the appropriate operation to complete.

Step 7: Introduce Appropriate Practice.   This involves a structured series of practice exercises that reinforces the correct computational procedure that has been taught.

Step 8: Identify and Apply Normative Standards.   Essentially, this refers to the establishment of criteria that the teacher feels are necessary to indicate that the child has mastered a particular computational procedure. In a sense, this is similar to establishing criteria for mastery noted in criterion-referenced testing.

FIGURE 13.2 Computation Error Chart

Student_____ Dates_____

Material_____ No. of Problems/Digits_____

Problem Class_____

	Error Type/Number	Corrective Strategy
Wrong Operation		
Computa-tional		
Defective Algorithm		
Grouping		
Random		
Other		

Beginning Time _____ Ending Time_____

Corrects per Minute _____ Errors per Minute_____

Peer Standards

High Performer—Corrects per Minute _____ Errors per Minute _____

Med Performer—Corrects per Minute _____ Errors per Minute _____

Low Performer—Corrects per Minute _____ Errors per Minute _____

Step 9: Evaluate Performance. This refers to the ongoing assessment that is necessary in the diagnostic remedial process. In addition to analyzing mathematics performance to determine an individual students's error patterns, teachers can also use error analysis with groups. Miller and Carr (1997) reported that using a technique called error ratio analysis was very helpful in assisting the teacher to make instructional decisions and monitoring class progress. This approach uses the number of different incorrect responses divided by the total number of incorrect responses.

Interviews

Interviewing a student about math performance is not really a typical interview. Enright, Gable, and Hendrikson (1988) described the diagnostic math interview as asking the students to "talk their way through" the arithmetic problems as they are solving them. In many cases, the examiner will clearly be able to see where and why the student is making an error. This is sometimes called the "think aloud" procedure. Take the following as an example:

$$\begin{array}{cccc} 12 & 13 & 47 & 13 \\ 3\sqrt{63} & 4\sqrt{124} & 2\sqrt{148} & 5\sqrt{155} \end{array}$$

The student commented, "Three into six is two, I put the 2 here (points); three into three is one, so I put that here." In this situation, the student understands division facts but probably is confused because addition, subtraction, and multiplication problems are all solved from right to left. He inappropriately generalized that procedure to division. The student responded in a similar fashion to the other three problems.

Howell and Nolet (2000) suggested that the student act like the teacher and show the examiner how to solve specific types of problems. They argued that this promotes student involvement and makes the thought processes more observable. Further, if this technique is not enough, more specific questions such as "What is the problem about?" "How would you check the steps you have taken or your answer?" and "How did you know you were done?" can be asked. Huinker (1993) noted the importance of using an interview because oftentimes a student who makes an error might lack the necessary conceptual knowledge or simply make a careless mistake. On the other hand, students sometimes might get the right answer for the wrong reason. Using interviews will help determine the process the student is using to solve problems. Similar to Enright and colleagues, Huinker recommends that the think-aloud procedure be used.

Authentic Assessment

Another helpful informal approach is authentic assessment (discussed in Chapter 6). Hopkins (1999) described the use of authentic assessment to measure students' knowledge of the concept of fractions. She noted that this is an area that is typically difficult for many students. She first developed a problem, called Ellen's Garden (see Figure 13.3) and had the students solve the problem. They were to show or tell the approach they used in solving it. Figure 13.4 shows one student's (Rose) solution to the problem. Hopkins noted from this solution that Rose did not have a grasp of the concept of fractions at an abstract level. She pointed out that Rose's visual approach was highly concrete. "She started the problem by tracing a whole bar, then she traced each fractional part of the garden onto that bar, and then she searched for a bar that matched the amount of garden left over. The need for twelfths as a common denominator was not evident in her solution and the fact that she chose to show the solution without words also indicates that she was not yet comfortable with this type of problem" (Hopkins, 1999, p. 25). Similar to error analysis, this is another assessment approach that allows the examiner to determine the strategies used in attempting to solve a problem.

Other Informal Approaches

One unique approach is the use of dynamic assessment to identify the cognitive deficiencies that result in math problems. This leads to an assessment-intervention link (see Focus on Diversity on p. 308). The area of mathematics also is one in

Interviews often use a "think aloud" procedure.

FIGURE 13.3 The Ellen's Garden Problem

Ellen's Garden

Ellen has 4 colors of flowers in her garden:

¼ of them are red.

⅙ of them are blue.

⅓ of them are orange.

The rest of them are yellow.

What fraction of her garden has yellow flowers? Show and/or tell how you solved the problem.

Source: M. Hopkins. Practicing What We Preach: Authentic Assessment in Mathematics. *Diagnostique, 25,* 24. Copyright © 1999 by Sage Publications Inc. Journals. Reprinted with permission of Sage Publications Inc. Journals in the format Textbook and Other book via Copyright Clearance Center.

which speed, as well as accuracy, is frequently a concern. For example, a teacher might be interested in increasing the speed with which a student can recognize or produce the correct answers to basic number facts (e.g., $12 - 8 = $ ____; $9 + 6 = $ ____). Again, criterion-referenced tests can be developed to incorporate both speed and accuracy. Another area that can be informally assessed is word problems.

FIGURE 13.4 Rose's Journal Entry for Ellen's Garden

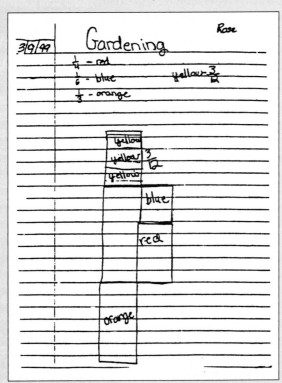

Source: M. Hopkins. Practicing What We Preach: Authentic Assessment in Mathematics. *Diagnostique, 25,* 25. Copyright © 1999 by Sage Publications Inc. Journals. Reprinted by permission of Sage Publications Inc. Journals in the format Textbook and Other book via Copyright Clearance Center.

focus on
Diversity

Linking Assessment to Intervention in Math

As noted in Chapter 7, dynamic assessment has been used to measure the process of intelligence, not the product of intelligence. A formal attempt to use dynamic assessment in combination with instrumental enrichment (an instructional mediation approach) was described by Jackson, Lewis, Feuerstein, and Samuda (1998). The students in the study were African American students from low socioeconomic families. The *Learning Potential Assessment Device* was administered "to isolate and identify the nature of deficient cognitive functions at the core of reduced cognitive performance" (p. 163). After these cognitive functions were identified, instrumental enrichment was used that provided an interactive and reflective process for the students to acquire skills and self-correction strategies. The results of the study clearly showed that the group receiving the assessment-intervention package made greater math gains than students receiving two other instructional programs.

Beyersdorfer (2003) noted that the "question–answer relationship (QAR)" technique (discussed in the reading assessment chapter) can be beneficial in determining how a student uses computation strategies to determine a response.

Clearly, informal assessment strategies, particularly when used in combination, can provide valuable information for the teacher. Curriculum-based assessment is also helpful. Jones (2001) described procedures to develop CBAs for math vocabulary and math comprehension. Enright (1995) suggested that a student summary sheet (see Figure 13.5) be used to help guide the teacher when conducting an informal assessment. This form requires the teacher to evaluate the errors in the areas of concern and to identify the specific skills to target for remediation. King-Sears (1994) described the use of the APPLY mnemonic (discussed in Chapter 5) as it relates to the assessment of math word problems. Note that this approach combines curriculum-based assessment with error analysis.

> The APPLY strategy might be helpful.

1. **Analyze** the curriculum.

   Mr. Huston is a teacher of students with mild and moderate disabilities in grades 4 through 6. Because there is a range of present levels of performance in his resource room class (that is, he manages instruction for students who are working toward mastery of curriculum objectives at their respective grade level, and each student is starting at a different point), mathematics is individualized for each student (shown in <u>underlined</u> portion of the behavioral objective). The instructional objective is: "Given a word problem that includes computations and reasoning with <u>addition and regrouping</u>, the student will earn 10 points for each problem solved according to the checklist of points earned."

2. **Prepare** items to meet the objectives.

   Mr. Huston has developed a large sampling of word problems that include computational skills appropriate for his students (whose present level of performance ranges from second to fourth grade, although they are chronologically in grades 4 to 6). On entering the classroom, students are instructed to select the word problem on a transparency for their group and solve the problem (a time-saver to prepare in advance to both relieve the teacher of writing problems on the board each assessment session and provide a reusable set of materials).

FIGURE 13.5   Student Summary Sheet for Basic Mathematics

Name_____   Date_____

A. Area of Concern (circle one or two)
  I. Readiness
  II. Number Facts
  III. Whole Number Operations
  IV. Fractions
  V. Decimals
  VI. Problem Solving

B. Specific Skills to Remediate
  1.
  2.
  3.
  4.
  5.

C. Types of Errors

COMPUTATION	PROBLEM SOLVING
1. Careless	1. Ignores question
2. Number facts	2. Uses extraneous data
3. Regrouping	3. Leaves out facts
4. Process substitution	4. Acts without a plan
5. Directional	5. Selects wrong operation
6. Omission	6. Doesn't check work
7. Placement	
8. Attention to sign	
9. Guessing	

Source: B. Enright. Basic Mathematics. In J. S. Choate, B. E. Enright, L. J. Miller, J. A. Poteet, and T. A. Rakes, *Curriculum-Based Assessment and Programming* (3rd ed.). Copyright © 1995. Reprinted by permission of Pearson Education, Inc., Upper Saddle River, New Jersey.

3. **Probe** frequently.

Two days each week, the transparencies provide "start-up" activities that students are expected to complete at the beginning of class. Mr. Huston collects the students' work at the end of two minutes (while he is taking attendance and conducting other class-keeping responsibilities).

Student work is scored on a 10-point scale, much like the evaluation criteria used by Montague, Bos, and Doucette (1991). The teacher's objective for each student can be individualized according to each youngster's instructional level in mathematics. One example of a behavioral objective is: "Given a word problem involving <u>fractional computations</u>, the student will write the correct answer by:

  a. Writing how they got the answer by describing the strategy they used—5 points possible,
  b. Showing the computation itself on the paper—3 points possible, and
  c. Writing the correct answer—2 points possible."

A total of 10 points is possible per word problem.

Because Mr. Huston uses word-problem transparencies at the beginning of class at least two days a week, he has the option of using other types of problems to begin class the other days of the week. He orients students to math instruction by having a set task for them to complete when they enter the classroom and begins instructional periods by discussing the problems and how students solve their problems.

4. **Load** data using a graph format.

   Students graph their performance on a 10-point scale, which represents the total number of possible points.

5. **Yield** to results—revisions and decisions.

   Mr. Huston and his students are able to conduct error analysis of specific problem areas. For Mr. Huston, this helps him to target key reteaching areas for the class, a group within the class, or individuals. Furthermore, he may enlist support from students in the class to work with each other when reteaching is necessary (King-Sears, 1994, pp. 106–107).

Diagnostic Mathematics Tests

Why Use Diagnostic Mathematics Tests?

Screening and identification; informal determination of objectives and teaching strategies; documentation of educational need; establishment of IEP goals.

Who Should Use Them?

Teachers; diagnostic specialists.

Key Math 3–Diagnostic Assessment

The *Key Math 3–Diagnostic Assessment* (Key Math 3-DA) (Connolly, 2007) is used with individuals ages 4½–21. Most of the items are presented orally by the examiner, using colored plates as a visual stimulus. There are two forms, A and B.

Description.   The Key Math 3-DA includes ten subtests that measure the areas of basic concepts, operations, and applications. The subtests that measure each are described next.

Basic Concepts

Numeration. Measures areas such as place value and number sense, decimals, and fractions.

Algebra. Includes areas such as early algebraic awareness and coordinate graphing.

Geometry. Measures areas such as two- and three-dimensional shapes, and lines and angles.

Measurement. Includes items measuring areas such as time and money.

Data Analysis and Probability. Measures areas such as charts, tables, graphs, and statistics.

Operations

Mental Companion and Estimation. Includes areas such as mental computation with whole numbers and estimation, and rational numbers.

Addition and subtraction. This written subtest requires the student to solve addition and subtraction problems of differing difficulty.

Multiplication and Division. Similar to the previous subtest, using multiplication and division problems.

Applications

Foundations of Problem Solving. According to the author, this subtest measures a student's "readiness" for applied problem solving.

Applied Problem Solving. Measures the application of many areas included in the Basic Concepts subtests such as algebra, geometry, and data analysis and probability.

Interpretation of Results.   The Key Math 3-DA includes scaled scores for each subtest (mean = 10, SD = 3) and standard scores (mean = 100, SD = 15) for the three content areas and the total test. Percentiles, age and grade equivalents, and growth-scale values are also available, The latter scores, which are used to monitor progress on different administrations of the Key Math 3-DA, are only available using *Assist,* the computer software program for scoring and profiling a student's test results.

Technical Characteristics

Normative Sample.   Age norms are based on 3,630 individuals. Of those, 3,105 were in kindergarten through grade 12 and were used for the grade norms. The sample was stratified according to geographic region, gender, race/ethnicity, and socioeconomic status, based on 2004 census data. In addition, students receiving special education were included, based on U.S. Department of Education data, and the educational status of those ages 18–21 was considered. For example, students who did not graduate from high school and those who were attending postsecondary institutions were both included.

Reliability.   Split-half reliabilities for the subtests were primarily in the .70s and .80s, with somewhat lower correlations for younger students. The split-half correlations for the content areas were primarily in the .80s and .90s, with slightly lower correlations for the Application area. Total test correlations were mainly above .95. Test-retest reliability coefficients by grade were primarily in the .80s and .90s for the subtests and content areas and was .97 for the total test. Alternate-form reliability coefficients were above .90 for the total test for all grades reported.

Validity.   Validity coefficients with several criterion measures are reported, including the *Key Math–Revised* and the KTEA-II. These coefficients were moderate, generally in the .60–.80 range. Construct validity was established by showing increase in raw score with age. The author gives a good description of how content validity was maximized, including consideration of the NCTM Standards.

Review of Relevant Research.   Because of the recency of publication of the Key Math 3-DA, no research was located in the professional literature. In fact, little research was found on the *Key Math–Revised,* its predecessor. Bachor (1990) did note that the *Key Math–Revised* was a substantial improvement over its predecessor. Rivera, Taylor, and Bryant (1995) evaluated the *Key Math–Revised* in relation to the National Council of Teachers of Mathematics *Curriculum and Evaluation Standards.* They reported that it met several of the standards with younger students but not for those in grade 5 or higher. Bachor (1998–1999) reviewed the updated norms for the *Key Math–Revised.* He noted that there were no substantial improvements over previous editions, since only the normative information was updated. He felt that a more extensive revision would have been appropriate. He particularly was critical of the fact that there were not enough items to cover the curriculum content in mathematics of the upper grades (grade 10 and above). The Key Math 3-DA seems to have addressed these shortcomings. Hopefully, research will be forthcoming.

Overview: Key Math 3–Diagnostic Assessment

- *Age level*—Kindergarten to grade 12, ages 4½ through 21 years.
- *Type of administration*—Individual.
- *Technical adequacy*—Adequate reliability (total score) and validity.
- *Scores yielded*—Standard scores, age and grade equivalents, percentile ranks, stanines.
- *Suggested use*—The *Key Math 3-DA* includes ten subtests that measure the major areas of Basic Concepts, Operations, and Applications. The five subtests that measure Basic Concepts were aligned with the NCTM standards. This required the addition of some new subtests and the elimination of others from the *Key Math–Revised.* According to the author, the instrument can be used to measure math proficiency, measure student progress, support educational placement, and support instructional development. This last purpose of accomplished through the use of the *Key Math 3–Essential Resources,* which is an instructional program that has a lesson linked to every item on the *Key Math 3-DA.* Users must keep in mind the visual (and largely nonwritten) format of the test. This has its advantages and disadvantages. It might be appropriate to measure the mathematical skills of a student with writing problems. On the other hand, the format requires skills that are dissimilar to the majority of skills required of students during classroom activities.

Stanford Diagnostic Mathematics Test–4

The *Stanford Diagnostic Mathematics Test–4* (SDMT-4; Harcourt Educational Measurement, 1996) is a group-administered or individually administered instrument designed to measure basic mathematic concepts and skills from grade 1 through grade 12. The SDMT-4 is divided into six levels. There are both multiple-choice and free-response items for each level. For the last three levels, there are two alternate forms. The suggested grade levels for each level follow.

The SDMT-4 can be group administered.

Red Level—grades 1.5 to 2.5
Orange Level—grades 2.5 to 3.5
Green Level—grades 3.5 to 4.5
Purple Level—grades 4.5 to 6.5
Brown Level—grades 6.5 to 8.9
Blue Level—grades 9.0 to 12.9

The SDMT-4 has six color-coded levels.

Each level contains items that measure a student's knowledge in two areas: (1) Concepts and Applications and (2) Computation. The tests themselves are used as diagnostic instruments to determine a student's strengths and weaknesses in math.

Description

Red Level

Concepts and Applications. This test measures the child's knowledge of areas such as basic numeration, problem solving, graphs and tables, and geometry and measurement.

Computation. This test includes addition and subtraction of whole numbers.

Orange Level

The Orange Level includes the same type and number of items found in the Red Level.

Green Level

Concepts and Applications. Same number and type of items as previous levels.

Computation. This test includes addition, subtraction, multiplication, and division of whole numbers.

Purple Level

The Purple Level includes the same type of items as the Green Level except that probability and statistics are included in the Concepts and Applications area.

Brown Level and Blue Level

The Brown Level and Blue Level include the same type and number of items as the Purple Level.

Interpretation of Results. Raw scores from the SDMT-4 can be transformed into a number of norm-referenced measures. Tables for percentile ranks, stanines, grade equivalents, and scaled scores can be found in the manuals for each level. Like the SDRT, computer scoring can also provide percentiles and stanines compared to both local and national norms. In addition to these, the SDMT-4 offers a progress-indicator (Pi) score that, essentially, is a criterion-referenced cutoff point. Its purpose is to help teachers identify students who have reached the level of competence necessary to achieve success in the instructional goals of the individual classroom. Each test can be either hand scored or computer scored. Each level includes an instructional-placement report that summarizes the results for an entire class. There is also a three-step test-plan-teach process and services and materials to facilitate this process.

Technical Characteristics

Normative Sample. A large, stratified, nationally representative sample of approximately 88,000 was used.

Reliability. Internal consistency was generally good; coefficients were mostly above .90. Alternate form reliability coefficients were generally above .80. Inter-rater reliability was .97 or higher.

Validity. Information related to content and concurrent validity is available (with the earlier version of the SDMT) in the manual. Data are generally lacking.

Review of Relevant Research.   The SDMT-4 has not been studied. Two reviewers of the 1976 SDMT had different opinions about the diagnostic utility of the instrument. Sowder (1978) indicated that it gave a "not too specific" indication of strengths and weaknesses and that it should be used for comparison rather than for educational programming. Lappan (1978), on the other hand, considered it adequate to identify strengths and weaknesses and to group students for instructional purposes. The format and items of the earlier versions of the SDMT and the SDMT-4 are somewhat different, however. In particular, the free-response items are new to the SDMT-4.

Overview: Stanford Diagnostic Mathematics Test–4

- *Age levels*—Grades 1 through 12.
- *Type of administration*—Group.
- *Technical adequacy*—Good standardization and reliability, limited validity data.
- *Scores yielded*—Percentile ranks, stanines, grade equivalent, scaled scores, progress indicator.
- *Suggested use*—The SDMT-4 is a well-constructed test. It can be used to identify general strengths and weaknesses in the areas of number concepts, computation, and application. The SDMT-4 is more appropriate as a general comparative test than as a specific test to determine instructional goals and objectives.

The SDMT-4 measures general strengths and weaknesses.

Test of Mathematical Abilities–2

The *Test of Mathematical Abilities–2* (TOMA-2; Brown, Cronin, & McEntire, 1994) includes five subtests that provide standardized information about two major skill areas—story problems and computation—and related information about attitude, vocabulary, and the general application of information. It is a norm-referenced test designed for use with students ages 8 through 18. The subtests may be either group or individually administered. Administration takes approximately one to two hours, although no time limits are imposed.

Description

Vocabulary. This subtest lists math-related vocabulary words that the subject must briefly define in writing.

Computation. This subtest is a paper-and-pencil test of math computation. Problems are arranged in order of difficulty.

General Information. This is an orally administered subtest of general mathematical knowledge. It requires some subjectivity in the scoring.

Story Problems. This subtest includes problems that the subject must read and complete. Nonreaders' scores should not be included, although the problems can be read aloud as part of a separate diagnostic analysis.

Attitude toward Math. This optional subtest requires the subject to decide what he or she thinks of each math-related sentence. The student indicates "agree," "disagree," or "don't know." Sentences are usually read to the subject, but good readers may proceed independently.

An Attitude toward Math subtest is optional.

Interpretation of Results. The TOMA-2 provides standard scores for all subtests, as well as percentiles and a Total Math Quotient that incorporates standard scores for the first four subtests. The manual includes suggestions for proper interpretation and use, and a list of resources is included for further assessment and programming of mathematical difficulties.

Technical Characteristics

Normative Sample. The sample included 2,082 students residing in twenty-six states. The characteristics of the sample compare favorably with those of the general U.S. population. Eleven percent of the sample were students with disabilities.

Reliability. Coefficient alpha for all subtests showed adequate internal consistency ranging from .84 (Attitude toward Math) to .97 (Math Quotient). Test-retest reliability was not as strong among subtests with coefficients ranging from .70 to .85 (Total Score yielded .92).

Validity. Criterion-related validity was demonstrated through correlations with the *SRA Achievement Series, Peabody Individual Achievement Test* (PIAT), *Wide Range Achievement Test* (WRAT), and the *Key Math.* Correlations were generally in the moderate range. A discussion of content validity is also presented in the manual.

Review of Relevant Research. No empirical studies on the TOMA-2 or its predecessor, the TOMA, were located. Howell (1990), in a review of the TOMA, noted, "The TOMA seems more notable for what it attempts to do than for what it actually does. For example, while a major strength of the test is its innovative conceptualization of mathematics, a major weakness is the attempt to validate this conceptualization through correlations with more typical measures" (p. 216). Griffin (1997) reviewed the TOMA-2 and concluded that it was useful in identifying students who are significantly below or above their peers in mathematics and in documenting progress in intervention programs.

Overview: Test of Mathematical Abilities–2

- *Age level*—8½ through 18 years.
- *Type of administration*—Individual or small group (individual recommended).
- *Technical adequacy*—Adequate standardization, questionable reliability and validity.
- *Scores yielded*—Standard scores, percentiles, and an overall quotient.
- *Suggested use*—Properly used, the TOMA-2 can be a useful tool to diagnose mathematical abilities and disabilities, but results should be followed by additional study of mathematical abilities (such as testing, observation, interview). The scores do not provide a sufficient basis for planning instructional programs on IEPs. Individual subtests are not appropriate for certain subjects (such as nonreaders, deaf) and should be eliminated from their assessments. Further validity data are necessary before its potential use can be determined.

TOMA-2 also measures math vocabulary and knowledge.

Other Diagnostic Mathematics Tests

Comprehensive Mathematical Abilities Test

- *Age level*—7 through 18.
- *Type of administration*—Individual.
- *Technical adequacy*—Good reliability (Composites) and validity.
- *Scores yielded*—Standard scores for subtests and composites.
- *Description*—The Comprehensive Mathematical Abilities Test (CMAT; Hresko, Schlieve, Herron, Swain, & Sherbenou, 2002) consists of six core subtests and six supplemental subtests. These subtests can be combined to form three core composites and three supplemental composites. The Core Composites are Basic Calculation, Mathematical Reasoning, and General Mathematics. The Supplemental Composites are Advanced Calculations, Practical Applications, and Overall Mathematic Abilities. The CMAT was developed using the National Council of Teachers of Mathematics (NCTM, 2000) standards. The authors state that the items are based on actual math teaching materials and represent real-world problems using current information. Calculators are allowed for all subtests except those measuring math computation. Raw scores can be compared to both age-based norms and grade-based norms.

Group Mathematics Assessment and Diagnostic Evaluation

- *Age level*—Kindergarten through grade 12.
- *Type of administration*—Group.
- *Technical adequacy*—Good standardization and reliability; adequate validity.
- *Scores yielded*—Standard scores, percentiles, stanines, normal curve equivalents, growth scores.
- *Description*—The *Group Mathematics Assessment and Diagnostic Evaluation* (G-MADE; Williams, 2004) is a group-administered test designed to measure the NCTM Standards. There are nine levels of the test, and all but the lowest level include three subtests. In the Concepts and Communication subtest, students are presented with words, symbols, or short phrases and must indicate which of four choices represents the stimulus presented. The Process and Applications subtest requires the student to solve word problems in a multiple-choice format. The Operations and Computation subtest (which is not included in the lowest level of the test) measures addition, subtraction, multiplication, and division and is also presented in a multiple-choice format.

Test of Early Mathematics Ability–Third Edition

- *Age level*—3 through 8 years.
- *Type of administration*—Individual.
- *Technical adequacy*—Adequate reliability and validity.
- *Scores yielded*—Standard scores, percentile ranks, age and grade equivalents.
- *Description*—The *Test of Early Mathematics Ability–Third Edition* (TEMA-3; Ginsburg & Baroody, 2003) includes seventy-two items measuring the areas of numbering skills, number-comparison facility, numerical literacy, mastery of number facts, calculation skills, and understanding of concepts. There are two alternative forms of the TEMA-3 that can be used either as a norm-referenced instrument or as an informal instrument to determine specific

strengths and weaknesses. Also included are additional assessment probes and instruction activities for skill development in the areas indicated by the child's performance.

Criterion-Referenced Mathematics Instruments

Why Use Criterion-Referenced Mathematics Instruments?

Identification of areas for further evaluation or remediation; informal determination of objectives and teaching strategies; development and evaluation of IEPs.

Who Should Use Them?

Teachers.

Diagnostic Assessment of Computation Skills

The *Diagnostic Assessment of Computation Skills* (Enright, 2002) is an interactive CD-ROM software package designed for elementary, middle, and junior high school students who have specific problems with arithmetic computation skills. The inventory consists of thirteen sections, including basic computation (adding, subtracting, multiplying, dividing) with whole numbers, fractions, and decimals, as well as conversions of fractions. Items in the inventory are based on a task analysis of each computational skill area. The inventory can be either individually or group administered. It includes three types of tests: basic facts, wide-range placement, and skill placement.

This inventory is now an interactive CD-ROM.

Description

Basic Facts.   This section includes two forms that each measure basic arithmetic facts in the areas of addition, subtraction, multiplication, and division.

Wide-Range Placement.   This section includes two forms that each include two items from each of the thirteen computation sections. This can be administered to determine a starting place for the more in-depth skill placement test.

Skill Placement.   This section includes thirteen tests, each with two forms, that measure the computation sections. A total of 144 skill sequences are included. (Table 13.1 shows the skill sequences for the multiplication of whole numbers.) A brief description follows.

- *Addition of Whole Numbers.* Twelve skill sequences ranging from "two-digit numbers with sum less than ten" to "two three-digit numbers, regrouping ones and tens."
- *Subtraction of Whole Numbers.* Fifteen sequences ranging from "one-digit number from a one-digit number" to "three-digit number from a three-digit number with zeros in the ones and tens places."
- *Multiplication of Whole Numbers.* Eighteen sequences ranging from "two one-digit numbers" to "three-digit number with zero in the tens place by a two-digit number."
- *Division of Whole Numbers.* Twenty-two sequences ranging from "one-digit number by a one-digit number with no remainder" to "five-digit number by a three-digit number with remainder."

- *Conversion of Fractions.* Eight sequences ranging from "improper fraction to a whole number" to "three fractions to the lowest common denominator (LCD) with the LCD not included."
- *Addition of Fractions.* Ten sequences ranging from "two like fractions (in horizontal form)" to "two mixed numbers."
- *Subtraction of Fractions.* Nine sequences ranging from "fraction from a like fraction" to "mixed number from a mixed number, with regrouping (in horizontal form)."
- *Multiplication of Fractions.* Six sequences ranging from "fraction by a like fraction" to "mixed number by a mixed number."
- *Division of Fractions.* Six sequences ranging from "fraction by a like fraction" to "mixed number by a mixed number."
- *Addition of Decimals.* Eleven sequences ranging from "two tenths decimals with no regrouping" to "two mixed decimals with regrouping (in horizontal form)."
- *Subtraction of Decimals.* Eleven sequences ranging from "tenths decimal from a tenths decimal with no regrouping" to "mixed decimal from a mixed decimal, with regrouping."
- *Multiplication of Decimals.* Six sequences ranging from "whole number times a tenths decimal" to "mixed number times a mixed number with regrouping."
- *Division of Decimals.* Ten sequences ranging from "tenths decimal by a one-digit number with no regrouping" to "mixed number by a mixed number."

TABLE 13.1   Example of Skill Sequences from the *Diagnostic Assessment of Computation Skills*

C. Multiplication of Whole Numbers

	Introduction
C-1	Two 1-Digit Numbers
C-2	2-Digit Number by a 1-Digit Number, with No Regrouping
C-3	3-Digit Number by a 1-Digit Number, with No Regrouping
C-4	2-Digit Number by a 1-Digit Number, Regrouping Ones
C-5	2-Digit Number by a 1-Digit Number, Regrouping Ones and Tens
C-6	3-Digit Number by a 1-Digit Number, Regrouping Ones
C-7	3-Digit Number by a 1-Digit Number, Regrouping Tens
C-8	3-Digit Number by a 1-Digit Number, Regrouping Ones and Tens
C-9	3-Digit Number by a 1-Digit Number, Regrouping Ones, Tens, and Hundreds
C-10	2-Digit Number by a 2-Digit Number, with No Regrouping
C-11	2-Digit Number by a 2-Digit Number, with Regrouping Caused by the Ones Place Digit of the Multiplier
C-12	2-Digit Number by a 2-Digit Number, with Regrouping
C-13	3-Digit Number by a 2-Digit Number, with No Regrouping
C-14	3-Digit Number by a 2-Digit Number, with Regrouping
C-15	3-Digit Number by a 3-Digit Number, with No Regrouping
C-16	3-Digit Number by a 3-Digit Number, with Regrouping Caused by the Ones Place Digit and the Tens Place Digit of the Multiplier
C-17	3-Digit Number by a 3-Digit Number, with Regrouping Caused by All Digits of the Multiplier
C-18	3-Digit Number with Zero in the Tens Place by a 2-Digit Number

Source: B. Enright. *Diagnostic Assessment of Computation Skills.* Copyright © 2002 by National Training Network. Reprinted by permission.

Interpretation of Results.   According to the author, the *Diagnostic Assessment of Computation Skills* provides three types of information. First, it provides specific information on which computational skills the student has mastered. A criterion level of 80 percent (four out of five items for each of the skills) is suggested for assuming mastery. Second, each of the 144 skill areas are correlated with the grade levels in which they are taught in five separate basal mathematics series. Finally, a valuable feature is the inclusion of guidelines to perform an error analysis. The author identified 233 discrete error patterns that could be grouped together into seven error clusters: regrouping, process substitution, omission, directional, placement, attention to sign, and guessing. Figure 13.6 shows an example of some of the process-substitution error patterns.

Overview: Diagnostic Assessment of Computation Skills

- *Age level*—Elementary to junior high.
- *Suggested use*—The *Diagnostic Assessment of Computation Skills* is a comprehensive, well-constructed instrument now available as an interactive CD-ROM. The inventory includes items related to basic computation of whole numbers, fractions, and decimals. The skill areas are sequential, so that information from the test can be used to identify appropriate objectives for an IEP. The error analysis also yields information important in choosing teaching strategies. Individual progress report sheets and class record sheets are available to summarize and clarify the test data. Although the level and detail of information provided by this instrument might not be necessary for the average student, it is quite appropriate for those for whom more complete information is warranted.

The built-in error analysis is very helpful.

Mathematics Test Builder and Test Banks

The *Mathematics Test Builder and Test Banks* (William K. Bradford Publishing Company, 2001) allows the teacher great flexibility in determining the content of the areas to be measured. The *Mathematics Test Builder* combines word processing, a database, and layout capabilities. It allows a teacher to develop questions, store and categorize them, and create tests and worksheets printed in several forms. It also has other capabilities, such as developing graphs and equations. The *Mathematics Test Builder* can be particularly helpful in developing curriculum-based assessment instruments because it allows the teacher to use his or her own questions in developing the tests. Also available are the Test Banks, which are a series of prepared question files. There are over twenty-five separate Test Banks available that measure a wide variety of areas from basic math to algebra to trigonometry and calculus. There are also Test Banks available that measure the previously discussed NCTM Standards. For example, the Standards Level I Test Bank includes 500 questions directly correlated to the grades K–4 Standards, the Standards Level II Test Bank includes 750 questions correlated to the grades 5–8 Standards, and the Standards Level III Test Bank also includes 750 questions correlated with the grades 9–12 Standards. All the questions in these three test banks are labeled according to their level of difficulty (easy, medium, or hard). Of particular relevance to the special education student are the Basic Math Test Banks that are also available for different grade levels. These include over a thousand items per grade range that are offered in a multiple-choice format and are cross-referenced to objectives in a number of skill areas. The use of these Test Banks would be very helpful in the development of criterion-referenced instruments described in Chapter 5.

Test Banks are available that measure the NCTM Standards.

FIGURE 13.6   Example of Error Patterns from the *Diagnostic Assessment of Computational Skills*

Process substitution 76:
(Doesn't find LCD.) Copies denominator of first fraction as numerator, and copies denominator of second fraction as denominator.

$$4\tfrac{1}{4} \text{ (first)}$$
$$+2\tfrac{3}{5} \text{ (second)}$$
$$\overline{6\tfrac{4}{5}}$$

Process substitution 77: Adds numerators, and copies larger denominator.

$$\tfrac{2}{5} \!>\! 3$$
$$+\tfrac{1}{10} \text{ (larger)}$$
$$\overline{\tfrac{3}{10}}$$

Process substitution 78:
(Doesn't find LCD.) Adds numerators, and copies denominator of second fraction.

$$\tfrac{2}{5} \!>\! 4$$
$$+\tfrac{2}{3} \text{ (second)}$$
$$\overline{\tfrac{4}{3}}$$

Process substitution 79:
Subtracts denominators.

$$\tfrac{3}{4} \!>\! 0$$
$$-\tfrac{1}{4}$$
$$\overline{\tfrac{2}{0}}$$

Process substitution 80:
Multiplies numerators, but keeps common denominator.

$$\tfrac{3}{4} \!\times\! 3$$
$$-\tfrac{1}{4}$$
$$\overline{\tfrac{3}{4}}$$

Process substitution 81:
Subtracts numerators and multiplies denominators.

$$\tfrac{3}{4} \!>\! 2$$
$$-\tfrac{1}{2} \!\times\! 8$$
$$\overline{\tfrac{2}{8}}$$

Process substitution 82:
(Doesn't find LCD) Ignores numerators, and writes difference of denominators as whole number.

$$\tfrac{③}{4}$$
$$-\tfrac{①}{2} \!>\! 2$$
$$\overline{2}$$

Process substitution 83:
(Doesn't find LCD.) Multiplies numerators, and subtracts denominators.

$$\tfrac{3}{4} \!\times\! 3$$
$$-\tfrac{1}{2} \!>\! 2$$
$$\overline{\tfrac{3}{2}}$$

Process substitution 84:
(Doesn't find LCD.) Subtracts numerators, and subtracts denominators.

$$\tfrac{3}{4} \!>\! 2$$
$$-\tfrac{1}{2} \!>\! 2$$
$$\overline{\tfrac{2}{2}}$$

Process substitution 85:
Writes product of numerator and denominator of first fraction as numerator, and writes product of numerator and denominator of second fraction as denominator.

(first) $\tfrac{3}{4} \!>\! 12$

(second) $-\tfrac{1}{2} \!>\! 2$

$$\overline{\tfrac{12}{2}}$$

Process substitution 86:
(Doesn't find LCD. Doesn't convert mixed numbers to improper fractions.) Subtracts whole numbers, subtracts numerators, and multiplies denominators.

$$7\tfrac{1}{2} - 2\tfrac{3}{4} = 5\tfrac{2}{8}$$

Process substitution 87:
(Doesn't find LCD.) Subtracts numerators, subtracts denominators, and writes differences as whole number.

$$\tfrac{3}{9} \!>\! 2$$
$$-\tfrac{1}{6} \!>\! 3$$
$$\overline{23}$$

Possible Answers to the Questions

1. **Why assess Zandra?** The primary reason to assess Zandra is to gather information to answer two math-related questions—"What to teach?" and "How to teach?" In other words, specific information about what Zandra does and doesn't know in math should be determined. In addition, possible teaching strategies should also be delineated. If it is determined that Zandra is having a significant problem in math, then IEP goals could also be identified.

2. **Who should assess Zandra?** More than likely, Zandra would be assessed by one or both of her teachers, particularly if more informal approaches are used. If the school has an educational diagnostician, then that person might also be used.

3. **What procedure(s)/test(s) should be used?** Because she is having difficulty with computation skills, the *Diagnostic Assessment of Computation Skills* might be administered. This inventory would identify both appropriate educational objectives (What to teach?) and suggested teaching strategies (How to teach?). The latter could be accomplished through the use of the error analysis guidelines. Informal error analysis of work products and the use of an interview (think aloud) would also be helpful. Because Zandra is reportedly also having problems applying math concepts, authentic assessment might be helpful. If necessary, a more formal test such as the *Key Math 3-DA* that includes application items could also be administered.

4. **What other areas would you assess?** Given the description of Zandra, it does not appear that any other area needs to be assessed at this time. Continuous monitoring of her math performance (as well as reading performance), of course, would be warranted.

STUDENT PROFILE DATA

Zandra

Zandra was administered the Key Math 3-DA by Ms. Rivera, her special education teacher. The following results were reported:

Area/Subtest	Standard/Scaled Score
Basic Concepts	**95**
Numeration	11
Algebra	8
Geometry	9
Measurement	8
Data Analysis and Probability	10
Operations	**78**
Mental Computation and Estimation	6
Addition and Subtraction	8
Multiplication and Division	5
Applications	**81**
Foundations of Problem Solving	8
Applied Problem Solving	6

These results indicate that Zandra understands the basic concepts of math but is having difficulty with computation skills, particularly in multiplication and division. She also is having some difficulty applying math concepts.

CASE STUDY *June*

Based on June's description, do you think any of the approaches and/or instruments described in this chapter would be used? If so, what?

Reflections

1. Do you think the NCTM Standards have impacted and will continue to impact math assessment instruments and practices? If so, how?
2. Why might informal assessment procedures (e.g., error analysis, authentic assessment) yield more instructionally relevant information than the use of a standardized test?
3. If you were a teacher in an inclusion classroom that had several students with identified math disabilities, would you choose to administer the Key Math 3-DA or the SDMT-4 ? Why?

Summary Matrix

Instrument or Technique	Prereferral: Screening and Initial Identification	Prereferral: Informal Determination and Evaluation of Teaching Programs and Strategies	Determination of Current Performance Level and Educational Need	Decisions about Classification and Program Placement	Postreferral: IEP Goals	Postreferral: IEP Objectives	Postreferral: IEP Evaluation	Target: Mild/Moderate	Target: Severe/Profound	Target: Preschool	Target: Elementary Age	Target: Secondary Age	Target: Adult	Special Considerations	Educational Relevance for Exceptional Students
Informal Assessment	X	X						X			X	X	X	Includes error analysis, interviews, and authentic assessment.	Very Useful
Key Math 3–Diagnostic Assessment	X	X	X		X			X			X			A new version of a popular test; the format should be considered in its interpretation.	Useful
Stanford Diagnostic Mathematics Test-4	X		X		X			X			X	X		Good technical aspects; computer scoring available.	Useful
Test of Mathematical Abilities-2	X	X	X					X			X	X		Has sections on attitude toward math and math vocabulary.	Adequate
Comprehensive Mathematical Abilities Test	X	X	X		X			X			X	X		Based on NCTM Standards; includes items based on actual teaching materials.	Adequate/Useful
Group Mathemitics Assessment and Diagnostic Evaluation	X	X						X			X	X		A group-administred test designed to measure the NCTM Standards.	Adequate
Test of Early Mathematical Ability–Third Edition	X	X	X					X		X	X			Includes probes and instructional activities.	Adequate
Diagnostic Assessment of Computation Skills	X	X	X		X	X	X	X			X			CD-ROM used to determine specific math objectives; error analysis is recommended.	Very Useful
Mathematics Test Builder and Test Banks	X	X	X		X	X	X	X			X	X		Teacher can develop computerized tests or use prepared test banks.	Useful

chapter fourteen

Assessment of Written Expression

STUDENT PROFILE

Ed

Ed is a fifth-grade student who, according to his teacher, Ms. Warde, "just doesn't like to write." He has been receiving services as a student with learning disabilities for two years in the area of reading. In previous years there had not been many writing demands in class; further, he frequently dictated his writing homework assignments, which would be typed by his mother. Ed's mother commented that it wouldn't get done if it was done any other way. Ms. Warde, however, has started to require more and more writing assignments during the school day. She has noted that Ed's writing samples typically include numerous problems in spelling, punctuation, and capitalization. In addition, he tends to write short passages. Ms. Warde is particularly concerned that when Ed goes to middle school he will have even more difficulty because of the increased writing demands. The following is an example of Ed's writing. The assignment was to take thirty minutes and write an essay on "If you could have one day at school to do whatever you want, what would you do?"

> *Ed*
>
> *I feel happy if no Teachers so we can do whitever and play nintendo and games and parties. No math or reading or homework. I would eat pizza and candy and doncits but I would not eat veglabls I go outside and play and jump around. I would go to office use the phone and call my friends. I wish school like that, it would make me happy*

Sarah

Sarah is in the sixth grade in a private school. Her spelling ability is weak and she tries to avoid situations that require her to spell. Her parents often remark that she is lucky that there's such a thing as Spellcheck. Her parents and teacher have noted that her spelling is inconsistent. She will misspell some easy words and then spell more difficult words correctly. For example, she recently spelled *even* as *evan* and *moshun* for *motion* in a sentence but correctly spelled *ambulance*. She is reported to be a good reader but does not spend a lot of time reading. The following is a written response to the question "What do you want to do when you are an adult?"

> Sarah,
>
> I am pleesed to say that I want to be an actrice. I have been in sevral plays and musicals. However, I know I need more expiereunce. My favoret musical is South Pacific. I played Nellie Forbush. My favoret person was Billis. He dansed the hoole with a pare of cocanuts. He was funny. I also liked to sing about washing the man out of my hair. Maybe I will go to Brawdway some day.

Think about These Questions as You Read This Chapter:

1. Why assess Ed and Sarah? (There could be more than one reason.)
2. Who should assess Ed and Sarah? (There could be more than one person.)
3. What procedure(s)/test(s) should be used?
4. What other areas (if any) should be assessed?

(Suggested answers appear at the end of this chapter.)

As noted in Chapter 10, the primary function of language is communication. This is true for written language as well as oral language. Clearly, the ability to express oneself in writing is a necessary skill related to school success. Pino (1998), in fact, reported that problems in written expression are second only to reading problems as the reason that teachers refer students for special education. Although experts disagree as to the number of components of written expression, the general consensus is that there are at least five major components. Those are handwriting, spelling, mechanics, usage, and ideation (Poteet, 1992). *Handwriting* is the visible product of written expression; if handwriting is not

There are at least five major components of written expression.

readable, then the goal of written expression, namely communication, is affected. Similarly, *spelling* is an important component of the communication process. As Poteet (1992) noted, "when reading incorrectly spelled words, our attention is diverted from the message of the communication to decoding what was written." *Mechanics* refers to the rules of language, such as capitalization, punctuation, and abbreviation, whereas *usage* refers to how the various areas of written language are chosen and combined for written expressive purposes. Table 14.1 shows the elements of usage that are included in the area of written expression. *Ideation* involves the ideas related to the writer's purpose and intent. Table 14.2 shows the various elements of ideation included in written expression. These elements are manipulated based on the intent of the writer. For example, ideation would be different if a person were writing a business letter than if the person were writing a short story or a poem.

Procedures for assessing the five components of written expression include informal techniques such as the analysis of writing samples as well as the use of more formal tests that measure the various components of written language. Also

TABLE 14.1 Elements of Usage of Written Expression

Element	Usage
Words	When words are used correctly, the writing flows smoothly and is easy to understand.
Phrases	Phrases are groups of words that belong together logically but cannot function as sentences because they do not contain a subject and predicate. The correct use and placement of phrases within sentences aid comprehension of the writing.
Clauses	Clauses have a subject and a predicate. They increase the maturity level of the writing, and they help the writer focus on the precise intent of the communication.
Sentences	A sentence is a logically related group of words containing a subject and predicate. It expresses a complete thought and can function independently of other groups of words to be understood. The sentence must be properly constructed for the writing to be clear to the reader.
Paragraphs	A paragraph is a group of related sentences, usually about one topic, often set off by an indent. Correct structure and transition between paragraphs makes the writing flow smoothly and easy to understand.

Source: J. Poteet. Written Expression. In J. S. Choate, B. E. Enright, L. J. Miller, J. A. Poteet, and T. A. Rakes. *Curriculum-Based Assessment and Programming* (3rd ed.). Copyright © 1995. Reprinted by permission of Pearson Education, Inc., Upper Saddle River, New Jersey.

TABLE 14.2   Elements of Ideation in Written Expression

Element	Ideation
Fluency	An appropriate number of words must be written to clearly express the writer's intent. Otherwise, the reader is left with a sense of emptiness. However, superfluous words detract from the clarity of the writing. The number of words written varies with the type of writing, but generally it increases with the age of the writer (Poteet, 1979).
Four Levels of Writing Maturity	1. Level 1, *naming,* is characterized by the writer simply naming objects or people. A beginning narrative might be "There is a boy, a girl, a cat, a dog, and a house." 2. Level 2, *description,* simply describes something. An example might be "The boy is running. The dog is barking. It is raining." 3. Level 3, *plot,* is a good story with a beginning, middle, and end. A more sophisticated story would present a conflict, problem, or complication that is resolved (Newcomer, Barenbaum, & Nodine, 1988). 4. Level 4, *issue,* is the most mature level of writing. The main purpose is the discussion of some issue, which can be social, personal, political, or philosophical.
Word Choice	The competent writer will choose words carefully to achieve the major purpose of the writing. Trite and mundane expressions will be avoided; words that create excitement, anticipation, and awareness of physical senses and emotions will be used.
Style	Probably the most personal of all elements of written expression, style is how the writer puts it all together. Although there are guidelines for improving the overall quality of the writing, it is the personal approach taken by the writer that ultimately establishes the style. The writing must be comprehensible, well organized, and well developed. Style is the personal trademark of the writer.

Source: J. Poteet. Written Expression. In J. S. Choate, B. E. Enright, L. J. Miller, J. A. Poteet, and T. A. Rakes, *Curriculum-Based Assessment and Programming* (3rd ed.). Copyright © 1995. Reprinted by permission of Pearson Education, Inc., Upper Saddle River, New Jersey.

available are both formal and informal diagnostic spelling tests that focus on only one component of the writing process.

Informal Assessment

Why Use Informal Written Expression Assessment?

Screening and identification of written language problems; informal determination of objectives and teaching strategies; analysis of spontaneous use of written language.

Who Should Use It?

Teachers; speech and language clinicians.

Just as important as the evaluation of oral language in the natural setting is the evaluation of written language using the student's actual work products. Gregg and Mather (2002) also pointed out that the *task format* is important when evaluating written language. For instance, it is possible to evaluate a student's copied work, written samples taken from dictation, and spontaneous written samples.

Portfolio assessment of written expression can be helpful.

Portfolio assessment has been suggested as a valuable method for written language skills as well (Jochum, Curan, & Reetz, 1998). In fact, using a writing assessment rubric similar to the one presented in Chapter 6, Schirmer and Bailey (2000) provided a convincing argument regarding its value as a feedback/instructional tool. Another technique related to portfolio assessment is the use of dialogue journals, particularly for students with the limited English proficiency (see Focus on Diversity). Curriculum-based measurement has also been used. Although the total words written or number of correct word sequences have been used as a measure of the student's skill level, the number of correct punctuation marks has also shown promise as a sensitive measure (Gansle, Noell, VanDerHeyden, Naquin, & Slider, 2002).

Another extremely valuable procedure is error analysis. According to Rousseau (1990), the analysis of written products should focus on the following types of errors: careless, excessive usage, verbs, nouns, pronouns, punctuation, capitalization, and paragraphs. Much of the analysis should focus on the *T-unit*, which is defined as "an independent clause including any dependent clauses attached to or embedded in it" (Rousseau, 1990, p. 94). For example, "The batter hit the baseball and the third baseman tried to catch it" is considered two T-units. Figure 14.1 provides an example of scoring procedures based on the eight previously mentioned error types.

Other areas of written language have also been recommended for error analysis. Isaacson (1988) suggested that fluency (number of words written), content (e.g., coherence and organization), convention (including spelling and handwriting), syntax, and vocabulary should be evaluated. Salvia and Hughes (1990) suggested that the two major areas of *content* and *style* be evaluated. They noted that the most common errors related to content are incomplete learning or poor proofreading skills. In the area of style, errors might be located in grammar, mechanics (e.g., punctuation and capitalization), diction (word usage), and diversity (e.g., use of grammatical transformations). Identification of errors in these areas can be used to provide feedback about the incorrect aspects of the student's writing (student product) as well as the appropriate aspects (teacher model). Luts (1991) attempted to determine the most common errors in written expression made by a group of second-grade students. She found that spelling was the most common error, followed by capitalization, punctuation, grammar, and context errors.

It is possible that the informal assessment of written expression could also directly address the five components of handwriting, spelling, mechanics, usage,

focus on Diversity

Using a Dialogue Journal to Assess and Improve Writing

When working with students with limited English proficiency, teachers can make use of dialogue journals. Willig and Ortiz (1991) described this process. The student writes a personal letter to the teacher who responds in writing on a daily basis. The response might be answering any student questions, asking the student questions, and expressing views. The teacher focuses on the communicative intent of the writing and even though writing errors might be noted, they are not corrected. Rather, correct written form is modeled by the teacher in a reciprocal fashion. Willig and Ortiz pointed out that these journals not only establish a line of communication between student and teacher, but also allow the student to explore his or her concerns and adjustments to a new culture.

FIGURE 14.1   Error Analysis Scoring Instructions

Enter the name of the *Student, Age* (years and months), *Grade,* and the *Date* the student wrote the sample.
Writing Time: Record the total number of minutes allowed for writing, and the actual number of minutes the student wrote.
Picture # of Topic #: List the picture or topic number used for the writing stimulus.

1. *Total Words:* Draw a line through the title, sound effects, and end markers such as "The End." Count the total words written. Exclude words marked out.
2. *Garbled Words:* Circle garbled words. Enter the total in the space provided.
3. *Readable Words:* Subtract the number of garbled words from the total words and enter in the space provided.
4. *T-Unit:* Mark the end of each T-unit with a slash mark (/) and number the T-unit. Enter the number of T-units.
5. *Average Number of Words per T-Unit:* Divide the total readable words by the number of T-units. Round off to the nearest hundredth.
6. *Scorer:* Sign your name.

Note: FOR ALL ERROR TYPES BEGINNING WITH *OMITTED* WORDS THROUGH *INAPPROPRIATE CAPITALS* COUNT THE TOTAL ERRORS AND DIVIDE BY THE TOTAL T-UNITS TO FIND THE NUMBER PER T-UNIT.

1. *Careless Errors:*
   Omitted Words: Write omitted words in pencil above the appropriate space. Write only words that are obvious (such as *and, he, the*) and that do not change the meaning of the T-unit.
   Substituted Words: Write *sub* above substituted words.
2. *Excessive Usage:*
   Beginning of T-Unit: Count the number of T-units that begin with conjunctions.
   Within T-Unit: Underline each use of conjunctions if they appear more than once for coordination within the T-unit. Do not count conjunctions at the beginning of the T-unit in this count.
3. *Verbs:*
   Inflections: Write in the correct verb ending.
   Subject-Verb Agreement: Write *s-v* above the verb for every subject-verb errors.
   Verb Tense Changes: Place a check mark (✓) at the end of each T-unit in which the verb tense is different from the verb tense in the previous T-unit. If there are tense changes within a T-unit, place a check mark in the margin for each change. An exception is if the verb tense change occurs with a change from narrative to direct quotation.
4. *Nouns:*
   Number: Underline nouns that show incorrect form for number.
   Possession: Write *NP* above the error.
5. *Pronouns:* Write the correct pronoun above each incorrect use.
6. *Punctuation:*
   End: Write in the correct form for the omitted or incorrect punctuation and circle it.
   Within T-Units: Using a red pencil, write in the correct form for the omitted or incorrect punctuation.
7. *Capitalization:*
   Beginning: Write correct uppercase letters over lowercase letters used at the beginning of T-units.
   Proper Nouns: Write correct uppercase letters over lowercase letters used for proper nouns.
   Inappropriate: Draw an X through the incorrectly capitalized letter.
8. *Paragraphs:*
   Extraneous T-Units: Underline extraneous T-units.
   New Line for Each T-Unit: Circle *Yes* or *No.*

Summary: Count the number of each type of error and enter in the appropriate row under "# per T-unit" on the Error Analysis Form. Divide the number of each error type by the number of T-units, and enter the result in the space provided.

Source: Robert A. Gable and Jo M. Hendrickson. *Assessing Students with Special Needs: A Sourcebook for Analyzing and Correcting Errors in Academics.* Copyright © 1990 by Pearson Education. Reprinted with permission.

and ideation. Figure 14.2 provides a checklist for evaluating the areas of ideation that were noted in Table 14.2. Spelling is a frequently analyzed component. A tremendous amount of information can be gleaned from looking at types of spelling errors. As in the analysis of arithmetic errors, spelling-error analysis is also relatively easy because a written product is usually available. Perhaps the most common types of spelling errors are phonological substitutions (such as *desishun* for *decision*) and omissions (such as *namly* for *namely*). Other errors included confused pronunciation (such as *denist* for *dentist*), doubling (such as *citty* for *city*), insertions (such as *biteing* for *biting*), transpositions (such as *freind* for *friend*) and homonyms (such as *see* for *sea*), and unclassified errors.

The information obtained from a careful look at error types suggests certain remedial strategies. For example, a student with transpositional errors might have difficulty learning or remembering spelling rules. A student with homonym errors might have problems attending to or understanding the meaning of words.

The following misspelled words provide an exercise for conducting an error analysis:

Actual Word	Student's Spelling	Type of Error
1. Enough	Enuff	_____
2. Believe	Belive	_____
3. Motel	Mottel	_____
4. Nerve	Nerv	_____
5. Has	Haz	_____
6. Good	Goode	_____
7. Carrying	Carring	_____
8. Eight	Ate	_____
9. Towel	Towle	_____
10. Girls	Grils	_____

Answers: (1) PS (2) O (3) D (4) O (5) PS (6) I/A (7) O (8) H (9) T (10) T

Key: PS—phonological substitution   O—omission
D—doubling   I—insertion
A—addition   H—homonym
T—transposition

Analyze writing samples, not just words.

Silva and Yarborough (1990) also provided a model for understanding and analyzing spelling errors. In their model, they encourage the analysis of actual writing samples rather than isolated spelling words.

To conduct a spelling error analysis, Hendrickson and Gable (1990) suggested a five-step process:

Step 1: Obtain a Sample. The teacher should dictate word lists, paragraphs, or stories to the student.

Step 2: Interview the Student. The teacher can use this procedure to identify spelling strategies that the student uses. Asking questions such as, "How do you remember how to spell new words that you learn?" can help better determine how the student approaches the reading process.

Step 3: Analyze and Classify the Errors. The analysis might involve some method of objectively scoring the errors. This is particularly helpful if the number of words sampled remains constant and the student is frequently

FIGURE 14.2 Ideation Evaluation Questions

Student's Name _____

Check the type of writing that is being evaluated:

____Friendly letter ____Narrative ____Expository ____Descriptive ____Story

____Report ____Review ____Essay ____Business letter ____Poem ____Other

A. **FLUENCY**—Are enough words and sentences written to:

    1. *adequately* convey the writer's ideas and purpose?   ____YES____SOMEWHAT____NO

    2. *appropriately* represent fluency for:

      (a) an average, nondisabled student of the writer's same age in the regular curriculum?

                      ____YES____SOMEWHAT____NO

      (b) the writer?   ____YES____SOMEWHAT____NO

          (Number of words written ____)

          (Number of sentences written ____)

B. **LEVEL OF MATURITY**—(Check only if writing is a narrative)

    ____Level I—Naming   ____Level II—Description

    ____Level III—Plot   ____Level IV—Issue

    Is the level appropriate for age/grade placement?   ____YES____SOMEWHAT____NO

C. **WORD CHOICE**—Are specific words expressly chosen to achieve the writer's *purpose* for a specific *audience,* on a specific *occasion*?   ____YES____SOMEWHAT____NO

D. **STYLE**—

    1. *Organization:* Is the writing well organized with a clear beginning, middle, and end?

                      ____YES____SOMEWHAT____NO

    2. *Development:* Are the *main idea* and *purpose* clear, accurate, and complete?

                      ____YES____SOMEWHAT____NO

      Is the *sequence* logical and orderly?   ____YES____SOMEWHAT____NO

      Is the composition *cohesive* (no superfluous ideas and no errors in logic)?   ____YES____SOMEWHAT____NO

      Are sufficient *details* (examples, proofs, reasons) and *supplementary ideas* used to support or develop the main idea or purpose?   ____YES____SOMEWHAT____NO

    3. *Comprehensibility:*

      Is the composition easily understood (no shift in tense, person, number, or point of view; no split infinitives; clear pronoun reference; proper location of modifiers, prepositional phrases, adjective clauses)?   ____YES____SOMEWHAT____NO

E. **OVERALL IMPRESSION**

    Is the overall impression favorable (effective, interesting, creative)?

                      ____YES____SOMEWHAT____NO

    Check any area below that requires remedial attention:

    ____Spelling   ____Handwriting   ____Capitalization   ____Punctuation

    ____Abbreviations   ____Numbers   ____Other (specify)

NOTES:

reevaluated. They summarized five approaches that can be used in scoring spelling errors. These are whole word, syllables, sound cluster, letters in place, and letter sequences. These approaches differ in the extent to which the spelling error is analyzed and scored. For example, using the syllable approach the word *city* would be scored 1/2 if it were spelled *cite* (ci/*te* note: underlined portion is scored as an error). If the word were spelled *site* the score would be 0/2 (*si*/*te*). Using the letter-in-place approach, *cite* would be scored 3/4 (c/i/t/*e*) and *site* would be scored 2/4 (*s*/i/t/*e*). Hendrickson and Gable note that the whole-word approach (the word is scored right or wrong) is the most logical for typical classroom use but that the others are more precise and might be helpful for more serious spelling problems.

Regardless of the scoring system used, it is important to look at the *pattern* of the errors. They suggest using a spelling error chart that indicates the *type* of errors (vowels, consonants, or rules and patterns) and whether the error *tendency* is to omit, delete, or substitute letters, or to change their order.

Step 4: Select a Corrective Strategy. The teacher can decide which instructional strategies to use by classifying the words misspelled as regular, irregular, or predictable. For example, if a student consistently missed predictable words (those that conform to traditional spelling words), the instructional strategy would be different than for irregular words that might require the use of certain memory strategies. Also, certain transposition errors (e.g., *freind* for *friend, maet* for *meat*) might require teaching certain spelling rules such as "Most of the time, i before e except after c" or "When two vowels go walking, the first usually does the talking." Hendrickson and Gable (1990) also provide guidelines for selecting and implementing instructional strategies that are beyond the scope of this discussion.

Step 5: Implement Strategy and Evaluate Its Effect. This would involve continuous monitoring to determine the effectiveness of the instructional program.

> Analyzing spelling errors should lead to a corrective strategy.

Written Expression and Language Tests

Why Use Tests of Written Expression and Language?

Screening and identification; informal determination of objectives and teaching strategies; documentation of educational need; establishment of IEP goals.

Who Should Use Them?

Teachers; diagnostic specialists.

Oral and Written Language Scales (Written Expression Scale)

> The Written Expression Scale is part of OWLS.

The written component of the *Oral and Written Language Scales* (OWLS; Carrow-Woolfolk, 1995) can be used by itself or combined with the Oral Scales discussed in Chapter 10. The Written Expression Scale is designed for individuals ages 5 through 21 (the Oral Scales are for ages 3 through 21). It is usually administered individually, although it can also be given to small groups. It measures the individual's ability to communicate using written linguistic forms. The test measures written expression in three areas using two different methods. The three areas are

Conventions (e.g., spelling, punctuation, capitalization), Linguistics (e.g., using complex sentences, different verb forms), and Content (e.g., appropriate word choice, subject matter). These areas are measured through indirect writing tasks, such as writing dictated sentences or combining sentences, and direct writing tasks. These require the individual to complete or retell a story in writing. One interesting feature is the use of age-appropriate item sets rather than basals and ceilings. Supposedly, the examiner chooses the item set that results in only developmentally appropriate items being administered to an individual.

Interpretation of Results.   There are scoring rules that are applied to each item and are based on the intent of the item (i.e., measurement of Conventions, Linguistics, Content). Examples are provided for each scoring rule. Raw scores can be converted to standard scores (mean = 100; standard deviation = 15), age equivalents, grade equivalents, stanines, normal curve equivalents, and percentiles. In addition, Descriptive Analysis Worksheets assist the examiner in determining the strengths and weaknesses in written expression. A computer scoring program, ASSIST, is available that provides a profile, suggested exercises, and a descriptive analysis.

Technical Characteristics

Normative Sample.   A total of 1,373 individuals were included in the standardization of the Written Expression Scale. This was the same group that was included in the standardization of the Oral Scales of the OWLS (not including the 3- and 4-year-old children). Characteristics of the sample were matched with the 1991 census data on variables such as gender, race, geographic region, and parent education level.

Reliability.   The mean internal reliability coefficient, test-retest coefficient, and interrater reliability coefficients were .87, .88, and .95 respectively.

Validity.   The Written Expression scale correlated .84–.88 with the global scores on the K-TEA, PIAT-R, and WRMT-R and the .50–.60s range with receptive language and verbal intelligence measures. Validity data with other measures of written expression are necessary.

Review of Relevant Research.   No research literature on the Written Expression scale of the OWLS was located. In a review, Goldblatt and Friedman (1998–1999) noted that the Written Expression Scales were very user friendly and easy to administer.

Overview: Oral and Written Language Scales (Written Expression Scale)

- *Age level*—5 through 21 years.
- *Type of administration*—Individual (small group possible).
- *Technical adequacy*—Good standardization, adequate reliability, questionable validity.
- *Scores yielded*—Standard scores, percentiles, age and grade equivalents, normal curve equivalents, stanines.
- *Suggested use*—The Written Expression Scale from the OWLS provides a potentially valuable measure of both the mechanics and fluency of writing. A wide variety of derived scores are available for comparison purposes. One disadvantage is that the Written Expression Scale is packaged

The Written Expression Scale can be used with the Oral Language Scale.

and sold separately from the Oral Scales of the OWLS. It would seem that the advantage of the OWLS is in giving an overall picture of language using the same comparison group. Having to use two separate tests tends to discourage that purpose. More validity data are also necessary.

Test of Written Expression

The *Test of Written Expression* (TOWE; McGhee, Bryant, Larsen, & Rivera, 1995) is an individually administered instrument that measures the six areas of ideation, semantics, syntax, spelling, capitalization, and punctuation (small-group administration is possible). The TOWE is designed for use with students from ages 6½ years through 14 years, 11 months. According to the TOWE authors, the test can be used to identify students who have writing problems and to discover their writing strengths and weaknesses. It can also be used to help evaluate a student's progress and can be used by researchers who are interested in studying the area of written expression. The test includes two major sections: the Items section (76 items) and the Essay section. Some items measure more than one of the six skill areas. A list of skills and item examples follow.

Six skill areas are measured in the TOWE.

Description of Items Section.   (Note: Directions are presented orally.)

Ideation. Mary is writing instructions on how to boil an egg. She wrote, "First you put water in a pot then you put the pot on the stove and turn on the burner." What did Mary forget to write in her directions?

Semantics. Write the word that completes this sentence, "The opposite of southern is _____."

Syntax. Write the preposition in this sentence: "The beautiful flowers flourished under the elm tree."

Capitalization. Write the following sentence: "The Girl Scout leader introduced the group's newest member, P. J. Winters." (Also score for spelling and punctuation.)

Punctuation. See capitalization example.

Spelling. See capitalization example.

Description of Essay Section.   The second component of the TOWE requires the student to write an essay based on a story in which the beginning is provided. In other words, the student must continue writing the story to its conclusion. The essay also is scored using criteria that represent the six skill areas previously noted. There is a possibility of 30 points on the essay portion.

Interpretation of Results.   Raw scores are determined for both the Items section and the Essay section (the Items section uses basal and ceiling rules for ease of administration). Total possible scores of 76 and 30 are available for those two sections, respectively. Each raw score can then be converted into a standard score (mean = 100, standard deviation = 15), percentile rank, and age equivalent. An overall descriptive rating for the student's performance on each section (e.g., poor, below average, average) is also available. These normative data can be displayed on a visual profile provided in the test protocol (see Figure 14.3). Finally, an informal analysis of the Items section can be conducted through the use of forms provided that allow the plotting of the person's performance in the six skill

FIGURE 14.3   TOWE Profile/Examiner Record Form

	Section I. Identifying Information

TOWE

Test of Written Expression

PROFILE/EXAMINER RECORD FORM

Name _____ Male ___ Female ___

	Year	Month	Day

Date of Testing ___ ___ ___
Date of Birth ___ ___ ___
Chronological Age ___ ___ ___
School _____ Grade _____
Examiner's Name _____
Examiner's Title _____

Section II. Record of TOWE Scores

Score	Raw Score	Std. Score	Grade Equiv.	%ile Rank	Rating
Items	___	___	___	___	___
Essay	___	___	___	___	___

Section III. Record of Other Test Scores

Test Name	Adm. Date	Score	TOWE Equiv.
1.			
2.			
3.			
4.			

Section IV. Profile of Test Scores

Std. Score	Items	Essay	1	2	3	4	Std. Score
150	•	•	•	•	•	•	150
145	•	•	•	•	•	•	145
140	•	•	•	•	•	•	140
135	•	•	•	•	•	•	135
130	•	•	•	•	•	•	130
125	•	•	•	•	•	•	125
120	•	•	•	•	•	•	120
115	•	•	•	•	•	•	115
110	•	•	•	•	•	•	110
105	•	•	•	•	•	•	105
100	•	•	•	•	•	•	100
95	•	•	•	•	•	•	95
90	•	•	•	•	•	•	90
85	•	•	•	•	•	•	85
80	•	•	•	•	•	•	80
75	•	•	•	•	•	•	75
70	•	•	•	•	•	•	70
65	•	•	•	•	•	•	65
60	•	•	•	•	•	•	60
55	•	•	•	•	•	•	55

Section V. Comments/Recommendations

Source: R. McGhee, B. Bryant, S. Larsen, and D. Rivera. _Test of Written Expression._ Austin, TX: Pro-Ed, Inc. Copyright © 1995 by Pro-Ed, Inc.

areas. These data are presented in terms of percentage of correct responses for each skill area.

Technical Characteristics

Normative Sample.   The TOWE was standardized on 1,355 students from twenty states. The percentage of students in the sample was similar to the percentage of the school-age population (based on the 1990 census) regarding race, ethnicity, gender, geographic region, and residence (there was a slight underrepresentation of urban students and overrepresentation of rural students).

Reliability.   The average internal consistency reliability coefficients were .92 and .90 for the Items and Essay sections, respectively. The reliability tended to increase slightly as a function of age. Test-retest reliability was determined using a relatively small sample and resulted in coefficients of .73 for the Items section and .78 for the Essay section. The authors do provide a method of determining the variance attributable to only test-retest reliability after other sources of error variance have been extracted. Those adjusted coefficients are .83 for the Items and .99 for the Essay. Interscorer reliability was also determined by having two examiners score the TOWE. The resulting coefficients were .98 for the Items and .89 for the Essay.

Validity.　Criterion-related validity coefficients were computed using a number of measures of written language, including other test results and ratings of written language. The median coefficients reported were .68 for the Items section and .61 for the Essay section. The authors also provide an argument for both content and construct validity. In the latter area, data indicating age differentiation and the relationship of the TOWE to general tests of mental ability and achievement are provided.

Review of Relevant Research.　Although no empirical studies on the TOWE were found, a review by Ehrler (1996) was located. He was impressed by the high reliability coefficients, particularly for the Essay section. He did feel, however, that the format of the test might make it uninteresting to some younger students.

Overview: Test of Written Expression

- *Age level*—6½ to 15 years.
- *Type of administration*—Individual (small group possible).
- *Technical adequacy*—Good reliability, adequate standardization and validity.
- *Scores yielded*—Standard scores, percentile ranks, age equivalents.
- *Suggested use*—The TOWE is a welcome addition to the limited number of instruments measuring written language and written expression. The test measures the areas of ideation, semantics, syntax, spelling, capitalization, and punctuation. Research should be conducted to provide additional information regarding its validity.

Test of Written Language–3

The *Test of Written Language–3* (TOWL-3; Hammill & Larsen, 1996) was developed to identify students who have problems with written expression, to indicate strengths and weaknesses in written language skills, to document progress, and to aid in research studies related to the writing process. The TOWL–3 can be administered either individually or in small groups and is designed to be used with students ages 7 through 17. The authors divide the area of written language into three components: conventional, linguistic, and cognitive. They also refer to two formats or methods of eliciting writing samples: contrived and spontaneous. The eight subtests on the TOWL–3 measure the various components in the authors' model (see Table 14.3).Two equivalent forms, A and B, are available.

The TOWL-3 measures both contrived and spontaneous written language.

Description.　There are eight subtests on the TOWL–3. The first five are considered contrived, and the second three are considered spontaneous. Although the contrived subtests are administered before the spontaneous ones, the student first writes a story using the picture depicted in Figure 14.4 (or a futuristic space scene for Form B). This story is the basis for the three spontaneous subtests, which can be scored at a later time.

TABLE 14.3   Component and Format Characteristics of the TOWL-3
Subtests

| | Format | |
| | Contrived | Spontaneous |
Component		
Conventional	Spelling Style	Contextual conventions
Linguistic	Vocabulary Sentence combining	Contextual language
Cognitive	Logical sentences	Story construction

Source: D. Hammill and S. Larsen. *Test of Written Language–3.* Copyright © 1996 by Pro-Ed, Austin, TX. Reprinted with permission.

Contrived Subtests

Vocabulary. This requires the student to write a sentence using a word (e.g., *night, umbrage*) supplied by the examiner.

Spelling. This subtest is scored along with subtest three, Style.

Style. The student is read a series of sentences that must be written with correct spelling, punctuation, and capitalization. Performance on this subtest also results in a score for subtest two, Spelling.

Logical Sentences. The student is given sentences that do not make sense and is told to rewrite them so that they do. For example, "Abbey reads the radio" should be written as "Abbey reads the book" or "Abbey listens to the radio."

Sentence Combining. The student is given several individual sentences and must combine them to make one sentence.

Spontaneous Subtests

Contextual Conventions. The student's freely written story is scored in the areas of capitalization, punctuation, and spelling using twelve criteria such as "All sentences begin with a capital letter" and "Uses quotation marks."

A picture is used to elicit a written story.

Contextual Language. The student's story is scored in the areas of sentence structure, grammar, and vocabulary using fourteen criteria.

Story Construction. This subtest uses eleven criteria to evaluate the student's use of prose, action, sequencing, and themes in the story.

Interpretation of Results.   The TOWL–3 includes standard scores and percentile ranks for subtests and three composites: Contrived Writing (first five subtests), Spontaneous Writing (last three subtests), and Overall Written Language (all eight subtests). The standard scores for the subtests have a mean of 10 and a standard deviation of 3. The composite standard scores have a mean of 100 and a standard deviation of 15. All data are placed on a summary-and-profile sheet that presents a visual display of the scores from all ten subtests.

Technical Characteristics

Normative Sample.   Approximately 2,200 subjects from nineteen states were included in the sample. Several demographic variables such as race, geographic

FIGURE 14.4   Stimulus for the Spontaneous Writing Sample from the Test of Written Language–3

Source: D. Hammill and S. Larsen. *Test of Written Language–3.* Copyright © 1996 by Pro-Ed, Austin, TX. Reprinted with permission.

region, ethnicity, gender, and urban or rural residence were considered in the selection of subjects and matched to the 1990 census data.

Reliability.   Internal reliability coefficients ranged from .70 (Contextual Conventions) to .90 (Story Construction) for the subtests and from .91 to .97 for the composites. Alternate-form reliability coefficients ranged from .71 (Contextual Conventions) to .90 (Vocabulary) and from .83 to .93 for the subtests and composites, respectively. Test-retest coefficients ranged from .75 (Contextual Convention) to .87 (spelling). The composites were between .86 and .89. Finally, interrater reliability was determined using two scorers with 38 test protocols. Those coefficients were in the .80s and .90s.

Validity.   A discussion of the test's content and construct validity is provided in the manual. Concurrent validity coefficients measuring reading, math, and general facts yielded correlations in the .40s, .50s, and .60s. Finally, correlations with the *Comprehensive Test of Nonverbal Intelligence* resulted in lower coefficients in the .30s to the .50s.

Review of Relevant Research.   In one study of the TOWL-3, Burns and Symington (2003) found only low to moderate correlations between the Spontaneous Writing Quotient and teacher ratings of writing progress. This suggests the need to investigate a school district's writing curriculum before using the TOWL-3. One study on the original TOWL (which was considerably different from the TOWL-3) by Poplin, Gray, Larsen, Banikowski, and Mehring (1980) found that students with learning disabilities score lower than students without learning disabilities on most subtests, particularly in the areas of spelling, punctuation, and word usage. More research that investigates the constructs and the psychological properties of the TOWL-3 needs to be conducted.

Research on the TOWL-3 is needed.

Overview: Test of Written Language–3

- *Age level*—7 to 18 years.
- *Type of administration*—Individual (small group possible).
- *Technical adequacy*—Adequate reliability (composites), questionable validity.
- *Scores yielded*—Standard scores and percentile ranks (subtests and composites).
- *Suggested use*—The capacity to use written language is, unfortunately, often overlooked in educational assessment. The TOWL–3 was developed to offer the special educator a measure in that area. The TOWL–3 measures several components of written language and appears to be a considerable improvement over its predecessors. The reliability of several of the subtests, particularly Contextual Conventions, is relatively low. In addition, the alternate form reliability is lower than that reported for many instruments. Using the different forms in test-retest situations should be done cautiously. Although the arguments for construct and content validity are sound, more criterion-related validity data with more appropriate criterion measures are necessary. Until further research is conducted in these areas, it is probably best to use the composite scores.

Additional Written Language Instruments

In addition to the previously described instruments, others are available, both norm-referenced and criterion-referenced, that directly measure written expression through the use of writing samples and other procedures. These are the *Mather-Woodcock Group Writing Tests, Test of Written English, Writing Process Test,* and the *Written Language Assessment.* Another instrument, the *Test of Early Written Language,* measures the emerging skills of young children. Yet another, the *Test of Handwriting Skills,* measures one specific component of written expression.

Mather-Woodcock Group Writing Tests

- *Age level*—Grade 2 through college.
- *Type of administration*—Group.
- *Technical adequacy*—Good standardization, adequate reliability and validity.
- *Scores yielded*—Standard scores, percentiles, proficiency levels.
- *Suggested use*—The *Mather-Woodcock Group Writing Tests* (Mather & Woodcock, 1997) is a modification of the writing tests from the *Woodcock-Johnson–Revised,* the predecessor to the WJ-III (discussed in Chapter 11). There are three forms

of the test, Basic, Intermediate, and Advanced, that are based on the grades for which it is to be used. Each form has four subtests: Dictation Spelling, Writing Samples (expression of ideas), Editing (ability to detect and correct punctuation, capitalization, and spelling errors in written text), and Writing Fluency (writing simple sentences correctly and quickly). The test can be administered in less than an hour and a computer scoring and reporting program is available, which must be used to generate derived scores.

Test of Early Written Language–2

- *Age level*—3 through 10 years.
- *Type of administration*—Individual.
- *Technical adequacy*—Adequate standardization, reliability, and validity.
- *Scores yielded*—Standard scores, percentiles, age equivalents, normal curve equivalents.
- *Suggested use*—The *Test of Early Written Language–2* (TEWL-2; Hresko, Herron, & Peak, 1996) focuses on the emerging written language skills of young children. It measures the areas of basic writing and contextual writing. It should be used for research purposes only for children under age 4. It is considered a companion instrument to the TOWL-3.

Test of Handwriting Skills

- *Age level*—5 to 11 years old.
- *Type of administration*—Individual or small groups.
- *Technical adequacy*—Adequate standardization, reliability, and validity.
- *Scores yielded*—Standard scores, scaled scores, percentiles, and stanines.
- *Suggested use*—The *Test of Handwriting Skills* (Gardner, 1998) measures both manuscript and cursive writing and includes both lower-case and upper-case forms. The test measures writing letters in alphabetical order, writing letters randomly from dictation, writing randomly presented numbers, copying lower-case and upper-case letters, copying words and sentences, and writing words from dictation. The test takes approximately thirty minutes to administer.

Test of Written English

- *Age level*—Grades 1 to 6.
- *Type of administration*—Group or individual.
- *Technical adequacy*—The *Test of Written English* is a criterion-referenced instrument.
- *Scores yielded*—Approximate grade-level placement.
- *Suggested use*—The *Test of Written English* (TWE; Andersen & Thompson, 1991) is a criterion-referenced test designed to measure four areas: Capitalization, Punctuation, Written Expression, and Paragraph Writing. The test was designed for use by teachers and diagnostic specialists. The Capitalization, Punctuation, and Usage items require the student to correct various errors made in sentences on the test form. The student also is required to write a brief paragraph.

Many tests use writing samples that are analyzed.

Writing Process Test

- *Age level*—Grades 2 to 12.
- *Type of administration*—Individual.

- *Technical adequacy*—Adequate reliability and validity.
- *Scores yielded*—Standard scores, percentile ranks.
- *Suggested use*—The *Writing Process Test* (WPT; Warden & Hutchison, 1992) is a direct measure of writing that requires the student to plan and compose an article for a specific audience. There is an optional component that requires the student to edit and revise the original article. One unique feature is the comparison of ratings from the teacher and the student with guidelines for identifying significant discrepancies. Scores are provided for two composite areas, Development and Fluency, based on ten criteria.

Written Language Assessment

- *Age level*—8 to 18 and older.
- *Type of administration*—Individual or group.
- *Technical adequacy*—Adequate standardization, limited reliability (subtests), adequate reliability (total score), adequate validity.
- *Scores yielded*—Standard scores.
- *Suggested use*—The *Written Language Assessment* (WLA; Grill & Kirwin, 1995) offers a direct measurement of written language through the use of writing samples. These writing samples are classified according to expressive, instructive, and creative writing. Scores are available in the areas of General Writing Ability, Productivity, Word Complexity, and Readability. An overall Written Language Quotient is also available that is a composite of the four subscores. One advantage of the Written Language Assessment is that it uses real writing tasks in a natural setting.

Diagnostic Spelling Tests

Why Use Diagnostic Spelling Tests?

Identification of areas for further evaluation or remediation; informal determination of objectives and teaching strategies; development and evaluation of IEPs.

Who Should Use Them?

Teachers.

Test of Written Spelling–4

The *Test of Written Spelling–4* (TWS-4; Larsen, Hammill, & Moats, 1999) is an individually administered or group-administered test designed to pinpoint a child's written spelling level and to specify the types of words with which a child is having problems. Its use as a group-administered instrument is somewhat limited, however. It is designed for use with students from grades 1 through 12 (ages 6 through 18).

Description. The TWS-4 includes fifty spelling words in increasing level of difficulty. It uses a dictated word format in which the examiner reads each word and the student provides a written response. The earlier editions of the TWS had separate word lists called Predictable and Unpredictable, but the fourth edition has abandoned that feature and now has two alternate forms (A and B) of

The TWS-4 now has two alternate forms.

fifty-item word lists. To demonstrate the appropriateness of the words selected, these words were cross-referenced to six basal spelling series with the results reported in the manual. According to the authors, the TWS-4 can be used to help identify a learning disorder, to document progress in spelling, and to serve as a research tool. In fact, research is cited in the manual about the relationship of spelling problems with a number of other areas such as reading disability, written language disorders, and attention-based learning problems. The authors do state that results from the TWS-4 should not be used for instructional planning. Rather, they suggest that users supplement the results with information from error analysis, informal surveys, and criterion-referenced testing.

Interpretation of Results. The TWS-4 yields a standard score (Quotient; mean = 100; SD = 15), a percentile rank, a spelling age, and a grade equivalent for the total score for Form A and/or B.

Technical Characteristics

Normative Sample. The sample used for the TWS-4 is actually the same as those from the TWS-2 and TWS-3. This included almost 5,000 individuals from twenty-three states. Geographic location, gender, residence (urban-rural), race, and ethnicity percentages are presented in the manual, comparing them with the 1997 census data and the projected 2000 data. Although the percentages are similar, the norms are still over twenty years old for the most part.

Reliability. Internal consistency was good; coefficients ranged from .87 to .96 for Form A and from .89 to .97 for Form B. Alternate-form reliability coefficients were all above .95 except for age 6 (.89) and age 7 (.91). Test-retest coefficients were also high (.95–.97) but were based on a restricted sample of forty-one children.

Validity. As noted earlier, the authors provide data to support its content validity by cross-referencing the words with spelling basal series. They also report impressive data to support the lack of item bias. In one study, scores were correlated with the spelling scores of group achievement tests. Correlations ranged from .78 (SRA) to .97 (California). In another study, the TWS-4 was correlated with the spelling subtests of the *Metropolitan Achievement Test* and the *Norm-referenced Assessment Program for Texas*. Those correlations were lower (e.g., .59 between Form A and the MAT). Finally, TWS-4 scores were correlated with teachers' rankings of their students' spelling. These were also only moderate (.60 for Form A, .55 for Form B). A discussion of construct validity is also presented in the manual.

Review of Relevant Research. No empirical studies on the TWS-4 were located. In reviews of the TWS-2, Erickson (1989) reported that it was an excellent screening instrument and Noyce (1989) noted that it was well constructed and easily administered. Because the format of the TWS-4 has changed, research on previous editions may or may not have relevance. Those limited studies and reviews were generally supportive of its use. Research needs to be conducted on the TWS-4, particularly in the area of validity.

Overview: Test of Written Spelling–4

- *Age level*—6 through 18 years.
- *Type of administration*—Individual (small group possible).
- *Technical adequacy*—Representative but dated norms, good reliability, limited validity (more data needed).

- *Scores yielded*—Standard score (Quotient), percentile, age and grade equivalent.
- *Suggested use*—The TWS-4 uses the identical items from previous editions but has grouped them as Form A and Form B instead of Predictable and Unpredictable. This was done in response to reviews and input from users. The authors should be commended for being responsive to suggestions. The uncertainty lies in the fact that the norms used for the TWS-4 are the same as previous editions, and there is little additional validity data to support its use. This does not mean that the test has significant limitations in these areas. It does suggest that further validity studies should be conducted to ensure that it is providing relevant, meaningful information. It remains as the major norm-referenced spelling test, although it should not be used as the only measure to develop instructional plans. Finally, as with any test like this, careful error analysis of the missed items might provide helpful information.

SuperSpell Assessment Disk

SuperSpell (Hoopers Multimedia, 2001) is a computerized, comprehensive spelling program used with students from kindergarten through grade 6. It includes an interactive CD-ROM called "A Day at the Beach," which involves a series of spelling games that use either the system's spelling lists or word lists provided by the teacher. The games are fully animated and reinforce the student for correct responses using cartoons. Also included are spelling worksheets that can be printed. Finally, there is an interactive assessment CD-ROM software package (described next).

Description.   The *SuperSpell Assessment Disk* includes four separate tests: a placement test and three diagnostic tests. The tests are criterion referenced rather than norm referenced. Each user of the *SuperSpell Assessment Module* is required to log in every time they use the program. Performances on the placement test and the three diagnostic tests and the date the test(s) were conducted are stored under the student's name.

SuperSpell includes a placement test and three diagnostic tests.

Placement Test.   The purpose of the placement test is not to diagnose specific spelling skills or to provide grade placements. Rather, it is used to determine the most appropriate diagnostic test for the student to take. The student is presented with 50 words randomly generated from a database of 250 words. The screen shows a scene related to a sentence in which a word is missing (e.g., We always _____ the animals in the afternoon). The program, which has full speech capability, has a woman's voice say the word to be spelled (in this example "feed"). The cursor is positioned where the word is to be typed, and the student types the spelling of the word. The delete key can be used to make any corrections. There also are opportunities for the student to hear the word again before typing the word.

If the student misspells at least five of the first twenty words, the placement test is terminated and she or he is directed to take Diagnostic Test 1. If the student misspells at least five of the first thirty-five words the recommendation is to take Diagnostic Test 2. Finally, if the student completes the test (all fifty words) and accumulates fewer than five errors, she or he would be advised to proceed to Diagnostic Test 3.

Diagnostic Test 1. This test, which includes fifty words, is used to evaluate the following spelling skills: regular consonant/short vowel/regular consonant words, initial and final consonant blends, consonant digraphs, digraph–consonant blends, double consonants, forming plurals, and simple multisyllabic words. The student either types in the whole word or only a part of the word that is pinpointing a particular phonic/letter pattern or spelling skill.

Diagnostic Test 2. This test, containing sixty words, measures the following spelling skills: long vowel sounds, vowel digraphs and dipthongs, vowels before *r*, silent consonants, soft consonant sounds, verb endings, and harder plurals.

Diagnostic Test 3. The purpose of this test, which includes fifty words, is to measure the student's knowledge of prefixes, suffixes, prefix and suffix in the same word, homophones, and commonly confused words. The user is required to type in the whole word.

Interpretation of Results. For each test the results can be printed and can be used to conduct an error analysis (see Figure 14.5). The words in the three diagnostic

FIGURE 14.5   Printout of Completed Diagnostic Test 1 from SuperSpell

Diagnostic Test 1

Name: Jackie   *Date:* 16 September 2007

1	lid	✓	18	hand	✓	35	srunk (shrunk)	✗
2	tin	✓	19	risk	✓	36	saded (sadden)	✗
3	pan	✓	20	dust	✓	37	bluf (bluff)	✗
4	mug	✓	21	spiny (spent)	✗	38	comon (common)	✗
5	tap	✓	22	drif (drift)	✗	39	hapen (happen)	✗
6	box	✓	23	swappe (swept)	✗	40	coton (cotton)	✗
7	wax	✓	24	crust	✓	41	bunshes (bunches)	✗
8	fix	✓	25	prank	✓	42	boses (bosses)	✗
9	yak	✓	26	blok (block)	✗	43	foxes (foxes)	✗
10	hat	✓	27	crush	✓	44	looves (loaves)	✗
11	flop	✓	28	wiff (whiff)	✗	45	entres (entries)	✗
12	twig	✓	29	thick	✓	46	canun (canyon)	✗
13	clap	✓	30	pinc (pinch)	✗	47	cammil (camel)	✗
14	scruub (scrub)	✗	31	trift (thrift)	✗	48	limon (Lemon)	✗
15	spung (sprung)	✗	32	scrub (shrub)	✗	49	pannil (panel)	✗
16	left	✓	33	crunsh (crunch)	✗	50	signul (signal)	✗
17	kepd (kept)	✗	34	patsh (patch)	✗			

Source: G. Leary. *SuperSpell.* Copyright © 2001 by Hoopers Multimedia, Ulverstone, Tasmania, Australia. Reprinted with permission.

tests are grouped together based on the specific spelling skills that they measure (such as two-letter final consonant blends). Student performance on each spelling skill is described as competent, partially established, or not established. Also, each test word in the three diagnostic tests is linked to one of the 160 *SuperSpell* word lists that are used for the activities and games in the *SuperSpell* "A Day at the Beach," and the appropriate lists are recommended (see Figure 14.6). The results can be either viewed on screen or printed. The authors recommend that the student or teacher print these results so progress can be monitored and comparisons can be made with earlier or later tests.

Overview: SuperSpell Assessment Disk
- *Age level*—Kindergarten through grade 6.
- *Suggested use*—The *SuperSpell Assessment Disk* is part of a comprehensive, computer-based spelling program. It includes four separate tests—a placement test and three diagnostic tests. The placement test is used to determine which of the three diagnostic tests is most appropriate for a given student. Words in the diagnostic tests are grouped together according to the type of spelling skill they measure. Results indicate the level of

The Assessment disk is part of a comprehensive spelling program.

FIGURE 14.6   Skills and Spelling Lists Identified from Test in Figure 14.5

SuperSpell

Results Sheet

Diagnostic Test 1

Name: Jackie   **Date:** 16 September 2007

Number of Words Spelled Correctly: 21/50

Percentage: 42%

Spelling Skills Established
3 Letter words (CVC)

Spelling Skills Partially Established
2 and 3L Consonant initial blends
2L Consonant final blends

Spelling Skills Not Established
Initial and final blends in the same word
Consonant digraphs
Digraph—consonant blends
Double consonants
Plurals
Multisyllabic words (short vowel sound)

SuperSpell Word Lists Recommended
9, 10, 11, 12, 14, 15, 17, 18, 19, 20, 21, 22,
23, 24, 25, 26, 27, 28, 29, 30, 31, 32

Source: G. Leary. *SuperSpell.* Copyright © 2001 by Hoopers Multimedia, Ulverstone, Tasmania, Australia. Reprinted with permission.

competence a student has for each spelling skill assessed. Also provided are the appropriate word lists to use within the teaching CD-ROM that is part of the system. Overall, the type of results yielded by the *SuperSpell Assessment Disk* provides a teacher with valuable information as well as a link with an instructional program to remediate spelling deficits.

BACK TO THE PROFILES

Possible Answers to the Questions

1. **Why assess Ed?** Because Ed has already met eligibility criteria for a learning disability, those procedures do not have to be duplicated. However, if Ed has problems in written expression as well as in reading, those should be documented and indicated as goals on his IEP. In addition, assessment could focus on identifying specific strengths and weaknesses and possible patterns.

2. **Who should assess Ed?** His teacher, Ms. Warde, should certainly be involved in the assessment, particularly if informal procedures are used. Others who might be involved would be a diagnostic specialist or school psychologist. It is possible that a speech/language clinician might do some testing. This would be dependent on the policies, philosophies, and resources of the school and school district.

3. **What procedure(s)/test(s) should be used?** To document the problem and to provide information that might be used to identify IEP goals, a test such as the TOWL-3 or TOWE might be administered. This would also provide information about whether the problem is more "mechanical" or emerges when he is required to write spontaneously. Another technique that should prove invaluable is error analysis. Even an analysis of Ed's brief passage at the beginning of the chapter indicates several patterns. For instance, he uses conjunctions instead of commas ("I would eat pizza and candy and donuts but I would not. . . ."). He also started almost every sentence with "I" and omitted verbs ("I feel happy if *there were* not teachers. . . . " and "I wish school *was* like that."). He had one incomplete sentence and made spelling errors indicating either omissions or phonetic substitutions. Obviously, more consistent patterns could be determined by analyzing more samples.

4. **What other areas should be assessed?** From the description in the vignette, there is no other obvious area that needs to be assessed. As noted earlier, Ed has already met eligibility criteria for learning disabilities so intelligence testing would not be necessary.

1. **Why assess Sarah?** The primary reason to assess Sarah is to gather information that could be incorporated into some type of remedial program. It might be appropriate to determine the extent of her spelling problem, but that information would not really provide instructional information.

2. **Who should assess Sarah?** Sarah's teacher would be the logical person to assess her. If there were some type of consulting teacher or resource person at her private school, that person might also assist the teacher.

3. **What procedure(s)/test(s) should be used?** Two approaches might be taken. First, the *SuperSpell Assessment Disk* could be used to help identify the types of words she is struggling with and to identify word lists for remediation. In addition, error analysis of her spelling using spontaneous writing samples would prove valuable. Sarah's short sample at the beginning of the chapter suggests that she might be spelling phonetically (e.g., *actrice* for *actress*, *Favoret* for *favorite*, *dansed* for *danced*). Further, the more

difficult words that she spelled—*Pacific, Forbush, Billis*—might be words that she has seen repeatedly. For example, she would have to have read those words repeatedly when memorizing her lines for the musical.

4. **What other areas should be assessed?** The vignette does not suggest that any other area should be assessed. It mentioned that Sarah is a good reader but does not read much. It might be a good suggestion for Sarah to read her own passages to see if some of the words "don't look right" and see if she could self-correct.

STUDENT PROFILE DATA

Ed

The *Test of Written Language–3* was administered to Ed. The following results were obtained:

Composite/Subtests	Standard/Scaled Score
Overall Written Language	**76**
Contrived Writing	**71**
Vocabulary	9
Spelling	6
Style	6
Logical Sentences	8
Sentence Combining	7
Spontaneous Writing	**79**
Contextual Conventions	6
Contextual Language	7
Story Construction	9

These results confirm Ms. Warde's observation that Ed was having difficulty with the more mechanical aspects of writing, including spelling, punctuation, and capitalization. As a result, his writing sample was relatively short, with numerous errors in the above areas. His vocabulary and thematic development were relatively high, particularly given his limited writing sample. An error analysis of his written sample also confirmed Ms. Warde's observations about the types of problems he was displaying in writing in general and in spelling in particular. She is planning to administer *SuperSpell* to get more information for instructional purposes.

CASE STUDY *June*

As part of the portfolio Mrs. Dunn submitted, there were several samples of June's essays and stories that she has written in class. One story was selected to be analyzed as part of the evaluation process. You have been asked to do that analysis. To help you with this analysis, complete the activities and questions that follow June's story. These activities include:

- An evaluation of the composition
- Comparing informal and formal assessment results
- Recommendations for further assessment

Here is the story. The directions to the students were to write a story including the story elements of setting, characters, and plot. The story was to be about a toy and was to be a minimum of two paragraphs long. The students had thirty minutes to complete the assignment.

The doll

Once upon a time their was a lovely doll. She belonged to a little girl who lived in a castle. Their was a mean which who lived in a dark cave not far from the castle. She did'nt like the girl. One day she flew to the castle on her black broom. She saw the lovely doll on the bed and she grabed it. The little girl saw the mean which fly away with her doll. She ran to tell her dad that the which took her doll. Her dad was the king so he sent his gards to the cave. When they got to the cave they saw the doll on the floor. They quickly grabed it and took it back to the girl. The girl thanked the gards and huged her dad.

- Evaluate the story and make comments about June's spelling, capitalization, and punctuation.

- Comparing informal and formal assessment results: Look at previous assessments that have provided information on June's oral and written language abilities. What conclusions can you now draw? Support your statements with specific examples. (Refer to June's Cumulative Assessment File on the Companion Website, www.prenhall.com/taylor8e.)

- Recommendations for further assessment: What other assessments in written expression might be utilized?

Reflections

1. Why do you think it is important to consider the area of ideation when evaluating written expression?
2. In this era of computers, do you think it is still important to evaluate spelling, when programs such as *Spellcheck* are readily available? Why or why not?
3. If you had a student with writing problems, would you administer the TOWE or the TOWL-3? Why?

Summary Matrix

Instrument or Technique	Screening and Initial Identification	Informal Determination and Evaluation of Teaching Programs and Strategies	Determination of Current Performance Level and Educational Need	Decisions about Classification and Program Placement	IEP Goals	IEP Objectives	IEP Evaluation	Mild/Moderate	Severe/Profound	Preschool	Elementary Age	Secondary Age	Adult	Special Considerations	Educational Relevance for Exceptional Students
	Prereferral	Prereferral			Postreferral	Postreferral	Postreferral	Target Population	Target Population	Target Population	Target Population	Target Population	Target Population		
Written Language Sampling	X	X			X	X	X	X			X	X	X	Helpful and easy to do because of availability of written products.	Very Useful
Oral and Written Language Scales (Written Expression Scale)	X	X	X	X	X			X			X	X		Can be combined with Oral Scales to get a comprehensive language measure.	Useful
Test of Written Expression	X	X	X	X	X			X				X		Measures six areas of written expression; includes an essay section.	Useful
Test of Written Language–3	X	X	X	X	X			X			X	X		Measures an important and often overlooked area; technical aspects are somewhat limited.	Useful
Mather-Woodcock Group Writing Tests	X	X	X		X			X			X	X		Measures four areas of both mechanical and fluency aspects of written language.	Adequate/Useful
Test of Early Written Language–2	X	X	X		X			X		X	X			Measures emerging writing skills; limited usefulness with very young children.	Adequate
Test of Handwriting Skills	X	X			X			X			X			Measures both manuscript and cursive writing in lowercase and uppercase forms.	Adequate
Test of Written English		X	X		X			X			X			A criterion-referenced test that measures four areas.	Adequate
Writing Process Test	X	X	X		X			X			X	X		Student writes and then edits and revises an article.	Useful
Written Language Assessment	X	X	X		X			X			X	X		Uses writing samples to measure skill areas.	Adequate/Useful
Test of Written Spelling–4	X	X	X		X			X			X			One of the few tests that yields normative information on spelling.	Useful
SuperSpell Assessment Disk	X	X			X	X		X			X			Computerized system; includes a placement test and three diagnostic tests.	Useful

part five

Special Assessment Considerations

This part addresses two assessment areas, each in its own chapter. These are *early childhood assessment* (Chapter 15) and *career/vocational/transitional assessment* (Chapter 16). These areas have become increasingly important because of legislation that has mandated educational services for infants and toddlers (Public Law 99-457) and transitional services for secondary students (IDEA 04). The Carl D. Perkins Act also brought increased attention to vocational services for students with disabilities.

In addition to a description of a variety of instruments (formal and informal) used with these populations, discussions will also center on the type of assessment process (e.g., team assessment) and alternative procedures (e.g., play-based assessment, analysis of work samples) that should be considered. The format for describing instruments will be similar to the chapters in Parts III and IV. That includes the following:

1. A summary matrix presents information about specific instruments and techniques in a format that allows easy comparison of the instruments for suggested use and target population. The matrix also includes a statement of any special considerations of which a user should be aware. In addition, for each instrument, the matrix gives the educational relevance for exceptional students. The matrices are directly related to the assessment model proposed in Chapter 2.

2. A thorough review of relevant research for each major norm-referenced instrument emphasizes use of the test with exceptional students.

3. An overview box for each test summarizes the age range, technical adequacy (for norm-referenced tests), and suggested use for each instrument.

AFTER READING PART FIVE
You Should Be Able To:

- Identify the reasons for needing team assessment for young children.

- Identify the importance of using play-based assessment for young children.

- Identify the strengths and weaknesses of a variety of screening and developmental tests.

- Identify the importance of developing transitional programs for secondary students.

- Identify the need for analyzing work samples and on-the-job assessment.

- Identify the strengths and weaknesses of a variety of vocational interest and aptitude measures.

chapter fifteen

Early Childhood Assessment

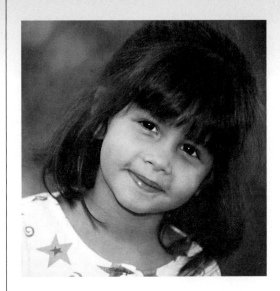

CHILD PROFILE

Mary

Mary is a 4-year-old girl, the only child in a single-parent household. Mary has been in daycare for over a year to allow her mother to work after she and Mary's father divorced. Staff at the daycare center were concerned that Mary's developmental skills were lagging behind her peers. In addition, she was having difficulty in the area of joint play and other socialization skills. Mary's mother was aware of some of these problems but attributed them to the unsettled nature of her home situation. She also had a difficult time finding a permanent daycare situation for Mary; her mother felt that this lack of consistency also may have affected her. Since the time daycare center staff brought this to her attention, Mary's mother began to observe her more closely and talk to some of the others in her "Mommy and Me" class. She did notice that Mary had a more limited vocabulary than her peers and seemed to depend on her for daily activities. Again, however, she felt that she was perhaps "babying" Mary a little too much because she was not with her as often as she would like. She contacted the local school district to ask if they could provide assistance. She was told that the district was sponsoring a large-scale developmental screening. After Mary was screened, the results indicated that she was, in fact, lagging behind in both language and motor skills.

Think about These Questions as You Read This Chapter:

1. Why assess Mary? (There could be more than one reason.)
2. Who should assess Mary? (There could be more than one person.)
3. What procedure(s)/test(s) should be used?
4. What other area(s) (if any) should be assessed?

(Suggested answers appear at the end of this chapter.)

Interest in the area of early childhood assessment has increased over the past 25 years. This popularity is partly due to legislation that provided increased awareness of, and mandated increased responsibility for, the educational needs of children from birth to 5 years old. For example, Public Law 98-199 (the Education of the Handicapped Amendment Act of 1983) targeted the expansion and improvement of services to preschool children with disabilities as one of its primary initiatives. Public Law 99-457 (discussed in Chapter 1) outlined specific responsibilities for the identification and appropriate educational programming for children from birth.

Important Components of Early Childhood Assessment

Use a team approach with young children.

Young children should be evaluated using a team approach. Frequently, for example, infants who have disabilities or are suspected of having a disability have medical problems that require evaluation from appropriate medical personnel. Others who might be involved are parents, psychologists, speech-language pathologists, audiologists, and physical and occupational therapists. It is important that these professionals, in conjunction with the teacher, work together to coordinate assessment results into the most viable overall educational plan. Older preschool children might be evaluated for many purposes, including screening and eligibility decisions when a less severe problem is suspected. Consequently, optimal communication is paramount among the various team members so that appropriate decisions can be made. Again, the teacher should be an active member of that team. Given the multidisciplinary nature of the assessment procedures used with young children, the instruments and techniques discussed in this chapter will focus on those used by teachers and other educational personnel.

The instruments used (norm-referenced and criterion-referenced) for infants and toddlers can be primarily considered *developmental*. Those for preschool children can be considered *developmental* (both norm-referenced and criterion-referenced), *screening,* or *preacademic.* It should be noted that many tests used in early childhood extend the entire preschool age range (usually birth to age 6 or 7).

Specific guidelines should be followed when preschool children are evaluated. First, the rapid developmental changes that occur during the preschool years make reevaluations and continuous monitoring extremely important. Second, it is necessary to address environmental variables that have a significant influence on young children and to evaluate the home environment. Third, any decision should be based on multiple scores and multiple sources and never on the basis of a single test. Fourth, tests should match the philosophy and goals of the educational program in which a child might be placed. Finally, as in all assessment, there should be sensitivity to individual diversity, both cultural and linguistic.

Other guidelines relate to the testing session itself. First, it should be structured in a way that allows for optimal response from the child. Subsequently, issues such as length of testing, establishing rapport, nature of instructions, and type of directions must be given extra consideration. Also, if possible, the child should not be subjected to multiple testing sessions with a number of different examiners. This may require that more than one person see the child at the same time. Next, it might be advantageous to make the testing sessions more playlike

focus on
Diversity

Should We Assess Young Children within a Cultural Context?

Meller, Ohr, and Marcus (2001) described an approach to evaluate the development of infants, toddlers, and preschool children within a cultural context. This approach is called Family-Oriented, Culturally Sensitive Assessment (FOCUS). One emphasis of this approach is input from the family regarding important and necessary cultural considerations in the assessment and intervention of their child. There are five steps of FOCUS:

1. Adequate training in assessing young children from diverse cultural backgrounds through coursework and/or professional development.
2. Assessing family characteristics, resources, competencies, and needs.

3. Assessing all areas of developmental competencies and needs using a variety of approaches over time and across settings.
4. Ongoing evaluation of both the child and family when developing and implementing a family intervention plan.
5. Ongoing evaluation and planning.

The FOCUS model, as noted in #3 above, involves numerous types of assessment procedures including interviews, formal and informal observation, norm-referenced and criterion-referenced testing, surveys, and arena (a type of team) assessment. It incorporates many of the best practices discussed in this chapter.

to sustain the child's attention. In fact, it is important to observe play behavior as part of the evaluation process. Finally, as in all assessment, the cultural backgrounds of the individual should be considered (see Focus on Diversity). These suggestions should be considered best practice for *all* individuals; they emphasize the importance of carefully planning and conducting an evaluation with young children.

Types of Early Childhood Assessment Procedures

In this chapter, the first area to be discussed will be *general assessment procedures,* including those areas such as team assessment models and the assessment of play behavior. Next, the specific area of *developmental screening* will be discussed. Developmental screening tests provide a brief assessment of a child's abilities that are highly associated with future skills. These tests are usually administered to identify children who may need early intervention or special education services. Because of the nature of the decision being made, the issue of predictive validity is important because those decisions related to a child's future performance are made on the basis of the test results. Most developmental screening tests are quick and easy to administer and include typical developmental skills such as gross motor, fine motor, language, and conceptual skills. It should be noted that two possible erroneous outcomes can result from using developmental screening tests. These are (1) identifying as high risk a child who does not have a problem (false positive) and (2) identifying as low risk a child who does have a problem (false negative). The first type of error can lead to a waste of time and money and might result in undue anxiety for the parents and the child. The second type of error results in the lack or postponement of a necessary prevention or remediation program.

False positive and false negative screening decisions can be made.

The third area that will be discussed is that of *norm-referenced developmental testing*. Specifically, the *Battelle Developmental Inventory–2* will be presented. The next area to be described is that of *preacademic and readiness testing*. These tests include items specifically designed to measure skills that students need to perform adequately in the early school years. Obviously, the content of many of these instruments will overlap with developmental screening tests, particularly regarding perceptual and fine motor skills that are normally developing in the preschool years. Preacademic and readiness tests, however, are more concerned with curriculum-related skills that a child has already acquired and are prerequisite for specific instructional programs.

The last area to be discussed will be *testing for educational programming*. The available tools are primarily criterion-referenced inventories that have been developed specifically for the preschool age range. These instruments provide detailed skill sequences in a variety of developmental areas. It is important that those using these instruments focus only on those areas in which educational programming is necessary. In other words, the entire instrument is not administered; rather, based on data gathered from the home environment, observation, and formal test results, the appropriate areas are identified and subsequently evaluated.

Many of the instruments and techniques discussed in other chapters in this book are also applicable to young children. Losardo and Notari-Syverson (2001) strongly recommended the use of alternative assessment procedures such as performance assessment and portfolio assessment (Chapter 6) and dynamic assessment (Chapter 7). In addition, young children are represented in the standardization sample in many norm-referenced tests, making it possible to obtain scores that can be applied to that age group. Examples of this are the *Kaufman Assessment Battery for Children–II* and the *Scales of Independent Behavior–Revised*. Still other instruments include a separate preschool version (usually a downward extension). Examples are the *Test of Language Development–Primary* and the *Detroit Tests of Learning Aptitude–Primary*. Several assessment devices, however, are designed specifically for use with infants, toddlers, and preschool children.

Team Assessment: A Collaborative Effort

As noted previously, the evaluation of preschool children involves a number of professionals. It is extremely important that these individuals work as a team, communicating with each other to streamline the evaluation and to coordinate decision making. In some situations the child might be evaluated by an entire team. This is known as **arena assessment.** Buck and Schock (1995) noted that in addition to the various professionals (e.g., teachers, therapists, psychologist), the parent or primary caregiver should also be a member of the team. That individual can provide important information and can facilitate the observation when necessary. An example of this approach is the Natural Assessment Model.

Natural Assessment Model

The Natural Assessment Model was developed and implemented in the Schaumburg, Illinois, school district. In this model, the evaluation team is composed of members from different disciplines who observe the child's performance in a variety of developmental domains. Each team member receives training in the areas of intellectual, language, social-emotional, and motor development. The

ARENA ASSESSMENT
A young child is evaluated simultaneously by an entire team.

assessment is carried out in a play setting and involves interaction with peers, thus focusing on the child's natural interaction with the environment. Four or five children are observed simultaneously by the evaluation team for one hour. At the same time, the parent is interviewed and histories are obtained. The observation room is supplied with a variety of toys and large motor equipment.

Each team member completes a developmental checklist called the *Mini-wheel of Developmental Milestones.* The areas on the Mini-wheel are primarily based on Piaget's work and measure the four major areas of intellectual, language, motor, and social-emotional development. Each area is further broken down into twelve specific skills that have accompanying definitions. The team is trained in each of the areas. Other notes are also taken by the team members related to the child's quality of performance. Ongoing communication between team members ensures that each area on the wheel is being evaluated for each child. The usual team members and their respective roles are:

Speech-language pathologist. Interacts with the child and records a spontaneous language sample, observes phonological processing, and is primarily responsible for language scores on the Mini-wheel.

Preschool teacher. Observes the child's interactions, problem-solving abilities, and drawing/fine-motor ability and is primarily responsible for the social, emotional, and motor scores on the Mini-wheel.

Psychologist. Assists in determining the intellectual score on the Mini-wheel and meets with the parents, acting as the school district liaison.

Teacher assistant. Collects information from the parent and engages in motor activities with the child.

Social worker. Meets with the parents to explain the Mini-wheel and the evaluation procedures, interviews them, and obtains developmental histories.

Nurse. Conducts initial screening for vision and hearing prior to the evaluation.

After the evaluation there is a twenty- to thirty-minute meeting for the team and parents to gather and share information. Each team member relates his or her observations and ratings on the Mini-wheel, and a consensus on the child's performance is reached.

Play-Based Assessment

The area of play-based assessment is extremely important when considering the overall developmental status of young children. Although many states require the use of standardized tests (particularly for eligibility decisions), play-based assessment should be incorporated into any evaluation. Linder (1993) in her book, *Transdisciplinary Play-Based Assessment,* provides a comprehensive and meaningful discussion of the informal and formal guidelines to follow when conducting a play-based assessment. For example, Linder suggests the following sequence of activities (although she notes that flexibility is a key to a successful assessment):

Play-based assessment is a very valuable procedure.

Phase I: Unstructured Facilitation. This twenty- to twenty-five-minute period allows the child to take the lead and to choose his or her own activities.

Phase II: Structured Facilitation. This ten- to fifteen-minute period allows the evaluator to observe such skills as puzzle making, drawing, or other areas not exhibited during the unstructured situation.

Phase III: Child–Child Interaction. In this five- to ten-minute period two children are allowed to play in an unstructured situation. If no interaction occurs, more structure (e.g., toys, prompts) is added.

Phase IV: Parent–Child Interaction. In this phase the parent interacts with the child for five minutes in an unstructured situation. At that point, the parent is asked to leave, and the child's reaction to the separation is observed. Finally, the parent is brought back for another five minutes in a more structured situation.

Phase V: Motor Play. This involves a ten- to twenty-minute session of both structured and unstructured play.

Phase VI: Snack. This final phase allows for additional observation of social interaction, self-help skills, and adaptive behavior, as well as motor skills.

Linder also provides observational guidelines as well as checklists for the areas of cognitive development, social-emotional development, communication and language development, and sensorimotor development. Interested readers are encouraged to consult her book for more detailed information regarding this area. Interestingly, in a review of transdisciplinary play-based assessment, Roszmann-Millican (1998–1999) noted two problems: (1) the fact that it doesn't yield standard scores required by many states for eligibility purposes, and (2) that it takes a considerable amount of time to complete. She pointed out, however, that this approach better represents the best practices in early childhood assessment.

Screening Instruments

Why Use Screening Instruments?

Screening.

Who Should Use Them?

Teachers; social workers; school psychologists; parent participation (often a team approach).

Early childhood screening tests are frequently administered to large groups of children. Often the child and a parent will come to a school or other area in which stations are set up where different developmental skills are assessed. The child and the parent go through the stations performing a variety of activities or answering questions. Subsequently, the test is scored and a decision is made about referring the child for further evaluation. Two popular norm-referenced instruments that are used for this purpose are the *AGS Early Screening Profiles* and the *Developmental Indicators for the Assessment of Learning–3.* Two terms that are used to evaluate the appropriateness of a screening test are sensitivity and specificity. A screening test that has good **sensitivity** will accurately identify children who, in fact, are found to have a problem after diagnostic testing. Conversely, a test with poor sensitivity will identify many children as having problems when they actually don't have any. A test with good **specificity** will not identify children who, in fact, don't have problems. Conversely, a test with poor specificity will fail to identify many children who actually do have problems.

SENSITIVITY
The percentage of children with problems who are accurately detected.

SPECIFICITY
The percentage of children without problems who are accurately identified.

AGS Early Screening Profiles

The *AGS Early Screening Profiles* (ESP; Harrison, 1991) is designed for use with children ages 2 through 6. Its primary purpose is to aid in the identification of those children with possible disabilities or, conversely, those who might be potentially gifted. The ESP uses an ecological approach to screening whereby numerous areas are measured and several individuals are involved in the assessment process. The child, parent, and teacher are all evaluated in the ESP. The evaluation time for children ranges from fifteen to thirty minutes, while the parent and teacher questionnaires can be completed in approximately fifteen minutes. The seven sections included (Figure 15.1) are the Cognitive/Language, Motor, and Self-Help/Social Profiles, and the Articulation, Home, Health History, and Behavior Surveys. Each of these will be described.

The ESP uses an ecological approach.

Description

Cognitive/Language Profile. This profile includes four subtests that are administered directly to the child. Those are verbal concepts, visual discrimination, logical relations, and basic school skills.

FIGURE 15.1 Components of the AGS Early Screening Profile

Components

ESP's three basic components, called Profiles, are supplemented by four Surveys. For most children, the total time needed for the three Profiles is under *30 minutes*. The Surveys, completed by a parent, teacher, or screening examiner, require an additional *15–20 minutes*.

Profiles

- The **Cognitive/Language Profile** is administered individually to the child. Tasks assess reasoning skills, visual organization and discrimination, receptive and expressive vocabulary, and basic preacademic and school skills. The Profile can be separated into Cognitive (nonverbal) and Language (verbal) subscales, a useful feature for screening children with language difficulties, hearing problems, or limited English proficiency.

- The **Motor Profile,** also individually administered, assesses both gross and fine motor skills.

- The **Self-Help/Social Profile** is a questionnaire that is completed by the child's parent, teacher, or daycare provider. It assesses the child's typical performance in the areas of communication, daily living skills, socialization, and motor skills.

Surveys

- The **Articulation Survey** measures the child's ability to pronounce 20 words selected to test common articulation problems in the initial, medial, and final positions of words.

- The **Home Survey** is completed by the parent and asks nonintrusive questions about the child's home environment.

- The **Health History Survey,** also completed by the child's parent, is a brief checklist summarizing any health problems the child has had.

- The **Behavior Survey** is used by the examiner to rate the child's behavior during administration of the Cognitive/Language and Motor Profiles. The child is rated in categories such as attention span, frustration tolerance, and response style.

Source: P. Harrison. *AGS Early Screening Profile.* Circle Pines, MN: American Guidance Service. Copyright © 1991 by American Guidance Service. Reprinted with permission.

Motor Profile. This section includes both gross-motor and fine-motor areas. A limited number of items, however, are used in this profile (five in gross motor, three in fine motor).

Self-Help/Social Profile. This information is gathered through both parent and teacher reports and measures four domains. Those are communication, daily living skills, socialization, and motor skills.

Articulation Survey. In this survey the child is required to identify twenty common objects. The examiner notes the initial, medial, and final sounds of those words.

Home Survey. This questionnaire is completed by the parent and addresses such issues as types of play materials available, numbers of books in the home, and the amount of responsibility that is given to the child.

Health History Survey. This also is completed by the parent and simply provides a general indication of the child's medical history, including information related to the birth of the child.

Behavior Survey. This survey is completed by the test administrator after the cognitive/language and motor profiles have been administered. This section can be completed in approximately two minutes and provides information related to such areas as attention span, activity level, and cooperativeness.

Two levels of scoring are available for the ESP.

Interpretation of Results.   The ESP has two levels of scoring. In Level I, the individual profiles and total screening are reported in screening indexes that range from one to six. Each index represents a range of performance expressed in various standard deviation units from the mean. For example, a screening index of 1 represents performance that is two standard deviations or more below the mean, whereas a screening index of 5 represents a performance one to two standard deviations above the mean. For Level II, a variety of derived scores are available, including standard scores (mean = 100; standard deviation = 15), percentile ranks, normal curve equivalents, stanines, and age equivalents. Scores for the individual subtests and domains and the profiles are also available (both Level I and Level II scoring). Scoring of the surveys result in descriptive categories of "above average," "average," and "below average." The Health History Survey is not scored. The manual provides suggestions on ways of combining profiles and the effect this has on the referral rate. Overall, the manual discusses the issue of interpretation to a significant extent.

Technical Characteristics

Normative Sample.   More than 1,100 children, ages 2 through 6, were included in the standardization. The sample was stratified based on gender, geographic region, socioeconomic status, and race or ethnic group. The percentage of children in the sample was similar to the 1990 U.S. census data.

Reliability.   Internal consistencies using coefficient alpha were reported in the .80s and .90s range for all Profiles and Surveys with the exception of the Motor Profile (.60s and .70s), the Home Survey (.30s to .50s), and the Behavior Survey (primarily .70s). Test-retest reliability was determined for the profiles and total screening excluding the teacher-completed Self-Help/Social Profile. Again, the coefficients were in the .80s to .90s range except for Motor, which was reported at .70. Delayed test-retest reliability coefficients were somewhat lower than expected and were primarily in the .70s and .80s range except for Motor, which was .55. Interrater reliability was determined for the Motor Profile. Those correlations were acceptable, ranging from .80 to .99 for the various items.

Validity. A thorough discussion of validity can be found in the manual. Results of concurrent validity studies indicated moderate to good correlations with a variety of criterion measures. Results of predictive validity studies generally indicated good correlations (usually .60s and .70s). Statistical evidence of construct validity is also provided.

Review of Relevant Research. A few research studies were located in the professional literature. In one, Hall, Bramlett, Barnett, and Cox (1994) found that ESP had a moderate agreement with the *Developmental Indicators for the Assessment of Learning–Revised* when identifying children who were educationally at risk. Similarly, Lenkarski, Singer, Peters, and McIntosh (2001) found that ESP correctly classified 81 percent of preschoolers at risk for cognitive delay. McIntosh, Gibney, Quinn, and Kundert (2000) reported that it was a good predictor of the *Differential Ability Scales* total score. Emmons and Alfonso (2005) reported that it has adequate technical characteristics but that the norms need to be updated. Glascoe (2005) pointed out, however, that the ESP has very poor sensitivity.

Overview: AGS Early Screening Profiles

- *Age level*—2 through 6 years.
- *Type of administration*—Individual (child is tested, parent and teacher interviewed).
- *Technical adequacy*—Good reliability (except for Motor); good validity.
- *Scores yielded*—Screening indexes, standard scores, percentile ranks, normal curve equivalents, stanines, age equivalents.
- *Suggested use*—The AGS ESP provides an ecological screening that involves direct testing of the child and participation from the parent and teacher. A close inspection of the technical data indicates that the correlations between the teacher-completed and the parent-completed Self-Help/Social Profiles were relatively low. Subsequently, the choice of informant might affect screening decisions. Another technical issue is the low correlations between the motor domain of the Self-Help/Social Profile and the Motor Profile. The relatively poor reliability of the Motor Profile adds to its questionable use.

  Several features, however, make the ESP a valuable instrument. These include the use of multiple domains and sources of information; ease of administration and scoring; and compatibility with more inclusive instruments such as the KABC–II, the *Vineland Adaptive Behavior Scales–II*, and the *Bruininks-Oseretsky Test of Motor Proficiency.* (The individual authors of many of the Profiles and Surveys are the same as those of these more comprehensive instruments.) The idea of receiving multiple sources of information on which to base screening decisions is a good one. When interpreting the results of the ESP, the use of subtest scores (using Level II scoring) should probably be discouraged because of the lack of supportive reliability data. A training videotape is available for the AGS ESP that should assist in increasing its reliability.

The Motor Profile has some limitations.

Developmental Indicators for the Assessment of Learning–3

The *Development Indicators for the Assessment of Learning–3* (DIAL-3; Mardell-Czudnowski & Goldenberg, 1998) is the latest revision of this popular test. The DIAL-3 is easy and quick to administer (approximately thirty minutes). It is individually administered to identify children ages 3 through 6 who are in need of a more comprehensive evaluation. There is both an English and a Spanish version of the instrument. The DIAL-3 is often used in large screenings in which stations are set up for each set of tasks in a domain and the children and their parents circulate among the stations.

The DIAL-3 uses both direct testing and parent input.

Description.   The DIAL-3 consists of items that measure the areas of Language, Concepts, Motor Skills, Self-Help Development, and Social Development. These reflect the five domains that were identified for assessment in Public Law 99-457. The items in the Language domain measure both expressive and receptive skills. The Concepts domain focuses on skills such as counting. Both fine-motor and gross-motor items are included in the Motor domain. Self-Help assesses the child's adaptive behavior such as eating and dressing. Finally, the Social area focuses on the child's interactions with parents, siblings, peers, and teachers. There is also an abbreviated version of the DIAL-3 called the Speed DIAL, which includes selected items from the Language, Concepts, and Motor domains. This can be administered in approximately fifteen minutes. Finally, there are supplemental, shorter rating scales for the areas of social/emotional and intelligibility.

Interpretation of Results.   A five-point scale (0–4) is used to obtain item scores for the Language, Concepts, and Motor areas. These scores are combined to determine the DIAL-3 total score. The Self-Help and Social items are scored as 0, 1, or 2 and are added to obtain the raw score for each area. Percentile ranks and standard scores are available for both the total test and for the five areas. One advantage of the DIAL-3 is the use of cutoff scores for ± 1, $1\frac{1}{2}$, and 2 standard deviations.

Technical Characteristics

Normative Sample.   A stratified sample of 1,560 English-speaking and 605 Spanish-speaking children were included in the standardization of the different versions and components of the DIAL-3. The children were matched with the 1994 census data related to gender, geographic region, ethnic background, and parents' education.

Reliability.   Internal consistency coefficients ranged from .66 to .85 for the areas and was .87 for the total score. The speed DIAL coefficient was .80. Test-retest coefficients were generally in the .70s and .80s for the areas and averaged .86 and .83 for the total score and the Speed DIAL score in samples from two age groups.

Validity.   Results of several studies determining the criterion-related validity of the DIAL-3 are reported in the manual. These studies generally show a moderate correlation with a variety of criterion measures, including language tests and intelligence tests. In addition, higher coefficients are reported with other developmental instruments. The manual also includes discussions regarding the content validity and construct validity of the instrument.

Review of Relevant Research.   A few reviews and empirical studies on the 1983 DIAL-R were found. Most of those studies cautioned against using the area scores to obtain a developmental profile (e.g. Barnett, Faust, & Sarmir, 1988). The DIAL-3, however, has vastly improved its technical characteristics, including the standardization, in the two revisions since that edition. In a review of the DIAL-3, Strawser and Sileo (1998–1999) felt that it was a comprehensive screening test with many desirable features. Two in particular were the availability of the Speed DIAL for a quick assessment of developmental skills and the Spanish version of the DIAL-3. There is a limited amount of research on the DIAL-3. Emmons and Alfonso (2005) reported that it has adequate technical characteristics but that the norms need to be updated. Glascoe (2005) did note, however, that the DIAL-3 does not report any sensitivity or specificity information. In addition, it appears that the DIAL-3 (Anthony, Assel, & Williams, 2007) and the DIAL-3 Spanish Version (Anthony & Assel, 2007) measure three factors: verbal ability, nonverbal ability, and achievement.

Overview: Developmental Indicators for the Assessment of Learning–3

- *Age level*—2 through 6 years.
- *Type of administration*—Individual.
- *Technical adequacy*—Good standardization; acceptable reliability and validity (particularly for total score).
- *Scores yielded*—Cutoff scores, standard scores, percentile ranks.
- *Suggested use*—The DIAL-3 is a quick screening device for the identification of gifted children and those with disabilities. The items on the DIAL-3 are a typical sample of those found on most developmental tests.

    The DIAL-3 added the areas of Self-Help and Social to be consistent with the assessment areas identified in P.L. 99-457. The Speed DIAL can be helpful when a very quick developmental screening is needed. For example, many districts have a two-tiered screening, in which a quick screen such as the Speed DIAL is administered initially. Those who fail that screen get a more comprehensive screen. This actually saves time because not all the children have to receive the more comprehensive screen. Finally, the fact that all of the DIAL-3 components have been translated into Spanish is a nice feature. Also available is a training video, a report to parents, and computer scoring software.

Developmental Inventories (Norm-Referenced)

Why Use Norm-Referenced Developmental Tests?

Screening; establishment of educational need (developmental lag); assistance in eligibility decisions; establishment of IEP goals.

Who Should Use Them?

Teachers, school psychologists, social workers.

Battelle Developmental Inventory–2

The *Battelle Developmental Inventory–2* (BDI-2; Newborg, 2004) is a revision of an instrument that was initially developed through funding from the U.S.

Department of Education. It is designed to measure developmental skills in children birth to age 8. It can be used for a variety of purposes, including:

1. Assessment of typically developing children
2. Assessment and identification of children with disabilities or developmental delay
3. Planning and providing instruction and intervention
4. Evaluating early childhood programs

The BDI-2 measures five domains.

Description.   The BDI-2 consists of 450 items that measure thirteen areas (subdomains) that are grouped into five separate domains: Adaptive, Personal-Social, Communication, Motor, and Cognitive. A screening version of the BDI-2 is also available that can be used as a quicker assessment of the five domains. The screening version includes 100 of the 450 items found in the BDI-2.

> *Adaptive.* Measures Self-Care and Personal Responsibility.
>
> *Personal-Social.* Includes the subdomains of Adult Interaction, Peer Interaction, and Self-Concept and Social Role.
>
> *Communication.* Measures both Receptive and Expressive Communication.
>
> *Motor.* Includes the subdomains of Gross Motor, Fine Motor, and Perceptual Motor.
>
> *Cognitive.* Includes the subdomains of Attention and Memory, Reasoning and Academic Skills, and Perception and Concepts.

Interpretation of Results.   Raw scores from the BDI-2 can be converted to a variety of scores including developmental quotients, scaled scores, percentile ranks, and age equivalents. The scaled scores for the subdomains have a mean of 10 and a standard of deviation of 3. The developmental quotients for the five domains and the total score have a mean of 100 and a standard deviation of 15. For the BDI-2 Screening Test, scores are also provided to assist in the identification of children who need additional evaluation. A summary page provides a visual representation of the child's developmental strengths and weaknesses (see Figure 15.2). Computer software and a Web-based scoring option are available as well as an electronic record form that eliminates paperwork.

Technical Characteristics

Normative Sample.   A total of 2,500 children from birth to age 8 were included. The normative sample was stratified according to geographic region, sex, race/ethnicity, and socioeconomic status (determined by mothers' educational level). The percentages were compared to the 2001 Census.

Reliability.   Internal reliability coefficients (split-half) for the domains ranged from .90 (Adaptive) to .96 (Personal-Social). The coefficient for the total BDI-2 Developmental Quotient was .99. Test-retest coefficients ranged from .87 (Cognitive) to .92 (Adaptive and Motor) and was .94 for the total score. Interscorer reliability was determined for 17 items that required subjective scoring and ranged from 94 to 99 percent.

Validity.   The author says that content validity was addressed through professional judgments, coverage of important constructs, and empirical item analysis. Criterion-related validity was determined using the orignal BDI and the *Bayley*

FIGURE 15.2   Summary Sheet from the Battelle Developmental Inventory–2

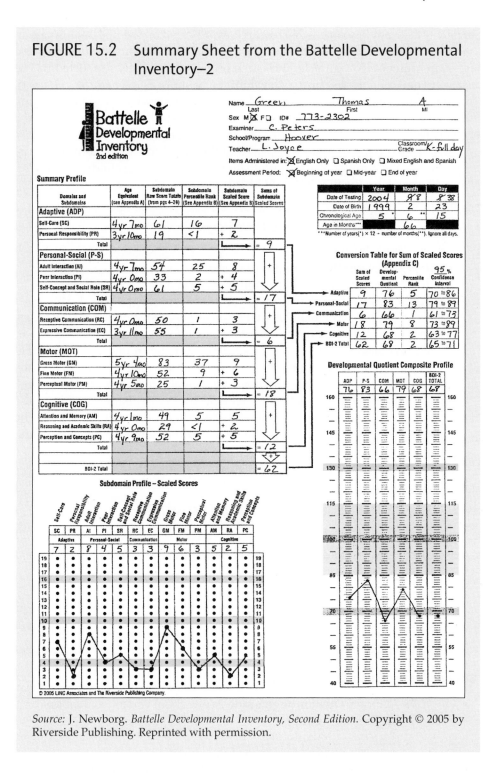

Source: J. Newborg. *Battelle Developmental Inventory, Second Edition.* Copyright © 2005 by Riverside Publishing. Reprinted with permission.

Scales of Infant Development–2. Coefficients for like areas were generally in the .60s and the .70s. Correlations with a number of instruments that measure specific domains were also reported. Evidence that the test discriminates between typically developing children and special populations is also provided. Finally, construct validity was determined by showing increases in scores as a function of age as well as factor analysis.

Review of Relevant Research.   No research was located on the BDI-2, although in one review, Bliss (2007) pointed out that the reliability data are strong and it is a useful instrument to administer. Research on the original BDI supported its use as a valid and reliable measure of developmental skills. The screening version of the BDI, however, was shown to significantly overidentify children as needing further evaluation. Summaries of several research studies can be found at the Earlier Research link for Chapter 15 on the Companion Website (www .prenhall.com/taylor8e). It does appear that the BDI-2 addressed some of the issues (such as the number of appropriate items for very young children) in the revision. Research on the BDI-2 should be forthcoming.

Overview: Battelle Developmental Inventory-2

- *Age level*—Birth to 8 years.
- *Type of administration*—Individual.
- *Technical adequacy*—Good reliability and validity.
- *Scores yielded*—Standard scores, percentile ranks, age equivalents.
- *Suggested use*—The BDI-2 is a well constructed developmental inventory that provides a helpful profile of a child's developmental strengths and weaknesses. Several improvements were made in the revised edition. These included additional items, expanded normative sample, and the option of an electronic record form. One helpful feature is an "item page" that is available for each item that specifically explains everything the examiner needs to know about administering and scoring that item. The BDI-2 promises to be one of the better norm-referenced developmental inventories.

The item page assists in the administration and scoring.

Readiness and Preacademic Instruments

Why Use Readiness and Preacademic Instruments?
Screening; establishment of IEP goals; grouping for instruction.

Who Should Use Them?
Teachers.

Boehm Test of Basic Concepts–3

- *Age level*—Kindergarten through grade 2 (preschool version available).
- *Type of administration*—Group.
- *Technical adequacy*—Limited.
- *Scores yielded*—Percentiles, performance ranges.
- *Description*—The *Boehm Test of Basic Concepts–3* (Boehm-3; Boehm, 2000) is a group-administered instrument designed to measure a child's mastery of concepts that are necessary for successful performance early in school. It is used with children in kindergarten and first and second grades. The author states that the test can be used both to identify children who have problems in the tested area and to identify specific concepts that need to be emphasized or taught. A separate preschool version called the *Boehm–3 Preschool* (Boehm, 2001) includes twenty-six items designed for children ages 3 to 5.

In general, the concept categories of space, quantity, and time are measured, as well as a miscellaneous category. Both the *Boehm-3* and the *Boehm-3 Preschool* are available in Spanish.

Bracken Basic Concept Scales–Third Edition

- *Age level*—3 through 6 years.
- *Type of administration*—Individual.
- *Technical adequacy*—Good standardization, reliability, and validity.
- *Scores yielded*—Standard scores, percentile ranks, concept age equivalents, descriptive classification.
- *Description*—The *Bracken Basic Concept Scale–Third Edition–Receptive* (Bracken, 2006a) and the *Bracken Basic Concept Scale–Third Edition–Expressive* (Bracken, 2006b) are complementary instruments designed to measure receptive and expressive concepts necessary for academic success. According to the publisher, these instruments are aligned with states' early childhood standards. The publisher provides a Website so users can see how the tests are aligned with their state's standards. The concepts that are measured include colors, letters/sounds, numbers/counting, size comparisons, shapes, direction/position, self-/social awareness, texture/material, quantity, and time/sequence. Also available is the *Bracken Concept Development Program* that provides activities, worksheets, and lesson plans correlated with the assessment instruments.

Metropolitan Readiness Tests–Sixth Edition

- *Age level*—Preschool to beginning first grade.
- *Type of administration*—Group or individual.
- *Technical adequacy*—Excellent standardization, adequate reliability, questionable validity.
- *Scores yielded*—Percentile ranks, stanines, performance ratings, scaled scores, normal curve equivalents.
- *Description*—The *Metropolitan Readiness Tests–Sixth Edition* (MRT-6; Nurss, 1994) is the oldest and most widely used readiness test. The 1994 edition has maintained many of the features of earlier editions. It is heavily weighted toward preacademic skills (e.g., beginning consonants) as opposed to perceptual or developmental skills. The standardization sample was large and representative. The MRT-6 has many nice features, including two levels and both norm-referenced and criterion-referenced scoring options. An easel kit is available for individual testing.

> The MRT-6 can be group administered.

Developmental Inventories (Criterion-Referenced)

Why Use Criterion-Referenced Developmental Tests?
Development of IEP goals and objectives; IEP evaluation.

Who Should Use Them?
Teachers.

Behavioral Characteristics Progression–Revised

The BCP-R has over 2,300 items.

The *Behavioral Characteristics Progression*–Revised (BCP-R; Vort Corporation, 2001) is a continuum of behaviors in chart form. It contains more than 2,300 observable traits referred to as behavioral characteristics. These behavioral characteristics are grouped into fifty-six criterion-referenced categories called *strands.*

This tool was intended to assist teachers of exceptional children to structure the teaching of the various areas they are asked to cover into a more coherent and manageable sequence. Particular care was taken to address the self-help, emotional, and practically oriented academic skills commonly needed by the special education student. Many of the strands are appropriate for older individuals with severe or profound disabilities as well.

As an *assessment* tool, the BCP-R provides the teacher with a comprehensive chart of pupil behaviors to aid in identifying which behavioral characteristics a pupil displays or does not display. As an *instructional* tool, the BCP assists the teacher in developing individualized, appropriate learner objectives for each student. As a *communication* tool, the BCP-R offers a historical recording device that, throughout the education of the student, can be used to indicate progress.

Description. Each strand contains up to fifty behaviors to measure the areas of cognition, language, gross-motor, fine-motor, social, self-help, and vocational skills. The evaluator chooses the strand or strands most appropriate for the person being evaluated. One nice feature is the inclusion of instructional activities that are correlated with the specific behaviors located in the strands. There are literally thousands of teacher-developed instructional activities for 1,900 of the behavior characteristics included in the BCP-R.

Interpretation of Results. For each student, the strands selected are noted in an individual record booklet. A baseline for each strand is determined by measuring the behavior characteristics. The behavior characteristics are scored according to the following system: (−), behavior not displayed; (½), behavior exhibited, but less frequently than the recommended 75 percent required incidence level; (✓), behavior displayed at the 75 percent level with no assistance; (H), physical disability prevents demonstrations of behavior. From this information, objectives can be delineated, and progress toward them can be monitored.

Overview: Behavioral Characteristic Progression–Revised

Booklets of instructional suggestions are available.

- *Age level*—No age provided.
- *Suggested use*—The BCP-R is a comprehensive criterion-referenced instrument. Although it is designed for individuals with a wide range of abilities, a number of its items deal with lower-level skills. Booklets of instructional suggestions that are correlated with the strands are also available. One potential disadvantage of the test is that it can be cumbersome if the number of strands is not limited.

Brigance Inventory of Early Development–II

The *Brigance Inventory of Early Development–II* (Brigance, 2004) was designed for use with individuals below developmental age 7. It can be used to identify strengths and weaknesses, to determine instructional objectives, and to indicate the individual's approximate developmental level in various areas. It can also be used as an ongoing evaluation system to monitor progress.

Description. The *Brigance Inventory of Early Development–II* measures abilities in eleven skill areas. These eleven areas include numerous *assessments,* which are essentially task analyses of the skill areas. A number of supplemental sequences are also available. One feature of the revised inventory is the inclusion of *comprehensive skill sequences.* These are more detailed sequences that can be used with children with more severe disabilities or others for whom the need for smaller steps is apparent. A nice feature is the option of obtaining normative information for forty-six of the assessments. Available are age equivalents and standard scores for five domains and ten subdomains.

Following is a list of the eleven skill areas:

Preambulatory Motor Skills and Behaviors
Gross-Motor Skills and Behaviors
Fine-Motor Skills and Behaviors
Self-Help Skills
Speech and Language Skills
General Knowledge and Comprehension
Social and Emotional Development
Readiness
Basic Reading Skills
Manuscript Writing
Basic Math

Interpretation of Results. Most notable in the interpretation of results are the instructional objectives that are spelled out based on the student's performance. As noted earlier, age equivalents and standard scores are also available for some of the assessments.

Overview: Brigance Inventory of Early Development–II

- *Age level*—Birth to 7 years.
- *Suggested use*—The *Brigance Inventory of Early Development–II* is a comprehensive test measuring eleven major skill areas. The test should not be given in its entirety; rather, the evaluator should choose the most appropriate areas to measure. The addition of the comprehensive sequences is a nice feature. The newest version of the *Brigance Inventory of Early Development* does provide some norm-referenced information.

There is now a normative scoring option for some areas.

Vulpé Assessment Battery–Revised

The *Vulpé Assessment Battery–Revised* (Vulpé-R; Vulpé, 1996) is a developmentally based system for measuring behaviors of children from birth to age 6. Information from the Vulpé can be used to determine an appropriate specific teaching approach, to indicate program goals and objectives, and to provide an accountability system for individual programs. The author states that the assessment battery is applicable to all children, including those who have multiple disabilities, are at-risk, and are typically developing. She further states that the battery is extremely comprehensive, individualized, and competency-oriented. The Vulpé-R is divided into six developmental skill areas or sections, and further divided into subskill areas or subsections. Each developmental skill area is sequentially based.

Description.   Many items on the *Vulpé Assessment Battery–Revised* appear in more than one of the instrument's six skill areas or sections. In order to eliminate the need to administer an item more than once, those that are included in more than one section are cross-referenced on the assessment form. In addition, all the equipment necessary and the instructions for administering each item are included on the record form. The skill areas are as follows:

> Gross Motor Behaviors
> Fine Motor Behaviors
> Language
> Cognitive Processes
> Activities of Daily Living
> Adaptive Behaviors

The Vulpé-R has a unique and valuable scoring system.

Interpretation of Results.   Each item on the Vulpé-R is given one of seven possible scores. A *no* score is given if the child has no apparent interest or motivation to participate in the task or cannot attend to the task. An *attention* score is given when a child shows any interest in any part of the activity but does not actively participate, whether because of physical incapacity or insufficient attention. A *physical assistance* score is used if a child actively participates in the activity when the task or environment is modified. A *social-emotional assistance* score is given when the child participates in the task when given more feedback, reinforcement, or reassurance. A *verbal assistance* score is given when the child's performance changes if verbal cues are given or the instructions repeated. An *independent* score is assigned when the student succeeds with no assistance within familiar surroundings. Finally, a *transfer* score is given when the student can perform tasks of similar complexity in different environments.

These scores can be marked directly on the Performance Analysis/Developmental Assessment scoring pad (Figure 15.3). In addition, comments about a child's performance (such as "did not perform due to sensory impairment") can be included. Age levels are provided for the items, but they represent gross indicators and should be used only to evaluate relative strengths and weaknesses.

Overview: Vulpé Assessment Battery–Revised

- *Age level*—Birth to 6 years.
- *Suggested use*—The Vulpé-R offers a highly comprehensive assessment of developmental skills of children between birth and age 6. Its comprehensiveness, in fact, might be considered one of its faults. It takes a good deal of time to administer and score all the appropriate items using the Vulpé-R system. The results, however, are more meaningful than those yielded from most developmental tests, particularly for use in educational programming. On the other hand, the relatively few items in certain subsections is a limitation.

FIGURE 15.3   Scoring Sheet from the Vulpé Assessment Battery

Performance analysis/developmental assessment

Name _____   Birthdate _____

Developmental area _____

Date _____   Manual page _____

Comments

Scale score   Information processing and activity analysis

No	Attention	Phys. assis.	Soc./emot. assis.	Verbal assis.	Independent	Transfer
1	2	3	4	5	6	7

1. Analyze activities considering component parts of each and relationship to: Basic Senses and Functions, Organizational Behaviors, Cognitive Processes and Specific Concepts, Auditory Language, Gross and Fine Motor

2. Information processing Consider:
Input
Integration
Feedback
Assimilation
Output

Activity (item number)

1 2 3 4 5 6 7

Activity (item number)

1 2 3 4 5 6 7

Activity (item number)

1 2 3 4 5 6 7

Activity (item number)

1 2 3 4 5 6 7

Activity (item number)

1 2 3 4 5 6 7

Source: S. Vulpé. *Vulpé Assessment Battery.* Copyright © 1979 by the National Institute on Mental Retardation, Ontario, Canada. Reprinted with permission.

Additional Developmental Inventories

Assessment Log and Developmental Progress Chart–Infants

- *Age level*—Birth to 24 months.
- *Description*—The *Assessment Log and Developmental Progress Chart–Infants* (Johnson-Martin, Jens, Attermeier, & Hecker, 2004) is part of the *Carolina Curriculum for Infants and Toddlers with Special Needs*. It includes items that are correlated with twenty-four curriculum sequences and is presented in checklist format. The instrument is largely based on Piaget's theory. There is also a separate *Assessment Log and Developmental Progress Chart–Preschoolers* (Johnson-Martin, Attermeier, & Hecker, 2004) that consists of twenty-five skills sequences. The instrument is based on a well-researched model that shows promise in determining instructional goals as well as providing instructional procedures. It should be noted, however, that many of the items might need to be adapted and that care should be taken to choose the areas that are adaptive (functional for the child). There also is a general lack of data about the use of the curriculum and, subsequently, the assessment component with older students with severe or profound disabilities. There is mention in the manual of field test data that it did not find the use of the curriculum effective with this population on a short-term basis.

Callier–Azusa Scale

- *Age level*—Birth to 9 years.
- *Description*—The *Callier–Azusa Scale* (Stillman, 1978) is an individually administered instrument designed to assess the developmental level of children who are deaf, blind, or who have severe disabilities. It is designed to be administered by teachers or other individuals who are thoroughly familiar with the child. The author states that the child should be observed for at least two weeks, preferably in a classroom setting. It is one of the few scales specifically designed to use with individuals with sensory or motor deficits. Also, some of its items are designed for individuals with significant intellectual impairments. The tests should be used to determine strengths and weaknesses and to identify general educational goals rather than to assess an individual's developmental level. It measures five major areas broken down into eighteen subscales. The five areas are motor development, perceptual development, daily living skills, cognition, communication and language, and social development. More information about the subscales can be found in the case study of James in Chapter 17.

BACK TO THE PROFILE

Possible Answers to the Questions

1. **Why assess Mary?** There are perhaps a number of reasons to evaluate Mary. The fact that the screening indicated a developmental lag in a number of areas would justify a more comprehensive developmental evaluation to determine if she might qualify for a preschool special education program. In addition, if she did qualify, information would need to be gathered to assist in developing the IEP.

2. **Who should assess Mary?** Ideally, Mary would be evaluated by a team of professionals. This might include a preschool special education teacher, a speech/language clinician, a school psychologist trained in working with preschool children, and, if available, a

social worker and a physical therapist. Mary's mother would also be involved in the evaluation, providing information about Mary's developmental status.

3. **What procedure(s)/test(s) should be used?** The *Battelle Developmental Inventory–2* might be an appropriate instrument to use. It provides normative information that might be required in a number of states for eligibility decisions. It also measures a number of areas and could provide a developmental profile that indicates Mary's relative strengths and weaknesses. The appropriate developmental areas could be evaluated by the appropriate professional (i.e., Communication = speech-language clinician, Cognition = psychologist, Motor = physical therapist). The social worker could also interview Mary's mother about the Personal-Social and Adaptive domains while Mary is being tested. Ideally, this would be done as a team approach so each professional can see all of Mary's performance. Play-based assessment could also be used to provide additional information. For the development of the IEP, a more comprehensive criterion-referenced inventory such as the *Behavior Characteristics Progression–Revised* or the *Vulpé Assessment Battery–Revised* should be used. As with any instrument of this type, only those portions of the inventory that correspond to her problem areas would be administered.

4. **What other area(s) (if any) should be assessed?** If the above procedures were used, a comprehensive evaluation that provides information for eligibility and educational programming would have occurred. It is possible, however, that one or more of the professionals might have observed some area that needs additional assessment. For example, the speech-language clinician might have noticed problems in some language areas, such as phonology or syntax, that might warrant further testing.

CHILD PROFILE DATA

Mary

Mary and her mother were evaluated by the school district's early childhood assessment team, consisting of a psychologist, speech and language pathologist, early childhood special education teacher, and a social worker. Each team member administered the subtests from the *Battelle Developmental Inventory–2* unique to their discipline. The following results were obtained:

Domain/Subdomain	Standard/Scaled Score
Adaptive	78
Self-Care	6
Personal Responsibility	8
Personal-Social	77
Adult Interaction	7
Peer Interaction	8
Self-Concept and Social Role	8
Communication	71
Receptive	7
Expressive	6
Motor	75
Gross Motor	8
Fine Motor	6
Perceptual Motor	7
Cognitive	85
Attention and Memory	9
Reasoning and Academic Skills	7
Perception and Concepts	7

These results indicate that Mary is below average in every area measured. Her lowest scores were in self-care, expressive communication, and fine motor skills. A relative strength was noted in attention and memory. Depending on the criteria that Mary's state uses, it is likely that she might qualify for IDEA 04 services under a category such as Developmental Delay.

CASE STUDY *June*

- After reviewing the nature of the assessment instruments and procedures in this chapter, would it be appropriate to give any of them to June? Why or why not?

Reflections

1. Can you think of any disadvantages of using play-based assessment exclusively to evaluate a 3-year-old child with apparent developmental problems? If so, what are they?

2. If you had to make a screening decision about a young child, knowing that some error exists, would you rather make a false positive error or a false negative error? Why?

3. In some states, results of a developmental inventory such as the *Battelle Developmental Inventory–2* may be enough to qualify the child for special education services. Do you think this is a good idea? Why or why not?

Summary Matrix

Instrument or Technique	Suggested Use: Screening and Initial Identification (Preferral)	Informal Determination and Evaluation of Teaching Programs and Strategies	Determination of Current Performance Level and Educational Need (Postreferral)	Decisions about Classification and Program Placement	IEP Goals	IEP Objectives	IEP Evaluation	Target Population: Mild/Moderate	Severe/Profound	Preschool	Elementary Age	Secondary Age	Adult	Special Considerations	Educational Relevance for Exceptional Students
AGS Early Screening Profiles	X							X		X				Uses a team approach including information from the parent; motor section limited.	Useful
Developmental Indicators for the Assessment of Learning–3	X							X		X				Has been used for early identification of disabled and gifted; quick to administer.	Adequate/Useful
Battelle Developmental Inventory–2	X	X			X			X	X	X	X			Well constructed; measures five developmental domains; limited with very young children.	Useful
Boehm Test of Basic Concepts–3	X	X			X			X		X	X			Best used informally; normative information of questionable relevance.	Useful
Bracken Basic Concept Scales–Third Edition	X	X			X			X		X	X			Well constructed; has a receptive and expressive scale.	Useful
Metropolitan Readiness Tests–Sixth Edition	X							X		X	X			Good technical aspects; comprehensive.	Useful
Behavioral Characteristics Progression–Revised			X		X	X	X	X	X	X				Instructional suggestions that are correlated with most items are available.	Useful
Brigance Inventory of Early Development–II			X		X	X	X	X	X	X				Includes objectives for each item; developmental age equivalents should be used informally only.	Adequate
Vulpé Assessment Battery–Revised			X		X	X	X	X	X	X				Has a tedious scoring system that yields important programmatic information.	Useful
Assessment Log and Developmental Progress Chart–Infants			X		X	X	X	X	X	X				Used in conjunction with the Carolina curriculum.	Useful
Callier–Azusa Scale			X		X				X	X				Designed for use with children who are deaf-blind.	Adequate

chapter sixteen

Career/Vocational/ Transition Assessment

STUDENT PROFILE

Jill

Jill is a seventh-grade student with Down syndrome who is receiving services as a student with moderate mental retardation. Her educational program has focused primarily on functional academics. She is in an inclusion classroom that uses a collaborative model. Within this system, Jill receives most of her instruction from the special education teacher who is in the room. Both her parents and teachers feel that it is important to begin a vocational program to give her some job skills. Jill is very interested in working in a factory like her dad.

STUDENT PROFILE

Sue

Sue is a senior in high school who has a learning disability, primarily in math. She is doing well in all of her other subjects and is in an honors English class. Her transition statements in her IEP all indicate that Sue could pursue postsecondary education. Lately, however, she is having second thoughts and is fearful of college math. She also doesn't know what she would major in. During the summer, she worked for a large video store taking inventory. She is afraid, however, that if she goes back she will be asked to run the cash register.

Think about the Following Questions as You Read This Chapter:

1. Why assess Jill and Sue? (There could be more than one reason.)
2. Who should assess Jill and Sue? (There could be more than one person.)
3. What procedure(s)/test(s) should be used?
4. What other area(s) (if any) should be assessed?

(Suggested answers appear at the end of this chapter.)

The emphasis on vocational/transitional programs, particularly for secondary-level students, continues to increase. As noted in Chapter 1, transition must be included in a student's IEP by the age of 16. Along with increased emphasis on transitional/vocational programming comes an increased emphasis on transitional/ vocational assessment. Recently, the Division on Career Development and Transition of the Council for Exceptional Children stressed that vocational assessment should be integrated with mandated statewide assessments and alternate assessments. Also, each assessment situation presents an opportunity for students with disabilities to learn to advocate for the types of accommodations needed in various assessments (Blalock et al., 2003).

Although in the past the focus of vocational assessment was on the use of formal instruments, current trends in the field are toward more informal techniques that help develop a more encompassing database that can and should stretch across a student's school career. Although traditional assessment procedures have not been abandoned, this shift has led to a more transdisciplinary approach to vocational assessment. In turn, this has led to shared responsibilities and cooperative planning and programming that are necessary to achieve successful postschool adjustments for students with disabilities (Gil, 2007). Although the specific role that vocational assessment and education specialists might play is dictated by funding and various state and local program needs, the special education teacher can and should be familiar with the techniques included in this chapter. Aside from some of the specific tests and inventories, virtually all other procedures can be implemented by classroom teachers although special education teachers may not be in a position to coordinate all the complex processes involved in transition planning and programming (Blalock et al., 2003).

If vocational assessment is conducted and the information is used appropriately, it is logical to assume that vocational programming goals on IEPs, vocational programs, and curricula and the quality of transition services will improve. With these improvements, we should also see much more positive postschool results for students with disabilities. Sitlington and Clark (2001) gave an overview of the overall purposes of career/vocational assessment. They stated:

> Career/vocational assessment is a planned, continuous process of obtaining, organizing, and using information on an individual's strengths, needs, preferences, and interests as they relate to his/her career choices and employment. This process includes gathering information in the areas of employment, self-determination, inter-personal relationships, and communication and academic performance. The purpose of this assessment is to assist each individual and his/her family in making all critical transitions related to career paths and employment both successful and satisfying. (p. 5)

It is apparent then, that career/vocational/transition assessment incorporates many procedures previously discussed related to areas such as academics, communication skills, and social and personal adjustment. It also involves procedures and instruments more specific to vocational and transition service delivery.

Career/vocational assessment has evolved from and employs the talents of several professional discipline areas (Sitlington & Clark, 2006). Not surprisingly then, vocational assessment has traditionally involved a wide variety of procedures. These have included describing a student's strengths, needs, interests and preferences, vocational training, personal, social, and educational goals, ability to

Three levels of vocational assessment have been suggested.

live independently, and function in the community (Sitlington & Clark, 2006). More specifically, vocational assessment may rely on the use of interviews and rating scales, psychometric testing, the use of work samples, curriculum-based assessment techniques, and situational assessment (Sitlington & Clark, 2006).

Michaels (1998) noted that most states conceptualize career/vocational assessment in terms of three levels of intensity. Level I assessments are given to all students with disabilities and typically prior to age 14 years. At this level, data gathered previously in the school career are often reviewed. At Level II, assessments are conducted for the specific purpose of developing goals and objectives related to the transition planning process. Paper-and-pencil inventories and aptitude tests would be examples of this level of assessment. Level III assessments focus on vocational outcomes and might include work samples, situations, and authentic assessments (Michaels, 1998). Curriculum-based vocational assessments might prove useful at all three levels. Additionally, person-centered vocational assessment and career planning have emerged to facilitate personal choice and empowerment of people with disabilities (Menchetti & Piland, 1998).

In this chapter, the current trends in transition planning and programming will be discussed with particular reference to federal mandates that influence vocational assessment and education for students with disabilities. The steps in developing transition goals and the role of vocational assessment in that process will also be addressed. The development and use of work samples are included, as well as the basis and strategies for the use of curriculum-based vocational assessment and direct observation of students on the job. Finally, information concerning a number of relevant and commonly used psychometric instruments used in assessing students' vocational interests and aptitude will be provided.

It is worth noting that some experts differentiate between vocational assessment and career assessment (a focus on life-long career development) (Sitlington & Clark, 2006). In this chapter, the terms will be used interchangeably and are intended to include both processes.

Support for Transition Services

Interest has increased in and requirements developed for providing transition services for students with disabilities that will better prepare them for the world of work. In 1984, Madeleine Will, then director of the Office of Special Education and Rehabilitative Services, wrote a position statement concerning the delivery of transition services to individuals with disabilities. She noted that the transition period includes high school, graduation, postsecondary placement, and initial years of employment. Transition planning and programming is a process that requires sound preparation and adequate support. Will stated that successful transitions require an effort that emphasizes shared responsibilities among service agencies.

Several legislative acts have supported the need for cooperative planning and service delivery to ensure successful transition programs. Such legislation has been necessary because the assimilation of people with disabilities into the mainstream workforce has yet to reach an optimal level (Johnson & Rusch, 1993; Rusch & Phelps, 1987). Many educators, however, believe that in addition to legislative mandates, actual transition planning and programming will be required to provide better opportunities for individual students with disabilities who are leaving school and entering the "real world."

In 1983, Public Law 98-199, Section 626, "Secondary Education and Transitional Services for Handicapped Youth," was enacted specifically to increase the likelihood of successful school-to-work transitions for students with disabilities. Other legislative acts such as the Americans with Disabilities Act (P.L. 101-336) provide protection against discrimination and require reasonable accommodations in the workplace for people with handicaps (Linthicum, Cole, & D'Alonzo, 1991). In 1984, the Carl D. Perkins Vocational Education Act expanded the services provided to students with disabilities through vocational education and assessment to include transition planning and programming.

The Carl D. Perkins Act expanded vocational and transition services.

Carl D. Perkins Vocational and Applied Technology Education Act

The Carl D. Perkins Act provided for an increase in the accessibility to vocational education services for special education students. Wehman, Moon, Everson, Wood, and Barcus (1988) outlined the following provisions of the Act that affect services to youths with disabilities: (1) 10 percent of a state's grant allotment be used to provide services to students with disabilities, (2) each student and his/her parents be informed of vocational opportunities available at least one year before the provision of vocational education services (or by the time the student reaches ninth grade), and (3) equal access be provided to vocational educational services as deemed appropriate through the IEP process. These services may include (1) vocational assessment, (2) guidance and career counseling and development, (3) adaptation of curriculum and provision of special services to meet individual needs, and/or (4) staff and counseling services to facilitate successful transitions.

More recently, the reauthorization of the Carl D. Perkins Career and Technical Education Act of 2006 included the following provisions related to students with disabilities (Association for Career and Technical Education & Brustein, 2006):

- Performance on state achievement and graduation tests to be reported to the federal government.
- The extent to which students with disabilities are prepared for subsequent employment in high-skill, high-wage occupations or are prepared for post-secondary education.
- Carry out scientifically based research and evaluation for the purpose of developing, improving, and identifying successful methods for the education, employment, and training of students with disabilities.
- Ensure that faculty and support personnel in the area of career and technical education, career guidance, and academic counseling are prepared to assist students with disabilities and their families.
- Ensure equal access and equal opportunity to education and training for students with disabilities.

This reauthorization emphasizes that students with disabilities should be given the best possible assessment and career educational opportunities to succeed as adults.

Other Important Legislative Acts

Amendments to the Rehabilitation Act of 1992 stressed the need for supported employment services (including students with the most severe disabilities) that could include vocational/transitional assessment (West, Johnson, Cone, Hernandez, & Revell, 1998). Of importance in establishing effective vocational/transitional programs is the development of vocational assessment and job development skills among transition specialists (DeFur & Taymans, 1995). Also, the 2004 reauthorization of the Individuals with Disabilities Education Act (IDEA) requires transition planning to begin no later than age 16. The School to Work Opportunities Act of 1994 stressed efforts to improve postschool outcomes for all youth.

Special education teachers should be capable of implementing, modifying, or adapting many of these practices in order to obtain vocational assessment data. Under current laws, students with disabilities and their families should also be involved in directing transition planning and programming that includes career/vocational education and assessment (Sitlington & Clark, 2006).

Guidelines for Establishing Transition Services: Importance of Career/Transition Assessment

Schriner and Bellini (1994) noted the emphasis that federal legislation places on transition services being based on individual need and being referenced to student preferences and interests. Services may include community-based experiences, training in adult living and daily living skills, and career/transition assessment. The Division on Career Development and Transition (DCDT) of the Council for Exceptional Children (n.d.) issued a position statement on age-appropriate transition assessment that reflects changes made in IDEA 04. The DCDT emphasizes that transition assessments should be related to the training, education, employment outcomes, and, when appropriate, independent living skills of students. The DCDT emphasizes that whatever specific assessment techniques are used, the results should:

- Help to construct realistic and meaningful IEP goals and objectives
- Inform programming decisions
- Provide information about a student's academic and other strengths, needs, interests, and preferences
- Help determine a student's career ambitions
- Assist students in making connections between their career ambitions and their academic program
- Assist in summarizing overall student performance

Other general guidelines include the following:

1. *Transition planning should begin no later than age 16, but can begin earlier.* The more barriers a student faces (e.g., behavioral difficulties, limited employment skills), the earlier the process should begin. Parents of students with severe disabilities and their teachers may wish to begin transition planning as early as the elementary school years. Transition values that focus on adult outcomes can provide guidance in developing appropriate educational programs and in what, when, and where to assess student performance, strengths, interests, preferences, and needs (Elrod, Isbell, & Braziel, 1989; Stodden & Leake, 1994).

2. *Career/vocational assessment becomes critical to the transition process as the student prepares for postsecondary adjustment.* During IEP discussions, a written vocational assessment report may be reviewed if available; otherwise relevant vocational assessment data should be discussed. That information should be used in deciding on vocationally-related goals and objectives, daily classroom activities implemented, vocational education, and vocational training placements (Meehan & Hodell, 1986; Wisniewski, Alper, & Schloss, 1991). Wisniewski and colleagues also stressed that systematic assessment by a transition specialist

Transition planning often starts before high school.

may assist in guiding community-based instruction, as well as ensure that the vocational curriculum is functional and relevant. One manner in which this may be accomplished is through curriculum-based vocational assessment (CBVA; Bisconer, Stodden, & Porter, 1993). Bisconer and colleagues noted that CBVA is "a process for determining the career/vocational needs of students based on their ongoing classroom and work experience activities and performances." CBVA is discussed in greater detail in a later section. Vocational assessment data are combined with those of other assessment specialists and educators to provide a total picture of the student's abilities, interests, and skills that might affect his or her postschool performance.

Other Important Considerations

Leconte and Neubert (1997) noted that when assessment information is not accurate, current, and relevant, transition planning falls apart. This necessitates the assessment process be ongoing and a shared responsibility. The DCDT (n.d.) emphasizes that assessment techniques may be formal or informal. Formal techniques can include: (1) adaptive behavior/daily living skills assessments to determine how much assistance a student might need; (2) aptitude tests to measure specific skills or abilities; (3) interest inventories to determine preferences for careers, employment activities, and different types of employment; (4) intelligence and achievement tests to determine cognitive and academic performance; (5) temperament inventories to determine dispositions toward different careers (such as whether one likes to work with other people); (6) self-determination assessments to determine the degree to which an individual is prepared to make decisions; and (7) transition planning inventories that address strengths and needs in areas such as postsecondary education and employment, community participation, and independent living.

Informal techniques may include: (1) interviews and questionnaires to determine a student's and others' perceptions regarding the student's performance, interests, needs, and so on; (2) direct observation of performance in school, employment, and other community settings; (3) curriculum-based assessments; and (4) ecological inventories/environmental analysis to examine strengths, needs, and skills required in various school, employment, and community environments (DCDT, n.d.).

Gil (2007) emphasized that the assessment process itself should involve the student with disabilities. The student should be taught whenever possible to examine and evaluate his or her own performance in academic, vocational, independent living, and personal/social skills. Gil noted that the assessment procedure should involve teaching self-evaluation and, when a student's disabilities do not permit this, the locus should shift to the parent if possible.

Students should be involved in self-assessment.

A 1998 position statement by the DCDT noted that self-determination and self-advocacy are important skills for all students. The DCDT noted that self-determination is promoted by having students and their families decide what needs to be assessed, how assessments will be conducted, and how results will be used (Field, Martin, Miller, Ward, & Wehmeyer, 1998). More specifically, the DCDT suggested that students may (1) reach agreement with educators and parents on assessment needs, (2) help decide what questions will be answered, (3) actively participate in data gathering, (4) offer suggestions and approve involvement from others engaged in assessment activities, (5) participate or conduct interviews to collect information for answering assessment questions, (6) assemble portfolio information, and (7) use assessment data to inform decisions and refine educational goals (Field et al., 1998). Wehmeyer (2001) stressed that assessment in self-determination must occur within an empowerment evaluation framework. That means, it is a collaborative assessment that focuses on the student with disabilities as both a self-evaluator and self-director of assessment. In this way, students are encouraged to assess themselves and develop goals that will help themselves and that will focus on their vision for the future.

Additionally, students should be assessed on social competence and social skills. Assessment of social competence refers to overall general quality of social performance whereas assessment of social skills refers to assessment of specific, observable interpersonal target behaviors. Both skills and competence should be assessed in reference to use in various settings and situations (Black & Ornelles, 2001).

Developing Transition Goals for the IEP

Transitions occur in or out of school regardless of whether there has been careful assessment-based planning (Thurlow & Elliott, 1998). Therefore, it is important that career/vocational assessment data be provided by a variety of individuals at the IEP meeting in order to develop desired outcomes and specific goals and objectives. The following are suggested steps adapted from Wehman and colleagues (1988) for implementing transition planning and programming. First, school/community/family teams may be organized that include school staff (e.g., transition specialists, vocational evaluators), community agency personnel (e.g., vocational rehabilitation counselors), and advocates involved with families and students with disabilities. These team members may serve on many IEP teams with the common purpose of transition planning and programming. These local interagency teams may facilitate coordination of transition services and vocational assessment activities for many students. Second, the IEP team meets as discussed in Chapter 2. Of importance is that all students 16 years of age or older must have a statement of needed transition services. At the IEP meeting (although team members may meet more frequently than for an annual review to ensure a smooth transition), emphasis should be on students participating in planning and decision making to the extent appropriate (Wehmeyer, 1998). Wehmeyer notes that involvement in the transition planning and programming is the "intuitive antecedent" to student-directed learning. Konrad and Test (2004) suggested that students can be involved in the IEP process through: (1) planning the IEP; (2) drafting the IEP; (3) meeting to revise the draft; and (4) implementing the IEP. The ability to use self-advocacy strategies in transition and IEP planning and programming are important areas of development for students with disabilities (DCDT, n.d.).

Following development of the transition goals, the IEP is implemented and progress monitored regularly. Of some importance is to schedule an exit meeting just before the student leaves school to discuss and ensure the continued provision of services as needed (Wehman et al., 1988). Followup assessments should be conducted to evaluate the effectiveness of the transition services for both the individual student and for the district/program in general (Johnson & Rusch, 1993). Outcomes assessment is discussed in greater detail in the Informal Procedures section that follows.

The statement of needed transition services may span a multiyear period, and IEP transition goals may involve adult service providers, family members, and other interested individuals. Transition goals are now part of the IEP process. They typically address at least three broad areas of long-term outcomes: employment/

Followup assessment is extremely important.

postsecondary education, residential/independent living, and community participation. IEP goals should be related to these long-term outcomes and support their achievement. Examples of specific activities related to these long-term outcome areas are investigating higher education institution options, possible living arrangements after graduation, and obtaining a driver's license and registering to vote. Persons responsible for each activity (such as parent and student, school counselor) are also identified, as well as the expected duration of the activities.

Sitlington, Neubert, and LeConte (1997) authored a position paper on transition assessment for the DCDT. DCDT stressed that transition assessment is ongoing and focuses on the needs, preferences, and interests of the individual as they relate to current and future working, educational, living, personal, and social environments. The data serve as the thread that forms the basis for defining goals to be included in the IEP. Therefore, transition assessment encompasses myriad variables. A variety of informal and formal assessment methods for assessing those variables will be discussed.

Informal Procedures

Checklists and Rating Scales

Why Use Checklists and Rating Scales?

Screening for career/vocational preferences, interests, and aptitudes; developing educational and vocational programs.

Who Should Use Them?

Teachers.

A variety of informal procedures might be used to evaluate career/vocational skills. Elrod and colleagues (1989) suggested that observational data and anecdotal records might be compiled and informal interviews conducted. Sample questions might include "What job would you like to have when you finish your education?" "Do you like to work alone or with others?" and "Would you prefer a desk job or a job where you can use your physical skills?" Elrod and colleagues pointed out that the *Brigance Diagnostic Inventory of Essential Skills* (discussed in Chapter 11) includes components in the vocational subtest that might serve as bases for either individual or group paper-and-pencil tasks or for interviewing. They also suggested that informal assessment of prevocational aptitudes (for grades 7 to 12) might involve the use of rating scales completed by the teacher that include items related to placement in vocational education or in private employment. Figure 16.1 shows an example of such a rating scale. Similar rating scales might be employed at actual job placements. For example, Burnham and Housley (1992) used a different survey, but one similar to that depicted in Figure 16.1, to compare perceptions of employers, adult service providers, and students with mental or learning disabilities. They found similarities and differences in the emphasis placed by each group on various dimensions of work behavior. Although checklists and rating scales may be easily employed by teachers, the information gleaned from such assessments might not provide a complete portrait of a student's aptitudes and abilities. Work samples, both commercially produced and locally validated, are an example of a more formal technique that might also provide useful information.

Informal rating scales can provide valuable information.

FIGURE 16.1   Prevocational Aptitude Rating Scale

Work Behavior		Rating			
1. Dresses appropriately	1	2	3	4	5
2. Is well groomed	1	2	3	4	5
3. Attends class regularly	1	2	3	4	5
4. Is punctual	1	2	3	4	5
5. Demonstrates initiative	1	2	3	4	5
6. Works well independently	1	2	3	4	5
7. Works well with peers	1	2	3	4	5
8. Works well with authority figures	1	2	3	4	5
9. Is receptive to constructive criticism	1	2	3	4	5
10. Shows pride in work	1	2	3	4	5
11. Keeps neat work area	1	2	3	4	5
12. Completes tasks on time	1	2	3	4	5
13. Asks questions, if needed	1	2	3	4	5
14. Accepts new responsibilities	1	2	3	4	5
15. Solicits additional duties when finished with a task	1	2	3	4	5

Rating Scale: 1 = Never observed; 2 = Observed sometimes; 3 = Observed about half of the time; 4 = Observed often; 5 = Always observed.

Source: G. Elrod, C. Isbell, and P. Braziel. Assessing Transition-Related Variables from Kindergarten through Grade 12. *Diagnostique, 14,* 259. Copyright © 1989 by Sage Publications Inc. Journals. Reprinted with permission of Sage Publications Inc. Journals in the format Textbook and Other book via Copyright Clearance Center.

Work Samples

Why Use Work Samples?

Evaluate performance of specific and general work skills and worker traits and characteristics.

Who Should Use Them?

Vocational assessment personnel.

Work samples are situational assessment tools used to simulate tasks associated with jobs in the labor market. The success of the use of work samples depends on the student's readiness for this type of assessment, the content of the sample, and the usefulness of the information gleaned for transition planning and programming (Thurlow & Elliott, 1998). These assessments are useful for determining an individual's interests, abilities, work habits, and social skills. A key to their administration is noting a student's interest level, attention to tasks, and requests for help or clarification, in addition to actual performance (Sitlington & Clark, 2001).

Work samples are both commercially and locally developed. Local development may allow for a better match between the work sample and actual jobs available in the local economy (Sitlington & Clark, 2006). Work samples are project- or product-oriented and allow the vocational evaluator to use systematic observation to record whether the student is able to perform on-the-job task requirements (Thurlow & Elliott, 1998). Such data might be useful in assessing a student's level

Locally developed work samples may be the most beneficial type.

of interest and attention to the task, requests for clarification or assistance, as well as the student's performance on the task. Work samples usually have standard directions, tasks, materials, and specific behaviors that the evaluator should be observing (Sitlington & Clark, 2006).

Curriculum-Based Vocational Assessment

Why Use Curriculum-Based Vocational Assessment?

Evaluate acquisition of vocational and related skills embedded within content and applied courses.

Who Should Use It?

Teachers; vocational assessment personnel.

Historically, vocational assessments were conducted without appropriate collaboration among student and their families, educators, adult service providers, and vocational evaluators. As a result, various difficulties emerged that resulted in fragmentation of services, substandard service delivery, and lack of coordination in referral, assessment, and programming efforts (Ianacone & LeConte, 1986). To address these problems, interested parties developed systems change projects resulting in better planning and service delivery as well as improved methods of assessment. One of those methods is curriculum-based vocational assessment (CBVA). CBVA can be conceived as an assessment approach as well as a specific method. It can, in fact, include criterion-referenced testing as well as portfolio assessment among other methods (Sitlington & Clark, 2001).

Thurlow and Elliot (1998) noted that CBVA may be used within existing resources, administered through performance-based activities, and provided within a vocational framework. For example, the student can be assessed on vocational/transitional skills present within the standard curriculum at school or within a vocational/transitional curriculum and/or in an individualized functional curriculum at school or in the community. Thus CBVA allows for assessing and planning within a variety of settings and contexts (Thurlow & Elliott, 1998). Kohler (1994) reported on a program in Florida that incorporated the use of CBVA to determine the effectiveness of classroom- and community-based instruction. The classroom-based component focused on employment-related skills taught in school. The community-based component focused on skill development and concurrent work experiences. Kohler noted that CBVA was a useful analytical tool for measuring curricular impact on student outcomes, strengths, and weaknesses. It also allowed educators to make individualized adjustments within the curriculum and vocational program.

CBVA requires training for general and special educators, as well as career/transition evaluators and specialists (Pierangelo & Giuliani, 2004). Figure 16.2 shows the key steps to developing a CBVA model. It is important to note that CBVA, as is curriculum-based assessment in general, is only as valid as the curriculum itself (Taylor, Willits, & Richards, 1988). That is, if the career/vocational course content is not meeting the needs of students, the assessment information may prove of little use. Additionally, students with more severe disabilities may not be participants in vocational education as experienced by students with milder disabilities. For these students (and for students with mild disabilities as noted earlier), direct observation of student performance at community-based work-experience sites yields data that may require fewer inferences about actual

CBVA provides a great deal of flexibility.

FIGURE 16.2   Key Steps to Curriculum-Based Vocational Assessment

1. Identify key development personnel.
   - Who are the key personnel needed to conceptualize, develop, and validate a curriculum-based vocational assessment model?
   - Who are the key personnel needed to operate and develop the vocational assessment model?
   - What disciplines and administrative personnel are critical to implementation and need to be represented?
2. Conduct a comprehensive search of program models, research literature, vocational evaluation/assessment instrumentation, and pertinent legislation.
   - What research is available concerning the efficacy of vocational assessment services in school-based settings?
   - What program models currently exist and what factors have influenced their effectiveness within the local education community and employment settings?
   - What factors influence validity and reliability in the collection of assessment data?
3. Establish basic considerations for the model based on previous research; analyze and synthesize the programmative needs. These considerations include tenants, i.e., vocational assessment:
   - Should be an integrated part of the total delivery of career/vocational services.
   - Should reflect preassessment readiness needs of the student and provide developmental growth information.
   - Should be a student-centered process with a career development orientation consisting of experiences to increase one's awareness, exploration, and understanding rather than a strict predictive procedure providing isolated ability data.
   - Should be based on the assessed employment needs of the local community and the applicable skills of the student to ensure key validity and efficacy factors contributing to the structure of the model.
   - Should measure key situational factors specific to work roles that can be critical determinants of interest and performance.
   - Should produce a wide variety of demonstratively useful information that can be assessed and used by several disciplines, the student, and the parents.
   - Who should coordinate and use the assessment information to make placement and programming decisions?
   - How will this information be applied to the development of individualized educational and vocational planning and program development?
4. Establish an operational plan to implement the process.
   - Where will vocational assessment activities occur?
   - Who will be assessed?
   - What information will be collected?
   - How will vocational assessment information be collected (instruments, activities, techniques)?
   - Who will conduct vocational assessment activities?
   - How will the vocational assessment information be gathered and organized?
   - Who will be responsible for coordinating information gathering, which includes facilitating, providing support, and monitoring?
   - Who will analyze, synthesize, and interpret vocational assessment findings to appropriate decision-making groups?
   - What time frame will be used for vocational assessment activities?
   - How will data collection be integrated and formalized as part of the instructional process?
   - How will the vocational assessment instrumentation be developed?
   - What specific competencies and specific related behaviors will be assessed?
   - How should the collected data be formatted and displayed for optimal application and use?
   - What evaluation criteria will be used to measure competency attainment and behaviors?
5. Pilot and evaluate the CBVA implementation activities.
   - What school(s) and personnel should be involved in field testing?
   - What steps need to be taken (additional inservice training, technical assistance, and ongoing support) to ensure the appropriate climate and expertise for full integration and application of the vocational assessment process in the pilot sites?

(continued)

FIGURE 16.2 *Continued*

- What criteria will be used to evaluate the process, instrumentation, and overall impact at the pilot site?
- What modifications need to be made to the process, instrumentation, or support mechanisms as a result of the pilot test?
- Who will make the modifications?
6. Implement, evaluate, and expand options.
- What additional steps need to be taken on a systemwide basis for full integration and application of the curriculum-based vocational assessment model and process?
- What specific evaluation data will be collected?
- What implementation and evaluation checkpoints need to be established?
- What additional course and activity settings would yield relevant career and vocational assessment information?
- What additional steps are needed to assist teachers to view their instructional processes and outcomes in a career or vocational context?

vocational interests, strengths, and weaknesses. Direct observation also provides information concerning behaviors (e.g., social interaction) that affect employability as well as the specific performance of the job itself.

Direct Observation and Ecological Assessment

Why Use Direct Observation and Ecological Assessment?

Evaluate performance of specific and general work skills and work-related behaviors; determine modifications for instruction.

Who Should Use Them?

Teachers, vocational assessment personnel, transition personnel.

In general, ecological assessment may involve quantitative measures (e.g., baseline and treatment measures of how often or how long a behavior occurs) or qualitative measures (e.g., adult demands, peer expectations, and conditions in the environment) (Evans, Gable, & Evans, 1993). Evans and colleagues emphasized that ecological assessment allows the teacher or evaluator to socially validate that a problem exists (e.g., an increase in undesirable interactions at a workplace), analyze setting events (e.g., occurrence of teasing by a coworker), and analyze consequent events (e.g., student is reprimanded by the supervisor but coworker goes unpunished).

Subsequent analyses of assessment information facilitates the identification of appropriate target behaviors that are likely to be naturally reinforced and maintained (Evans et al., 1993). Ecological assessment is a multidirectional procedure. Following are more specific strategies for the use of direct observation and ecological assessment, particularly in vocational environments. The first step involved in direct observation involves activities in the actual worksite and matching the requirements of the job to the individual student. This process is referred to as the "job match" (Falvey, 1989). As Falvey noted, it is critical that the student's abilities be adequate to the demands of the employment situation. This includes not only the specific skill requirements, but a host of other variables that may affect successful employment. A work-site analysis is then conducted to gather more in-depth information (Falvey, 1989). A job-site analysis involves determining knowledge and skills needed, job procedures (e.g., clocking in), communication skills, clothing needed, safety requirements, and areas such as pay and benefits. Once this information is gathered, the job coach (the individual providing direct training at a job) or teacher may then proceed with breaking down activities and skills into teachable components as required by the student's rate of learning.

Although originally developed for students with severe disabilities, the use of ecological and student repertoire inventories (Brown et al., 1979; Brown et al., 1980; Falvey, Brown, Lyon, Baumgart, & Schroeder, 1980) are applicable to this type of training situation and with students with disabilities in general. During this process, the teacher or assessment specialist analyzes the environment in terms of what skills are required to be successful in the activities occurring in that environment and then assesses the student's performance of those skills. For example, when performing an ecological inventory, Brown and colleagues (1979) outlined the following general steps. First, delineate the environment itself (e.g., a fast-food restaurant). Second, delineate subenvironments where the student will be required to function successfully (e.g., up front where orders are to be taken, in the cooking area, in the storeroom, outside on the restaurant grounds and parking area). Third, the specialist delineates the activities that occur in each of those environments (e.g., taking orders, filling orders, cooking french fries and sandwiches, assembling and wrapping sandwiches, stocking shelves, picking up trash). Fourth, the specialist delineates the particular skills required to participate in each activity (e.g., greeting the customer, listening to the order, inspecting to see if the items are available or must be ordered from the cooks, telling the customer the cost, ringing up items on the cash register, giving change). The similarity between this process and task analysis discussed in Chapter 5 should not be overlooked. In fact, a completed ecological inventory may resemble an assortment of task analyses related to each of the activities and skills involved in the job. Also noted in Chapter 5, the degree to which activities and skills would be broken down would depend on the severity of the student's disability. For example, a student with a mild disability may require fewer and "larger" steps than would an individual with a moderate or severe disability.

Falvey and colleagues (1980) stressed that when the ecological inventory is completed, a **student repertoire inventory** must be implemented. The student repertoire inventory is used to assess the student's performance compared to that of peers without disabilities on the ecologically inventoried skills. Falvey (1989) listed the following steps in conducting the student repertoire inventory. First, complete the ecological inventory delineating the skills performed by individuals without disabilities. Second, observe and record whether the student is able to perform the skills exhibited by the individuals without disabilities for a given activity. These observations should be systematic and the recording procedures suggested in Chapter 4 may be used (e.g., event recording, duration recording). Third, conduct a discrepancy analysis. This step involves analyzing whether the student is or is not able to perform the inventoried skills. If the student is not able to perform, the assessment specialist should observe and analyze all aspects of that skill (e.g., antecedents, consequences, criteria). The student's performance is further analyzed to determine which aspects of the skill are presenting difficulty. Finally, the teacher provides intervention for these same skills using one of the following three options: teaching the skill directly, making adaptations in the skill

STUDENT REPERTOIRE INVENTORY
Used to assess a student's performance compared to peers without disabilities on ecologically inventoried skills.

or in how the student performs the skill, or teaching the student to perform a related skill. Suppose a student working at a fast-food restaurant is having difficulty with the skills necessary for cooking french fries. The student might be taught how to cook the potatoes through direct instruction and task analysis. The student might be provided with some adaptive device (e.g., to assist in emptying the fry basket) or taught to perform another skill that would free another worker to fry potatoes.

The advantages of using ecological and student repertoire inventories are that they assess functional skills in the actual environment where those skills will be used and that the performance is assessed in the presence of naturally occurring conditions. It should be added that this type of assessment may be used to evaluate student performance in other areas related to successful functioning such as home-living and community-living skills. This type of assessment is not, however, the only type of assessment that might be used in a vocational setting. Clearly, in an actual paid work or community-based training situation, input from the employer would also be desirable and might be obtained from a simple 1-to-5 scale that is completed by the supervisor and the employee together. It may be necessary for the teacher or trainer to spend some time with the employer or supervisor to ensure the scale is filled out as objectively as possible. It is certainly not unheard of for an employer or supervisor to either underrate or overrate a student's performance due to unduly low or high expectations. Additional types of information that might be gathered could include production rates, accuracy rate, or rate at which new skills are learned. This information could be obtained using the same observational techniques discussed in Chapter 4. Another direct observation method related to ecological assessment is **situational assessment.** In situational assessment, the evaluator assesses the student's performance in settings and situations as close as possible to an individual's future work environments. Therefore, the student is not actually working but being assessed under similar circumstances as the actual work setting. Demands such as the work tasks, interpersonal skills, and communication skills can be varied as well as the situations in which observations occur. Situational assessment is useful in planning other assessments, determining instructional plans and programs, and determining interests, abilities, and needs in school-based and community-based work sites among other uses (Sitlington & Clark, 2001).

Two final procedures for informal assessment, portfolio assessment and outcomes assessment, may utilize many of the informal techniques already discussed. Each is closely related to CBVA in particular; both do, however, also include noteworthy characteristics aside from those discussed elsewhere.

> **SITUATIONAL ASSESSMENT**
> A direct observation method in which the evaluator assesses the student's performance in settings and situations as close as possible to the individual's future work environment.

Portfolio Assessment

Why Use Portfolio Assessment?

To construct a record over time of content and skills acquire; document job experiences; evaluation of progress.

Who Should Use It?

Teachers; vocational assessment personnel.

As noted in Chapter 6, portfolio assessment is one component of the overall current movement toward classroom- and community-based assessments (Nolet, 1992). For example, Sarkees-Wircenski and Wircenski (1994) reported on a project

Career portfolios address many assessment goals.

in Texas in which students with disabilities were involved in constructing a "Career Portfolio" that could be used by educators and adult service providers to prepare the students for postschool opportunities. First, appropriate competencies for successful transitions were identified (e.g., employability skills, work-related social skills, independent-living skills, generalized skills such as reading or writing, and job-specific skills). Next, these competencies were validated by a variety of educators, administrators, and adult service representatives. Ultimately, the number of competencies across the abovementioned areas was reduced to 108. On each competency students were rated on a five-point continuum from having had no exposure to the competency to requiring differing degrees of supervision to achieving independence. Students and teachers would include samples of work from a variety of sources to demonstrate status on any particular competency. Sarkees-Wircenski and Wircenski suggested a number of potential uses for a career portfolio. A portfolio could be used for informal individual assessment prior to placement in a program. Competencies could form the basis for short- or long-term instructional objectives. Competencies could be used to formulate a "job match" between student strengths and job requirements. The portfolio could be used for vocational counseling. Students could select samples of their work. The portfolio could serve as documentation of accomplishments to a prospective employer. Finally, the portfolio could be used as a cooperative planning tool that would allow educators, service providers, and employers to identify those competencies most important for vocational success and target those same competencies for intervention (Sarkees-Wircenski & Wircenski, 1994). It should be noted that commercially published career portfolios are now available.

Career portfolios are one example of how portfolios may be used in assessing, planning, and programming. There may be other uses, and these should reflect the nature of the student's plans for postsecondary life. For example, if the student is going to college, the portfolio contents should address the requirements of the admission/interview process (Thurlow & Elliott, 1998). The use of portfolio assessment is not universal but its use is likely to continue. A related form of assessment is outcomes assessment.

Outcomes Assessment

Why Use Outcomes Assessment?

To evaluate both individual vocational/educational outcomes and overall program effectiveness.

Who Should Use It?

Teachers; program evaluators; administrators; vocational assessment personnel.

There does not appear to be a clear consensus on exactly what constitutes outcomes assessment. DeStefano and Wagner (1993) stated that despite individual differences in design, measures, and data collection approaches, outcomes assessment models focus on individual achievements, statuses, or behaviors. Again, the relationship to CBVA for the case of the individual student is a close one. For the purpose of this chapter, the focus regarding outcomes assessment will be on adult outcomes and their importance in vocational/transitional assessment and programming. That is, the follow-up assessment of students who have exited from school will be highlighted.

As noted during the discussion of transition planning and assessment, the importance of determining postschool outcomes (e.g., employment status, behaviors leading to maintenance of or loss of employment, residential arrangements, accessibility of recreational opportunities, and degree of ongoing supervision required to live in the community) are essential to determining program effectiveness and instructional modification. Such information also indicates areas of need for individuals as well as within communities at large.

DeStefano and Wagner (1993) outlined a number of potential uses for outcomes assessment. Vocational rehabilitation agencies may use the assessment of outcomes achieved at exiting school and afterwards to (1) facilitate a smooth "hand off" of the student with disabilities from supervision by educators to the adult service provider, (2) determine if the linkage between vocational rehabilitation and school programs is strong and well coordinated, (3) anticipate personnel and service needs and to document systems change, and (4) provide information for long-term planning and program improvement. These same authors also posed questions of concern. First, who will be responsible for collecting and compiling outcome data? As planning and programming issues and concerns arise, what is the process for altering the focus of the outcomes assessment? Who will provide the resources necessary to conduct outcomes assessment? How much information is needed to effectively plan, implement, and modify programs (DeStefano & Wagner, 1993)? Clearly, the answers to these questions must be determined within the cohort of educators and adult service providers in each community, but overall guidance in what and how to assess does exist in the literature. For example, Rusch, Enchelmaier, and Kohler (1994) compiled results from questionnaires completed by 106 transition project directors. These researchers (along with a panel of experts they employed) identified both outcomes and activities within those outcomes for transition to work programs. The outcomes to be assessed included those at the family and student level (e.g., placement in competitive and integrated employment), program level (e.g., upgrade skills of professionals), organization level (e.g., develop materials to encourage replication of successful practices), and at the community level (e.g., document the formal interface between school and community services). Johnson and colleagues (1993) listed four essential questions that may serve as the basis for formulating an individually localized outcomes assessment:

Outcomes assessment makes use of followup data.

1. What are the desired outcomes for students to achieve after being out of school for one year?
2. What aspects or characteristics of current programs and transition planning support or limit students in achieving those outcomes?
3. What fundamental changes need to be made to improve outcomes?
4. What types of information should be collected and compiled to aid decision making in improving the educational and transition process?

Many models for follow-up studies that employ outcomes assessments exist in the literature (e.g., see Johnson & Rusch, 1993, for a review of twenty-four follow-up studies). The key to outcomes assessment is that data collection must not cease at the end of school careers if vocational and special education programs are to remain resilient and responsive to changes in education, technology, the economy, and the local community. Readers might wish to visit the home page of the *National Longitudinal Transition Study–2* (www.nlts2.org). This Webpage describes the outcomes of a national followup study funded by the U.S. Department of Education. This study provides national perspective on the adult outcomes of youths and adults with disabilities.

Although the focus has been on informal assessment processes to this point, the use of formal assessment procedures remains common. Data from such procedures are often incorporated into the vocational/transition counseling, planning, and programming of students with disabilities. These data are typically used to complement those obtained through informal assessments.

Interest and Aptitude Instruments

Why Use Interest and Aptitude Instruments?

Screening for vocational/career interests and vocational aptitudes; developing educational/vocational programs.

Who Should Use Them?

Vocational assessment personnel.

Many formal instruments have been designed to evaluate an individual's vocational interests and aptitude. These instruments are usually administered by a guidance counselor, school psychologist, or other professional involved in helping students determine their best career options.

It should be noted that most traditional instruments of this type are pencil-and-paper tests that provide scores in various aptitude areas (e.g., verbal reasoning, mechanical reasoning) and/or career–occupational interest areas of the student. There are some different approaches that are being offered, however. For example, in 1997, Pro-Ed published the *Career IQ and Interest Test* (CIQIT). The CIQIT is an interactive CD-ROM that allows self-administration of both aptitude and interest measures. However, it also includes a searchable database that includes the entire 1996–1997 *Occupational Outlook Handbook,* published by the U.S. Department of Labor. A different type of approach is the *Transition Planning Inventory–2* (Clark & Patton, 2007), which is actually a system to address a student's transition needs. Consistent with IDEA 04, it provides linkages from assessment to program planning, including linkages with postschool agencies. It is completed by a number of individuals, including the student, parents, and school personnel. This results in a team consensus regarding transition goals. A third approach to career planning is offered by Gilliam (1994). His *Work Adjustment Inventory* measures work-related temperament, the student's ability to adjust to work. The area of job-related temperament is an important one and should not be overlooked. Also available is the *Brigance Employability Skills Inventory* (Brigance, 1995), a criterion-referenced inventory that identifies specific skills.

A brief description of several instruments that are used for career guidance purposes follows. This is only a brief sampling of the many instruments available.

Differential Aptitude Tests

- *Age level*—16 years or older.
- *Technical adequacy*—Validity and reliability have been supported in the technical manual and in the professional literature.
- *Areas measured*—Verbal Reasoning, Numerical Ability, Abstract Reasoning, Mechanical Reasoning, Space Relations.
- *Types of scores*—Percentile ranks, stanines, and standard scores for males, females, and combined.

- *Suggested use*—The *Differential Aptitude Tests* (DAT; Bennett, Seashore, & Wesman, 1990) are currently among the most widely used measures of multiple abilities. The battery is intended primarily for use in educational and vocational counseling with students in grades 7 to 12, although it is also appropriate for young adults not in school. There are two levels of the test—Level I for students in grades 7 to 9 and Level II for students in grades 10 to 12. A special large-print edition is available for the visually impaired, and several versions have been developed in other languages for use outside the United States.

  The battery is designed for group administration. It should be administered in two or more sessions because the total procedure takes approximately two to three hours. A supplemental test, the *Career Interest Inventory*, is designed to be used with the DAT to allow the students to explore their interest in various fields of employment. The battery yields nine scores, one for each test, with an additional combined score of Verbal Reasoning and Numerical Reasoning. This combined score is used as a measure of scholastic ability and correlates highly with measures of intelligence.

The DAT can be group-administered.

Job Observation and Behavior Scale

- *Age level*—15 years and older.
- *Technical adequacy*—Adequate; interrater and test-retest reliability as well as concurrent validity studies were conducted.
- *Areas measured*—Work-required daily living activities, work-required behaviors, and work-required job duties.
- *Types of scores*—Raw scores only.
- *Suggested use*—The *Job Observation and Behavior Scale* (JOBS; Rosenberg & Brady, 2000) is a somewhat different instrument from others discussed in this chapter because it actually evaluates job performance. It is an employee performance assessment designed for those who work with the training and placement of secondary students and adults in the work force. Among the specific purposes of JOBS are the determination of the quality of work performance, the types of needed supports, and the worker's growth and development in the job over time. The Work-Required Daily Living Activities subtest includes thirteen items such as "Punctuality: Employee arrives at work on time, clocks in, telephones supervisor if delayed, returns from breaks and lunch on time." The Work-Required Behavior subtest includes eight items such as "Changes in Routines: Employee maintains quality and quantity of work productivity when faced with change of supervisor, work task, schedule, or production criteria." The Work-Required Job Duties subtest has nine items, including "Safety Procedures: Employee comprehends work hazards, follows standard safety procedures, handles tools and materials safely, and reports unsafe conditions to supervisor." Each of the thirty items is rated on a 1-to-5 scale.

Occupational Aptitude Survey and Interest Schedule–3

- *Age level*—Grades 8 to 12 and adult.
- *Technical adequacy*—Adequate reliability and validity for both Aptitude and Interest Surveys.
- *Areas measured*—Aptitude Survey (General Ability, Verbal Aptitude, Numerical Aptitude, Spatial Aptitude, Perceptual Aptitude, Manual Dexterity). The Interest Schedule measures twelve factors such as Artistic and Scientific.
- *Types of scores*—Standard scores, percentiles.

- *Suggested use*—The *Occupational Aptitude Survey and Interest Schedule–3* (OA-SIS-3; Parker, 2001) measures both aptitude and interest. The six aptitude scales are related to more than 20,000 jobs listed in the *Dictionary of Occupational Titles* and the interest factors are related to jobs listed in the *Guide for Occupational Exploration*. Profile forms are available to provide a visual summary of the student's aptitude and interests. The instrument is easy to administer; the student booklets have been reformatted in the revised edition to improve their readability. Machine scoring options are available.

Strong-Campbell Interest Inventory

- *Age level*—Ages 16 and older.
- *Technical adequacy*—Test-retest coefficients were moderate to strong; validity data were supportive of its use.
- *Areas measured*—Occupational Themes; Basic Interests; Occupational Scales; Special Scales (academic comfort, introversion, extroversion); Administrative Indexes.
- *Types of scores*—A variety of scores including T-scores are generated (through computer scoring only) for a variety of scales such as Basic Interest and Occupation.
- *Suggested use*—The *Strong-Campbell Interest Inventory* (Strong, Campbell, & Hansen, 1984) is intended to measure an individual's interest (not aptitude or intelligence) in various occupations. The theoretical foundation for developing the test is based on the assumption that individuals with the same occupations will have similar interests and personality characteristics. The instrument is easy to administer and can be given individually, in groups, or by mail. It takes an average of twenty-five to thirty-five minutes to complete. A computerized version is also available.

  The Strong-Campbell is considered by many to be one of the best interest inventories available and is also one of the most widely used instruments for adult assessment (Harrison, Kaufman, Hickman, & Kaufman, 1988). Changes were made to make it more gender specific (see Focus on Diversity). There have been some weaknesses, however. Tzeng (1985), for example, noted some inconsistencies between the Basic Interest and Occupational Scales and that more data supporting its construct validity are needed. Also, care should be taken when different editions of the Strong-Campbell are used, because they yield considerably different profiles (Creaser & Jacobs, 1987).

Vocational Preference Inventory–Revised

- *Age level*—Ages 14 to adult.
- *Technical adequacy*—Limited; available data support validity and reliability of earlier versions; more current research is needed to establish its technical characteristics.
- *Areas measured*—Personality and Vocational Interests, Realistic, Investigative, Artistic, Social, Enterprising, Conventional, Self-Control, Masculinity-Femininity, Status, Infrequency, Acquiescence.
- *Types of scores*—Standard scores (T-scores).
- *Suggested use*—The *Vocational Preference Inventory–Revised* (VPI-R; Holland, 1985) was designed to measure an individual's personality and vocational interests. It is based on Holland's six work typologies (first six scales listed above). The instrument is easy to administer and score. Shepard (1989) noted

focus on Diversity

Are Vocational Interest Inventories Gender-Biased?

When the Strong-Campbell Interest Inventory was revised in the mid 1980s, significant changes were made primarily as a result of the women's movement, during which the participants were very vocal about inequities in the job market. There was also criticism about the nature of the separate Occupational Scales for men and women. Although these scales were revised, separate male and female scales were retained. The test authors argued that this was necessary to expand options rather than to limit them. They did encourage both men and women to consider occupations that are frequently dominated by the opposite gender (Sodowsky, Gonzalez, & Kuo-Jackson, 1998).

that it was one of the more time- and cost-efficient inventories, although it lacked current technical data. In general, support for its claim as a vocational interest inventory is greater than its claim as a personality measure.

Wide Range Interest and Occupation Test–2

- *Age level*—Ages 9 through 80.
- *Technical adequacy*—Adequate standardization, limited validity and reliability data.
- *Types of scores*—Graphic profile analysis.
- *Suggested use*—The *Wide Range Interest and Occupation Test*–2 (WRIOT-2; Glutting & Wilkinson, 2003) is a reading-free instrument in which examinees must indicate whether they like, dislike, or are undecided about different jobs depicted on 238 full-color cards. Computer administration is also available through a CD that also depicts the pictures. Results provide a profile in seventeen occupational and sixteen interest areas. The WRIOT-2 can be individually or group-administered.

The WRIOT-2 does not require reading.

BACK TO THE PROFILES

Possible Answers to the Questions

1. **Why assess Jill?** Jill should be assessed to determine appropriate and realistic vocational goals. By at least age 16, she must have a statement of her transition service needs within the curriculum in her IEP. However, these goals should be included as soon as possible. At this point she might also be assessed to determine what interagency linkages, if any, she needs.

2. **Who should assess Jill?** Jill would be assessed most appropriately by her teacher, a vocational assessment specialist, a transition specialist, and by herself and her parents. If Jill's teacher is familiar with the procedures in this chapter, he or she might adequately assume the roles of the vocational assessment specialist and transition specialist.

3. **What procedure(s)/test(s) should be used?** Jill's records should be reviewed (e.g., former IEPs) for information concerning past career education/prevocational skill development. Additionally, Jill and her parents could be interviewed or given interest

inventories to determine what, if any, career/vocational interests Jill might possess. Overall, present levels in areas such as physical skills, dexterity, work capacity, stamina, attitude, interpersonal skills, and communication skills might also be derived from past records and checklists and observations. Because goals for Jill at this point would likely focus on general vocational/transitional skills, ecological inventories might be used to analyze specific school environments (e.g., school office, media center) where Jill might obtain some prevocational skill training. Portfolio development might begin at this point as Jill begins to develop interests and skills in this area.

4. **What other areas should be assessed?** Jill could be assessed with work samples or via CBVA to determine her proficiency at the entry-level skills for current and future school vocational/transitional programs. Also, outcomes based assessments might be examined for former students to determine what have been successful and less successful practices in this area to increase the likelihood of providing an appropriate program for Jill.

---

1. **Why assess Sue?** Sue's case is interesting because she is so close to graduation. Assessment in math skills would be appropriate, but such an academic assessment should focus on those skills needed to pursue her postsecondary interests and specific job skills needed in the meantime (e.g., on her after-school job). Sue is capable of postsecondary education, but given her fears, she needs to be assessed to ensure she would pursue an appropriate college major or postsecondary career opinion. Additionally, it is clear Sue has a strength in the area of English; finding other areas of strength is important also to determine what would be an appropriate postsecondary path.

2. **Who should assess Sue?** Sue and her parents should be major participants in the vocational/transitional assessment, planning, and programming. A career counselor/college counselor and/or vocational assessment specialist might be involved in helping Sue determine viable options for the future. Sue's teacher could also be involved in assisting with assessment in the workplace as well as in her educational skills. Sue and her parents could be involved in all areas, but they would also assess the availability and affordability of postsecondary options. If Sue would qualify, a vocational rehabilitation counselor would be helpful as well.

3. **What procedure(s)/test(s) should be used?** Interest inventories could prove helpful in pinpointing specific areas of interest (clearly areas related to English skills should be evident). An aptitude test such as the *Differential Aptitude Test*, which indicates specific career choices, could be used by a vocational assessment specialist, career counselor, or vocational rehabilitation counselor. The OASIS-3 would provide information for interests and aptitude. Tests such as the SAT or ACT commonly taken by seniors could be appropriate (with appropriate accommodations). The teacher could employ ecological inventory techniques for use in the workplace for determining and teaching specific math skills needed. Interviews and examination of existing Websites and materials would be useful for Sue and her parents in determining what colleges/universities might be more accommodating to Sue and provide adequate support services and career guidance to students with disabilities. Sue, her parents, and teachers as well as others could construct a portfolio whose contents reflected the admission requirements to programs of interest.

4. **What other areas should be assessed?** Math was noted in question 1. Other areas of academic strengths in addition to English might also be probed. Another area would be to assess Sue's abilities in learning strategies, study skills, and organization/management. Finally, Sue's ability to advocate for herself (self-determination) might be informally assessed so that skills necessary for living/learning more independently in a college/university setting could be addressed in her final months in high school.

STUDENT PROFILE DATA

Sue

Sue was initially administered the OASIS-3 by her high school career counselor to determine her interests and aptitude in a number of areas. The following results were obtained:

Aptitude Survey

Factor	Percentile Rank
General Ability	56
Verbal Aptitude	98
Numerical Aptitude	32
Spatial Aptitude	44
Perceptual Aptitude	50
Manual Dexterity	42

Interest Schedule

Scale	Percentile
Artistic	58
Scientific	35
Nature	25
Protective	47
Mechanical	21
Industrial	28
Business Detail	44
Selling	38
Accommodating	65
Humanitarian	69
Leading-Influencing	70
Physical Performing	21

Note: Some percentiles are based on the total test standardization and others on just the female subjects (where applicable).

The results from the Aptitude Survey verify the observations reported; Sue's obvious strength is verbal aptitude, and her weakness is numerical aptitude. Results from the Interest Schedule were interesting. In general, she was not interested in most areas. Her highest scores were in Leading-Influencing (jobs such as librarian and lawyer), Humanitarian (jobs such as school counselor), and Artistic (jobs such as writer/novelist). These interests reflect areas in which she might apply her strong verbal skills.

CASE STUDY *June*

Transition needs of students with disabilities must be addressed beginning at the age of 16. June is only 10 years old and in the fourth grade. However, it is never too early to think abut a child's transition needs. Transitions occur throughout the school years. At the end of fifth grade (in one year), June will transition to middle school. Elementary school and middle school are very different education and social settings (as well you may remember).

- Given her anxiety about school, make a list of suggestions you would have for June's teachers and parents that might ease this transition for June.

Reflections

1. If you had a high school student with a severe disability who required an alternate assessment, what procedures would you recommend to document his vocational/transition needs? Why did you choose these?
2. IDEA 04 required that student's transition needs must be addressed in the IEP by age 16. Earlier versions of IDEA required (1) a separate Transition Plan and (2) that those needs be addressed by age 14. Which of these options do you think is most appropriate? Why?
3. Why do you think it is important to measure both a student's interests and aptitude?

Summary Matrix

Instrument or Technique	Preferral — Screening and Initial Identification	Preferral — Informal Determination and Evaluation of Teaching Programs and Strategies	Postreferral — Determination of Current Performance Level and Educational Need	Postreferral — Decisions about Classification and Program Placement	Postreferral — IEP Goals	Postreferral — IEP Objectives	Postreferral — IEP Evaluation	Target Population — Mild/Moderate	Target Population — Severe/Profound	Target Population — Preschool	Target Population — Elementary Age	Target Population — Secondary Age	Target Population — Adult	Special Considerations	Educational Relevance for Exceptional Students
Checklists and Rating Scales		X						X			X	X		Informal techniques that provide preliminary data but require additional techniques for complete data.	Adequate
Work Samples			X		X	X						X	X	Combination of commercial and locally developed instruments is suggested although cost is a concern.	Useful
Curriculum-Based Vocational Assessment		X	X		X	X	X	X				X	X	Validity of vocational curriculum must be considered.	Very Useful
Direct Observation and Ecological Assessment		X	X		X	X	X	X	X		X	X	X	Probably most adaptable and widely applicable technique.	Very Useful
Portfolio Assessment		X	X		X	X	X	X	X		X	X	X	See Chapter 6; use of a career portfolio is helpful.	Useful
Outcomes Assessment		X	X				X	X	X				X	Emphasizes importance of determining postschool outcomes.	Useful
Differential Aptitude Tests						X		X				X	X	Widely used instrument; time consuming; computerized version available.	Adequate
Job Observation and Behavior Scale					X		X	X				X	X	Actually measures on-the-job performance.	Useful
Occupational Aptitude Survey and Interest Schedule-3						X		X				X	X	Measures aptitude and interests.	Adequate
Strong-Campbell Interest Inventory					X			X				X	X	A popular instrument that is widely researched.	Adequate
Vocational Preference Inventory-Revised												X	X	Based on Holland's six work typologies.	Limited
Wide Range Interest and Occupation Test-2						X		X			X	X	X	Is a reading-free instrument.	Adequate

Examples

In Chapter 2, a pragmatic approach to the assessment process was discussed and an assessment model provided. Throughout this book, a variety of assessment procedures have been described that can be used to implement that model. This has included both informal and formal procedures that are used for a variety of purposes. Also included has been a description of assessment instruments that are used to evaluate a variety of areas.

In this section (Chapter 17), two examples of the assessment process (from initial identification through the development and evaluation of the IEP) are presented. Both examples use a case study approach; one follows a student with mild disabilities and includes prereferral assessment data and test scores and their interpretation for documentation of educational need. The use of those test scores for eligibility is also discussed. Finally, the use of assessment data to develop the IEP is presented. The second case study involves a student with severe disabilities to permit a comparison of the similarities and differences of the assessment process with that of the student with mild disabilities.

chapter seventeen

Examples

Putting It All Together

This chapter includes two case studies that follow a student with mild disabilities and a student with severe disabilities from the beginning of the assessment process (initial identification) through development of the IEP. The procedures and instruments are typical of those used in many states (although some variation, of course, will exist). These examples are meant to show the uses, as well as the limitations, of various types of assessment instruments and data.

Case Study: Frank, a Student with Mild Disabilities

Frank, a 10-year-old fourth-grader, could not concentrate on most tasks for more than two or three minutes at a time. Every ten minutes or so he would turn around and talk to and bother the student behind him. His teacher had to stand over him and tap his desk every time he became disruptive. Writing was painstakingly difficult for Frank. It took him five minutes to write a five-word sentence. Most of the time he began sentences in the middle of the page. The letters were usually written very small, and some were written backwards. His script e looked like an i, and he did not dot his i's or cross his t's. When doing tasks of this type, he often got frustrated and tore his paper up. His teacher noted that Frank was a "different boy" when he was working on his science lessons. He would sit quietly, read his assignment, and wait for his turn to present the information to the rest of the class. His teacher wanted an evaluation to determine why Frank performed so well in some areas and so poorly in others. She wanted information that might help her to motivate him or accommodate his learning style. In addition, she thought that he might benefit from special education.

Step One: Initial Identification

Routine curriculum-based assessment indicated that Frank was having considerable difficulty in language arts. He was significantly behind the rest of the class regarding the appropriate placement within the school's language arts curriculum. Through the use of the CBA results, observation, and evaluation of Frank's work products (including portfolio assessment), his teacher decided that further assessment was needed. One thing she noted was that Frank appeared to be off task quite often, and he frequently failed to complete assignments, particularly written assignments.

Step Two: Prereferral Assessment: Developing and Evaluating Teaching Programs and Strategies

Frank's teacher decided to use informal techniques to collect information before a formal referral. Specifically, she used observational data to document his off-task behavior and to evaluate various intervention strategies. She decided to use momentary time sampling, twice a day (during language arts and during science) for a ten-minute period. She took the following steps: (1) define off-task behavior (no eye contact during verbal tasks, not working at written task), (2) determine schedule for time samples (every fifteen seconds), (3) develop charts, (4) collect baseline data, (5) implement intervention program, (6) observe behavior to evaluate program.

After three days, a specific pattern emerged for Frank; the baseline data are shown in Figure 17.1. This information indicated that Frank was off task approximately 30 percent of the time during the language arts sessions and only about

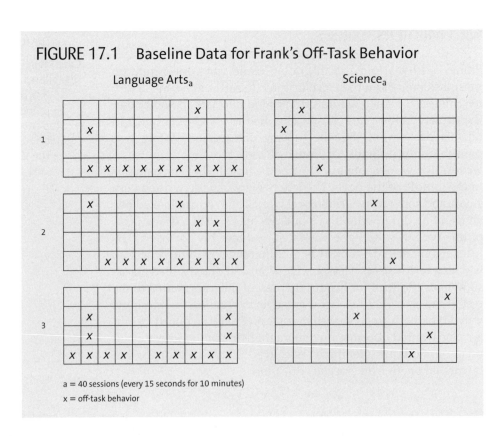

FIGURE 17.1   Baseline Data for Frank's Off-Task Behavior

Language Arts$_a$ Science$_a$

a = 40 sessions (every 15 seconds for 10 minutes)

x = off-task behavior

7 percent of the time during the science sessions. Further, it appeared that he was off task primarily near the end of the sessions.

On the basis of these observations, Frank's teacher decided to initiate a pre-referral intervention program during the language arts period. This consisted of changing the task (from spelling exercises to dictionary work). Figure 17.2 shows the results of that intervention. This had some effect, but he was still off task approximately 15 percent of the time. His teacher then initiated a reinforcement system, whereby Frank received extra privileges for increasing his on-task behavior each day. Although this decreased his off-task behavior, Frank's teacher noted that he still was not completing the tasks. Further, his written assignments in other subjects were not being completed. She decided, therefore, to refer Frank for further evaluation.

Step Three: Referral

Frank's teacher completed the required referral form and attached the observational data that she had collected as well as results from the CBA and examples of his work in language arts.

Step Four: Obtaining Parental Permission

Before formal assessment was initiated, it was necessary to obtain parent permission.

Step Five: Formal Assessment Procedures—The IEP Process

Formal evaluation was initiated to document Frank's educational needs and to provide information for eligibility and placement decisions. The following tests

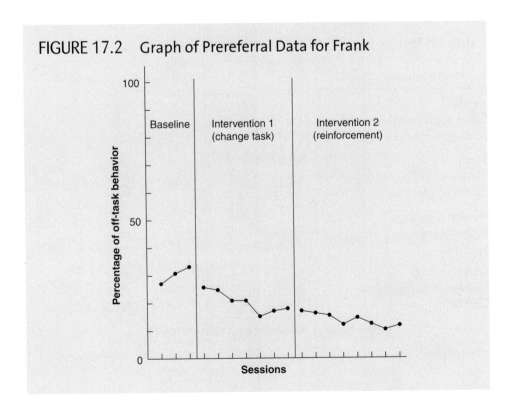

FIGURE 17.2   Graph of Prereferral Data for Frank

were administered initially: *Wechsler Intelligence Scale for Children–IV* (discussed in Chapter 7), *Kaufman Test of Educational Achievement–II* (discussed in Chapter 11), *Test of Written Language–3* (discussed in Chapter 14), and the *Test of Written Spelling–4* (discussed in Chapter 14). The following data were collected.

Wechsler Intelligence Scale for Children–Fourth Edition (WISC-IV)

Index/Subtest	Quotient/Scaled Scores
Verbal Comprehension	**110**
Similarities	13
Vocabulary	9
Comprehension	13
Perceptual Reasoning	**109**
Matrix Reasoning	11
Block Design	11
Picture Concepts	12
Working Memory	**82**
Letter-Number Sequencing	8
Digit Span	7
Processing Speed	**75**
Symbol Search	7
Coding	6

Full Scale IQ—95

Kaufman Test of Educational Achievement–II (KTEA-II)

Subtest/Composite	Quotient/Standard Score
Reading	**99**
Letter and Word Recognition	97
Reading Comprehension	96
Math	**96**
Mathematics Concepts and Applications	101
Math Computation	89
Written Language	**70**
Written Language	69
Spelling	73
Oral Language	**90**
Listening Comprehension	95
Oral Expression	84

Comprehensive Achievement Composite—81

Test of Written Language–3 (TOWL-3)

Subtests/Composite	Scaled/Standard Scores
Vocabulary	7
Spelling	6
Style	9
Logical Sentences	9
Sentence Combining	9
Contextual Conventions	5
Contextual Language	6
Story Construction	6
Contrived Writing	83
Spontaneous Writing	73
Overall Written Language	77

Test of Written Spelling–4 (TWS-4)

Spelling Quotient—74

Interpretation of Results.   The WISC-IV and the KTEA-II were administered by the school psychologist. She stated,

> On the basis of the WISC-IV data, the following comments are warranted. Frank is performing within the average range of intelligence. He demonstrated relative strengths in the areas of verbal comprehension and perceptual reasoning, most notably in abstract thinking, social judgment, and conceptual knowledge. He had difficulty with tasks requiring memory, concentration, and writing. On the KTEA-II, his scores indicate average reading skills and slightly below average oral language skills. He appears to be stronger in receptive language than expressive language. In math, he has a relative strength in conceptual knowledge and a relative weakness in computation skills. This latter finding might be due to the writing component involved. His lowest area is written language in which he scored two standard deviations below average. Using the KTEA-II error analysis, it seemed that spelling is his major problem.

The learning disabilities specialist administered the TOWL-3 and TWS-4. She noted that Frank "scored below average on skills involving writing. The results from the TOWL-3 indicate that the overall quality and quantity of his written language production were below average. He scored particularly low in the area of spelling. The TWS-4 confirms his deficit in this area."

Use of Evaluation Data in Making Decisions

Determining Eligibility and Placement.   A case study conference was held that included the school psychologist, the counselor, the learning disabilities specialist, Frank's parents, and the general classroom teacher. On the basis of this available information, it was decided that Frank qualified under IDEA 04 as a student with a learning disability.[1] He met all of the eligibility criteria for learning disabilities,

---

[1]In actuality, Frank would need to meet the eligibility criteria established by his state.

and the test data were consistent with the prereferral information and the referral concern. The IEP team also felt that Frank could and should be placed in an inclusion classroom. Thus the goal was to keep Frank in the general education curriculum with accommodations and supplementary services.

Development of Goals and Objectives.[2]   Next, it was necessary to identify appropriate goals and objectives as well as time lines, types of services, and how the school will monitor the student's progress. First, however, a criterion-referenced test was developed that included several of the basic spelling skills. The skills were chosen primarily on an error analysis of his spelling performance on the tests administered as well as his work products in school.

Area Measured	*Results*
Writing cursive letters—lowercase	Wrote every letter except *i*, *t*, and *e* correctly.
Writing cursive letters—uppercase	Wrote eight letters correctly (A, B, C, D, E, I, O, and P), but missed all the others.
Spelling—initial consonants	Correctly wrote the beginning consonant for nineteen of twenty-one words presented. He wrote *k* for *car* and *c* for *quit*.
Spelling—initial clusters	Missed three of twenty-six 2-letter initial blends. He wrote su for *swell*, sc for *sky*, and *kr* for *crack*. He missed seven out of seven 3-letter initial blends. Examples include *trl* for *thrill* and *stg* for *string*.
Spelling—suffixes	Missed twenty-five out of thirty-six different suffix additions. Basically, he correctly answered only those suffixes that could be added without applying rules.
Alphabetical order	He was able to alphabetize the letters and words with 100 percent accuracy. He did, however, take a long time to complete the task.

Decisions about the IEP.   During the IEP conference, the following observations and decisions were made:

From teacher's input and observational data. Frank is a distractible student, particularly during certain activities. These activities seem to be related to language arts, particularly when some type of written response is required. It is possible to increase his on-task behavior using reinforcement procedures, but he still does not complete the tasks.

From formal evaluation data for eligibility. Frank's profile is most consistent with that of a student with learning disabilities. He has average overall intelligence but has some significant academic weaknesses, most notably in spelling and other aspects of written language. Further, his problems seem to be related to the production of written language rather than to a visual-perceptual problem. (Note: These data alone were insufficient in establishing relevant educational objectives.)

[2]Although IDEA 04 does not require objectives be written in the IEP for students with mild disabilities, the process of developing those objectives for Frank is presented to demonstrate how more educationally relevant information can be obtained from assessment data.

From criterion-referenced testing. Frank was able to write all but two lowercase letters cursively. He had more difficulty with uppercase letters (he missed eighteen of twenty-six). In terms of spelling, two patterns emerged. First, he made phonetic substitutions (e.g., *k* for *c* and vice versa). Second, he had difficulty with spelling rules (e.g., he wrote *hoping* for *hopping*). On a specific language arts task of alphabetizing letters and words, Frank performed at 100 percent accuracy, although it took him a long time to complete the task. This could explain why, during the prereferral observation, he was able to decrease off-task behavior yet still not complete the task.

In Frank's IEP, therefore, the following goals were included:

Annual Goals	*Evaluation Schedule*
1. The student will increase his spelling grade level score.	Annual/Use a norm-referenced test.
2. When presented with pencil and paper and requested to write the lowercase and uppercase cursive letters, the student will correctly and legibly write all twenty-six letters (uppercase and lowercase) in cursive script.	Annual/Use a criterion-referenced test.

In addition, even though they were not required for Frank's IEP, the following general and short-term instructional objectives were determined to help the teacher meet his goals.

General Instructional Objectives

1. *Objective:* When the examiner pronounces words that begin with consonants, the student will demonstrate his ability to recognize initial consonant sounds auditorily by writing the correct initial consonant for twenty-one out of twenty-one different consonants.	Every three months/Use a criterion-referenced test.
2. *Objective:* When the examiner pronounces words with initial blends and digraphs (clusters), the student will demonstrate his ability to recognize the initial blend and digraph sounds auditorily by writing the letters that make up the cluster for thirty-three out of thirty-three different blends and digraphs.	Every three months/Use a criterion-referenced test.
3. *Objective:* When the examiner presents the student with a printed stimulus root word and requests the student to write the same root word plus a designated suffix, the student will correctly write the altered word. This task will be performed correctly for twenty-seven out of thirty-six different suffix additions (75 percent accuracy).	Every three months/Use a criterion-referenced test.

Short-Term Objectives

When the examiner pronounces fifteen words with the initial consonants *k*, *g*, and *c*, the	Weekly/Use a criterion-referenced test.

student will demonstrate his ability to recognize initial consonant sounds by writing the correct initial consonant with 100 percent accuracy.	
When the examiner pronounces fifteen words with initial blends *sw, sk,* and *cr,* the student will demonstrate his ability to recognize the initial blend by writing the correct two letters with 100 percent accuracy.	Weekly/Use a criterion-referenced test.
When the examiner pronounces ten words with initial three-letter blends (for example, *thr, str*), the student will demonstrate his ability to recognize each blend by writing the correct three letters with 50 percent accuracy.	Weekly/Use a criterion-referenced test.
When presented with three printed stimulus root words and requested to add a designated suffix (*ing* with doubled consonants; *ed* with doubled consonants; *ed* to words ending in silent *e*) to that root word, the student will correctly write the requested word with 100 percent accuracy.	Weekly/Use a criterion-referenced test.
When presented with pencil and paper, the student will correctly write all the lowercase letters in cursive script.	Weekly/Use a criterion-referenced test.
When presented with pencil and paper, the student will correctly write the uppercase letters A, B, C, D, E, F, G, H, I, J, K, L, M in cursive script.	Weekly/Use a criterion-referenced test.

Note: This section includes examples of teaching objectives. Objectives of this type are changed and updated frequently, and they are typically found in lesson plans.

The decision was also made to have his special education teacher work with Frank for one hour each school day in the inclusion setting. During this time, he would receive structured one-to-one tutoring in handwriting (using stencils that would be faded gradually) and in spelling rules. In addition, his special education teacher would work with his general education teacher to incorporate the recommendations in his inclusive setting. Initially, he would be requested to complete the tasks with no time limit. After he met the criteria for mastering the skill, however, he would be required to gradually decrease the time he needed to complete the task. After one year, his progress toward the goals would be evaluated, and decisions about further steps would be made on the basis of the evaluation.

Determining Participation in Large-Scale Assessments.   The IEP team determined that Frank could participate in any district- or statewide assessment program but that accommodations were necessary. Specifically, they determined that additional time should be allowed and that oral responses could be substituted for written responses unless the goal of the assessment was to evaluate writing skills.

Case Study: James, a Student with Severe Disabilities

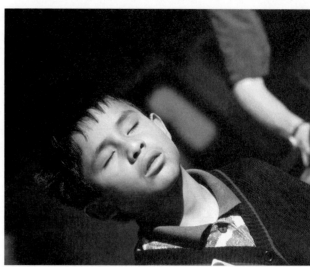

James is a 6-year-old boy who has a medical diagnosis of "severe brain damage from anoxia at birth." James is nonambulatory and visually impaired, and he has an extremely limited range of motion. He is also heavily medicated for control of seizures. James has been enrolled in a preschool program for children with disabilities for the past four years. He is no longer eligible for this program because of his age.

Step One: Initial Identification

James was identified as having severe disabilities shortly after birth. Extensive documentation from physicians, physical therapists, and other medical personnel accompanied him when he began receiving services for infants and toddlers (Part C of IDEA 04). That information, as well as assessment data gathered during his five years of early intervention services, indicated the need for James to continue in some type of special program.

Step Two: Referral

James was referred for evaluation so that the appropriate placement and educational program could be determined and carried out.

Step Three: Obtaining Parental Permission

Step Four: Formal Assessment Procedures—The IEP Process

A formal evaluation was conducted to determine James's ability level in a number of cognitive, social, self-help, motor, and communication areas. The following instruments were administered: *Vineland–II (Survey Interview Form)* (discussed in Chapter 8) and *Battelle Developmental Inventory–2* (discussed in Chapter 15). The following data were collected.

Vineland–II (Survey Interview Form)

Domain	Percentile
Communication	2
Daily Living Skills	3
Socialization	4
Motor Skills	1
Maladaptive Behavior	2
Total Adaptive Behavior	2

Battelle Developmental Inventory–2

Domain	Standard Score	Age Equivalent
Personal/Social	60	2–1
Adaptive	55	1–3
Motor	<55	0–9
Communication*	<55	1–4
Cognitive*	<55	1–6

*Scores affected by visual impairment.

Use of Evaluation Data in Making Decisions

Determining Eligibility and Placement.   On the basis of the available information, the IEP team determined that James qualified for special education services under the primary category of mental retardation. Because of the potential medical complications and the need for significant related services, they decided to place James in a self-contained class with children with similar needs.

Development of Goals and Objectives.   Additional information was needed to determine the goals and objectives for James. The psychologist decided to administer the *Callier-Azusa Scale* and portions of the *Brigance Inventory of Early Development–II* (based in part on the Callier-Azusa results), both of which are discussed in Chapter 15.

Callier-Azusa Scale

Motor Development
1. Postural Control—Holds head up for indefinite periods; turns head from side to side.
2. Locomotion—Rolls from stomach to back and from side to back.
3. Fine Motor—Has a reflex grasp of small objects.
4. Visual-Motor—Does not respond to any visual stimulus.

Perceptual Development
1. Visual Development—Does not respond to any visual stimulus.
2. Auditory Development—Turns head and eyes in the direction of an auditory stimulus.
3. Tactile Development—Reacts to tactile stimulation but does not localize the source.

Daily Living Skills
1. Undressing and Dressing—Resists being undressed or dressed.
2. Personal Hygiene—Plays with toys, soap, and washcloth while being bathed.
3. Feeding Skills—Allows being fed from spoon.
4. Toileting—Reacts negatively to wet pants.

Cognition, Communication, and Language
1. Cognitive Development—Recognizes and reacts to familiar objects (tactilely).
2. Receptive Communication—Understands simple signals that are tactilely presented.
3. Expressive Communication—Nonverbally signals to indicate needs (for example, holds out arms to be picked up).

Social Development
1. Interaction with Adults—Differentiates familiar and unfamiliar adults (auditorily).
2. Interaction with Peers—Responds to peers' presence.
3. Interaction with Environment—Differentiates familiar and unfamiliar environments.

At this point, James's current performance level was documented, and the IEP goals, time lines, types of services, and evaluation schedule could be determined. It was decided that James would also benefit from physical therapy and speech and communication therapy as part of his overall educational program. The severity of James's problems precluded his ability to continue in the general education curriculum. The following goals were adopted:

Annual Goals	*Evaluation Schedule*
1. The student will sit when supported. His head will be in midline and erect with upper trunk rounded and shoulders forward.	Annual observation by physical therapist or teacher.
2. The student will crawl forward or backward on his stomach by pulling with his forearm and pushing with his foot from the opposite side.	Annual observation by physical therapist or teacher.
3. The student will eat from spoon (independently, with considerable spilling) after food has been placed on it.	Annual observation by teacher.
4. The student will respond appropriately to simple one-word commands.	Annual observation by teacher.
5. The student will use simple gestures, signs, or vocalizations to indicate his needs (situation-specific and probably will not generalize).	Annual observation by speech therapist or teacher.

Once the goals had been adopted, portions of the *Brigance Inventory of Early Development–II* were administered to obtain more information. On the basis of results of this and the previously mentioned tests, the following objectives were determined in relation to James's annual goals:

Objectives	*Evaluation Schedule*
1a. When placed in a sitting position, the student remains momentarily but head sags forward.	Weekly observation by the physical therapist or teacher.
1b. When placed in a sitting position, the student remains momentarily; head bobs forward, but student demonstrates some evidence of support or control.	Every three months/observation by the physical therapist or teacher.
1c. Same as above; head steady but not erect.	Same as above.
1d. Same as above; head erect and steady.	Same as above.
2a. When placed in a prone position, the student will raise chest with arm support.	Weekly/observation by the physical therapist or teacher.
2b. When placed in a prone position, the student will support most body weight with hands rather than arms.	Every three months/observation by the physical therapist or teacher.

2c. When placed in a prone position, the student will turn on his stomach to face in a different direction.	Same as above.
3a. The student will feed himself a cracker or cookie.	Weekly/observation by the teacher.
3b. The student will feed himself small pieces of food such as raisins.	Every three months/observation by the teacher.
3c. The student will hold a spoon independently.	Same as above.
3d. The student will put spoon to mouth (with physical guidance).	Same as above.
4a. The student will respond to a few simple commands that are tactilely presented.	Weekly/observation by the teacher.
4b. The student will imitate a gesture with objects present (e.g., rolling a ball if the teacher makes a pushing motion).	Every three months/observation by the teacher.
4c. The student will understand a gesture without objects present (e.g., will find a ball to roll if teacher makes a pushing motion).	Same as above.
5a. The student will imitate a gesture *while* the teacher is gesturing.	Weekly/observation by the teacher.
5b. The student will imitate a gesture after the teacher stops by the teacher (prompting necessary).	Every three months/observation by the teacher.
5c. The student will initiate a gesture without a prompt.	Same as above.

Determining Participation in Large-Scale Assessments.   Based on the severity of James's problems, it was decided that participation in any large-scale assessment would not be appropriate because it would be based on curricular material not within James's exposure. Subsequently, an alternate assessment focusing on independent living skills was developed.

CASE STUDY *June*

Now that you have seen an example of the assessment process applied for both James and Frank, you can make your own decisions about June, whose case has been presented throughout this text. By following June's story in each chapter and participating in the activities, you have had the opportunity to be involved in the process students, parents, and teachers follow when a student is referred for special education services. The Cumulative Assessment Profile on the Companion Website contains June's complete file. The format in which the information is presented follows the assessment process model discussed in Chapter 2 of the textbook.

- In a paragraph, summarize the results of June's assessment.
- On the basis of the available information, does June meet the eligibility criteria for any disability category under IDEA? If so, which one? Justify your answer.
- What do you think is the appropriate placement for June? Why?
- June's IEP goals need to be determined. Given all that you now know about June, what recommendations would you make to be included in her IEP goals?

Summary

The case studies of Frank and James were intended to provide examples of the overall assessment process. As noted earlier, the choice of instruments and techniques will vary. In addition, eligibility criteria will differ from state to state. With Frank, who has a mild disability, the prereferral component and the postreferral component of the assessment model were included. On the other hand, only the postreferral component was used with James because of the severity of his disabilities.

Functional Behavior Assessment Form

FUNCTIONAL BEHAVIOR ASSESSMENT

Part One: Assessing the Behavior

1. Specific Target Behavior (include topography; include frequency, duration, or intensity)

   _____

   _____

2. Setting(s) in Which Behavior Occurs _____

   _____

   _____

3. Activities during Which the Behavior Occurs _____

   _____

   _____

4. Time of Day Behavior Occurs _____

   _____

   _____

5. Person(s) around Whom the Behavior Occurs _____

   _____

   _____

6. Factors That Appear to Set off or Precede the Behavior

Teacher Factors

_____ Task Explanation	_____ Performance Feedback
_____ Lesson Presentation	_____ Teacher Reprimand
_____ Teacher Praise	_____ Individual Attention
_____ Lack of Attention	_____ Task Demands
_____ Teacher Request	_____ Consequence Imposed for Negative Behavior
_____ Other _____	

Peer Factors

_____ Peer Attention (Positive)

_____ Peer Attention (Negative)

_____ Other _____

Setting Factors

_____ Transition (Task; Routine)	_____ Transition (Setting; Routine)
_____ Transition (Task; Unexpected)	_____ Transition (Setting; Unexpected)
_____ Elevated Noise Levels	_____ Presence of Unfamiliar Adults
_____ Presence of Unfamiliar Peers	_____ Other _____

7. Factors That Appear to Be Present When the Behavior Occurs

Student Factors

_____ Drowsy/Sleepy Appearance	_____ Physical Complaints (e.g., hunger, pain)
_____ Disturbed Affect (e.g., sad, angry)	_____ Excessive Motor Activity

_____ Other _____

Setting Factors

_____ Independent Seat Work	_____ Group Instruction
_____ Crowded Setting	_____ One-to-One Instruction
_____ Unstructured Setting	_____ Unstructured Activity

_____ Other _____

8. Factors That Appear to Follow the Behavior

Teacher Factor

_____ Teacher Reprimand	_____ Teacher Praise
_____ Task Removal	_____ Withdrawal of Attention
_____ Teacher Warning	_____ Time-Out
_____ Response Cost	_____ Sent to Office
_____ Communication with Parent	_____ Predetermined Contingency Imposed
_____ In-School Suspension	_____ Out-of-School Suspension

_____ Other _____

Peer Factors

_____ Peer Attention (Positive)

_____ Peer Attention (Negative)

_____ Other _____

9. Behavioral Intent or Function(s) That the Behavior Appeared to Serve

_____ Power/Control

      _____ Over Teachers

      _____ Over Peers

      _____ Over Parents

      _____ Other _____

_____ Escape/Avoidance

      _____ From an Activity/Task

      _____ From a Person

      _____ From the Classroom

      _____ From the School

      _____ Other _____

_____ Attention

      _____ Teacher

      _____ Peer

      _____ Parent

      _____ Other _____

_____ Expression of Self

_____ Gratification (Self-Reward)

_____ Acceptance/Affiliation (More Formal Than Immediate Peer Attention)

_____ Justice/Revenge

_____ Other _____

Part Two: Formulation of Hypotheses

Based on Information from Part One:

1. What Appears to Be the Predominant Setting/Activity in Which the Behavior Occurs?

_____

2. What Time(s) of Day Does the Behavior Typically Occur?_____

_____

3. Around What Person(s) Does the Behavior Typically Occur? _____

_____

4. What Seems to Immediately Precede or Set Off the Behavior? _____

_____

5. What Seems to Be the Immediate Consequence of the Behavior?_____

_____

6. What Function or Purpose Does the Behavior Seem to Serve? _____

_____

Functional Hypothesis

Indicate both (a) the conditions in which the behavior occurs and (b) the function that the behavior seems to serve.

_____

_____

_____

Part Three: Development of Behavior Intervention Plan

Prevention of Behavior

Based on the available information, list steps that could be taken to prevent the target behavior from occurring (e.g., avoidance of certain tasks and/or types of instructional delivery, seating arrangement)

_____

_____

Replacement Behavior

Based on the available information, what behavior needs to be taught to allow the student to have a successful adaptation (e.g., requesting assistance to replace tantruming as a means of gathering attention)

_____

_____

Identification of Reinforcers

List all reinforcers, including preferred activities that are appropriate for this student

_____

_____

Implementation of Behavior Intervention Plan

Goal:

_____

Prevention Strategies for Target Behavior

Strategy	Date	Person(s) Responsible	Outcome

Intervention Strategies for Replacement Behavior

Strategy	Date	Person(s) Responsible	Outcome

Criteria for Program Discontinuation

_____

_____

_____

References

Abedi, J. (2003). *Impact of student language background on content-based performance: Analyses of extant data. CSE report.* ERIC Document Reproduction Service No. ED 480903.

Abedi, J. (2006). Psychometric issues in the ELL assessment and special education eligibility. *Teachers College Record, 108,* 2282–2303.

Acevedo-Polakovich, I., Reynaga-Abiko, G., Garriot, P., Derefinko, K., Wimsatt, M., Gudonis, L., & Brown, T. (2007). Beyond instrument selection: Cultural considerations in the psychological assessment of U.S. Latinas/os. *Professional Psychology: Research and Practice, 38,* 375–384.

Achenbach, T. M. (1991, 1997, 2000, 2001, 2003, 2007). *Achenbach System of Empirically Based Assessment.* Burlington, VT: Research Center for Children, Youth and Families, Inc.

Achenbach, T. M., & Rescorla, L. A. (2001). *Manual for the ASEBA School-Age Forms & Profiles.* Burlington, VT: University of Vermont Research Center for Children, Youth, and Families.

Adams, G. (1986). *Normative Adaptive Behavior Checklist.* San Antonio, TX: The Psychological Corporation.

Alberto, P., & Troutman, A. (2006). *Applied behavior analysis for teachers* (6th ed.). Columbus, OH: Charles E. Merrill.

Alessi, G. (1980). Behavioral observation for the school psychologist: Responsive discrepancy model. *School Psychology Review, 9,* 31–45.

Algozzine, B., Christenson, S., & Ysseldyke, J. (1982). Probabilities associated with the referral to placement process. *Teacher Education and Special Education, 5,* 19–23.

Allinder, R. (1996). When some is better than none: Effects of differential implementation of curriculum-based measurement. *Exceptional Children, 62,* 525–535.

Allinder, R., Bolling, R., Oats, R., & Gagnon, W. (2000). Effects of teacher self-monitoring on implementation of curriculum-based measurement and mathematics computation achievement of students with disabilities. *Remedial and Special Education, 21,* 219–226.

Allinder, R., & Eccarius, M. (1999). Exploring the technical adequacy of curriculum-based measurement in reading for children who use manually coded English. *Exceptional Children, 65,* 271–282.

Allinder, R., Fuchs, L., & Fuchs, D. (1998). Curriculum-based assessment. In H. B. Vance (Ed.), *Psychological assessment of children* (2nd ed.; pp. 106–127). New York: John Wiley & Sons.

Allinder, R., & Oats, R. (1997). Effects of acceptability on teachers' implementation of curriculum-based measurement and student achievement in mathematics computation. *Remedial and Special Education, 18,* 113–120.

American Educational Research Association (AERA). (1999). *Standards for educational and psychological testing.* Washington, DC: Author.

American Psychological Association. (1992). *Ethical principles of psychologists and code of conduct.* Washington, DC: Author.

Anastasi, A., & Urbina, S. (1997). *Psychological testing* (7th ed.). Englewood Cliffs, NJ: Prentice-Hall.

Andersen, V., & Thompson, S. (1991). *Test of Written English.* Novato, CA: Academic Therapy.

Anderson, V., & Roit, M. (1998). Reading as a gateway to language proficiency for language-minority students in elementary grades. In R. Gersten & R. Jimeniz (Eds.), *Promoting language for culturally and linguistically diverse students* (pp. 42–56). Belmont, CA: Wadsworth.

Anthony, J., & Assel, M. (2007). A first look at the validity of the DIAL-3 Spanish version. *Journal of Psychoeducational Assessment, 25,* 165–179.

Anthony, J., Assel, M., & Williams, J. (2007). Exploratory and confirmatory factor analysis of the DIAL-3: What does this "developmental screener" really measure? *Journal of School Psychology, 45,* 423–438.

Applegate, M. D., Quinn, K. B., & Applegate, A. J. (2002). Levels of thinking required by comprehension questions in informal reading inventories. *Reading Teacher, 56,* 174–180.

Arter, J., & Jenkins, J. (1977). Examining the benefits and prevalences of modality considerations in special education. *Journal of Special Education, 11,* 281–298.

Arthaud, T., Vasa, S., & Steckelberg, A. (2000). Reading assessment and instructional practices in special education. *Diagnostique, 25,* 205–228.

Ashlock, R. (2006). *Error patterns in computation* (9th ed.). Upper Saddle River, NJ: Merrill Prentice-Hall.

Association for Career and Technical Education, & Brustein, M. (2006). *Perkins Act of 2006: The official guide: The authoritative guide to federal legislation for career and technical education.* Alexandria, VA: ACTE.

Bachor, D. (1990). Review of KeyMath–Revised. *Diagnostique, 15,* 87–98.

Bachor, D. (1998–1999). Review of the KeyMath–Revised/Normative Update. *Diagnostique, 24,* 161–182.

Bacon, E. (1989). Review of Behavior Rating Profile. In J. Conoley & J. Kramer (Eds.), *Tenth mental measurements yearbook* (pp. 84–86). Lincoln, NE: University of Nebraska Press.

Bagnato, S., & Neisworth J. (1991). *Assessment for early intervention: Best practices for professionals.* New York: Guilford Press.

Bain, S., & Allin, J. (2005). Review of the Stanford-Binet Intelligence Scale, Fifth Edition. *Journal of Psychoeducational Assessment, 23,* 87–95.

Baker, E. L. (1993). Questioning the technical quality of performance assessment. *The School Administrator, 50*(11), 12–16.

Baker, J. J. (2003). Dispositional coping strategies, optimism, and test anxiety as predictors of specific responses and performance in an exam situation. *Dissertation Abstracts International: Section B. The Sciences & Engineering, 64*(3–8), 1537.

Baker, S., Plasencia-Peinado, J., & Lezcano-Lytle, V. (1998). The use of curriculum-based measurement with language minority students. In M. Shinn (Ed.), *Advanced applications of curriculum-based measurement* (pp. 175–213). New York: Guilford Press.

Balthazar, E. (1976). *Balthazar Scales of Adaptive Behavior.* Palo Alto, CA: Consulting Psychologists Press.

Barnett, D. W., Faust, J., & Sarmir, M. A. (1988). A validity study of two preschool screening instruments: The LAP-D and DIAL-R. *Contemporary Educational Psychology, 13,* 26–32.

Barnhill, G., Hagiwara, T., Myles, B., Simpson, R., Brick, M., & Griswold, D. (2000). Parent, teacher, and self-report of problem and adaptive behaviors in children and adolescents with Asperger's disorder. *Diagnostique, 25,* 47–67.

Baron, I. (2005). Test review: Wechsler Intelligence Scale for Children–Fourth Edition (WISC-IV). *Child Neuropsychology, 11,* 471–475.

Barrera, M. (2003). Curriculum-based dynamic assessment for new or second-language learners with learning disabilities in secondary education settings. *Assessment for Effective Intervention, 29,* 69–84.

Barton, N. (2000). Depression in adolescence with attention deficit hyperactivity disorder: Using conditional probabilities based on teacher ratings from the Behavior Assessment System for Children. *Dissertation Abstracts International, 60*(8-a), 2861.

Beattie, J., & Enright, B. (1993). Problem solving: Verify the plan with action. *Teaching Exceptional Children, 26,* 60–62.

Beaver, B., & Busse, R. (2000). Informant reports: Conceptual and research bases of interviews with parents and teachers. In E. Shapiro & T. Kratochwill (Eds.), *Behavioral assessment in schools* (2nd ed.; pp. 257–287). New York: Guilford Press.

Beck, J., Beck, A., & Jolly, J. (2005). *Beck Youth Inventories* (2nd ed.). San Antonio: Psychological Corporation.

Beckmann, J. (2006). Superiority: Always and everywhere? On some misconceptions in the validation of dynamic testing. *Educational and Child Psychology, 23,* 35–49.

Belk, M. S., LoBello, S. G., Ray, G. E., & Zachar, P. (2002). WISC-III administration, clerical, and scoring errors made by student examiners. *Journal of Psychoeducational Assessment, 20,* 290–300.

Bell, N. L., Rucker, M., Finch Jr., A. J., & Alexander, I. (2002). Concurrent validity of the Slosson Full-Range Intelligence Test: Comparison with the Wechsler Intelligence Scale for Children–Third Edition and the Woodcock-Johnson Tests of Achievement–Revised. *Psychology in the Schools, 39,* 31–38.

Bellak, L., & Bellak, S. (1991). *Children's Apperception Test.* San Antonio: Psychological Corporation.

Bender, W., & Shores, C. (2007). *Response to intervention: A practical guide for every teacher.* Thousand Oaks, CA: Corwin Press.

Bennett, G., Seashore, H., & Wesman, A. (1990). *Differential Aptitude Tests* (5th ed.). San Antonio: Psychological Corporation.

Bentz, J., & Pavri, S. (2000). Curriculum-based measurement in assessing bilingual students: A promising new direction. *Diagnostique, 25,* 229–238.

Berends, M., & Koretz, D. (1996). Reporting minority students' test scores: How well can the National Assessment of Educational Progress account for differences in social context? *Educational Assessment, 3,* 249–285.

Berninger, V. (2000). *Process Assessment of the Learner: Test Battery for Reading and Writing.* San Antonio: Psychological Corporation.

Betts, E. (1946). *Foundations of reading instruction.* New York: American Book Co.

Beyersdorfer, J. (2003). *QARs + tables = successful comprehension of math word problems.* Urbana, IL: International Reading Association, ERIC Document Reproduction Service No. ED 482396.

Bigge, J., & Stump, C. (1999). *Curriculum, assessment, and instruction.* Belmont, CA: Wadsworth.

Bisconer, S. W., Stodden, R. A., & Porter, M. E. (1993). A psychometric evaluation of curriculum-based vocational assessment rating instruments used with students in mainstream vocational courses. *Career Development for Exceptional Individuals, 16,* 19–26.

Black, R., & Ornelles, C. (2001). Assessment of social competence and social networks for transition. *Assessment for Effective Intervention, 26,* 23–39.

Blalock, G., Kochhar-Bryant, C. A., Test, D. W., Kohler, P., White, W., Lehmann, J., Bassett, D., & Patton, J. (2003). The need for comprehensive personnel preparation in transition and career development: A position statement of the Division on Career Development and Transition. *Career Development for Exceptional Individuals, 26*(2), 207–226.

Blankenship, C. (1985). Using curriculum-based assessment data to make instructional decisions. *Exceptional Children, 52,* 233–238.

Bliss, S. (2007). Review of Battelle Developmental Inventory–Second Edition. *Journal of Psychoeducational Assessment, 25,* 409–415.

Block, R. (2003). Evaluation of a day treatment program for mentally disabled/severely emotionally disturbed adolescents. *Dissertation Abstracts International, 63*(11-B), 5504.

Boan, C., & Harrison, P. (1997). Adaptive behavior assessment and individuals with mental retardation. In R. Taylor (Ed.), *Assessment of individuals with mental retardation* (pp. 33–54). San Diego: Singular Publishing Group.

Boardman, A., & Woodruff, A. (2004). Teacher change and "high-stakes" assessment: What happens to professional development? *Teaching and Teacher Education, 20,* 545–557.

Boehm, A. (2000). *Boehm Test of Basic Concepts–3.* San Antonio: Psychological Corporation.

Boehm, A. (2001). *Boehm-3 Preschool.* San Antonio: Psychological Corporation.

Boehm, A., & Weinberg, R. (1997). *The classroom observer: Developing observation skills in early childhood settings* (3rd ed.). New York: Teachers College Press.

Boelte, S., & Poustka, F. (2002). The relation between general cognitive level and adaptive behavior domains in individuals with autism with and without co-morbid mental retardation. *Child Psychiatry and Human Development, 33,* 165–172.

Bolt, S., & Ysseldyke, J. (2006). Comparing DIF across math and reading/language arts tests for students receiving a read-aloud accommodation. *Applied Measurement in Education, 19,* 329–355.

Boney, T. (2003). Race, gender, and parental education differences in children's scores on the Adaptive Behavior Assessment System. *Dissertation Abstracts International, 63*(10-A), 3515.

Borich, G. (2007). *Observation skills for effective teaching* (5th ed.). Columbus, OH: Merrill.

Bosley, M. (1998). An analysis of language maturity, verbal aggression, argumentativeness, and propensity to violence in middle school adolescence. *Dissertation Abstracts International, 58*(10-a), 3773.

Bowers, L., Huisingh, R., Barrett, M., Orman, J., & LoGiudice, C. (2006). *Test of Problem Solving–3 (Elementary).* East Moline, IL: LinguiSystems.

Bracken, B. (2006a). *Bracken Basic Concept Scale–Third Edition Receptive.* San Antonio, TX: Psychological Corporation.

Bracken, B. (2006b). *Bracken Basic Concept Scale–Third Edition Expressive.* San Antonio, TX: Psychological Corporation.

Bracken, B., & Boatwright, B. (2005). *Clinical Assessment of Attention Deficit–Child.* Lutz, FL: Psychological Assessment Resources.

Bracken, B., Keith, L., & Walker, K. (1998). Assessment of preschool behavior in social-emotional functioning: A review of thirteen third-party instruments. *Journal of Psychoeducational Assessment, 16,* 153–168.

Bracken, B., & McCallum, R. (1998). *Universal Nonverbal Intelligence Test.* Itasca, IL: Riverside.

Braden, J. S., & Sabers, D. L. (2001). Test Reviews: Hammill, D. D., Bryant, B. R., & Pearson, N. A. (1998). Hammill Multiability Intelligence Test (HAMIT). *Journal of Psychoeducational Assessment, 19,* 383–391.

Bradley, A., & Scott, J. (2006). Tests of achievement useful, but beware of bias. *PsycCritiques, 51*(9).

Bradley-Johnson, S. (1997). Review of the Comprehensive Test of Nonverbal Intelligence. *Psychology in the Schools, 34,* 289–292.

Bradley-Johnson, S. (1998a). Review of the Oral and Written Language Scales. *Psychology in the Schools, 35,* 96–99.

Bradley-Johnson, S. (1998b). Review of the Test of Language Development–Primary: Third Edition. *Psychology in the Schools, 35,* 93–95.

Bradley-Johnson, S. (1999a). Review of the Brigance Diagnostic Comprehensive Inventory of Basic Skills–Revised. *Psychology in the Schools, 36,* 523–528.

Bradley-Johnson, S. (1999b). Review of the Bracken Basic Concept Scale–Revised. *Psychology in the Schools, 36,* 269–273.

Bradley-Klug, K., Shapiro, E., Lutz, J., & DuPaul, G. (1998). Evaluation of oral reading rate as a curriculum-based measure within literature-based curriculum. *Journal of School Psychology, 25,* 183–197.

Bramlett, R. K., & Barnett, D. W. (1993). The development of a direct observation code for use in preschool settings. *School Psychology Review, 22*(1), 49–62.

Bricker, D., Yovanoff, P., Capt, B., & Allen, D. (2003). Use of a curriculum-based measure to corroborate eligibility decisions. *Journal of Early Intervention, 26,* 20–30.

Bridgeman, B., Lennon, M. L., & Jackenthal, A. (2003). Effects of screen size, screen resolution, and display rate on computer-based test performance. *Applied Measurement in Education, 16,* 191–205.

Brigance, A. (1981). *Brigance Diagnostic Inventory of Essential Skills.* North Billerica, MA: Curriculum Associates.

Brigance, A. (1994). *Brigance Life Skills Inventory.* North Billerica, MA: Curriculum Associates.

Brigance, A. (1995). *Employability Skills Inventory.* North Billerica, MA: Curriculum Associates.

Brigance, A. (1999). *Brigance Comprehensive Inventory of Basic Skills–Revised.* North Billerica, MA: Curriculum Associates.

Brigance, A. (2004). *Inventory of Early Development–II.* North Billerica, MA: Curriculum Associates.

Browder, D. M., Fallin, K., Davis, S., & Karvonen, M. (2003). Consideration of what may influence student outcomes on alternate assessment. *Education and Training in Developmental Disabilities, 38,* 255.

Brown, J., Fishco, V., & Hanna, G. (2000). *Nelson-Denny Reading Test* (CD-ROM). Circle Pines, MN: American Guidance Service.

Brown, L., Branston, M. B., Hamre-Nietupski, S., Pumpian, I., Certo, N., & Gruenwald, L. (1979). A strategy for developing chronological age appropriate and functional curricular content for severely handicapped adolescents and young adults. *Journal of Special Education, 13,* 81–90.

Brown, L., Falvey, M., Vincent, L., Kaye, N., Johnson, F., Ferrara-Parrish, P., & Gruenwald, L. (1980). Strategies for generating comprehensive, longitudinal, and chronological age-appropriate individualized education programs for adolescent and young-adult severely handicapped students. *Journal of Special Education, 14,* 199–215.

Brown, L., & Hammill, D. (1990). *Behavior Rating Profile–2.* Austin, TX: Pro-Ed.

Brown, L., & Leigh, J. (1986). *Adaptive Behavior Inventory.* Austin, TX: Pro-Ed.

Brown, L., Sherbenou, R., & Johnsen, S. (1997) . *Test of Nonverbal Intelligence–3.* Austin, TX: Pro-Ed.

Brown, M., Giandenoto, M., & Bolen, L. (2000). Diagnosing written language disabilities using the Woodcock-Johnson Tests of Educational Achievement–Revised and the Wechsler Individual Achievement Test. *Psychological Reports, 87,* 197–204.

Brown, V., Cronin, M., & McEntire, E. (1994). *Test of Mathematical Abilities–2.* Austin, TX: Pro-Ed.

Brown, V., Hammill, D., & Wiederholt, J. L. (1995). *Test of Reading Comprehension–3.* Austin, TX: Pro-Ed.

Brownell, R. (2000a). *Expressive One-Word Vocabulary Test.* Novato, CA: Academic Therapy Press.

Brownell, R. (2000b). *Receptive One-Word Vocabulary Test.* Novato, CA: Academic Therapy Press.

Bruininks, R., Woodcock, R., Weatherman, R., & Hill, B. (1996). *The Scales of Independent Behavior–Revised.* Allen, TX: DLM Teaching Resources.

Bruno, R., & Walker, S. (1998–1999). Review of the Comprehensive Test of Phonological Processing. *Diagnostique, 24,* 69–82.

Bryant, B., Wiederholt, J., & Bryant, D. (2004). *Gray Diagnostic Reading Test–Second Edition*. Austin, TX: Pro-Ed.

Buck, K., & Schock, H. (1995). What is arena assessment? *Journal of Child Assessment News, 4*, 1–3.

Budoff, M. (1973). *Learning potential and educability among the educable mentally retarded* (Progress report, Grant No. OEG-0-8-080506-4597 from the National Institute of Education, HEW). Cambridge, MA: Research Institute for Educational Problems.

Bullock, A., & Hawk, P. (2005). *Developing a teaching portfolio.* (2nd ed.). Upper Saddle River, NJ: Prentice-Hall.

Bullock, L., Wilson, M., & Campbell, R. (1990). Inquiry into the commonality of items from seven behavior rating scales: A preliminary examination. *Behavioral Disorders, 15*, 87–99.

Bulotsky-Shearer, R., & Fantuzzo, J. (2004). Adjustment scales for preschool intervention: Extending validity and relevance across multiple perspectives. *Psychology in the Schools, 41*, 725–736.

Burgemeister, B., Blum, L., & Lorge, I. (1972). *Columbia Mental Maturity Scale* (3rd ed.). New York: Harcourt Brace Jovanovich.

Burger, S. E., & Burger, D. L. (1994). Determining the validity of performance-based assessment. *Educational Measurement, 13*, 9–15.

Burke, M. D., Hagan-Burke, S., Sugai, G. (2003). The efficacy of function-based interventions for students with learning disabilities who exhibit escape-maintained problem behaviors: Preliminary results from a single-case experiment. *Learning Disability Quarterly, 26*, 15–25.

Burnham, S. C., & Housley, W. F. (1992). Pride in work: Perceptions of employers, service providers and students who are mentally retarded and learning disabled. *Career Development for Exceptional Individuals, 15*, 101–108.

Burns, E. (1982). The use and interpretation of standardized grade equivalents. *Journal of Learning Disabilities, 15*, 17–18.

Burns, M., & Symington, T. (2003). A comparison of the Spontaneous Writing Quotient from the *Test of Written Language* (*3rd ed.*) and teacher ratings of writing progress. *Assessment for Effective Intervention, 28*, 29–34.

Butcher, J., Dahlstrom, W., Graham, A., & Kaemmer, B. (1989). *MMPI-2: Manual for administration and scoring*. Minneapolis: University of Minnesota Press.

Byrnaldyssen, S. (2002). *Recent reading initiatives. Examples of national state and professional organizations efforts.* Bloomington, IN: Family Learning Association. ERIC Document Reproduction Service No. ED 469927.

Cabrera, P., Grimes-Gaa, L., & Thyer, B. (1999). Social work assessment of adaptive functioning using the Vineland Adaptive Behavior Scales: Issues of reliability and validity. *Journal of Human Behavior in the Social Environment, 2*, 33–50.

Calhoun, M. B., & Fuchs, L. S. (2003). The effects of peer-assisted learning strategies and curriculum-based measurement on the mathematics performance of secondary students with disabilities. *Remedial and Special Education, 24*, 235–245.

Calhoun, M., Fuchs, L., & Hamlett, C. (2000). Effects of computer-based test accommodations on mathematics performance assessment for secondary students with learning disabilities. *Learning Disability Quarterly, 23*, 271–282.

Campbell, C., & Ashmore, R. (1995). Test review: The Slosson Intelligence Test–Revised. *Measurement and Evaluation in Counseling and Development, 28*, 116–118.

Campbell, J., Bell, S., & Keith, L. (2001). Concurrent validity of the Picture Vocabulary Test–Third Edition as an intelligence and achievement screener for low SES African American children. *Assessment, 8*, 85–94.

Campione, J. (1989). Assisted assessment: A taxonomy of approaches and an outline of strengths and weaknesses. *Journal of Learning Disabilities, 22*, 151–165.

Canter, M., Bennett, B., Jones, S., & Nagy, T. (1994). *Ethics for psychologists: A commentary on the APA ethics code.* Washington, DC: American Psychological Association.

Carlisle, J. (1999). Free recall as a test of reading comprehension for students with learning disabilities. *Learning Disability Quarterly, 22*, 11–22.

Carothers, D. E., & Taylor, R. L. (2005). Using portfolio assessment to develop transition programs for students with mental retardation. *Assessment for Effective Intervention, 30*(4), 33–39.

Carr, E., & Durand, V. (1985). Reducing behavior problems through functional communication training. *Journal of Applied Behavior Analysis, 18*, 111–126.

Carrow, S. (1994). *Carrow Elicited Language Inventory.* McAllen, TX: DLM Resources.

Carrow-Woolfolk, E. (1995). *Oral and Written Language Scales.* Circle Pines, MN: American Guidance Service.

Carrow-Woolfolk, E. (1999a). *Comprehensive Assessment of Spoken Language.* Circle Pines, MN: American Guidance Service.

Carrow-Woolfolk, E. (1999b). *Test for Auditory Comprehension of Language–Third Edition.* Austin, TX: Pro-Ed.

Cartwright, C., & Cartwright, G. (1984). *Developing observational skills* (2nd ed.). New York: McGraw-Hill.

Cashel, M. L. (2003). Validity of self-reports of delinquency and socio-emotional functioning among youth on probation. *Journal of Offender Rehabilitation, 37*, 11–23.

Cattell, R., Cattell, A., & Cattell, H. (1993). *Sixteen Personality Factor Questionnaire* (5th ed.). San Antonio, TX: Psychological Corporation.

Chafouleas, S. M., Riley-Tillman, C., & Eckert, T. L. (2003). A comparison of school psychologists' acceptability, training, and use of norm-referenced, curriculum-based, and brief experimental analysis methods to assess reading. *School Psychology Review, 32*, 272–281.

Champion, T. B., Hyter, Y. D., McCabe, A., & Bland-Stewart, L. M. (2003). "A matter of vocabulary": Performances of low-income African American Head Start children on the Peabody Picture Vocabulary Test–III. *Communication Disorders Quarterly, 24*, 121–127.

Child Assessment News. (1997). The consistency of cross-informant inconsistency. *Child Assessment News, 6*, 10–12.

Chin, C., Ledesma, H., Cirino, P., Sevcik, R., Morris, R., Fritjers, J., & Lovett, M. (2001). Relationship between the Kaufman Brief Intelligence Test and WISC-II scores of children with learning disabilities. *Journal of Learning Disabilities, 34*, 2–8.

Chittooran, M., & Miller, T. (1998). Informal assessment. In H. B. Vance (Ed.), *Psychological assessment of children* (2nd ed.; pp. 13–59). New York: John Wiley & Sons.

Christ, T. (2006). Short-term estimates of growth using curriculum-based measurement of oral reading fluency: Estimating standard error of the slope to construct confidence intervals. *School Psychology Review, 35,* 128–133.

Ciardi, E. (1990). Reading comprehension and the SAT. *Journal of Reading, 33,* 558–559.

Clarizio, H. (1982). Intellectual assessment of Hispanic children. *Psychology in the Schools, 33,* 558–559.

Clark, G., & Patton, J. (2006). *Transition Planning Inventory–2.* Austin, TX: Pro-Ed.

Cloud, N. (1991). Educational assessment. In E. Hamayan & J. Damico (Eds.), *Limited bias in the assessment of bilingual students* (pp. 219–246). Austin, TX: Pro-Ed.

Cobb, N., & Ray, R. (1975). *Manual for coding discrete behaviors in the school setting.* Eugene, OR: Oregon Research Bulletin.

Cohen, L., & Spence, S. (1990). Fundamental considerations of curriculum-based assessment. In L. Cohen & J. Spruill (Eds.), *A practical guide to curriculum-based assessment for special educators* (pp. 3–14). Springfield, IL: Charles Thomas.

Colarusso, R., & Hammill, D. (2002). *The Motor-Free Test of Visual Perception Test–Third Edition.* Austin, TX: Pro-Ed.

Cole, J., D'Alonzo, B., Gallegos, A., Giordano, G., & Stile, S. (1992). Test biases that hamper learners with disabilities. *Diagnostique, 17,* 209–225.

Coleman, L. J. (1994). Portfolio assessment: A key to identifying hidden talents and empowering teachers of young children. *Gifted Child Quarterly, 38,* 65–69.

Colón, E., & Kranzler, J. (2006). Effect of instructions on curriculum-based measurement of reading. *Journal of Psychoeducational Assessment, 24,* 318–328.

Conners, C. K. (1997). *Conners Rating Scales–Revised.* N. Tonawanda, NY: Multi-Health Systems.

Connolly, A. (2007). *KeyMath–3–DA.* Circle Pines, MN: American Guidance Service.

Connor-Smith, J. K., & Compas, B. E. (2003). Analogue measures of DSM-IV mood and anxiety disorders based on behavior checklists. *Journal of Psychopathology and Behavioral Assessment, 25,* 37–48.

Costantino, G., Flanagan, R., & Malgady, R. (2001). Narrative assessments: TAT, CAT, TEMAS. In L. Suzuki, J. Ponterotto, & P. Meller (Eds.), *Handbook of multicultural assessment* (2nd ed; pp. 217–236). San Francisco, CA: Jossey-Bass.

Council for Exceptional Children. (1997). Making assessments of diverse students meaningful. *CEC Today, 4,* 1, 9.

Council for Exceptional Children. (2006–2007). *Learning disabilities.* www.cec.sped.org/AM/Template.cfm?Section=Identifying_Learning_Disabilities. Retrieved 3/12/2007.

Coutinho, M., & Malouf, D. (1993). Performance assessment and children with disabilities: Issues and possibilities. *Teaching Exceptional Children, 25*(4), 62–67.

Crawford, L., Helwig, R., & Tindal, G. (2004). Writing performance assessmments: How important is extended time? *Journal of Learning Disabilities, 37,* 132–142.

Creaser, J., & Jacobs, M. (1987). Score discrepancies between the 1981 and 1985 editions of the Strong-Campbell Interest Inventory. *Journal of Counseling Psychology, 34,* 288–292.

CTB/McGraw-Hill. (2001). *TerraNova–Second Edition.* New York: Author.

CTB/McGraw-Hill. (2004). *Guidelines for inclusive test administration.* Monterey, CA: Author.

Daly, E., & Murdoch, A. (2000). Direct observation in the assessment of academic skills problems. In E. Shapiro & T. Kratochwill (Eds.), *Behavioral assessment in schools* (2nd ed.; pp. 46–77). New York: Guilford Press.

Dana, R. (1996). Culturally competent assessment practices in the United States. *Journal of Personality Assessment, 66,* 472–487.

Dana, R. (1999). Cross-cultural-multicultural use of the Thematic Apperception Test. In L. Gieser and M. Stein (Eds). *Evocative images: The Thematic Apperception Test and the art of projection* (pp. 177–190). Washington, DC: American Psychological Association.

Davenport, R. (2002). *Miscues, not mistakes. Reading assessment in the classroom.* ERIC Document Reproduction Service No. ED 472803.

Davis, C. (1980). *Perkins-Binet Intelligence Scale.* Watertown, MA: Perkins School for the Blind.

Day, V., & Skidmore, M (1996). Linking performance assessment and curricular goals. *Teaching Exceptional Children, 29,* 59–64.

DeFur, S. H., & Taymans, J. M. (1995). Competencies needed for transition specialists in vocational rehabilitation, vocational education, and special education. *Exceptional Children, 62,* 38–51.

Denham, A., Bennett, D., Edyburn, D., Lahm, E., & Kleinert, H. (2001). Implementing technology to demonstrate higher levels of learning. In H. L. Kleinert & J. F. Kearns (Eds.), *Alternative assessment: Measuring outcomes and supports for students with disabilities* (pp. 148–154). Baltimore: Paul H. Brookes.

Deno, S. (1985). Curriculum-based measurement: The emerging alternative. *Exceptional Children, 52,* 219–232.

Deno, S. (2003). Developments in curriculum-based measurement. *Journal of Special Education, 37,* 184–192.

Deno, S., & Fuchs, L. (1987). Developing curriculum-based measurement systems for data based special education problem solving. *Focus on Exceptional Children, 19,* 1–16.

DeStefano, L., Shriner, J., & Lloyd, C. (2001). Teacher decision making in participation of students with disabilities in large scale assessment. *Exceptional Children, 68,* 7–22.

DeStefano, L., & Wagner, M. (1993). Outcome assessment in special education: Implications for decision-making and long-term planning in vocational rehabilitation. *Career Development for Exceptional Individuals, 16,* 147–158.

Dicerbo, K. (2003). English language proficiency and tests of intelligence and academic achievement. *Dissertation Abstracts International, 64*(3-A), 793.

DiPerna, J., & Elliott, S. (2000). *Academic Competence Evaluation Scales.* San Antonio: Psychological Corporation.

DiPerna, J., & Volpe, R. (2005). Self-report on the Social Skills Rating System: An analysis of reliability and validity for an elementary sample. *Psychology in the Schools, 42,* 345.

DiStefano, C., & Dombrowski, S. (2006). Investigating the theoretical structure of the Stanford-Binet–Fifth Edition. *Journal of Psychoeducational Assessment, 24,* 123–136.

Division on Career Development and Transistion. (n.d.). *Student involvement in the IEP process.* www.dcdt.org/pdf/DCDT_Fact_Sheet_IEP_Process.pdf. Retrieved 01/04/2008.

Division on Career Development and Transistion. (n.d.). *Age appropriate transition assessment.* www.dcdt.org/pdf/Trans_Assess_Fact_Sheet%20.pdf. Retrieved 01/04/2008.

Dombrowski, S., DiStefano, C., & Noonan, K. (2004). Review of the Stanford-Binet Intelligence Scale: Fifth edition (SB5). *Communique, 33,* 32–34.

Duckworth, J. C. (1991). The Minnesota Multiphasic Personality Inventory–2: A review. *Journal of Counseling and Development, 69,* 564–567.

Dufflemeyer, F., & Dufflemeyer, B. (1989). Are informal reading inventories passages suitable for assessing main idea comprehension? *The Reading Teacher, 42,* 358–363.

Dufflemeyer, F., Robinson, S., & Squier, S. (1989). Vocabulary questions on informal reading inventories. *The Reading Teacher, 43,* 142–148.

Duffy, M., Jones, J., & Thomas, S. (1999). Using portfolios to foster independent thinking. *Intervention in School and Clinic, 35,* 34–37.

Dunn, L., & Dunn, G. (2007). *Peabody Picture Vocabulary Test–4.* Circle Pines, MN: American Guidance Service.

Duran, R., Brown, C., & McCall, M. (2002). Assessment of English-language learners in the Oregon statewide assessment system: National and state prospectives. In G. Tindal & T. Haladyna (Eds.), *Large scale assessment programs for all students* (pp. 371–394). Mahwah, NJ: Lawrence Erlbaum.

Eaves, R., Campbell-Whatley, G., Dunn, C., Reilly, A., & Tate-Braxton, C. (1995). Statistically significant differences between standard scores on the Woodcock Reading Mastery Tests. *Diagnostique, 21,* 1–5.

Eaves, R., & Milner, B., (1993). The criterion related validity of the Childhood Autism Rating Scale and the Autism Behavior Checklist. *Journal of Abnormal Child Psychology, 21,* 481–491.

Eaves, R., Woods-Groves, S., Williams, T., & Fall, A. (2006). Reliability and validity of the Pervasive Developmental Disorders Rating Scale and the Gilliam Autism Rating Scale. *Education and Training in Developmental Disabilities, 41,* 300–309.

Edwards, O. (2006). Special education disproportionality and the influence of intelligence test selection. *Journal of Intellectual and Developmental Disability, 31,* 246–248.

Edwards, O., & Oakland, T. (2006). Factorial invariance of Woodcock-Johnson III scores for African Americans and Caucasian Americans. *Journal of Psychoeducational Assessment, 24,* 358–366.

Edyburn, D. L. (1994). An equation to consider: The portfolio assessment knowledge base and technology = The Grady Profile. *LD Forum, 19*(4), 35–38.

Ehly, S. (1989). Review of Adaptive Behavior Inventory. In J. Conoley & J. Kramer (Eds.), *Tenth mental measurements yearbook* (pp. 20–21). Lincoln, NE: University of Nebraska Press.

Ehrler, D. (1996). Test of Written Expression: A critical review. *Journal of School Psychology, 34,* 387–391.

Ekwall, E. (1993). *Locating and correcting reading difficulties* (6th ed.). New York: Maxwell Macmillan International.

Ekwall, E., & Shanker, J. (1988). *Diagnosis and remediation of the disabled reader* (3rd ed.). Boston: Allyn and Bacon.

Ellers, R., Ellers, S., & Bradley-Johnson, S. (1989). Stability reliability of the Behavior Rating Profile. *Journal of School Psychology, 27*(3), 257–263.

Elliott, S., DiPerna, J., & Shapiro, E. (2000). *Academic Intervention Monitoring System.* San Antonio: Psychological Corporation.

Elliott, S., & Fuchs, L. (1997). The utility of curriculum-based measurement and performance assessment as alternatives to traditional intelligence and achievement tests. *School Psychology Review, 26,* 224–233.

Elliott, S., Kratochwill, T., & McKevitt, B. (2001). Experimental analysis of the effects of testing accommodations on the scores of students with and without disabilities. *Journal of School Psychology, 38,* 3–24.

Elliott, S., & Roach, A. (April, 2002). *The impact of providing testing accommodations to students with disabilities.* Paper presented at the annual convention of the American Educational Research Association, New Orleans, LA.

Elrod, G., Isbell, C., & Braziel, P. (1989). Assessing transition-related variables from kindergarten through grade 12: Practical applications. *Diagnostique, 14,* 247–261.

Emmons, M., & Alfonso, V. (2005). A critical review of the technical characteristics of current preschool screening batteries. *Journal of Psychoeducational Assessment, 23,* 111–127.

Enright, B. (1995). Basic mathematics. In J. Choate, B. Enright, L. Miller, J. Poteet, & T. Rakes (Eds.), *Curriculum-based assessment and programming.* (2nd ed.; pp. 197–230). Boston: Allyn and Bacon.

Enright, B. (2002). *Diagnostic Assessment of Computation Skills* (CD-ROM). Greensboro, NC: National Training Network.

Enright, B., Beattie, J., & Algozzine, B. (1992). Helping mainstreamed students develop successful test-taking skills. *Diagnostique, 17,* 128–136.

Enright, B., Gable, R., & Hendrickson, J. (1988). How do students get answers like these? Nine steps in diagnosing computation errors. *Diagnostique, 13,* 55–63.

Epstein, M. (2004). *Behavioral and Emotional Rating Scale.* (2nd ed.). Austin, TX: Pro-Ed.

Erickson, D. (1989). Review of Test of Written Spelling–2. In J. Conoley & J. Kramer (Eds.), *Tenth mental measurements yearbook* (pp. 858–859). Lincoln, NE: University of Nebraska Press.

Espin, C., Shin, J., Deno, S., Skare, S., Robinson, S., & Benner, B. (2000). Identifying indicators of written expression proficiency for middle school students. *Journal of Special Education, 34,* 140–153.

Evans, S., Evans, W., & Mercer, C. (1986). *Assessment for instruction.* Boston: Allyn and Bacon.

Evans, W. H., Gable, R. A., & Evans, S. S. (1993). Making something out of everything: The promise of ecological assessment. *Diagnostique, 18,* 175–185.

Ezell, D., & Klein, C. (2003). Impact of portfolio assessment on locus of control of students with and without disabilities. *Education and Training in Development Disabilities, 38,* 220–227.

Ezell, D., Klein, C., & Ezell-Powell, S. (1999). Empowering students with mental retardation through portfolio assessment: A tool for fostering self determination skills.

Education and Training in Mental Retardation and Developmental Disabilities, 34, 453–463.

Falvey, M. (1989). *Community-based curriculum* (2nd ed.). Baltimore: Paul H. Brookes.

Falvey, M., Brown, L., Lyon, S., Baumgart, D., & Schroeder, J. (1980). Strategies for using cues and correction procedures. In W. Sailor, B. Wilcox, & L. Brown (Eds.), *Methods of instruction for severely handicapped students* (pp. 109–133). Baltimore: Paul H. Brookes.

Farhady, H., & Keramati, M. (1996). A text-driven method for the deletion procedure in cloze passages. *Language Testing, 13,* 190–207.

Farr, R., & Tone, B. (1998). *Portfolio and performance assessment: Helping students evaluate their progress as readers and writers* (2nd ed.). Fort Worth, TX: Harcourt Brace College Publishers.

Faykus, S., & McCurdy, B. (1998). Evaluting the sensitivity of the maze as an index of reading proficiency for students who are severely deficient in reading. *Education and Treatment of Children, 21,* 1–21.

Federal Register. (1977). Washington, DC: U.S. Government Printing Office, August 23, 1977.

Federal Register. (1997). Washington, DC: U.S. Government Printing Office, June 4, 1997.

Ferdinand, R. F., van Der Ende, J., & Verhulst, F. (2004). Parent-adolescent disagreement regarding psychopathology in adolescents from the general population as a risk factor for adverse outcome. *Journal of Abnormal Psychology, 113,* 198–206.

Ferguson, J., & Kerstig, F. (1988). Comparison of diagnostic inventories used in special education with state-approved essential skills tests. *Journal of Human Behavior and Learning, 5,* 39–42.

Fernsten, L., & Fernsten, J. (2005). Portfolio assessment and reflection: Enhancing learning through effective practice. *Reflective Practice, 6,* 303–309.

Feuerstein, R., Haywood, H., Rand, Y., Hoffman, M., & Jensen, B. (1984). *Examiner manuals for the Learning Potential Assessment Device.* Jerusalem: Hadassah-WIZO-Canada Research Institute.

Fewster, S., & MacMillan, P. D. (2002). School-based evidence for the validity of curriculum-based measurement of reading and writing. *Remedial and Special Education, 23,* 149–156.

Field, S., Martin, J., Miller, R., Ward, M., & Wehmeyer, M. (1998). Self-determination of persons with disabilities: A position statement of the Division on Career Development and Transition. *Career Development for Exceptional Individuals, 21,* 113–128.

Fielding-Barnsley, R., & Purdie, N. (2003). Early intervention in the home for children at risk of reading failure. *Support for Learning, 18,* 77–82.

Figueroa, R., & Newsome, P. (2006). The diagnosis of LD in English learners: Is it nondiscriminatory? *Journal of Learning Disabilities, 39,* 206–214.

Fischer, C., & King, R. (1995). *Authentic assessment: A guide to implementation.* Thousand Oaks, CA: Corwin Press.

Flanagan, D., McGrew, K., Abramowitz, E., Lehner, L., Untiedt, S., Berger, D., & Armstrong, H. (1997). Improvement in academic screening instruments? A concurrent validity investigation of the K-FAST, MBA, and WRAT-3. *Journal of Psychoeducational Assessment, 15,* 99–112.

Flanagan, D., McGrew, K., Abramowitz, E., & Untiedt, S. (1997). Improvement in academic screening instruments? A concurrent validity investigation of the K-FAST, MBA, and WRAT-III. *Journal of Psychoeducational Assessment, 15,* 99–112.

Flanagan, D., Ortiz, S., Alfonso, V., & Dynda, A. (2006). Integration of response to intervention and norm-referenced tests in learning disability identification: Learning from the tower of Babel. *Psychology in the Schools, 43,* 807–825.

Fleege, P. O., Charlesworth, R., Burts, D. C., & Hart, C. H. (1992). Stress begins in kindergarten: A look at behavior during standardized testing. *Journal of Research in Childhood Education, 7*(1), 20–26.

Flippo, R., Becker, M., & Wark, D. (2000). Preparing for and taking tests. In R. Flippo & D. Caverly (Eds.), *Education handbook of college reading and study strategy research* (pp. 221–260). Mahwah, NJ: Lawrence Erlbaum.

Florida Department of Education. (1989). *Prekindergarten assessment and training of the handicapped.* Tallahassee, FL: Author.

Floyd, R., & Bose, J. E. (2003). Behavior rating scales for assessment of emotional disturbance: A critical review of measurement characteristics. *Journal of Psychoeducational Assessment, 21,* 43–78.

Floyd, R., Evans, J., McGrew, K. (2003). Relations between measures of Cattell-Horn-Carroll (CHC) cognitive abilities and mathematics achievement across the school year. *Psychology in the Schools, 40,* 155–171.

Floyd, R., McCormack, A., Ingram, E., Davis, A., Bergeron, R., & Hamilton, G. (2006). Relations between the Woodcock-Johnson–III and measures of executive functions from the Delis-Kaplan Executive Function System. *Journal of Psychoeducational Assessment, 24,* 303–317.

Fodness, R., McNeilly, J., & Bradley-Johnson, S. (1991). Relationship of the Test of Language Development–2 Primary and the Test of Language Development–2 Intermediate. *Journal of School Psychology, 29,* 167–176.

Foegen, A., Espin, C., Allinder, R., & Markell, M. (2001). Translating research into practice: Preservice teacher's belief about curriculum-based measurement. *Journal of Special Education, 34,* 226–236.

Forbes, G. B. (2001). A comparison of the Conners' Parent and Teacher Rating Scales, the ADD-H Comprehensive Teacher's Rating Scale, and the Child Behavior Checklist in the clinical diagnosis of ADHD. *Journal of Attention Disorders, 5,* 25–40.

Forbey, J., & Ben-Porath, Y. (2007). Computerized adaptive personality testing: A review and illustration with the MMPI-2 computerized adaptive version. *Psychological Assessment, 19,* 14–24.

Forsyth, R., Ansley, T., Feldt, L., & Alnot, S. (2001). *Iowa Tests of Educational Development, Form A.* Chicago: Riverside.

Frank, A. (1973). Breaking down learning tasks: A sequence approach. *Teaching Exceptional Children, 6,* 16–21.

Frank, A., & Gerken, K. (1990). Case studies in curriculum-based measurement. *Education and Training in Mental Retardation, 25,* 113–119.

Frank, L. (1939). Projective methods for the study of personality. *Journal of Psychology, 8,* 389–413.

French, J. (2001). *Pictorial Test of Intelligence–Second Edition.* Austin: TX: Pro-Ed.

Frisby, C. L., & Braden, J. P. (1992). Feuerstein's dynamic assessment approach: A semantic, logical, and empirical critique. *Journal of Special Education, 26*(3), 281–301.

Frostig, M., Lefever, W., & Whittlesey, J. (1966). *Administration and scoring manual: Marianne Frostig Developmental Test of Visual Perception.* Palo Alto, CA: Consulting Psychologists Press.

Fuchs, D., & Fuchs, L. (1989). Effects of examiner familiarity on black, Caucasian, and Hispanic children: A metanalysis. *Exceptional Children, 55,* 303–308.

Fuchs, L. (1994). *Connecting performance assessment to instruction.* Reston, VA: Council for Exceptional Children. (Abstracted in *Diagnostique, 20*).

Fuchs, L., & Fuchs, D. (1990). Traditional academic assessment: An overview. In R. Gable & J. Hendrickson (Eds.), *Assessing students with special needs* (pp. 1–13). New York: Longman.

Fuchs, L., & Fuchs, D. (2000). Analogue assessment of academic skills: Curriculum-based measurement and performance assessment. In E. Shapiro & T. Kratchowill (Eds.), *Behavioral assessment in schools* (2nd ed.; pp. 168–201). New York: Guilford Press.

Fuchs, L., & Fuchs, D. (2002). Curriculum-based measurement: Describing competence, enhancing outcomes, evaluating treatment effects, and identifying treatment nonresponsers. *Peabody Journal of Education, 77,* 64–84.

Fuchs, L., Fuchs, D., Eaton, S., & Hamlett, C. (2003). *Dynamic Assessment of Test Accommodations.* San Antonio: Psychological Corporation.

Fuch, L., Fuchs, D., Eaton, S., Hamlett, C., & Karns, K. (2000). Supplementing teacher judgements of mathematics test accommodations with objective data sources. *School Psychology Review, 29,* 65–85.

Fuchs, L., Fuchs, D., & Hamlett, C. (1989). Computers and curriculum based measurement: Effects of teacher feedback systems. *School Psychology Review, 18,* 112–125.

Fuchs, L. S., Fuchs, D., & Hamlett, C. L. (1993). Technological advances linking the assessment of students' academic proficiency to instructional planning. *Journal of Special Education Technology, 12,* 49–62.

Fuchs, L., Fuchs, D., Hamlett, C., & Allinder, R. (1991). The contribution of skills analysis to curriculum-based measurement in spelling. *Exceptional Children, 57,* 443–452.

Fuchs, L., Fuchs, D., Hamlett, C., & Ferguson, C. (1992). Effects of expert system consultation within curriculum-based management using a reading maze task. *Exceptional Children, 58,* 436–450.

Fuchs, L., Fuchs, D., Hamlett, C. L., Phillips, N., & Bentz, J. (1994). Classroom curriculum-based measurement: Helping general educators meet the challenge of student diversity. *Exceptional Children, 60,* 518–537.

Fuchs, L. S., Fuchs, D., Hosp, M. K., & Hamlett, C. L. (2003). The potential for diagnostic analysis within curriculum-based measurement. *Assessment for Effective Intervention, 28,* 13–22.

Fuchs, L., Fuchs, D., Karns, K., Hamlett, C., Dutka, S., & Katzaroff, M. (2000). The importance of providing background information on the structure and scoring of performance assessment. *Applied Measurement in Education, 13,* 1–34.

Fuchs, L., Fuchs, D., Karns, K., Hamlett, C., & Katzaroff, M. (1999). Mathematics performance assessment in the classroom: Effects on teacher planning and student problem solving. *American Educational Research Journal, 36,* 609–646.

Fuchs, L., Hamlett, C., & Fuchs, D. (1997). *Monitoring Basic Skills Progress—Reading.* Austin, TX: Pro-Ed.

Fuchs, L., Hamlett, C., & Fuchs, D. (1998). *Monitoring Basic Skills Progress—Math.* Austin, TX: Pro-Ed.

Fuchs, L., Hamlett, C., & Fuchs, D. (1999). *Monitoring Basic Skills Progress—Math Concepts and Applications.* Austin, TX: Pro-Ed.

Fujiki, M. (1989). Review of Test of Pragmatic Skills. In J. Conoley & J. Kramer (Eds). *Tenth mental measurement yearbook* (pp. 847–848). Lincoln: University of Nebraska Press.

Gable, R. (1990). Curriculum-based measurement of oral reading: Linking assessment and instruction. *Preventing School Failure, 35,* 37–42.

Gable, R., & Coben, S. (1990). Errors in arithmetic. In R. Gable & J. Hendrickson (Eds.), *Assessing students with special needs* (pp. 30–45). New York: Longman.

Gable, R., & Hendrickson, J. (1990). *Assessing students with special needs.* New York: Longman.

Galagan, J. (1985). Psychoeducational testing: Turn out the light the party's over. *Exceptional Children, 52,* 288–299.

Gall, M. (1990). *Tools for learning: A guide to teaching study skills* (ED 320126). Alexandria, VA: Association for Supervision and Curriculum Development.

Gansle, K. A., Noell, G. H., VanDerHeyden, A. M., Naquin, G. M., & Slider, N. J. (2002). Moving beyond total words written: The reliability, criterion validity, and time cost of alternate measures for curriculum-based measurement in writing. *School Psychology Review, 31,* 477–497.

Gansle, K., VanDerHeyden, A., Noell, G., Resetar, J., & Williams, K. (2006). The technical adequacy of curriculum-based and rating-based measures of written expression for elementary school students. *School Psychology Review, 35,* 435–450.

Gardner, H. (1993). *Frames of mind: The theory of multiple intelligences.* New York: Basic Books.

Gardner, M. (1998). *Test of Handwriting Skills.* Austin, TX: Pro-Ed.

German, D. (2000). *Test of Word Finding–2.* Austin, TX: Pro-Ed.

Gettinger, M., & Seibert, J. (2000). Analogue assessment: Research and practice in evaluating academic skills problems. In E. Shapiro & T. Kratchwill (Eds.), *Behavioral assessment in schools* (2nd ed.; pp. 139–167). New York: Guilford Press.

Gettinger, M., & Stoiber, K. (2006). Functional assessment, collaboration, and evidence-based treatment: Analysis of a team approach for addressing challenging behavior in young children. *Journal of School Psychology, 44,* 231–252.

Giacobbe, G., & Traynelis-Yurek, E. (1989). Undergraduate students' errors in the administration of standardized tests. *Diagnostique, 14,* 174–182.

Gibb, G., & Dyches, T. (2007). *Guide to writing quality individualized programs* (2nd ed.). Boston: Allyn and Bacon.

Gickling, E., & Thompson, J. (1985). A personal view of curriculum-based assessment. *Exceptional Children, 52,* 205–218.

Gil, L. A. (2007). Bridging the transition gap from high school to college. Preparing students with disabilities for a successful postsecondary experience. *Teaching Exceptional Children, 40*(2), 12–15.

Gillam, R. B., Crofford, J. A., Gale, M. A., & Hoffman, L. M. (2001). Language change following computer-assisted language instruction with Fast ForWord or Laureate Learning Systems software. *American Journal of Speech-Language Pathology 10,* 231–247.

Gillham, J., Carter, A., Volkmar, F., & Sparrow, S. (2000). Toward a developmental operational definition of autism. *Journal of Autism and Developmental Disorders, 30,* 269–278.

Gilliam, J. (1994). *Work Adjustment Inventory.* Austin, TX: Pro-Ed.

Gilliam, J. (1995). *Attention Deficit/Hyperactivity Disorder Test.* Austin, TX: Pro-Ed.

Gilliam, J. (2001). *Gilliam Autism Disorder Scale.* Austin, TX: Pro-Ed.

Gilliam, J. (2006). *Gilliam Asperger Rating Scale-2.* Austin, TX: Pro-Ed.

Gilotty, L., Kenworthy, L., Sirian, L., Black, D. O., & Wagner, A. E. (2002). Adaptive skills and executive function in autism spectrum disorders. *Child Neuropsychology, 8,* 241–248.

Gimpel, G., & Nagle, R. (1999). Psychometric properties of the Devereux Scales of Mental Disorders. *Journal of Psychoeducational Assessment, 17,* 127–144.

Ginsburg, H., & Baroody, A. (2003). *Test of Early Mathematics Ability–3.* Austin, TX: Pro-Ed.

Giordano, L. (2000). Effects of test anxiety control training on the anxious behaviors and academic performances in college students with learning disabilities. *Dissertations Abstracts International, 60*(8-b), 41–96.

Giordano, F., Schwiebert, V., & Brotherton, W. (1997). School counselors' perceptions of the usefulness of standardized tests, frequency of their use, and assessment training needs. *School Counselor, 44,* 198–205.

Glanz, J. (1994). Effects of stress reduction on reducing test anxiety among learning disabled students. *Journal of Instructional Psychology, 21,* 313–317.

Glascoe, F. (1997). Do the Brigance Screens detect developmental and academic problems? *Diagnostique, 22,* 87–99.

Glascoe, F. (2005). Screening for developmental and behavioral problems. *Mental Retardation and Developmental Disabilities, 11,* 173–179.

Glutting, J., Watkins, M., Konold, T., & McDermott, P. (2006). Distinctions without a difference: The utility of observed versus latent factors from the WISC-IV in estimating reading and math achievement on the WIAT-II. *Journal of Special Education, 40,* 203–114.

Glutting, J., & Wilkinson, G. (2003). *Wide Range Interest and Occupational Test–2.* Austin, TX: Pro-Ed.

Glutting, J., & Wilkinson, G. (2007). *Wide Range Achievement Test–4.* Austin, TX: Pro-Ed.

Goldblatt, J., & Friedman, F. (1998–1999). Review of the Oral and Written Language Scales. *Diagnostique, 24,* 197–210.

Goldman, R., & Fristoe, M. (2000). *Goldman-Fristoe Test of Articulation–2.* Circle Pines, MN: American Guidance Service.

Good, R. H., & Kaminski, R. A. (Eds.). (2002). *Dynamic indicators of basic literacy skills* (6th ed.). Eugene, OR: Institute for the Development of Educational Achievement.

Goodman, Y., & Burke, C. (1972). *Reading Miscue Inventory.* New York: Macmillan.

Goodman, Y., Watson, D., & Burke, C. (1987). *Reading miscue inventory: Alternative procedures.* New York: Richard C. Owen, Publisher.

Gonzalez, L., & Robison, D. (2003). Early reading intervention in the home for children at risk of reading failure. *Support for Learning, 18,* 77–82.

Gordon, L. (1981). *Gordon Occupational Check List II.* San Antonio: Psychological Corporation.

Grados, J., & Russo-Garcia, K. (1999). Comparison of the Kaufman Brief Intelligence Test and the Wechsler Intelligence Scale for Children–Third Edition and economically disadvantaged African-American youth. *Journal of Clinical Psychology, 55,* 1063–1071.

Grady, M. (1999). *Grady profile* (computer software). St. Louis: Aurbach and Associates.

Graziano, W. (1982). Race of the examiner effects and the validity of intelligence tests. *Review of Education Research, 52,* 469–497.

Greenwood, C., Carta, J., Kamps, D., Terry, B., & Delquadri, A. (1994). Development and validation of standard classroom observation systems for school practitioners: Ecobehavioral Assessment Systems Software (EBASS). *Exceptional Children, 61,* 197–210.

Gregg, N., & Mather, N. (2002). School is fun at recess: Informal analyses of of written language for students with learning disabilities. *Journal of Learning Disabilities, 35,* 7–22.

Gresham, F. (2001, August). *Responsiveness to intervention: An alternative approach to the identification of learning disabilities.* Paper presented at the Learning Disabilities Summit: Building a foundation for the future, Washington, DC.

Gresham, F. (2003). Establishing the technical adequacy of functional behavioral assessment: Conceptual and measurement challenges. *Behavioral Disorders, 28,* 282–298.

Gresham, F., & Elliot, S. (1990). *Social Skills Rating System.* Circle Pines, MN: American Guidance Service.

Griffin, H. (1997). Review of the Test of Mathematical Abilities–2. *Measurement and Evaluation in Counseling and Development, 29,* 242–247.

Grill, J., & Kirwin, M. (1995). *Written Language Assessment.* Novato, CA: Academic Therapy.

Gronlund, N. (1973). *Preparing criterion-referenced tests for classroom instruction.* New York: Macmillan.

Gronlund, N. (1988). *How to construct achievement tests* (4th ed.). Englewood Cliffs, NJ: Prentice-Hall.

Gronlund, N. (2006). *Assessment of student achievement* (8th ed.). Boston: Allyn and Bacon.

Grubb, D., & Courtney, A. (1996, March). *Developmentally appropriate assessment of young children: The role of portfolio assessments.* Paper presented at the annual conference of the Southern Early Childhood Association, Little Rock, AK. (ERIC Document Reproduction Service No. ED 400114).

Gullo, D. (2006). Alternative means of assessing children's learning in early childhood classrooms. In B. Spodak and O. Saracho (Eds.), *Handbook of research on the education of young children* (2nd ed.; pp. 443–455). Mahwah, NJ: Erlbaum.

Gunning, M., & D'Amato, R. (1998). Review of the Student Self-Concept Scale. *Journal of Psychoeducational Assessment, 16,* 181–186.

Guthke, J., & Beckmann, J. (2003). Dynamic assessment with diagnostic problems. In R. Sternberg and J. Laudrey (Eds.) *Models of intelligence: International perspectives* (pp. 227–242). Washington, DC: American Psychological Association.

Guthke, J., Beckmann, J., & Dobat, H. (1997). Dynamic testing—Problems, uses, trends, and evidence of validity. *Educational and Child Psychology, 14,* 17–32.

Hadaway, N. L., & Marek-Schroer, M. (1994). Student portfolios: Toward equitable assessments for gifted students. *Equity and Excellence in Education, 27,* 70–74.

Haladyna, T. (2002). *Essentials of standardized achievement testing validity and accountability.* Boston: Allyn and Bacon.

Haley, J. (1963). *Strategies of psychotherapy.* New York: Grune & Stratton.

Hall, J., Bramlett, R., Barnett, D., & Cox, F. (1994). Classification of risk status in kindergarten screening: A comparison of alternative measures. *Journal of Psychoeducational Assessment, 12,* 154–164.

Hallahan, D., & Cruickshank, W. (1973). *Psychoeducational foundations of learning disabilities.* Englewood Cliffs, NJ: Prentice-Hall.

Hallahan, D., & Kauffman, J. (2004). *Exceptional learners* (9th ed.). Boston: Allyn and Bacon.

Halpern, A. S. (1994). The transition of youth with disabilities to adult life: A position statement of the Division on Career Development and Transition. *Career Development for Exceptional Individuals, 17,* 115–124.

Hammill, D. (1998). *Detroit Tests of Learning Aptitude–4.* Austin, TX: Pro-Ed.

Hammill, D., Brown, V., Larsen, S., & Weiderholt, L. (2007). *Test of Adolescent and Adult Language–4.* Austin, TX: Pro-Ed.

Hammill, D., Bryant, B., & Pearson, N. (1998). *Hammill Multiability Intelligence Test.* Austin, TX: Pro-Ed.

Hammill, D., Hresko, W., Ammer, J., Cronin, M., & Quinby, S. (1998). *Hammill Multiability Achievement Test.* Austin, TX: Pro-Ed.

Hammill, D., & Larsen, S. (1996). *Test of Written Language–3.* Austin, TX: Pro-Ed.

Hammill, D., Mather, N., & Roberts, R. (2001). *The Illinois Test of Psycholinguistic Abilities–Third Edition.* Austin, TX: Pro-Ed.

Hammill, D., & Newcomer, P. (1997). *Test of Language Development: 3 (Intermediate).* Austin, TX: Pro-Ed.

Hammill, D., Pearson, N., & Voress, J. (1993). *Developmental Test of Visual Perception–2.* Austin, TX: Pro-Ed.

Hammill, D., Pearson, N., & Wiederholt, L. (1997). *Comprehensive Test of Nonverbal Intelligence–Computer Administered.* Austin, TX: Pro-Ed.

Hammill, D., & Wiederholt, L. (2001). *Illinois Test of Psycholinguistic Abilities–3.* Austin, TX: Pro-Ed.

Hammill, D., Wiederholt, L., & Pearson, N. (1996). *Comprehensive Test of Nonverbal Intelligence.* Austin, TX: Pro-Ed.

Haney, M., & Evans, J. (1999). National survey of school psychologists regarding use of dynamic assessment and other traditional assessment techniques. *Psychology in the Schools, 36,* 295–304.

Harcourt Educational Measurement. (1996). *Stanford Diagnostic Mathematics Tests: 4.* San Antonio, TX: Author.

Harcourt Educational Measurement (2002). *Metropolitan Achievement Tests, Eighth Edition.* San Antonio, TX: Author.

Harcourt Educational Measurement. (2003a). *Stanford Early School Achievement Test.* San Antonio, TX: Author.

Harcourt Educational Measurement. (2003b). *Stanford Achievement Test.* San Antonio, TX: Author.

Harcourt Educational Measurement (2003c). *Stanford Test of Academic Skills.* San Antonio, TX: Author.

Hardman, M., Drew, C., & Egan, M. (2006). *Human exceptionality* (8th ed.). Boston: Allyn and Bacon.

Harrington, R. (1985). Review of Battelle Developmental Inventory. In D. Keyser & R. Sweetland (Eds.), *Test critiques, 2* (pp. 72–82). Kansas City: Test Corp. of America.

Harris, D. (1963). *Children's drawings as measures of intellectual maturity.* New York: Harcourt Brace Jovanovich.

Harris, J. G., Tulsky, D. S., & Schultheis, M. T. (2003). Assessment of the non-native English speaker: Assimilating history and research findings to guide clinical practice. In D. S. Tulsky, & D. H. Saklofske (Eds.), *Clinical interpretation of the WAIS-III and WMS III* (pp. 343–359). San Diego, CA: Academic Press.

Harris, M., & Curran, C. (1998). Knowledge, attitudes, and concerns about portfolio assessment: An exploratory study. *Teacher Education and Special Education, 21,* 83–94.

Harrison, P. (1990). Adaptive behavior, mental retardation, and giftedness. In A. Kaufman (Ed.), *Assessing adolescent and adult intelligence* (pp. 533–585). Boston: Allyn and Bacon.

Harrison, P. (1991). *Early Screening Profiles.* Circle Pines, MN: American Guidance Service.

Harrison, P., Kaufman, A., Hickman, J., & Kaufman, N. (1988). A survey of tests used for adult assessment. *Journal of Psychoeducational Assessment, 6,* 188–198.

Harrison, P., & Oakland, T. (2003). *Adaptive Behavior Assessment System–Revised.* San Antonio: Psychological Corporation.

Hart, D. (1994). *Authentic assessment.* New York: Addison-Wesley.

Hart, E., & Lahey, B. (1999). General child behavior rating scales. In D. Shaffer, C. Lucas, & J. Richters (Eds.), *Diagnostic assessment in child and adolescent psychology* (pp. 65–90). New York: Guilford Press.

Hasbrouk, J., Woldbeck, T., Ibnot, C., & Parker, R. (1999). One teacher's use of curriculum-based measurement: A changed opinion. *Learning Disabilities Research and Practice, 14,* 118–126.

Hasselbring, T., & Moore, P. (1990). Computer-based assessment and error analysis. In R. Gable & J. Hendrickson (Eds.), *Assessing students with special needs* (pp. 102–116). New York: Longman.

Hathaway, S., & Meehl, P. (1951). *An atlas for the clinical use of the Minnesota Multiphasic Personality Inventory.* Minneapolis, MN: University of Minnesota Press.

Hatton, D. D., Wheeler, A. C., Skinner, M. L., Bailey, D. B., Sullivan, K. M., Roberts, J. E., Mirrett, P., & Clark, R. D. (2003). Adaptive behavior in children with fragile

X syndrome. *American Journal on Mental Retardation, 108,* 373–390.

Havey, J. (1999). School psychologists' involvement in special education due process hearings. *Psychology in the Schools, 36,* 117–127.

Havey, J. M., Story, N., & Buker, K. (2002). Convergent and concurrent validity of two measures of phonological processing. *Psychology in the Schools, 39,* 507–514.

Haywood, H. C. & Lidz, C. (2007). *Dynamic assessment in practice: Clinical and educational applications.* New York: Cambridge University Press.

Hendrickson, J., & Gable, R. (1990). Errors in spelling. In R. Gable & J. Hendrickson (Eds.), *Assessing students with special needs* (pp. 78–88). New York: Longman.

Henley, S., Klebe, K., McBride, J., & Cudeck, R. (1989). Adaptive and conventional versions of the DAT: The first complete test battery comparison. *Applied Psychological Measurement, 13,* 363–371.

Herman, J., Gearhart, M., & Baker, E. (1993). Assessing writing portfolios: Issues in the validity and meaning of scores. *Educational Assessment, 1,* 201–224.

Heshusius, L. (1991). Curriculum based assessment and direct instruction: Critical reflections on fundamental assumptions. *Exceptional Children, 57,* 315–328.

Hessels-Schlatter, C. (2002). A dynamic test to assess learning capacity in people with severe impairments. *American Journal on Mental Retardation, 107,* 340–351.

Hetzroni, O. E., & Roth, T. (2003). Effects of a positive support approach to enhance communicative behaviors of children with mental retardation who have challenging behaviors. *Education and Training in Mental Retardation and Developmental Disabilities, 38,* 95–105.

Hewett, S. (2007). Electronic portfolios and education: A different way to assess academic success. In L. Tan Wee Hin & R. Subramaniam (Eds.), *Handbook of research on literacy in technology at the K–12 level* (pp. 437–450). Hershey, PA: Idea Group Reference/IGI Global.

Hewitt, G. (1995). *A portfolio primer.* Portsmouth, NH: Heinemann.

Hilton, L. M. (1991). Cultural bias and ecological validity in testing rural children. *Rural Educator, 12*(3), 16–20.

Hing-McGowan, J. (1994). The multicultural vocational classroom: Strategies for improving student achievement. *Journal for Vocational Special Needs Education, 16*(2), 10–15.

Hinshaw, S., & Nigg, J. (1999). Behavior rating scales in the assessment of disruptive behavior problems in children. In D. Shaffer, C. Lucas, & J. Richters (Eds.), *Diagnostic assessment in child and adolescent psychology* (pp. 91–126). New York: Guilford Press.

Hintze, J. M., Ryan, A. L., & Stoner, G. (2003). Concurrent validity and diagnostic accuracy of the Dynamic Indicators of Basic Early Literacy Skills and the Comprehensive Test of Phonological Processing. *School Psychology Review, 32,* 541–556.

Hintze, J., Stoner, G., & Bull, M. (2000). Analogue assessment: Research and practice in evaluating emotional and behavioral problems. In E. Shapiro & T. Kratochwill (Eds.), *Behavioral assessment in schools* (2nd ed.; pp. 104–138). New York: Guilford Press.

Hishinuma, E., & Tadaki, S. (1997). The problem with grade and age equivalents: The WIAT as a case in point. *Journal of Psychoeducational Assessment, 15,* 214–225.

Hiskey, M. (1966). *Hiskey-Nebraska Test of Learning Aptitude.* Lincoln, NE: Union College Press.

Hobbs, N. (1975). *Issues in the classification of children* (2 vols.). San Francisco: Jossey-Bass.

Hodapp, A., & Gerken, K. (1999). Correlations between scores for the Peabody Picture Vocabulary Test–III and the Wechsler Intelligence Scale for Children–III. *Psychological Reports, 84,* 1139–1142.

Hoffman v. Board of Education. (1979) NY 2d 121, 400 N.E. 2d 317, 424 N.Y.S. 2d 376.

Holdnack, J., & Weiss, L. (2006). IDEA 2004: Anticipated implications for clinical practice—Integrating assessment and intervention. *Psychology in the Schools, 43,* 871.

Holland, J. (1985). *Vocational Preference Inventory–Revised.* Odessa, FL: Psychological Assessment Resources.

Hoopers Multimedia. (2001). *SuperSpell Assessment Disk.* East Dorset, VT: Tool Factory.

Hoover, H., Dunbar, S., & Frisbie, D. (2001). *Iowa Test of Basic Skills.* Itasca, IL: Riverside.

Hopkins, M. (1999). Practicing what we preach: Authentic assessment in math. *Diagnostique, 25,* 24.

Hosp, M., Hosp, J., & Howell, K. (2007). *The ABCs of CBM: A practical guide to curriculum-based measurement.* New York: Guilford Press.

Howell, K. (1990). Review of Test of Mathematical Abilities. *Diagnostique, 15,* 210–217.

Howell, K. W., Bigelow, S. S., Moore, E. L., & Evoy, A. M. (1993). Bias in authentic assessment. *Diagnostique, 19*(1), 387–400.

Howell, K., Fox, S., & Morehead, M. (1993). *Curriculum-based evaluation: Teaching and decision making* (2nd ed.). Pacific Grove, CA: Brooks/Cole.

Howell, K., & Morehead, M. (1987). *Curriculum-based evaluation for special and remedial education.* Columbus, OH: Charles E. Merrill.

Howell, K., & Nolet, V. (2000). *Curriculum-based evaluation.* Belmont, CA: Wadsworth.

Howell, K., Zucker, S., & Morehead, M. (1985). *Multilevel Academic Skills Test.* San Antonio: Psychological Corporation.

Hresko, W., Herron, S., & Peak, P. (1996). *Test of Early Written Language–Second Edition.* Austin, TX: Pro-Ed.

Hresko, W., Reid, D., & Hammill, D. (1999). *Test of Early Language Development–Third Edition.* Austin, TX: Pro-Ed.

Hresko, W., Schlieve, P., Herron, S., Swain, C., & Sherbenou, R. (2002). *Comprehensive Mathematical Abilities Test,* Austin, TX: Pro-Ed.

Hughes, S. (1988). Adaptive Behavior Inventory. In D. Keyser & R. Sweetland (Eds.), *Test critiques* (v. 7; pp. 3–9). Kansas City, MO: Test Corporation of America.

Huinker, D. (1993). Interviews: A window to students' conceptual knowledge of the operations. In N. Web & A. Coxford (Eds.), *Assessment in the mathematics classroom* (pp. 80–86.) Washington, DC: National Council of Teachers of Mathematics.

Hunnicutt, L., Slate, J., Gamble, C., & Wheeler, M. (1990). Examiner errors on the Kaufman Assessment Battery for

Children: A preliminary investigation. *Journal of School Psychology, 28,* 271–278.

Ianacone, R. N., & Leconte, P. J. (1986). Curriculum-based vocational assessment: A viable response to a school-based service delivery issue. *Career Development for Exceptional Individuals, 9,* 113–120.

Ice, G. (2004). Technological advances in observational data collection: The advantages and limitations of computer-assisted data collection. *Field Methods, 16,* 352–375.

Idol, L., Nevin, A., & Paolucci-Whitcomb, P. (1999). *Models of curriculum-based assessment* (3rd ed.). Austin, TX: Pro-Ed.

Isaacson, S. (1988). Assessing the writing product: Qualitative and quantitative measures. *Exceptional Children, 54*(b), 528–534.

Jackson, D. (1998). *Multidimensional Aptitude Battery–II.* Port Huron, MI: Sigma Assessment Systems.

Jackson, Y., Lewis, J., Feuerstein, R., & Samuda, R. (1998). Linking assessments to intervention with an instrumental enrichment. In R. Samuda, R. Feuerstein, A. Kaufman, J. Lewis, & R. Sternberg (Eds.), *Advances in cross-cultural assessment* (pp. 162–196). Thousand Oaks, CA: Sage Publications.

Jacob-Timm, S. (1999). Ethically challenging situations encountered by school psychologists. *Psychology in the Schools, 36,* 205–212.

Jastak, J., & Jastak, S. (1979). *Wide Range Interest-Opinion Test.* Wilmington, DE: Jastak Associates.

Javorsky, J. (1998–1999). Review of the Behavior Rating Profile–2. *Diagnostique, 24,* 33–40.

Jayanthi, M., Epstein, M., Polloway, E., & Bursuck, W. (1996). A national survey of general education teachers' perceptions of testing adaptations. *Journal of Special Education, 30,* 99–115.

Jenkins, J. R., & Jewell, M. (1993). Examining the validity of two measures for formative teaching: Reading aloud and maze. *Exceptional Children, 59,* 421–432.

Jitendra, A. K., & Kameenui, E. J. (1993). Dynamic assessment as a compensatory assessment approach: A description and analysis. *Remedial and Special Education, 14*(5), 6–18.

Jochum, J., Curran, C., & Reetz, L. (1998). Creating individual educational portfolios in written language. *Reading and Writing Quarterly: Overcoming Learning Disabilities, 14,* 283–306.

Johns, J. (2001). *Basic Reading Inventory.* Dubuque, IA: Kendall/Hunt.

Johns, J., & VanLeirsburg, P. (1992). Teaching test-wiseness: Can test scores of special populations be improved? *Reading Psychology, 13*(1), 99–103.

Johnson, D. R., Thompson, S. J., Sinclair, M., Krantz, G. C., Evelo, S., Stolte, K., & Thompson, J. R. (1993). Considerations in the design of follow-up and follow-along systems for improving transition programs and services. *Career Development for Exceptional Individuals, 16,* 225–238.

Johnson, E. (2000). The effects of accommodations on performance assessments. *Remedial and Special Education, 21,* 261–267.

Johnson, E., & Arnold, N. (2007). Examining an alternate assessment: What are we testing? *Journal of Disability Policy Studies, 18,* 23–31.

Johnson, E., Kimball, K., Brown, S., & Anderson, D. (2001). A statewide review of the use of accommodations in large scale, high stakes assessments. *Exceptional Children, 67,* 251–264.

Johnson, E., & Monroe, B. (2004). Simplified language as an accommodation on math tests. *Assessment for Effective Intervention, 29,* 35–46.

Johnson, H., Blackhurst, A., Maley, K., Cox-Cruey, T., & Dell, A. (1995). Development of a computer-based system for the unobtrusive collection of direct observational data. *Journal of Special Education Technology, 12,* 291–300.

Johnson, J., Bardos, A., & Tayebi, K. (2003). *Relationships between written expression achievement and the Cognitive Assessment System.* ERIC Document Reproductive Service No. ED 480487.

Johnson, J. R., & Rusch, F. R. (1993). Secondary special education and transition services: Identification and recommendations for future research and demonstration. *Career Development for Exceptional Individuals, 16,* 1–18.

Johnson, R. L., McDaniel II, F., & Willeke, M. J. (2000). Using portfolios in program evaluation: An investigation of inter-rater reliability. *American Journal of Evaluation, 21,* 65–80.

Johnson-Martin, N., Attermeier, S., & Hecker, B. (2004). *Assessment Log and Developmental Progress Chart–Preschool.* Baltimore: Paul H. Brookes.

Johnson-Martin, N., Jens, K., Attermeier, S., & Hecker, B. (2004). *Assessment Log and Developmental Progress Chart—Infant.* Baltimore: Paul H. Brookes.

Johnstone, C., Thurlow, M., Moore, M., & Altman, J. (2006). *Using systematic item selection methods to improve universal design of assessments.* www.education.umn.edu/nceo/OnlinePubs/Policy18/default.html. Retrieved 3/12/2007.

Jones, C. (2001). CBAs that work. *Teaching Exceptional Children, 34,* 24–29.

Jonz, J. (1990). Another turn in the conversation: What does Cloze measure? *TESOL Quarterly, 24,* 61–83.

Kaiser, A. P., Cai, X., Hancock, T. B., & Foster, E. M. (2002). Teacher-reported behavior problems and language delays in boys and girls enrolled in Head Start. *Behavioral Disorders, 28,* 23–39.

Kamphaus, R., Petoskey, M., & Rowe, E. (2000). Current trends in psychological testing of children. *Professional Psychology: Research and Practice, 31,* 155–164.

Karlsen, B., & Gardner, E. (1996). *Stanford Diagnostic Reading Test–4.* San Antonio, TX: Harcourt-Brace Educational Measurement.

Kass, R., & Fish, J. (1991). Positive reframing and the test performance of test anxious children. *Psychology in the Schools, 28,* 43–52.

Kaufman, A., Flanagan, D., Alfonso, V., & Mascolo, J. (2006). Review of the Wechsler Intelligence Scale for Children–Fourth Edition (WISC-IV). *Journal of Psychoeducational Assessment, 24,* 278–295.

Kaufman, A., & Kaufman, N. (1995). *Kaufman Functional Assessment Skills Test.* Circle Pines, MN: American Guidance Service.

Kaufman, A., & Kaufman, N. (2004a). *Kaufman Brief Intelligence Test–II.* Circle Pines, MN: American Guidance Service.

Kaufman, A., & Kaufman, N. (2004b). *The Kaufman Test of Educational Achievement–II.* Circle Pines, MN: American Guidance Service.

Kaufman, A., & Kaufman, N. (2004c). *The Kaufman Assessment Battery for Children–II.* Circle Pines, MN: American Guidance Service.

Kaufman, A., Lichtenberger, E., Fletcher-Jansen, E., & Kaufman, N. (2005). *Essentials of KABC-II assessment.* Hoboken, NJ: John Wiley and Sons.

Keefe, C. (1999). Responsive reading assessment: An alternative. *Diagnostique, 25,* 5–13.

Kehrer, C., Sanchez, P., Habif, U., Rosenbaum, J., & Townes, B. (2000). Effects of a significant other observer on neuropsychological test performance. *Clinical Neuropsychologist, 14,* 67–71.

Keith, T., Fine, J., Taub, G., Reynolds, M., & Kranzler, J. (2006). Higher order, multisample, confirmatory factor analysis of the Wechsler Intelligence Scale for Children–Fourth Edition: What does it measure? *School Psychology Review, 35,* 108–127.

Keith, T., Kranzler, J., & Flanagan, D. (2001). What does the Cognitive Ability Scale measure? *School Psychology Review, 30.*

Kerka, S. (1995). *Techniques for authentic assessment: Practice application brief.* Columbus: OH: Ohio State University. (ERIC Reproduction Service No. ED 381688).

Kerlinger, F., & Lee, H. (2000). *Foundations of behavioral research* (5th ed.). New York: Holt, Rinehart & Winston.

King-Sears, P. (1994). *Curriculum-based assessment in special education.* San Diego: Singular Publishing Group.

Kirk, S., McCarthy, J., & Kirk, W. (1968). *Illinois Test of Psycholinguistic Abilities.* Urbana: University of Illinois Press.

Kirschenbaum, R. (1998). Dynamic assessment and its use with underserved gifted and talented populations. *Gifted Child Quarterly, 42,* 140–147.

Klein-Ezell, C., & Ezell, D. (2005). Use of portfolio assessment with students with cognitive disabilities/mental retardation. *Assessment for Effective Intervention, 31,* 15–24.

Kleinert, H., Haig, J., Kearns, J., & Kennedy, S. (2000). Alternate assessments: Lessons learned and roads to be taken. *Exceptional Children, 67,* 51–67.

Kleinert, H. L., & Kearns, J. F. (2001). *Alternate assessment: Measuring outcomes and supports for students with disabilities.* Baltimore, MD: Paul H. Brookes.

Kleinert, H., Kennedy, S., & Kearns, J. (1999). The impact of alternate assessments: A statewide teacher survey. *Journal of Special Education, 33,* 93–102.

Klimczak, N., Bradford, K., Burright, R., & Donovick, P. (2000). K-FAST and WRAT-III: Are they really different? *Clinical Neuropsychologist, 14,* 135–138.

Knight, P. (1992). How I use portfolios in mathematics. *Educational Leadership, 49*(8), 71–72.

Knoff, H., & Prout, H. (1985). *Kinetic Drawing System for Family and School: A Handbook.* Los Angeles: Western Psychological Services.

Kohler, P. D. (1994). On-the-job training: A curricular approach to employment. *Career Development for Exceptional Individuals, 17,* 29–40.

Konald, T. (1999). Evaluating discrepancy analyses with the WISC-III and WIAT. *Journal of Psychoeducational Assessment, 17,* 24–35.

Konrad, M., & Test, D. W. (2004). Teaching middle-school students with disabilities to use an IEP template. *Test Career Development for Exceptional Individuals, 27*(1), 101–124.

Koppitz, E. (1968). *Human Figure Drawing Test.* New York: Grune & Stratton.

Kovaleski, J., Gickling, E., Morrow, H., & Swank, P. (1999). High vs. low implementation of instructional support teams: A case for maintaining program fidelity. *Remedial and Special Education, 20,* 120–183.

Kranzler, J., Brownell, M., & Miller, M. (1998). The construct validity of curriculum-based measurement of reading: An empirical test of a plausible rival hypothesis. *Journal of School Psychology, 25,* 399–415.

Kranzler, J., Miller, D., & Jordan, L. (1999). An examination of racial/ethnic and gender bias on curriculum-based measurement or reading. *School Psychology Quarterly, 14,* 327–342.

Krasa, N. (2007). Is the Woodcock-Johnson–III a test for all seasons? Ceiling and item gradient considerations in its use with older students. *Journal of Psychoeducational Assessment, 25,* 3–16.

Krug, D., Arick, J., & Almond, P. (1993). *Autism Screening Instrument for Educational Planning–2.* Austin, TX: Pro-Ed.

Kuhlmann, F., & Anderson, R. (1997). *Kuhlmann Anderson Test-Revised.* Bensenville, IL: Scholastic Testing Service.

Kveton, P., Jelinek, M., Voboril, D., & Klimusova, H. (2007). Computer-based tests: The impact of test design and problem of equivalency. *Computers in Human Behavior, 23*(1), 32–51.

Lachar, D., & Gruber, C. (1995). *Personality Inventory for Youth.* Los Angeles, CA: Western Psychological Services.

Lachar, D., & Gruber, C. (2001). *Personality Inventory for Children–Second Edition.* Los Angeles: Western Psychological Services.

Lachar, D., Wingenfeld, S., Kline, R., & Gruber, C. (2000). *Student Behavior Survey.* Los Angeles: Western Psychological Services.

Lambert, N., Leland, H., & Nihira, K. (1993). *AAMR Adaptive Behavior Scale–School Edition (Second Edition).* Austin, TX: Pro-Ed.

Lang, S., Kumke, P., Ray, C., Cowell, E., Elliott, S., Kratochwill, T., Thomas, R., & Bolt, D. (2005). Consequences of using test accommodations: Student, teacher, and parent perceptions of and reactions to testing accommodations. *Assessment for Effective Intervention, 31,* 49–62.

Lappan, G. (1978). Review of Stanford Diagnostic Mathematics Test. In O. Buros (Ed.), *The eighth mental measurement yearbook* (pp. 436–437). Highland Park, NJ: Gryphon Press.

Larry P. et al. v. *Wilson Riles et al.* (1979). United States District Court, Northern District of California, Case No. C-71–2270-RFP.

Larsen, S., & Hammill, D. (1975). The relationship of selected visual perceptual abilities to school learning. *Journal of Special Education, 9,* 281–291.

Larsen, S., Hammill, D., & Moats, L. (1999). *Test of Written Spelling–4*. Austin, TX: Pro-Ed.

Laughon, P. (1990). The dynamic assessment of intelligence: A review of three approaches. *School Psychology Review, 14,* 459–470.

Launey, K., Carroll, J., & van Horn, K. R. (2007). Concurrent validity of the WISC-IV in eligibility decisions for students with educable mental disabilities. *Psychological Reports, 100,* 1165–1170.

Law, N. (1995). *On the relevance of intelligence: Applications for classrooms? Intelligence testing: The good, the bad, and the ugly.* Paper presented at the annual meeting of the American Educational Research Association, San Francisco. (ERIC Reproduction No. ED 387503).

Lazarus, B., McKenna, N., & Lynch, D. (1990). Peabody Individual Achievement Test–Revised. *Diagnostique, 15,* 135–148.

Leconte, P. J., & Neubert, D. A. (1997). Vocational assessment: The kick-off point for successful transitions. *Alliance: The Newsletter of the National Transition Alliance, 2*(2), 1–8.

Lee, L. (1974). *Developmental Sentence Analysis*. Evanston, IL: Northwestern University Press.

Lee, O. K. (2003). Rasch simultaneous vertical equating for measuring reading growth. *Journal of Applied Measurement, 4,* 10–23.

Lenkarski, S., Singer, M., Peters, M., & McIntosh, D. (2001). Utility of the Early Screening Profile in identifying preschoolers at risk for cognitive delay. *Psychology in the Schools, 38,* 17–24.

Leung, B. (1996). Quality assessment practices in a diverse society. *Teaching Exceptional Children, 28,* 42–45.

Lewandowski, L., & Martens, B. (1990). Selecting and evaluating standardized reading tests (test review). *Journal of Reading, 33,* 384–388.

Lichtenberger, E. (2005). General measures of cognition for the preschool child. *Mental Retardation and Developmental Disabilities, 11,* 197–208.

Linchenberger, E., & Smith, D. (2005). *Essentials of WIAT-II and K-TEA-II assessment*. Hoboken, NJ: Wiley.

Lidz, C. S. (2002). Mediated learning experience (MLE) as a basis for an alternative approach to assessment. *School Psychology International, 23,* 68–84.

Lignugaris-Kraft, B., Marchand-Martella, N., & Martella, R. (2001). Writing better goals and short-term objectives or benchmarks. *Teaching Exceptional Children, 34,* 52–59.

Linder, T. (1993). *Transdisciplinary play-based assessment* (2nd ed.). Baltimore: Paul H. Brookes.

Lindsley, O. (1964). Direct measurement and prosthesis of retarded behavior. *Journal of Education, 14,* 62–81.

Linthicum, E., Cole, J. T., & D'Alonzo, B. (1991). Employment and the Americans with Disabilities Act of 1991. *Career Development for Exceptional Individuals, 14,* 1–13.

Lipson, M., & Wixson, K. (2003). *Assessment and instruction of reading and writing difficulty: An interactive approach* (3rd ed.). New York: Allyn and Bacon.

LoBello, S., & Holley, G. (1999). WPPSI-R administration, clerical, and scoring errors by student examiners. *Journal of Psychoeducational Assessment, 17,* 15–23.

Loe, S., Kadlubek, R., & Marks, W. (2007). Administration and scoring errors on the WISC-IV among graduate student examiners. *Journal of Psychoeducational Assessment, 25,* 237–247.

Lohman, D., & Hagen, E. (2001). *Cognitive Abilities Test, Form 6*. Chicago: Riverside.

Lombardino, L., Lieberman, J., & Brown, J. (2005). *Assessment of Literacy and Language*. San Antonio, TX: Psychological Corporation.

Lonigan, C., Wagner, R., Torgesen, J., & Rashotte, C. (2007). *Test of Preschool Early Literacy*. Austin, TX: Pro-Ed.

Losardo, A., & Notari-Syverson, A. (2001). *Alternative approaches to assessing young children*. Baltimore: Paul H. Brookes.

Luckasson, R., Borthwick-Duffy, S., Buntinx, W., Coulter, D., Craig, E., Reeve, A., Schalock, R., Snell, N., Spitalnik, D., Spreat, S., & Tasse, M. (2002). *Mental retardation: Definition, classification and systems of support* (10th ed.). Washington, DC: American Association on Mental Retardation.

Luckasson, R., Coulter, D., Polloway, E., Reiss, S., Schalock, R., Snell, N., Spitalnik, D., & Stark, J. (1992). *Mental retardation: Definition, classification, and systems of support* (9th ed.). Washington, DC: American Association on Mental Retardation.

Lund, N., & Duchan, J. (1993). *Assessing children's language in naturalistic contexts* (3rd ed.). Englewood Cliffs, NJ: Prentice-Hall.

Luts, N. C. (1991). *The most common errors of second-grade story-writers*. (ERIC Document Reproduction Service No. ED 329 995).

Maag, J. (2004). *Behavior management: From theoretical implications to practical applications*. (2nd ed.). Belmont, CA: Wadsworth.

Maddox, C., & Johnson, L. (1998). Computer-assisted assessment. In H. B. Vance (Ed.), *Psychological assessment of children* (2nd ed.; pp. 87–105). New York: John Wiley & Sons.

Madelaine, A., & Wheldall, K. (1999). Curriculum-based measurement of reading: A critical review. *International Journal of Disability, Development, and Education, 46,* 71–85.

Madelaine, A., & Wheldall, K. (2004). Curriculum-based measurement of reading: Recent advances. *International Journal of Disability, Development, and Education, 51,* 57–82.

Mantzicopoulas, P. (1999). Reliability and validity estimates of the Brigance K and 1 screen based on a sample of disadvantaged preschoolers. *Psychology in the Schools, 36,* 11–19.

March, R. E., & Horner, R. H. (2002). Feasibility and contributions of functional behavioral assessment in schools. *Journal of Emotional and Behavioral Disorders, 10,* 158–170.

Mardell-Czudnowski, C., & Goldenberg, D. (1998). *Developmental Indicators for the Assessment of Learning–3*. Circle Pines, MN: American Guidance Service.

Markwardt, F. (1998). *Peabody Individual Achievement Test–Revised*. Circle Pines, MN: American Guidance Service.

Marlow, A., & Edwards, R. (1998). Test review: Gray Oral Reading Test, Third Edition. *Journal of Psychoeducational Assessment, 16,* 90–94.

Marshall, N. (1983). Using story grammar to assess reading comprehension. *The Reading Teacher, 36,* 16–20.

Marston, D., & Magnusson, D. (1985). Implementing curriculum based measurement in special and regular education settings. *Exceptional Children, 52,* 266–276.

Mather, N., Hammill, D., Allen, E., & Roberts, R. (2004). *Test of Silent Word Reading Fluency.* Austin, TX: Pro-Ed.

Mather, N., & Woodcock, R. (1997). *Group Writing Test.* Chicago: Riverside.

Mathes, P., Fuchs, D., Roberts, P., & Fuchs, L. (1998). Preparing students with special needs for reintegration: Curriculum-based measurement impact on transenvironmental programming. *Journal of Learning Disabilities, 31,* 615–624.

Mathews, J. (1990). From computer management to portfolio assessment. *The Reading Teacher, 43,* 420–421.

Matto, H., & Naglieri, J. (2005). Race and ethnic differences and human figure drawings: Clinical utility of the DAP: SPED. *Journal of Clinical Child and Adolescent Psychology, 34,* 706–711.

Mazefsky, C., & Oswald, D. (2006). The discriminative ability and diagnostic utility of the ADOS-G, ADI-R and GARS for children in a clinical setting. *Autism, 10,* 533–549.

McCarney, S. (1993). *The prereferral intervention manual:* Columbia, MO: Hawthorne Educational Systems.

McCarney, S. (1995). *Attention Deficit Disorders Evaluation Scale–2.* Columbia, MO: Hawthorne.

McCarney, S., & Arthaud, T. (2003). *The Emotional or Behavioral Disorder Scale.* Columbia, MO: Hawthorne.

McCarney, S., Jackson, M., & Leigh, J. (1990). *Behavior Evaluation Scale–2.* Columbia, MO: Hawthorne.

McCarthy, D. (1972). *Manual for the McCarthy Scales of Children's Abilities.* New York: Psychological Corporation.

McCloskey, D., & Athanasiou, M. (2000). Assessment and intervention practices with second language learners among school psychologists. *Psychology in the Schools, 37,* 209–225.

McConnell, K., Patton, J. R., & Polloway, E. A. (2007). *BIP-3: Behavioral Intervention Planning–Third Edition.* Austin, TX: Pro-Ed.

McCullough, C. S. (1995). Overcoming QWERTY. *Child Assessment News, 4,* 11–12.

McDermott, P. (1981). Sources of error in the psychoeducational diagnosis of children. *Journal of School Psychology, 19,* 31–44.

McDougal, J., Moody-Clonon, S., & Martens, B. (2000). Using organizational change procedures to promote the acceptability of prereferral intervention services: The school-based intervention team project. *School Psychology Quarterly, 15,* 149–171.

McGhee, R., Bryant, B., Larsen, S., & Rivera, D. (1995). *Test of Written Expression.* Austin, TX: Pro-Ed.

McGivern, J., & Marquart, A. (2000). Legal and ethical issues in child and adolescent assessment. In E. Shapiro & T. Kratochwill (Eds.), *Behavioral assessment in schools* (2nd ed.; pp. 387–434). New York: Guilford Press.

McIntosh, D., Gibney, L., Quinn, K., & Kundert, D. (2000). Concurrent validity of the Early Screening Profile and the Differential Ability Scales with an at risk preschool sample. *Psychology in the Schools, 37,* 201–208.

McIntyre, L., Blacher, J., & Baker, B. (2002). Behaviour/mental health problems in young adults with intellectual disability: The impact on families. *Journal of Intellectual Disability Research, 46,* 239–249.

McKevitt, B. C., & Elliott, S. N. (2003). Effects and perceived consequences of using read-aloud and teacher-recommended testing accommodations on a reading achievement test. *School Psychology Review, 32,* 583–600.

McLaughlin, M., & Warren, S. (1995). *Using performance assessment in outcome-based accountability systems.* Reston, VA: Council for Exceptional Children. (ERIC Reproduction Services No. ED 381987).

McMillan, J. (2004). *Classroom assessment* (2nd ed.). Boston: Allyn and Bacon.

Mealey, D. L., & Host, T. R. (1992). Coping with test anxiety. *College Teaching, 40*(4), 147–150.

Meehan, K. A., & Hodell, S. (1986). Measuring the impact of vocational assessment activites upon program decision. *Career Development for Exceptional Standards, 9,* 106–112.

Mehrens, W. A. (1992). Using performance assessment for accountability purposes. *Educational Measurement: Issues and Practice, 11,* 3–9, 20.

Mehrens, W. A. (2002). Consequences of assessment: What is the evidence? In G. Tindal & T. Haladyna (Eds.), *Large scale assessment programs for all students* (pp. 149–177). Mahwah, NJ: Lawrence Erlbaum.

Mehrens, W. A., & Clarizio, H. F. (1993). Curriculum-based measurement: Conceptual and psychometric considerations. *Psychology in the Schools, 30,* 241–254.

Mellar, P. J., Ohr, P. S., & Marcus, R. A. (2001). Family-Oriented, Culturally Sensitive (FOCUS) assessment of young children. In L. A. Suzuki, J. G. Ponterotto, & P. J. Meller (Eds.), *Handbook of multicultural assessment: Clinical, psychological, and educational applications* (2nd ed.). San Francisco: Jossey-Bass.

Meltzer, L., & Reid, D. K. (1994). New directions in the assessment of students with special needs: The shift toward a constructivist perspective. *Journal of Special Education, 28,* 338–355.

Menchetti, B. M., & Piland, V. C. (1998). The personal career plan: A person-centered approach to vocational evaluation and career planning. In F. R. Rusch & J. R. Chadsey (Eds.), *Beyond high school: transition from school to work* (pp. 319–330). Belmont, CA: Wadsworth.

Mercer, J. (1972). IQ: The lethal label. *Psychology Today, 6,* 44–47, 95–97.

Mercer, J., & Lewis, J. (1977). *System of Multicultural Pluralistic Assessment.* New York: Psychological Corporation.

Merrell, K. (2000). Informant reports: Theory and research in using child behavior rating scales in school settings. In E. Shapiro & T. Kratochwill (Eds.), *Behavioral assessment in schools* (2nd ed.; pp. 233–256). New York: Guilford Press.

Merydith, S. (2001). Temporal stability and convergent validity of the Behavior Assessment System for Children. *Journal of School Psychology, 27,* 253–265.

Meyers, J., & Lytle, S. (1986). Assessment of the learning process. *Exceptional Children, 53,* 138–144.

Michaels, C. A. (1998). *Transition to employment.* Austin, TX: Pro-Ed.

Mieko, A., & Burns, T. (2005). Review of Stanford-Binet Intelligence Scales. *Applied Neuropsychology, 12,* 179–180.

Miller, J., & Carr, S. (1997). Error ratio analysis: Alternate mathematics assessment for general and special educators. *Diagnostique, 23,* 225–231.

Miller, M., & Seraphine, A. (1993). Can test scores remain authentic when teaching to the test? *Educational Assessment, 1,* 119–130.

Miller, W. (1986). *Reading diagnosis kit.* West Nyack, NY: The Center for Applied Research in Education.

Minton, B., & Pratt, S. (2006). Gifted and highly gifted students: How do they score on the SB5? *Roeper Review, 28,* 232–236.

Montague, M., Bos, C., & Doucette, M. (1991). Affective, cognitive, and metacognitive attributes of eighth-grade mathematical problem solvers. *Learning Disabilities Research and Practice, 6,* 219–224.

Mori, L. T., & Armendariz, G. M. (2001). Analogue assessment of child behavior problems. *Psychological Assessment, 13,* 36–45.

Morrison, R. (1999). Picture this! Using portfolios to facilitate the inclusion of children in preschool settings. *Early Childhood Education Journal, 27,* 45–48.

Morrow, L. (1989). Creating a bridge to children's literature. In P. Winograd, K. Wixson, & M. Lipson (Eds.), *Improving basal reading instruction* (pp. 210–230). New York: Teachers College Press.

Morse, D. (1998). The relative difficulty of selected test-wiseness skills among college students. *Educational and Psychological Measurement, 58,* 399–408.

Morsink, C., & Gable, R. (1990). Errors in reading. In R. Gable & J. Hendrickson (Eds.), *Assessing students with special needs* (pp. 46–62). New York: Longman.

Moskal, B. (2003). *Developing classroom performance assessments and scoring rubrics–Part I.* ERIC Document Reproduction Service No. ED 481714.

Motta, R. W., Little, A., & Tobin, J. (1993). The use and abuse of human figure drawings. *School Psychology Quarterly, 8,* 162–169.

Muenz, T., Ouchi, B., & Cole, J. (1999). Item analysis of written expression scoring systems from the *PIAT-R* and WIAT. *Psychology in the Schools, 36*(1), 31–40.

Muller (2007). Reporting on the state assessment data for students with disabilities: Synthesis of the 2007 NCEO report. *Project Forum at NASDE,* February, 1–7.

Munoz-Sandoval, A., Woodcock, R., McGrew, K., & Mather, N. (2007). Bateria III Woodcock-Munoz NU. Rolling Meadows, IL: Riverside Publishing.

Murray, H. (1943). *Thematic Apperception Test.* Cambridge, MA: Harvard University.

Murray, H., & Bellak, L. (1973). *Thematic Apperception Test.* San Antonio, TX: Psychological Corporation.

Naglieri, J. (1988). *Draw-a-Person: A Quantitative Scoring System.* San Antonio: Psychological Corporation.

Naglieri, J. (2003). *Naglieri Nonverbal Ability Test.* San Antonio, TX: Harcourt Educational Measurement.

Naglieri, J., & Das, J. (1997). *Das-Naglieri Cognitive Assessment System.* Chicago: Riverside.

Naglieri, J., Das, J., & Jarman, R. (1990). Planning, attention, simultaneous, and successive processes as a model for assessment. *School Psychology Review, 19,* 423–442.

Naglieri, J., LeBuffe, P., & Pfeiffer, S. (1993). *Devereux Behavior Rating Scales–School Form.* San Antonio, TX: Psychological Corporation.

Naglieri, J., McNeish, T., & Bardos, A. (1991). *Draw-a-Person: Screening Procedure for Emotional Disturbance.* San Antonio: Psychological Corporation.

Naglieri, J., & Paolitto, A. (2005). Ipsative comparisons of WISC-IV index scores. *Applied Neuropsychology, 12,* 208–211.

Naglieri, J., & Rojahn, J. (2001). Intellectual classification of black and white children in special education programs using the WISC-III and the Cognitive Assessment System. *American Journal on Mental Retardation, 106,* 359–367.

National Association of School Psychologists. (2003). *Position statement on using large scale assessment for high-stakes decisions.* Bethesda, MD: Author.

National Association of School Psychologists. (2007). *NASP position paper on identification of students with specific learning disabilities.* Bethesda, MD.

National Council for Teachers of Mathematics (NCTM). (2000). *Principles and standards for school mathematics: An overview.* Washington, DC: Author.

National Excellence: A case for developing America's talent (1993). Washington, DC: U.S. Dept. of Education, Office of Educational Research and Improvement.

Needelman, H., Schnoes, C., & Ellis, C. (2006). The new WISC-IV. *Journal of Developmental and Behavioral Pediatrics, 27,* 127–128.

Neel, R., & Cessna, K. (1993). Behavioral intent: Instructional content for students with behavior disorders. In K. Cessna (Ed.), *Instructional differentiated programming: A needs-based approach for students with behavior disorders* (pp. 31–39). Denver, CO: Colorado Department of Education.

Neubert, D. A. (2006). Legislation and guidelines for secondary special and transition services. In P. Sitlington & G. M. Clark (Eds.), *Transition education and service for students with disabilities* (4th ed.; pp. 35–71). Boston: Pearson.

Newborg, J. (2004). *Battelle Developmental Inventory-2.* Chicago, IL: Riverside Publishing.

Newcomer, P. (1985). A comparison of two published reading inventories. *Remedial and Special Education, 6,* 31–36.

Newcomer, P. (2001). *Diagnostic Achievement Battery–3.* Austin, TX: Pro-Ed.

Newcomer, P., & Barenbaum, E. (2003). *Test of Phonological Awareness Skills.* Austin, TX: Pro-Ed.

Newcomer, P., Barenbaum, E., & Nodine, B. (1988). Teaching writing to exceptional children: Reaction and recommendations. *Exceptional Children, 54,* 559–564.

Newcomer, P., & Bryant, B. (1993). *Diagnostic Achievement Test for Adolescents–2* Austin, TX: Pro-Ed.

Newcomer, P., & Hammill, D. (1997). *Tests of Language Development: 3 (Primary).* Austin, TX: Pro-Ed.

Newland, T. E. (1969). *Manual for the Blind Learning Aptitude Test: Experimental Edition.* Urbana, IL: T. Ernest Newland.

Nickerson, A. B., & Nagle, R. J. (2001). Interrater reliability of the Devereux Behavior Rating Scale-School Form: The influence of teacher frame of reference. *Journal of Psychoeducational Assessment, 19,* 299–316.

Nihira, K., Leland, H., & Lambert, N. (1993). *AAMR Adaptive Behavior Scale—Residential and Community Edition (Second Edition).* Austin, TX: Pro-Ed.

Njardvik, U., Matson, J., & Cherry, K. (1999). A comparison of social skills in adults with autistic disorder, pervasive developmental disorder not otherwise specified, and mental retardation. *Journal of Autism and Developmental Disorders, 29,* 287–295.

Nolet, V. (1992). Classroom-based measurement and portfolio assessment. *Diagnostique, 18*(1), 5–26.

Norton, P. J., & Hope, D. A. (2001). Analogue observational methods in the assessment of social functioning in adults. *Psychological Assessment, 13,* 59–72.

Noyce, R. (1989). Review of Test of Written Spelling–2. In J. Conoley & J. Kramer (Eds.), *Tenth mental measurements yearbook* (pp. 860–861). Lincoln, NE: University of Nebraska Press.

Nurss, J. (1994). *Metropolitan Readiness Tests.* San Antonio, TX: Harcourt Brace Educational Measurement.

Oakland, T. (1977). *Pluralistic norms and estimated learning potential.* Paper presented at the annual meeting of the American Psychological Association, San Francisco.

O'Leary, K., & Johnson, S. (1979). Psychological assessment. In H. Quay & J. Werry (Eds.), *Psychopathological disorders of childhood* (pp. 210–246). New York: John Wiley & Sons.

Olmi, J. (1994). Review of the Behavior Evaluation Scale–2. In J. Mitchell & J. Impara (Eds.), *The eleventh mental measurement yearbook* (Supplement; pp. 74–76). Lincoln, NE: University of Nebraska Press.

O'Neill, R., Horner, R., Albin, R., Storey, K., & Sprague, J. (1997). *Functional analysis of problem behavior: A practical assessment guide* (2nd ed.). Pacific Grove, CA: Brooks/Cole.

O'Reilly, C. (1989). The confirmation bias in special education eligibility decisions. *School Psychology Review, 18,* 126–135.

Otis, A., & Lennon, R. (2003). *Otis-Lennon School Ability Test–8.* San Antonio, TX: Harcourt Brace Jovanovich.

Overton, T., Fielding, C., & Simonsson, M. (2004). Decision making in determining eligibility of culturally and linguistically diverse learners: Reasons given by assessment personnel. *Journal of Learning Disabilities, 37,* 319–340.

Padilla, A. (2001). Issues in culturally appropriate assessment. In L. Suzuki, J. Ponterotto, & P. Meller (Eds.), *Handbook of multicultural assessment* (2nd ed.; pp. 5–28) San Francisco, CA: Jossey-Bass.

Padilla, A., & Garza, B. (1975). IQ tests: A case of cultural myopia. *National Elementary Principal, 54,* 53–58.

Pankratz, M., Morrison, A., & Plante, E. (2004). Difference in standard scores of adults on the Peabody Picture Vocabulary Test (Revised and Third Edition). *Journal of Speech, Language, and Hearing Research, 47,* 714–718.

Paris, S. G., & Carpenter, R. D. (2003). FAQs about IRIs. *Reading Teacher, 56,* 578–80.

Parker, R. (2001). *Occupational Aptitude Survey and Interest Schedule–3.* Austin, TX: Pro-Ed.

Parker, R., Hasbrouck, J., & Tindal, G. (1992). The maze as a classroom-based reading measure: Construction methods, reliability, and validity. *Journal of Special Education, 26,* 195–218.

Parrish, B. (1982). A test to test test-wiseness. *Journal of Reading, 25,* 672–675.

Partenio, I., & Taylor, R. (1985). The relationship of teacher ratings and IQ: A question of bias? *School Psychology Review, 14,* 79–83.

Pase v. *Hannon,* 506 F. Supp. 831 (N. D. Ill. 1980).

Patterson, G., Reid, J., Jones, R., & Conger, R. (1975). *A social learning approach to family intervention, V. 1: Families with aggressive children.* Eugene, OR: Castalia Publishing.

Paul, R., Miles, S., Cicchetti, D., Sparrow, S., Klin, A., Volkmar, F., Coflin, M., & Booker, S. (2004). Adaptive behavior in autism and pervasive developmental disorder—not otherwise specified: Microanalysis of scores on the Vineland Adaptive Behavior Scales. *Journal of Autism and Developmental Disorders, 34,* 223–228.

Paulson, F. L., Paulson, P. R., & Meyer, C. A. (1991). What makes a portfolio a portfolio? *Educational Leadership, 48*(5), 60–63.

Payette, K., & Clarizio, H. (1994). Discrepant team decisions: The effects of race, gender, school and IQ on LD eligibility. *Psychology in the Schools, 31,* 40–48.

Pehrsson, R. (1994). Challenging frustration level. *Reading and Writing Quarterly, 10,* 201–208.

Pena, E., Quinn, R., & Iglesias, A. (1992). The application of dynamic methods to language assessment: A nonbiased procedure. *Journal of Special Education, 26,* 269–280.

Perlman, C. (2003). *Performance assessment: Designing appropriate performance tasks and scoring rubrics.* ERIC Document Reproduction Service No. ED 480073.

Petot, J. (2000). Interest and limitations of projective techniques in the assessment of personality disorders. *European Psychiatry, 15,* 11–14.

Peverly, S., & Kitzen, K. (1998). Curriculum-based assessment of reading skills: Considerations and caveats for school psychologists. *Psychology in the Schools, 35,* 29–48.

Pierangelo, R., & Giuliani, G. A. (2004). *Transition services in special education. A practical approach.* Boston: Pearson.

Pierangelo, R., & Giuliani, G. (2006). *Assessment in special education.* San Francisco, CA: Jossey-Bass.

Pikulski, J. (1990). Informal reading inventories. *The Reading Teacher, 43,* 514–516.

Pikulski, J., & Pikulski, E. (1977). Cloze, maze, and teacher judgment. *The Reading Teacher, 30,* 766–770.

Pino, D. (1998). The effects of story grammar instruction in learning disabled students' performance on the Test of Written Language–3. *Dissertation Abstracts International, 59*(3-a), 0726.

Pipho, C. (1997). Standards, assessment, accountability: The tangled triumvirate. *Phi Delta Kappan, 78,* 673–674.

Plass, J., & Hill, K. (1986). Children's achievement strategies and test performance: The role of time pressure, evaluation anxiety, and sex. *Developmental Psychology, 22,* 31–36.

Platt, T., Zachar, P., Ray, G., Underhill, A., & LoBello, S. (2007). Does Wechsler Intelligence Scale administration and scoring proficiency improve during assessment training? *Psychological Reports, 100,* 547–555.

Plotts, C., & Webber, J. (2001–2002). The role of developmental histories in the screening and diagnosis of autism spectrum disorders. *Assessment for Effective Intervention, 27,* 19–26.

Plucker, J., Callahan, C., & Tomchin, E. (1996). Where for art thou, multi-intelligences? Alternative assessments for identifying talent in ethnically diverse and low income students. *Gifted Child Quarterly, 40,* 81–88.

Polotsky, L. (1992). Test anxiety among children administered screening tests for giftedness. In F. Moenks, W. Peters, & A. Willy (Eds.), *Social and personality development of gifted children* (pp. 240–247). Assen, Netherlands: Van Gorcum & Co.

Pomplun, M., & Custer, M. (2005). The construct validity of the Stanford-Binet 5 measures of working; memory. *Assessment, 12,* 338–346.

Poplin, M., Gray, R., Larsen, S., Banikowski, A., & Mehring, T. (1980). A comparison of written expression abilities in learning disabled and non-learning disabled students at three grade levels. *Learning Disability Quarterly, 3,* 46–53.

Posey, C. (1989). Review of Behavior Rating Profile. In J. Conoley & J. Kramer (Eds.), *Tenth mental measurements yearbook* (pp. 86–88). Lincoln: University of Nebraska Press.

Poteet, J. (1992). Written expression. In J. Choate, B. Enright, L. Miller, J. Poteet, & T. Rakes (Eds.), *Curriculum-based assessment and programming*. Boston: Allyn and Bacon.

Powell-Smith, K., & Stewart, L. (1998). The use of curriculum-based measurement in the reintegration of students with mild disabilities. In M. Shinn (Ed.), *Advanced applications of curriculum-based measurement* (pp. 254–307). New York: Guilford Press.

Prasad, S. (1994). Assessing social interaction skills of children with disabilities. *Teaching Exceptional Children, 26,* 23–25.

Pretti-Frontczak, K., & Bricker, D. (2000). Enhancing the quality of individualized education plan (IEP) goals and objectives. *Journal of Early Intervention, 23,* 92–105.

Pro-Ed. (1997). *Career IQ and Interest Test.* Austin, TX: Author.

Psychological Corporation. (2001). *Wechsler Individual Achievement Test–II.* San Antonio, TX: Author.

Psychological Corporation. (2003a). *Early Reading Diagnostic Assessment-Second Edition.* San Antonio, TX: Author.

Psychological Corporation. (2003b). *Pre-Reading Inventory of Phonological Awareness.* San Antonio, TX: Author.

Psychological Corporation. (2004). *Early Reading Success Indicator.* San Antonio, TX: Author.

Putnam, M. L. (1992). The testing practices of mainstream secondary classroom teachers. *Remedial and Special Education, 13*(5), 11–21.

Quay, H., & Peterson, D. (1987). *Revised Behavior Problem Checklist.* Miami: Author.

Quereshi, M. (2003). Absence of parallel forms for the traditional intelligence tests. *Current Psychology: Developmental, Learning, Personality, Social, 22,* 149–154.

Quintana, S., Castillo, E., & Zamarripa, M. (2000). Assessment of ethnic and linguistic minority children. In E. Shapiro & T. Kratochwill (Eds.), *Behavioral assessment in schools* (2nd ed.; pp. 435–463). New York: Guilford Press.

Raphael, T. (1999). Teaching question-answer-relationships, revisited. *The Reading Teacher, 39,* 516–522.

Rasinski, T. (1999). Exploring a method for estimating independent and instructional and frustration reading rates. *Reading Psychology, 20,* 61–69.

Raven, J. (1956). *Progressive Matrices.* London: H. K. Lewis & Co., Ltd.

Reich, W. (1996). *Diagnostic Interview for Children and Adults–Revised.* St. Louis: Washington University.

Reid, D. K., Hresko, W., & Hammill, D. (2001). *Test of Early Reading Ability–3.* Austin, TX: Pro-Ed.

Reid, R., Epstein, M., Pastor, D., & Ryser, G. (2000). Strength-based assessment differences across students with LD and EBD. *Remedial and Special Education, 21,* 346–355.

Repetto, J. B., Tulbert, B. L., & Schwartz, S. E. (1993). A statewide transition base: What's happening in Florida. *Career Development for Exceptional Individuals, 16,* 27–38.

Repp, A., Nieminen, G., Olinger, E., & Brusca, R. (1988). Direct observation: Factors affecting the accuracy of observers. *Exceptional Children, 55,* 29–36.

Reschly, D. (1979). Nonbiased assessment. In G. Phye & D. Reschly (Eds.), *School psychology: Perspectives and issues.* New York: Academic Press.

Reschly, D. (1980). *Nonbiased assessment.* Ames, IA: Iowa State University, ERIC Document Reproduction Service No. ED 209810 and ERIC EC 140324.

Reschly, D. (1991). The effects of placement litigation on psychological and educational classification. *Diagnostique, 17,* 6–20.

Reschly, D., Kicklighter, R., & McKee, P. (1988). Recent placement litigation part III: Analysis of differences in *Larry P.* v. *Marshall* and *S-1* and implications for future practices. *School Psychology Review, 17,* 39–50.

Reschly, D., & Reschly, J. (1979). Validity of WISC-R factor scores in predicting teacher ratings of achievement and attention among four groups. *Journal of School Psychology, 17,* 355–361.

Rescorla, L. (2005). Assessment of young children using the Achenbach System of Empirically Based Assessment (ASEBA). *Mental Retardation and Developmental Disabilities, 11,* 226–237.

Reynolds, C., & Kamphaus, R. (2004). *Behavior Assessment System for Children–2.* Circle Pines, MN: American Guidance Service.

Reynolds, C., Pearson, N., & Voress, J. (2002). *Developmental Tests of Visual Perception—Adolescent and Adult.* Austin. TX: Pro-Ed.

Richard, G., & Hanner, M. (2005). *Language Processing Test–3.* Moline, IL: Linguisystems.

Richards, S., Taylor, R., Ramasamy, R., & Richards, R. (1999). *Single subject research: Applications in educational and clinical settings.* San Diego, CA: Singular Publishing Group.

Ritzler, B. (1993). Test review: TEMAS (Tell-Me-A-Story). *Journal of Psychoeducational Assessment, 11,* 381–389.

Rivera, D. (1993). Performance, authentic and portfolio assessment: Emerging alternative assessment options in search of an empirical basis. *Diagnostique, 18,* 325–348.

Rivera, D., Taylor, R., & Bryant, B. (1995). Review of current trends in mathematics assessment for students with mild disabilities. *Diagnostique, 20,* 143–174.

Riverside Publishing Company. (2002). *Basic Early Assessment of Reading.* Chicago, IL: Author.

Roach, A. (2005). Alternate assessment as the "ultimate accommodation": Four challenges for policy and practice. *Assessment for Effective Intervention, 31,* 73–78.

Robertson, G. (2004). *Wide Range Achievement Test Expanded Early Reading Assessment.* Wilmington, DE: Wide Range.

Roe, B. (2006). *Burns-Roe Reading Inventory.* Boston: Houghton Mifflin.

Rogers, M. (1998). Psychoeducational assessment of culturally and linguistically diverse children and youth. In H. B. Vance (Ed.), *Psychological assessment of children* (2nd ed.; pp. 355–384). New York: John Wiley & Sons.

Rogers, R., & Sewell, K. (2006). MMPI-2 at the crossroads: Aging technology or radical retrofitting. *Assessment, 13,* 175–178.

Rogers, W., & Yang, P. (1996). Test wiseness: Its nature and application. *European Journal of Psychological Assessment, 12,* 247–259.

Roid, G. (2003). *Stanford-Binet Intelligence Scales–Fifth Edition.* Chicago, IL: Riverside.

Roid, G., & Miller, L. (1997). *Leiter International Performance Scale–Revised.* Wood Dale, IL: Stoelting.

Roid, G., & Miller, L. (2000). *Stoelting Brief Nonverbal Intelligence Test.* Wood Dale, IL: Stoelting Company.

Rorschach, H. (1932). *Psychodiagnostik: Methodik und Ergebnisse eines Wahrnehmungsdiagnostischen Experiments* (ed. 2). Bern, Switzerland: Huber.

Rosenberg, H., & Brady, M. (2000). *Job Observation and Behavior Scale.* Wood Dale, IL: Stoelting.

Roszmann-Millican, M. (1998–1999). Review of Transdisciplinary Play-Based Assessment. *Diagnostique, 24,* 241–248.

Rotholz, D. A., Kamps, D., & Greenwood, C. (1989). Ecobehavioral assessment and analysis in special education settings for students with autism. *Journal of Special Education, 23*(1), 59–81.

Rothstein, L. (2000). *Special education law* (3rd ed.). New York: Longman.

Rousseau, M. (1990). Errors in written language. In R. Gable & J. Hendrickson (Eds.), *Assessing students with special needs* (pp. 89–101). New York: Longman.

Rueda, R., & Garcia, E. (1997). Do portfolios make a difference for diverse students? The influence of type of data on making instructional decisions. *Learning Disabilities Research and Practice, 12,* 114–122.

Rusch, F. R., Enchelmaier, J. F., & Kohler, P. D. (1994). Employment outcomes and activities for youths in transition. *Career Development for Exceptional Individuals, 17,* 1–16.

Rusch, F. R., & Phelps, L. A. (1987). Secondary special education and transition from school to work: A national priority. *Exceptional Children, 53,* 487–492.

Rust, J., & Wallace, M. (2004). Adaptive Behavior Assessment System–Second Edition. *Journal of Psychoeducational Assessment, 22,* 367–373.

Ryan, J., & Glass, L. (2006). Substituting supplementary subtests for core subtests on reliability of WISC-IV indexes and full scale IQ. *Psychological Reports, 98,* 187–190.

Ryan, J., Glass, L., & Brown, C. (2007). Administration time estimates for Wechsler Intelligence Scale for Children–IV subtests, composites, and short forms. *Journal of Clinical Psychology, 63,* 309–318.

Ryser, G., & McConnell, K. (2001). *Diagnostic Assessment Scales for Attention Deficit/Hyperactivity Disorder.* Austin, TX: Pro-Ed.

Saemundsen, E., Magnusson, P., Smari, J., & Sigurdardottir, S. (2003). Autism Diagnostic Interview–Revised and the Childhood Autism Rating Scale: Convergence and discrepancy in diagnosing autism. *Journal of Autism and Developmental Disorders, 33,* 319–328.

Saenz, T. I., & Huer, M. B. (2003). Testing strategies involving least biased language assessment of bilingual children. *Communication Disorders Quarterly, 24,* 184–193.

Salend, S. (1998). Using portfolios to assess student performance. *Teaching Exceptional Children, 31,* 36–43.

Salvia, J., & Hughes, C. (1990). *Curriculum-based assessment: Testing what is taught.* New York: Macmillan.

Salvia, J., Neisworth, J., & Schmidt, M. (1990). *Responsibility and Independence Scale for Adolescents.* Chicago: Riverside.

Salvia, J., Ysseldyke, J., & Bolt, S. (2007). *Assessment in special and remedial education* (10th ed.). Boston: Houghton Mifflin.

Samuda, R. (1975). *Psychological testing of American minorities: Issues and consequences.* New York: Dodd, Mead.

Sanders, S., McIntosh, D., Dunham, M., Rothlisberg, B., & Finch, H. (2007). Joint confirmatory factor analysis of the Differential Ability Scales and the Woodcock-Johnson Tests of Cognitive Abilities–Third Edition. *Psychology in the schools, 44,* 119–138.

Sarkees-Wircenski, M., & Wircenski, J. (1994). Transition planning: Developing a career portfolio for students with disabilities. *Career Development for Exceptional Individuals, 17,* 203–214.

Sarouphim, K. (1999). Discovering multiple intelligences through a performance based assessment: Consistency with independent ratings. *Exceptional Children, 65,* 151–161.

Sattler, J., & Gwynne, J. (1982). White examiners generally do not impede the intelligence test performance of black children: To debunk a myth. *Journal of Consulting and Clinical Psychology, 50,* 196–208.

Scannell, D. (1996). *Tests of Achievement and Proficiency.* Chicago: Riverside.

Schirmer, B., & Bailey, J. (2000). Writing assessment rubric. *Teaching Exceptional Children, 33,* 52–58

Schopler, E., Reichler, R., & Renner, B. (1988). *The Childhood Autism Rating Scale.* Los Angeles: Western Psychological Services.

Schriner, K. F., & Bellini, J. L. (1994). Analyzing transition policy implementation: A conceptual approach. *Career Development for Exceptional Individuals, 17,* 17–27.

Schwean, V., Burt, K., & Saklofske, D. (1999). Correlates of mother and teacher ratings of hyperactivity-impulsivity and inattention in children with AD/HD. *Canadian Journal of School Psychology, 15,* 43–62.

Schweiker-Marra, K., & Marra, W. (2000). Investigating the effects of prewriting activities on writing performance and anxiety of at risk students. *Reading Psychology, 21,* 99–114.

Scruggs, T., & Mastropieri, M. (1986). Improving the test-taking skills of behavior-disordered and learning disabled children. *Exceptional Children, 53,* 63–68.

Scruggs, T., Mastropieri, M., & Tolfa-Veit, D. (1986). The effects of coaching on the standardized test performance of learning disabled and behavior disordered students. *Remedial and Special Education, 7,* 37–41.

Seagle, D., & Rust, J. (1996) Concurrent validity of the K-BIT using the WISC-III as the criterion. (Eric Document Reproduction Service No. ED 403288).

Semel, E., Wiig, E., & Secord, W. (2003). *Clinical Evaluation of Language Fundamentals–4.* San Antonio, TX: Psychological Corporation.

Sepassi, F. (2003). How do learners of different language ability perform on the cloze? A verbal protocol analysis of EFL test takers performance on cloze tests. *Indian Journal of Applied Linguistics, 29,* 5–33.

Shankar, J., & Ekwall, E. (2000). *Ekwall/Shanker Reading Inventory.* Boston: Allyn and Bacon.

Shapiro, E. (1990). An integrated model for curriculum-based assessment. *School Psychology Review, 19,* 331–349.

Shapiro, E. (2003). *Behavioral assessment in school psychology.* Hillsdale, NJ: Erlbaum.

Shapiro, E., & Eckert, T. L. (1994). Acceptability of curriculum-based assessment by school psychologists. *Journal of School Psychology, 32*(2), 167–183.

Shapiro, E., Keller, M., Lutz, J. G., Santoro, L., & Hintze, J. (2006). Curriculum-based measures and performance on state assessment and standardized tests. *Journal of Psychoeducational Assessment, 24,* 19–35.

Shepard, J. (1989). Review of the Vocational Preference Inventory. In J. Conoley & J. Kramer (Eds.), *Tenth mental measurements yearbook* (pp. 882–883). Lincoln: University of Nebraska Press.

Sherrets, S., Gard, G., & Langner, H. (1979). Frequency of clerical errors on WISC protocols. *Psychology in the Schools, 16,* 495–496.

Shin, J., Deno, S., & Espin, C. (2000). Technical adequacy of the maze test for curriculum-based measurement of reading growth. *Journal of Special Education, 34,* 164–172.

Shinn, M., & Bamonto, S. (1998). Advanced applications of curriculum-based measurement: "Big ideas" and avoiding confusion. In M. Shinn (Ed.), *Advanced applications of curriculum-based measurement* (pp. 1–31). New York: Guilford Press.

Shinn, M., Collins, V., & Gallagher, S. (1998). Curriculum-based measurement and its use in a problem-solving model with students from minority backgrounds. In M. Shinn (Ed.), *Advanced applications of curriculum-based measurement* (pp. 143–174). New York: Guilford Press.

Shinn, M. R., Habedank, L., Rodden-Nord, R., & Knutson, P. (1993). Using curriculum-based measurement to identify potential candidates for reintegration into general education. *Journal of Special Education, 27*(2), 202–221.

Shipley, K., Stone, T., & Sue, M. (1983). *Test for Examining Expressive Morphology.* Tucson, AZ: Communication Skill Builders.

Shurrager, H., & Shurrager, P. (1964). *Haptic Intelligence Scale.* Chicago: Institute of Technology.

Siegel, E., & Allinder, R. (2005). Review of assessment procedures for students with moderate and severe disabilities. *Education and Training in Developmental Disabilities, 40,* 343–351.

Siegel-Causey, E., & Allinder, R. (1998). Using alternative assessment for students with severe disabilities: Alignment with best practices. *Education and Training in Mental Retardation and Developmental Disabilities, 33,* 168–178.

Silva, C., & Yarborough, R. (1990). Help for young writers with spelling difficulties. *The Reading Teacher, 34,* 48–53.

Silvaroli, N. (2001). *Silvaroli/Wheelock Classroom Reading Inventory.* Boston: McGraw-Hill.

Silverthorne, P. (1994). Assessment of ADHD using ADDES. *Child Assessment News, 4,* 1–3.

Simon, J. (1998–1999). Review of the Woodcock Diagnostic Reading Battery. *Diagnostique, 24,* 285–198.

Simpson, R., Smith, S., Johnson, T., & Halpin, G. (2003). The psychometric effects of altering the ceiling criterion on the Passage Comprehension test of the Woodcock Reading Mastery Tests–Revised/NU. *Assessment for Effective Intervention, 28,* 35–40.

Sitlington, P., & Clark, G. M. (2001). Career/vocational assessment: A critical component of transition planning. *Assessment for Effective Intervention 26*(4), 5–22.

Sitlington, P. L., & Clark, G. M. (2006). *Transition educaton and services for students with disabilities* (4th ed.). Boston: Pearson.

Sitlington, P., Neubert, D., & LeConte, P. (1997). Transition assessment: The position of the Division on Career Development and Transition. *Career Development for Exceptional Individuals, 20,* 69–79.

Skinner, C., Dittmer, K., & Howell, L. (2000). Direct observation in school settings: Theoretical issues. In E. Shapiro & T. Kratochwill (Eds.), *Behavioral assessment in schools* (2nd ed.; pp. 19–45). New York: Guilford Press.

Slate, J., & Jones, C. (1990). Identifying students' errors in administering the WAIS-R. *Psychology in the Schools, 27,* 83–87.

Slate, J. R., Jones, C. H., Murray, R. A., & Coulter, C. (1993). Evidence that practitioners err in administering and scoring the WAIS-R. *Measurement and Evaluation in Counseling and Development, 25.*

Slosson, R., Nicholson, C., & Hibpshamn, T. (1998). *Slosson Intelligence Test-Revised 3,* East Aurora, NY: Slosson Educational Publishers.

Smiley, L., & Goldstein, P. (1998). *Language disorders.* San Diego: Singular Publishing Company.

Smith, S. R., & Reddy, L. A. (2002). The concurrent validity of the Devereux Scales of Mental Disorders. *Journal of Psychoeducational Assessment, 20,* 112–127.

Smith, T. T., Bradham, T., Chandler, L., & Wells, C. (2000). The effect of examiner's race on the performance of African American children on the SCAN. *Language, Speech, and Hearing Services in Schools, 31,* 116–125.

Smith, T., Smith, B. L., Eichler, J. B., & Pollard, A. G. (2002). Validity of the Comprehensive Receptive and Expressive Vocabulary Test in assessment of children with speech and learning problems. *Psychology in the Schools, 39,* 613–619.

Snider, M., Lima, S., & DeVito, P. (1994). Rhode Island's Literacy Portfolio Assessment Project. In S. Valencia, E. Hiebert, & P. Afflerbach (Eds.), *Authentic reading assessment: Practices and possibilities.* Newark, DE: International Reading Association.

Sodowsky, G., Gonzalez, J., & Kuo-Jackson, P. (1998). Multicultural assessment and the Buros Institute of Mental Measurements: On the cutting edge of measurement concerns. In R. Samuda, R. Feuerstein, A. Kaufman, J. Lewis and R. Sternberg (Eds.), *Advances in cross-cultural assessment* (pp. 242–273). Thousand Oaks, CA: Sage Publications.

Sofie, A., & Riccio, C. A. (2002). A comparison of multiple methods for the identification of children with reading disabilities. *Journal of Learning Disabilities, 35,* 234–244.

Soodak, L. (2000). Performance assessments and students with learning problems: Promising practice or reform rhetoric? *Reading and Writing Quarterly: Overcoming Learning Difficulties, 16,* 257–280.

South, M., Williams, J., McMahon, W. M., Owley, T., Filipek, P., Shernoff, E., Corsello, C., Lainhart, J. E., Landa, R., & Ozonoff, S. (2002). Utility of the Gilliam Autism Rating Scale in research and clinical populations. *Journal of Autism and Developmental Disorders, 32,* 593–599.

Sowder, L. (1978). Review of Stanford Diagnostic Mathematics Test. In O. Buros (Ed.), *The eighth mental measurement yearbook* (pp. 437–439). Highland Park, NJ: Gryphon Press.

Sparrow, S., Balla, D., & Cicchetti, D. (2007). *Vineland Adaptive Behavior Scales–2.* Circle Pines, MN: American Guidance Service.

Spector, J. (2005). How reliable are informal reading inventories? *Psychology in the Schools, 42,* 593–603.

Stainback, S., & Stainback, W. (1992). Schools as inclusive communities. In W. Stainback & S. Stainback (Eds.), *Controversial issues confronting special education.* Boston: Allyn and Bacon.

Stecker, P. (2006). Using curriculum-based measurement to monitor reading progress in inclusive elementary settings. *Reading & Writing Quarterly, 22,* 91–97.

Stecker, P., & Fuchs, L. (2000). Effecting superior achievement using curriculum-based measurement: The importance of individual progress monitoring. *Learning Disabilities Research and Practice, 15,* 128–134.

Stella, J., Mundy, P., & Tuchman, R. (1999). Social and non-social factors in the Childhood Autism Rating Scale, *Journal of Autism and Developmental Disorders, 29,* 307–317.

Stephens, K., & Karnes, F. (2000). State definitions for the gifted and talented revisited. *Exceptional Children, 66,* 219–238.

Sternberg, R. (1993). *Sternberg Triarchic Abilities Test.* New Haven, CT: Unpublished.

Sternberg, R. (1999). A triarchic approach to the understanding and assessment of intelligence in multicultural populations. *Journal of School Psychology, 37,* 145–159.

Stillman, R. (1978). *Callier-Azusa Scale.* Dallas: University of Texas at Dallas Center of Communication Disorders.

Stinnett, T. (1997). Review of the AAMR Adaptive Behavior Scale–School (2nd ed.). *Journal of Psychoeducational Assessment, 15,* 361–372.

Stinnett, T., Fuqua, D., & Coombs, W. (1999). Construct validity of the AAMR Adaptive Behavior Scales–School Edition: 2. *School Psychology Review, 28,* 31–43.

Stodden, R. A., & Leake, D. W. (1994). Getting to the core of transition: A reassessment of old wine in new bottles. *Career Development for Exceptional Individuals, 17,* 65–76.

Stoiber, K. (2003). *Functional assessment and intervention system: Improving school behavior.* San Antonio: Psychological Corporation.

Stone, W., Ousley, O., Hepburn, S., Hogan, K., & Brown, C. (1999). Patterns of adaptive behavior in very young children with autism. *American Journal on Mental Retardation, 104,* 187–199.

Stowitschek, J. J., & Kelso, C. A. (1989). Are we in danger of making the same mistakes with ITPs as were made with IEPs? *Career Development for Exceptional Individuals, 12,* 139–151.

Strawser, S., & Sileo, N. (1998–1999). Review of the Developmental Indicators for the Assessment of Learning–3. *Diagnostique, 24,* 99–114.

Strickland, B., & Turnbull, A. (1993). *Developing and implementing IEPs* (3rd ed.). Columbus, OH: Charles E. Merrill.

Strong, E., Campbell, D., & Hansen, J. (1984). *Strong-Campbell Interest Inventory.* Palo Alto, CA: Consulting Psychologists Press.

Suporitz, J., & Brennan, R. (1997). Mirror, mirror on the wall, which is the fairest test of all? An examination of the equitability of portfolio assessment relative to standardized tests. *Harvard Educational Review, 67,* 472–506.

Sutton, J. (1998–1999). Review of the Woodcock Reading Mystery Test–Revised/Normative Update. *Diagnostique, 24,* 299–316.

Swain, K., & Allinder, R. (1996). The effects of repeated reading on two types of CBM: Computer maze and oral reading with second grade students with learning disabilities. *Diagnostique, 21,* 51–66.

Swanson, H. L., & Howard, C. (2005). Children with disabilities: Does dynamic assessment help in the classification? *Learning Disability Quarterly, 28,* 17–34.

Swanson, S., & Howell, C. (1996). Test anxiety in adolescents with learning disabilities and behavior disorders. *Exceptional Children, 62,* 383–397.

Swezey, R. (1981). *Individual performance assessment.* Reston, VA: Reston Publishing Company.

Swicegood, P. (1994). Portfolio-based assessment practices. *Intervention, 30*(1), 6–15.

Synhorst, L., Buckley, J., Reid, R., Epstein, M., & Ryser, G. (2005). Cross-informant agreement of the Behavioral and Emotional Rating Scales–2nd edition (BERS-2) parent and youth rating scales. *Child and Family Behavior Therapy, 27,* 1–11.

Tackett, J. L., Krueger, R. F., Sawyer, M. G., & Graetz, B. W. (2003). Subfactors of DSM-IV conduct disorder: Evidence and connections with syndromes from the Child Behavior Checklist. *Journal of Abnormal Child Psychology, 31,* 647–654.

Tan, C. S. (2007) Test review: Behavior Assessment System for Children (2nd ed.). *Assessment for Effective Instruction, 32,* 121–124.

Taylor, R. (1984). *Assessment of exceptional students: Educational and psychological procedures.* Englewood Cliffs, NJ: Prentice-Hall.

Taylor, R. (1997). Nondiscriminatory evaluation. In R. Taylor (Ed.), *Assessment of individuals with mental retardation* (pp. 55–72). San Diego, CA: Singular Publishing Group.

Taylor, R. L., Willits, P., & Richards, S. B. (1988). Curriculum-based assessment: Considerations and concerns. *Diagnostique, 14,* 14–21.

Taub, G., & McGrew, K. (2004). A confirmatory factor analysis of Cattell-Horn-Carroll theory and age invariance of the Woodcock-Johnson Test of Cognitive Abilities–III. *School Psychology Quarterly, 19,* 72–57.

Tenopyr, M. (1989). Review of the Kuder Occupational Interest Survey. In J. Conoley & J. Kramer (Eds.), *Tenth mental measurements yearbook* (pp. 427–429). Lincoln: University of Nebraska Press.

Terrell, S. L., Daniloff, R., Garden, M., Flint-Shaw, L., & Flowers, T. (2001). The effect of speech clinician race and Afro-American students' cultural mistrust of clinician-child conversation. *Clinical Linguistics and Phonetics, 15,* 169–175.

Theriot, J. A., Franco, S. M., Sisson, B. A, Metcalf S. C., Kennedy, M. A., & Bada, H. S. (2003). The impact of early literacy guidance on language skills of 3-year-olds. *Clinical Pediatrics, 42,* 165–172.

Thompson, S., & Thurlow, M. (2001). *State special education outcomes, 2001: A report on state activities at the beginning of a new decade.* Minneapolis, MN: National Center for Educational Outcomes. ERIC Reproduction No. ED 455626.

Thurlow, M., & Elliot, J. (1998). Student assessment and evaluation. In F. Rusch & J. Chadsey (Eds.), *Beyond high school: Transition from school to work.* Belmont, CA: Wadsworth.

Thurlow, M., House, A., Scott, D., & Ysseldyke, J. (2000). Students with disabilities in large-scale assessments. *Journal of Special Education, 34,* 154–163.

Tindal, G., Heath, B., Hollenbeck, K., Almond, P., & Harniss, M. (1998). Accomodating students with disabilities on large-scale tests: An experimental study. *Exceptional Children, 64,* 439–450.

Torgesen, J., & Bryant, B. (2004). *Test of Phonological Awareness–Second Edition.* Austin, TX: Pro-Ed.

Touchette, P., MacDonald, R., & Langer, S. (1985). A scatter plot for identifying stimulus control of problem behavior. *Journal of Applied Behavior Analysis, 18,* 343–351.

Trout, A. L., Ryan, J. B., La Vigne, S. P., & Epstein, M. H. (2003). Behavioral and Emotional Rating Scale: Two studies of convergent validity. *Journal of Child and Family Studies, 12,* 399–410.

Truscott, S., & Frank, A. (2001). Does the Flynn effect affect IQ scores of students classified as LD? *Journal of School Psychology, 39,* 319–334.

Tucker, J. (1985). Curriculum-based assessment: An introduction. *Exceptional Children, 52,* 199–204.

Tukey, J. (1977). *Exploratory data analysis.* Reading, MA: Addison-Wesley.

Turner, B., Beidel, D., Hughes, S., & Turner, M. (1993). Test anxiety in African American school children. *School Psychology Quarterly, 8,* 140–152.

Tymitz-Wolf, B. (1982). Guidelines for assessing goals and objectives. *Teaching Exceptional Children, 14,* 198–201.

Tzeng, O. (1985). Review of the Strong-Campbell Interest Inventory. In D. Keyser & R. Sweetland (Eds.), *Test critiques,* v. 2 (pp. 737–749). Kansas City, MO: Test Corporation of America.

Tzuriel, D., & Shamir, A. (2002). The effects of mediation in computer assisted dynamic assessment. *Journal of Computer Assisted Learning, 18,* 21–32.

Ukrainetz, T. A., & Blomquist, C. (2002). The criterion validity of four vocabulary tests compared to a language sample. *Child Language Teaching and Therapy, 18,* 59–78.

Ullman, R., Sleator, E., & Sprague, R. (1991). *ADD-H Comprehensive Teacher's Rating Scale–Second Editon.* Los Angeles: Western Psychological Services.

Underwood, J., & Mead, J. (1995). *Legal aspects of special education and pupil services.* Boston: Allyn and Bacon.

U.S. Department of Education. (2004). *A blueprint for preparing America's future: Summary: The Carl D. Perkins Secondary and Technical Education Excellence Act of 2004.* Washington, DC: U.S. Government Printing Office.

Urbina, S. (2004). *Essentials of psychological testing.* Hoboken, NJ: John Wiley & Sons.

Valencia, S. (1990). A portfolio approach to classroom reading assessment: The why's, what's, and how's. *The Reading Teacher, 43,* 142–148.

Valencia, S. (1997). Authentic classroom assessment of early reading: Alternatives to standardized tests. *Preventing School Failure, 41,* 63–70.

van Keulen, J., Weddington, G., & DeBose, C. (1998). *Speech, language, learning, and the African American child.* Boston: Allyn and Bacon.

Vaughn, S., & Fuchs, L. S. (2003). Redefining learning disabilities as inadequate response to instruction: The promise and potential problem. *Learning Disabilities Research & Practice, 18*(3), 137–146.

Vavrus, L. (1990). Put portfolios to the test. *Instructor, 100*(1), 48–53.

Vitale, G. J. (1993). *Factors influencing teachers' assessment and instructional practices in an assessment-driven educational reform.* Doctoral dissertation, University of Kentucky.

Vladescu, J. (2007). Review of Kaufman Test of Educational Achievement–Second Edition. *Journal of Psychoeducational Assessment, 25,* 92–100.

Volkmar, F., & Marans, W. (1999). In D. Shaffer, C. Lucas, & J. Richters (Eds.), *Diagnostic assessment in child and adolescent psychology* (pp. 167–208). New York: Guilford Press.

VORT Corporation. (2001). *Behavioral Characteristics Progression–Revised.* Palo Alto, CA: VORT Corporation.

Vulpé, S. (1996). *Vulpé Assessment Battery–Revised.* Toronto, Canada: National Institute on Mental Retardation.

Wagner, R., Torgesen, J., & Rashotte, C. (1999). *Comprehensive Test of Phonological Processing.* Austin, TX: Pro-Ed.

Walker, H., & McConnell, S. (1995). *Walker-McConnell Scale of Social Competence and School Adjustment.* San Diego: Singular Publishing Group.

Wallace, G., & Hammill, D. (1997a). *Comprehensive Receptive and Expressive Vocabulary Test–Adult.* Austin, TX: Pro-Ed.

Wallace, G., & Hammill, D. (1997b). *Comprehensive Receptive and Expressive Vocabulary Test–Computer Administered.* Austin, TX: Pro-Ed.

Wallace, G., & Hammill, D. (2001). *Comprehensive Receptive and Expressive Vocabulary Test–2.* Austin, TX: Pro-Ed.

Wallace, T., Anderson, A. R., Bartholomay, T., & Hupp, S. (2002). An ecobehavioral examination of high school classrooms that include students with disabilities. *Exceptional Children, 68,* 345–359.

Wallingford, E., & Prout, H. (2000). The relationship of season of birth and special education referral. *Psychology in the Schools, 37,* 379–387.

Warden, M. R., & Hutchison, T. (1992). *Writing Process Test.* Chicago: Riverside Publishing Company.

Warlick, K., & Olsen, K. (1999). How to conduct alternate assessments: Practices in nine states. (ERIC Document Reproduction Number ED 431 261).

Washington, J., & Craig, H. (1999). Performance of at risk African American preschoolers on the Peabody Picture Vocabulary Test–III. *Language, Speech, and Hearing Services in Schools, 30,* 75–82.

Watkins, M. W., Ravert, C. M., & Crosby, E. G. (2002). Normative factor structure of the AAMR Adaptive Behavior Scale–School, Second Edition. *Journal of Psychoeducational Assessment, 20,* 337–345.

Watkins, M., Wilson, S., Kotz, K., Carbone, M., & Babula, T. (2006). Factor structure of the Wechsler Intelligence Scale for Children–Fourth Edition among referred students. *Educational and Psychological Measurement, 66,* 975–983.

Wechsler, D. (2003). *Manual for the Wechsler Intelligence Scale for Children–Fourth Edition.* San Antonio: Psychological Corporation.

Wechsler, D. (2007). *Wechsler Essential Academic Skills Inventory.* San Antonio, TX: Harcourt Assessment.

Wehman, P., Moon, M. S., Everson, J. M., Wood, W., & Barcus, J. M. (1988). *Transition from school to work.* Baltimore, MD: Paul H. Brookes.

Wehmeyer, M. (1998). Student involvement in transition planning in transition program implementation. In F. Rusch & J. Chadsey (Eds.), *Beyond high school: Transition from school to work* (pp. 206–233). Belmont, CA: Wadsworth.

Wehmeyer, M. (2001). Assessment in self-determination: Guiding instruction and transition planning. *Assessment for Effective Intervention, 26*(4), 21–49.

Wepman, J., & Reynolds, J. (1986). *Auditory Discrimination Test.* Chicago: Language Research Associates.

Wesson, C. L., & King, R. P. (1992). The role of curriculum-based measurement in portfolio assessment. *Diagnostique, 18*(1), 27–38.

Wesson, C., & King, R. (1996). Portfolio assessment and special education students. *Teaching Exceptional Children, 28,* 44–49.

Wesson, C., Vierthaler, J., & Haubrich, P. (1989). The discriminant validity of curriculum-based measures for establishing reading groups. *Reading Research and Instruction, 29,* 23–32.

West, M., Johnson, A., Cone, A., Hernandez, A., & Revell, G. (1998). Extended employment support: Analysis of implementation and funding issues. *Education and Training in Mental Retardation and Developmental Disabilities, 33,* 357–366.

Wheldall, K., & Madelaine, A. (2000). A curriculum-based passage reading test for monitoring the performance of low progress readers: The development of the WARP. *International Journal of Disability, Development, and Education, 47,* 371–382.

White, O., & Haring, N. (1980). *Exceptional teaching* (2nd ed.). Columbus, OH: Charles E. Merrill.

Wickes, K., & Slate, J. (1999). Math and reading tests: Dissimilar scores provided by similar tests for African American students. *Research in Schools, 6,* 41–45.

Wiederman, M. (1999). A classroom demonstration of potential biases in the subjective interpretation of projective tests. *Teaching of Psychology, 26,* 37–39.

Wiggins, G. (1989). A true test: Toward more authentic and equitable assessment. *Phi Delta Kappan, 70,* 703–713.

Wilkinson, G. S., & Robertson, G. J. (2007). *Wide Range Achievement Test–4 (WRAT-4).* Los Angeles: Western Psychological Services.

Will, M. (1986). Educating children with learning problems: A shared responsibility. *Exceptional Children, 52,* 411–416.

William K. Bradford Publishing Company. (2001). *Mathematics Test Builder and Test Banks.* Concord, MA: Author.

Williams, K. (2004). *Group Mathematics Assessment and Diagnostic Evaluation.* Circle Pines, MN: American Guidance Service.

Williams, K. (2007). *Expressive Vocabulary Test–2.* Circle Pines, MN: American Guidance Service.

Williams, R. (1972). *Black Intelligence Test of Cultural Homogeneity.* St. Louis, MO: Williams and Associates.

Willig, A., & Ortiz, A. (1991). The nonbiased individualized educational program: Linking assessment to instruction. In E. Hamian & J. Damico (Eds.), *Limited bias in the assessment of bilingual students* (pp. 281–302). Austin. TX: Pro-Ed.

Willis, J., Dumont, R., & Cruse, C. (1997). Review of the Mini-Battery of Achievement. *Journal of Psychoeducational Assessment, 15,* 270–280.

Wisniewski, L. A., Alper, S., & Schloss, P. (1991). Work-experience and work-study programs for students with special needs. *Career Development for Exceptional Individuals, 14,* 43–58.

Wolf, D. P., LeMahieu, P. G., & Eresh, J. (1992). Good measure: Assessment as a tool for educational reform. *Educational Leadership, 49*(8), 8–13.

Wolfram, W. (1990). *Dialect differences and testing.* Washington, DC: Office of Educational Research and Improvement (ED 323813).

Woodcock, R. (1998). *Woodcock Reading Mastery Tests–Revised.* Circle Pines, MN: American Guidance Service.

Woodcock, R., Mather, N., & Schrank, F. (2004). *The WJ-III Diagnostic Reading Battery.* Chicago: Riverside.

Woodcock, R., McGrew, K., Mather, N., Shrank, F. (2007). *Woodcock-Johnson III– Normative Update.* Itasca, IL: Riverside.

Woodcock, R., McGrew, K., & Werder, J. (1994). *Woodcock-McGrew-Werder Mini-Battery of Achievement.* Chicago: Riverside.

Woods, M., & Moe, A. (1999). *Analytical Reading Inventory.* Englewood Cliffs, NJ: Charles E. Merrill.

Wrightson, L., & Saklofske, D. (2000). Validity and reliability of the Draw a Person Screening Procedure for emotional disturbance with adolescent students. *Canadian Journal of School Psychology, 16,* 95–102.

Wyss, C. A., Voelker, S. L., Cornock, B. L., & Hakim-Larson, J. (2003). Psychometric properties of a French-Canadian translation of Achenbach's Youth Self-Report. *Canadian Journal of Behavioural Science, 35,* 67–71.

Yang, P. (2001). Effects of test-wiseness on the Test of English as a Foreign Language. *Dissertation Abstracts, International Section A. Humanities and Social Sciences, 62*(5A), 1724.

Yell, M., Deno, S., & Marston, D. (1992). Barriers to implementation of curriculum-based measurements. *Diagnostique, 18,* 99–112.

Yell, M. L., & Stecker, P. M. (2003). Developing legally correct and educationally meaningful IEPs using curriculum-based measurement. *Assessment for Effective Intervention, 28,* 73–88.

Ysseldyke, J., & Christenson, S. (1992). *The Instructional Environment Scale.* Longmont, CO: Sopris West.

Ysseldyke, J., & Olsen, K. (1999). Putting alternate assessments into practice: What to measure and possible sources of data. *Exceptional Children, 65,* 175–185.

Ysseldyke, J., Thurlow, M., Bielenski, J., House, A., Moody, M., & Haigh, J. (2001). The relationship between instructional and assessment accommodations in an inclusive state accountability system. *Journal of Learning Disabilities, 34,* 212–220.

Ysseldyke, J., Vanderwood, M., & Shriner, J. (1997). Changes over the past decade in special education referral to placement probability: An incredibly reliable practice. *Diagnostique, 23,* 193–202.

Yzquierdo, Z., Blalock, G., & Torres-Velasquez, D. (2004). Language-appropriate assessments for determining eligibility of English language learners for special education services. *Assessment for Effective Intervention, 29,* 17–30.

Zeidner, M. (1998). *Test anxiety: State of the art.* New York: Plenum.

Author Index

Abedi, J., 69
Abramowitz, E., 189, 263
Acevedo-Polakovich, I., 16
Achenbach, T. M., 196, 198
Adams, G., 189
Alberto, P., 80, 82
Albin, R., 93, 95–96
Alessi, G., 81
Alfonso, V., 23, 163, 361, 363
Algozzine, B., 55
Allen, D., 121
Allen, E., 294
Allin, J., 160
Allinder, R., 114–115, 119, 121, 122, 129, 176
Almond, P., 20, 214
Alnot, S., 251
Alper, S., 380–381
Altman, J., 59
Ammer, J., 262
Andersen, V., 340
Anderson, A. R., 91
Anderson, D., 58
Anderson, R., 155
Anderson, V., 281
Ansley, T., 251
Anthony, J., 363
Applegate, A. J., 279
Applegate, M. D., 279
Arick, J., 214
Armendariz, G. M., 79
Arnold, N., 134
Arter, J., 5
Arthaud, T., 209, 276, 292
Ashlock, R., 302
Ashmore, R., 170
Assel, M., 363
Athanasiou, M., 128
Attermeier, S., 372

Babula, T., 163
Bachor, D., 311, 312
Bailey, D. B., 188
Bailey, J., 328
Bain, S., 160
Baker, B., 185
Baker, E. L., 130, 134
Baker, J. J., 54
Baker, S., 121
Balla, D., 185
Balthazar, E., 176
Bamonto, S., 114
Banikowski, A., 339
Barcus, J. M., 379, 382
Bardos, A., 217

Barenbaum, E., 225, 327
Barnett, D. W., 88, 361, 363
Barnhill, G., 205
Baron, I., 162
Baroody, A., 316
Barrera, M., 153
Barrett, M., 240
Bartholomay, T., 91
Barton, N., 205
Bassett, D., 377
Baumgart, D., 388
Beattie, J., 54, 55
Beaver, B., 44–45
Beck, A., 218
Beck, J., 218
Becker, M., 54
Beckmann, J., 153
Beidel, D., 54
Bell, S., 233
Bellak, L., 216
Bellak, S., 216
Bellini, J. L., 380
Bender, W., 23, 121
Benner, B., 114
Bennett, D., 136
Bennett, G., 393
Ben-Porath, Y., 59
Bentz, J., 121
Berends, M., 249
Bergeron, R., 167
Berninger, V., 5
Betts, E., 278
Beyersdorfer, J., 307–308
Bielenski, J., 56
Bigelow, S., 132
Bigge, J., 44, 47, 152, 153
Binet, A., 4
Bisconer, S. W., 381
Blacher, J., 185
Black, D. O., 187
Black, R., 382
Blackhurst, A., 81
Blair, T. R., 281
Blalock, G., 16, 377
Bland-Stewart, L. M., 233
Blankenship, C., 109, 110
Bliss, S., 366
Block, R., 185
Blomquist, C., 233
Boan, C., 175, 176–177
Boardman, A., 13
Boatwright, B., 213
Boehm, A., 78, 366
Boelte, S., 188

Bolen, L., 258
Bolling, R., 122
Bolt, D., 58
Bolt, S., 56, 65, 66
Boney, T., 189
Booker, S., 188
Borich, G., 90
Borthwick-Duffy, S., 30, 175
Bos, C., 309
Bosley, M., 230
Bowers, L., 240
Bracken, B., 195–196, 213, 367
Braden, J. P., 154
Bradford, K., 189
Bradham, T., 61
Bradley, A., 255
Bradley-Johnson, S., 231, 235
Bradley-Klug, K., 115
Brady, M., 393
Bramlett, R. K., 88, 361
Branston, M. B., 388
Braziel, P., 380, 383, 384
Brennan, R., 146
Brick, M., 205
Bricker, D., 121
Bridgeman, B., 60
Brigance, A., 265, 267, 368, 392
Brotherton, W., 217
Browder, D. M., 22
Brown, C., 56, 163, 187
Brown, J., 60, 285
Brown, L., 177, 388
Brown, M., 258
Brown, S., 58
Brown, T., 16
Brown, V., 239, 293, 314
Brownell, M., 115
Brownell, R., 226
Bruininks, R., 183
Bruno, R., 236
Brustein, M., 379
Bryant, B., 169, 225, 293, 311, 334, 335
Bryant, D., 293
Buck, K., 356
Buckley, J., 209
Budoff, M., 153–154
Buker, K., 236
Bull, M., 79
Bullock, A., 134
Bulotsky-Shearer, R., 199
Buntinx, W., 30, 175
Burger, D. L., 130
Burger, S. E., 130
Burke, C., 284

Subject Index

Accommodations
    decision-making process for, 57
    guidelines for using, 21
    in high-stakes assessments, 58–59
    nature of, 19–20
    as practical consideration, 55–59
    for students with limited English
      proficiency, 56
    types of, 21
Accuracy, 105
Adaptive behavior assessment, 174–193
    adaptive behavior, defined, 175
    cultural bias and, 176
    instruments for, 176–190, 193
    nature of, 175–176
    summary matrix, 193
Adequate yearly progress (AYP), 13–14
Administration
    of criterion-referenced tests, 107–108
    differences in, 59–60
African Americans
    adaptive behavior scales and, 176
    item bias and, 70
    linking assessment to intervention in
      math, 308
Age equivalents, 38–39
Alternate-form reliability, 66–67
Alternative assessment, 6–7, 20–23. *See also*
    Authentic assessment; Informal
    assessment; Performance assessment;
    Portfolio assessment
    defined, 129
    of intelligence, 152–154
    methods of, 43–48
Amendments to the Rehabilitation Act of
    1992, 379–380
American Association on Intellectual and
    Developmental Disabilities, 30
American Association on Mental Deficiency
    (AAMD), 177
American Association on Mental
    Retardation (AAMR), 30, 175, 176,
    178–183
American Counseling Association, 71–72
American Education Research Association
    (AERA), 17
American Psychiatric Association (APA),
    211, 212, 215
American Psychological Association (APA),
    17, 71–72
Analogue assessment, 79
Anxiety, of examinee, 53–54
Application, mathematical, 300
APPLY mnemonic, 308–310

Appropriate achievement, 248
Arts, portfolio assessment, 133
Assessment
    of adaptive behavior. *See* Adaptive
      behavior assessment
    of behavioral and emotional status. *See*
      Behavioral and emotional assessment
    career/vocational/transition. *See*
      Career/vocational/transition
      assessment
    defined, 3
    early childhood. *See* Early childhood
      assessment
    of general achievement. *See* General
      achievement tests
    historical background of, 4–8
    of intelligence. *See* Intelligence testing
    legislation concerning, 10–23, 164
    litigation concerning, 8–10
    of mathematics. *See* Mathematics
      assessment
    of oral language. *See* Oral language
      assessment
    process of. *See* Assessment process
    of reading. *See* Reading assessment
    testing versus, 3
    of written expression. *See* Written
      expression assessment
Assessment portfolio, 135
Assessment process, 26–52
    assessment model, 50–51
    case studies, 403–415
    decisions about program placement, 36
    ethical considerations, 71–73
    examinee factors, 53–59, 72
    examiner factors, 48, 59–63, 72
    initiation of, 36–37
    practical considerations, 53–71
    procedures used in, 37–48
    purposes of assessment, 26–36
    results of, 49–50
    technical factors, 63–71
    timing of, 48–49
ASSIST software, 186, 240, 333
Attention-deficit/hyperactivity disorder
    (AD/HD)
    defined, 195
    instruments to measure, 211–213, 223
    key characteristics, 211
Authentic assessment
    areas for, 132
    defined, 129, 131–132
    in mathematics, 306
    summary matrix, 147

Autism
    defined, 195
    instruments to measure, 213–215, 223
    student observation and, 88
Autism Society of America, 215

Basal, of a test, 68
Behavioral and emotional assessment, 4, 88,
    194–223
    attention-deficit hyperactivity disorder
      (AD/HD), 195, 211–213, 223
    autism, 88, 195, 213–215, 223
    behavior-rating scales/assessment
      systems, 195–196
    classroom/home behavior instruments,
      196–209
    measuring emotional status, 215–220
    personality inventories, 4, 218–220, 223
    projective measures, 4, 216–218, 223
    social skills instruments, 195, 209–210
    summary matrix, 223
Behavioral Graphing 99, 115–117
Behavioral intervention plan (BIP), 91, 92
*Behavioral Intervention Planning—Third
    Edition* (McConnell et al.), 92
Behavioral Observation of Students in Schools,
    82
Behavior Evaluation Strategies and Taxonomies
    (BEST), 81–82
Behavior-rating scales/assessment systems,
    195–196
Behaviors, defining, in functional behavior
    assessment, 92–93
Behavior-specific interviews, 45
Benchmarking, 33–34, 141
Benchmark objectives, 33–34
Bias
    cultural, 176
    examiner, 61
    factor-analysis, 70–71
    gender, 395
    item, 70
    mean-difference, 70
    psychometric, 70–71
    test, 69–71

Career/vocational/transition assessment,
    376–399
    guidelines for establishing transition
      services, 380–383
    informal procedures, 381, 383–392
    interest and aptitude instruments,
      392–395, 399
    legislation concerning, 379–380

Test Index